Basic Media Writing

Fifth Edition

Basic Media Writing

Melvin Mencher
Columbia University

Brown & Benchmark
PUBLISHERS

Madison   Dubuque, IA   Guilford, CT   Chicago   Toronto London
Caracas   Mexico City   Buenos Aires   Madrid   Bogota Sydney

Book Team

Executive Publisher *Edgar J. Laube*
Acquisitions Editor *Eric Ziegler*
Developmental Editor *Mary Rossa*
Publishing Services Coordinator *Peggy Selle*
Proofreading Coordinator *Carrie Barker*
Production Manager *Beth Kundert*
Production/Costing Manager *Sherry Padden*
Visuals/Design Freelance Specialist *Mary L. Christianson*
Marketing Manager *Katie Rose*
Copywriter *M. J. Kelly*

Basal Text *10/12 Times Roman*
Display Type *Insignia*
Typesetting System *Mac/Quark XPress*
Paper Stock *50# Restorecote*
Production Services *Edwards Brothers*

President and Chief Executive Officer *Thomas E. Doran*
Vice President of Production and Business Development *Vickie Putman*
Vice President of Sales and Marketing *Bob McLaughlin*
Director of Marketing *John Finn*

A Times Mirror Company

The credits section for this book begins on page 465 and is considered an extension of the copyright page.

Cover design by Lesiak/Crampton Design, Inc.

Photo research by Shirley Lanners

Copyedited by Sarah Lane; Proofread by Patsy A. Adams

Printed in the United States of America by Times Mirror Higher Education Group, Inc., 2460 Kerper Boulevard, Dubuque, IA 52001

10 9 8 7 6 5 4 3 2 1

On the Cover: Journalists at Work

The front and back covers illustrate some of the work of media journalists. The photograph on the front by Charlie Neuman of *The San
Diego Union-Tribune* led off the newspaper's articles and photographs
describing a 24-hour period at the busiest land crossing in the world, the
border between Mexico and the United States at San Ysidro. The woman
stands between lines of cars in Mexico, hoping for a handout.

On the back cover, Cathie Lynn Rowand of *The Journal-Gazette*
took this photo just as the steeple on one of Fort Wayne's oldest churches
collapsed after a fire caused by lightning.

The Mud Couple Hug, which is how AP photographer Stephan
Savola describes this photo, was taken at the 25th anniversary celebration of Woodstock. "I went to the first Woodstock as a 16-year-old participant," says Savola. "Having that experience to draw upon, I was
looking for contrast and comparison all weekend. I found very little to
rekindle the sense of community I experienced 25 years earlier until I
stumbled across this couple covered in mud." More than a thousand journalists slogged through muddy fields to cover the event.

The Super Bowl is the most widely viewed event on television, and
it draws hundreds of reporters and photographers. Here, Bob Galbraith
of the AP uses the NC 2000 to record the action.

Bob Thayer snapped this photo of a student practicing a facial mas-
sage at a beauty school for his photo-essay for the *Providence Journal
Sunday Magazine*.

Contents

Preface   xv

Acknowledgments   xviii

Part One   Journalists in Action

1   The Media's Wide Compass   2

Looking Ahead   2
Handling a Big Story—Alone   3
   Racing the Clock   3
   Writethru   5
The Scope of the Media   6
   The Need to Know   7
   Nothing Is Routine   7
A California Daily Newspaper   7
   A Questionable Photograph   8
   Designer at Work   8
   Planning Coverage   8
   Budget Meeting   9
Bullets, Tanks and Torture   10
A 10-Alarm Fire   11
Inside a Newsroom   12
   A Fatal Accident   12
   At City Hall   12
   An Obituary   13
   A Hurricane and Canned Tuna   13

   Approaching Deadline   13
   On the Copy Desk   14
   The Cartoonist   15
Helicopter Newsman   16
   Looking for O.J.   16
   A Street Corner Beating   17
Newsletters, Desktop Publishing   17
Free-Lancing   18
The Dividing Line   19
Criticism and Reviews   20
   Two Duds   20
   The Dean Speaks Out   21
The Columnists   21
   In the Pew   21
   On the Playing Field   22
   At the Police Station   22
On the Editorial Page   23
Some Other Persuaders   24
   In the Advertising Department   24

Up in the Air   25
At a PR Agency   26
The Underpinning   **26**
Reporting   **27**

Proving Your Point   27
Collecting Information   28
The Journalistic Process   **28**
Suggested Reading   **29**

2 The Journalist: Traits and Characteristics 30

Looking Ahead   **30**
The Curious Sophomore   **31**
A Dog's Tale   31
Independence   **32**
Skepticism   **33**
Savvy   **34**
Knowledge   34
Street Smarts   35
Integrity   **35**
Desecrated Bodies   35
Composure   **36**
Creativity, Ingenuity   **38**
Perseverance   **40**
Arrival in Tunica   41
Commitment   **44**
A Career of Exposés   45
Piercing the Bamboo Curtain   46
Native-American Concerns   48
The Copy Editor   48
Completeness   **50**
Photo Fallout   51

Rape Data: Real or Magnified?   52
Twenty-Eight Years
    Behind Walls   53
Dependability, Initiative   **56**
Pinpoint Accuracy   **56**
Objectivity, Interpretation   **56**
Involvement   **57**
Discipline   **58**
Courage, Stamina   **58**
Death in the Afternoon   59
Some Realities   **63**
A Variety of Jobs   63
A Job Tryout   64
Satisfaction . . .   66
. . . and Frustration   66
Women in Journalism   67
Minorities in Journalism   67
Group Ownership   67
Truth Seekers   **68**
Suggested Reading   **68**

Part Two Writing

3 Rudiments of the Story 70

Looking Ahead   **70**
Accuracy   **71**
Attribution   **73**
Placement   74
Verbs of Attribution   75
Anonymous Sources   75

Background   **77**
Balance and Fairness   **77**
Stereotypes and Sexism   79
Brevity   **80**
Content   80
Word Choice   81

Clarity	82	Objectivity	89
Completeness	83	Opinion	90
Human Interest	83	Verification	93
Identification	85	Hoaxes	94
News Point	87	Seeking Truths	94
Novelty	89	Suggested Reading	95

4 Writing 96

Looking Ahead	**96**	**Errors Galore**	**111**
The Ingredients	**97**	Muddy Thinking = Mistakes	113
Simple Sentences	97	Redundancies	114
Simple Words	99	Clichés	114
Conviction	100	Journalese	115
Natural Style	106	Synonyms for *said*	115
Some Guides	**108**	**Summing Up**	**116**
Storytelling	109	**Suggested Reading**	**117**

5 Values and Beginnings 118

Looking Ahead	**118**	**Creating the Lead**	**131**
What Is News?	**119**	Cancer Outrage	133
Three Basic Determinants	120	Direct and Delayed Leads	134
Other Determinants	122	Writing the Lead	135
Other Factors	125	Take 10	136
Gatekeeping	125	Straight News Lead	141
Summing Up	126	Feature Lead	144
Beginning the Story	**126**	Hard, Soft; Direct or	
Finding the Focus	127	Delayed?	146
Finding the Purpose	130	**Suggested Reading**	**148**

6 Structuring the Story 149

Looking Ahead	**149**	The Three-Element Story	157
Story Building	**150**	**The Feature**	**161**
The Straight News Story	**150**	Choosing a Style	161
The Single-Element Story	151	Focusing on a Theme	162
The Two-Element Story	152	Accentuating the Ending	164

The News Feature	**164**
Volunteers to the Dying	167
Structuring the Feature and	
News Feature	168
Summing Up	**169**

Some Tips for Good Writing	169
Major Problems	170
Copy Check	170
Suggested Reading	**170**

Part Three
Reporting

7 Finding Information and Gathering Facts   172

Looking Ahead	**172**
Foundations of Fact Gathering	**173**
Direct Observation	173
Interviews	177
Research	180
Taking Stock	**186**
What to Look For	186
Building Background	**187**
Learn the System, Know the	
Community	188

Study Press Law and History	189
Gather Specifics	191
Meet the Audience	192
Research	194
Keep on Learning	194
Develop Common Sense	196
Taking Notes	**198**
Marking Notes	198
Summing Up	**200**
Suggested Reading	**200**

8 Purposeful Reporting   201

Looking Ahead	**201**
Developing the Framework	**202**
Women as Victims	203
Profile of a Lawyer	204
Missing Mothers	205
Being Flexible	206
Knowing the Essentials	207
Developing Confidence	210
Fine-Tuning the Framework	**210**

Knowing the Beat	212
Building Relationships	213
Showing Enterprise	216
Investigative Reporting	218
Writing Interpretive Stories	218
Negotiating the Obstacles	**219**
Moral Indignation	219
Personal Biases	220
Suggested Reading	**221**

9 Capturing the Spoken Word   222

Looking Ahead	**222**
Interviews	**223**

Techniques	223
Spot News Interviews	223

Profiles	**227**
Guidelines	227
Preparations	228
Devising a Theme	229
Inducing Subjects to Talk	229
Asking Questions	230
Listening and Watching	231
Taking Notes	232
On- and Off-the-Record	232
Master of the Interview	233
Profile Essentials	234

Ending The Profile	238
Public Gatherings	**239**
Meetings	239
Panel Discussions and	
Symposia	**243**
News Conferences	**247**
Speeches	**248**
Leads	**249**
Summary	**252**
Suggested Reading	**252**

10 Story Essentials 253

Looking Ahead	**253**
Accident Stories	**254**
Fire Stories	**256**
Death of a Smoker	257
Crime Stories	**259**
Crime Reports	260
Robbery	261
Burglary	261
Investigation	262
Arrests	263
Law-Enforcement Agencies	265
Booking	266
Criminal Court Coverage	**266**
Pretrial	266
Plea Bargaining	269
Trial	270
Civil Court Coverage	**272**
Actions at Law	273
Equity Proceedings	273
Federal Court Coverage	**274**
Obituaries	**274**
Personal Details	275
Cause of Death	276
The Lead	277
Localizing the Obituary	278
Sports Coverage	**278**

High School and College	
Sports	279
The Lead	281
Imagination and Emotion	282
Structure	283
Restraint	284
Extra Dimension	284
More Than Only Games	286
Jocks No More	286
Women in the	
Locker Room	287
Covering Religion	**288**
Other Types of Stories	**289**
Briefs	289
Precedes	290
Personals	290
Brights	292
Localizing Stories	292
Follow-Up Stories	294
Sidebars	295
Roundups	296
Weather Stories	296
Rewriting Releases	**298**
The Roving Reporter	**299**
Summary	**300**
Suggested Reading	**300**

Part Four Specialties

11 Broadcast Writing 302

Looking Ahead	**302**
On-the-Scene Reporting	**303**
Human Guinea Pigs	304
Writing for Listeners	**307**
Clarity	307
Attribution and Leads	308
Immediacy	309
Summary	**309**
Rewriting the Wires	**310**
Under Pressure: 30 Minutes to Deadline	311

"CBS Evening News"	**313**
The Writers	313
Minutes to Go	313
On the Air	314
Preparing Broadcast Copy	**315**
Style Rules	315
Broadcast Career Necessities	**317**
Suggested Reading	**318**

12 Visual Reporting 319

Looking Ahead	**319**
The Picture Is Universal	**320**
The Ingredients of a Good Photo	**320**
The Tools of the Photojournalist	**321**
Content and Treatment	322
Starting Out	**323**
Know Everything	323
On the Job	**324**
Tension on Campus	325
Poverty in Appalachia	326
Violence at Florence and Normandie	328
From Vietnam to a Kansas Prison	329
The Photo Essay	331
Writing Captions	**331**
The Photo Editor	**333**
The Camera	**333**
Aperture	333

Shutter Speed	333
Lenses	334
Depth of Field	336
Film	337
Revolutionary Changes	**338**
The Photojournalist's Insight	**338**
Crusaders with Camera	**339**
Lewis Hine	340
Contemporary Documentarians	**341**
Documenting Domestic Violence	343
The Cracked Mirror	**344**
The Ethics of Changing Reality	344
Some Problems	**346**
What's Wrong with These Photographs?	346
What's Wrong? The Answers	**349**
A Home Study Course	**350**
Suggested Reading	**350**

13 Advertising 352

Looking Ahead   352
The Art of Persuasion   353
Looking Back   354
  Brand Identity   354
  Image Ads   355
  Competition   355
Newspaper Ad Departments   355
Advertising Agencies   356
  Account   356
  Research   357
  Creative and Media   358
  From Browning to Barkley   362
Media Selection   362
  Creating An Outdoor   364
  Tots, Teens, Travelers   364
  Super Costly Super Bowl   365

The Ratings Game   365
Unpredictable Audiences   366
The Content   366
  The Results   367
  Helping Dreams Come True   368
  Speaking to Runners   370
  Hype Is Out   371
  Some Constants   372
Regulation   373
Careers in Advertising   375
Summing Up   376
  The Objective   376
  The Strategy   376
  Content, Media Selection   376
  The Results   377
Suggested Reading   377

14 Public Relations 378

Looking Ahead   378
The Purpose: Advocacy   379
The Beginnings   379
  Robber Barons and
    Reformers   380
  A "Physician to Corporate
    Bodies"   381
  Rubber Whales and Salami
    Queens   382
The Quest for Legitimacy   383
The Scope   384
The Tasks   385
Sports Information   386

Corporate Public Relations   387
  Selling Cars   387
  Selling Tuna   388
Public Affairs   390
  In the County   390
  In the Capital   392
Political Public Relations   392
  Too Funny   392
  Too Bookish   393
A Reporter's View   393
Ethics   394
The Path to a Job   395
Suggested Reading   396

Part Five Laws and Codes

15 Libel, Privacy, Ethics and Taste   398

Looking Ahead	**398**	Gifts	408
Some Problems	**399**	Ethical Behavior	408
Libel	**399**	Personal Guides	408
Libel Defined	400	Poses and Disguises	413
Libel Defenses	401	**Taste**	**414**
Avoiding Libel Suits	402	The Double Standard	414
Privacy	**404**	Frank Language	416
Danger Areas	404	Changing Guidelines	417
Ethics	**406**	Offensive Subject Matter	418
Plagiarism	406	Questionable Photographs	419
Dishonesty	407	Summary	421
Conflict of Interest	407	**Suggested Reading**	**422**

Stylebook	**423**	**Appendix D Code of Ethics**	**446**
Punctuation	429	**Appendix E Grammar**	**449**
Appendix A Preparing Copy	**435**	Agreement	449
On a Typewriter	435	Dangling Modifier	450
On a Video Display Terminal	436	Misplaced Words	450
Appendix B Moving the Story	**437**	Parallel Construction	451
Newspaper Copy	437	Pronouns	451
Broadcast Copy	440	Sentence Fragments	452
Appendix C How to Use the		Sequence of Tenses	452
Freedom of Information		**Appendix F Copy Editing**	**453**
Act	**442**	Drunk Driver	455
Who Can Make a Request?	442	Stabbing	456
How Quickly Will an		Boots	457
Agency Respond?	442	**Glossary**	**459**
Where to Write	443	Print Terms	459
Describe What You Want	443	Broadcast Terms	464
Plan Your Request Strategy	443	**Credits**	**465**
Identify What You Want		**Name Index**	**469**
Clearly	444	**Subject Index**	**481**

Preface

Basic Media Writing is designed to help students survey the various fields in journalism and to show them how the practitioners in these fields do their work. Whether the practitioner is a reporter for a television station, a public relations specialist, a movie reviewer, an editorial writer or a courthouse reporter for the local newspaper, the work he or she does has a common core.

Media workers gather information, analyze it and shape the material into lean, accurate and clear writing. The gate to success in these fields admits those who can observe sharply, listen carefully and write pungently.

The everyday experiences of media practitioners provide the foundation on which *Basic* is built. Every technique, principle and concept is illustrated with an example from the work of a professional. For students considering careers in journalism, the work of these media professionals brings the faces and facets of journalism to life:

> The young woman just out of journalism school who is called on to cover a fire that kills 20 people; the television reporter who hears that human beings are being used as guinea pigs to test an insecticide; the movie reviewer who has just had to sit through two very bad films; the news photographer assigned to cover a volatile speaker on a college campus; the editorial writer who hopes to persuade his readers to support a school bond issue; the advertising copywriter working on a public service television spot for the United Negro College Fund; the public relations practitioner trying to persuade a community to adopt a project for the recycling of home waste; the photographer covering the defilement of a U.S. serviceman's body in Somalia.

We will also accompany a news magazine writer on an assignment, observe a foreign correspondent arrange an interview to avoid police spies and listen to a columnist talk about the job of banging out a column regularly. We will take a side excursion as well to look at how the people in design, layout and graphics work, and we'll watch a cartoonist at his work table.

The techniques described in this book are those followed by men and women who make words and images do their bidding. The professionals who have contributed to *Basic* know that their work is demanding. The writers understand how hard it is to whip words into submission so that they dance lightly or march somberly across the page. Those whose work reaches out to thousands, sometimes millions, have demanding taskmasters. But they learn their craft through patience, confidence and effort.

Patience is necessary because words have a tendency to go their own way, resisting our efforts to lock them into headlines, captions, sentences and paragraphs. Also, the event is fleeting; we have to learn how to grasp it in an instant.

Confidence is important because it seems that the right words will never come, that they refuse to blend smoothly and insist on zigzagging their way down the page—no matter how patient we are. But we all possess the creative instinct, the ability to make something of our experience and to tell and to show others what we have seen and heard. With confidence, we can do that.

Effort makes the patience pay off and the confidence hold true. The aspiring artist who seeks to transfer a sunset to canvas does not instinctively dip her brush into the precise colors on the palette, no matter how patiently she waits for inspiration. Through study and trial and error she learns just how much white to mix with red for the clouds. The singer cannot turn words and musical notes into a song of lost love the first time he sees the score, no matter how confident he is. It takes hours, sometimes days, before everything comes together and the performance is worth taping. The journalist is no different. Beginner or veteran, the journalist achieves success through hard work.

Unguided effort is wasted work, however. The purpose of *Basic* is to serve as compass and sextant. It provides the directions in which the student should point his or her efforts.

The philosophy of *Basic,* now in its fifth edition, is best summed up by Samuel Johnson's remark, "The end of writing is to enable the readers better to enjoy life, or better to endure it."

Johnson's approach to the world around him, wrote the essayist George Gordon, was based on "a habit of truth," which was "in all situations to insist on the facts, and to face them when found." Gordon says Johnson's attitude was "to refuse, at whatever cost, to make life seem better than it is . . . to practice true statement not only in the most important things, but in the least."

Truth telling is the journalist's compulsion and underlying ethic. It is the hallmark of those whose work merits our respect.

Truth is difficult to ferret out. We will watch several journalists try to find some truths in the face of sometimes overwhelming obstacles. Authority often wants us to see its truths, obliging journalists with ample material. The journalist true to his or her calling tries whenever possible to follow Peter Arnett's guideline: "simply to write only what I saw myself."

Unfortunately, truth is often annoying, sometimes ugly, and its unpleasantness reaches into the journalist's work so that the product reflects truth's irritability. "We have art in order not to die of the truth," Nietzsche wrote. Indeed, some within the journalistic fold urge on us artistic license to make our work more palatable, more popular.

Yet even the artist understands the necessity of telling untarnished truths, as Robert Lowell wrote in his *Epilogue:*

> But sometimes everything I write
> With the threadbare art of my eye
> Seems a snapshot,
> Lurid, rapid, garish, grouped,
> Heightened from life,
> Yet paralyzed by fact.
> All's misalliance.
> Yet why not say what happened?

If we know what is happening we can cope with the world around us, hold communal conversation on a realistic basis. Serviceable, workable truths—the kind the journalist can provide—enable us to work together to solve our problems.

For all its practicality, this textbook recognizes that journalism is more calling than trade. Kin to teaching, cousin to preaching, journalism is much more than the sum of its techniques and the advice of its practitioners. Through its many examples, *Basic* seeks to demonstrate the moral underpinnings of journalism.

Journalism's hope and inspiration are its young men and women. This book was written for them and especially in memory of two young men who were killed in Vietnam, Ron Gallagher and Peter Bushey. Ron was editor of the *University Daily Kansan* when I was its adviser at the University of Kansas, and Peter was one of my students at Columbia University. They loved journalism and had faith in what it could accomplish. They wrote, they took pictures and they aspired to make the world a better place for us all through journalism. To them, journalism was a noble calling.

Sheila Carney prepared the name and subject indexes. Many of my research tasks were aided by the enthusiastic assistance of Ms. Carney, Elizabeth A. Brennan and Steve Toth, both of the Columbia University Journalism Library. Helpful suggestions for this fifth edition were provided by John Mitchell of the Syracuse University journalism faculty and Douglas P. Starr of the journalism faculty at Texas A&M University. Design is by David Decker of Decker Decker & Associates. Wendy Shilton handled the copy editing and the proofreading.

Acknowledgments

The following people have provided help with the book. The affiliations listed applied at the time the individuals supplied material for *Basic Media Writing:*

Mervin Block
Television writer and broadcast workshop director

Harold Burson
Burson-Marsteller

Kirk Citron
Vice president, Hal Riney & Partners, San Francisco

Renee Edelman
Edelman Public Relations Worldwide

Heidi Evans
Daily News (New York)

Bob Gesslein
Sports Information Director, Long Island University

Mary Ann Giordano
Daily News (New York)

Jack Grinold
Sports Information Director, Northeastern University

Stephen Hartgen
The Times-News (Twin Falls, Idaho)

Barbara J. Hipsman
Kent State University

Robert E. Kollar
Chief Photographer, Tennessee Valley Authority

Jeff McAdory
The Commercial Appeal (Memphis, Tenn.)

Mitch Mendelson
The Birmingham Post-Herald

Carol Nation
Dept. Public Works, Arlington County, Va.

Marcia Parker
Contra Costa Times (Walnut Creek, Calif.)

Merrill Perlman
The New York Times

Susan J. Porter
Editor, *Scripps Howard News*

Ron Rapoport
Daily News, Los Angeles

Charlie Riedel
The Hays (Kan.) *Daily News*

Sam Roe
The Blade, (Toledo, Ohio)

Bob Rose
The Blade (Toledo, Ohio)

Michele Ruiz
KTLA-TV, Los Angeles

Andrea Sachs
Time magazine

Joel Sartore
The Wichita Eagle-Beacon

Christopher Scanlan
The Providence Journal; St. Petersburg Times

Barbara Shulgasser
San Francisco Examiner

Lena H. Sun
The Washington Post

Janet L. Taylor
The Times-News (Twin Falls, Idaho)

Kevin Tedesco
Young & Rubicam, NW Ayer

Bob Thayer
The Providence Journal–Bulletin

Bob Tur
Los Angeles News Service

Burt Unger
Mercedes-Benz of North America, Inc.

Keith Warren
The Commercial Dispatch (Columbus, Miss.)

Tim Weiner
The New York Times

Jan Wong
The Globe and Mail (Toronto)

Emerald Yeh
KRON-TV, San Francisco

Phoebe Zerwick
Winston-Salem (N.C.) *Journal*

PART ONE
Journalists in Action

The interview is a major source of information for all media workers. The news reporter questions a police officer at the scene of an accident. The advertising representative seeks information from a store owner about a Mother's Day special. An account executive for a public relations agency asks women in a focus group which painkiller they prefer.

1 The Media's Wide Compass

Media writers can be found at crime scenes, at city council meetings, in advertising and public relations agencies, at movies and at rock concerts. The number of jobs and tasks is enormous. *Susan Pollard, Contra Costa Times*

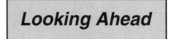

Looking Ahead

Media writers inform, entertain and persuade us. They strive to be interesting, accurate and thorough, which they accomplish by applying their skills and knowledge to their observations, interviews and research and, finally, to their writing. In their work, these professionals have to cope with deadline pressure and sometimes with hazardous circumstances.

Handling a Big Story—Alone

The lights are out in the fashionable stores along Fifth Avenue, and the tall buildings in Rockefeller Center loom over the deserted streets. Patrons have made their way home from Radio City Music Hall, a block away on Sixth Avenue. It is well past midnight in midtown New York.

Although the lights in one Rockefeller Center office building burn brightly, there is an unusual calm there, too. The reporters, editors and operators in the Associated Press newsroom have left for the night. The office is deserted—except for a young woman sitting at one of the desks.

Lindy Washburn is working the early shift—11:30 p.m. to 8 a.m.—in the New York City bureau of the Associated Press. She was hired as a summer vacation replacement after her graduation from journalism school. As the newcomer in the bureau, she has been taught the ropes: the need for speed, accuracy and brevity; which wires send out sports, radio, local and national news and the method for transmitting stories when the operators are not on duty.

Washburn is responsible for a large area of the East Coast, and she will be on her own for most of the shift. This is her first night alone on the early shift. As the old hands leave for home, one stops to reassure her. "Looks like a quiet night," he says.

For a while it is quiet. Suddenly, at 1:40 a.m., the stillness of the office is broken by the ring of the telephone. The night city editor of the *Daily News* is on the other end. Washburn senses the urgency in his voice.

"We have a tip there's a big fire in New Jersey," he says. "Have you got anything?" No, she hasn't, she says. She asks him where the fire is. "Bradley Beach," he replies.

Washburn looks at a map and sees that Bradley Beach is a town on the Atlantic shore and is near Asbury Park, a larger city.

She calls long-distance information and asks for the telephone numbers of the police and fire departments of Bradley Beach and Asbury Park. First, she calls the Bradley Beach fire department.

"Lady, we're busy," a man says and hangs up. He sounds frantic.

She telephones the Asbury Park fire department.

"What's happening in Bradley Beach?" she asks. "I can't get anything from the department there."

"That's some fire," the dispatcher answers. "We have departments from all over the state fighting it. It looks like a big one."

"Any deaths?" Washburn asks.

"I think it was 20 last time I checked. Could be more now."

Racing the Clock

Washburn's heart picks up a few beats. This is obviously a big story, one that is likely to be given play around the country. She knows that at this time—nearly 2 a.m.—morning newspapers in the West are readying their front pages. She will have to hurry to catch them.

Taking Notes

Lindy Washburn interviews a source for a story she will soon place on the AP wires for newspapers and broadcast stations all over the country. *John Titchen*

She asks the dispatcher for the address of the building, what it is used for, when the first alarm was received. She wants to know what the building looks like—is it wood, brick, stucco? The dispatcher says it's a wooden frame building called the Brinley Inn. No, he doesn't know the cause.

As she hangs up, another telephone rings. The call is from a radio station reporter in Asbury Park. He had called the AP's Newark bureau with information; a message had informed him that the bureau was closed for the night and that important stories should be phoned to the New York City bureau.

"Have you heard about the fire?" he asks Washburn. "Yes," she replies. "How many deaths are there?" The death toll is the key to the importance of her story, and she must have it confirmed.

"The hospital spokesman on the scene says 23," the reporter answers, and he confirms the address of the Brinley Inn that the dispatcher had provided.

The radio reporter then plays for Washburn a tape of his interview with a doctor from the medical examiner's office who was at the scene.

Washburn now has just about all she needs for a bulletin. After she sends it she will have to alert the AP New Jersey staff to start working on the fire.

She looks over the notes she has been taking during her telephone conversations. The death toll clearly is the heart of the story and will be placed in her first sentence, the **lead.** She rearranges her notes with the lead in mind and starts to write.

Satisfied with her story, although she realizes that she will have to gather additional information, Washburn types in the code for an all-points bulletin and relays the story:

o364
   B N ZYVVYXUIV
BNBX NRO7 NRO5
BNBX
BC-Bradley Beach Fire
   Bradley Beach, New Jersey (AP)—A major fire in Bradley Beach has killed 23 people, according to fire officials.
   The fire at Brinley Inn, 200 Brinley Ave., began at 11:20 P.M. and was brought under control at midnight, according to Chief Theodore A. Bianchi of the Bradley Beach Fire Department.
   The cause of the fire is undetermined, he said.
   The Brinley Inn, a three-story wood frame building, was reportedly occupied by 36 people at the time of the blaze. Many elderly persons and teen-agers were among those killed, the officials said.
   Dead and injured were taken to the Jersey Shore Medical Center and the Long Branch Medical Center.
   More
   AP-NY-07-27 0201EDT

Writethru

All of this is done in about 20 minutes, and Washburn is pleased by her ability to act quickly in a critical situation. (She later learns that she had beaten the opposition, UPI, by 35 minutes.) But she is not pleased with her story. There are some flubs.

She sees that she should have abbreviated *New Jersey* in the dateline, and she realizes that the adjective *major* in the lead is extraneous. She also realizes that she should have used *said* instead of *according to* in the lead.

Washburn resumes her reporting and learns that the Brinley Inn is a four-story—not a three-story—rooming house. She collects more details about the injured and where the dead had been trapped, and she learns the exact time the fire broke out.

She begins to write a new lead. Her focus will still be the most newsworthy fact she has, the 23 deaths. She will then use the new material she has gathered about those who were injured.

Her first story cleared at 2:01 a.m. Her second piece clears the wire at 3:26 a.m. Here is the beginning of her Writethru, which eliminates her earlier piece:

> o365
> B N ZYVVYXWYF
> AM-Beach Fire, Writethru, 400
> Eds: Updates, Corrects Building to four-story
> structure, adds color
> Bradley Beach, N.J. (AP)—At least 23 persons
> were killed Saturday in a fire at a rooming house in
> this seaside resort, hospital officials said.
> Two others suffered smoke inhalation and were
> admitted to the Jersey Shore Medical Center, said
> Hospital Administrator Ernest Kovats. An additional
> 13 people were examined at the hospital, Kovats
> said.
> As many as 36 people may have been inside
> The Brinley Inn when the fire broke out at 11:02
> P.M. and was brought under control about midnight,
> authorities said.
> Witnesses said most of the victims appeared to
> be elderly and appeared to be trapped on the top
> floors of the four-story wood-frame building.
> The cause of the fire was not determined, but
> there were some reports of an explosion, said Fire
> Chief Theodore A. Bianchi. . . .

We leave Washburn as she continues to work on her story. The next day, she will be complimented on her work, and a colleague will tell her that her steady performance probably earned her a job with the AP, a major supplier of news to newspapers and broadcast stations around the world.

Washburn is one of the many thousands of men and women whose handiwork fills the page, moves across the screen and goes out over the radio wires.

The Scope of the Media

We awaken to the clock radio that is broadcasting the day's weather and the news headlines. A commercial for a brand of coffee finally rouses us, and on our way to the kitchen we switch on the morning television news program.

Over breakfast, we look through the morning newspaper or finish the movie reviews in the news magazine we started reading the night before.

On the way to work or school, a billboard advising us to eat out catches our eye as we check the traffic situation on the local all-news radio station. A news story reports the resignation of the university president. He's going to Washington to work for the State Department. We wonder whether the criticism of the local newspaper has made him decide to seek other pastures for his talents, and we recall the cartoon in yesterday's paper that showed him handling some papers: His hands were drawn to consist of all thumbs.

In the hour or two between awakening and settling down to work or study, we have seen and heard the handiwork of hundreds of people who make a living working for the media.

As we settle in for the day, some media workers race to make a deadline with news of a new investigation involving the president. Others labor over reviews, press releases, page designs, advertisements and editorials. A young writer in Chicago tries to sell an editor on the profile of an up-and-coming singer who may be tomorrow's Michael Jackson. Two of the reporters we will be following are in China, trying to find out what is really going on despite being followed and harassed by government agents.

Some of these media workers write. Some, like Ron Tarver of *The Philadelphia Inquirer,* take pictures. We'll go along with Tarver as he explores the drug-infested Badlands of the city, and we will accompany a broadcast journalist who does his journalism from a helicopter. We will watch him as he hovers over a bloody street-corner scene in Los Angeles and then again on another day as he tries to track down a fleeing O.J. Simpson.

Some media workers design pages, and some sit for hours watching movies, many of which they will pan. Some are free-lance writers.

In New York, a former foreign correspondent for the United Press International is working on a biography, encouraged by the success of her first book, which was about the intrepid newspaperwoman Nellie Bly. Brooke Kroeger's biography of Bly was based on considerable investigative work since Bly left no diary and few letters.

Bly went to work for a Pittsburgh newspaper in 1886 at 21 and was soon hired by Pulitzer's *New York World.* Bly achieved instant fame when she feigned insanity, was committed to an insane asylum and wrote a scathing exposé of the inhumane treatment of patients. Two years later, Bly was circling the globe in an

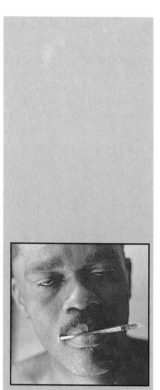

Works for Sale

Biscuit is an entrepreneur in Philadelphia's Badlands, offering syringes for $1 each to passersby. *Ron Tarver, The Philadelphia Inquirer*

Brooke Kroeger

© Lonny Kalfus

attempt to beat the time of the hero of Jules Verne's *Around the World in Eighty Days*. She made it in 72. The first of the so-called stunt reporters, Bly also covered strikes, World War I and the plight of unwed mothers and their children.

Kroeger spent three years on the Bly biography and says, "I never felt such deadline pressure." Her book immediately went into three printings.

In Evansville, Ind., the advertising copywriter whose billboard caught our eye is at work on another.

The Need to Know

These media workers are devoting their time and thinking to meeting the unquenchable need we have for information. Should we take umbrella and galoshes on the way out of the house? How is the league race shaping up after last night's games? What is happening to the peace process in eastern Europe? Which of the two movies we might see tonight is the better one? Will there be a sale on athletic shoes this weekend?

"What's new?" we ask when we greet a friend. If the answer sounds interesting, we press for details. If it's old stuff, we change the subject.

Put yourself in a newsroom, at a desk in an advertising or public relations agency. You know that the people out there want to know what's new, what's different, what's interesting that will affect them. Your job is to satisfy them. And good journalists do just that.

Nothing Is Routine

Bill Mertens, the editor of *The Hawk Eye* in Burlington, Iowa, recalls one of his first assignments as a reporter. He was sent to cover a high school graduation, "a routine assignment," Mertens thought. "I produced an equally routine story," he said.

Mertens' editor looked it over and shook his head. He asked his young reporter a few questions. Turns out the seniors had chosen as their commencement speaker a young man who had overcome a stuttering problem that had made him shy and reclusive.

"My story ignored what Mac (his editor) considered the obvious news peg," Mertens recalls, and he says he has never been able to forget his editor's disappointment at the "squandered opportunity" to tell a fascinating story.

A California Daily Newspaper

Let's move behind the scenes to look at the sources of this tide of information. Our first stop is Walnut Creek, Calif., headquarters of Lesher Communications, Inc., which publishes five San Francisco Bay Area daily newspapers, 13 weekly newspapers and four shoppers, which are freely circulated shopping newspapers. We'll focus on the group's flagship newspaper, the *Contra Costa Times,* circulation about 100,000, where a major news decision is in the making.

Journalism Majors. Almost all media workers are college graduates, and four of five of those hired are journalism majors.

Ruination. "More newspapermen have been ruined by self-importance than by liquor."
—*Walter Lippmann*

Responsibility. "Making a living is nothing; the great difficulty is making a point, making a difference—with words."
—*Elizabeth Hardwick*

A Questionable Photograph

A 12-year-old girl who had been abducted from her home at knifepoint was found alive 22 hours later in a field east of Lodi. A *Times* photographer was with the 100 law enforcement officers when they picked up the girl. He photographed her as she walked toward them, clad only in her socks.

The photograph was dramatic. It showed the youngster walking toward a police officer, her arms across the front of her body. Her nakedness was hardly visible, but the story indicated the state she was in.

Designer at Work

The Blend

Moving from art to headline to text smoothly. *Contra Costa Times*

While the editors are discussing the kidnap story, Sharon Henry is working on a design for the front page of the Monday business section, "Money Matters."

"There are three main ingredients that a designer works with to create a page," she tells an onlooker. "Headlines, copy and art."

The art, which may be an illustration or a photograph, "is the first item the reader will notice," Henry says. For the page she is working on, money management by women, she has made a drawing, an eye-catching illustration of a woman nurturing her money tree. "The art sets the mood for the page. It also 'drives' the page, meaning that its size and direction tell the designer where the headline and the copy will be placed."

In her illustration, the woman is looking to her right, and this is where the major headline and story begin.

"The headline has to sell the story as well as explain and complement the art," Henry continues. "Display or art type is used often in headlines for feature stories, but it is important that the headline design not compete with the art or be thought of as mere decoration. The headline's primary job is to supply information."

In the design she is working on, a four-word headline, "Financial Nurturing for Women," indicates the scope of the story.

"After the art and the headline are placed, the copy for the story is positioned, which involves a decision on how the text should be treated: Should it have oversize type, extra leading (the space between lines of type), white space?"

For the "Money Matters" cover page she decides the lead story will have large, heavily leaded type and run flush left and ragged right. The sidebar story will be set regular body type within the usual column width.

"While these activities are usually done independently and in this order," Henry says, it is important for the designer to be aware of how the different elements will play off each other. The aim is to have them make a smooth transition from art to headline to text.

"In the same way that a good architect designs a house with interesting shapes and ease of movement through rooms, a page designer should think of moving the reader through the page."

Planning Coverage

As this page is being designed, Marcia Parker, an assistant managing editor for business news and training, is balancing several activities. She has three reporting teams working on projects and she wants to discuss their progress with them.

Two reporters are working on a Sunday story about a nearby town's investments that have the smell of a scandal; a three-person team is planning a series on municipal finance for the fall and Parker will lay out an outline for the stories and a timetable; and for a Sunday package spurred by a freeze in the coffee growing countries, she wants one story on the consequences of the bad weather and two on the way the coffee trading market works, who the international coffee producers are, who other market players are and how they affect the price of a cup of coffee.

Budget Meeting

Along with all this, Parker is preparing for the 11 a.m. daily budget meeting, the session at which editors go through the stories and photos on hand and those that are anticipated and where they plan the contents and play of major stories.

The major items discussed at the budget meeting consisted of several local features and the possible imposition of parking fees in the garages of the BART commuter line. Also, the editors discussed the kidnapping story.

The possibility of paying for parking was news and would be the major story on page one. Many of the readers commute from their suburban homes to San Francisco and Oakland jobs, and they fill the 32,200 parking spots early, sometimes, as the story says, "long before sunrise."

Since many *Times* readers had been following the kidnapping story on radio and television, the child's rescue and the arrest of the 25-year-old who was suspected of kidnapping her were not new to them. This story would be given second position on page one but played prominently.

The third story on the page localizes an out-of-state traffic piece. It merits front-page play because of the 37 killed—14 were from California, 12 of them children.

The fourth piece is the mandatory July 4th holiday story, but from a different angle. Emily Gurnon describes what the holiday means to a city manager whose city attracts thousands of holiday celebrants.

Gurnon also has a short feature with a holiday twist. She wandered over to a Concord mall and asked teen-agers whether they knew what July 4th celebrates. Few did. Here is her story:

Page One Play
Contra Costa Times

For some teens, July 4 is just another day off

By EMILY GURNON
Staff writer

CONCORD—Few students are likely to crack the books this holiday weekend. But given their knowledge of Independence Day's history, maybe they should.

A startling number of young people at Sunvalley mall this week could not say why the United States celebrates the Fourth of July.

"I have no idea," said Michelle Markey, 13, of Walnut Creek. "I just knew it was a patriotic holiday."

"I don't know," said eighth-grader Amanda Coles, who lives in Italy and was in California for vacation. She turned to her friend, 12-year-old Angela Rosario of Pleasant Hill. "Didn't we learn this in social studies?"

Amanda wasn't sure either. "I don't really pay attention to it because my birthday's two days later."

Jason Alberts, 17, of Crockett thought about the question for a minute. "Um . . . Independence Day or something?" Did he know what country we were gaining independence from?

"I could guess. . . . Europe?"

France, guessed 17-year-old Charles Bowser of Concord. "I'm right, aren't I?" he said.

Brian Zaidel and Andrea McKee, 15-year-olds from Napa, didn't have a clue about the holiday's meaning. "Come on, Brian, think," Andrea said.

Brian was at a loss. "This is, like, fifth-grade stuff," he said.

"I don't know if we were signing something or what," said 15-year-old Brian Knight, who said he used to live in Concord and was now visiting from Texas. "It's summer. I don't remember anything."

Some of the young people got it exactly right. Others, at least, are trying.

Brita Rosenheim of Lafayette will be a senior at Acalanes High School in the fall. She said she has a summer class in history at Diablo Valley College.

The Fourth of July celebrates Independence Day, she said. "Freedom from Europe—France or whatever." She wasn't sure how long ago it was. "I haven't learned that yet."

The editors put this feature inside where they also decided to run a story by Joan Morris with a three-column photograph about the ninth annual Psychic and Healing Arts Fair. It begins:

PLEASANT HILL—Instead of the sterile, antiseptic smell of the doctor's office, there were flowery, sensual undertones. The "x-rays" were rainbow-hued and revealed vague, glowing misty shapes.

While the moods and methods were far removed from conventional medicine, the idea was the same. Those who came Sunday to the ninth annual Psychic and Healing Arts Fair were there for a spiritual health check.

People come to psychic fairs to have their auras read, their spines realigned, their inner selves sketched, their troubles massaged away and their futures read.

"Sometimes people come out just to see what we do," said Rose-Ellen Trebach, a San Francisco clairvoyant and spiritual healer. "But they're all looking for clarification about their lives, about problems they're having. My role as a healer is to find out what their blocks are, so they can then remove those limiting blocks. It's up to the person to do it, though. It's very empowering for them."

Let's continue west, across the Pacific to China. Jan Wong of *The Globe and Mail* of Toronto is on a balcony of the Beijing Hotel. She is watching history being made.

Bullets, Tanks and Torture

"Soldiers had entered the square from the west, out of our view, and we watched as they fired into the backs of terrified civilians trying to scale the hotel fence. Then, the tanks arrived, dozens of tanks, perhaps a hundred altogether."

Wong is looking down on Tiananmen Square. The Chinese government has decided to put a bloody end to the hopes of thousands of university students that democracy would come to their country. For almost a month, the students had conducted a hunger strike after proclaiming, "I swear to promote democracy and the prosperity of my country. I love my homeland more than rice."

In the square, the students had built a statue—the Goddess of Liberty—which was modeled after the Statue of Liberty.

"We watched the carnage below. Between cars in the hotel parking lot, a couple cowered with their young daughter to escape the hail of bullets. A cyclist was hit in the back just below my balcony, and brave strangers helped lift the wounded man onto the straw mat of a pedicab."

Wong watched, wrote and sent her dispatches to her newspaper. Trained as an economics reporter and sent to China to cover the growing business between China and Canada, Wong suddenly found herself in the middle of bloody tumult—tanks and heavily armed troops mowing down unarmed civilians. It was, she says, "a massacre."

After the students were routed from the square, the government relentlessly sought out the leaders and all of those who dared to criticize the government. These people were arrested, tortured for names of the leaders of the democracy movement and imprisoned.

Although she was under surveillance, Wong also looked for these dissidents for interviews, and some searched her out so that their stories could be heard. They wanted the world to know they would not give up, though they would have to go into hiding for a time. They sought out Wong to send the message.

In the accompanying photograph, Wong is interviewing Gao Xin, a teacher who took part in the hunger strike. Gao was arrested, tortured, jailed without charge and then released.

A 10-Alarm Fire

Next, we dart back to the United States, over to Boston where Lauren Thierry is in the master control room of WBZ-TV 4. She is watching videotape of a huge fire in nearby Revere. She is preparing the newscast she will anchor.

"After seeing just three or four minutes of this blaze, I knew the video would carry the horror of this firestorm," she said later. "But I also wanted the words to be compelling, to make people come closer to the set and crank up the volume."

Thierry writes her lead:

> The worst fire in his 35 years of fire fighting. That's how one Revere fire official is describing the inferno that is burning out of control in a four-block radius in Revere at this hour.

As the screen shows the fire filmed from a helicopter, Thierry picks up the account:

Park Rendezvous

To avoid wiretaps and to be able to spot inquisitive authorities, Jan Wong set up her interview with a Chinese dissident in a public park. The men and women working for a democratic China sought out Wong so that she could tell the world that despite intimidation, jail and torture, the democratic movement was alive. *Mark Avery*

No Shortcuts

Lauren Thierry spent six years at five different stations before reaching Boston. Along the way, she says, everyone had an opinion of her work, sometimes flattering sometimes critical. "I took no shortcuts to get here, and I can live with that," she says. *Jerry Margolycz*

> The Revere fire inspector says this fire now has gone to ten alarms . . . and that fire companies from as far away as western Massachusetts and New Hampshire are en route to help douse the flames.

The distinguishing feature of most of the newspapers and stations in the United States is their emphasis on local news. Unlike the newspapers in most nations of the world, which are national newspapers, our printed press is highly local, as are most of our stations.

Inside a Newsroom

If we could look in one of the 1,600-plus daily newspapers a few hours before press time, we might notice telephones ringing as reporters call in to speak to the city editor about their stories, teletype machines disgorging reams of AP and UPI copy. We could also see copy editors at their terminals, removing the word *felt* and inserting the word *said,* writing a headline for a page-one story about a fatal accident.

The news editor is chatting with the managing editor about a weather story out of Florida, and reporters are working at their terminals, looking up at the screen now and then to see whether the lead is just right.

A police siren pierces the evening's stillness outside, and soon the wail of an ambulance is heard. No one pays attention.

A Fatal Accident

The phone on the city editor's desk rings. The police reporter is calling from the police station. "Bad accident at an intersection with the bypass," he says. "You want me to get out there or cover from here? They think two people have been killed."

The city editor tells the reporter to sit tight, that with the rain-slick roads and the fog there may be other accidents. The editor doesn't want the reporter to lose touch with police headquarters for a while.

"Try to get a fix on it," the editor says. "If it's as bad as you say, I think you'd better get out there. I'm sending a photographer anyway."

For the next half-hour, the police reporter monitors the police radio. At the same time, he goes through the notes he has taken from police reports. He spots a burglary at the First Baptist Church. He recalls that he has notes somewhere in his pad about the theft of religious scrolls from a synagogue on Maple Avenue. He decides he will put the two thefts into one story. He makes a mental note to call the lieutenant to ask whether the same people could have been involved in both burglaries.

At City Hall

Three blocks away in city hall, another reporter is walking into the city council chambers. He greets the city clerk.

"Should be a good meeting tonight, Alice," he says. "The appeal on the zoning decision on Hale's will bring them out. I'm glad you gave me the background on that one."

He turns to chat with the manager of Hale's Department Store, who has entered the room with the store's lawyer. The reporter wants more background on Hale's plans to build a large store in a residential area.

An Obituary

In the newsroom, a young reporter is bent over several sheets of paper, copies of obituary notices from the advertising department. One of the notices is about the death of a retired school principal who had taught in local schools for 30 years and had been a principal for 13 years. She probably has many former students in town, the reporter thinks. She decides to obtain more information about the woman.

A telephone call interrupts her thoughts. The caller is the president of the United Way. He has the results of the fund drive just completed.

"We worked all day getting the field reports together, and I'm glad to say we've set a record," he says. The reporter asks how much was raised, what accounted for the record donations. Did any particular organization or event raise an unusually large amount of money? The questions continue.

In a corner of the newsroom, the news editor is looking over some wire service stories.

A Hurricane and Canned Tuna

"Hurricane expected to hit Florida," he tells the managing editor. "People boarding up. Worst in a decade, they think." The managing editor tells him to blend the AP and UPI stories. It could run on page one, he says. It's a good story because many local people have friends and relatives who have moved to Florida.

"Here's a piece that will interest the earth-first people," the news editor says. "StarKist is announcing it won't buy any tuna from fishermen who take dolphins in their nets." The managing editor nods. "Yep. We ran a piece a few months ago about local school kids writing the company protesting about the dolphins."

The city editor chimes in. "We gave it a good ride. I have a press release from StarKist that quotes the president of the company as saying that letters from school children made a difference. Let's localize the story."

Approaching Deadline

Not all the information and news being gathered will be used. The police reporter has had reports of two more accidents, and he knows that he will have little time to write up the minor burglaries, break-ins and arrests from his notes. He knows that he will have to spend the few hours before deadline on the accidents, rounding them up into a single story, probably for page one.

The reporter handling the obituaries has learned that a fund drive is being planned to raise money for a memorial scholarship in honor of the retired school principal who has just died. The scholarship will be called the *Rose Harriet Allen Memorial Scholarship,* and some of the city's leading citizens—her former students—are serving on the committee to raise money.

The reporter intends to interview these people, not only about their plans to raise money, but also about their recollections of their school days in Allen's classroom.

She looks at a batch of notes she has taken for several other obituaries. She will have little time for the calls she planned to make for additional material for some of them. Obituaries are among the newspaper's most-read items, she knows, and readers want the full stories on the deceased. If she can, she will spend time on the other obituaries once she has finished the Allen story. She will have to work at twice her usual pace, which is already twice as fast as she thought she'd work when she studied journalism in college.

On the Copy Desk

Over there, eyes intent on the screens before them, sit the copy editors, the men and women whose task is to insert commas, delete adjectives and help some helpless writer teetering on the edge of making a fool of himself in print.

Let's listen in as a copy editor reads some material and talks to herself as she edits:

"The house, on the corner of 4th Street . . ." Oh, oh. This guy won't use the stylebook; better read this copy carefully. Make it Fourth Street. Man's name is spelled Fehrback in the second graf and Fehrbach in the fifth. Send this story back. A mess.

"The principal's remarks brings the usual cheers. . . ." Remarks . . . brings . . . What kind of grammar is this? Zip off that s in brings.

"His expenditures for office supplies. . . ." Come on. Use everyday language. Make expenditures expenses.

"They set off for the factory in the morning, about 6 a.m." Extra words. Let's get rid of in the morning.

"Alot." One word? Are you kidding? A lot, pal. And this one: "Studies effect grades, she said." Affect grades.

This is a real lulu. Obviously, this reporter hasn't the foggiest idea of what he's writing about. Says the judge gave the defendant a 37-year-sentence. Period. Our policy is to talk about time served, and it's usually about a third of the sentence. So this guy, who's killed his girlfriend and her three children and her mother's companion, will get out of prison when he's 40-years-old. Ah, here in the last graf it says there was a "plea agreement." Let's make it plea bargain. But what was the original charge? And what was the bargain they struck? From murder to manslaughter? Questions, questions. Better send it back.

"About 1 percent of the 105 stores . . ." Come on. One percent of 105 is one, isn't it? Let's make that sentence begin "One store . . .".

"He trudged down the hallway to the director's door." Ah. Like that verb. Really shows the actor is weary, maybe even worried about what he'll find inside. Keeps the reader moving.

"Emil Ho and her children . . . . The Ho's . . ." Let's get with it, pal. The plural of Ho is Hos. At lunch I'll ask him if he makes the plural of dog into dog's.

Chapter One

"Harding, the grandson of black *migrant workers who . . ."* What's race doing here in this obit? Violates our policy.

We leave our friendly copy editor as she starts working on a headline for the obituary of Vincent Harding.

The Cartoonist

At another desk, an editor is making up Thursday's editorial page. He is looking at the syndicated cartoon for the page. He turns to a colleague. "He's in his 80's and still as tough as nails," the editor says. "I like what someone said about Herblock, that when he sits—" He reaches over for a clipping and reads: "When he sits down to his drawing board, his mind turns to the rascals, the phonies and the frauds."

And he shows his coworker another slip of paper, this a quote by Herbert Lawrence Block, the cartoonist known the world over as Herblock: "There's always somebody trying to do something, or somebody just not doing something when they ought to." Herblock describes himself as an "equal-opportunity" satirist. Of his work, often criticized as too relentlessly critical of presidents, he says, "It's not as if the person temporarily occupying the White House is some kind of holy icon."

Herblock has a thoughtful pen. He reads several daily newspapers and the news magazines, talks to reporters and has three assistants as fact checkers. "He's an absolute stickler for accuracy," says an aide.

Herblock began his career as a high school newspaper cartoonist and along the way has picked up three Pulitzer Prizes and the enmity of Presidents Johnson and Nixon and a multitude of senators, representatives and public figures, many of whom would have subjected him to the horsewhip if they could.

Getting Back   In some countries, that's precisely what happens to cartoonists too critical of their leaders or national customs. In Saudi Arabia, when *The Arab News* ran a "B.C." strip that authorities there considered as questioning the existence of God, the official reaction was swift: The features editor was sentenced to two years in prison and 500 lashes and the editor-in-chief one year and 300 lashes. An international furor led to a reduction of the sentences.

They were lucky. An Iranian cartoonist, whose drawing of a soccer player was seen as resembling the late Ayatollah Khomeini, received 50 lashes and 10 years in prison.

Getting There   Making it as a cartoonist is difficult, says Jerry King, who was a prizewinning college cartoonist at Ohio State University with ambitions to be a political cartoonist. He has had to move sideways in his career.

"Newspapers are relying on syndicates to provide cartoons," he says. "And a syndicate won't hire a cartoonist unless he's been with a newspaper."

King turned to greeting cards, children's books and free-lance cartooning. His first cartoon book was sold widely.

Prizewinner

Jerry King's college cartoons won awards. After graduation he became a freelance cartoonist, greeting card artist and author of children's books.

Syndicated

Marshall Ramsey moved from college cartoons to work on a Texas newspaper. His cartoons attracted the interest of other papers and he is now syndicated nationally.

Bob Tur

"Students who want to work in journalism must do three things," King says. "First, study, study, study and get a degree. Second, intern at a paper or station for the experience. Third, work at a paper, even if you work for nothing, just to gain the experience."

Marshall Ramsey, another prizewinning college cartoonist, did manage to make it to a newspaper. Ramsey, who drew biting cartoons as an undergraduate at the University of Tennessee and then as an art student at Kennesaw State College in Marietta, Ga., is an editorial cartoonist with the Copley News Service.

His first newspaper job was with *The Conroe Courier* in Texas where he also designed advertisements, helped with the editorial page design, created maps and graphics and worked on the newspaper's promotional campaigns.

Ramsey's work with the small Texas newspaper caught the eyes of editors at *The New York Times,* who selected some of his cartoons for reproduction in their Sunday roundup of cartoonists. It also attracted the Copley News Service editors who have syndicated Ramsey's drawings.

Helicopter Newsman

Next, out to southern California to watch Bob Tur, a helicopter newsman. After eight years as a ground-bound journalist, he decided to take to the skies, not a bad idea for covering news in spread-out Los Angeles, which has been described as seven suburbs in search of a city.

Looking for O.J.

It's late afternoon and Bob and his wife Marika, who has worked as a police reporter in Los Angeles and who handles the video camera from the helicopter, are at home trying to figure out the biggest puzzle of the day in what will develop into the biggest news event of the week, perhaps of the year: The search for O. J. Simpson whose ex-wife and a male friend were found brutally murdered.

Simpson, the former football star turned actor and television huckster, is wanted by the police. Tur knows that KCBS-TV, one of the major clients of his Los Angeles News Service, will want footage of Simpson's capture. "We've got to find him," Tur tells his wife.

They decide to put themselves in Simpson's place. "Where would we go if we were him?" Suddenly, the idea hits them. "The cemetery." The cemetery where his ex-wife is buried.

The Turs take off, but the police have staked out the cemetery and they turn the chopper away. As they do, there he is, Simpson in his white Bronco on the freeway, police squad cars trailing him. "So we flip on the switch and we're live," Tur says.

Maybe it's luck. Probably not. Tur knows his stuff, having been at it since 1983 when he founded the helicopter news service. "It's like the Wild West," he says, "with the police chasing cars, and the guys hanging out the windows shooting at them." Tur says he's covered 128 police pursuits.

This isn't the first time the couple has been at the center of a national news story.

A Street Corner Beating

After four white police officers were acquitted in a state trial of the beating of black motorist Rodney King in 1992, sections of Los Angeles erupted. Angry blacks and Hispanics took to the streets, and in the opening moments of the riots a group of black men noticed a white truck driver stopped at an intersection.

They pulled him from his gravel truck and began to beat him. One hurled a brick that hit the driver, Reginald Denny, in the face. One of them stomped on Denny's head, and another shot him in the leg. The men then proceeded to go through Denny's pockets as he lay dazed and bleeding.

Above this scene, which *Time* later called "the mirror-image replay of the King beating," the Turs and Robert E. Clark, a photographer for *The Outlook* of Santa Monica, Calif., circled in a helicopter. They came in closer. Bullets grazed the aircraft. Clark recalled his experience in Vietnam; he was aware of what bullets can do to human flesh. He unfastened his safety belt and placed himself behind Marika Tur, which allowed her to videotape the scene. Clark also continued to photograph the action.

Although Tur pleaded on his radio for the police to come and rescue Denny, none arrived. Tur radioed for "someone, anyone to please rescue this man from being killed below us." Four black men suddenly appeared at Normandie and Florence. They rushed Denny to a hospital.

"Doctors later said that if they had gotten him to the hospital even a few minutes later, he would have died," Clark said.

For his coverage of the Denny beating, Tur was awarded an Emmy and the Edward R. Murrow Award.

Newsletters, Desktop Publishing

Most journalists head for the tried and true—jobs at newspapers, magazines, the wire services, radio and television stations, advertising and public relations agencies. Yet other opportunities beckon.

Newsletter journalism is a fast-growing field of specialized publications. These subscription newsletters are a world apart from the PTA or church bulletins and the house organs of organizations. They cover areas of special concern to subscribers—the aerospace industry, education, medicare, public broadcasting, electronic communications. More than 4,000 newsletters are published, some daily, some less frequently. Subscribers pay from $600 to $4,000 a year and expect high-quality reporting.

The style is the same as newspaper writing, but it is more detailed, more analytical. David Baumann, a senior reporter for *Education Daily,* has investigated such subjects as the U.S. Education Department's failure to collect on millions of

The Beating of Reginald Denny

Robert E. Clark, The Outlook, Santa Monica, Calif.

Desktop Publishers

dollars in student loans, and Carol Sardinha has covered Medicare fraud for *Medicare Compliance Alert.*

Desktop publishing has attracted journalists who like the idea of handling their own enterprises, from graphics to writing in a vast variety of forms—posters, book jackets, brochures, newsletters, advertisements. They produce the material on the computer with various software programs. Service bureaus then take the output and generate the final product. A growing number of magazines use the technology, as does *USA Today.*

Jennifer and Donald Schwartz, who operate Imagelink out of Brooklyn, are recent entrepreneurs. Jennifer does the artwork and Donald handles the photography. They share an optimism with others in the field, and as the technology improves and costs decline they believe major publications will turn to DTP, as the process is known.

Eugene Barnes of the Allen Press Inc. in Lawrence, Kan., says, "For the first time, the tools required for typesetting, pasteup, illustration, layout, etc. are actually affordable.

"A desktop computer, laser printer and the required software to do the job cost roughly a tenth of what a former 'professional' system would have cost." Barnes puts the cost as low as $4,000 to $5,000.

Many of those who work at desktop publishing do so from their homes, as do Jennifer and Donald. So do free-lancers. Let's drop in on the Chicago home of one of the many media writers who free-lance, selling articles and other media work to a variety of clients.

Free-Lancing

Leslie Whitaker is sitting at her desk in an office whose windows overlook her garden. "It took six years at *Time*'s New York headquarters," she says, "before I was given an office with a window."

Whitaker tired of the life of a working mother in New York where she had to take her son in his stroller on the subway to the day-care center, take another subway to work, put in a full day, reverse the process and then cook dinner upon arriving at home.

After graduation from journalism school, Whitaker went to *Time,* and the years she put in there helped her to obtain the background and the contacts necessary for successful free-lancing. It was difficult at first, she says. "As a business person, you begin to think in quarters of the year. My first quarter as a free-lancer I made only $800. But it went up rapidly from there."

She does free-lance work for public relations firms, writes a weekly column for the real estate section of the *Chicago Tribune* and handles assignments for the Chicago *Time* bureau.

Her varied assignments while in New York with *Time* have given her the expertise to write for national publications: golfing for *Newsweek,* grandparenting for *McCall*'s, religion for *Modern Maturity,* and luxury real estate selling for *Selling.* She also is the co-author of a book on personal finance.

Her advice to those thinking of free-lancing: "It's ideal if you are experienced, disciplined and organized. And instead of slaving for one boss, you work for many clients. But at least you have some say about the hours you work and who those clients are."

The Dividing Line

Most of the journalists we have been watching work one side of the vast arena of media activity. They are the fact gatherers, the information purveyors. Their code of objectivity requires that they tell their stories without injecting their opinions.

On another side is a different group, the dispensers of judgments and opinions—the critics and reviewers, the columnists and the editorial writers.

The line that divides these two groups is a distinguishing characteristic of journalism in the United States, Canada and a few other western nations. Walter Lippmann, a columnist for 35 years and the author of important books about government and the forming of opinion, describes this division as an "old rule." The rule is that "reporters collect the news, which consists of facts, and that the editorial page then utters opinions approving or disapproving these facts."

Lippmann praises this separation, which he says is "the news writer's Bill of Rights." He continues:

> It encourages not only the energetic reporting of facts but also the honest search for the truth to which these facts belong. It imposes restraints upon owners and editors. It authorizes resistance, indeed in honor it calls for resistance, to the contamination of the news by special prejudices and by special interests.
>
> It proclaims the corporate opposition of our whole profession to the prostitution of the press by political parties and by political, economic and ideological pressure groups, and by social climbers and by adventurers on the make.

Now let's cross this dividing line to look over the shoulders of some of the reviewers, columnists and editorial writers. Later on, we will venture into the realm of the persuaders, where people like the writer of the billboard advertisement toil and the public relations specialists are at work. First, to the critics and reviewers.

Criticism and Reviews

Movies, books, TV series, plays, exhibits, albums, concerts, clothing and restaurants. Sylvester Stallone's latest, the new hemline from Paris and the addition of a salad bar to the menu of a national fast food chain. All are subjected to the scrutiny and the evaluation of a critic or a reviewer from a newspaper, magazine or broadcast station.

Reviewers are consumer reporters. They tell us whether we should spend our time and money on a product. Some reviewers carry tremendous power. A negative review by *The New York Times* theater critic can shut down a multimillion dollar musical in two weeks. A positive review in *The New Yorker* can put a book on the best-seller list.

A review has two parts: basic information about a work (straight reporting) and the reviewer's assessment (the criticism). The reviewer tells us whether the book is fiction or non-fiction, describes the plot or the area covered and gives us some background about the author's previous work.

"Like all good journalism," says Barbara Shulgasser of the *San Francisco Examiner,* "a review is based on a set of non-negotiable necessities. Any review starts with solid reporting. A critic is expected to get the basics right—the names of the actors, the director and the writer and the details of the plot.

"But similarities between criticism and straight reporting end there. The critic is biased, a subjective creature." But the reviewer cannot offer only offhand opinion. "A reviewer has to make a case," she says.

A solid case is made through the reviewer's knowledge of the field, clear, authoritative writing and proof in the review that the critic's standards are valid.

There is an underlying ethic for the critic, says Shulgasser. "The best the reviewer can do is to be honest with himself," she says. "Once he writes to be quoted in newspaper advertisements or to be revered as a visionary by future scholars, or to be loved by readers and the artists in the community, he'll never be more than an unreliable resource to those who read him."

Two Duds

Let's join Shulgasser at her keyboard in the *San Francisco Examiner* newsroom just after she has watched a couple of movies, neither of which impressed her. One, a documentary about New York City's underside, shows a nightclub performer biting the heads off white mice. "He reportedly has to have a tetanus shot after each performance," she writes. "Electroshock might be more appropriate." She reluctantly grants the film one star on her scale of one to four.

Shulgasser was even less impressed by the other film on which she bestows half a star. The female lead, she writes, is "an aspiring rock-star type girl, IQ approximately room temperature on a winter day, when the heat isn't working. . . ."

Shulgasser recently swapped seats for the other side of the movie camera: She and Robert Altman coauthored a movie, "Ready to Wear" ("Prêt-à-Porter"). She later wrote a piece about the making of the movie for *Vanity Fair.*

The Dean Speaks Out

Critics and reviewers are anxious to praise, but they do not hesitate to condemn the silly, the stupid and the exploitative. They pay a price for their criticism, though. Fans do not like their heroes and favorites slammed. Listen to Pauline Kael, often described as the dean of American film critics, as she summed up almost 25 years work at *The New Yorker:*

> I write assertively. I hate people who pussyfoot. I do it knowingly and people who disagree with me are absolutely enraged. They jump on me. The mail I got after "Dances with Wolves" (she wrote that Kevin Costner had feathers in his hair and feathers in his head) would bring a blush to your cheeks. . . . But I don't write like a little mouse, so I have to expect it. I take pride in my perceptions and statements.

Here are some of her judgments: "Tim Robbins is brilliant and not yet recognized. Michael Keaton is very exciting. Paul Newman, Sidney Poitier and Sean Connery have aged magnificently." She also likes Nicholas Cage, Jessica Lange, John Cusack, Debra Winger, Denzel Washington, Diane Keaton, Wesley Snipes, Sigourney Weaver, Keanu Reeves, Anjelica Huston, Kurt Russell, Michelle Pfeiffer and Tom Hanks, whom she describes as first rank.

The Columnists

If reader interest can be measured by the volume of mail and telephone calls, then columnists probably would finish first or close to the top. When the syndicated columnist Heloise asked her readers if anyone knew how to make a chocolate-sauerkraut cake, 5,000 recipes poured into the King Features Syndicate office.

Usually, it's the columnists' comments on social and political issues that arouse responses. William Raspberry says he was overwhelmed by the response to his column suggesting that white leaders should have expressed greater outrage at the verdict that cleared the officers who beat Rodney King.

In the Pew

Religion spurs many reactions, and an outspoken column by Bill Tammeus of *The Kansas City Star* about a plane crash stimulated some to thoughtful comments. Tammeus wrote that the people who had survived the crash and said that

God saved them were wrong, that plane crashes are caused by human factors, not God. What kind of God, he asked, would allow some people to die and others to survive?

Sara Engram of the Baltimore *Evening Sun* wrote in her syndicated column about the anti-Semitism of some famous Christian theologians. She received a variety of mail, from "long, scholarly letters" disagreeing with her to "hate mail from anti-Semites coming out of the woodwork."

On the Playing Field

Like Pauline Kael, Jim Murray does not hesitate to speak his mind. His vehicle is his sports column. Murray's columns for the *Los Angeles Times* won a Pulitzer Prize for commentary, a prize rarely awarded to sports writers; the Prize usually goes to commentators on national and international topics.

One of Murray's most famous columns is said to have cost the Alabama football team a trip to the Rose Bowl. Murray wrote that a team that would not allow black athletes to play should not be invited to play against UCLA's racially mixed team.

"So Alabama is the national champion," he wrote. "National champions of what, the Confederacy? This team hasn't poked its head above the Mason-Dixon Line since Appomattox."

Opinion makers not only tell us what they think; they also try to persuade us to act on their opinions: Don't waste your money on this book, that album, this bummer of a movie. Let's practice democracy on the playing field. Vote yes on the bond issue.

Sometimes they are successful. Just as often, people are deaf to their pleas and suggestions.

At the Police Station

Getting behind the badge is one of the toughest jobs for a reporter. Police are notoriously closemouthed, and they adhere to a chain of command as rigid as the army's. Cops don't talk. That's rule No. 1 on the force.

It's Leonard Levitt's job to break the code of silence for his *New York Newsday* column "One Police Plaza Confidential." And with old-fashioned digging journalism he succeeds most of the time.

"You have to know the turf, the players, the nuances so that you can speak boldly, with authority, as I have to use a lot of material without attribution," Levitt says. Levitt spent several years covering police and the courts, building up contacts and background.

Levitt has revealed that a top brass remarked that it's all right "to slap around" drug dealers, that a $50,000-a-year detective who made the jump to a $87,600 post as deputy commissioner had swung the police department's Hispanic Society to support the candidacy of the man elected mayor, that a police precinct was riddled with corruption—cops stole the money, guns and drugs of the drug dealers they investigated and then shared their loot with their sergeant.

On the Editorial Page

In his office just off the newsroom of *The Times-News* in Twin Falls, Idaho, Stephen Hartgen is going over an editorial to be published before Twin Falls residents vote on a big school bond issue. From the outset, Hartgen, publisher of the 22,000-circulation daily, knew he was waging an uphill battle.

Persuading people to pay higher taxes to finance the proposed $20 million high school would not be easy. Nevertheless, Hartgen, an activist publisher, devoted considerable news and editorial space to the issue. He ran scores of letters to the editor on the subject. Some writers complained that Hartgen had no business as a publisher serving on the school bond planning committee. But Hartgen did not apologize for supporting the bond issue on his editorial page and in the community.

"How can I criticize those who don't take part in community issues if I don't?" he asked.

Hartgen's editorial page does not run from controversial issues. "The town is accustomed to our taking a position on issues—strong on gun control, pro-choice on abortion, tough on the teachers' union."

This outspokenness angers many. After one editorial critical of a local congressman, a reader dropped a package on Hartgen's desk. "This," he told the publisher, "has the same ingredient as your editorial." Hartgen gingerly opened the package and reached in—it was a cow patty.

While reporter Kirk Mitchell wrote two or three stories a week about the school bond proposal—one story gave the total cost as $39 million, the result of interest added to the bond issue—Hartgen and his editor pumped out editorials pegged to the community's future. An improved educational system, one editorial stated, "turns out graduates better prepared to enter the work force." To those who said the 6.6 percent tax increase was too much and the large new school should be scaled down, the newspaper responded, "A new school should be like a child's new winter coat: Frugal parents buy one with room for growth."

Two days before the vote, an editorial declared, "It's an investment not only in your kids but in our community's economic health. Well-educated graduates are vital to any town's economic development. . . .

"We urge a yes vote on Tuesday."

The people decided otherwise. They rejected the proposal 2 to 1.

Hartgen was undaunted. He called in his editorial for continued work to remedy school overcrowding and asked opponents of the bond issue to serve "on the roster for the next citizen committee." Here's how the editorial concluded:

> For our part, we pledge to aid in the process by providing thorough news coverage of the debate—and by occasionally putting in our editorial two cents.
> What about you? What will your contribution be?

Stephen Hartgen

Overwhelming Defeat

Some Other Persuaders

Let's look in on some others who are engaged in the business of persuasion. First, we'll walk to the other side of *The Times-News* offices where the advertising department is located. Then we'll look in on some public relations practitioners.

In the Advertising Department

Jean Herrick is working on a display advertisement for a local home furnishing store. Herrick, an advertising representative for the newspaper, has discussed the idea for the ad with the store's advertising manager and has a good grasp of what the manager wants the ad to show.

The design she is finishing is a **spec,** so-called because it is speculative, subject to the advertiser's approval. Also known as a **rough,** the spec will be shown to the manager, Herrick says, and he will make additions if he wishes.

Designing an Advertisement

Advertising representative Jean Herrick goes over ideas for an advertisement with the advertising manager of a local home furnishings store.

The Finished Product

She and the newspaper's advertising designer came up with this conservative design for Mother's Day.

The salespeople and the designers are working on other ads, blending words and illustrations to inform and persuade readers. A Radio Shack ad features savings: "Save $400. $599.95. Reg. $999.95. Low as $20 a month."

The IGA attracts the sweet-toothed with a come-on: M&Ms and Mars candy bars are priced "3 for 99¢." Some ads suggest gift ideas. Mother's Day is approaching and Venzon Jewelry advises "a strand of pearls" for mom, a "pottery plate" for grandma and an "Idaho T-shirt" for auntie.

At the far end of the advertising department, several people are working on the newspaper's new section, "Ag Weekly," a tabloid-size insert targeted to farmers, ranchers, suppliers and others involved with the region's agricultural economy.

"We never had a separate publication devoted to agriculture," says Janet L. Taylor, the paper's advertising sales manager. To find out whether the idea was sound, the newspaper conducted considerable research. A dozen focus groups consisting of possible readers and advertisers were set up.

The newspaper concluded there would be sufficient advertising to justify publication, and a pilot edition was issued. It looked good and the "Ag Weekly" was off and running.

Up in the Air

That billboard our motorist saw a few pages back was for Hardee's, a fast-food chain. Here's Pat Fagan, the creative director for Keller Crescent Co. of Evansville, Ind., explaining how he created this outdoor advertisement:

> To increase traffic in Hardee's drive-through lanes, and to take advantage of the fact that competitive fast-food restaurants offer notoriously slow service, we created this board.

Keller Crescent Co.

Eye-Grabber

To catch the passing motorist's eye the graphic must be compelling, the message brief.

> The headline is short and to the point: Fast drive-thru. A hole was cut in the actual board to appear as though a driver took the message literally and drove his/her car through the board.
> This visual reinforcement of our message has real stopping power.

So much for the objectives and the realization of the advertisement. Has it been effective?

> Use of the drive-thru lane at Hardee's has increased dramatically. After four years the billboard is still being used. It is moved bimonthly from one location to another.

At a PR Agency

Back in New York, Terrie Williams was coaxing the musician Miles Davis to pose for an advertisement for a large clothing store. Williams, who was Davis' publicist, told him that the advertisement, which would appear when Davis' new album and book were introduced, would help sales.

"Wear a T-shirt with your bad jacket and bad leather pants," she told him. "It'll be fine."

Williams, president and founder of The Terrie Williams Agency at 60th Street and Broadway, runs what she calls a "full service public relations agency." She handles sports and entertainment clients such as Willie Stargell and Eddie Murphy.

Williams is an enthusiast, and her enthusiasm is contagious. She persuaded world-famous trumpeter Wynton Marsalis to play taps for the reinterment of 19 black soldiers although he had begged off, saying that the piece made him nervous.

"Wynton, Wynton, Wynton. You could do it. This is for your forefathers who died in the Civil War."

Terrie Williams

Williams snagged her first client, Eddie Murphy, by mailing him a set of ideas. He was impressed. "My sensibility as a woman has had a great impact on how I interact with people," she says.

The Underpinning

From the $1,000 for a 30-second spot on ABC's "Good Morning America" to the $1 million-plus for a commercial during the Super Bowl, the $325 for a 6½ inch deep advertisement that runs across the width of a page of the "Ag Weekly" and the $120,000 it takes to buy a page in *Sports Illustrated*—the revenue generated by advertising is the major support for the commercial media in the United States and Canada.

In most other countries, the government supports the major broadcast networks. Many newspapers are subsidized by government, unions and political parties. But in the United States advertising wholly supports commercial radio and television, makes up four-fifths of the income of newspapers and provides half of magazine income.

Even the college press in the United States has come to rely on advertising revenue. A third of all college and university newspapers receive more than half their finances from advertising. Rates range from $1 to $8 a column inch. A third have total annual revenues of more than $100,000, and several take in more than $1 million a year.

The increasing reliance of the mass media on the advertiser rather than on users or on special interests is a plus to some observers. But to others this dependence has altered the media's performance for the worse. Leo Bogart, a former advertising executive become public opinion specialist, says that the advertising underpinning of the media "means that the people who manage most media enterprises have, for many years, regarded advertisers, rather than the public, as their clients. . . . The structure and content of the media system is profoundly affected, if not actively controlled, by the judgments and practices of advertisers whose interest in media structure is entirely instrumental and pragmatic."

When Dan Rather was negotiating a contract with CBS, some executives balked at the multimillion dollar offer to the newsman. Then one who favored the deal wrote on a scrap of paper: "1 point = $5 million." The brief note, passed to other executives, meant that a loss of one point in the evening news ratings would result in a loss of $5 million in profits from advertisers. The deal was clinched.

Reporting

Reporting, says writer Tom Wolfe, "is the heart of everything." Informing, entertaining or persuading—whether done by reporters, columnists, reviewers or advertising copywriters—begins with information gathering, the assembling of factual material.

Jerry F. Dhonau, who has written editorials for several papers, says, "Editorial writers are like reporters. They rely on facts and fact-gathering, just like reporters. But then they carry the exercise an additional step or two, and this is what sets them apart."

"The opinion that an editorial writer expresses is enriched by background reading and experience that set the facts in perspective."

Proving Your Point

Though they differ in purpose, all of those who offer information to the public follow the same commandment: Prove your point.

The news story, for example, consists of two parts: the lead, which briefly summarizes the event, and the body of the story, which documents and buttresses the point made in the lead.

The review and the editorial also must prove their points, buttress their judgments and opinions. "A review offers a point of view," says Shulgasser, "but the reviewer has to make his case, prove his point."

Interview

Almost three-fourths of the material that journalists use in their work comes from interviews of the sort Ellen Perlman is conducting here with the mayor of Charlotte, N.C., for a profile. *Roy Karten*

The advertising copywriter who tries to persuade us to buy Dockers, donate to the United Way or vote for Sen. Ted Kennedy moves us to action with facts, not just clever phrase-making. Show me, says the reader. Prove your case, says the viewer.

Collecting Information

A wide variety of fact-gathering techniques makes up the business of reporting. Most reporting is a combination of interview, observation and research. The story of last night's basketball game, for example, includes the reporter's observation of the game, comments from players based on locker-room interviews and a check of standings and averages.

The interview is probably the most frequently used fact-gathering tool— employed by everyone from the entertainment reporter for *The Des Moines Register* profiling Prince to Jean Herrick talking to the manager of Cain's about its advertisement for next week.

Fact gathering also involves using clippings, references such as *Who's Who in America,* documents and data bases. What people see on television commercials and look at in their newspapers and magazines is the result of considerable research.

Levi's and Taco Bell, for example, decided on the basis of research findings to switch from the quick cuts and loud music of MTV-type commercials to storytelling. So did Budweiser, Mars candy and Procter & Gamble. Research told them that people remember more from a storytelling spot than from the tumult of an MTV-type commercial. Later, Taco Bell went back to the MTV format.

Not all fact gathering is easy going. Sometimes the material is buried, and sources are reluctant to reveal it. When Heidi Evans of the *Daily News* tried to find out what had happened to 2,000 Pap smears taken by the New York City Health Department, she ran into blank walls. With persistence, she discovered that the tests had been ignored for as long as a year, leaving hundreds of women at high risk of developing cervical cancer. Evans' reporting led to resignations and reforms. It also resulted in Evans winning a number of awards for her thorough, persevering journalism.

The Journalistic Process

We have been looking over the shoulders of a few of the 250,000 people who work for the 1,600 daily and 7,000 weekly newspapers, 10,000 radio and television stations and the other organizations and enterprises associated with informing the public through the mass media.

Veterans and novices, reviewers and reporters, copywriters and television anchors—they all follow the same process:

Information gathering—Observations, interviews, research.
Verifying—Checking to see that information is accurate, complete and relevant.
Planning—Plotting the story, editorial, review, advertisement, news release, spot, layout.

Writing—Putting the pieces together in a form that is interesting, clear and succinct.

Production—Fitting the final work into the whole—the newspaper, the broadcast, the video release.

In brief, this process consists of information gathering, information processing and information dissemination.

Writing isn't the easiest way to make a living. One of the great sports writers, Red Smith, once remarked, "Sure, writing is easy. You just sit at a typewriter until beads of blood form on your forehead."

That's the agony. But there is the ecstasy of telling others that you witnessed this event, spoke to those people, had such and such an experience. Everyone wants to be someone, to create an identity. We see initials carved on trees and park benches, pictures painted on cave walls, a palm print embedded in cement.

Writing is also a way to exercise power, and in journalism that power can be used to positive ends. We have seen some examples in this chapter of public service journalism. The mastery of language gives writers access to power.

Before we go into any more detail about the ways to make words do our bidding, let's take a closer look at journalists. We will next examine the traits and characteristics they have in common and the skills they are expected to have when they begin their careers.

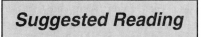

Suggested Reading

Commission on Freedom of the Press. *A Free and Responsible Press.* Chicago: University of Chicago Press, 1947.

Garcia, Mario. *Contemporary Newspaper Design . . . A Structural Approach,* 3d ed., Englewood Cliffs, N.J.: Prentice Hall, 1993.

Halberstam, David. *The Powers That Be.* New York: Alfred A. Knopf, 1979.

Kroeger, Brooke. *Nellie Bly. Daredevil, Reporter, Feminist.* New York: Times Books/Random House, 1994.

Lippmann, Walter. *Public Opinion.* New Brunswick, N.J.: Transaction Pubs., 1965.

Mayer, Martin. *About Television.* New York: Harper & Row, 1972.

Morris, Joe Alex. *Deadline Every Minute: The Story of the United Press.* New York: Doubleday, 1957.

Pierce, Robert N. *A Sacred Trust. Nelson Poynter and The St. Petersburg Times.* Gainesville, Fla.: University Press of Florida, 1994.

Swanberg, W.A. *Citizen Hearst.* New York: Charles Scribner's Sons, 1961.

Swanberg, W.A. *Pulitzer.* New York: Charles Scribner's Sons, 1967.

2 The Journalist: Traits and Characteristics

Media writers develop the ability to extract information from diverse sources: a witness to a kidnapping, an officer at an accident scene, people in a focus group. *Michael Lipack*

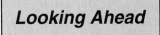

Looking Ahead

Journalists are committed to accuracy, fair play and the balanced and honest presentation of what they learn in their fact gathering. Whenever possible, they try to see events for themselves rather than rely on the accounts of others. Among the traits journalists share are curiosity, independence, creativity, skepticism and a commitment to helping people by offering them reliable information.

The Curious Sophomore

A Boston University sophomore, Nick Gage, was struck by one of the scenes in a new biography of the American playwright Eugene O'Neill. O'Neill is dying and he instructs his wife to burn the unfinished manuscripts of his plays in the fireplace of their Boston hotel room.

Gage knew that the hotel O'Neill lived in had become a student dormitory. What does the room look like now? he wondered. He decided to walk across the campus to find out. "To my surprise," he recalled later, "there was no evidence of a fireplace in the room. Out of curiosity, I looked up the blueprints of the building dating from its construction. Sure enough, there was no fireplace."

Gage, who was a reporter for his college newspaper, wrote a piece about his discovery. The authors of the biography heard about Gage's article and called him. Then they called O'Neill's widow, who said that on second thought she might have burned the manuscripts in the basement furnace. The authors corrected the book in its next edition.

Gage said he was "bitten by the investigative bug." After working for several newspapers, he sought a job with *The New York Times*. The man who interviewed and hired Gage was Arthur Gelb, then metropolitan editor of the *Times* and the coauthor, with his wife, of the O'Neill biography Gage had read and corrected.

You might say that what made Gage a natural for journalism was his curiosity plus a sense for what is new, interesting and different—in short, news sense.

A Dog's Tale

Journalists often find that curiosity pays off with good stories. What interests reporters usually interests readers and listeners. No good journalist could pass up this handbill on the wall of a parking garage:

Missing Dog

$50 Reward

Three Legs	Blind in Left Eye
Right Ear Missing	Broken Tail

Answers to the Name Lucky

Did the owner ever find Lucky, and how could one dog be the repository of such varied misfortunes? The answers to the reporter's questions would make a good story.

Writers also share various interests and concerns with their readers. They both want the same questions answered. Call it the feel for the public pulse or simply a commonality of interest. Whatever the description, the result is work that appeals to people.

Speed the Plow The snow was piling up around Washington, D.C. Carol Nation, who was handling public information for the Department of Public Works in Arlington County, Va., was curious: How does the county handle a snowstorm? A picture story would be informative. She decided to accompany a snowplow clearing roads.

"We had gone only a few miles from the equipment yard," she says, "when we were stranded on Columbia Pike, a heavily traveled corridor. There were so many cars stuck and stranded and spinning that we sat on that road for more than an hour. We couldn't get free to plow any streets because we were hemmed in. This was happening all over the area."

Instantly, Nation had an idea for a brochure that would be distributed to the public. The message would be simple: Stay home during a snowstorm so that snowfighters can do their job.

Seems obvious. So obvious no public works department had thought of it. But after Nation's brochure was designed and distributed, it became a model for similar information brochures throughout the United States and Canada.

On the Scene   Notice that Gage's discovery of the error in the O'Neill biography and Nation's widely copied brochure were the result of direct observation. Gage and Nation saw for themselves.

During the Vietnam War, a young reporter for a wire service sent out a story based on an Army press release. His story of a successful engagement by U.S. troops was played on page one of *The New York Times,* to the dismay of the paper's Vietnam correspondent, Homer Bigart.

Bigart had seen the actual situation. He knew the release was dead wrong. Bigart took the young reporter to the front and showed him. "That's what I wanted you to see—it isn't here," he said.

During the Persian Gulf War, most journalists were kept away from the front. The few who were allowed to go went in pools under the direction of service personnel. This rigid control over reporting led to press complaints that the public had no independent source of information about the war. The press presumed, no doubt accurately, that the armed forces still blamed the revelations of an independent press for U.S. withdrawal from Vietnam. The government wanted no interference this time.

Independence

The public has come to rely on the press as a counterweight to power, whether of government or commerce. This balancing role of the press was intended by those who wrote the Bill of Rights and established press freedom in the First Amendment. An independent press, they reasoned, would speak for the public, against concentrations of power.

Journalists understand that they serve best when they represent the public. One way to look at the tension between power and the press that the First Amendment deliberately establishes is to see the press as having an agenda of its own, a public agenda, distinct from the particular agendas of those it covers.

At a news conference, the speaker presents points that constitute his or her agenda. The reporters then ask questions from agendas they have established, agendas independently made of the issues they consider important.

The mayor's news is his appointment of a school superintendent and the decision to initiate a recycling program for home waste. Fine, say the reporters, dutifully taking notes. Then they ask him what he intends to do about the growing number of homeless people on the streets and how he responds to the governor's assertion that the city won't balance its budget unless it cuts the city payroll by 20 percent.

Implicit in the relationship between the press and power is the press's skepticism, a conviction that officials sometimes are unwilling to be open with the public, that they will put the best gloss they can on their actions.

Human progress can be described as the result of the interplay of authority and skepticism. Columbus and Magellan; Copernicus, Newton and Einstein; Beethoven and Rembrandt; Frederick Douglass, Susan B. Anthony and Martin Luther King Jr.—each ventured forth independently, skeptical of the established ways, and each forged new paths.

Skepticism

When Gerald Ford found himself in the presidency after the Watergate scandals, Washington reporters were concerned that he was not intellectually fit for the position. When their concern became manifest, Ford denied that he was too dumb to be president. He said he had finished in the upper third of his class. Whereupon reporters asked that he show them his college transcript.

In the best of worlds, everyone would be forthright, honest, aboveboard. But the stakes are so high, the prizes so great in politics and the marketplace that deception and lying are sometimes standard procedure for those in power.

When Chrysler was accused of selling as new the automobiles that its executives had been driving, the president of the corporation, Lee Iacocca, denied the charge. The media carried his vehement denial. A few days later, Chrysler admitted that it had been turning back the odometers on these cars.

Reporters learn to have faith in physical sources—their observations and the documents and records they dig up. They learn to be wary of human sources, but often they must use such sources for documentation and verification, for usually there is little time in the rush to print or to broadcast. They protect themselves by attributing material, but reporters know that readers and listeners tend to accept what they read and hear without making distinctions between what is attributed to a source and what is true.

Generally, reporters ignore material they know to be untrue, or they hold it until it can be verified. Some material can never be checked: Records are sealed or do not exist; the people involved will not comment. In those cases, the reporters' feel for news, their news sense, takes over.

Skeptics. Lyndon Johnson, no sweetheart of the press, once remarked that if one day he walked on top of the water across the Potomac River the headline would read, President Can't Swim.

Reporters talk about a *feeling* that something is wrong, unsound, incorrect. They have a gut reaction or a sixth sense that tells them to check, to ask some questions, to look again at the information.

When confronted by information that seems questionable, the standard procedure for the reporter is to ask the source for proof. If none is forthcoming, the reporter says so in the story.

Savvy

Some journalists say that the essential requirement for a young man or woman considering a career in journalism is savvy, by which they mean the combination of knowledge and street smarts, skepticism and judgment. No small order.

Knowledge

Since journalism consists of explaining events and ideas, the journalist must understand the material before it can be put into a story, review, release or advertisement. When a city council member says a proposed tax is regressive, the reporter knows at once that the councilwoman considers the tax injurious to those with low and moderate incomes.

If the campus security chief refuses to divulge information about a campus crime or supply data about total crimes on campus last year, the journalist knows that the chief cannot close his records, that he is acting illegally. The education reporter knows that any school that receives federal aid for students is required by law to provide graduation rates.

Spinach Computing   The advertiser who wants to say he has lowered the prices on canned tomatoes and spinach has to be asked if the presale and postsale cans are the same size. If there's no reply, the journalist has to do the figuring.

Figure it out with this can of spinach:

Old can—13 ounces; price 79 cents.
New can—11 ounces; price 75 cents.

The advertiser can rightly claim, "Save 4 cents a can." But the sharp advertising representative knows that the savvy reporter in town will jump on the advertiser. So she tells the advertiser, "Look, at 13 ounces for 79 cents, it cost the buyer 6.08 cents an ounce." (That's 79 cents divided by 13 ounces and rounded off.) "The new price is 75 cents divided by 11 ounces or 8.18 cents an ounce. The customer is paying more, not less."

Everyone is happy now. The advertiser because he's been saved from humiliation and the ad rep because she's cemented relations with her advertiser. Almost everyone but the reporter who missed a good story because of the ad rep's savvy.

Street Smarts

The woman cried bitterly. Her boy had disappeared the day before, she said on the evening television news. The child had wandered off while the mother and her boyfriend were shopping in a department store. It was a dramatic story. Too dramatic for Marcia Chambers of *The New York Times*. "The woman was too controlled, too ready to tell her story."

Chambers went to the precinct that was investigating the disappearance and asked the detective in charge, "Is her boyfriend a suspect?" A pause. The detective had no idea who had tipped off the reporter. Yes, he said, the child's body had been found badly burned in a lot near the family apartment and the boyfriend was a suspect.

It was no tip. Street smarts.

Skepticism figured in the reporter's calculations as well. Sad to say, reporters know that people are capable of unimaginable deeds.

It's hard to ask the 22-year-old starting a career to have the judgment of the veteran. Yet without the ability to make sound evaluations and lacking the shrewdness and intuition that journalists are supposed to have in abundance— without these, the journalist cannot tell the momentous from the minute, the manipulator from the crusader, the false article from the genuine.

Integrity

Journalists are faithful to the facts, whatever the consequences. When Dan Rather was covering the Nixon administration for CBS television, he was under enormous pressure to let up on his dogged coverage of the president.

He said later that the White House had a "journalistic goon squad" that pressured reporters who did not accept at face value the pronouncements from the president's office.

"If a truck runs over me tomorrow," he said once, "what I really would love to have someone tell my kids is that their father wouldn't buckle—not under Lyndon Johnson, not under Richard Nixon."

During the uprising of the Shiites in Iraq following the Gulf War, Salah Nasrawi of the AP filed a report on the destruction of the Shiite holy city of Karbala. He reported the damage that had been inflicted by Iraq's artillery and tanks. Iraqi censors ordered him to change his report, to blame the damage on allied bombing during the war.

He refused and Iraqi officials revoked his credentials, closed the AP office and took the AP's satellite phone.

Desecrated Bodies

In Somalia, Paul Watson of *The Toronto Star* was told the Pentagon was denying that the bodies of U.S. troops killed in Mogadishu were being mutilated by Somalis. He knew differently. He had seen the charred flesh and teeth being

Powerful Image

This photograph by Paul Watson of *The Toronto Star* ran on the front pages of many leading newspapers despite its horrifying nature. For this picture, Watson was awarded the Pulitzer Prize for spot news photography in 1994. *Paul Watson, The Toronto Star*

Holding Back. When Robert Kennedy was in Oregon on the campaign trail, Gail Sheehy was assigned to do a piece on his presidential campaign for *New York* magazine. "The day before my deadline," she recalls, "Kennedy was assassinated. That was my baptism. I had to become a professional at that moment.

"Overcome with personal as well as patriotic grief, I was writing through my tears, learning to be on deadline and do the job."

held like trophies after a U.S. helicopter was shot down. Next time, the photographer vowed, he would have the pictures to prove what he knew. And he did.

After two more helicopters were shot down, Watson saw the body of a U.S. soldier being pulled through the streets. He started to take pictures. The crowd grew hostile. He continued to shoot.

"If they wanted revenge," he said later, "I was it." But they left him alone, and his photographs became the subject of intense debate when they were published. Some newspapers refused to print them. Watson, who had covered Africa for four years for the newspaper, was awarded the Pulitzer Prize for photography for his graphic shots.

"If they were my soldiers," he says, "and I were back home, I'd sure as hell want to know about it so I could do something about it."

Public pressure caused the government to pull out the U.S. troops.

Honesty with Sources   Journalists often deal with people unaccustomed to being interviewed, people unwary of the ways some journalists have of extracting information. In her interviews for her series on abandoned infants, Sheryl James of the *St. Petersburg Times* said one of the most difficult aspects of reporting was "dealing with good but somewhat unsophisticated people who would have been easy to manipulate. It was a challenge to be sure they understood what I was doing and to keep promises made during the reporting process that I could have broken with impunity." Her reporting for the story, she says, was an ethical test for her.

Honesty with Language   The honest portrayal of reality extends to the use of language. News stories can be no more exciting—through the manipulation of words—than the event itself. The journalist matches language to the event. If the meeting of the city council was routine, the news writer does not try to dramatize it with hyperactive prose.

Composure

However knowledgeable, however talented, unless the writer can meet deadlines, he or she is of little use. The deadline is an absolute demand on the journalist. For the wire service reporter, there is a deadline every minute. As Lindy Washburn was writing her fire story, she was aware that some newspapers were readying their front pages for the press.

Sometimes deadlines can be devastating. "I do not know of one single reporter who likes covering the World Series any more," says Edwin Pope, the sports editor of *The Miami Herald.* Games start at night, some as late as 8:30, in order to sell commercial spots on television. When a game runs long, there is little time between its completion and the deadlines of morning newspapers in the East.

"It drove us to our knees," said George Solomon, the assistant managing editor for sports at *The Washington Post,* of one Series. Late starts and late endings had the sports staff pressed to the edge.

Chapter Two

Meeting the Deadline

Journalists move to the speed of the clock's second hand. When a woman tried to hold up a bank in Tallahassee, reporters and photographers were on the scene right after the arrival of law enforcement officers. The woman was captured outside the bank.
Phil Sears, Tallahassee Democrat

In the rush to make its deadline, *The Plain Dealer* in Cleveland, Ohio, ran this headline for a Sox-Mets Series game:

**Red Sox Win,
Take Series**

The headline should have read:

**Red Sox Win,
Take Series Lead**

But such blunders are rare. Journalists manage to do the job despite deadline pressures. Baseball or board meeting, profile or police drug raid, news release or advertising video release—there is always a deadline.

Leg warmers and Mohawk haircuts, drooping pants and caps turned backwards, feminism and careerism. Some become short-lived fads, and others develop into powerful movements. Media writers are able to discern the new and different as they go about their work. What's the subject of this campus petition? Are people excited about it, or is it of interest only to a few?

There are calmer moments, though. And when the writer has time, he or she puts it to good use by enterprising news and feature stories. The city hall reporter will do a feature on the mayor's hobby of raising roses. The education reporter will profile a day-care center volunteer worker, and the county courthouse reporter will interview a judge about his campaign for court reforms.

Creativity, Ingenuity

"Now and then the breaking news will save us from dullness and make the paper worth a quarter," says James K. Batten, president of the Knight-Ridder newspaper chain. "But most days it won't. And it's got to be our creativity, or ingenuity, especially on the typical slow days, that makes the paper so compelling, so indispensable. . . ."

Curiosity begets creativity.

"I was an inquisitive child and was constantly reprimanded for prying into the personal lives of visitors who stopped at our home," recalls Helen Thomas, senior White House correspondent for the United Press International. Thomas once asked what flavor of Jell-O Ronald Reagan had eaten during his hospitalization after he was shot in an assassination attempt.

Studies of creative people show that high IQ is not the only factor in creative work. While intelligence plays a part, imagination, perseverance and zeal are just as important. Creative people are hard workers.

In journalism, we say that the reporter who is creative and who shows ingenuity is a self-starter. This reporter does not have to wait for assignments but generates ideas on his or her own. The reporter who sees stories on her way to work, while chatting with a secretary on his beat, or on chance encounters in elevators, on the street and in lunchrooms—that reporter has a future.

Jim Dwyer found stories while riding the New York City subway. He found so many he became *Newsday*'s underground correspondent. He interviewed a subway platform guitarist, who told him, "People say, 'You got a million dollar voice; what you doing in the subway?' I got a wife and daughter, and I can put food on the table. I'm not rich. I know I been blessed, and I put my best foot forward." Dwyer catches the small scenes—a 4-year-old waves to a transit police officer, who salutes the child in return. Little boys still wave at police officers, the officer says. "It happens a lot. I like it."

Spotting Trends   One of the ways in which journalists show their ingenuity is by spotting trends, the undercurrents that create news. Take the growing interest in religion. Baby boomers—those born between 1946 and 1964—are taking an interest in religion that is more intense than that of their parents. Why? How is it manifesting itself? Are the baby boomers flocking to the charismatic and Pentecostal sects or staying with the mainline denominations?

Sheryl James says of her Pulitzer Prize-winning series, "A Gift Abandoned": "For more than a year, there had been a tragic trend, it seemed, of mothers abandoning babies in South Florida. It seemed a natural idea to pursue one of these cases." She told the story of a woman who left her newborn boy in a box near a dumpster in a Tampa suburb.

Looking for Ideas   Media writers develop story ideas by examining the concerns and interests of people. Here are some current concerns:

Health care—The U.S. is 25th in the world in its infant mortality rate. AIDS, alcohol and drugs have caused massive health problems in the inner city. People are living longer and require a greater share of an already overstretched tax-supported health program. Who is getting or deserves priority?

Family life—Since the 1950s, the number of women in the work force has more than tripled to 60 million. Today, 60 percent of women with children under 6 work outside the home. Seven percent of U.S. households include an at-home mother and a father who is the sole wage earner. Almost 2 million unmarried couples live together. Each year, there are some 1.2 million divorces involving 1 million children. Some groups want to toughen divorce laws. A fourth of all children under 18 live with a single parent; for black children, the figure is 60 percent. Half of those 18 to 24 live at home with parents, and 23 million Americans live alone.

Education—The lowest scoring students in a national test came from low-income homes with single parents. People believe that something is seriously wrong with the U.S. educational system: High schools graduate semiliterates; few students study science, mathematics or foreign languages. Only one of seven eighth graders in the U.S. is proficient in eighth-grade mathematics. Increasingly, the middle class sends its children to private schools with the subsequent loss of interest in the public schools by those traditionally most committed to its success. Educators are being asked to take on tasks usually assigned to the family, and, at the same time, taxpayers are rebelling at having to pay education bills.

Money—Everyone worries about it; no one seems to have quite enough, and some have none. Do people who make $100,000 or $500,000 a year pay their fair share of taxes? A fifth of all children grow up in poverty; teen-age pregnancy and out-of-wedlock births are common among some segments of society, the result, it is said, of the culture of poverty. On a larger scale, the U.S. economy is moving from manufacturing to services; white collar jobholders now outnumber blue collar workers.

Racism—Despite the civil rights movement, despite laws, despite education, racism is pervasive and may be increasing. Why is this so, and what are the consequences?

These seem to be enormous issues, too complicated for the journalist given two minutes on the evening news or 750 words in the newspaper to tackle them. Actually, it is not difficult to put these topics in human terms, to find individuals and groups that illustrate trends and developments.

For a story about poverty, find a family trying to get through the month on a working mother's slim paycheck or a welfare payment. What does the family eat?

Enterprise. When reporters converged on Washington for the funeral of President John Kennedy, one reporter separated himself from the pack. Jimmy Breslin of the *Daily News* went to Arlington National Cemetery and interviewed the gravedigger. His story about the man's sadness did a better job of summing up the nation's mourning than the other reporters' coverage of the funeral procession.

No to TV. The top 10 states in a national academic test were also the 10 states with the smallest percentage of students who reported watching television more than six hours a night.

Perseverance

When last we looked in on Lauren Thierry, a television journalist, she was covering a 10-alarm fire for a station in Boston. Now with the syndicated TV news program "American Journal" in New York, she is waiting outside a federal courthouse on Long Island, hoping to interview an assistant U.S. attorney.

But Thierry is not having luck. The prosecutor has eluded her and her crew. And now an official tells them to leave. They refuse, and the official urges the police and federal marshals to arrest Thierry. Suddenly, he shouts at Thierry: "I am telling you that if I am on film I'll sue your balls off." Thierry replies, "I don't happen to have any, but I'm holding on just fine anyway." She and the crew took their pictures.

Sometimes, coverage of an event requires more than hanging on for a few hours in the face of obstacles. Thomas French of the *St. Petersburg Times* spent a year at Largo High School for his series on the lives of students.

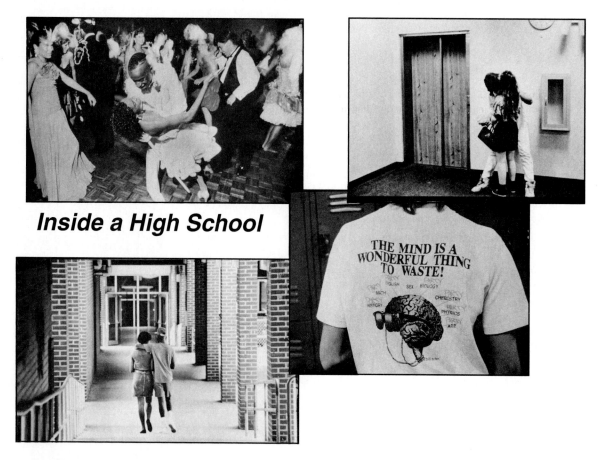

Inside a High School

Tom French, 33 and greying, stuck out at Largo High School. Gradually, they accepted him. "I wore my Nikes and stayed away from ties," he said. "Many students talked about intimate details of their lives." *Maurice Rivenbark, St. Petersburg Times*

The story, told in seven parts, described youths sporting gold jewelry and carrying beepers; a bright senior translating Cicero in Latin class; a group of young women talking about their visits to an abortion clinic; boys who have never known their fathers; youngsters with demanding, disciplining parents. The students' cars "pack monster stereos with up to 1000 watts, and what they're booming with these days is 2 Live Crew." The series later became a book.

Another extensive reporting project was carried out by staffers of *The Commercial Appeal* of Memphis. The newspaper sent two reporters and a photographer to Tunica, Miss., which had been described by Jesse Jackson as "America's Ethiopia," a symbol of poverty in the United States.

Two of the journalists were white: Jeff McAdory, the photographer, who was born in Mississippi, and Kevin Kittredge, who had been covering Tunica as part of his beat. The other reporter was Celeste Williams, a black woman born in New York City, graduated from high school in Detroit and from Ball State University in Muncie, Ind.

Arrival in Tunica

Here is Williams' first entry in her diary:

Arrived in Tunica. Felt a strange sensation in my gut, resembling what I feel when stepping into a darkened room—a strange sense of the unknown, maybe dread. Another strange feeling—leaving Memphis only 30 or so miles behind, yet feeling I have been planted in a foreign country. While unloading the car, three young folks—one young man, two young women—stopped in the street next to the house we were renting.

The young man—I think Derrick was his name—sucked on a straw dipped into his soft drink cup and grinned openly and warmly, while the girls stood to one side and smiled more shyly. Derrick said he was a senior at Rosa Fort. He said he wanted to get a good job, maybe start a construction company and rebuild houses in Tunica. I looked at the houses around him. I remembered Sugar Ditch. I wished him well.

The reporters looked at all the indicators of community life in the poorest county in the United States:

Income—The leading source of income is government assistance, welfare for most. Median household income, $6,620. U.S. median household income, $17,710.

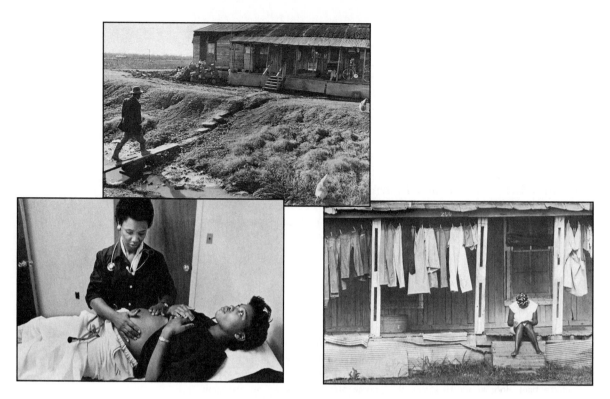

America's Ethiopia

One of the poorest communities in the country, Tunica became a symbol of the nation's underclass. Its residents had to cross an open sewage ditch to get to their homes; the infant mortality rate was three times that for white infants; income was a third of the national average. *Jeff McAdory, The Commercial Appeal*

Education—Still segregated—not by law, but by residence.

Health—The infant mortality rate among blacks is 31 deaths per 1,000 live births; among whites 11. The reasons—poverty and ignorance. Teen-age pregnancy is common.

"Teen-agers who get pregnant here are overwhelmingly black, poor and unmarried; they do not seek out available family planning information, and they wait months for prenatal care," writes Williams. " 'I've seen and heard everything,' says a health worker. But she admits, 'Twelve-year-olds delivering babies still throws me.' "

Employment—"Forty-five of every 100 families are officially in poverty. Almost all the poor people are black."

Politics—In a county with a 73 percent black population, whites are in the majority in all city and county boards but the county election commission. One article quotes a professor of history at the University of Mississippi: "As long as you've got an economically dependent population, then you're always vulnerable to at least informal, unspoken or unrecognized pressures if you start to exercise your political rights."

Cool Reception   The news team found that most blacks were glad to see them, but whites in official positions declined to be interviewed. The officials complained that previous news reports had stirred up trouble.

Nevertheless, the reporters were able to dig deeply into the separate worlds of white and black. They interviewed well-to-do whites and teen-agers with two and three children, and they went to church:

Let us pray.

The Rev. Holmes looks familiar: short, mustache, receding hairline, brow furrowed in perpetual concern. Still, I can't place him. I interrupt his Sunday school lesson at the African Methodist Episcopal Church, slipping in the back door about 10:45; at the front of the room are Rev. Holmes and Brother Peace—a plump black man with a sonorous voice. Rev. Holmes smiles a greeting nervously, smelling reporter.

I take a seat by Jeff and Celeste in the second row. The first two or three pews are half-filled with small children and a few adults—mostly female. The girl's choir, The Sunbeams, is already seated behind the pulpit for 11 o'clock service.

We are asked to introduce ourselves—Celeste warned me this would happen.

Jeff stands up, smiling.

"Good morning. My name is Jeff McAdory, I'm visiting in Tunica and I'm happy to be able to worship with you here on this fine Lord's Day."

That's a tough act to follow. When my turn comes I just say my name.

Services start. They sing a lot—three songs right off the bat. The church is still only half full, but the singers aren't timid and the songs come off good and strong. An enormous woman in front of me sings a low harmony, while Mrs. Grant, the funeral director's wife, adds a fine soprano.

During Rev. Holmes' sermon he adopts a sing-song style of speaking I've never heard before, though Celeste says it's common in black churches. A sentence begins on a relatively high note, then drops a third at the final syllable—gaining resonance throughout and trembling with vibrato. It is like an impromptu song.

At the end of the service nearly everyone there seeks us out to shake hands and say "hello."

I leave feeling fine.

—Kevin Kittredge

The Results   Press attention helped. The shacks that many blacks lived in were replaced, the open ditch that carried off human waste along Sugar Ditch Alley cleared. The improvements were personalized through the experiences of Tunica residents:

TUNICA, Miss.—Christine Bell's struggle to keep enough wood burning in a stove to warm her and her three children ended yesterday when the door opened to her new apartment at a housing project here. . . .

For some families, such as Andrew Jones and his wife, the new apartment means running water for the first time in 12 years. For others, such as Doris Moore and her 10-year-old son Adrian, it means the first living quarters they can call their own. . . .

Perseverance

From 1945 to 1947, a highly radioactive substance was injected into the veins of 18 people in an experiment to determine the effects of plutonium on the body. None of the people was informed of the nature of the experiment in what an official of a research group describes as "one of the great, dark stories of the nuclear era." Eileen Welsome of *The Albuquerque Tribune* spent seven years digging into the story. Her work was recognized with a Pulitzer Prize for national reporting and a summons to Washington to testify about the experiment and the government cover-up. *Scripps Howard News*

Commitment

Some people become journalists because they have a strong urge to reveal injustices, to change what to them seem dangerous or harmful situations. These people practice an activist journalism. They strive to move beyond the reporting of the actions and statements of the newsworthy to underlying causes and consequences.

Clearly, this was the thrust of the work by the staff members of *The Commercial Appeal.* The need to reveal hidden realities also motivates Tim Weiner of the Washington bureau of *The New York Times,* and it sends Lena H. Sun of *The Washington Post* out to interview those who, despite threats of jail, torture and worse, seek democracy for China.

Lena H. Sun

A Career of Exposés

"Our job—my job, as I see it, anyway—is not to entertain people," says Weiner, "but to explain complicated phenomena in clear language, to give people an understanding of unseen political and economic forces affecting their lives."

Not for the Money

Why do young men and women seek out careers in journalism? Not for big bucks. Few make it to the top tier of television and million-dollar salaries. From the time journalists take their first jobs to the period of maximum income, their salaries are on the low side of the professions.

Entry-level salaries in print range from $16,500 to $30,000 and in television from $15,500 to $35,000, depending on the size of the medium and the market. Experienced people in all media fields can earn as much as $100,000 in the larger cities, which is what most other professionals make after only a year or two in practice.

Weiner always had a hankering for the story under the surface. He began his career after journalism school with coverage of the federal court in New York City where, he says, "every issue imaginable winds up. The courts provide a continuing education in human folly. Moreover, they are the greatest repository of public records you can use to write eye-popping investigative and analytic stories."

He went on to *The Kansas City Times,* and when a new hotel collapsed, he was a major player on an investigative team that looked into the disaster that killed 114 people. "We dug into the rubble to discover the cost-cutting, shoddy work and corporate greed that had caused the collapse," he says. For the articles the *Times* won a Pulitzer Prize.

Explanatory Stories   Then he moved to *The Philadelphia Inquirer* where, under Gene Roberts, he continued to dig. "Roberts wanted stories that explained why the city's housing was falling apart, the ways in which the cops and the courts were corrupted, how the public schools failed to teach their students, why the rich got richer and the poor got poorer—extraordinarily complex stories told simply and directly.

"They took months, and they involved thousands of documents and hundreds of interviews." Weiner quotes Roberts: "Great stories don't break—they ooze."

From the *Inquirer,* Weiner went to *The New York Times* where he covers the intelligence community and does investigative projects. "If government—which is almost entirely invisible to most Americans—is the force that fascinates you, then you'll want to wind up in Washington," he says. Weiner has written one book—about the covert spending by the Pentagon that amounted to $36 billion one year—and is at work on another, which is about a CIA agent who spied for the Soviet Union.

Weiner was able to interview the spy, Aldrich H. Ames, for the *Times,* and in one piece he describes how Ames' Soviet case officer worried that the CIA had discovered the mole in their employ. Ames told Weiner he didn't worry. If he were discovered, he told Weiner, there was nothing he could do. But he wasn't discovered, and for another seven years Ames informed his Communist paymasters. The results: hundreds of classified documents sent to Moscow and perhaps a dozen double agents who worked for the U.S. executed by Moscow.

Ames' only worry when he heard about the executions was that they would blow his cover.

Weiner says, "Two paths exist for a reporter. Be a stenographer and a courtier to politicians. Or dig down into the workings of the great machine and see what's really going on."

Piercing the Bamboo Curtain

The reporter's instinct to see what's really going on pushed Lena H. Sun during her stint in China as the correspondent there for *The Washington Post.* "Every day," she wrote in one of her stories that infuriated the authorities, "individuals are arrested and sentenced for political crimes and may even be tortured, in total obscurity."

Dictatorships prefer darkness, and one of China's darkest secrets is just what happened at Tiananmen Square on the night of June 3, 1989. Sun sought out a mother who defied government harassment to find out what had happened to her son and to the others who had died there. "I don't care how long it takes," Sun quotes her, "I want the real truth to be known. I want to know how many were killed by the government."

The government says it had to use the army to quell a counterrevolutionary rebellion, Sun writes. "The civilians killed were 'counterrevolutionary rebels,' 'thugs,' or 'rioters,' authorities have said." Here is how Sun's story, headlined "A Mother's Crusade," begins:

BEIJING—On that night five years ago this week, high school sophomore Jiang Jielian decided to go to Tiananmen Square one last time. There, Beijing's students had camped at the gates of political power, demanding democracy in the most serious challenge to 40 years of China's Communist Party rule.

On June 3, 1989, Beijing was under martial law. Authorities had warned residents to stay home. But Jiang, who had marched in peaceful protests for democracy all spring, was

Crusader

To Chinese officials, the civilians who were shot down at Tiananmen Square—mostly young men and women—were "thugs" and "rioters." But to Ding Zilin, whose 17-year-old son was killed during the demonstration for democracy,. they were idealists. Here she goes through envelopes containing funds donated to the families of those who were killed in the Square. *Lena H. Sun, The Washington Post*

worried about the safety of the university students still in the square.

His mother begged him not to go. She bolted the front door of their ground-floor apartment. But Jiang came to her, kissed her on the cheek and said goodbye, using a Chinese phrase that means farewell forever. He then locked himself in the bathroom and jumped out the window.

"I remember saying to him, 'What can you do? You're only a high school student,' " his mother recalled, fighting back tears. "He said, 'If all parents were as selfish as you, there would be no hope left for our country.' "

Sun is relentless. In another story, three days later, she reports that the authorities have cut off all contact with the parents of the slain high school student. The couple had planned to begin a hunger strike to protest harassment.

"It was unclear if the couple's telephone service had been cut off or if they might have been detained," she writes. Journalists were prevented from entering the university campus where the parents teach, and one reporter, Sun writes, had been detained by the police earlier in the week after she chatted with students.

She goes on to provide background about China's situation:

Although security in Beijing always tightens before the June 3 date of the Tiananmen massacre, authorities seem particularly uneasy this year. Because of widespread corruption, high inflation and discontent among peasants, laid-off workers and others on fixed incomes, authorities fear that even small commemorative events can spark wider protests.

Sun's reporting has so irritated the government that security officers burst into her home one day in 1992, interrogated her for three hours and went through her files.

Interviewing Dissidents   Throughout the years of her China assignment, Sun cultivated dissidents and profiled some of them. About one such story, she said, "The decisions that went into that story illustrate one of the biggest problems about being a foreign correspondent here. You are constantly weighing the story against getting a source into trouble."

She went with one dissident as he talked to people about the arbitrary actions of the police and party bosses. She pointed out that the work of 31-year-old Zhang Lin in going into the countryside "is a change from the abstract calls for democracy that characterized the student-led movement crushed by the Chinese army in Beijing's Tiananmen Square on June 4, 1989. For a ruling party that for decades called itself the dictatorship of the proletariat, the dissidents' focus on workers and peasants strikes at the heart of the party's grip on power."

Sun decided to use his name in her story. "Because he had been arrested before, and because he was very open about what he was doing, I decided to go ahead and use his name and picture. He became even more active after the profile appeared, traveling around to other provinces to recruit people for his organization."

Eventually, the authorities acted, and in a story two months after her description of the activist's work, Sun wrote that Zhang Lin had been arrested. One of his

Activist

Zhang Lin allowed reporters to use his name, despite the probability of retaliation by Chinese authorities. Zhang, who traveled widely to enlist people in his campaign for democratic reforms, was arrested often. *Lena H. Sun, The Washington Post*

so-called crimes was associating with foreign journalists. "Mr. Zhang," Sun wrote, "a nuclear physics graduate from Qinghua University in Beijing, has been jailed five times." The authorities also decided that Sun had been too inquisitive, too diligent about revealing the repressive nature of the regime. The government refused to extend her credentials for one week, which would have allowed her to properly hand over the bureau to her successor. She was instead given 48 hours to leave the country.

Native-American Concerns

For Bunty Anquoe, the Washington correspondent for the weekly *Indian Country Today,* her job is to serve a readership the regular press passes by.

"Our issues aren't seen as important by the mainstream press," she says, "but to us they're life and death." When she learned that the federal budget had cut funds for the Indian Housing Authority, of no interest to most Washington journalists, she pursued the story.

"As a Native American," she said, her job is "to explore topics and news issues that affect all the Indian tribes in this country." She also has the task of educating non-Indian readers "about the realities of Indian life in the 20th century," one of these realities being the "mascot-nickname issue." Her newspaper has been crusading against the use of nicknames such as Redskins, Chiefs and Braves and has had some success with high school and college teams.

The Copy Editor

Commitment takes other forms. One is to the work itself, a concern to see that it is done right and done well. This is one aspect of what drives the conscientious copy editor, says Merrill Perlman, who helps to recruit copy editors for *The New York Times.*

The copy editor, she says, is concerned with the reader, the reporter, the medium for which she or he is working and language and history.

Reader Perlman has seen newspapering from both sides of the copy desk. After graduating from journalism school, she spent four years as a reporter with the *Southern Illinoisan* in Carbondale, Ill., and then moved to desk work with *The Des Moines Register.* She later joined *The New York Times* financial section copy desk and worked her way up to chief of the newspaper's Metro copy desk.

Perlman says the copy editor has to think of all the questions a reader might ask and to make sure the story answers them, or at least doesn't ignore them or leave them dangling.

"The city council raised the water levy by 1 mill. What does that mean for my taxes?" The reporter must be able to convert bureaucratic language into understandable terms, she says, and she recalls ruefully her failure to do just that.

"It took me six months to realize that the 'early school leavers' program at the local school district I covered was aimed at dropouts, not the students who went home at 2 p.m.

Bunty Anquoe

"I didn't know, the copy editor didn't ask, and the reader was ill served."

Reporter   If her editor had been thinking, Perlman would have been spared humiliation. "This means thinking the way the reporter thinks," she says. "What was this sentence trying to say? How can I say it the way the reporter would say it? If this were MY story, would I want to know about the change made by the copy editor here?"

The copy editor "must forget about making HIS mark on the story," she adds. "Any marks he does make should leave no scars. The best editors can make extensive changes in a story and have the reporter thank them the next morning for not changing much."

Newspaper   The copy editor has to know "the paper's style and tone, and enforce it," Perlman continues. "Consistency may be the hobgoblin of little minds, but it is the signature of a good newspaper. How can the reader trust the paper if four different stories use four different spellings of Moammar Khadafi? If a paper is known for its high moral ground, should an editor point out the overly grisly details of this murder or the insensitive stereotyping of that ethnic group?"

Language   "This means understanding it, cherishing it, protecting it against intrusions by fads and jargon. Will most of our readers know what 'ergo' means? If not, either explain it or find another term."

History   "That sounds lofty and arrogant, but it means protecting the integrity of the stories we print. 'If in doubt, take it out' is an old advisory to copy editors. Leave in an interesting but unverifiable statement and risk it becoming fact."

To protect the reader and the newspaper from being victimized by errors, the copy editor has "to know everything, or at least know enough to know what she doesn't know. And she knows how to find it."

What should the copy editor know?

"Math to figure percentages.

"English to iron out awkward sentences.

"Psychology to coax and flatter untrusting reporters.

"Philosophy to be able to joke about it.

"The dirtiest mind, the thickest skin, the highest ethical and moral standards, the best sense of humor in the newsroom.

"The ability to work long hours, nights, weekends and holidays with little recognition. And to be proud of it because, unlike the reporter who's responsible for just one or two stories, the copy editor is responsible for the whole paper." And that, Perlman says, is what "makes it the most rewarding job in the newsroom."

Portrait of a Journalist

Harrison Salisbury's writing, reporting and editing career spanned more than 60 years following his graduation from the University of Minnesota in 1930. In summing up Salisbury's work that included 29 books, domestic and foreign coverage for the United Press and *The New York Times* and various editing posts with the *Times,* a colleague described him as "intrepid, enterprising and indefatigable." Another *Times* reporter said, "He had physical and moral courage, a wonderfully suspicious mind, a remarkable instinct for detecting falsehood, and a delight in exposing lies in print."

His managing editor, Turner Catledge, said: "He can report, he can write, he can see story ideas, he can direct others. He can do all these things because, besides having natural talent, he has a passion to excel."

Working for Change   To Phoebe Zerwick the fact that North Carolina had the highest infant mortality rate in the nation was more than a statistic. It was a spur to action that could save lives. She described conditions in the eastern part of the state where the mortality rate was the highest. She found "a legacy of poverty, inadequate health care and hopelessness." Her stories for the *Winston-Salem Journal* brought a major problem to the attention of the public and its officials.

For Steve Jenning, reporting was not enough. He wanted a more active part in bringing about change. After working for the Associated Press for several years, he sought out a career in government and became staff director of a congressional subcommittee.

His work enabled him to call attention to the hazards of dieting, the inadequacies of medical testing laboratories and the dangerous dumping of medical waste.

Jenning's public affairs work led to major stories in *The Washington Post, The New York Times* and *The Wall Street Journal,* and it resulted in corrective legislation.

Completeness

Not only do media workers persevere in their pursuit of information, they make sure to complete the cycle. That is, if a story leaves something up in the air, the journalist's job is to find the source and document the material that will round out the picture, answer questions still hanging.

This striving for completeness involves reporters, reviewers, editorial writers—all hands. When the *Contra Costa Times* reported that BART, the Bay Area subway line that takes suburban dwellers into San Francisco and Oakland, was thinking of charging parking fees in its garages, the newspaper decided its readers would want to know what the paper thought of the proposal.

Readers did not have long to wait. A few days after the page-one story, the editorial page had this headline over an editorial: "No parking fees at BART lots."

Photo Fallout

The *Times* editorial page also was used as a forum following the newspaper's publication of the photograph that showed the rescue of a kidnapped 12-year-old girl. She was clad only in socks. After the photo of the youngster was published, the phone calls swamped the switchboard and the letters flooded the mailroom.

Clayton Haswell, the executive editor, said about 150 readers objected. Here is a typical letter:

Appalling photo

I was shocked and appalled at the front-page photo on July 4. The girl is a minor and deserves privacy and protection. Think of the humiliation and embarrassment she will suffer, having to know her nudity was exposed to everyone in the entire circulation area of the Times.

To top it off, you quoted the accused attacker as if to redeem this fellow for his thoughtfulness. Boy, did he get the coverage he wanted.
Teri Hernandez
Bethel Island

Controversial Photo

Many readers objected to this page-one photograph of a kidnapped girl running across a field toward a police officer. They said the picture violated the child's privacy. *Greg Stidham, Contra Costa Times*

Divided Staff. When the photo of the nude child came across her desk, Marcia Parker, the ranking editor on duty, was asked to decide whether to publish it. She conferred with staffers. She said there "was an intense staff discussion, with the newsroom almost evenly divided."

She listened and then made her decision and informed the news editor, who agreed with her, as did the executive editor later. The newsroom discussion continued through the next day, with staffers again divided on use.

Editor's Defense   In an editorial page column a few days later, Haswell defended his decision to use the photograph. A few callers, he said, objected to the paper's running the story, but most were offended by the photograph. Haswell wrote:

We at the Times have a responsibility to report the news. We don't consider ourselves to have divine wisdom, but we work hard at trying to cover the issues and events that are important to our readers.

We cover lots of good news, and go out of our way to report on people who make a difference in their communities, and who are positive forces for change. . . .

But often the news isn't good. And we will not cover that up or try to make it go away. We endeavor to look at the news with honesty and sensitivity. Sometimes I think we get it right. Sometimes we don't.

Then he went on to explain how the newspaper reached its decision. The kidnapping, he wrote, was the biggest news event of the day in Northern California, "a matter of great public interest and importance." Such stories, he continued, are covered "without fail, even when they are unpleasant for our staff and readers."

The paper did not identify the child because of the "strong likelihood that sexual assault charges would be filed." And although her name was used widely by other media, Haswell said, the *Times* stood by its policy of not identifying the victims of sex crimes.

The *Times'* photographer took many photos. Some were "compelling, but unpublishable" because the girl could be identified and her nakedness was revealed.

Assistant Managing Editor Marcia Parker called me at home and advised that one of Stidham's (the photographer) images showed the girl at sufficient distance that she was not identifiable, and her nakedness was not visually evident. She had conferred with Assistant Managing Editor Bill Walter. Both felt the photo should be used.

I made the decision to publish.

. . . our job is to cover the news, and that is really what this was about. The story was of transcendent importance, and as journalists our responsibility is to cover such stories as diligently and thoroughly as possible. This includes photographic as well as written coverage. . . .

Stidham's photo was a powerful image. It told the story in a way that thousands of words could not. And we believe it did so in a responsible way.

We know that many of our readers disagree with our decision. We have heard them, and will reaffirm our continuing commitment to sensitivity and privacy issues as we do our job.

Rape Data: Real or Magnified?

When Sam Roe of *The Blade* in Toledo read rape statistics he was confused. At the same time the government's annual crime reports were showing that one of 1,300 women reported rape to police, organizations were circulating frightening figures: one in three or four, some said, and others put the figure at one in six or eight. What is the risk of rape?

Roe and Nara Schoenberg, another *Blade* reporter, set out to find out. It took them six months to do the job.

Their reporting ranged from Toledo to college campuses. The story had ramifications. Roe and Schoenberg understood that rape is a rallying cry for many women. On campuses, women have organized "Take Back the Night" marches to protest what they consider the lack of awareness of dangers faced by women and problems with law enforcement.

In Toledo, they learned that 43 percent of the rapes reported over a five-year period were of victims under the age of 18 and that 11 percent of rapes involved girls under 12. Minority women suffered disproportionately from rape.

Despite assertions that college women are especially vulnerable, FBI data showed few cases. The reporters discussed the varying definitions of rape and saw in this disparity the possibility of inflated figures.

Nationally, reported rape is on the rise, they learned. But it is hardly affecting one of eight, much less one of three, they found. Their conclusion: "A conservative estimate is that one in 50 women are affected."

The results: The nation's leading campus anti-rape campaign pulled its "one in six" posters and literature after Roe and Schoenberg pointed out the discrepancy in the figures. The series was quoted in newspapers and on network newsmagazine shows.

Christina Hoff Sommers, the author of *Who Stole Feminism? How Women Have Betrayed Women* (New York: Simon & Schuster, 1994), writes of the work of Roe and Schoenberg:

> The *Blade* story on rape is unique in contemporary journalism because the authors dared to question the popular feminist statistics on this terribly sensitive problem. But to my mind, the important and intriguing story they tell about unreliable advocacy statistics is overshadowed by the even more important discoveries they made about the morally indefensible way that public funds for combatting rape are being allocated. Schoenberg and Roe studied Toledo neighborhoods and calculated that women in the poorer areas were nearly thirty times more likely to be raped than those in the wealthy areas. They also found that campus rape rates were thirty times lower than the rape rates for the general population of eighteen- to twenty-four-year-olds in Toledo. The attention and the money are disproportionately going to those least at risk. According to the *Blade* reporters, ". . . the new spending comes at a time when community rape programs—also dependent on tax dollars—are desperately scrambling for money to help populations at much higher risk than college students."

Like Roe and Schoenburg, Berkley Hudson was determined to find the truth. Let's listen to him.

Twenty-Eight Years Behind Walls

Berkley Hudson is talking about a story that began one day in the newsroom of *The Providence Journal*. "This man had sneaked off the grounds of a state mental hospital, managed to get a bus and walked into the newspaper to tell his story."

Confined for 28 Years

Berkley Hudson interviews a man he believes has been unjustly held in a state mental institution. *Bob Thayer, The Providence Journal*

The man had spent five years in the state penitentiary and 23 in a state mental hospital for shooting his wife. Most people confined to such places believe they are unjustly confined but the more the man talked the more Hudson felt that his confinement was unjust.

Hudson decided to look into Chester Jefferds' story.

From examining hospital records and interviewing social workers and administrators at the hospital, Hudson concluded that neither justice nor compassion would be served by keeping Jefferds locked away.

"He doesn't belong here," a social worker told Hudson. That quote was underlined in Hudson's notes. It would have to go high up in the story. He remembered a point his journalism instructor had driven home relentlessly: Good quotes up high.

Hudson was angry about what he found, but he knew that the best way to write the story would be to let it tell itself. The indignation would have to come from the reader. Hudson would lay out the facts and let the readers reach their own conclusions. The reporting took two weeks.

"When I had all the information I thought I needed, I decided to start writing," Hudson says. He went into the office at 10 a.m. and looked over his notes carefully. As often happens, he discovered he needed additional details.

"At 2 o'clock I had organized my notes and was ready to write." With a few breaks, he wrote until about midnight. He spent another hour with the Sunday editor, going over the story, making some changes in the copy. His story begins on the next page.

He survived inside; now he'd like to be free

By BERKLEY HUDSON
Journal-Bulletin Staff Writer

CRANSTON — Chester G. Jefferds Jr. has survived 28 years in confinement. His face has deep, bold wrinkles. His hazel eyes are murky.

He spent five years in the state prison, then 23 more in the state mental hospital. He has seen other prisoners kill themselves — and sometimes each other. His was a world of beatings and rape, strait jackets and electroshock therapy, nurse's needles and attendants' pills.

Chester Jefferds learned how a man labeled crazy stays sane in a mental institution. You keep quiet. You try to forget why you're there. You don't listen to the moans and screams around you.

"You go through the alphabet, saying the letters over and over," he says. "You go through the fraction tables. 7 into 100. 8 into 100."

He has one tooth left. The rest he lost in fights. He has a raspy voice.

"There's only one way to go in this place," he·says. "You keep your mouth shut."

Those who know him call him Jeff. He is 68. It has been 28 years since he was sentenced to life imprisonment for shooting his wife to death. Now he would like his freedom.

★ ★ ★

"HE DOESN'T belong here," says David J. Arone, a social worker at the state General Hospital. "There's plenty of evidence Chester has been able to take care of himself."

Since 1973, psychiatrists, social workers and nurses have been saying what Arone says: Jefferds is not sick, mentally or physically.

The problem, Arone says, is that Jefferds is unique among the 1,400 patients at the medical center. Like others there, he is elderly and has been in a mental hospital for many years, yet he is no longer ill. What makes him different is that he is under a life sentence for murder.

"He's still here because if he weren't here, he'd be at the prison," says Frederick Young, chief of social services at the General Hospital. Jefferds, Young says, doesn't belong in prison either. Mental-health laws require the release of anyone who is not ill, but hospital officials believe that if he were released from the hospital, he would be required to go back to prison.

"Had he been at the prison all this time as a lifer, he'd probably be free now," Young says. . . .

Six weeks after Hudson's story appeared, the state parole board decided to allow Jefferds to leave the hospital for a halfway house. After three months there, he would be a free man. Hudson went to the hospital to watch Jefferds pack and he described Jefferds packing his belongings and leaving.

Chester Jefferds stood next to his suitcase. It had a rope for a handle. Inside, among his few possessions, was a card from a friend. It read, "Good luck in your new venture." . . .

During the last four years, the Parole Board reviewed his case on 10 occasions. Once, in August, 1977, the board approved his removal from the locked wards for the criminally insane, but it required him to continue living at the mental institution. . . .

Dependability, Initiative

Sent out on an assignment, the journalist works at it until it is fit for broadcast or print. The public depends on the journalist, as it does on all professionals, to do his or her best, whatever the circumstance.

The journalist shows initiative in generating story ideas and is relentless and enterprising in pursuing a story. A few months after his graduation from Notre Dame, Phil Cackley was hired by *The Albuquerque Tribune* and given the University of New Mexico beat.

"When I got the beat, I didn't expect any major stories to result from it," Cackley said. "My first story was about a student who hatched a duck from an orphan egg."

But Cackley was a self-starter and a digger. Within a few months, he found that grades were being faked for some athletes to maintain their eligibility.

Pinpoint Accuracy

The knowledge that people act on what they read and hear drives journalists to a high standard of accuracy. Journalists try to give people information they need to live happy, complete lives, information that will enable them to spend money wisely, live in harmony with their neighbors, attain their goals.

The review that says the rock concert at $25 a ticket was a ripoff; the news story that describes the platform of the candidate for governor; the editorial that urges a yes vote on the school bonds; the advertisement of the one-week sale of automobile tires—all these provide people with accurate, useful information. And since we all need to laugh to remain human in a world often cruel and inhuman, the feature story about Lucky, the three-legged, half-blind dog, helps us, too.

Accuracy is a function of unfettered observation. Writers view the passing scene with a detachment that helps them see clearly, objectively and without the blinders of bias, personal involvement or prejudgment.

Objectivity, Interpretation

This detachment by the journalist leads to what we call objectivity, and it is this ingredient of news stories that allows the reader to have the facts without the writer's opinions, feelings, and guesswork. Despite their involvement in the affairs of other people, journalists are able to distance themselves from the people and the events they are observing.

Gary Trudeau, the creator of the comic strip "Doonesbury," says that he is able to develop ideas for his work by being an outsider rather than by fraternizing with important people. Trudeau says he wants his work to represent the outsider looking at the activities of people, a journalistic approach.

The line between personal feelings and objectivity in the presentation of material is described by Walter Lippmann as an "old rule" in journalism. We read his comments about this in the preceding chapter. Lippmann came to understand that mere facts were insufficient "to fit the conditions of the modern age." He amended his Bill of Rights for journalists to include interpretive reporting, which, he said, allows the journalist to evaluate, appraise and deduce from the factual material.

Lippmann understood the dangers of such freedom for the journalist. He said that interpretation does not mean "fitting the facts to a dogma," and he described the process of interpretive journalism:

> It is by proposing theories or hypotheses which are then tested by trial and error. We put forward the most plausible interpretation we can think of, the most plausible picture into which the raw news fits, and then we wait to see whether the later news fits into the interpretation. We do well if with only a little amendment, with only a minor change of the interpretation, the later news fits into it. If the later events do not fit, if the later news knocks down the earlier story, there are two things to be done. One is to scrap the theory and the interpretation, which is what liberal, honest men do. The other is to distort or suppress the unmanageable piece of news.

Involvement

In their openness to new ideas and a variety of experiences, journalists encounter people of all kinds. Those who write for a living are committed to involvement in the affairs of all sorts of people, for without knowledge of the human dimension, no writing can reach the heart and mind. The reporter, the reviewer and the advertising copywriter compose in a vacuum unless they know the interests and tastes of the people they are trying to reach.

People are found in factories and service stations, supermarkets and laundromats, unemployment offices and executive suites, schoolrooms and kitchens. By seeking out people at work, at play, wherever they may be, writers can hear their communities' heartbeats; they can understand the needs of people, listen in on their dreams.

When Christopher Scanlan and Mark Patinkin of the *Journal-Bulletin* in Providence wanted to know about the black communities in Rhode Island, they set out on a series of interviews that took them into the offices of black lawyers and to the homes of welfare mothers. They spoke to merchants and hookers. They went into housing projects—monuments of despair to some of the tenants, models of hope to others—and they visited the police station.

There is another aspect of the journalist's involvement with people. Contrary to the popular notion that media workers will do anything for a story, devise any ideas to please a client or hawk shoddy merchandise on demand, media professionals subscribe to an ethic of concern. Bob Tur, the helicopter newsman, for example, has received awards for rescuing people trapped in the storms he was filming for television, and during an earthquake he flew patients from the damaged Granada Hills Hospital to trauma centers.

Discipline

The ability to work steadily at a task is another trait common to all who work creatively—writers, musicians, painters, designers, builders, dancers, actors, teachers. Ernest Hemingway labored over his sentences and paragraphs until he was satisfied. He would rewrite a paragraph 20, 30 times until it did his bidding.

Advice from the Consummate Comic

W.C. Fields, one of the greatest film comedians ever, seemed to be a natural comic, his comedy effortless.

Actually, he labored at his craft.

"Show me a comic who isn't a perfectionist and I'll show you a starving man," he said. "You have to sweat and toil and practice indefinitely. A comic should suffer as much over a single line as a man with a hernia would in picking up a heavy barbell."

John McPhee, a *New Yorker* writer who describes himself as a "working journalist," walks into his office at 8:30 in the morning and leaves at 8:30 in the evening. He takes only a 90-minute break each day.

McPhee, considered one of the finest journalists in the country, disciplines himself to write.

"People want to be writers without writing," he says. Impossible. After he graduated from college he tried to write television plays. He was learning and so the task was arduous. The temptation to leave the typewriter was so great that he resorted to tying himself to a chair with his bathrobe sash.

Dan Rather enjoys hunting and fishing, but he has little time for recreation. "I work about 110 hours a week," he says. "It will eat you up, but if it doesn't you have a difficult time being good at it. I think you have to care that much."

Courage, Stamina

Despite practicing detachment, objectivity and discipline, journalists have feelings that can be touched. Some assignments are emotionally trying: interviewing the mother of the boy who drove his motorcycle into an oncoming ore truck; reviewing the unacceptable debut of the young musician who has invested years of study; choosing one of two excellent candidates to support in an editorial.

There are dangerous assignments as well. Correspondents have been maimed and murdered, shot by snipers, socked by irate fans.

Tough. "Talent is helpful in writing, but guts are absolutely necessary."
—*Jessamyn West*

Death Threat

Cincinnati Post reporter Lisa Popyk and photographer Bruce Crippen were threatened by a gun-toting drug dealer when they investigated a murder in a drug-plagued area of the city. "He was wearing a dark ski mask and a baggy sports coat and holding a silver, semi-automatic handgun," says Popyk. "He said, 'We don't need no cops here.' He raised his gun and pointed." Popyk dashed inside an apartment where children were lying on the floor, their hands covering their heads. "We heard gunshots. A couple of children started to scream; one was crying. Their mother was calm: 'Everyone stay on the floor. Get away from the windows. Do like always.'" *Scripps Howard News*

Death in the Afternoon

While in Liberia to cover the work of missionaries from the Southwestern Baptist Theological Seminary, the reporter-photographer team for the *Fort Worth Star-Telegram* was suddenly thrust into history's cauldron.

Liberia had erupted with savage violence. A young soldier, Master Sergeant Samuel K. Doe, had led his troops in a military coup. Under Doe's command, soldiers had assassinated the president and then set about eliminating the country's leaders. The executions were to be carried out on a hot afternoon on a Liberian beach, and the press was invited.

Larry C. Price, the photographer, and Paul Rowan, the reporter, made their way to the beach where thick, sturdy posts 10 feet high were being placed in the white sand. As the posts were being adjusted, Price broke away from the group of newsmen gathered 100 yards from the beach. Alone, he walked toward the posts anchored in the sand. As he walked, he snapped pictures. The heavily armed soldiers watched him but did nothing.

Rowan edged closer and took notes. The number of posts grew, Rowan noted on his pad, from four to five, from five to seven, seven to nine. In the middle of the work stood the 27-year-old photographer, snapping pictures.

The condemned leaders were then brought out.

Unsafe Terrain

Courage is a trait journalists are called upon to muster, even though they don't talk about it much. When reporters were sent to the South to cover the civil rights protests, many were abused. Bill Minor, who covered Mississippi for more than 40 years, recalled what happened in 1961 when a bus terminal in McComb was desegregated under a federal court order.

Black freedom riders were on their way to town and as arrival time drew near, "tension was thick as the Dixie dew," Minor said. In the July/August 1987 *QUILL* he describes the incident in his piece "Mississippi Dateline":

I had gone into the office of the local newspaper, the McComb *Enterprise-Journal,* with three guys from *Time* and *Life* who were friends of mine. As we stepped out on the sidewalk to leave, four young toughs jumped us. They had apparently fingered the three *Life* and *Time* fellows and went after them, leaving me alone.

The toughest of the lot, whom I later learned was something of an amateur fighter, went after Simmons Fentress, then an Atlanta-based correspondent for *Time,* hitting him with full fist on the side of the head with a resounding smack. Fentress, somewhat amazingly, did not go down.

Meanwhile, two of the other hoodlums rammed Don Urbrock, a stocky writer for *Life* out of Miami, into a plate glass storefront with such force that the glass cracked and came sliding down like a guillotine blade. Urbrock managed to pull himself away just in time to avoid the pane of glass as it came crashing down; it would have sliced him in two if he had been a little slower.

As the four toughs ran away, I shouted to the storekeeper whose plate glass window had been smashed, asking him if he knew who they were. He shook his head and said, "I've never seen them before in my life." That was a lie, of course. The leader of the gang, at least, was well known around town.

(There's a poetic postscript to that incident: Two years later, I learned, the storekeeper was shot to death at a roadside tavern by the same tough guy he could not recognize as the one who slugged Simmons Fentress.)

"They tied nine men, old-looking men, paunchy, gray-haired men, to the posts," Rowan wrote.

Then the shots rang out, and the bodies began to crumple into the sand. Price was so close an ejected shell casing struck him.

He continued to take pictures.

Price's photographs of the deaths of the old rulers won the Pulitzer Prize for spot news photography. The pictures grimly record men calculating the death of fellow men, the moment of death and the celebration of the kill.

Witness to History

Photojournalist Larry C. Price stood so close to soldiers in the firing squad that an ejected shell casing struck his cheek. The soldiers let him take pictures of them preparing government officials for their execution and then of the ensuing celebration. "The central thing in photojournalism is that you have to get it when it happens," Price says, "There are no second chances." These photographs won Price the first of his two Pulitzer Prizes for photography. ©*Larry C. Price, Fort Worth Star-Telegram*

Execution . . .

. . . and Celebration

Price and Rowan were appalled by what they saw. But their job was to record for their readers, and for history, the momentous event.

"I'm certainly not coldhearted," Price said later. "Taking pictures of tragedy does affect me."

Some Realities

As we have seen, journalism survives through the sale of space and time to advertisers. The consequence is that some publishers and editors pay more attention to the ledger than to the news. Increasingly, as newspapers and broadcast networks and stations become part of big business, the pressure from investors for larger and larger dividends leads to pressure to reduce news staffs, to rely on press releases rather than staff reporters, to give advertisers more space and time while cutting into news space and time and to emphasize entertainment at the expense of news.

The student thinking of a career in journalism should understand this and more: Much of the journalism of conscience is not rewarded by change. People often ignore what to the journalist is an obvious wrong. They return incompetents, sometimes convicted criminals, to office. They tolerate an educational or criminal justice system that does not work.

Despite newsroom politics—which can be bloody—publisher greed and public indifference, journalism can do good, as we have seen, and it continues to attract young men and women of conscience and ability.

A Variety of Jobs

For the well-trained young man or woman in journalism, a vast field beckons: newspapers, daily and weekly; magazines, general circulation and specialized; radio and television; public relations; advertising; newsletters. But competition is stiff.

You can be a specialist and cover the aerospace industry and defense for the newsletter *Aerospace Daily* or handle the KFC account for Young & Rubicam; attend international conferences for *Time* or cover the San Francisco Giants for the *Chronicle* or *Examiner;* sit at an anchor desk for ABC or cover fires, traffic accidents and city council meetings for KAIT-TV in Jonesboro, Ark.

Your career choice might land you a job in Washington handling press relations for a congresswoman or in Beijing reporting the tension between an aged leadership and young dissidents striving for democracy.

Most beginners start small, and this is the way it should be. The small beginning is where learning takes place.

"Working on a smaller paper and covering the police, the board of education and the council is invaluable experience," says Clyde Haberman, a foreign correspondent for *The New York Times*. "At one time or another there will be a fire in Tokyo, or there will be an earthquake, and what is needed out of me then is not someone who is a student of history or language, but someone who has covered a fire in his day, and someone who knows how to cover people in situations hav-

Protective. "When my office sued a car dealer who had violated our state's advertising laws—clearly a news story of interest to the state's consumers—one Connecticut radio station spiked the story for fear of alienating one of its major advertisers, the car dealership in question."

—*Joseph Lieberman, former attorney general of Connecticut*

Some Tips. The AP advises new reporters to be on time, to dress properly and to stay in touch with the desk while on assignment.

ing to deal with tragedy. It doesn't make a difference if it's happening in Tokyo or Newark."

After graduating from Georgetown University, Carol Sardinha went to the UPI. "I learned how to brave some very difficult situations at UPI," she said.

"You really have to go through trial by fire; you don't have time to be instructed when there are only two or three reporters covering everything that happens in the western part of Pennsylvania." Today, she is editor of *Medicare Compliance Alert* newsletter.

Not everyone aims for the big city. The journalist who likes to see the results of his or her work is happy to stay small.

Small-City Journalism "In a community like this," says Stephen Hartgen, publisher of the *Times-News* in Twin Falls, Idaho, population 30,000, "you can see the effect of your work. The attraction of places like this is that you can have an impact. Small-city journalism is a throwback to colonial journalism, when journalists had a direct effect."

At the *Times-News,* which has 24 full-time editorial and 30 advertising department employees, Hartgen says he looks for people with a good education, a strong sense of purpose, excellent command of writing, curiosity, a low threshold of indignation ("Passion. They have to feel, 'I want to do something about that.' ") and an appreciation, respect and feel for people.

At the Burson-Marsteller public relations agency, applicants are given a writing test that requires them to write a news release based on a speech, write a picture caption from a set of facts and organize a news story.

Arthur V. Ciervo, director of public information and relations for The Pennsylvania State University, advises his colleagues who hire college graduates, "Always give a writing test because writing is a large part of any staff member's work in a news bureau." The applicant, he says, "must be a good writer."

A Job Tryout

Let's look at the experience of a young man who got over the first hurdle of the newspaper's test and was put on the job on probation. We focus on a luncheonette in Gloucester, Mass., where Nicholas Trowbridge is recalling for a friend his first few days on the local daily, *The Gloucester Times*. He has just graduated from college, where he worked on his college weekly.

"I had a three-day tryout for the job," he says between bites into a ham sandwich. "The first day was a disaster. I was told to condense five stories to capsule length. After two hours, I had five two-page stories.

"The boss looked at them and said, 'When I said brief I meant two grafs, not two pages.'

"When the third day came and the paper's veteran reporter suggested I do a sidebar to go along with his story on a mayoral election debate at the local Legion Hall, I knew this was it.

"My assignment was to talk to people in the bar downstairs and ask them why they weren't upstairs listening to the debate. The reporter introduced me to the bartender and went upstairs.

The Wise Guys "I talked to a few of the regulars at the bar and had the beginnings of a story. Then I ran into the wise guys.

"They were playing pool in one of the rooms off the bar, and after I identified myself, one turned to me and said, 'You're new, aren't you?'

"When I told him I hadn't even been hired yet, that I was on trial, he said, 'Well if you want the job, the big story's in the bar. Jack's his name and he set a record last week.'

"The record, they told me with complete sincerity and honesty, was for not going to the toilet. It was going to be published in the *Guinness Book of World Records,* they said.

" 'Come on, you're kidding me,' I laughed.

"They assured me it was no lie. I went into the bar and asked if Jack was in.

" 'Why do you want Jack?' one woman asked as she cradled a Seven-and-Seven between her forearms.

" 'I hear he set a record, he's the one who didn't go . . . uh, forget it,' I stammered. 'Why aren't you upstairs, listening to the politicians at the debate?'

" 'One's an idiot and one's retarded,' she answered, probably angry at the choices offered the voters. 'No, that's not it, they're both retarded.'

"I put the quote high in my story and the editor ran it on page one. The next day he told me I had the job and said I could thank the woman in the bar for it. A few days later the paper received an angry letter on my story from one of the two mayoral aspirants who claimed the story was derogatory to those with mental handicaps.

"But it's lucky my story wasn't about a mythical Jack who avoided the call of nature for a record number of days. Had it been, I'd probably still be wandering through the South in search of a job, hitching with truckers through an endless succession of roadside truck stops and interviews."

Lost in the Crowd A few weeks later, as a wiser and tougher reporter (he thought), Trowbridge was assigned to accompany a busload of local parishioners who were going to see the Pope in Boston. They split into four groups to walk to Boston Common, where the Pope was to celebrate Mass.

"I decided to stick with the largest group for the day, listen to their comments, watch their reaction to the Pope.

"On the way to the Common, I ducked out for a cup of coffee. When I got out of the coffee shop, the group was gone.

"I raced to the Common. They were lost in a sea of people. After a two-hour search, I realized I was wasting my time.

"I went to a pay phone and called the boss, collect.

" 'I've lost them,' I said.

" 'Lost who, Nick?'

" 'The parishioners from St. Ann's. I went into this place to get some coffee, and when I came out they were gone, vanished,' I told him, thinking that his advice would be to head south to look for another job.

" 'Nick lost the parishioners and he's looking for them on Boston Common,' I could hear him telling the staff.

"I could hear laughter in the newsroom.

" 'Don't worry,' he told me. 'Just get some good quotes on the bus on the way back.

" 'And don't miss the bus.'

" 'No problem,' I told him. 'I've got it under control.' "

The young reporter's self-assurance may seem to have been built on a foundation of toothpicks. But he managed to hold his job and to do well.

Satisfaction . . .

In a study of reporters on Iowa daily newspapers, this is what reporters said they liked about their jobs:

- "We're beholden to nobody. This place has integrity."
- "I'm involved in what's going on in the community."
- "The camaraderie of the news staff."
- "Independence for creative writing."
- "Being where the action is."
- "Good discipline, effective on-the-job training."
- "Opportunity to express opinions on the editorial page."
- "The freedom of adventure a small newspaper affords."
- "The responsibility given to me and to each reporter by management."

. . . and Frustration

Charles M. Young is a worrier. He sweats and strains over his stories, never really happy about them. But his stories for *Rolling Stone* and other publications about rock groups and entertainers seem to flow like maple syrup over a short stack.

Despite his pain, Young enjoys writing. His delight in language and his subjects is evident in his piece "Carly Simon, Life, Liberty and the Pursuit of Roast Beef Hash" that begins:

Most rock writers, it has been observed, would rather be the people they write about; that is, trade in their typewriters to scream nonsense at 20,000 rioting lude freaks while Keith Richards powerchords their brains into Cool Whip. Not me. I don't want to be Mick Jagger. Nor do I want to be Carly Simon and have millions of college students think dirty thoughts about my album covers. I don't even want to be James Taylor, who is married to Carly Simon.

I would trade it all to be Benjamin Taylor. Here is someone with a good deal in life; all Benjamin Taylor has to do is cry and Carly Simon sticks her breast in his mouth. The other 4 billion of us on earth could cry for the rest of our lives and Carly Simon would not stick her breast in our mouths.

Greater injustices have marred human history, I suppose, but I can't think of them right now, because Carly Simon has just placed her breast in Benjamin Taylor's mouth. He is having a good time. I am breaking into a cold sweat, wondering if it is obvious from ten feet away that my eyes are dropping from Carly Simon's face to her uplifted blouse every three seconds.

"This is beginning to look obscene," says Carly Simon in the living room of her huge ten-room Central Park West apartment. Benjamin, a cuter-than-hell miniature of James Taylor, is gymnastically curled around his dinner, which he is clutching with both hands and both feet, as well as his mouth.

Women in Journalism

A majority of journalism majors are women. Seventy percent of public relations majors are women. For the other fields, the figure is about 60 percent.

Women are heavily represented on smaller newspapers, less so on the larger newspapers. Only 10 of every 100 editors and news executives are women, most of them on newspapers with circulations under 25,000. The same disparity exists in radio and television stations. The situation is gradually improving as more women move into executive posts.

Minorities in Journalism

The Associated Press Managing Editors organization found that the large newspapers—newspapers with circulations of more than 150,000—are hiring minority entry-level journalists at a 40 percent rate. "The route of entry of minority journalists differs from that of others," the APME says. "The majority of whites who get into the newsroom start at smaller newspapers. Minorities tend to get to larger papers more quickly."

The effort to hire black, Hispanic and Asian journalists began in the 1960s in response to the civil rights movement. Over the next decade, minority employment increased by 35 percent. In the 1960s, minority employment in newspaper editorial positions was estimated at 1 percent of the total. The figure stands at almost 11 percent today, still too low to suit many in journalism. Almost half the nation's newspapers employ no members of minority groups, and 75 percent have none in executive news positions.

Group Ownership

Most newspapers and many radio and television stations are owned by companies that have several media properties. Concentration of ownership in the newspaper industry is constantly increasing: Chain-owned newspapers represent 82 percent of total daily newspaper circulation and 76 percent of total daily newspapers.

The chains sell 50 million papers every day. The chains with the largest circulations are Knight-Ridder, 3.8 million, and the Gannett Company, which has a 6.3 million circulation of its more than 120 daily, semiweekly and weekly newspapers.

(Don't confuse buyers and readers. The circulation of a newspaper indicates buyers. For every buyer, though, one to two others read the newspaper that was purchased.)

The chains are aggressive buyers of newspapers, and some press critics contend that absentee ownership means less sensitivity to local affairs and greater concern with profits.

Truth Seekers

Journalists sometimes hear themselves described as truth tellers. They don't accept that description, for they know that truth is elusive, and that in the long run *your* truth may not be your *friend's* truth. But they would not quibble about being described as truth *seekers,* fully aware that truth is always just beyond their grasp. In fact, it's possible to describe the journalist's work with this formula:

Truth = Story + X

The story is never the full truth. There is always an X, a missing ingredient. Actually, there is not a single X but a series—X_1, X_2, X_3, X_4. . . .

For example, there is the deadline (X_1) that requires the material to be finished quickly, before all facts are in. Here are some other limitations, some other X's:

Availability of sources—Too often, the person the writer needs to complete the work is not available.

Nature of the medium—Television favors action over talk. Fine points are lost to vivid pictures.

Limitations of the reporter—The art of journalism consists of looking in the right direction at the right moment, asking the pertinent questions, having the background to put the story in perspective and then deciding what to include or what to leave out because of the pressures of time and space.

With all this facing the journalist only a fool would contend that the media-worker can find truth. Yet, journalism does come close, closer than any other institution we have, to presenting an accurate report of the passing scene. Much of journalism's reliability stems from its independence. More correctly put: Much of journalism's ability to approach a reasonable version of reality stems from the independence of the journalist, who owes no government, no party, no private interest any obligation to manipulate information.

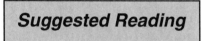

Suggested Reading

Bagdikian, Ben H. *The Media Monopoly,* 4th ed. Boston: Beacon Press, 1992.

Berkow, Ira. *Red: A Biography of Red Smith.* New York: Times Books, 1986.

Chancellor, John and Walter R. Mears. *The News Business.* New York: Harper and Row, 1983.

Crouse, Timothy. *The Boys on the Bus.* New York: Random House, 1973.

Mills, Kay. *A Place in the News: Women's Pages to the Front Page.* New York: Dodd, Mead, 1988.

Scanlan, Christopher. *How I Wrote the Story.* Providence, R.I.: Providence Journal Co., 1986.

Sheean, Vincent. *Personal History.* Boston: Houghton Mifflin Co., 1969.

Steffens, Lincoln. *The Autobiography of Lincoln Steffens.* New York: Harcourt, Brace and Co., Inc., 1931.

PART TWO Writing

Writing begins with a full grasp of the material at hand. Some writers devise outlines when they have time. Some construct their outlines while they gather information.

Writers know the major points they want to make in their stories and adopt a writing strategy to make them fit the nature of the event. *Michael Du Cille*

3 The Rudiments

The media writers' basic commandments require them to select the essential elements of the event they are portraying and to describe it accurately, thoroughly and briefly. *Bill Turnbull, Daily News*

Looking Ahead

Journalists, like other professionals, abide by the rules and customs of their work. These essentials of their practice include accuracy, attribution to sources, use of background information, balance and fairness, brevity, clarity, completeness, human interest whenever possible, full identification of those in the material, a focus on the theme or news point, novelty, objectivity and the verification of claims, and assertions.

Accuracy

Journalism's rudiments begin with accuracy. Unless accurate, articles, reviews, advertisements and news releases are misleading and, therefore, worthless. The media writer marches to a set of inflexible orders. Words and names must be spelled correctly. Addresses must be verified. Words must be used as the dictionary defines them. Sources must be quoted without distortion. Figures and computations must be double-checked.

Journalistic lore is filled with stories about practitioners who failed to abide by the rules of their calling. A *New York Times* reporter wrote that tobacco taxes would increase more than 3,000 percent if a bill were enacted into law. His computation was off by two zeroes. It should have been 30 percent.

In their lectures on libel law, instructors often reach into their bag of horror stories to find the one about the wrong initial. A courthouse reporter, it seems, used an *L* instead of a *T* in reporting a divorce action. A couple of days after the story ran, the newspaper received a note from the nondivorcing couple whose initial had been mistakenly used. A libel suit was on the way.

The story brings forth the shudders the instructor sought from his or her students. After a moment or two, however, the students shrug it off as just another of those stories they have been hearing all semester. Shrug away. The stories are

Check, Check Again

The telephone directory is used to verify the spelling of names and to check addresses as well as to find telephone numbers. In her first job after journalism school, Jan Wong verifies names of her sources for a story in *The Gazette* of Montreal. Wong later joined *The Wall Street Journal* staff and then became a foreign correspondent for *The Globe and Mail* of Toronto. *Jean Pierre Rivest, The Gazette*

In the lead story on page one describing the U.S. Senate vote of 76 to 24 in favor of the GATT agreement, a *New York Times* reporter wrote:

The House of Representatives approved the agreement by an even wider margin, 288 to 146.

Why is this an example of what critics say is growing innumeracy, the lack of competence in mathematics?

true. Most libel suits begin with a small mistake, a foolish error, a lapse in accuracy. The consequences can be serious.

Consider the advertising representative who drew up an advertisement based on his notes that the air conditioner was on sale for $99. He had to face a firestorm when the merchant complained people were demanding his $499 product at a fifth of the price.

Experienced journalists as well as beginners make mistakes. Look at what *Newsweek* did in a single issue: The name of a professor of political science at the University of Arizona was misspelled; *personal* bankruptcy was attributed to a man whose *corporation* had gone bankrupt; a former Air Force pilot was confused with a shadowy character in the Iran-Contra scandal with a similar name. These errors include only the ones that were caught by the people who were directly involved and who saw the issue.

Accuracy begins with painstaking attention to every detail when gathering information. Names, ages, addresses—check. The number of fire trucks that answered the alarm—check. Check and double-check.

Should there be an error, the writer must correct it. But the writer's task is not to make the mistake in the first place.

The Unforgiveable Inaccuracy

You do not misspell a person's name. This is Rule No. 1 for writers. And yet:

- The AP story looked back 40 years when several runners were threatening to break the 4-minute barrier for the mile run. One runner who had been given a good chance, reported the AP, was "Wes Santy in the United States."

Wrong. It's *Santee.*

How did it happen? The AP writer used as the source for his story a piece written by a runner who had run in the race in which Roger Bannister set the then-record time of 3:59.4. "That gave our writer an unjustified confidence," says an AP editor.

- The long article in *The New Republic* by Michael Lewis questioned the value of a journalism education. In describing a class Lewis thought wasteful, he referred to the instructor as Steven Isaacs.

Wrong. It's *Stephen.*

How did it happen? Hearing Isaacs' first name, Lewis made an assumption about its spelling, violating the cub reporter's maxim: Assume nothing; verify everything.

Next time you are too rushed to double-check an initial, too rushed to check a reference work, too tired to check a name, remember this correction:

> Mai Thai Finn is one of the students in the program and was in the center of the photo. We incorrectly listed her as one of the items on the menu.

Mercifully, no mention will be made of the reporter who committed this blunder, nor of the newspaper that printed it.

Attribution

Information and statements must be attributed to the source of the material:

> The police reported two people were killed when. . . .
> Mayor Sam Parnass today urged. . . .
> Childhood diseases are declining, the state health department said. . . .
> "College grades are meaningless," Professor Alvin Goodman told. . . .

However, no attribution is necessary for assertions that are obvious and for events that the reporter observes:

> July 4th falls on Tuesday this year.
> Lincoln was loved and hated in his day.
> The cost of living has steadily increased.
> The Tigers defeated the White Sox 3-2 last night.

"Obvious" means commonly accepted as true. When there is no absolute proof or common acceptance, there must be attribution.

Notice the use of attribution in the following lead:

> Police said today they expect major roads out of the city to be heavily traveled beginning Friday at midafternoon. The holiday weekend will run from Saturday through Monday.

The first statement is attributed to a source. The second is stated as fact because it is obvious.

Actions are attributed to the person or group committing or performing them:

> Mayor George Albritton today ordered all city offices closed next Monday in memory of the city's first mayor, Richard Beatty, who died last week at 104 years of age.

> The state Republican Party yesterday took the first steps toward holding its November state convention. The party . . .

Generally, when we speak of attribution, we refer to what is called *sourcing* a quote or statement. That is, responsibility for the material is given to the source. When there is no attribution, the reporter, newspaper or station is considered the source.

Attribution to a source does not guarantee that the statement is true. It places responsibility for the assertion with the source. When reporters doubt the accuracy or truth of a statement, they try to verify it.

Jeff Klinkenberg, outdoors writer for the *St. Petersburg Times,* was astonished at some of the things a shark fisherman was telling him in an interview. "Many of the things he told me I double-checked and found to be true. Things I couldn't check, I went with an attribution," he said.

People sometimes bend facts their way, and the writer may be obligated to use the material, especially if the statements are made by officials or public figures. Although the attribution clearly places responsibility with the source, the writer will try to include in the news story the truth when it is available. This way the source is on record, and so is the truth:

> The superintendent said the seniors' test scores last year were "the highest we've had in the past 10 years." Actually, school records show that scores six and eight years ago were higher.

Placement

Most of the time, attribution is placed in the lead. For print, the standard approach is to follow the assertion or action with the attribution. For broadcast, attribution usually precedes assertion and action.

Some news writers say that attribution in the lead sometimes makes the lead too long. They prefer to cite the source in the second or third paragraph. This approach works, but only if the material is from an official record or document or is not controversial. No source is necessary in this lead because the event is obviously on record with the police:

> Three dead men were found afloat—in two Dade canals and a lake—at midday Sunday by a fisherman, golfers and a scavenger in search of scrap metal.

Attribution is essential in any lead that contains accusations and charges:

> G. Arthur Levy, a local attorney, today charged the state liquor authority with "capricious decisions" in denying liquor licenses to two of his clients.

Chapter Three

Now and then, a reporter will try to make a lead to a story like this more exciting by writing something like this:

> The state liquor authority today stands accused of "capricious decisions" in denying two liquor licenses.

This kind of lead is unfair to the reader, who may conclude that the charge has been made in the courts or by some official body. When the source is finally revealed in the story, the reader may feel cheated.

Always identify the source in a story unless he or she is well-known. We don't need to identify Madonna, Bill Clinton or Mark Twain. But who is Sabrina Gallon? Look at this item from a television news script:

> Sabrina Gallon of Queens was as surprised as anyone to find out that a nude photograph of her appeared in Hustler magazine back in October of 1983. . . . Turns out, say the courts, that her ex-boyfriend sent in the photo with a forged consent form. . . . Gallon has been awarded 30-thousand dollars since Hustler never checked the authenticity of the form.

"Who is Sabrina Gallon?" asks Mervin Block, a broadcast writing coach. "A novice in a nunnery, a sergeant of gunnery, a purveyor of punnery? We don't want her *curriculum vitae,* but we do want to know who she is. Further, don't start a script with the name of an unknown."

Block's rule is: Always identify a person unless that individual has star quality.

Verbs of Attribution

The most frequently used verb of attribution is *said.* It is an invisible word in a sentence, not calling attention to itself as do *charged, whispered, shouted, pointed out.*

When a candidate says his opponent is "incapable of sober judgment," the reporter can write, "The candidate *charged* his opponent is . . ." And when someone does whisper or shout, we say so. But most of the time, the verb for attribution is *said.*

Anonymous Sources

Sources sometimes seek anonymity. They will offer information only if their identities are not disclosed. Newspapers and other news media are reluctant to run such material because anonymity absolves the source of responsibility for the material. When anonymity is promised to a source, the reporter may not use the source's name.

Some editors demand to be told the names of anonymous sources. When this is the case, the sources must be informed that their names will be given to the editor. The AP says its "basic rule is attribute and attribute by name. Anonymity is reserved for those cases in which the information is newsworthy, factual and not available from any source on the record. We use anonymous sources only on matters of fact, not on matters of opinion or judgment."

OK for Most. Of nine journalism reviews asked for their policy on the use of anonymous sources eight said they publish material from unnamed sources if that is the only way to obtain important information. The *Nieman Reports* said it does not use anonymous sources.

Attribution

Not Necessary

John Walker, The Fresno Bee

Necessary

Marc Ascher, The Home News

When reporters working on a story about the illegal use of child labor on farms and in fields see the youngsters at work, they can describe what they see without attribution.

But the reporter who is not present when a murder occurs must reconstruct the event from the reports of investigators and attribute their findings to them.

Background

When a writer provides material that helps readers or listeners to understand an event more fully, we say that the writer is providing background. This material comes from sources, from the reporter's own knowledge and from checking references and clips. (*Clips* are previously run stories filed in the broadcast or newspaper library.)

When the cardinal who heads the New York Roman Catholic archdiocese refused to go along with other prelates in suggesting the use of condoms to combat AIDS, reporters recalled that the Catholic Church in New York had lobbied successfully for years in the state legislature against the display of condoms in drugstores.

When President Reagan vainly sought the help of Republican senators to sustain his veto of an $88 billion highway and mass transit bill, Steven V. Roberts of *The New York Times* quoted several senators. Then, at the end of his piece, he cut to the heart of the issue with this paragraph:

Many conservative Republicans who have voted with the President when he wanted to cut welfare or food stamps were less eager to go along when the issue was roads and bridges used by middle-class voters.

This single sentence, brought up from Roberts's knowledge of politics, tells us a great many truths: who has political clout, how politicians are influenced and why certain bills become laws while others die of neglect. Roberts' paragraph is also an example of interpretative reporting, which experienced and trusted reporters are allowed to do.

Reporters sometimes seek the assistance of public relations personnel when an agency is involved in an event. When StarKist announced its decision not to can tuna caught with nets that also trapped dolphins, the Edelman Public Relations Worldwide agency knew reporters needed background, and the agency distributed press kits and fact sheets—the history of the opposition to such fishing by environmental groups, the industry's position, the reasons for StarKist's shift.

The Full Story

Events are rarely isolated but usually are part of a sequence. They have causes and consequences. Journalists who mine sources for background are able to provide readers and viewers with the full dimension of events.

Balance and Fairness

In the past, it was not unusual for newspaper publishers and editors to use the news columns of their newspapers to attack ideas, groups, individuals and officials. In his book *The Powers That Be* (New York: Alfred A. Knopf, 1979), David Halberstam describes a visit that a *New York Times* reporter made to California in 1934 to cover the campaign for governor. Upton Sinclair, the author of many books and a supporter of social and political change, was one of the candidates.

On his arrival in Los Angeles, the reporter picked up a copy of the *Los Angeles Times* to look for news about the campaign, especially to learn something about Sinclair, who was a national figure. The only story he could find about Sinclair was one saying that the candidate was un-Christian.

That night, the reporter went to dinner with the chief political correspondent of the *Los Angeles Times*. The reporter asked where Sinclair would be speaking so that he could cover some of his rallies.

As *The New York Times* reporter recalls, he was told, "Forget it. We don't go in for that kind of crap you have back in New York of being obliged to print both sides. We're going to beat this son of a bitch Sinclair any way we can. We're going to kill him." Halberstam adds, "Which they did."

A quarter of a century later, in 1958, another New York reporter went to California to cover the turbulent political scene. The same Los Angeles correspondent was directing political coverage. He helped his eastern colleague with background about the Republicans. "What about the Democrats?" asked his visitor. "Oh, we don't bother with them," was the answer.

The days of outrageous favoritism in the news are gone, except in some isolated instances. Today, the *Los Angeles Times* is among the best newspapers in the country, balanced and fair in its reporting.

Both Sides

Charge and counter-charge, point and counter-point. The writer provides both sides of the controversy, gives the accused a chance to reply, obtains background to round out the account. *Rafael Trias, The San Juan Star*

Balance means that both sides in a controversy are given their say. In a political campaign, for example, all candidates are given enough space and time to present their major points.

Fair means that all those involved in news events are treated without favoritism. If someone makes a charge against another person and newspapers or other news media carry the allegation, the news media are obliged to try to carry the response of the person charged. Fairness requires that the reporter tie charge and reply together whenever possible.

When a lawyer said his clients had been mistreated by the state liquor authority, the reporter sought the response of the authority and put the reply high in the story:

G. Arthur Levy, a local attorney, today charged the state liquor authority with "capricious decisions" in denying liquor licenses to two of his clients.

Levy said the authority had no reason to turn down Fred P. Schmidt and Alice Long, both of whom sought licenses for outlets in shopping centers north of the city.

The executive director of the authority, Theodore Landau, denied that the state agency had acted without reason. He said the applicants had failed to satisfy the authority about their backgrounds. . . .

The journalist is not a tennis ball, bouncing from charge to rebuttal as the sources volley away. As you saw a few pages back in the section on attribution, the journalist tries to check the truth or accuracy of material, and when a misstatement is made, the journalist provides the background that sets the record straight.

(Just a minute here for a sidestep. Note the next to last word in the previous paragraph: *record.* Journalists have to realize that their work is a record, that it is cited by people as authoritative. It may be history in a hurry, but it is part of the historical record.)

Fairness also involves the honest use of language. Look at these statements:

- Jones admitted he had seen the documents.
- Jones said he had seen the documents.

The first sentence implies that Jones is under attack for having done something wrong, whereas the second sentence is neutral. There are occasions when *admit, refuse, complain* and other words that imply an attitude or behavior can be used appropriately. But these are loaded words. They signal caution.

Stereotypes and Sexism

Fairness also demands of the journalist an awareness of the trap of the stereotype. The days are past when writers consciously used the thrifty Scotchman and the crafty Asian to make a point. Stereotypes are insidious. They can sneak into copy when the writer isn't watching:

- *Policeman* for police officer.
- *John Jacobs and Mrs. Jacobs* for John and Sarah Jacobs.

Words and descriptions that would never be used to describe men in similar situations creep into copy about women. Sen. Barbara Boxer of California was described by *The New York Times* as a "feisty little woman."

In looking for comments about issues, reporters often turn to men, even when the matter concerns women. During the debate about the safety of silicone breast implants, the *Times* ran a story quoting 23 male sources. No female source was cited.

Brevity

The art of media writing is knowing what to leave out and condensing what's left. The most effective writing makes its point succinctly, economically. Writers make a little go a long way by carefully selecting the material they use and by using words that work hard. They have trained themselves to stay on the major point, and they know that action verbs and concrete nouns are the backbone of crisp writing.

Content

The writing coach Donald M. Murray says the most effective stories make one dominant point. The writer's job is to decide on that point and to pare away everything else. Writers who insist on including most of what they find in their fact gathering and research find much of their labor wasted, cut away by their editors. If the material does make it into print, it sags with the overload, like a fullback who has trained on beer.

When space or air time costs money, writers don't waste words. This is why some print and broadcast writers say they study the advertisements and commercials of the best agencies.

When the writer has selected the single most important theme (occasionally two, rarely three themes), there may be interesting and relevant material remaining. To handle this leftover economically, writers use the summary:

> The city council also:
> 1. Appropriated $50,000 for paving Regis Street between Western and Indiana Avenues.
> 2. Approved the appointment of L.P. Potts of 52 Bradley Lane as Water Department superintendent.
> 3. Put off acting on a proposal for an anti-litter ordinance until next month.

This technique is also used for an interview piece when the source makes interesting statements that aren't directly related to the theme of the interview. Here's the way this can be done:

> Nelson ranged widely over the field of music in his remarks:
> "Country western will be around as long as people are romantics. . . .
>
> "The mainstream singers give people what they think people want. They're wrong. People want authenticity. . . .

Attention Getter

Media consumers have short attention spans, which leads media writers to compress their messages and to use bright writing to lure the consumer into tarrying a moment longer. *Livingston & Co.*

Terse. After Calvin Coolidge returned from a church service, a friend asked the president what the sermon was about.

"Sin," replied Coolidge.

The friend asked what the clergyman had said. Coolidge replied, "He said he was against it."

"Travel is no way to make a living, but it's our only way. We are today's minstrels. . . .

"Country music appeals to grandpa and his granddaughter."

Why Some Stories Are Too Long

It helps to know where you're heading when you set out to write. With a plan and a direction in mind, you will take the shortest path to your destination. Lewis Carroll makes the point in *Alice's Adventures in Wonderland* that without a plan the way will be long:

"Would you tell me, please, which way I ought to go from here?"

"That depends a good deal on where you want to get to," said the Cat.

"I don't much care where—" said Alice.

"Then it doesn't matter which way you go," said the Cat.

"—so long as I get *somewhere*," Alice added as an explanation.

"Oh, you're sure to do that," said the Cat, "if you only walk long enough."

Word Choice

When George Eliot, the English novelist, was writing *Daniel Deronda,* she wrote this sentence: "She began to sob hysterically." Eliot's manuscript shows that she crossed off the adverb *hysterically,* realizing that the verb *sob* was strong enough to carry the meaning she intended.

Writers make one word do the work of two or three. By choosing a concrete noun—a noun that refers to an actual person, place or thing—good writers avoid adjectives. By using action verbs that whisper, sing or shout, writers can avoid using adverbs. Good writers make their nouns and verbs work for them.

Look at these sentences. The weak ones are the wordy sentences. The strong sentences make their points succinctly by using action verbs:

Weak—He was hardly able to walk.
Strong—He staggered. (He stumbled. He faltered.)
Weak—He left the room as quickly as possible.
Strong—He ran out. (He rushed out. He dashed out.)

Concrete nouns are words that stand for something we can point to as real: table, desk, chalk, crayon, basket, Ted Kennedy, Prince Charles.

Abstract nouns have no physical reference: patriotism, feminism, freedom, hope. These words have different meanings to different people. The writer avoids using abstract nouns, except in direct quotes.

The approach to making copy concise is to ask, are these words or ideas essential? Here are some cuts the AP suggested to its reporters:

Sentence—A national homosexual rights law group said Wednesday it is suing several federal agencies for failing to make more AIDS treatment drugs available to victims of the fatal disease.

Suggestion—Period needed after *available*. They wouldn't be complaining about nonvictims.

Sentence—A man whose eight-year reign as chief of the state Department of Natural Resources ended in scandal pleaded innocent Wednesday to extortion charges and said he had no doubt he would be cleared.

Suggestion—Period needed after *charges*. What else would he say?

Sentence—The American Medical Association has called for a ban on smoking on all commercial U.S. aircraft, citing the dangers of secondhand smoke and accidental fire inside a sealed cabin.

Suggestion—Too wordy. Make it: The American Medical Association wants smoking banned on U.S. commercial flights because of health and fire hazards.

"Use little words," says a managing editor. "No one wants to know how extensive your vocabulary is."

Some writing coaches advise their charges to study advertisements. "After all," said one coach, "the advertiser is paying for every word, and he wants to make that word count. There's little waste in good ads."

"Brevity," says Simon Jenkins, the editor of *The Times* of London, "is the key to clarity. Without clarity a newspaper is useless." And so, for that matter, is the wordy review, news release, editorial or broadcast news item.

Clarity

Everyone—readers, listeners, editors—agrees: After making sure a story is accurate, the most important job of the writer is to be clear, to make the information understandable. The article, editorial or review must be clear on the first reading.

Unclear stories often are the result of muddy thinking. George Orwell knew this, and he knew the signs: "purple passages, sentences without meaning, decorative adjectives and humbug generally."

The economist and author John Kenneth Galbraith said that no matter how complicated and obscure the subject, the matter can be "stated in plain language." But he added, "It is impossible to be wholly clear on something you don't understand."

Once the subject is understood, the writer must organize the material. The theme that best summarizes the situation is selected. Then the supporting material is arranged in an organized fashion. Writers see themselves as guides leading the reader through a thicket. Inept guides lead their followers in circles or into a forest of confusion.

Short, crisp, to-the-point beginnings and logical story structure make for clarity. We can add another essential guideline: the S-V-O sentence structure

(Subject-Verb-Object). The sentence that has someone saying or doing something is usually clear. Here are some additional tips:

- Avoid excess punctuation. Too many commas confuse readers.
- Stay away from adjectives and adverbs. Mark Twain said, "One can seldom run his pen through an adjective without improving his manuscript."
- Watch out for long sentences linked with the words *and, but* and *for* and with other conjunctions. Usually, long sentences can be broken into two sentences with a period in place of the connecting words.

Completeness

At this point you may have the impression that media writers strive to be as brief as possible. True enough, but not at the expense of giving complete information. Just as inexcusable as the overwritten, flabby piece is the underwritten, anemic piece. People want the full story, and it's the writer's task to do that.

If the information cannot be relayed satisfactorily in four paragraphs, then make it six. An editor can slash away unnecessary words and facts. But the editor cannot add relevant information to the piece. All the editor can do is ask you to fill the holes in the piece you've written.

The news item that says the AIDS Awareness Group will meet next month, period, is insufficient. What are the date and time, and where will the meeting be held? People may want to attend. The news release that says General Motors is awarding its advertising account to NW Ayer must say who lost the account, why and how much it's worth.

To guard against uninformative copy, keep in mind some catchwords: background, cause, consequence. These help flesh out the too-skimpy piece.

Prove It. One way to look at media writing is to see the headline or the lead of the story as the premise and the body of the material as the proof. If the body doesn't deliver satisfactory buttressing material, the piece is incomplete.

Human Interest

The campus correspondent for a local newspaper showed the city editor a story he had written for his college newspaper. He wanted to know whether it would interest the editor. The story began this way:

College students face problems ranging from alcohol abuse to loneliness, but the difficulties can be handled with a little friendly assistance, say members of the Campus Ministerial Association.

The organization's members, composed of ministers representing six denominations, say that students here are like other young people.

"Students are not that different from anyone else," the Rev. . . .

The city editor looked up after reading the story. The piece has possibilities, he told the student. "You've done a lot of work. You quote the director of the Wesley Foundation, the director of the Baptist Student Center, a Catholic priest and an Episcopal vicar. They have interesting things to say about students experimenting with drugs, sex and alcohol and then feeling guilty or lost.

"But the story is missing a key element. It's about the problems of students, but there are no students in it. You haven't talked to any students.

"The story lacks human interest. It moves all around the subject but never shows us the people who are directly involved."

He suggested the student reporter interview several students. The reporter could promise not to use names if requested.

We want to get behind the walls and fences that people construct around themselves, to pierce the anonymity of the city. We want to know what went on inside a room down the hall last night when someone screamed. Or whose 10-speed bike left chained to a post was stripped of every part but the frame. Or what happened to the family whose home burned last night. Who took them in? Have they any clothing?

The story reports the sermon, but says nothing about what the 7-year-old child or the old woman in the black shawl are praying for. The newlyweds are honeymooning at the Lake of the Ozarks, but the wedding story says nothing about why they chose this particular place.

Since the human element catches the reader's interest, it is often put high in the story. When postal workers went on strike, Marcia Chambers, then with *The News Tribune* in Perth Amboy, N.J., dug beneath the union and government statements to look into the life of a striking worker. Here is how her story began:

This March Joe Capik will have worked as a mail carrier in Perth Amboy for 20 years. He takes care of his wife and four children on $110 a week.

Mostly he and his four children, who live at 56 Maplewood Ave. in a Cape Cod bungalow in Keasbey, eat dinners of stews and soups and spaghetti. Things were bad enough

Lifeless. . .   *. . . Lively*

Photograph or news story, press release or advertisement, editorial or review, column or feature—all reach people better when they have human interest.

last year, he said, that he applied for food stamps. But the county turned him down.

Last week Joe Capik went out on strike for the first time in his life. He joined 49 letter carriers who were on strike for the first time in the 195-year history of the postal system.

"I don't feel right about striking. I really don't," he said outside the deserted post office in Perth Amboy.

"But it's a question of desperation. The situation has been forced upon us," he said. . . .

Human interest can also be put into a story through the use of personal pronouns and concrete nouns:

1. Johnson put the pencil down and closed the book.
2. Johnson put **his** pencil down and closed **his** book.
3. He said his textbook was as lively as a good lecture.
4. He said his textbook was as lively as one of **Professor Albrecht's** good lectures.

Similes, metaphors and colorful phrases and quotations that involve the senses and feelings also add human interest. Compare these sets of sentences:

5. It had a bad odor.
6. It smelled liked burned rubber.
7. His back ached.
8. His back felt like the football team had practiced on it.
9. Jim Thorpe, the great American Indian athlete, was an especially adept runner.
10. Jim Thorpe described his running technique: "I give 'em the hip, then I take it away."

Hold it. Look at the examples, strong and weak, in the last couple of pages. The college journalist failed to interview students. Marcia Chambers' story was successful because she interviewed a specific postal worker. The failure or the success of these stories hinged on reporting, fact gathering. And so we come to a fundamental truth about writing: No writing can be any better than the quality of the information that supports it.

Identification

Writers describe the people they are writing about so that readers and listeners can visualize, locate and identify these people. Identification is a quick portrait. The basic identifying material is **name, age, address, occupation.**

Name—The best source for the proper spelling of a person's name is that person. Also, the telephone book and city directory are usually accurate. If a person uses a middle initial, include that in the story. Nicknames are rarely used except in sports stories or features.

Age—A person's age should be used only when it bears directly on the story. It is always used in obituaries and in stories about the victims of accidents and fires. Age is also used when it helps to make the point of the story. The youth of John Kennedy and the age of Ronald Reagan were relevant in their presidential campaigns, for example.

In this youth-conscious culture, some older people are reticent about revealing their age. When it is relevant, the reporter is obligated to put it in the story. This can be done with tact:

> She graduated from high school in 1932.

Address—Where a person lives can tell the reader a great deal. An address in a high-income neighborhood sends one kind of message, an address in a poor neighborhood another. An address helps the reader visualize a neighborhood—large lawns and single residence homes or low-income city projects.

Occupation—Work defines many people. That is, jobs can describe character and personality. Think of the images that you build from the following job titles: hotel maid, film producer, grocer, commercial fisherman, teacher, actor. Obviously, those pictures are general and we cannot push them too far or we will stereotype individuals.

Other Indicators—We can use more identifying information: height, weight, hair color, distinguishing physical characteristics. How a person speaks, his or her posture and mannerisms. All these help us see a person. Such descriptive detail is necessary in profiles and feature stories when the writer is trying to draw a portrait of the subject.

Race, religion and national origin are sometimes essential to a story, but too often they are injected when they have no bearing on the situation.

The New York Times Manual of Style and Usage cautions writers:

> Race should be specified only if it is truly pertinent. The same stricture applies to ethnic and religious identifications.

When the Roman Catholic Church appointed an archbishop in France, news stories pointed out that he was born a Jew. To keep him from death in the Nazi concentration camps, his parents turned him over to a Catholic family, which reared him in the Catholic faith. His parents died in the Holocaust. Obviously, his religion was pertinent.

Another kind of identification is essential when a source is quoted as an authority. In this situation, the source is identified by title or background to give the person the authority to speak on the subject on which he or she is being quoted:

> "Freedom of the press is guaranteed only to those who own one," A.J. Liebling wrote. Liebling, a newspaper reporter who turned to magazine and book writing, was a staunch critic of the press. For years he wrote a column called "Wayward Press" for *The New Yorker* magazine.

News Point

In journalism, the key message is called the *news point* or the *focus* of the information. Usually, the point is put in the lead of a news release or story, the headline in an advertisement, the first few words in a newscast.

Even when the information is presented in a feature story, review or editorial and the writer purposely delays the theme—sometimes placing it at the end of the piece—the point is clearly stated. (In feature writing, the paragraph in which the theme or point is presented is called a *nut graph*.)

Writers try to determine the news points or leads in their assignments as early as possible. The sooner they grasp the central idea or theme of the event, the more time they have to gather the supporting material to buttress and to illustrate their themes.

Clearly, Marcia Chambers knew before she wrote the story of the postal strike that she wanted to describe the economic consequences of a strike for a particular worker.

Although experienced reporters usually have a good idea of their stories early on, they are alert to the possibility of contradicting material. When their reporting reveals information that negates their ideas about the story, reporters develop new ideas that are consistent with their observations. Reporters are aware of the danger of seeing and hearing only what they set out to see and hear.

Charlie Riedel, The Hays Daily News

First the Theme

Maryanne Russell © 1991

Every time media writer's put words on paper they have a point to make, whether the words are for a headline and story about the consequences of a fire, a television commercial for KFC, or about a devastating riot that shook Los Angeles. (See next page.)

The Outlook

A Multitude of Facts . . .One Focus

When a jury acquitted four white police officers accused of beating Rodney King, a black motorist they had pulled over, Los Angeles became a nightmare of anger. People were attacked, stores looted, buildings set afire. Officials counted a billion dollars in damaged property, and more than 50 people lost their lives. Racial animosity flared into beatings and shootings.

Novelty

When we pick up a newspaper, tune in the evening newscast or look over the day's advertising specials, we are usually on the prowl for something new, something different. We expect the writer to tell us something we hadn't known or heard before, something that may bring us up-to-date.

The new excites us. The different interests us. No one in the writer's trade can make a living at it peddling stale information.

> Dog bites man—page 27, one paragraph. Man bites dog—page 1B, half a column.
>
> Playwright says he is enjoying visiting local town, likes people, scenery—ho-hum, 30 seconds at end of the 6:30 p.m. news. Noel Coward interviewed by reporter for the *Star* is asked, "Sir, would you like to say something to the *Star?*"
>
> "Of course," replies Coward. "Twinkle."
>
> Reply makes page-one feature and anthologies as well.

Colin Martindale, a member of the psychology department of the University of Maine, writes of the "need for novelty," which, he says, is a historical constant that has spurred creative people in their work. We see this every day on the pages of our newspapers, on our newscasts, in advertisements. Some brilliant advertising slogans have brief, shining moments in the sun and then fade away. The advertising agency NW Ayer began Bell System ads with the signature line: *One policy. One system. Universal service.* Then came others: *Weavers of Speech . . . Long distance is the next best thing to being there . . . The voice with a smile . . . Reach out and touch someone.*

Objectivity

The great strength of journalism in the United States, Canada and a number of western European countries is its objectivity. Readers and listeners and viewers expect their news to be written by journalists who are impartial and independent.

Objectivity has two meanings:

The work itself—A story is objective when it is balanced and impersonal; the reporter does not include his or her opinions, feelings, biases.
Information is verified through the reporter's direct observation of the event or through documents and records to which the reporter can point as proof of his or her account. The objective writer subordinates feelings to facts.

The tradition—Journalism in the so-called free world represents "an impartial third party, the one that speaks for the general interest," says James Boylan, former editor of *The Columbia Journalism Review*. Walter Lippmann, the philosopher of journalistic objectivity, "depicted journalism as an institution apart, charged with supplying society with reliable, impartial information," says Boylan.

Demanding Discipline. "Probably the hardest thing in the world for a man is the simple observation and acceptance of what is. Always we warp our pictures with what we hoped, expected, or were afraid of."

—*John Steinbeck*

Checked Feelings

The writer may have strong feelings about some of his or her subjects. A crime reporter may have seen too many horrible scenes of violence to be objective about criminal suspects. Or the journalist may consider criminals the victims of circumstances. Whatever the belief, the writer keeps it inside and writes the account as objectively as possible. *Joseph Noble, The Stuart News*

Opinion

Beginning writers have a difficult time keeping their enthusiasms, feelings and opinions out of their news stories. How do these sentences differ?

1. The city council last night gave city workers an extravagant wage increase of 15 percent.
2. The city council last night gave city workers a wage increase of only 15 percent.
3. The city council last night gave city workers a 15 percent wage increase.

If your answer is that sentences 1 and 2 express opinions, you are right. Opinion does not belong in a news story, unless attributed to a source. The opinion in the first sentence is obvious. The use of the word *extravagant* reveals that the news writer believes the workers should not have been given such an increase. The second sentence implies with the word *only* that the workers deserve more than the 15 percent increase granted to them. The third sentence is acceptable because it states the fact without an opinion. Readers can draw their own conclusions from it.

Opinions seem to flow from the keyboards of broadcast writers as they try to spruce up their opening lines:

> Good news from the state highway patrol, at least less bad news than expected. There were only nine highway deaths in North Carolina this holiday weekend, half the number predicted.

As Mervin Block wrote in his column "WordWatching" for the magazine *Communicator,* "For nine families, the news is not good or bad; it's catastrophic. *Only* nine deaths? *Only* is a qualifier to use with caution. . . ."

Now, look over these sentences and try to spot where the writer has intruded:

1. The women's fencing team won its first match of the year under its outstanding new coach, Alice Meyers.

2. His reluctance to speak about the crime indicated his fear of being trapped by the police.

3. The building was the fourth in the area this month to suffer fire damage, and, like the three others, the fire was probably the handiwork of an arsonist.

4. The Democratic candidate, like others of his party, favors spending on social issues, which invariably leads to an unbalanced budget.

Here is how an editor analyzed these sentences:

1. "Be careful of adjectives. Every time you use one make sure it is justified, that you can prove it. The first sentence says the coach is 'outstanding.' Also that she is 'new.' Clearly, if this is her first year, she is new. But 'outstanding'? What does that mean? That she is good? Here we have the reporter's enthusiasm taking over. You could quote the athletic director if he says Alice Meyers is outstanding, but you cannot say it yourself."

2. "All we know is that he didn't answer police questions. How does the reporter know what was on the guy's mind? Has the reporter 20-20 X-ray vision that can bore into the guy's head? Maybe he was taking his lawyer's advice to be mum. Who knows? Of course, if a police officer says to you, 'The guy wouldn't talk—afraid of getting himself in a bind,' then you might want to quote the officer. You have someone to pin that conclusion or inference on. The question, though, is whether it's fair to use the officer's quote. I wouldn't. After all, how does he know? And he is implying guilt. Only a jury can determine that."

3. "Reporters don't guess or deal in probabilities. Even if this were the hundredth building to burn and 99 had been torched by an arsonist, reporters can't make the inference about the hundredth. When we talk about inferences we mean that the person who makes an inference jumps from what is known to the unknown. We know three fires were caused by arson, but we know nothing about the cause of the fourth. All we can say is that the three others resulted from arson, and if the reader wants to infer arson for the fourth, well that's OK."

4. "No opinions, please. There are two in the sentence. The reporter says, 'like others of his party.' Well, it is true that Democrats historically have been more open-handed on social issues than Republicans. But not all

Democrats follow this philosophy, as is obvious from reading the papers. The second opinion is that spending for social purposes leads to an unbalanced budget. There are many causes of an unbalanced budget—huge defense spending and low taxes, for example."

Before we let the editor persuade us that a journalist can be as detached as an engineer designing a bridge, let's admit that journalists have opinions and that they can jump to conclusions as rapidly as a fan leaps to his feet when his team scores a basket. In fact, opinions, feelings and biases can direct the journalist to rewarding stories.

But the opinions, personal inferences and emotions of the journalist cannot be inserted in the news story. That's the province of the reviewer, the columnist, the editorial writer and a few others.

"Every good journalist I know has convictions," says Thomas Griffith, a veteran reporter and editor with *Time*. "But it is in his capacity to separate his beliefs from his reporting that a journalist should be judged."

Shades of Opinion

"We are proud not of our objectivity but of our independence. Readers know the views of the reporter and expect them to be reflected in their stories."

—An editor of *Le Monde*

"I have found that a story leaves a deeper impression when it is impossible to tell which side the author is on."

—Leo Tolstoy

"Why should freedom of speech be allowed? Why should a government which is doing what it believes to be right allow itself to be criticized?" Journalists should be "agitators, propagandists and agents of the state."

—Lenin

"We shut them [the newspaper *Ayendegan*] up because we knew who they were and what they were after. And this is not contrary to freedom. This is done everywhere. . . ."

—Ayatollah Khomeini

"The press is the chief democratic instrument of freedom."

—Alexis de Tocqueville

"The theory of a free press is that the truth will emerge from free reporting and free discussion, not that it will be presented perfectly and instantly in any one account."

—Walter Lippmann

"The majority of the countries in the world have no free press. In only a fourth are newspapers and broadcast stations free to carry what journalists write. In countries where journalists challenge censorship, they are arrested, tortured and murdered."

—Freedom House

Carried Away

Enthusiasm is expected at football games and at rock concerts. But journalists check their emotions and their passions when they are on the job. They know that these can influence what they see and hear. And sometimes these strong feelings blind journalists to the need to verify what they do not see first-hand. *Michael Patrick, The Knoxville News-Sentinel*

Useful Feelings

The writer whose compassion leads him to do a piece about children in poverty; the reporter whose anger leads her to write about sexism in pay scales and promotions—clearly, strong feelings can point the way to important stories. The articles are written objectively as news stories; the writer lets the facts speak for themselves. *Joel Strasser*

Verification

When a writer checks his or her information against some kind of objective source, we say that the material has been verified.

The New York Times says, "Don't trust anybody on anything that is check-able." This rule applies even to the most trustworthy sources. They can make mistakes, such as the artists representative's press release that reported a show at a gallery on East 66th Street. The reporter given the release made a routine check in the phone book. The gallery was on East 61st Street.

Mary Hargrove, special-projects editor of *The Tulsa Tribune,* describes what happens when a source has his or her way with a reporter—chagrin and embarrassment result. She interviewed officials of the Penn Square Bank of Oklahoma City after the bank was reported to be in trouble.

No problems, bank officials told her. "I go on my way, fat, dumb and happy," she said. She checked no further. She wrote a page-one story about the soundness of the bank. That was on the July 4th weekend.

Mom? Newsroom veterans tell beginners, "If your mother calls you sonny, check it out."

Sad, very sad, the journalism instructor said to himself as he read a student's story about a homeless young man who said he was a graduate of West Point.

The instructor was even sadder the week after the piece had been distributed to newspaper subscribers of the student news service.

The West Point public information officer called to say no person by that name had ever attended West Point. The moral: People make all sorts of assertions. Check them out.

"After the holiday, the bank is closed," she said.

When the writer knows that the material he or she is given is wrong, the writer says so. Paul Lewis of *The New York Times* visited the twin gilded mosques in Karabala, Iraq, that were damaged when Saddam Hussein's forces put down a Shiite revolt. The area around the mosques was levelled as well. Lewis quotes a clergyman of the mosque as saying the damage was caused by "the bombs and rockets of the American aggression." Lewis continues: "He was referring to the gulf air war, although the allies did not bomb anywhere near these religious sites."

Hoaxes

Although reporters often are warned about shooting from the hip, about going with what they've got before verification, even the most sophisticated are taken in now and then. One day, a messenger showed up in the New York UPI newsroom with a death announcement from a law firm. The obituary was on the firm's letterhead, and the packet included a biographical sketch and a photograph of the deceased. The dead man was L. Dennis Plunkett, age 31, editor-in-chief of *National Lampoon,* according to the announcement. Plunkett died, the note said, after addressing about 300 students at Cornell University the previous evening. The cause of death was undetermined.

The UPI desk moved the obituary on the wires, and within a short time, the UPI's Chicago bureau called New York and said the obituary sounded fishy. New York killed the story and checked with the magazine, which informed the UPI it had no one named Plunkett on its staff and no such title as editor-in-chief. At the New York AP bureau, the staff was trying to verify the obituary when the UPI called to warn the agency about the hoax.

UPI tightened its procedures to require verification of all obituaries.

Seeking Truths

The point of verifying or confirming material is to try to guarantee its truth for the reader or listener. Accuracy is important, but it is not enough.

When President Clinton flew west aboard Air Force One, news reports stated that because he had a haircut aboard the plane air traffic was tied up at Los Angeles International Airport. In referring to the incident later, a reporter for *The New York Times,* stated:

> Indeed, although Mr. Clinton did get the haircut, he did not tie up air traffic.

Note that the reporter took it upon himself to set the record straight. No one was quoted as saying airport traffic was not tied up. The reporter stated it himself.

"The fact without the truth is futile; indeed, the fact without the truth is false." The source is G.K. Chesterton, an English writer who lanced shams and charlatans. This same idea was taken up in the 1950s by Elmer Davis, a radio journalist who was one of the few journalists who sought to determine the truth of the charges of treason and subversion made by Sen. Joseph McCarthy of Wisconsin.

While it is a fact that McCarthy said many people prominent in government were members of or sympathizers with the Communist Party, which the press dutifully reported, Davis took a next step. He asked, "Is it true?" He asked further, "Does the press have an obligation to tell people the truth of the fact?"

Attribution does take the responsibility of assertions, charges and declarations from the shoulders of the press. But in serious matters, shouldn't the press try to find the truth on its own?

Davis said yes, and the press, through the years, has come to agree with him. Reporters have made independent verification of charges, statements and accusations and even of convictions in court. Paul Henderson of *The Seattle Times* took seriously the protestations of innocence of a man convicted of first-degree rape. Henderson dug into the story and, five days before the man was to be sentenced, presented evidence that set the man free.

Next, we turn to starting the story, and then we'll look at how news stories are constructed.

Suggested Reading

Bernstein, Theodore. *Watch Your Language.* Great Neck, N.Y.: Channel Press, 1958.

Davis, Elmer. *But We Were Born Free.* New York: The Bobbs-Merrill Co., 1954.

White, E.B. *Essays of E.B. White.* New York: Harper & Row, 1977.

What's Wrong?
(See page 72.)

True, the yes vote in the Senate was 52 votes greater than the no vote, whereas in the House the yes vote was 142 votes greater than the no vote. But this kind of comparison is misleading since the Senate has fewer members than the House.

It's not the "margin" the *Times* writer cites that is relevant but the percentages or ratios:

Percentages
House: Yes, 66%; No, 34%.
Senate: Yes, 76%; No, 24%.

Ratios
House: 288 to 146 is a ratio of 2:1.
Senate: 76 to 24 is a ratio of 3:1.

Thus, the *Times* gave to its readers exactly the opposite impression than it should have of the voting in Congress.

4 Writing

The writer's task is to find the words, the form and the style that will enable people to see, hear and understand situations such as the sorrow of the trainers of a race horse that collapsed on the track and had to be put down. *Bill Frakes, The Miami Herald*

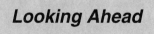

Looking Ahead

Good writing makes for good reading. Media writers make their writing interesting and effortless reading by using everyday words in short sentences and by including quotations and dialogue, incidents and anecdotes. They give their stories life by showing the human dimension of the event and conviction by fully documenting the event. Good writing depends on accurate observation. No story can be better than the reporting that supports it.

The Ingredients

When he was a young journalist struggling to make a name for himself during the rough-and-tumble days of New York tabloid journalism, Jim Bishop was taken aside by a famous columnist and given some advice.

"If you want to write," Mark Hellinger told him, "you are going to have to learn to pound out terse sentences composed of small words."

Bishop took the advice and applied it to all he wrote. He became a successful reporter and then a syndicated columnist and the author of such books as *The Day Lincoln Died* and *A Day in the Life of President Kennedy.* In his stories, columns and books, Bishop wrote short sentences and he used the language of daily life.

Successful writers have mastered the ingredients of good writing. They are:

1. **Simple sentences.** Writers follow the advice of the great Russian short story writer, Isaac Babel: "Not more than one idea and one image to a sentence."

2. **Simple words.** Media writers reach out to their readers by using everyday language. The fewer big words, the better. George Orwell put it simply: "Never use a long word where a short one will do." The words must also be apt for the situation.

3. **Conviction.** The point of the piece must be so well-documented the reader or viewer comes away convinced the writer has caught the event accurately and thoroughly.

4. **Natural style.** The manner of telling about the event should be appropriate to it; the event and its description should have a close fit.

Writers have at their command a battery of writing techniques they can set off to dazzle their readers. First, there is the language itself and its astonishingly rich array of colorful and vibrant verbs and nouns. Second, there are the fiction writer's narrative techniques and the use of dialogue and critical observation adopted by journalists to characterize people.

Sometimes writers perceive clever and dazzling writing as an end itself instead of as a means to an end. The end of writing, its purpose, is to tell us something useful about the world we live in. Colorful writing should not be used to camouflage inadequate fact gathering and observation. It should not be used to give certainty to what can only be conjecture. It should not be used to trivialize and oversimplify the serious and complex.

Simple Sentences

As a rewriteman, Robert Peck's job was to make cloudy stories clear. One of his major problems was the long sentence, which was the result, he said, of writers trying to include too much information in the sentence. Peck, acknowledged to have been one of the finest rewritemen ever to work in New York, pared away

> **Action.** "I recall an assistant city editor on one occasion chastising me: 'Remember that short you did about the window cleaner falling to his death from the 10th story. He didn't fall—he PLUNGED. Make the verbs count.'"
> —*Fletcher P. Martin,*
> *Chicago Sun-Times*

word after word. He cut the sentences "to little more than subject, verb and object," he said.

What emerged, he said, was a story that gained "grace and speed," a story that was well told and moved quickly and gracefully from beginning to end.

Writers gather large amounts of information in their reporting, and they are reluctant to discard any of it. But if the story is about a speaker discussing the need for science and mathematics requirements for college graduation, then his remarks about the beauty of the campus and the bracing spring weather are irrelevant, no matter how clever and complimentary.

Rhythm   We say that short sentences help achieve clarity. But a parade of 10- and 15-word sentences would be as irritable as the two-note phoebe announcing itself the afternoon long. The writer needs to establish a rhythm with sentences—long, short, a bit longer, very short. On the whole the average sentence length should be on the short side, under 20 words. Close to 15. (The average sentence length of this paragraph is 12 to 13 words.)

Frederick C. Othman, a master reporter for the UPI, was asked to give advice to colleagues about the art of journalistic writing. He said, "I shall not repeat any warnings about the need for keeping sentences simple, but I do urge you to count words. If you've got a long sentence, make the next one short. Like this.

"The idea is to produce variety, but if your average is more than 25 words per sentence, your reader will desert you. That's been proven scientifically."

Look at the first three sentences in this story from *The Washington Post:*

> They came in darkness before the dawn of Dec. 11, 1978. There were six or seven of them, with ski masks over their heads and guns in their hands, and they knew what was supposed to be in the Lufthansa cargo terminal that morning.
> Millions.

The sentence lengths are 11, 33, 1. That's 45 words in three sentences, average length 15 words. Just as important, there is a balance—short, long, very short.

Readability   This table is given to wire service reporters:

Average Sentence Length	Readability
8 words or less	Very easy to read
11 words	Easy to read
14 words	Fairly easy to read
17 words	Standard
21 words	Fairly difficult to read
25 words	Difficult to read
29 words or more	Very difficult to read

If the sentences are long, one way out of the trouble is to remember the advice of the English author George Orwell: "If it is possible to cut a word out, always cut it out." Watch for the conjunctions *and* and *but.* These words sometimes introduce a second idea. Try putting a period before the *and* or *but.* There's nothing grammatically wrong with beginning a sentence with a conjunction. But it can be overdone.

Paragraphs should not be long. A long paragraph can discourage a reader. By dividing the number of words in the article by the number of paragraphs, an average paragraph length is obtained. Some editors say they prefer no more than 50 to 70 words to a paragraph. One way to keep paragraph length down is to limit paragraphs to no more than three or four sentences.

Simple Words

Our language has a vast array of short, vivid words that everyone understands. But writers sometimes grandstand. Here's a sentence from the news script for a New York City television station:

> In the Bronx, precipitation is delaying the Yanks-Red Sox game.

Precipitation? Oh, you mean *rain*.
Or this from a news release:

> At this point in time, the users of fossil fuel have . . .

At this point in time? You mean *now* or *these days?*

It does not take a writing coach to make the point that the English language has useful verbs and nouns for the plucking. They are all there for your use.

Carl Sandburg, the poet and biographer of Abraham Lincoln, said at age 75, "I'm still studying verbs and the mystery of how they connect nouns. I am more suspicious of adjectives than at any time in all my born days." We could add another suspect: adverbs.

Adjectives and adverbs are the crutch of the inadequate writer, the writer who cannot reach for the concrete nouns and the action verbs that enliven and propel writing. Adjectives and adverbs are props used to hold up shaky nouns and verbs. They get in the way of story movement.

Look at this sentence:

> The harried man hurriedly ate his lunch, quickly swallowed his soft drink, made a hurried lunge for his jacket and speedily exited.

Now let's use concrete nouns and action verbs to get rid of the adjectives and adverbs:

> The lawyer gobbled his sandwich, gulped down his Coke, grabbed his jacket and plunged out the door.

Hold it—how do we know he's a lawyer, that he ate a sandwich and drank a Coke? We know because we asked and we observed. We followed this rule: Good reporting precedes good writing.

Quote Him

The words of the flood survivor carry greater conviction than the writer's paraphrase. Also, they reach readers and listeners with greater intensity than does the description of an observer. Quotation marks shout for the reader's attention.
Craig Lee, San Francisco Examiner

The Right Words   It's not enough to use simple words. We had better be sure we are using the right words, the words that accurately describe the situation or person. Did she run, jog, amble, walk, trot to the scene? Was her hair tinted a bright orange, a dull red, close to yellow?

Mark Twain urged the writer to "say what he is proposing to say, not merely come near it; use the right word, not its second cousin. . . ."

In what may be the most frequently quoted bit of advice about word selection, Twain said, "The difference between the right word and the almost right word is really a large matter—'tis the difference between the lightning and the lightning bug." And when the writer does hit the right word, the effect, said Twain, "is physical as well as spiritual and electrically prompt."

Well, our words may not jolt our readers with Twain's 220-volt prose, but we can be accurate in their selection, and we can start with the correct grammar and common sense:

> . . . the shoe company sunk 25-million dollars into an advertising campaign centered around Dan and Dave. . . .

That's from a network newscast. The past tense of sink is *sank*, not *sunk*. And how can you center around anything?

Conviction

When Joan E. Rigdon of *The Wall Street Journal* wanted to describe the effect of the increasing cost of college, she had plenty of convincing data:

> There are almost 5 million student borrowers, and they owe $12.5 billion.

The result, she found, is that some students change career plans to enable them to pay back their loans. To dramatize her data, she selected a student who typified the situation. When he graduated from Boston College Law School, Liam C. Floyd wanted to work for the district attorney's office.

"Now," writes Rigdon, "he's interviewing with bankruptcy firms. The reason, he says, is purely financial. About to graduate with $51,000 in student loan debts, the 28-year-old Mr. Floyd figures he needs a more lucrative job to meet his $550 monthly payments."

Not only is the vignette of Floyd persuasive because of the specific figures about his financial plight, its use of an individual in trouble offers evidence of the truth of the generality.

The anchorwoman on the network news show "A Current Affair" closed out her story by saying, "Our hearts go out to everyone affected by this tragedy." That's hardly convincing. Who is the mysterious "our"? The network, the people on her show, all of us watching? "Anyway," says Emerson Stone, who worked for CBS for many years, "the anchorwoman's own unnatural wording (no one talks like that) confirms her unbelievability."

For decades, advertising copywriters outdid each other in their claims for the products they were pushing. These excessive and exaggerated ads became increasingly unconvincing. The public resentment was caught by a *New Yorker* cartoon that showed a well-fed gentleman shouting at the image on his television set of an advertising pitchman holding up a bottle and extolling its virtues. Says the irate viewer: "A quart is a quart, damn it! How can it be a big, jumbo quart?"

Using Quotes   Quotes carry conviction. Mervin Block, a newspaper and television writer, was assigned to do a magazine piece about the newspaper war between the *Daily News* and *The New York Post.*

He used a quote:

"What competition?" snaps the Post's metropolitan editor, Steve Dunleavy. "If it's war, it's a massacre—by the Post. We're gaining two to every one they lose . . . we're so confident we walk around the trenches with our helmets off."

We can visualize the colorful, confident, cocky editor.

Radio journalist Studs Terkel interviewed a telephone solicitor. Enid Du Bois' job was to call people to ask them to subscribe to a Chicago newspaper. She talks to Terkel:

At first I liked the idea of talking to people. But pretty soon, knowing the area I was calling—they couldn't afford to eat, let alone buy a newspaper—my job was getting me down. They'd say, "Lady, I have nine to feed or I would help you." What can you say? One woman I had called early in the morning, she had just gotten out of the hospital. She had to get up and answer the phone.

They would tell me their problems. Some of them couldn't read, honest to God. They weren't educated enough to read a newspaper. Know what I would say? "If you don't read anything but the comic strips . . ." "If you got kids, they have to learn how to read the paper." I'm so ashamed thinking of it.

In the middle-class area, the people were busy and they couldn't talk. But in the poor area, the people really wanted to help the charity I talked about. They said I sounded so nice, they would take it anyway. A lot of them were so happy that someone actually called. They could talk all day long to me. They told me all their problems and I'd listen.

They were so elated to hear someone nice, someone just to listen a few minutes to something that had happened to them. Somehow to show concern about them. I didn't care if there was no order. So I'd listen. I heard a lot of their life stories on the phone. I didn't care if the supervisor clicked in.

In these quotes, so much is revealed: the compassion of Du Bois, her disgust with her job, the generosity of the poor, the terrible loneliness of people. All of this in just four paragraphs.

When to Use Quotes

Handling quotes can be an art—the art of knowing when to use direct quotes and when to paraphrase. Not everything a person says should be quoted directly. Use a direct quotation when:

• It's important to put a person on the record with his or her own words.

• The quotation sums up what the person is saying.

• The quotation lets the reader or listener visualize the person or situation.

• The quotations are essential in question and answer stories such as those about meetings, trials and confrontations.

Costly Quote   During a gubernatorial race in Texas, the Republican candidate cast himself as a "good ole boy," to contrast his candidacy with that of his Democratic opponent, a witty woman who, the reports had it, had experimented with pot. She was seen by some conservatives as the embodiment of the New Woman. Listen to what he told some reporters in a chat about the lousy weather the state was experiencing:

Bad weather is like rape, he said. "If it's inevitable, relax and enjoy it."

Some say that this single quote might have cost the good ole boy the governorship.

Show First, Then Tell   The phrase, she knew at once, would have to be in her lead. Ellen Perlman was interviewing the New Hampshire director of Medicaid for her story on the increasing drain of Medicaid on state budgets when he remarked:

"If expectant mothers received the kind of prenatal care they need, there wouldn't be so many million-dollar babies with low birthweight in expectant care."

These babies, he said, were a big part of the state's almost $100 million Medicaid expenses.

"Million-dollar babies." The phrase hit Perlman.

"The more he talked," says Perlman, "the more I probed for details so I could transfer onto paper the image I was developing of a tiny infant in a hospital costing a lot of money to care for." The director would not supply any infant's name, but he did give one baby's initial and that was enough to make a complex subject come alive.

Perlman found the state had 137 others like Baby S:

Baby S is about to become a million-dollar baby.

Weighing in at less than two pounds when she was born 14 months ago, the tiny baby's huge medical expenses resulting from her premature birth will exhaust the $1 million lifetime limit on her parents' health insurance policy in a few weeks.

From then on, New Hampshire's public health-care system will pay for the space-age medical gadgetry—an estimated $500,000 next year alone—required to keep Baby S alive until she can survive on her own.

Perlman, a staff writer for *City & State* magazine, said, "If I'd just written, 'The state of New Hampshire pays XXX dollars for the care of 138 severely disabled infants'—a straight news lead—I might have lost a lot of my reading audience. You have to grab the reader right away with a compelling reason to keep reading."

The story did go into figures, quoted a number of sources and gave differing views on who is responsible for the nation's health care—which required calls to dozens of sources. But the documentation came only after Perlman had allowed the reader to see Baby S in her incubator.

A reporter on assignment in a Central American country that had been ruled by three generations of dictators wanted to learn what people thought of the present head of state. The president's grandfather had been ruthless. One of his favorite methods of torturing opponents was to dip them head down in a well. The grandson supposedly was enlightened.

The reporter went into the countryside to find out what the campesinos thought. In one of his interviews, he asked an elderly farm worker whether there was any difference among the three presidents.

"Un arbol no puede dar tres clases de frutas," the laborer replied, and the reporter wrote this in his story, along with the English translation, "One tree cannot give three kinds of fruits."

Despite the president's elaborate and expensive public relations apparatus in the United States, directed at painting him as democratic, the homespun saying of the farm laborer carried more weight than presidential press releases.

Showing vs. Telling When Jeff Klinkenberg wrote his story about a shark fisherman, he began it by showing us his man fishing from a bridge:

> Ron Swint moaned in the dark about the shark called Old Hitler, the largest shark in Tampa Bay, as traffic roared by on the Skyway Bridge. Somebody in a car shouted and Swint automatically winced. . . .

The reader is put on the bridge with Swint, in the dark, in the middle of traffic, hearing Swint moan, seeing the traffic roar past.

Telling the story would have led to something like this:

> Ron Swint is after the largest shark in Tampa Bay, Old Hitler, and he fishes from the Skyway Bridge in the dark, as traffic roars by.

That's not the worst beginning that can be written, but it pales beside Klinkenberg's.

Showing lets the reader see, feel, smell and even taste:

> The food at political picnics in Vadonia County starts with chowder, large bowls of it with the clams so thick you can hardly see the broth. Then there are the vegetables—green beans, long and slender; zucchini, sliced lengthwise and—take your pick—fried or boiled; corn, heaped in bowls, a large gob of butter slowly melting into the kernels; beets, red and succulent, sweet as candy. . . .

Simply **telling** the reader takes away the joy of feeling, smelling, tasting:

> The food at political picnics in Vadonia County is plentiful. There are various vegetables, clam chowder and several kinds of meat to choose from.

Center on Quotes. Klinkenberg likes to structure his stories around quotations. When he organizes his story, he underlines his "best quotes," he says.

"When I have the time, I'll type them out, and then I'll assign different values to different quotes. My best quotes I'll try to get high in the story and then proceed in a kind of descending order.

"I'll try to save a couple of good ones for the end. I think it's a good way to organize a story."

A guideline: Good quotes up high.

Details Count

This shark, the story reports, was 12 feet 7 inches long and weighed 732 pounds. The specifics sound convincing. But there are sharks and then there are sharks. What kind did this fisherman hook on his first shark-fishing venture? (It was a tiger shark.) *St. Petersburg Times*

With a touch like that, this writer might as well be typing out menus for the fast-food outfit down the street.

Providing Specifics   One reporter wrote, "There were about a dozen people in the courtroom to hear the verdict." Another wrote, "There were 11 people in the courtroom, including the defendant's girlfriend."

It doesn't require much thought to understand which reporter has the convincing detail. We know the second reporter was there, on the scene.

If the book that was stolen from the library was 4 inches by 6 inches, say so. Don't write, "It was a small book." Write, "The valuable book was 4 inches by 6 inches, small enough to fit into a coat pocket." This is a specific detail plus an image. We can see the book nestled in the thief's coat pocket.

Readers love details that help them visualize events and people: "The suspect is a 5-foot-4-inch woman who wore blue jogging shoes, a tight yellow blouse and blue denim jeans. Her brown hair was close-cropped. She used a small handgun that fit in the palm of her hand."

Look at how a *Miami Herald* reporter began a story of a youth's murder:

Sixteen-year-old Kenneth Richardson was killed Thursday over a floppy brown hat, police said.

The reporter notes sizes, weights, numbers of things, colors, smells. Was it as large as a baseball or a basketball, as heavy as a letter or a book? Did it smell like onions, garlic or newly cut grass? Was it a deep blue, almost black, or the light blue of a sky after a rainstorm? Did it sound like the snap of a firecracker or the bang of a backfire?

Notice that in these questions the specifics are linked to things that can be seen, touched, smelled, heard.

Just as we avoid saying *around a dozen* or *small,* we do not use abstractions, such as *patriotism, equality, affection,* unless they are tied directly to a specific event or situation or we are quoting someone. Abstractions have no agreed-upon meaning. For example, what is obscenity? As a federal judge observed, "One man's lyric is another man's obscenity."

Words must be anchored to real things in nature. Should the source talk of the rights of the unborn, the meaning of the Constitution, the immorality of the young, the reporter is immediately alert. The reporter knows that these words mean different things to different people. Their meanings are elusive. The reporter has to grab the slippery words and tie them down, anchor them to real things.

The reporter will ask the source, "Can you give me an example of what you mean by a fair and decent wage?" As one reporter put it, "I always ask anyone who speaks in generalities for a 'for-instance.' "

"Make Me See"

"My first editor in the newspaper business was blind. . . . His name was Henry Belk. He was the editor of the Goldsboro (N.C.) *News Argus,* which then had a circulation of 9,000. He was a tall man, six foot seven, I believe, and he walked with a stretch aluminum cane. He wore a battered fedora, which must have been bought at a time when he had his vision and saw movies like "The Front Page." . . . Lucille, his wife, and a succession of high school students read to him every word of every issue of both the *News Argus* and the *Raleigh News and Observer.* And many, many days—I still wince at the thought of how many times—he would summon me into his cubicle after having heard my stories word by word and say, 'You aren't making me see. Make me see.'

"It took me years to realize it, but no one ever handed down the prescription for good writing more succinctly or better than Henry Belk in those three words, 'Make me see.'

"There is not much left to say. That is, after all, what good writing is all about—good reporting, too, for that matter. It is putting the reader on the scene, making him see, making him hear, making him understand. The task, of course, of every editor who wants to improve the quality of newspaper writing is to make reporters see that what they have to do is to make the reader see. It is that simple and, alas, that complex."

—Gene Roberts, managing editor, *The New York Times*

"We were developing a nice little collection of chalk outlines on the street." The quotation is from an interview with a Muskegon Heights, Mich., housing commissioner. He is talking about a city housing project ravaged by drugs and the consequence—death. The chalk marked the outlines of victims' bodies.

Lisa Perlman of the Associated Press knew that the quote would hit home. It was a dramatic image for her readers. You see the sidewalk and the markings—an urban epitaph.

Writers are on the lookout for the words that will paint pictures. For her story in the *Sun Times* of Old Orchard Beach, Maine, about church healing services, Melinda Vercini Noonan begins:

Pain always takes prisoners.

Anyone who has suffered, from a headache to a heartache, knows what it is to be encircled, bound and trapped by unceasing pain. Yes, you are a prisoner. The image is just right.

Make Me Care. Unsafe bridges in Tulsa was the subject of *The Tulsa Tribune* reporter's study. Some of the bridges were used by school buses. Mary Hargrove, the special projects editor of the newspaper, suggested that the reporter ride on a school bus before filing the story. "Put me on that bus," she said. "Make me care."

Stacatto and Solemn

Every piece of writing has a tone, a voice appropriate to the action being described. The basketball story is fast paced with short sentences. The piece about the Bible group is relaxed with long sentences.

Charlie Riedel, The Hays Daily News

Ken Elkins, The Anniston Star

Natural Style

Our fourth ingredient of the well-written story is a writing style appropriate for the event. That is, the style of writing should fit the subject.

Style for the writer has several meanings. We talk of *broadcast writing style,* by which we mean that the writing is attuned to the ear. Sentences are short, the present tense is used and details that might confuse the listener are avoided.

We also talk of *style* as in the stylebook: Abbreviate the word *street* in an exact address, but spell out when there is no street number. Thus, the textbook has it as *1314 Kentucky St.,* but *Kentucky Street* without the specific address. The AP does not use the courtesy title Mr. on second reference, but *The Wall Street Journal,* as you read in the piece about the debt-burdened Mr. Floyd, does.

But here we are talking about something less certain, less exact. *Style* is also the feel, the tone of the story. Put it this way: When you catch a snatch of a tune, chances are you know whether it's Streisand or Madonna. You look at a painting in a museum and you can tell whether it is a Picasso or a Rembrandt. Style. The individual's touch.

Now it's true that many writers have a style of their own. Hemingway's was brusque, mostly show, little tell. Henry James' style was circular, triangular, dense. He told, constantly.

Listen to Your Words

"When you write, you make a sound in the reader's head. It can be a dull mumble—that's why so much government prose makes you sleepy—or it can be a joyful noise, a sly whisper, a throb of passion.

"Listen to a voice trembling in a haunted room:

" 'And the silken, sad, uncertain rustling of each purple curtain thrilled me—filled me with fantastic terrors never felt before. . . .'

"That's Edgar Allan Poe, a master. Few of us can make paper speak as vividly as Poe could, but even beginners will write better once they start listening to the sound their writing makes."

—Russell Baker, columnist

But the journalist on the beat, the writer of news releases and the advertising copywriter adapt their style to the particular nature of the situations they are describing. Most media writers have a hundred voices: An obituary—tell it with solemnity. A close football game—tell it breathlessly. The company president's annual report to stockholders—tell it matter-of-factly.

The profile of a young woman who has just won a beauty contest will not be written with the same somber style as the obituary of a local resident. The profile will be breezy:

Evelyn Marie Welton woke up yesterday morning with a headache.

Last night she went to bed with a head full of dreams.

The 19-year-old Mason City college sophomore was crowned Miss Douglas County at the Civic Auditorium last night. Next month, she goes to the state finals.

"I felt terrible, just terrible all day," Welton said after her victory. "But as soon as I walked into the auditorium, something happened. Like, you know, it snapped."

The lights, the excitement of competition, the possibility of going all the way to the top had its effect.

"I just knew I could do it," she said. . . .

On the other hand, the obituary will be somber and reserved:

Albert Funnel, 78, of 45 East Alpine Ave., who served as city clerk for 46 years before retiring, died yesterday after a long illness.

Funnel had been hospitalized a week ago with lung cancer.

The former city worker was known throughout the state for his innovations in the office of city clerk. He instituted a new system of . . .

Most news stories report events that have occurred within the past 24 hours. These stories rely for their effect on their immediacy, and they get right to the point with direct leads:

CLEVELAND—Neck-and-neck heading into Tuesday's U.S. Senate primary, Democrats Joel Hyatt and Mary Boyle clashed on crime yesterday, angrily accusing each other of lying.

—*The Blade*, Toledo

HUBER HEIGHTS (AP)—Thirty vehicles were involved in a pileup yesterday on Interstate 70 near this Dayton suburb, police said.

No fatalities were reported.

Rolaids makes an annual award to the best relief pitchers in baseball, and the company uses the award in its advertising. Kevin O'Donoghue of Young & Rubicam knew that the announcement of the award would interest sports fans.

He created an ad of two sections: one with 28 baseballs and under each ball the name of an award winner, and the other with one large Rolaid. The sections were headed: "All time great relievers" and "All time great relief."

A Grim Story   Mitch Mendelson had a tragic story to cover, a house fire in which five people died. The style of his story is simple and direct. Long sentences alternate with short ones. The average sentence length is 13 words. He lets the facts show the tragedy. He gives them no adornment. Here is the beginning of his understated story, which appeared in the *Birmingham Post-Herald*:

The use of a delayed lead puts the reader on the scene.

A coroner stood in the rain yesterday afternoon and poked through the smoldering rubble of what had been a house. She was looking for the bodies of four young children and their great-grandmother.

A helper standing nearby shivered.

One by one, the tiny, charred figures were carefully zipped into black vinyl body bags and carried away.

A chilling quote sums up the tragic event.

As the coroner, Dale Cunningham, was leaving, a passer-by asked if there were any bodies left in the ruins. "Five is all," she said. "Five is too many."

Reginald, 4, Stephanie, 2, Roderick, 2, and Amanda Gardner, 6 months, and Fannie Harvell, 88, were killed by a fire that destroyed their Dolomite home yesterday morning.

The essential facts fill in the story.

The children's mother, Sandra Gardner, 23, was reportedly visiting neighbors when the fire started. Her 19-year-old brother escaped the house. Ms. Gardner was treated for shock at Lloyd Nolan Hospital in Fairfield.

All four children were in the same room. One body was found in a corner, another under a bed.

Mrs. Harvell died near the back door. . . .

Some Guides

We've seen the ingredients of the writing that people will want to read or listen to. And we have seen some examples of how these principles are used. Most of the writers whose work has been used in this textbook so far did not become media writers the day they first confronted a keyboard. They learned, and for many it was a struggle.

Most of them who studied writing were given two rules about writing news stories:

1. Structure all stories in the form of an inverted pyramid. This means that all important material should be placed high in the story, preferably at the beginning.

2. The beginning of the story should answer these questions:

Where?   Who?
Why?   What?
How?   When?

The rules work well enough, as we can see in these leads:

Gov. Janet Kocienowski will speak tomorrow at 7:30 p.m. in the Civic Auditorium on methods of reducing the number of violent crimes in the state, which increased 22 percent last year over the previous year.

John Whitticomb, 22, of Hampton, a Mallory College senior, was seriously injured last night when the motorcycle he was driving struck a tree after he lost control of the vehicle on a section of Highway 28 that had recently been damaged by a washout.

These leads hold so much information they can just about stand alone to tell the story. For brief items, for news roundups and when space is at a premium, the old formulas still work and work well. They help us find out what is happening, quickly.

Storytelling

But when people settle back for a good read, they want more than telegrams in their reading matter. Writers are told these days to tell stories.

One way to hold on to readers—and this is serious business for newspapers and magazines—is to make the straight news item into a news feature, when appropriate. Which of these two accounts do you prefer?

Straight News Lead

City officials said today Miami's public pools will close at 5 p.m. this summer instead of at 8 p.m. because of a shortage of lifeguards.

News Feature Lead

Miamians seeking cool, wet relief on hot summer evenings won't find it this year at the city's public pools. For the first time in years, they are closing at 5 p.m.

It isn't a tight budget that is forcing the pools, traditionally open until 8 p.m., to close early in this summer of high inner-city unemployment. It's precisely the opposite.

The city can't hire enough certified lifeguards to staff them, said Brian Finnicum. . . .

The news feature lead was used by *The Miami Herald* and we'd all agree that it is more entertaining. It doesn't tell us any more than the brief version. In fact, some might say it is an accessory to denuding Canadian forests. Be that as it may, the trend in journalism is toward storytelling, even if it takes more space.

As a consequence of the interest in storytelling, some writing coaches have interred the two old guides. Not so fast, folks. First, they remain useful for many kinds of basic news events. Second, they are excellent as starting points for apprentices.

Clutter

Clutter is the enemy of clarity. Sentences that bump and grind their way from capital letter to period without regard for clarity and directness are like franchise city—an incoherent mix of competing signals. The sentence makes a single point. Each word is chosen to contribute to that point, and every sentence builds the case for the story's theme.
Mike McClure

Too many beginning writers figuring they can fly free of formulas write what they take to be splendid prose only to find they've left out the location of the accident (where), the date of the meeting (when) or the reason the singer failed to show (why).

Only the rare genius needs no learning period. No apprenticeship. For the rest of us, learning by following formulas isn't a bad idea. Then we can fly free. And therein lies a modern morality tale.

Elvis and His Songwriter   After five years of writing successful songs for Elvis Presley, one of his songwriters found he was repeating himself. The songs were successful enough, he knew. But they were being ground out to a formula, and he was bored.

Presley had no reason to change his style since it continued to be a huge financial success. However, the writer felt he was not being challenged. His musicianship was not growing. He decided to leave Presley, to move on.

Much of what's been prescribed so far in this textbook may seem to the aspiring writer as much a formula as the ingredients of Presley's songs. But for the ambitious, for those who aspire to stand out, it is sometimes necessary to move beyond formulas and set ways. It's possible to do this but only after mastering the basics. And that is hard work.

Early on, writers discover that exciting, fascinating prose doesn't flow like water from a faucet. It must be coaxed forth. Writing is hard work at the beginning of a career, in the middle and to the end.

Joyful Agony Everyone who writes for a living—poets, novelists, critics, advertising copywriters, public relations practitioners—knows the joy of making ideas come to life . . . and each knows the agony. Especially the pain of rewriting.

Kirk Citron, a senior writer with the Hal Riney & Partners advertising agency in San Francisco, wrote 300 headlines for the California prune growers before he was happy with one. It was a prizewinner. Good writing is rewriting.

Henry David Thoreau produced seven versions of *Walden* in the six years he worked on the book. Behind the beautiful and clear story of his two years alone by a Concord pond are years of toil.

Caskie Stinnett, an essayist and critic, says Thoreau "stopped and started, tinkered and rearranged, selected and discarded, chose and reconsidered, and fought with the English language until he forced it to come to terms with him."

Errors Galore

No matter how thorough the reporting and checking may be, however interesting the writing, all this work can be undone by a small slip, an error in spelling, a misplaced comma. Errors are like mosquitoes at a campsite. No matter how careful we are, they manage to infiltrate our tent. There are just too many of them, and their determination exceeds our precautions. They surround us—incorrect and inappropriate word use, misspellings, clichés, poor grammar, misdirected apostrophes and commas.

Let's stroll around the states and Canada and see what we find. Before we take off, here's something from the U.S. Postal Service that came in this morning's mail:

> By using this address information correctly, it will enable new automation equipment to sort your mail to it's proper destination.

Oh, oh. That's one *oh* for each mistake. Can you spot the two errors?

A circular distributed in Tecopa Hot Springs, Calif., announces that a pancake and sausage breakfast will be **sponsered** by the junior high school.

Signs on highways near Uvalde, Tex., and Hot Springs, S.D., invite travelers to visit the **tradeing** posts in town.

A poster in Roosevelt Hospital in New York City invites patients to a special clinic with this question:

> Want to **loose** weight?

The sign on the canopy over the pumps at an Exxon service station in Batavia, N.Y., reads:

> **CLEARENCE** 12′9″

The Lakeside Motel in Parry Sound, Ontario, lures travelers to stop with a sign offering the use of **peddle** boats.

Along Interstate 90 east of Mitchell, S.D., motorists in trouble are advised of a 24-hour **toe** service.

A sign at the entrance to the Publix Supermarket in Homestead, Fla., warns customers:

> According to our license, alcoholic beverages may not be **drank** in this store or on the parking lot.

A tourist brochure for the Copper Queen Hotel in Bisbee, Ariz., says the town "remains architecturally as it stood in **it's** heyday."

The AAA Tour Book for three southern states contains an advertisement for a motel in Myrtle Beach, S.C., that boasts of a "**seperate** meeting room."

In its brochure, the Stihl company warns users of its chainsaws about "the **occurance** called 'kickback.' "

New York University's School of Continuing Education advertises its writing courses: "NYU has something for every**one** who wants to insure that words never fail **them.**"

Not to be outdone, the New York University Department of Applied Psychology has a form for recommendations supporting applicants. It states, "Feel free to use your own **stationary** and attach to this form. . . ."

A poster in Bloomingdale's department store asks, "What **does** an old farm and Bloomingdale's have in common?"

But who can blame the folks who committed these errors when in newspapers and on television errors of this sort abound?

A Dunkin' Donuts television commercial says, "The problem with supermarket doughnuts is there's no telling how long they've been **laying** there."

At the St. Patrick's Day Parade, the *Savannah Morning News* recalls, 86 of the 87 females in the parade had "stripped to the **waste.**"

The network sports announcer comments that Notre Dame is completing many passes because the pass defenders "have **overran** the receivers."

The Boston Globe referred to a man who had been arraigned on a charge of "**negligible** homicide."

A TV script described a man who "was found **hanged to death.**"

The Milwaukee Journal ran a story about tourists who "**pour** over English lessons."

Editor & Publisher reported that the faculty of Boston University's School of Public Communication found "the Pakistan environment **teaming** with secret agents. . . ."

The New York Times contained this quote: "But I have **alot** of respect for the people."

The Washington Post described attempts to keep Northern Virginia's **principle** reservoir from drying up. It mentioned a company that has **became** the first to put a new machine to use.

The *Eugene Register-Guard* said a conductor stopped "at a Christmas **bizarre**."

The Beaufort (S.C.) *Gazette* said, "Despite the **bazaar** delay, the 'Brigadoon' was the first boat to pass the finish line."

The AP wrote of the "**first annual** International Congress."

The *San Francisco Examiner* wrote, "When your best player is out, and a lot of teams are **effected** that way now . . ."

The Assn. of Independent Colleges and Universities sent this out in a news release: "There is also a substantial reduction in grants to part-time students ($1.1 million **effecting** 2,500 students)."

The Iona College news office printed this headline:

Westchester-Rockland School Districts **Effected**

James Reston, the respected columnist for *The New York Times,* told his readers of a "**serious crisis**" abroad.

If carpenters treated their tools the way too many journalists treat language, their walls would sag, their floors would slope and the carpenters would be on the unemployment line before long.

Granted, language does change. But some things never change. Periods will always be used to end sentences, and the verb will always have to agree with the subject. The spelling of *grammar* will always have *ar* at the end, not *er,* and *sophomore* will undoubtedly always be spelled that way and never *sophmore.*

An important point needs to be made about why these mistakes occur. Much of the time they are the result of poor thinking or no thinking at all.

Muddy Thinking = Mistakes

Every person who works with tools knows just what each tool can do. The auto mechanic would not think of using an air pressure gauge to measure the gap of a spark plug. It would make no sense. But writers sometimes fling words around with little regard for their use. They reach into their word kit and haul out something that looks or sounds as though it could do the job.

TWO SOVIET COSMONAUTS SUCCESSFULLY DOCKED THEIR SOYUZ 35 SPACE CAPSULE. . . .

GOSSIPOL WAS FIRST DISCOVERED IN 1971 AFTER PEASANTS IN . . .

ARMED GUNMEN SUNDAY KIDNAPPED THE OWNER AND EDITOR OF THE WORLD'S LARGEST CIRCULATION. . . .

These are from wire service stories.

The fact that the capsule was docked indicates it was a successful venture. The modifier *successfully* is a wasted word.

The second excerpt also has an unnecessary modifying word, *first.* When something is discovered, it is obviously for the first time. Could Columbus discover America in 1492 and then discover it again a few years later on another voyage?

As for the third sentence, ask your friends if they have ever heard of an *unarmed* gunman.

These three sentences are examples of redundancies, needlessly repetitive words.

Redundancies

What do these phrases have in common: serious crisis; trudged slowly; ran quickly; ominous portent; carefully scrutinized?

They belong to the same family as *totally destroyed* and *first annual,* the family of redundancies. The parents of these awkward children, these needless repetitions, conceived them in a passion of adjectivitis and adverbitis. Redundancies are also the offspring of muddy thinking.

Serious crisis—What crisis is trivial (adj.)?
Trudged slowly—You cannot trudge rapidly (adv.).
Ran quickly—Try any other way to run (adv.).
Ominous portent—See dictionary for *portent* (adj.).
Carefully scrutinized—Ditto for *scrutinize* (adv.).

Here is a list of the most common redundancies. It was compiled by the Minnesota Newspaper Association.

absolutely necessary	enclosed you will find	reasonable and fair
advance planning	exactly identical	redo again
ask the question	fair and just	refer back
assemble together	fall down	refuse and decline
at a later day	first and foremost	revert back
attached hereto	friend of mine	right and proper
at the present time	gathered together	rise up
canceled out	honest truth	rules and regulations
city of Chicago	important essentials	send in
close proximity	necessary requirements	small in size
consensus of opinion	open up	still remain
carbon copy	other alternative	temporarily suspended
continue on	patently obvious	totally unnecessary
cooperate together	plain and simple	true facts
each and every	postpone until later	various and sundry

Clichés

If at first you don't succeed, try, try again. Hit the nail on the head. Cool as a cucumber. Out of the frying pan into the fire. Sadder but wiser. Make hay while the sun shines. Love makes the world go 'round.

At one time these were original and picturesque expressions. But their novelty was their undoing. Writers picked them up and used them and overused them. These expressions have been ground down to the humdrum and dull, so today phrases like these are known as *clichés.* No writer who is proud of his or her writing will resort to using these stale and tired expressions.

Because these sentences and phrases are heard everywhere, all the time, writers have them imprinted in their memory banks, and in the struggle to find an apt expression the clichés pop out. Shove them back in again.

Here is a small part of a list of clichés Block put together one day from the wires of the press services. Block says these are a small portion of those he gathered:

CHICAGO—THIS IS THE UNKINDEST CUT OF
ALL. . . .
NEW YORK—THE FIGHT FOR THE
NOMINATIONS SEEMS TO BE ALL OVER SAVE THE
SHOUTING.
FORT WAYNE, IND.—MARTHA COLEMAN . . .
MET WITH FEDERAL AGENTS BEHIND CLOSED
DOORS. . . .
NEW YORK—ABC AND NBC BELIEVE COMEDY
IS THE WAY TO KEEP LAUGHING ALL THE WAY TO
THE BANK.
UNIONDALE, L.I.—THE NEW YORK ISLANDERS
COMPLETE A RAGS-TO-RICHES CLIMB TO . . .

Block says the most breathtaking set of clichés he heard came from the keyboard of a radio news writer describing the entry of a reluctant candidate into a race: "Jones dropped the other shoe, threw his hat in the ring and now it's a whole new ball game."

Journalese

The dictionary defines *journalese* as the language style characteristic of news writing. Among journalists, *journalese* is known as the combination of clichés, hack writing, overwriting, exhausted phrases and supercharged prose that is the sign of the hopeful beginner or the hopeless veteran.

In journalese, costs and the crime rate are always *skyrocketing,* and officials who worry about problems often *raise the red flag.*

When a group meets for any period longer than an hour, the meeting is said to last *long hours.* The facts raised in meetings are *cold facts,* sometimes *hard facts.*

Close elections are always *cliff-hangers,* and when someone is elected he or she may *kick off* the term with an inaugural speech. An official who does something unusual is said to have *written a page in the political history books.*

People often *hail* the actions or statements that please them. The AP polled its correspondents to determine the most overworked word or phrase, and the winner was *to hail.* Or, as journalese would have it, *to hail took the honors.*

Synonyms for *said*

Another strong entry in the AP poll was the variety of synonyms for the word *said.* For some reason, writers prefer *declared, stated, asserted; whispered,*

Temptation. "When the facts themselves don't make the reader's pulse beat faster, the journalist thinks it his duty to apply the whip and spur of breathless words and phrases. Since they exist only in finite numbers, they get repeated, and repetition begets their weakening, their descent into journalese."

—Wilson Follett, Modern American Usage

shouted, declaimed; repeated, recalled, remembered; inquired, asked; pronounced, related and *announced.*

The reluctance to use the word *said* has at least two causes. One is a fear of using the same word twice in a news story. If a news writer is doing a piece about Expo '96 it's perfectly all right to use synonyms—exposition, event, exhibition, display, presentation. But *said* catches no one's attention, no matter how often it is used, and substitutes for it usually exaggerate the nature of the statement and mislead the reader.

The other cause is the inherent desire of writers to strut their stuff. Anyone can use the verb *said.* "Look at how many words I can think of to dazzle you," says the writer. True, a barrage of *police said, he said, she said* is unappealing. To make their stories move faster, careful writers will use a phrase that avoids this repetition: *Police gave this account, he offered these suggestions, she made these points.* These phrases are followed by the points the source made or the information that was offered.

Journalese is contagious. "She was credited with the murder of her son." This sentence is from a wire service story. The phrase *credited with* makes the sentence grotesque. Even so, some reporters use it to express causation. A similar phrase is *thanks to,* as in this one from a southern newspaper: "Thanks to the recent storm, 600 people were left homeless in the delta area." Soon we may expect to see sports writers writing, "Thanks to Johnson's tackle, Simms suffered three broken ribs and a fractured nose." Simms' parents will have to send Johnson a thank-you note.

Summing Up

This is a chapter of do's and don'ts, too much for anyone to swallow in a gulp. And as if what's gone before is not enough, here is some closing advice from Charlotte Evans, who helps to direct the training program for young reporters at *The New York Times.* Evans says the two most common mistakes of beginners are:

1. Lack of details in the story to support the lead.
2. Generalities rather than specifics.

Look at these two points again. Yes, the major writing failures can be tracked to reporting failures. No amount of showing, of simple language and of stylistic excellence can compensate for the eyes that do not see, the ears that do not hear.

Presuming, then, that your fact gathering is operating in top form, let's move on to examine in detail two important tasks of the media writer: how to begin the account and how to structure the form.

Suggested Reading

Capon, Rene J. *The Word*. New York: Associated Press, 1982.

Clark, Roy Peter, ed. *Best Newspaper Writing for (year)*. St. Petersburg, Fla.: Poynter Institute for Media Studies (year). (Annual anthology.)

Howarth, W.L. *The John McPhee Reader*. New York: Vintage Books, 1977.

Strunk, William Jr. and E.B. White. *The Elements of Style*. New York: The Macmillan Co., 3d Edition, 1979.

Terkel, Studs. *Working People Talk About What They Do All Day and What They Think of While They Do It*. New York: Pantheon Books, 1972.

Terkel, Studs. *An Oral History of World War II*. New York: Pantheon Books, 1984.

5 Values and Beginnings

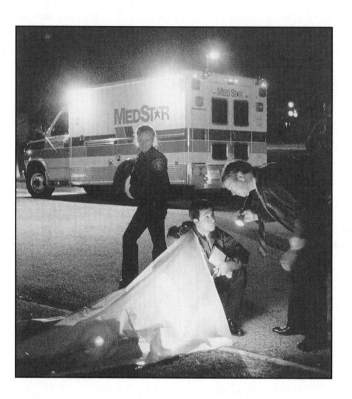

Our interest is aroused when something new, important or different strikes us. Media writers make use of this human response. Fort Worth residents were shocked to learn from their newspaper that their city's crime rate is among the highest in the nation. *Rodger Mallison, Fort Worth Star-Telegram*

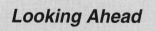

Looking Ahead

The news value of an event is determined by its impact on people, the unusual nature of the event and the prominence of the people involved. Factors that add to news value are conflict, proximity, timeliness and currency.

The beginning of the story takes its shape and content from a determination of how best to tell the story—directly as straight news or indirectly as a feature.

What Is News?

Our examination of the news story begins in a stately old building, the county courthouse. On the second floor, in a large room filled with metal file cabinets, a young woman is standing at a long counter looking over some documents. She is the county courthouse reporter for the local newspaper.

As she examines the records, she places them in two piles. The larger pile consists of court documents that she has looked through for news and has rejected. The other pile includes material she has set aside to take notes from for news stories.

She reads rapidly, but the damage suits, pleadings and other documents seem inexhaustible. At one sheaf of papers, she hesitates. Then she studies the pages closely. She tosses the document on her newsworthy pile. A new reporter learning the beat asks her why she decided to take a second look at the document.

"It seems to be important," she answers.

"I have two guides I use to separate material. Either the material is important or it's so unusual that it will make an interesting story.

"This one is important because it is a request by a big developer to have the court force the county to issue a building permit for a shopping mall north of town. It means a battle is shaping up between developers and people who want to keep the area green."

She picks up two pages stapled together from her pile of possible news stories. "Here's one that isn't important at all. But it will make a good little story. It's wild." The papers describe a suit for damages of several thousand dollars by a woman who accused a department store Santa Claus of slapping her 6-year-old son.

"Whoever heard of someone suing Santa Claus?" she says. "This is the kind of story readers enjoy."

That evening, the novice reporter thought about what the courthouse reporter had told him. A recent journalism graduate, he was being given a tryout by the newspaper. He realized he had to sharpen his news sense so that he could distinguish between what is newsworthy and what isn't.

He wrote down two definitions:

1. News is material that the public must have because it's important.
2. News is material that is entertaining, that is fun to read.

He recalled reading something that illustrated his first definition of news:

> News is information that helps people solve their problems intelligently.

But what about the second category of news, entertainment? Well, as his grandfather used to say, people do not live by bread alone—they need an occasional delicacy.

The courthouse reporter's guidelines help us to know the range of news. Let's go a step further. If we were to examine newspapers and the transcripts of newscasts, we would find that news falls into three general categories.

Who's News? A rule of thumb for determining what is newsworthy: The smaller the community or the audience, the greater the amount of personal news. Make an illegal left turn and you may find your name in the small-town newspaper next day, alongside the day's hospital admissions, marriages, divorces, births and deaths. The newspaper will name all the high school graduates.

The big-city newspaper will not carry every murder, will mention the hospitalization of the mayor, marriage of the governor, divorce of the junior U.S. senator and will pass on 95 percent of the deaths that day.

Three Basic Determinants

Most news stories (1) are about events that have an **impact** on many people, (2) describe **unusual** or exceptional situations or events or (3) are about widely known or **prominent** people. The length of a news story is usually determined by the number of people affected by the event and/or the number of people interested in the event.

Impact By *impact,* we mean importance or significance. One way to judge impact is to figure out what the results or consequences of a news story might be. The more people affected, the more important the story.

The Unusual An interruption of life's routine makes news. If something makes a reporter stop and stare, wonder and exclaim, then the reporter knows that what he or she is looking at may be newsworthy.

Prominence People who are widely known or who have positions of authority are said to be prominent. These are the newsmakers. They may be politicians or car dealers, priests or labor leaders, entertainers or cabinet members. If you recognize a person's name and think your readers will, chances are that the person is prominent. What prominent people do, even if it is unimportant, is often newsworthy. Names make news.

U.S. Navy

Shattering Events: Public and Personal

World events and personal problems affect us. We want to know more, and often we want to find out what we can do. Media writers supply such information.

The battleship USS Arizona, shown here after the surprise attack on Pearl Harbor on Dec. 7, 1941, went down with 1,100 men entombed in its hull. The story is retold to this day, and the site is a shrine.

Changing social and sexual customs have consequences. This public service advertisement suggests a solution to one problem.

Planned Parenthood Federation of America

Impact

The publication of this photograph by the *Missoulian* in Missoula, Mont., so outraged the public that it brought about a change in policy. The state had allowed hunters to shoot buffalo, and more than 520 were killed at the time the newspaper ran this picture. Embarrassed by the outcry, the state halted the killing. *Kurt Wilson, the Missoulian*

News Is . . .

"News is what interests a good newspaperman."

—Gerald Johnson, *The Sun*

"News is anything that will make people talk."

—Charles A. Dana, editor, *New York Sun,* 1869–1897

"News is anything that makes the reader say, 'Gee whiz.' "

—Arthur McEwen, longtime editor

Journalists, like historians, prefer dramatic events to the "great constants of the human condition—birth, childhood, marriage, old age and death."

—Robert Darnton, professor of history, Princeton University

Other Determinants

We need to examine four other factors that heighten the news value of an event: **conflict, proximity, timeliness** and **currency.**

Conflict   Conflict underlies our lives. There are internal conflicts with which we are all familiar. The student must master a list of Spanish verbs for a test the following day, but his friends are leaving for a movie. Conflict. The car owner notices that her car battery is running down. A new battery will cost $75. She has the money, but she had planned to use it for a cabinet she saw advertised. Conflict.

Eternal Struggles

Conflict is part of the human condition. People fight with each other, and they battle against the elements. After the U.S. Supreme Court declared school segregation unconstitutional and black youngsters tried to attend all-white public schools, violence erupted. One of the worst confrontations occurred in Little Rock in 1957 when whites attacked black parents taking their children to school.

The battle against inhospitable nature is symbolized in the famous photograph of a farm family in Cimarron County, Okla., during the 1930s when drought ravaged the land and created the Dust Bowl.

Wilmer Counts, The Arkansas Democrat

Arthur Rothstein, the Library of Congress

Almost every meeting of the city council, state legislature or Congress involves conflicts. The U.S. Constitution purposely sets governmental powers in conflict so that no one branch of government can dominate the others.

Probably because we are so familiar with strife, we overlook its drama except for the most obvious confrontations: strikes, political campaigns, courtroom confrontations, wars.

Less-evident conflicts are newsworthy too: the struggles of individuals against adversity, the woman trying to hold a family together on $100 a week, the historian with a view of Thomas Jefferson that conflicts with the established perception, the handicapped youngster trying to play baseball. Some of the best stories a reporter can dig up are the attempts by groups, organizations or individuals to contest prevailing attitudes. When women banded together in the 70s to protest what they called a sexist society, few reporters paid attention. In fact, the women were ridiculed as "bra burners." The few reporters who recognized the movement became acquainted at the onset with what was to become a massive and effective drive for sexual equality.

Proximity   "Anything that is close to my readers or listeners is more important than something remote." This is how one reporter defines proximity. When sociology students at the local college stage mock marriages for a class project, that's news in the local newspaper. It's of no interest to newspaper readers in a neighboring state, unless one of the couples elopes there.

Proximity usually refers to something physically or geographically close. A fatal accident at an intersection near a town interests local readers but is of no interest to people 100 miles away, unless the victims lived there.

Proximity has another meaning. People feel attached to those like themselves and to those with whom they share common interests. Catholics want to read about the activities of the Pope, and many Jews are interested in events in Israel. When a plane crashes in Cyprus, newspapers and broadcast stations will tell readers and listeners whether any Americans were aboard. The fewer Americans, the less relevant and important the story will be in the United States.

Timeliness   We always want to know the latest. We race to the minute hand on the clock. Our all-news radio stations, our newspapers and our television stations beat out a drumfire of news for us. We awake to the morning news, and we eat lunch to news and music. Dinner is scheduled around—sometimes with— the evening news.

News has a short life in this barrage. What occurs today has greater impact than an event that occurred yesterday, even if the event was not reported at that time. To impress their readers with the timeliness of their stories, news writers usually put the word *today* in their leads.

Journalism does a good job with the big event, with the new personality that looms up today on our screens. It is not so good at making news out of continuing situations. We jump when the thermometer spurts to 105. But when it stays at 100 and life goes on, no one pays attention.

We are now ready for the last of our determinants.

First Off.   "When people wake up in the morning, they want to know who died last night and whether it's going to rain. It's always been that way."
—*Reuven Frank, television news pioneer*

Prominence and Proximity—
Willie Nelson and Distant Death

The United Press International ran these two stories on its major news wire on the same day:

> LOUISVILLE, KY. (UPI)—Country music singer Willie Nelson canceled his scheduled appearance Saturday night at the Kentucky State Fair's closing concert because he is hospitalized with a lung ailment.
>
> Julie Shaw, Manager of the 10-day fair, said Sunday that Nelson—the top drawing card at last year's fair—had been hospitalized in another state for a serious respiratory ailment.
>
> Mrs. Shaw said she hoped to announce today a replacement for Nelson.
>
> 10:21 AED

The story above is not important, but Nelson's **prominence** led the UPI to give it this much space on its wire.

The following story is certainly more important than the illness of a country music singer, but its impact is diminished by its lack of **proximity** to readers in the United States. UPI gave it half the length of the Willie Nelson story.

> NEW DELHI, INDIA (UPI)—A bus fell into a canal today in the northern state of Kashmir killing 22 people, the Press Trust of India reported.
>
> The accident occurred near Pahalgaon, about 400 miles northwest of New Delhi.

Currency   One way to define *currency* is to say that it is a situation that's been around for a while whose time has finally come. Why? We're not sure. For poverty, it was a book President Kennedy read and made into a political crusade. For starvation in Ethiopia, it was a documentary made by a news team that was so poignant it broke the hearts of viewers, and starvation in Africa became news. Hunger was suddenly current.

In September 1989, President Bush declared war on drugs. Television and newspapers ran stories about drug abuse. The news weeklies put the war on their covers. Polls showed drugs were one of the two or three most important issues facing people. Drugs, a problem for at least two decades, suddenly became big news.

By the 1990s, however, the issue eased onto back pages and rarely made the evening news. Whereas 70 percent of those polled in 1989 picked drugs as a major national problem, only 25 percent cited drugs as a leading threat the following year. Why? Certainly, there has been no letup in drug trafficking and other crimes associated with narcotics. In fact, more than a million men and women continue to march through the courts each year on drug charges. And each year 300,000 drug-addicted babies are born.

The answer to our question takes us to a blurry area of journalism.

Other Factors

In the case of distant deaths, as in Ethiopia, proximity is at work. But we also seem to have a short attention span for death and poverty around the corner from our homes. Twenty-four countries have a lower infant mortality rate than the United States, the world's richest nation. Yet only the determination of a few committed reporters persuades editors to run a story on U.S. infant mortality. And 30 million people continue to live in poverty in this, the world's wealthiest country.

Why is it that after a spurt of interest in a continuing story the story is put to rest without resolution? One answer is that news is nervous. It shines its light here, now there, remaining nowhere for very long. Some say this characteristic reflects the public's short attention span, its need for novelty. Others contend that the media nourish this need, creating a public that hungers for something new and different daily, if not hourly.

As for drugs and poverty, sociologists tell us that middle-class people lose interest in a social problem that does not threaten them or their children. The media, of course, cater to the interests of the middle class. Also, news budgets determine what is news. A newspaper with a state capital bureau and a foreign staff will have much statehouse and foreign news, more than the paper that lacks such bureaus. When ABC closed bureaus in three Central American countries, its coverage there declined. We also know that when a newspaper is thick with advertising, more space is available for news and items appear in its news columns that on thin advertising days would be ignored. What's not news on Saturday or Monday is big news Thursday and Friday when the grocery and department store ads give the paper more space for news matter.

Gatekeeping

News floods into newsrooms in near-overwhelming cascades, and only the discernment of editor-gatekeepers prevents the staff from being engulfed. These editors understand the news needs of their communities and the limitations of their news operations. They are skilled decision makers.

In addition to understanding what makes news, they are aware of two other factors: Their need to match important news used by their competitors and the changing nature of the public's appetite for news.

All the Elements

The Pope's visit to Denver provided local media with elements that make for a newsworthy event—impact, prominence, timeliness, proximity. The *Rocky Mountain News* assigned 22 reporters, eight editors and 18 photographers to cover the visit, and it printed extra copies.

For many years, the Associated Press ran on its news wire a summary of the news on the front page of the first edition of *The New York Times.* The news judgment of *Times* editors was a guide to editors who made up the evening network newscasts and to newspaper editors everywhere. Nowadays, editors monitor all sorts of competitors, from the regional newspapers and local weeklies to cable television and radio talk shows.

One of the consequences of this sensitivity to competition is that some editors feel forced to run material they would prefer to ignore. The *Times,* for example, broke long-time policy to run the name of a woman who accused a member of the Kennedy clan of rape. It did so, editors said, because NBC News had done so.

Another factor affecting news decisions is the popularity of the nightly television syndicated magazine shows, shows whose editors, writes David Shaw, media critic of *The Los Angeles Times,* "seem willing to broadcast virtually any story, the sexier and the stranger the better, if only to fill that nightly void (and, not incidentally, drive those nightly ratings)."

The result, says Shaw, is that some editors "seem terrified of ignoring" these so-called news items.

Summing Up

We have sketched out the seven determinants of news: impact, rarity, prominence, conflict, proximity, timeliness and currency. The first three are the more important, and the remaining four extend or diminish the news value of the event through their presence or absence.

A brief word here about how these determinants are used. The first guideline, impact or consequence, implies that the event is so important readers or viewers should know about it. The event calls for the kind of telling that imparts the information effectively. This telling is done with the form we call the straight news story. The story begins with the most important fact or facts—the information that the writer considers will have major impact on the public.

The second guideline, the unusual or the bizarre, calls for another approach. The writer wants the reader or listener to slow down, to relax and enjoy this tale. And so, the form is the feature story with an inviting start that cajoles the reader into sitting a while as the story unfolds. The news point or lead is sometimes placed at the end of the piece as a *kicker.*

Service. "The primary purpose of gathering and distributing news and opinions is to serve the general welfare by informing the people and enabling them to make judgments on the issues of the time."

—*The American Society of Newspaper Editors*

Beginning the Story

We are now ready to use these news determinants or news values to write. But first, let's stop at a newsroom in California where the city editor is striding past the desks of reporters and editors. Although he holds no lash, only some papers, George's steely eyes and rasping voice make all hands squirm. George is one of the last of the old-fashioned city editors who believe that might is right.

The final edition has been put to bed and reporters are looking it over. George spots one reporter, a new man, who is sitting at his desk and staring at the ceiling.

"What do you think you're doing?" George snarls.

"Thinking, George," the reporter answers calmly.

"You're paid to write, not to think," George shoots back.

"George, you can't write if you can't think," says the reporter, and he resumes his communion with the ceiling.

For the first time in the memory of the oldest reporter on the staff, George is speechless. His mouth opens, shuts. Opens. Shuts. George walks back to his desk, sits down, stares out a window.

They say in that newsroom that on that fateful day George had come across something so true, so profound—for him—that he ceased his thunderous newsroom wanderings thereafter.

The reporter knew what he was talking about. Clear thinking underlies clear writing.

A plan, an approach precedes writing. Before writing, writers ask themselves:

1. What's the main point or focus of the story? What's the event about? First, is it about a person or an event?

2. Does this event make for a straight news story or a feature story?

3. What kind of lead should I use, a direct or a delayed lead?

4. If this is a straight news story and I use a direct lead, what major fact should I put in the lead?

5. If this is a feature story and I use a delayed lead, what anecdote or illustration will I use at the beginning to lure the reader into the story?

6. How do I structure the piece? What goes where?

These preparations may seem as intricate as those of a surgeon preparing for a brain surgery. Not at all. With practice, the steps become easier. And some stories seem to write themselves, even for the most inexperienced writer. But for now, keep these steps in mind before writing.

Finding the Focus

Boiled down to its essentials, every story is about either:

1. A **person** who has said or done something important or interesting or a **person** to whom something important or interesting has happened.

2. An **event** of importance or interest to many people.

The beginning of the news story, or the **lead,** usually summarizes the story's main theme. Look at a batch of news stories. Almost all of them will begin with a lead that answers one of these two questions:

1. **Who** said, did or experienced something?

2. **What** happened?

These questions take us to the heart of news writing. When a reporter sits down to write, there are almost always two choices:

1. If a person is central to an event, the writer answers the question:
What did the person say, do or experience?

Not That Way. "When I look at stories written by college students, the lead very frequently will be something like: 'The faculty committee met Wednesday.' Period. The story goes on to say that the committee decided something, and I say, Wait a minute, what the committee decided is the lead."

—*Walter Mears, AP*

Subway Saxophonist

The person need not be a headliner to merit attention. The entertainer who plays for dimes and quarters on a street corner or subway platform can make an interesting profile. "It's not Carnegie Hall or the Cow Palace," says the subway musician. "But it's a living."
Alejandro Videla

2. When an event is important or unusual, the writer answers the question: **What happened that was significant, exceptional or unusual?**

Look closely at the numbered items and you will see that they embody the three key news determinants—impact or consequence, the unusual and prominence.

Focusing on the Person   When an event involves an individual saying or doing something, or when an individual has something happen to him or her, the writer first must decide whether readers and listeners recognize the individual's name.

Is the singer Michael Jackson or Ralph Martin? If it is Jackson, most people will recognize the name, and *Jackson* will go into the lead. If it is *Martin,* few will know that name, and some kind of **identifying label** will have to be used: *A 26-year-old rock singer,* for example.

Here are some leads using the **name** of the person involved in the news event:

Who did what?

MALDEN, Mass. (AP)—*Malden Police Commissioner William A. Davidson* yesterday *ordered two police officers fired* after they arrested him for drunk driving.

Who said what?

SPRINGFIELD—*Chancellor William E. Barnes told* entering freshmen today *the way to academic success is through "unstinting effort."*

If the person central to the event is not well-known to the news writer's audience, a label must be used that allows readers or listeners to visualize the person quickly. The label can be **age** and **address** or **home town:**

Who experienced something?

A 39-year-old Kansas City, Kansas, man was charged Monday in Wyandotte County District Court *with the fatal shooting* early Saturday *of a patron* at a tavern in that city.
—*Kansas City Star*

The label can also be the **occupation** or **title** of the person:

Who experienced something?

A Kentucky State Police detective was shot to death yesterday afternoon while searching for marijuana in a field in rural Edmonson County.
—*Lexington Herald*

Who had something happen to him?

JACKSON, Miss. (AP)—*A high school principal* who was dismissed for letting students read prayers over the school's intercom system *has been ordered reinstated* at the end of the school year.

—*Los Angeles Times*

When a person's **connection to the event** identifies him or her, that relationship can be used as the identifying label:

Who experienced something?

HOUSTON (UPI)—*A Rolling Stones fan was stabbed to death* during the British rock group's near-sellout show at the Astrodome, police said Thursday.

Focusing on O.J.

The leads to the flood of stories about the pursuit, arrest and trial of O.J. Simpson, the ex-football star turned television sports commentator, movie actor and advertising celebrity, indicate the powerful pull of a well-known name to lead a story:

LOS ANGELES (AP)—An ex-wife of Hall of Fame football player O.J. Simpson and a man were found dead early Monday outside her condominium.

Football great O.J. Simpson's former wife and a 25-year-old man were found apparently stabbed to death outside her Brentwood townhouse early Monday morning.

—*Broadcast Bulletin*

Focusing on the Event When the **event** is the most important aspect of the story, the writer uses the lead to describe what occurred in the briefest way possible:

What happened?

A supply ship was blown to bits today when it hit a mine in the Gulf of Oman.
—"NBC Nightly News"

What happened?

THROOP, Pa. (AP)—*Eight teenage party-goers were crushed to death* when their car swerved into a guard rail, plunged some 190 feet through the air and crashed on its roof, officials said Friday.

What happened?

CHICAGO (AP)—*DePaul University's student newspaper was shut down* Friday after printing a story about a rape on campus, in defiance of orders from the director of student publications, the editor said.

Rescue—Event

When a blizzard struck Kansas pastures, endangering cattle, the National Guard dropped bales of hay to the stranded animals. *Charlie Riedel, The Hays Daily News*

Notice that these are all straight news leads. This is the type of story the reporter most frequently writes, and its mastery is important. When the event is unusual, the reporter writes another type of story, the feature.

Finding the Purpose

The second of the six questions we ask before writing is, "What is the purpose of the story?" The answer is important because a story takes its form from its purpose. We need to decide if the event makes for a straight news story or a feature story. If our purpose is to inform, we write one way; if it is to entertain, we write another way.

Let's imagine that you have been told about a fire that damaged a student hangout, the Pork Parlor, located near the campus. You are to write a story for class. You gather information from the fire department and the owner. Here is the story you write:

> A favorite student dining spot, the Pork Parlor, at 150 College Lane, was damaged today by a fire that started in the kitchen.
> The fire destroyed the kitchen and caused some damage in the dining area. Fire department officials said fat in a frying pan caught fire at around 6:30 a.m.
> The fire was under control in about 15 minutes, an official said. No one was hurt.
> Damage was estimated at $50,000. The owner, Steve Poulton, said insurance covered the loss. He said he plans to reopen in three weeks.

This is a straightforward news story. But suppose you also heard that one of the part-time employees, a college student, lost something valuable in the fire. A fire department official says he recalls her looking through some charred equipment in the kitchen. He thinks he heard her ask about a manuscript she had left there. You call Poulton and learn the student's name, Karen Yount.

You manage to reach Karen. She says she had just finished a term paper for her English class, had taken the disk to work and had put it in a cabinet in a corner of the kitchen. The paper would have been the basis of her grade in the course. She is an English major and needs the course credit to graduate. But now. . . . Her voice trails off.

What would you do? You might still write a straight news story and add Karen's loss to the piece with this paragraph at the end:

> But Karen Yount, a college senior, has no insurance for her loss. Her term paper for an English class was destroyed in the fire. She had put it in a kitchen cabinet when she went to work this morning at the Pork Parlor.

That's not a bad ending to the story. But would it make a better beginning? Should Karen's misfortune go into the lead of a straight news story? No, that would overplay her loss, which obviously has less impact on the community than the damage to the restaurant.

On the other hand, the fire was not serious. No one was hurt and $50,000 in damage is not large. As fires go, it was routine. What makes this fire different from others is Yount's loss.

All this reasoning could lead you to conclude that the incident might make a better news-feature story than a straight news account. You call Yount and obtain more information, and you write the following:

> For three months, Karen Yount spent most of her evenings in the library and at a word processor.
>
> A college senior, she was writing a term paper on the novelist George Eliot. It was to be the basis of her grade in the class and, she hoped, strong enough to impress the admissions committee at the University of Michigan, where she hopes to do graduate work.
>
> But her disk, and perhaps her grade and her hopes, went up in flames this morning.
>
> A fire at the Pork Parlor at 150 College Lane, where Yount works, destroyed the kitchen. Yount had put her term paper disk and books in a kitchen cabinet. She had failed to make a backup of her paper.
>
> The fire broke out at . . .

Most editors would prefer this approach to that of the straight news account.

Creating the Lead

Let's look closely at the beginning of a news story, the first words in a feature, review, editorial, broadcast story or news release. If we were to clock writers at work we'd see that they spend more time on their leads than on any other part of the piece. All writers know it's important to start off smartly.

Newly minted writers are surprised at how important lead writing is on the job. Editors often toss back stories after glancing at the lead only. But when they read a good lead, the lines around their mouths relax. The fastest way to success is through a good lead.

The lead has to accomplish a lot. First, of course, it must attract the readers or listeners, usually by informing them of what's ahead, what the piece is about. To attract and keep the reader, the writer pulls out all stops in the lead:

> Of all the men running for President in 1988, only two were forced, by the birth dates of their children, to admit having had sex with their wives before marriage—and those two, Pat Robertson and Jesse Jackson, were the only preachers in the race.

This is how Garry Wills begins his review of three books about the evangelical movement and the Christian right wing in *The New York Review of Books*.

Who could resist reading a book that begins this way?:

> Mom and pop were just a couple of kids when they got married. He was eighteen, she was sixteen and I was three.

This is the way jazz singer Billie Holiday started her book of recollections.

Not only does a good beginning grab the reader, viewer or listener, it helps the writer keep the theme or focus in view and the rest of the story on track.

Robert Schumann, the composer, advised his fellow composer, Johannes Brahms, to study the "beginning of the Beethoven symphonies . . . to try to make something like them."

"The beginning is the main thing; if only one makes the beginning, then the end comes of itself."

As experienced writers know, if the beginning is clearly in mind everything else goes well. When AP staff correspondent Edie Lederer was covering the tribal battles in Somalia, she came across a sight that she knew at once she would use to begin her story of what such strife meant:

> Habiba Tuhow insisted on climbing onto the
> death truck making its morning rounds so she could
> watch over her 5-year-old daughter Fardoza,
> wrapped in a small shroud on her final journey to the
> cemetery.

Look back at that sentence, that lead again. The picture it draws is truly terrible:

- Notice the verb *insisted*. We can see the anguished mother arguing with officers that she must be with her child during their last moments together.
- The phrase *morning rounds* tells us that death is routine in this situation, as commonplace as picking up the morning trash.
- The verb *watch over* suggests the tenderness this grieving mother holds for *Fardoza*. Lederer does not write *her daughter* but uses the name of the child to establish an intimacy with the reader.
- Another powerful verb—the child is *wrapped* in a small shroud. What does the verb show us? What is wrapped? Groceries and such are routinely wrapped. Is the writer trying to show us that death, even for a child, is ordinary here? It would seem so, that the verb carries out the concept of *morning rounds,* of death as part of the daily routine in Somalia.

The rest of the story flows naturally from these key elements in Lederer's lead—the daily death toll and its causes, the unsparing hand of death that takes children along with adults.

Cancer Outrage

When Heidi Evans of the *Daily News* discovered a potentially fatal blunder by the New York City Health Department, she began her story by getting right to the point:

What happened?

More than 2,000 Pap smears languished in a city health department laboratory for as long as a year, leaving hundreds of women at high risk of developing cervical cancer without knowing it.

The mayor reacted quickly, and the next day Evans told readers about the mayor's action:

Who did what?

Outraged that the Health Department allowed 2,000 Pap smears to sit unread in a city lab, Mayor Dinkins yesterday ordered the department to track down immediately the women whose tests have since shown they are at risk for cervical cancer.

The next day, Evans had another story on this fast-breaking series of events, and again she began her story with a direct account of what happened:

Who said what?

The city health commissioner yesterday pledged that by June 1 the city will find all the women who were put at risk of developing cervical cancer because their Pap tests were allowed to languish in a laboratory.

Promises and pledges make for reassuring reading, but reporters know that reality may be much different, and Evans checked on the commissioner's pledge and the next day wrote this lead:

Who said what?

Despite the city health commissioner's pledge to find all the women at risk of developing cervical cancer because their Pap tests sat unread in a city lab, clinic doctors said yesterday it is already too late to locate many of them.

In her journalism classes, Evans had learned that most situations require peeling away layers to get at the essentials. Her digging resulted in another major revelation:

What happened?

Top city officials knew early in 1989 that voluminous backlogs of Pap smear specimens had placed women in jeopardy of cervical cancer, according to documents obtained by the Daily News.

Evans continued to investigate. She learned that there were 3,000, not 2,000, backlogged cases and that 93 of the smears indicated health problems. These

Daily News
Inaction

Daily News
Assistance

Daily News
Negligence

Values and Beginnings   133

women were told to seek immediate medical attention. Evans decided to seek out some of the women involved to give the story a human dimension. She found the lucky and the unfortunate:

Who experienced something?

Like thousands of women who have turned to one of the city's sexually transmitted disease clinics for a checkup and a Pap smear, the shy high school junior was told to assume all was fine if she didn't hear back otherwise.

That was last July.

So when she reached home from school April 16 and found a Mailgram saying it was urgent she contact the Health Department about her Pap test, she feared the worst—that she had been diagnosed as having cervical cancer.

The student, the story related, was fortunate. She did not have cancer. Suspecting that some of the women involved wouldn't be as lucky, Evans continued to dig:

Who experienced something?

When Mary Pollack got the Mailgram it was Friday evening, too late to call the Health Department to have someone explain the message, "Urgent!! Concerning Your Health! Medical Emergency!"

On Monday morning, as Pollack held the Mailgram in her shaking hands, the doctor at the city's Jamaica, Queens, clinic gave her the scare of her life.

"You have cancer," he told her.

Now, look over the seven leads Evans created. The first five go directly to the point in the first paragraph. The last two hint at something to come later in the story. The point is delayed. We are now ready to discuss the two kinds of leads: direct and delayed.

Direct and Delayed Leads

There are few rules for leads. Generally, we say leads should be short, less than 35 words, if possible. From here, the rules depend on whether the story is a straight news piece or a feature.

The straight news story forces writers to fashion a lead that moves **directly** to the news point or focus of the event. If the writer decides to tell a feature story, he or she need not get right to the point; the lead may be **delayed** for effect.

There we have the two types of leads, the only two you need to think about. All other types fall into these two categories: *direct* and *delayed*. Don't fret about the long lists of lead types you will sometimes see—contrast, narrative, staccato,

Forget It. "Brevity (in leads) is not the primary goal. Clarity is. The old rule holds that the shorter the lead, the better. That's old enough to be forgotten. There are limits, but a 25- or 30-word lead is not necessarily better than one 35 or 40 words long. It needs to be simple and understandable, not necessarily short."

—*Walter Mears, AP*

direct address, etc. No one in the newsroom talks this way. You may hear the terms *hard* and *soft*. These terms are synonymous with *direct* and *delayed.*

Marianne, the courthouse reporter we encountered at the beginning of the chapter, knew that the Santa Claus damage suit would be a change of pace for readers. It was a soft story, so she began it with a delayed lead:

> Santa Claus is a child's best friend. The kindly old gent pats little boys on the head and little girls on the cheek.
>
> But two weeks ago, says Carolyn Elliott, a Zale's Department Store Santa whacked her 6-year-old son Dennis on the head.

Marianne had written about another damage suit, this one involving fatal burns that resulted from an office building fire. This time, she used a direct lead:

> An elderly couple filed suit today for $1 million against the Franklin Realty Co. in whose downtown offices the couple's daughter was fatally burned last August.
>
> Mr. and Mrs. Grant Foster, 22 Eastern Ave., claimed the company was negligent in. . . .

Deciding whether the news event calls for a feature or straight news treatment is not a simple or rote matter. Some writers seem inclined toward writing features, and others have a tendency to see events as straight news stories.

What would you have done when faced with this report?: A man had resisted having his pit bull quarantined after it had bitten three people and in a struggle with police, the owner, his father and a police officer were killed. Would you write a news feature beginning with the arrival of the officer with an order for the quarantine and then moving into a narrative of the events that followed?

Here is how the AP began its story:

> OAKLAND, Calif. (AP)—A police officer who was 11 months from retirement was killed Wednesday in a gunfight over a dog, along with the dog's owner and the owner's father.

The AP decided on a direct lead because of the gravity of the situation—three deaths. A news feature might trivialize the tragedy. This line of thought gives us a rule of thumb for leads: When the event is serious and has important consequences, get to the heart of the situation at once with a direct lead. When the event or situation is entertaining, diverting, the lead can be delayed in favor of an inviting beginning.

Writing the Lead

Let's presume you have decided whether the piece is a news story or a feature, whether you want a direct or delayed lead and how long the piece will be. Now you're ready to write.

Grab the Reader

"Some writers like to begin a story with some kind of jolting word play, and still others like to begin with some sort of description setting the mood. You have to allow your material to dictate what kind of lead you will use.

"The only rule is that you get the reader involved in the story and that you get him involved quickly.

"I think a reader will consider a novel some kind of investment and will not be dismayed that he is not quite grabbed by page 10. He will give the novelist or short story writer a lot of room and time to make himself clear and to make his book interesting.

"A newspaper doesn't have that kind of luxury. You've got to get the reader's attention very quickly."

—*Clyde Haberman, The New York Times*

Put It Off. Sometimes, the lead just won't come. Gladwin Hill, for many years with *The New York Times,* suggests that if the lead does not pop into mind quickly, "skip over it and jump right into the body of the piece. By the time you get to the end, a workable introduction will have occurred to you."

First, you should know that most sentences in the news story—certainly at least three-fourths of them—are simple, declarative sentences. They begin with a subject, which is followed closely by a verb and then an object. To put it another way, these sentences describe someone doing or saying something, or they show something happening:

• Chancellor Robert Hartmann asked the legislature to approve a $50 million university building program to meet the demands of increased enrollment.

• The state legislature last night defeated the $50 million university building bill by a vote of 67-13.

Let's apply the subject-verb-object (S-V-O) structure to these leads:

Who said or did what?

S—Chancellor Robert Hartmann
V—asked
O—legislature

What happened?

S—The state legislature
V—defeated
O—bill

Now that you can see the structure of the lead, it follows that to write a lead you look at the theme or focus and break it into its S-V-O components. Then you build the lead on this foundation.

Another approach is the time-tested *Five W's and an H.* Some beginners list these and answer the questions:

Who—Chancellor Robert Hartmann
What—asked the legislature to approve program
When—today
Where—(not in lead)
Why—to meet increased enrollment
How—(not in lead)

Take 10

Here are 10 notes you have on your notepad. Try to write leads from them. Then read on and we will see what news writers have done with these notes.

1. A Trans-American jetliner on a flight from Los Angeles to Miami runs out of fuel and must land in Tampa.

2. Disturbances occur in Worcester, Mass., when it is revealed that the Cockroaches, a rock group giving a concert at a local night spot, are actually the Rolling Stones practicing for their first American tour in three years.

3. A group of women blocks the approach to a nuclear reactor in Diablo Canyon, Calif.

4. A company makes a wage offer to striking steel workers.

5. More city jobs will be eliminated Friday to balance the budget.

6. An 18-year-old high-school student in Wisconsin devises a program to teach youngsters about the dangers of alcohol.

7. A New York City radio station switches music formats and becomes the most-listened-to station in the nation.

8. A state law passed last September sends youngsters into the adult court system.

9. A figure skating champion is superstitious.

10. A blind man sails a 35-foot sailboat.

Number 1   The writer doing a straight news story knows he or she must get to the point at once. Since the lead will include someone saying, doing or experiencing something, the writer begins with the person or the event—Who or What.

If the writer is working from the S-V-O summary, the **subject** will begin the lead. If the Five W's and an H are being used, **who** or **what** will start the lead.

Here is the S-V-O of number 1 of our list:

S—Jet
V—makes
O—emergency landing

The five W's and an H give us a more complete set of facts from which to work:

Who—Jetliner
What—made emergency landing
When—today
Where—in Tampa
Why—ran out of fuel
How—unknown

From either the S-V-O skeleton or the answers to the Five W's and an H, the lead is built. First, the **who** or **subject** of the sentence is written:

A Trans-American jetliner on a flight from Los
Angeles to Miami.

Notice that we say as much about the jetliner as possible to identify it, to separate this jetliner from the thousands that were flying on that day. We do the same thing when the **who** or the **subject** is a person. We don't say a man or a woman. We say *a 29-year-old steel worker* or *Mildred Sherman, 69, of 166 Chapel St.*

Next, we move to the **what** or the **verb** and the **object:**

made an emergency landing in Tampa today

Notice that we added the **where** and the **when** here. Place and time are usually placed near the verb or the object.

We could stop here, but the lead would leave people wondering about the cause of the emergency, the **why.** So we add the following:

> after it ran out of fuel.

Now we have:

> A Trans-American jetliner on a flight from Los
> Angeles to Miami made an emergency landing in Tampa
> today after it ran out of fuel.

This is a word-for-word duplicate of the wire service lead on the story.

Number 2   Our presumption in number 1 was that this was a news story that required a direct lead. But what about number 2?

Our first reaction is that this could be serious business—news story, direct lead. But the damage was minor and no one was hurt. The newsroom rule is: When in doubt, play it straight. That is, if the choice is not obvious, the best way to write the story is with a news approach and a direct lead. This is the safe way. To make light of a serious matter could be offensive. But how serious is this incident?

Numbers 3–5   Number 2 was played straight by most newspapers, which was safe but silly. Numbers 3 and 4 are straight news stories that took direct leads. Number 5, at first glance, seems like a straight news story. Is it?

A tipoff to the nature of number 5 is the word *more.* This means the layoffs are part of a series of layoffs. Words such as *again, still, continued* indicate there is not much new. Thus we lose the news determinant of timeliness.

Bob Rose of *The Blade* in Toledo made the event into a news feature with some enterprising reporting. In his story, he used a delayed lead. The theme does not come until the sixth paragraph:

Delayed lead: use of incidents to begin the story

One night this week, some Mabel Street residents went hunting for rats that had moved into their North Toledo neighborhood.

"I called rodent control, and they're closed up," Tom Munger said. "I talked to the mayor's office and the woman who answered the phone said she didn't know what I could do about it. She said I should have voted."

Mr. Munger, who admitted he did not cast a ballot on the payroll-income tax increase issue last month, said he and a neighbor took the problem into their own hands. "I think we got one," he said of the pests.

Delayed lead (continued)	One night later, L. Michael Duckworth, assistant city manager, got a telephone call at home from someone asking when the city's swimming pools would open.
Transition to theme	City officials know it, but some citizens apparently do not: With 846 layoffs in the last two years, Toledo cannot control rats and it cannot open the pools. It cannot do a lot of things it used to do.
Theme: news point	When 262 more city jobs are eliminated Friday, the city will have taken another step toward balancing its budget by bringing the work force down to 2,875. But the list of what it cannot do will grow longer.

Number 6   Number 6 obviously does not require a *today* in the lead. It is a news feature, so the AP put a delayed lead on it:

> FOND DU LAC, WIS. (AP)—Sometimes the best help a junior high school student can receive comes not from a teacher or parent but from a senior high school student.
>
> That theory, "Kids Helping Kids," is the idea behind a new alcohol awareness program developed by a St. Mary's Springs High School student for elementary and junior high school students.
>
> The program was developed by Jeff Weinshrott, an 18-year-old Springs senior. . . .

Here is the lead idea: High school student develops program to combat alcoholism among youth. The AP writer realized that the unique or unusual aspect of the event was a student teaching students about the dangers of alcohol. The writer used the idea to begin the story. The specific theme follows quickly in the second and third paragraphs.

Number 7   What happened in number 7? An FM station switched from mellow music to disco and its ratings jumped. Significant or entertaining? For a magazine devoted to reporting broadcast news, this is significant and a direct lead is in order. Something like this:

> By switching to disco, New York radio station WKTU-FM has become the most-listened-to station in the country.

But for a general audience, the reaction to that lead may well be, "So what?" For Geoff Walden, a student who wrote this story on assignment for a journalism class, it was an entertaining story, and so he used a delayed lead. He dramatized the switch this way:

NEW YORK—Last July 24th, at 5:59 p.m., WKTU-FM "Mellow 92" was playing Neil Young's soft-rock song, "It's Over."

At 6 p.m., WKTU-FM, "The new Disco 92," was playing Donna Summer's "The Last Dance."

For Donna Summer, the song went on to win this year's Oscar for the Best Original Song, for the movie "Thank God It's Friday." For the radio station, the song was the start of an all-disco format that has made WKTU the most-listened-to station in America, with an average of 275,000 people tuning in every quarter hour. . . .

The direct lead tells readers, "Here comes something important." Walden's beginning tells them, "Relax, I'm going to entertain you." But notice that the theme or central idea is exactly the same for both the direct and delayed leads:

S—Radio station
V—makes
O—format change

Number 8   Number 8 involves a law that was passed a while back. How should the story be approached?

Richard Higgins, another journalism student, reasoned that his story should describe the law in action with a strong human-interest element. So he began his story by portraying two young offenders in the new courtroom setting.

NEW YORK—Rafael Torres and Hector Valdez sat at the brown wooden table, playing with Superman coloring books, combing their hair, waving and occasionally shouting to friends in the room.

It could have been a scene out of the South Bronx junior high school where they are enrolled in the eighth grade. But it was the beginning of an arson and multiple murder trial in the Bronx Criminal Courthouse and the two skinny, squirming boys were not there to learn; they were the defendants. . . .

In the next paragraph Higgins introduces the central theme that tells the reader that these adolescents are among the first juveniles being tried in the adult courts. He makes a news feature out of his material.

Number 9   For this kind of feature, Linda Kramer, an AP reporter, says she gathers "piles of material for a story." When she writes, she tries to "weed out the non-essential copy. I want to choose the anecdote that best reflects and highlights what I want to say."

This is a precise description of how the writer must select an anecdote or incident to begin a feature or news feature story. The anecdote must feed directly into the theme or central idea.

"In writing about figure-skating champion Linda Fratianne, I led with a description of a lucky charm she pins to her costume during competition. To me, this little touch of superstitiousness illustrated the 17-year-old behind the star," Kramer says. This, then, was her theme: Although Fratianne's magnificent presence on the ice makes her seem almost regal, the real Linda Fratianne is a teenager with a young woman's feelings. Here is Kramer's first paragraph in her delayed lead:

> Tucked in a tiny blue pouch pinned to Linda Fratianne's sequined skating costume are two four-leaf clovers, a piece of gold foil, and a snip of green yarn.

Number 10   In number 10 the news writer takes the reader aboard the blind man's sailboat with this delayed lead:

> Keeping a grip on the sheet, Albert Adams draws the maximum amount of speed from his 35-foot sailboat.
>
> The yellow-hulled boat responds to Adams' touch and picks up speed. Adams turns to his crew—his wife and two teen-age sons—and asks them to lend a hand.
>
> Adams has been blind since birth. The 33-year-old accountant sails regularly. He can tell from which direction the wind is coming by ear. . . .

Like the beginning of many features, this one **shows** the subject doing something.

Straight News Lead

Let's look further at the spot news story, which is also called the straight news story, or simply the news story.

In Chapter 1, we watched a reporter write the obituary of Rose Harriet Allen. The event contains one major news determinant, prominence. There is some impact in the fact that a fund drive will be launched that will involve the public. The reporter decided to make this a straight news story, as most obituaries are.

Two strong elements are involved, each one a possible theme for the lead—the death, the fund drive. Should the lead contain the death only or both elements? Let's listen to the writer's thinking:

> *Everyone in town knows Allen, so I'll start with that and immediately go to the fund drive. The lead will include both elements.*

Here is the reporter's lead:

> Rose Harriet Allen, 71, of 33 Fulton Ave., who taught in Freeport schools for 30 years and was a school principal for 13 years before her retirement, died yesterday in the Community Hospital. A fund drive will be . . . .

The reporter continues to analyze her lead:

No, that won't do. The first paragraph will be a blockbuster, much too long. Maybe the better lead is the fund drive since that has lasting significance. Obviously, with that as a beginning, Allen's name will be worked into the story since the drive is in her memory.

A college scholarship fund is being set up in memory of Rose Harriet Allen, 71, who died yesterday after a career of 43 years in the Freeport public schools.

That's better. It's shorter and it combines the two elements.

She continues to write, and in the middle of the fourth paragraph she suddenly stops and slowly reads what she has written.

This is becoming a story about a fund drive, not the death of a well-known teacher who probably has thousands of friends in town. The impact, the real significance, is not the fund drive but her death. Allen's death will affect many of our readers who knew her as a teacher and principal.

The lead should concentrate on Allen's death and the fund drive should go lower in the story.

She starts over:

Rose Harriet Allen, whose teaching and administrative career spanned 43 years in Freeport public schools, died here yesterday at the age of 71.

Allen died in the Community Hospital where she had been since suffering a heart attack last week in her home at 33 Fulton Ave.

For 30 years, Allen taught in several of the city's elementary schools. For the next 13 years of her education career, she was the principal of the Lincoln School. She retired six years ago.

She is remembered as a friendly, outgoing teacher. As a principal, she delighted in taking a class for a teacher who was ill.

"She was strict," recalled Albert Green, a local lawyer. "If you didn't do your homework, she wanted to see your parents in school the next day."

Green and some of Allen's other former students said they are planning to establish a college scholarship fund in her memory.

"Miss Allen came from a poor farm family," Green said. "She used to tell us how hard it was for her to stay in school at State Teachers College, how she worked for a family for her room and board and did chores six hours a day, went to class and studied."

This version satisfies the reporter. It balances both important elements of the story, Allen's death and the fund drive. She has good quotes that tell something of Allen's personality. The personal details about Allen help the reader to visualize the kind of person Allen had been.

Presidential Assassinations

The direct lead tells the reader or listener what happened in as few words as possible. This has always been the reporter's purpose in covering breaking news stories, as the following leads about two presidential assassinations illustrate:

TO THE ASSOCIATED PRESS
THE PRESIDENT WAS SHOT
IN A THEATRE TONIGHT AND
PERHAPS MORTALLY WOUNDED.
—Lawrence A. Gobright, April 14,
1865.

———

UPI A7N DA
PRECEDE KENNEDY
DALLAS, NOV. 22
(UPI)—THREE SHOTS WERE
FIRED AT PRESIDENT KENNEDY'S
MOTORCADE IN DOWNTOWN
DALLAS.
JT1234PCS..

UPI ASN DA
URGENT
1ST ADD SHOTS, DALLAS (A7N)
XXX DOWNTOWN DALLAS
NO CASUALTIES WERE
REPORTED
THE INCIDENT OCCURRED
NEAR THE COUNTY SHERIFF'S
OFFICE ON MAIN STREET, JUST
EAST OF AN UNDERPASS LEADING
TOWARD THE TRADE MART WHERE
THE PRESIDENT WAS TO MA

FLASH
KENNEDY SERIOUSLY WOUNDED
PERHAPS SERIOUSLY
PERHAPS FATALLY SHOT BY
ASSASSINS BULLET
JT1239PCS
—Merriman Smith, Nov. 22, 1963.

Feature Lead

When David Stacks was sent to cover an arm-wrestling tournament, he knew that his story for *The Anniston Star* probably would not be the most important in the newspaper the next day. He knew he would be writing a feature story, which meant he would need to watch for a good incident to begin his story:

Sweat beaded on Bruce Jernigan's forehead. His biceps swelled as blood rushed through his strong chest and into his right arm. His face grimaced with exertion.

Bruce's opponent, Claude Bradford, smiled in seeming defiance as the two boys' fists—locked in an arm-wrestler's grip—teetered slowly back and forth over the tabletop.

Then, with a burst of energy, 14-year-old Claude overcame his opponent's balanced show of strength. Both boys fell from near exhaustion as the referee declared the match concluded.

Theirs was a test of strength, endurance and will. In the end, Claude managed to wear down his friend and adversary Bruce, 14, in the Anniston Park and Recreation Department's first

Gotcha

Contests, games and rivalries far from the big playing fields can make good features. There is drama in a Little League game and in the neighborhood bowling alley. An arm wrestling tournament provided a writer with a feature story about an ancient sporting tradition. *Ken Elkins, The Anniston Star*

arm-wrestling tournament Saturday morning at Carver Community Center on West 14th Street.

"It's all in the way you move," Claude said afterwards.

Arm-wrestling is an ancient con-test of power in which two opponents grasp each other's hands with their elbows resting on a flat surface. The one who forces the other's arm down to the surface wins. . . .

A Major League Blooper

Editors are always on the lookout for the briefest of features, what are known as brighteners or brights, those short, humorous pieces that lighten our day:

MONTREAL—Randy Holcombe had his big chance last night. The relief pitcher, who had been called up Tuesday, dashed to the mound in the eighth inning to try to extinguish a Pirates rally.

The manager handed him the ball, turned toward the dugout, turned back and began waving his arms.

In his eagerness to get into the game, Holcombe had left his glove behind in the bullpen.

Santa Claus   Let's look closer at how the courthouse reporter settled on the start of her story about the suit involving a department store Santa Claus. When Marianne came across the suit in the courthouse, she knew at once that she would write a short feature story. Her problem was how to write an entertaining lead. She had a few ideas. The best, she thought, was that although most of us visualize Santa as a kindly old man, here he is accused of a cruel act. Marianne decided to put this idea of contrasts into her lead:

Santa Claus, that paragon of kindness, is being sued for cruelty to a child.

As with most first efforts, hers wasn't exactly right. The idea was sound, she still felt, but not the way she had put it. Writers should use simple language, but here she was using the word *paragon,* which some people might not understand. She tried again:

Kindly Santa Claus is being sued for being cruel to a youngster.

The lead was still too close to a straight news lead and it sounded dull. The beginning of a feature should beckon readers and say to them, "Slow down a minute—I've got something funny I want to tell you."

Suddenly, she realized there was a more serious problem than her choice of words and tone. In her effort to be entertaining, Marianne had neglected to be scrupulously careful about the facts. Her lead mistakenly identified the party the suit was brought against, the defendant. It was not Santa Claus, as both drafts of her lead had stated. It was the department store.

That disaster averted, she turned to another problem—brevity. She knew she did not have much space, so she could not spin out the tale for more than five or six paragraphs. After her leisurely beginning, she would have to give the facts succinctly—name and address of mother, description of the incident, damages sought. She wrote the following:

Santa Claus is a child's best friend.

The kindly old gent pats little boys on the head and little girls on the cheek.

But two weeks ago, says Carolyn Elliott, a Zale's Department Store Santa whacked her 6-year-old son Dennis on the head.

Mrs. Elliott, of 49 East End Ave., wants $10,000 for her "humiliation and embarrassment" and her son's "nervous reaction." She filed suit against the store in the Grant County District Court yesterday.

The department store had no comment.

Hard, Soft; Direct or Delayed?

When the *Reader's Digest* published a streamlined version of the Bible, the Associated Press sent out a story that began this way:

NEW YORK (AP)—In the beginning the scribe condensed the books of Daniel, First Samuel and Acts. And the editors of the Reader's Digest saw it and said it was good. Then they said to the scribe, "Take six others like you and condense the whole Bible."

And so it came to pass after seven years, in the second year of the presidency of Ronald Reagan, that their work was done, and on the Sabbath the scribes rested while the fruit of their labor was released to the multitudes.

The Reader's Digest Bible is 40 percent shorter than the 850,000-word Revised Standard Version, and "smoother, more inviting, more readable," according to Jack Walsh, the scribe who began editing the first three books of the new Bible in 1975.

About half an hour later, the AP sent this over its wires:

Condensed Bible 2nd Ld-Writethru
Eds: SUBS grafs 1–3 with 2 grafs to recast for
editors who may prefer a harder news approach.

NEW YORK (AP)—Reader's Digest, no stranger
to boiling down popular books, has condensed the
biggest best seller of them all—the Bible.
The Reader's Digest Bible released Sunday is
40 percent shorter than the 850,000-word Revised
Standard Version, and "smoother. . . .

The AP apparently decided that the first version might offend some of its members and ordered the less featurized direct news lead. This brings us to an important factor in deciding how to begin our pieces, for what we say at the outset not only indicates whether the piece is straight news or a feature but gives it a tone as well.

When we write we must be conscious of the audience, the people for whom we are writing. Here are the beginnings of two versions of the same event. They differ because of the nature of the audience.

The first beginning is by Mike Wilkinson of *The Blade* in Toledo and followed a city-wide discussion about the appearance in Toledo of Louis Farrakhan:

When Jews use hate as a tool to make sure the world doesn't forget the Holocaust, no one screams in indignation.

But when Minister Louis Farrakhan hints at it, he says he's wrongfully vilified as a hatemonger.

In a two-hour, 15-minute lecture at the University of Toledo yesterday, the controversial leader of the Nation of Islam rejected claims that he is a bigot, racist, and an anti-Semite.

"Is it wrong for me to remind you what you have suffered at the hands of white people?" he asked the nearly all-black crowd of 3,500 in Savage Hall.

"No sir!" they shouted back.

"If I don't remind my people of what you people have done, you might get the mind to do it again," Mr. Farrakhan said. "I want to make sure it's over with."

Mr. Farrakhan, 61, visited Toledo and talked yesterday as part of a "Stop the Killing" rally sponsored by UT's Black Student Union. His appearance sparked an outcry among a number of Toledo religious and civic leaders.

More than 100 individuals and 17 organizations, including Mayor Carty Finkbeiner, signed a full-page newspaper advertisement that criticized him. . . .

Here is how the AP began its account of the same speech:

TOLEDO, Ohio, May 1 (AP)— Louis Farrakhan, the minister of the Nation of Islam, asserted in a speech on Saturday that whites would not stop black-on-black violence because it provided organ donations.

When a rich white needs a kidney or a heart, they say, "Get us a nigger," Mr. Farrakhan told a mostly black audience at an anti-violence rally on Saturday night at the University of Toledo.

"When you're killing each other, they can't wait for you to die," he told the crowd of about 6,000. "You've become good for parts."

Mr. Farrakhan's appearance was preceded by an advertisement in the local newspaper, The Blade, that about 100 people and 17 organizations had signed to protest his "words of intolerance, prejudice and bigotry." Signers included Mayor Carty Finkbeiner; Representative Marcy Kaptur, Democrat of Ohio; Bishop James Hoffman of the Roman Catholic Diocese of Toledo, and two black officials. . . .

The subject of transplants was in the 20th paragraph of *The Blade*'s 25-paragraph story. Why the vastly different approaches?

The first is a local story, written for people who had been reading about the charges of racism made by some Toledo residents against the Nation of Islam. The AP story is written for a wider audience that had seen a number of stories about the Nation and its position on Jews, Catholics and whites but had not heard about Farrakhan's assertions about transplants.

Now that we have watched how writers approach their stories and how they construct their beginnings, our trek through story writing takes us to putting a lead and a body together into a smoothly written, flowing narrative.

Suggested Reading

Broder, David S. *Behind the Front Page, a Candid Look at How the News Is Made*. New York: Simon & Schuster, 1987.

Gans, Herbert J. *Deciding What's News*. New York: Random House, 1980.

Westin, Av. *Newswatch: How TV Decides the News*. New York: Simon & Schuster, 1983.

 Structuring the Story

The well-structured piece of writing is like a perfectly composed picture: It is balanced and has movement and momentum. Structuring begins with a recognition of the theme or central idea the writer wants to communicate. *Bob Thayer, The Providence Journal*

Looking Ahead

News stories are structured logically: The most important material is presented first and then it is elaborated. Material of secondary importance follows. For feature stories, a delayed lead may be used to draw the reader or listener into the story. The main theme may be delayed until the very end to provide a dramatic conclusion.

Story Building

The writer is a builder. Like any builder, the writer works from a set of plans. Just as the builder has one set of plans for an office building, another for a three-bedroom home and still another for an apartment building, so the writer of news has different plans for different types of stories.

Generally, the plan is based on two decisions the writer makes:

1. Straight news story or feature? For the former, the piece is top heavy with facts. The feature may be more leisurely told, strung out, the theme at the end.

2. How many themes or major elements are essential for this piece? The single-element story includes the facts, quotes and incidents that explain and support the element used in the lead. The body of the two- and three-element stories explains each element in order. Few stories contain more than three major elements.

For both single- and multi-element stories, secondary matter is placed at the bottom.

The Straight News Story

Our writer has decided that the situation she wants to describe calls for a straightforward account. Her next step is to examine her notes to determine how many major elements or themes she will emphasize.

When we talk about themes or elements we don't mean individual facts. A story may contain many facts but only one, two or three major themes or elements. You might say that a theme or element is a summary of a set of related facts. Here is a reporter's summary of the major action taken at a city council meeting:

> The city council voted 4-3 in favor of spending $1 million on a citywide street-paving program.

That summary becomes the major element for the lead. The arguments for and against the program, the present condition of city streets, the city engineer's recommendation that twice the proposed amount is needed to fix the streets—all these are facts that go into the body of the story to support the major element in the lead.

The city council also discussed but took no action on other items that the writer will include in the story—hiring a director for the city recreation department, building a $500,000 addition to the solid waste disposal plant and planning city holidays so that employees can have three-day weekends. These themes are secondary in importance, and they are included in the story after the writer has given sufficient attention in the body of the story to the street-paving program, which is the major theme.

Let's have another scenario. Suppose the city council had *approved* the $500,000 addition to the waste disposal plant. That's a big step and deserves consideration as a major element along with the street-paving program. The writer would have a two-element lead in this case. After these elements were adequately explained in the body of the story, the writer would turn to the proposed appointment of the recreation director and the holiday proposal.

Donald M. Murray, a writing coach, says the lead can be thought of as a promise and the body the material that makes good on that promise. The lead says to the reader or listener, "Hey, look what I found out." The body says, "Now, I'll explain it to you."

The Single-Element Story

A plane crash kills three people. A local clothing store is swept by fire. The president flies to Mexico for a conference. A former school principal dies. The Bulls beat the Lakers. A bank names a new president.

These are spot news stories, and like most spot news stories they make for single-element news stories. Single-element news stories take the basic structure shown here.

The first paragraph contains the lead. The second paragraph either elaborates on the lead or provides the necessary background. The story continues with supporting information about the lead element. When the writer has finished with the relevant material that supports the main element of the story, secondary themes are added.

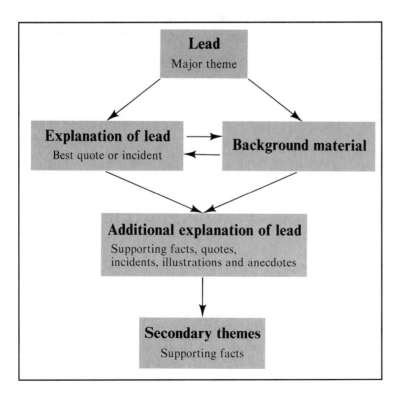

Single-element Story Structure

The following is an example of a spot news story with a single major theme, a one-element story:

Lead—Fire may spread

A fire in the Daniel Boone National Forest that destroyed 500 acres of woodland is threatening to spread to private lands.

Explanation of the lead—High winds causing fire to spread

The Kentucky Division of Forestry reported today that high winds have made control of the blaze difficult. The winds are pushing the fire toward timberlands to the northeast, agency officials said.

Background—When fire started, its cause, weather conditions

The fire broke out Thursday. The cause is undetermined. Forest fires are common during periods of dry, warm weather such as the area is now experiencing, an official said.

Additional explanation of the lead—Firefighters hampered

The forestry division has sent 40 firefighters to the area to try to contain the fire. But they have been hampered by the lack of access roads.

More explanation of the lead—Which areas in danger

No inhabited areas are threatened by the fire, the official said. But there are valuable timberlands to the northeast owned by private growers.

Secondary theme—New strategy used

The forestry division is trying a new form of forest-fire spray that was developed by the state's engineers. In addition to digging trenches and felling trees in the path of the fire, the firefighters are using a spray that temporarily causes leaves and needles to drop, thus making it more difficult for the fire to spread.

The Two-Element Story

The governor announces that because of financial problems he must take drastic action on two educational matters. He is ordering an immediate halt in the $25 million construction program on college and university campuses. He also says he will recommend to the state board of education that all salaries for public school teachers in the state be frozen for next year.

As a reporter on your college newspaper, you want to know whether construction will be halted on your campus. You discover that the order eliminates a plan for a $3 million dormitory to be built with state funds. This gives you a good single-element story. The freezing of salaries for public school teachers does not directly affect your readers, so it becomes secondary material.

Crammed with Action

Bank Robbery: Police officer wounded in shootout. Four-hour standoff with the suspect. Surrender. A major story opportunity with several possible lead elements. The writer's job is to reduce these elements to the fewest possible for the start of the story. One option: The surrender of the suspect who wounded an officer. *Jack Kirkland, The Knoxville News-Sentinel*

On the other hand, press association reporters and state capital bureau reporters from large daily newspapers and stations realize that both announcements will interest their readers. Because these reporters consider the items of equal importance, they will construct their stories on a two-element lead.

There are three ways to structure the two-element story:

1. If the two elements conveniently fit into a single sentence, the writer can put them both in the first paragraph.

2. If combining both elements into a single sentence requires more than 35 or 40 words, the writer will give each element a sentence of its own. This option allows the writer to place both sentences in the first paragraph or to make each sentence into a separate paragraph.

3. If the two elements cannot be squeezed into a sentence (option one) and the writer does not want to write a two-sentence or two-paragraph lead (option two) because it would be too long and cumbersome, a third option is available—the summary lead. A summary lead is just what its name implies: It sums up the two elements.

The Options: Money Troubles Let's see what a news writer for a daily in the state capital does with the governor's announcement. He considers his options in order. He would prefer a lead that can handle both elements in fewer than 35 words (the first option):

> Gov. Mark Acosta said today financial problems necessitate an immediate halt to a $25 million state college construction program, and he also said he will recommend no salary increases next year for public school teachers.

The lead just makes it by word count, but it has a jammed-up feel. He decides to try the second option, two sentences:

> Gov. Mark Acosta said today financial problems necessitate an immediate halt to a $25 million state college construction program. He also said he will recommend no salary increases next year for public school teachers.

No. Still jammed-up. What's more, he suddenly sees he has the lead turned around. He should put the wage freeze first since many people have children in public school and the action will have consequences in all cities.

Even if he does reverse the elements, he still has a bulky lead. As for making each sentence into a paragraph, he does not like two-paragraph leads unless he is forced to use them.

Can he cut down on the number of words? Yes, he can put the reason for the governor's drastic actions in the second paragraph:

> Gov. Mark Acosta said today he will recommend a freeze in salaries for public school teachers next year, and he ordered an immediate halt to a $25 million state college construction program.
>
> The governor said financial problems necessitated his actions. He said that cutbacks in federal aid for education had not been anticipated when the construction program was adopted.

That's better, he thinks. He has also managed to insert background material into the second paragraph. But the city editor is a short-lead advocate who likes leads under 25 words. The reporter now must try a summary lead, the third option. In writing a summary lead, the trick is to find something common to both elements. The state's financial troubles tie in both elements here.

No, and Another No

When a union spokeswoman comments on the governor's salary and construction freeze, another element is added to the story. *Leslie Jean-Bart*

The reporter also notes that the actions were described by the governor as "drastic," and so he decides to use that idea as the basis of his summary lead:

> Gov. Mark Acosta said today financial problems have forced him to take "drastic" action on teacher salaries and the state college construction program.
>
> The governor said he will recommend a freeze on next year's salaries of public school teachers. And he ordered an immediate halt to the $25 million college construction program.
>
> The governor said unforeseen federal cutbacks necessitated his actions. . . .

More Options: Trouble at the Dump   Here is a two-paragraph lead (the second option) that a reporter wrote because she decided the two major elements that developed at a city council meeting could not be squeezed into a lead sentence:

> The city council last night voted to postpone a decision on the purchase of acreage north of the city for a garbage dump after angry residents in the area disrupted the council meeting.
>
> In another action, the council voted 4-3 to end financing of the city's summer educational programs despite protests from parent groups.

Too much action for the reader to grasp, the writer thinks. She decides to use a summary lead (the third option). She has to find a common idea that links the two elements. Obviously, one common idea is that the two actions were taken by the city council. But that's so broad it says next to nothing. Another idea is that the actions are important, but that's too broad as well. There is another common idea, the protesting groups. She tries to make something of this:

> One group of residents had their way with the city council last night, but a second group of angry protesters lost out.

Not too bad. Let's accept this, then see what comes next. The writer must immediately elaborate on the two actions in order:

> The successful protest was aimed at the council's consideration of the purchase of acreage north of the city for a garbage dump. Residents from the area disrupted the council meeting with their protest.
>
> The council postponed a decision.
>
> In the other action, the council voted 4-3 to end financing of the city's summer educational programs despite the protests of parent groups.

Although the summary lead takes a while to get the reader to the heart of the story, it is preferred by many newspapers and is the way broadcast leads for complex stories are written. The summary lead does not overwhelm the reader or listener. It beckons the reader to come into the story.

Zigzagging   Most of us spend a bit of the day trying to put order into our lives. We straighten out the papers strewn on our desk. We arrange the clothes in our closet, put our tapes in alphabetical order, decide to pay the dentist bill first and put off the telephone company since the dentist is being persistent. In our reading as in our lives, we want order. The last thing we need in our reading material is chaos, facts tossed this way and that.

This is why writers spend a lot of time organizing their stories. They know that readers, listeners and viewers will turn to less arduous pursuits than trying to follow the piece that zigs to this and zags to that and zigs back to this.

Organizing the single-element story is simple: Give the theme first, buttress it at once and then move on to secondary material. The same concept holds true for multiple-element stories. For these stories, the body buttresses the major themes in the order in which they are presented at the beginning of the piece.

The best approach is to put similar material together. Put all the supporting material about lead element A together before you begin to elaborate on element B. In the city council meeting story, the body includes material about the garbage dump first since that was the first element mentioned in the lead. After the supporting material about the dump, the reporter writes a transition or swing paragraph introducing the summer program, and then uses the buttressing material for the vote on the summer program.

Here is a possible transition in the council meeting story from the explanation of element A (successful protest against the garbage dump) to the explanation of element B (vote to end the city's summer programs):

> Although the garbage-dump protesters were pleased by the council action, the parents hoping to retain the summer programs were disappointed.

A good transition tells readers where they have been (action on dump) and then informs them where they are being taken (action on summer program).

Notice the word *although*—it serves as a transition in the sentence. *Although* is a conjunction, a word or phrase that serves as a connector. Connectors join the different elements in a story and give the piece a well-knit structure. Here are some other conjunctions:

after	meanwhile
although	moreover
and	nevertheless
before	next
but	now
furthermore	on the other hand
however	then
in addition to	while
later	

You can see that these words are two directional, taking the reader back and then projecting the reader forward. Notice their use in these transitional sentences:

- The Hawks had no trouble with tonight's opponents, *but* tomorrow's game should be another story.
- *In addition to* commenting on the high price of fuel, she discussed the need for home insulation.
- *Next* in his list of objections was the department's action on street repairs.

No reporter should be a slave to a formula. Sometimes, a news writer handling a two-element story will amplify A and B with a paragraph or two for each before moving into the fairly rigid compartmentalizing of the supporting material for each.

Some news writers will bring up secondary material before they have finished with all the supporting material for the lead elements. They do this when they consider the secondary material to be important but not important enough for the lead.

Occasionally, the writer of a long piece has to contend with a three-element event, A, B and C. The organizing concept is no different: The body of the story elaborates on each element in the order it was stated at the top of the piece.

The Three-Element Story

The city editor has just finished reading a story in the Sunday *New York Times* about teen-agers and marijuana. He calls over a reporter and tells her, "Boil this down and give the *Times* full credit. We're going to have a series on the local drug scene among youngsters and I want to show the scope of the problem."

The reporter reads through the story and sees that there are three elements: Teen-agers can find pot easily, don't feel guilty about using it and have no fear of arrest.

The reporter takes three sheets of paper and puts one element at the top of each sheet. Under each element, she lists the supporting data. (Yes, even professionals make outlines for their long pieces.)

On her first sheet, under the heading **Find Easily,** she writes the following:

> Buy from classmates.
> Buy from street sellers.
> Even pushers at famous Public Library.
> Cocaine and heroin also sold here.

She makes similar lists on the other two sheets. On a fourth sheet she lists the secondary material, such as the increase in drinking among teen-agers.

She is now ready to write. She would like to put all three elements in the lead for emphasis, to show the scope of the situation:

> New York teen-agers who smoke marijuana can find it easily, do not feel guilty about using it and have little fear of being arrested.

Judy in Custody

"I recognized from the start this was extraordinary material," Sheryl James says of her series on an abandoned child. "When it all came together I realized I was looking at a chronological narrative series." She began with the discovery of the infant. She covered the mother's arrest and she ended with a scene half a year later at the home of the mother who abandoned him:

Judy says she hopes Rusty never has to know about the day he was born. She hopes that by then, no one will remember it. . . .
Yes, it's possible someone will say something. Or Rusty will ask questions.
"I'd just tell him there was a big mistake made," Judy says. "You know. Something happened."

Jim Stem
© St. Petersburg Times

These are the findings of a survey of 1,000 high school students as reported in "The New York Times" Sunday . . .

Now, all she need do is go to her first sheet and elaborate on the availability of pot. When that task is finished, she will write a transition and go to the second sheet on lack of guilt, and so on until she has completed the secondary material.

The 1, 2, 3 Approach   Reporters occasionally use a variation of the summary lead for a story with three elements. The 1, 2, 3 approach looks something like this:

> The city council took three far-reaching actions at its meeting last night.
> The council voted to:
> 1. Open bids on the controversial community center whose construction has been stalled in court.
> 2. Buy three parcels of land for a new downtown mass transit center.
> 3. Construct a pedestrian overpass over Highway 28 where the Arden Hills Shopping Center will be built.

Caution: Leads with two and three elements can be the lazy writer's way out of making tough decisions, and editors know this. Most events have one important element, not two or three, and it's up to the news writer to figure out which element stands out. The two- and three-element lead is used only when the struggle for the single-element lead fails to fix on the one element.

The Chronological Approach   Since prehistoric times, people have gathered around fires in caves to listen to storytellers. Even when the listeners know the outcome, they will hear the speaker to the end of the tale. Appreciation for a well-told tale is the principle behind the chronological approach to the breaking news story.

In this approach, the story usually is told twice. The lead tells the reader what happened, and a few paragraphs of buttressing material amplify the lead. Then there is a transition and the writer turns back to give an account of how the situation occurred—the day the crime was committed, the excitement of two couples as they set out for a wedding party, the first play of the last two minutes of the game.

Here is how the story of a frightening ride on a school bus began in *The Advocate* of Stamford, Conn.:

> Forty junior high school students on school bus 10 were terrified Friday afternoon.
> Their normal 15-minute ride home from Cloonan Middle School to the Westover and Long Ridge sections took more than an hour. The students said they spent the hour watching the bus careen around curves and listening to drivers of oncoming cars honk warnings to slow down.
> Some believed they were being kidnapped by their driver, but the school bus company said the man was merely lost.

"All the kids were screaming and some of the kids were crying," said Karen Seren, a seventh-grader. "We screamed to a policeman out the window, but he didn't believe us."

In their fear, eight students jumped out the rear door when the bus stopped at Rippowam High School, and they flagged down a police car for help. All the students eventually were returned home, late but safe.

Allen Graften, assistant superintendent of schools, said he will look into the incident and have some answers by Monday.

In these six paragraphs of this spot news story, Rita Jensen and Kevin Flynn have described the climax and the essentials of the event. The account could stop here. But there is so much local interest in an event of this kind, the writers knew, that they decided to go on. They wrote a transition paragraph and then began their chronological account this way:

From accounts of the parents and children who called "The Advocate" and from the manager of ARA bus operations here, the ride of terror and confusion began when. . . .

Notice the word *began*. This word tells the reader to sit back while the writer spins out the tale.

The Inverted Pyramid Approach   The story about the terrifying bus ride climaxes at the beginning, in the lead. The writers gave the major material first and then the secondary information. This approach results in a traditional story structure—the inverted pyramid.

The inverted pyramid is a perfectly good approach to the straight news story. When it comes to important events, readers and listeners want to know what happened—now.

However, use of the inverted pyramid does limit the storytelling abilities of the writer. Sometimes the writer may want to withhold the key element for a few paragraphs, or even until the end of the story. Sometimes the story is better told when the climax is at the end than when it is at the beginning.

For a long time, writers struggled with the restrictions of the inverted pyramid. In fact, they made it the symbol of the limitations of journalistic writing. It became fashionable for gifted writers to scoff at the inverted pyramid.

Their scoffing was valid—to a point. Actually, news writers who had mastered the inverted pyramid had for years been able to transcend it and the traditional structures of the news story—when the occasion permitted it. The last clause bears repeating—when the occasion permitted it.

The inverted pyramid approach works well for the majority of stories and news releases. Despite its limitations, it is still widely used for spot news stories.

. . . and Something Different   But when possible, media writers turn from following formulas like the inverted pyramid to using the storytelling approach.

The Old Standby

Generations of media writers have been trained to make their news writing conform to the structure of the inverted pyramid, so named because the major information is clustered at the top of the story. As the diagram illustrates, this approach results in a top-heavy story. Some writers prefer a linear approach, replacing the pyramid with a straight-line narrative that gradually develops the point. However, most news stories and releases use the pyramid form.

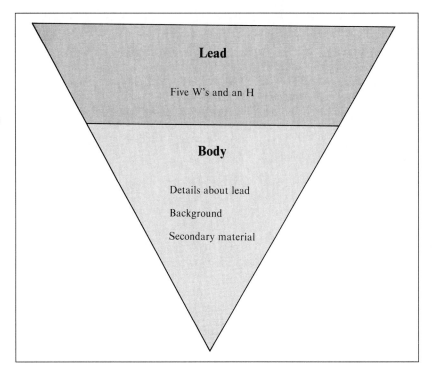

Lead

Five W's and an H

Body

Details about lead

Background

Secondary material

The appearance of Miss America in California on her personal tour was the occasion one writer grabbed for an inventive story approach.

"I was sent out to a motel where Miss America was to hold a news conference," the former reporter-turned-journalism teacher recalls. "She had just been crowned and she was making a national tour. That was news in those days in small and medium-size towns."

Two print reporters and a television camera crew and reporter awaited her arrival in one of the rooms of her suite. In a corner was Miss America's mother, ironing a dress. They waited. After a five- or 10-minute delay, Miss America entered.

"She was holding a Pepsi, as I recall. Clutching it to her, unopened. On one of the bureaus was a cardboard poster advertising another sponsor of the Miss America pageant," he said. "The whole business seemed arranged, staged."

At that point, the reporter had the idea for his story about Miss America's visit. It would be in the form of a stage play.

He began his story with stage directions:

Stage right: Mother ironing blue evening gown. Advertising poster on bureau to left.

Opened luggage on low racks. Reporters and camera crew sitting, chatting quietly.

Enter from rear of center stage:

Miss America. She enters slowly, holding an unopened a soda bottle. There is a moment of silence. She speaks.

Miss America: "Thank you for coming. I have something to say and then I will answer questions. . . .

He says that when he handed in his story the city editor laughed, started to hand it back and then decided to run it. "It was a one-day stand. I never wrote another play, but not because the idea was bad. The right occasion never came up again."

These days, most editors want imaginative and colorful writing, and when the event allows it, they urge their reporters to use the techniques of the feature writer, even on straight news stories. Enter the news feature.

Before we examine the news feature in detail, let's look at the other parent that produced the hybrid we call the news feature—the feature.

The Feature

The feature is journalism's grab bag. It can be about anything under the sun—even the sun itself. The feature can be as light and fluffy as a cream puff or as solid and substantial as a rib roast. It can make us cry or laugh. A basic difference between the straight news story and the feature is that whereas the news story informs us, the feature is usually intended to entertain us. The news story has immediacy and must be used right away, whereas the feature has currency and can be used almost any time. Some features are explanatory, intended to expand a subject. Most often, these are news features, a category we will get to in a few pages.

Another distinctive mark of the feature is its style. The straight news story is just that, a straightforward account of an event. The feature is . . . well, there is no telling what form the feature may take. And this characteristic may well be its trademark. Some features are humorous, some somber. And some cannot be catalogued, like this one:

Ramble, Yes Rambling, No

The feature takes the reader on an entertaining stroll. Sometimes, the walk is along a sun-drenched beach, and the writing is heated. And then there is the intimate walk around the pond in a mist, and the writing is leisurely. Often, there's a surprise at the end of the walk. *Bob Thayer, The Providence Journal*

Six-year-old Brian Waters spotted a fence down the street from school yesterday and made a detour from his usual way home.

He stared at the iron fence: IIIIIII.

Then he decided to look into the yard through the fence: IIIoIII. But when Brian had seen enough he couldn't pull his head back.

A passer-by called the fire department and a fireman approached the fence with a sledgehammer: /.

In short order, he had pried apart a couple of the bars: II(o)II. Freed, Brian wiped his tears and went on home.

Choosing a Style

The style of the feature is, as we can see, simple and relaxed. The following feature by Mike Stanton that moved over the AP wires roams around almost as much as its subject—a college student who rode the rails to gather information for a term paper. Despite the rolling, informal style, Stanton gives us enough information by the end of the sixth paragraph that we have a solid picture of the student and what he did.

Here is the beginning of the story:

AMHERST, MASS. (AP)—Ted Conover's classroom was a rolling boxcar, his first big test a fight with a drunken hobo. He fell off a train, foraged through garbage cans for food and got lice in his hair.

The Amherst College student rode the rails for 3 1/2 months, living the life of a railroad tramp, to research his senior thesis.

He found that it wasn't all bad.

"There's something about jumping on a freight train that just feels right," said Conover, a 23-year-old anthropology major from Denver.

"It's the feeling of the wind in your face and the train pulling you along. I think there's some truth to the saying that every red-blooded American boy should hop a train."

Conover rode the rails for 10,000 miles last fall, criss-crossing the American West to study what author John Steinbeck called "the last free men."

Conover said he didn't want to "suffer in the library" researching his thesis, so he spent a semester observing or interviewing 460 tramps. He estimates there are at least 10,000 hobos living in the United States today. . . .

Feature Facts

Style—Relaxed, informal. Let the people in the story do things; let them talk. Underwrite. Keep the story moving with quotes and incidents. Use dialogue. Have people talk to each other. Listen to them at work or play. Tom Wolfe, master of the profile, says "realistic dialogue" fascinates readers. Use verbs that make pictures for the reader. When possible, use the present tense to give the reader a sense of continuing action or of being present at the scene.

Lead—Delayed leads are preferred. An anecdote or incident can be used to begin. Stress human interest in the lead by using someone directly involved in the situation. Make sure the lead fits into the main theme.

Body—Avoid overwhelming the reader with detail. A few well-chosen quotes and incidents tell the story. Selection is the essence of the feature. A Zen saying makes the point: "To make a vase, you need both clay and the absence of clay." You are not obligated to use everything a source has given you.

Focusing on a Theme

Because the feature has a relaxed, leisurely approach and contains many quotes and several interesting incidents, beginners think all that is necessary to write one is to pile on quotes and anecdotes and then glue them together with a few transitions.

Finding the Theme

Some writers pinpoint the themes of their pieces by first choosing a word or two that best describe the event and then writing sentences around the words. A piece about a riding school for youngsters might be built around the word *turn* because of the difficulty the young riders had making their mounts turn left or right. Or the word could be *excitement* to reflect the thrill city children had when they first saw their horses. *Joe Luper*

Not so. The writer must have a specific theme in mind and use only those quotes, anecdotes and incidents that amplify the theme. The writer Tom Wolfe says that too many feature writers think "that somehow if you get in enough details, enough random fact—somehow this *trenchant portrait* is going to rise up off the pages."

Yes, he agrees, detail and dialogue are essential, but the good feature writer "piles it all up *very carefully,* building up toward a single point. . . ."

Wolfe's "single point" is the theme or point of the article.

In this respect, a feature is no different from any news story. It must have a main theme. The main theme is always the spine of the story. Everything else branches from it.

The reporter who interviews a rock singer who has just been released from a clinic for alcoholics and drug addicts has a good idea of the questions she needs answered for her feature. So does the sports writer who is to do a piece about the 38-year-old pitcher who has been named Comeback Player of the Year.

The rock singer may surprise the reporter and say, "I'm through with music. With it, I'll be back on the habit. Without it, I'll be poor, but alive." The pitcher may be petulant and angry instead of being happy about his award. He may take off about his salary, fellow players and the baseball commissioner. The unexpected material becomes the main theme of these stories.

The Wall Street Journal Formula

Here is a structure for features that *The Wall Street Journal* has used successfully for many years:

Beginning—Start with an anecdote or illustration of the theme.
Theme—Shortly after the beginning, state the point of the piece. Don't drop this point lower than the sixth paragraph.
Body—Provide details that elaborate on the theme. Tell the reader what is happening and why and what's being done about the situation.

Accentuating the Ending

Rather than conclude on a secondary piece of information as do most news stories, the feature may have what is called a kicker, a punch at the end that drives home the theme.

In a story about a woman who visits prisoners in the Dade County Jail to help them with their problems, *Miami Herald* reporter Shula Beyer describes Georgia Jones Ayers as being sympathetic to prisoners she believes to have been unjustly accused and imprisoned. But Ayers is no bleeding heart. She does not tolerate crime. To make this point about Ayers, Beyer ends her story with this dramatic incident and quote:

One of the stories people tell about Georgia Ayers is that she turned over a drug pusher to the police. He was sentenced to eight years. The pusher was her son, Cecil.

"When my own children do wrong, I don't uphold them. The law is the law. He respects me for what I did. I couldn't afford to see him destroy himself.

"I would rather see him behind bars than for someone to call me to identify his body in a morgue."

The News Feature

Early one cold Saturday morning, as Bob Rose was at home preparing to go to work at *The Blade* in Toledo, the telephone rang. It was his editor. A house a few blocks from Rose's apartment on Parkwood Avenue had caught fire. Could he get over there? Yes, he could. He left in minutes.

He tried to drive, but the frost on his car window was unyielding and after a few blocks, he hopped out of the car and ran the rest of the way.

"I arrived in time to see the fireman carry a child out of the house," he said. He spent about an hour at the scene gathering information from fire department officials and from the people who had been driven out of their home.

At the office, he checked the hospital where the injured had been taken, and by early afternoon he had finished his story. But he was not happy with it.

"Somehow it didn't seem right," Rose recalled. He asked the assistant city editor what she thought of the story, and she told him it lacked drama. He worked on it some more and left the office feeling somewhat satisfied.

Soon, he had another call. Ed Whipple, an assistant managing editor, had made a change. "He wanted to bring the reader right into the story. My lead ended up being the third graph, and the scene of a tearful firefighter with the dead girl went first," Rose said. The story was put on page one.

In the past, most editors would have wanted Rose's straight news lead. But Whipple wanted a news feature. Rose's story as it appeared in *The Blade* is on the next page.

The news feature emphasizes human interest and drama. The dramatic quote and the telling incident point up the major theme. The news feature may use the delayed lead to lure the reader into the story, and then get to the point of the piece after several paragraphs, or it may put the lead theme in a kicker at the end.

Rose's story puts the reader on the scene at once. We visualize this large man in his dark cold-weather clothing clutching a small figure. The second paragraph stuns the reader with a brief quote.

The way the story is told reflects the poignancy of the event more closely than would a straight news story with a direct lead such as this:

> A 4-year-old child died and two other family members were hospitalized when their home at 2346 Lawrence Ave. was damaged by a fire this morning.

This straight lead is satisfactory, but the point of this fire is the tragedy of a child's death. Why not show the reader this and let the reader share the grief? The lead on the published story fits the event.

Neighbors Aid Firemen

Girl, 4, Dies In Fire; 8 In House Rescued

By BOB ROSE
Blade Staff Writer

It was 7:50 a.m. Saturday when fireman Jack Rynn carried 4-year-old Quanous Russell out of a burning house at 2346 Lawrence Ave.

"She's gone," he said minutes later of the bundle in the blue baby blanket, his eyes welling with tears.

Fighting zero-degree weather and their own emotions, Toledo firemen — aided by alert neighbors — helped save eight other family members in the house.

Timmy Hicks, 2, was rescued by fireman Fred White, who, like Mr. Rynn, struggled through thick smoke and flames to take the child from an upstairs bedroom.

Timmy had stopped breathing, but paramedic Larry LaVigne revived him en route to St. Vincent Hospital, where he was in serious condition Saturday.

Neighbors Help

Before firemen arrived, neighbors had helped others from the home.

Paula Russell, 26, the mother of the dead girl, jumped from a second-floor window into the arms of Bruce Ethridge, who heard her screams from a block away. She was in fair condition at St. Vincent Saturday.

Johnny Hicks, 4, was found on steps in the house by Eron Villanveva, who lives next door. He had summoned firemen after hearing screams and breaking glass.

Others escaped through the front door or were pulled from the roof of the house by firemen who arrived at 7:33 a.m., two minutes after the alarm sounded.

Curtain Was Burning

Kevin Russell, 19, said he was the first to be wakened by the blaze. "Something told me to wake up," he said at a neighbor's house after other family members were taken to the hospital. "When I woke up, my curtain was burning down the side."

An electric space heater in his room had ignited the curtain. He struggled to put the fire out, first by stamping on the curtain and then by running for buckets of water, but the fire was winning.

"It happened so quick, I couldn't even get everybody woke," he said.

His father, Clinton Russell, 72, wearing a tattered coat zipped over his pajama top, shivered as he watched firemen work on the white frame house he has owned since the 1960s. He was the only family member sleeping on the first floor.

"I can't think," he finally said after trying to name other family members who had gone to sleep in the house the night before.

All But 2 Released

They were identified by hospital and fire officials as his daughter, Elizabeth Hicks, 23, who was visiting from Cincinnati with sons Timmy and Johnny. Others were Clinton's wife, Lois, 52, and son, Quincy, 16.

All but Timmy Hicks and Paula Russell were released after treatment.

Toledo Fire Chief William Winkle arrived soon after he was called at home by firemen. "Those guys did a hell of a job," he said of the men who were directed in the freezing weather by acting deputy chief Ron Sturgill.

Chief Sturgill, who estimated damage at $18,000, said the two closest fire hydrants were frozen and water from pumper trucks had to be used while another hydrant was hooked up.

"The first guys there ran into the house without masks (for air) and got to the top of the stairs," Chief Winkle said. "But they couldn't go farther. Guys with masks had to go in to get the kids."

Chief Winkle kicked a snow bank when he talked about the year's first fatal fire. "Damn," he said.

The news feature is built around incidents, examples, anecdotes and quotes. Human interest is a major factor in the news feature as well as in the feature.

Volunteers to the Dying

Rick Sluder, a reporter for *The News and Observer* in Raleigh, N.C., built his news feature about a hospice around the people involved. A hospice is an organization that serves the needs of the dying and their families.

The story originated in a press release from the Hospice of Wake County. "My editor felt this was a worthwhile organization and that I should look into it," Sluder said. "Getting the lowdown on how the organization worked was the easy part. Volunteers and officials were eager to meet with me."

Sluder decided that this kind of information was only part of the story. He knew he needed the human element. The story should be about the people the hospice volunteers worked with, the dying. He wanted to **show** the hospice at work, not **tell** about it through the words of officials.

"This caused officials to rub their hands for a moment," he said. "Their concern was understandable. Relationships in situations like this are confidential." They did agree to reach some families to ask whether Sluder could talk to them.

"A day or two later, I got the names of the Silvers and the Voelkers. And that's when it became a bit sticky for me. I found myself phoning these people to ask if they would talk to me, a stranger, about the deaths of their loved ones."

Sluder learned what many young reporters find surprising. Despite their tragedies, some people are willing to talk to reporters if they believe the reporters are sincere and want to perform a service by writing the story.

Notice how Sluder structures the beginning of his story. He uses an illustration, with quotations, of the point he will be making—that the dedicated volunteers ease the pain of the dying:

Three-year-old Bethany Voelker was sick, and she didn't want any visitors. When Elizabeth Hernandez appeared, she said so.

"Would it be all right if I came to visit you?" Ms. Hernandez asked.

"No," Bethany said. "I'll throw you out."

"I'm going to come anyway."

"Well, I'll throw you out again."

Undaunted, Ms. Hernandez came—and she visited again and again. As days passed, Bethany's uneasiness gave way to tolerance. Friendship followed, and finally, surely, love.

One day the two were together and Bethany was feeling worse than usual. They talked little. As Ms. Hernandez bent to kiss her, Bethany whispered with childhood's sincerity: "I'll be your friend forever."

The bond was sealed. And though Bethany died of leukemia a few weeks ago, it remains strong. Loved ones are not forgotten.

Bethany's parents, Robert and Darlene Voelker of Raleigh, are certain the friendship brightened their daughter's last days of life, just as Ms. Hernandez says she is richer for having known Bethany.

It's a sentiment shared by most of the volunteers with Hospice of Wake County, an organization intended to minister to the needs—physical and emotional—of the dying and their families.

But it's hard to think of Hospice as an organization, with budgets and letterheads and articles of incorporation. Instead, Hospice is people, caring people, who celebrate each second of life by meeting moments of death, accepting death for what it is, refusing to turn away. It is, by any reckoning, in the major leagues of human interaction.

Hospice of Wake County began accepting clients in April. So far it is serving six families; deaths have occurred in five of them.

Its mission is simple, said Dr. William R. Berry, medical director. "We provide medical care for terminally ill patients in the home setting," he said. We help them and their families any way we can to meet their needs."

In the first nine paragraphs, Sluder shows us how a hospice works, though he never uses that word. It is not until the 10th paragraph that he introduces the hospice, and this and the next three paragraphs provide the lead and background. No question that this is an effective way to begin the story.

Unlike the straight news story, which stops when the writer runs out of secondary material, the ending of the feature must leave the reader or listener with a reminder of the point of the piece. Sluder does this with a vivid combination of incidents about and quotations from the two families in which deaths occurred. Here is the end of his story:

Bethany turned 4 shortly before she died. She got a birthday party her little friends are still talking about. Uncle Paul from TV and Guppy the clown were there. So were many of the Hospice workers, who with some others helped arrange it.

James Silver had a birthday party, too, the Friday before his death on Monday. He had planned it and left instructions it was to be held even if he couldn't attend. "He wanted his friends, the ones who had done so much for him, to have a good time," Mrs. Silver said. The Hospice people were there.

They were there at the two funerals, too. And they're still there, the families said, calling, dropping by, sharing lunch and memories and hopes for the future.

"Sometimes you forget how wonderful people can be," Mrs. Silver said, "but I guess it's like James always said. It isn't how long you're on Earth, it's what you do while you're

Structuring the Feature and News Feature

The structures of the feature and news feature depend on whether the writer chooses to get to the point immediately or to hold the reader in suspense. After making this decision, the writer has three options: Sometimes the lead will be up high, in the first paragraph or two (first option). Often, the lead comes after an introductory section, as in Sluder's piece about the hospice (second option). Or it may be placed at the end (third option).

These alternatives are diagrammed on the opposite page.

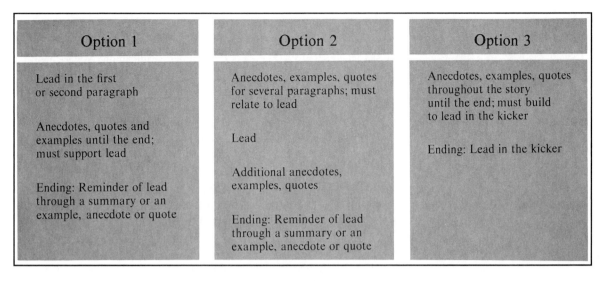

Option 1	Option 2	Option 3
Lead in the first or second paragraph	Anecdotes, examples, quotes for several paragraphs; must relate to lead	Anecdotes, examples, quotes throughout the story until the end; must build to lead in the kicker
Anecdotes, quotes and examples until the end; must support lead	Lead	Ending: Lead in the kicker
Ending: Reminder of lead through a summary or an example, anecdote or quote	Additional anecdotes, examples, quotes	
	Ending: Reminder of lead through a summary or an example, anecdote or quote	

Three Routes to the Feature Story

Summing Up

Chapters 3 through 6 should give you a good start on writing for the media. Before we move on to the next section on fact gathering, here are three sets of suggestions. The first is a summary of what writing coaches, editors and journalism instructors suggest as your approach to good writing.

Some Tips for Good Writing

1. Make the lead inviting, clear and simple.
2. Use quotes when they speak louder than a paraphrase. Place good quotes up high in the story.
3. Use examples, anecdotes, details when they help make the point of the piece. Show, don't tell.
4. Give the story movement by blending paragraphs with transitions, by using short words and by varying sentence rhythm.
5. Good writing is built on a foundation of solid reporting: Go to the scene, talk to the source personally.
6. Start writing only after you know what you want to say. If you have time, write an outline, which need consist of only a few key words that remind you of your story structure.

Next is the deficiency list, a compilation of the most frequent problems one editor says he sees in the copy that moves to his desk.

Perishable Prose. "Anyone can write. Only the real writer knows how to erase."
—*Anonymous*

Major Problems

1. **Not enough self-editing.** Reporters fight so hard to put their words on paper, they have a vested interest in them and are reluctant to change them. But no story is perfect on first writing. Don't cherish every word you write. Always ask, "Does this word, this sentence, this paragraph move the story forward?"

2. **Wrong lead.** The writer has used a secondary theme for the main point of the story. The writer has to keep asking, "What made this event different from all others like it?" The answer is placed in the lead.

3. **Poor organization.** This is often a result of not identifying the main theme and not knowing where it should be placed—at the start of the news story or later on in the news feature or feature.

4. **Misuse of the delayed lead.** Too many hard news stories are given a soft news approach.

5. **Overwriting.** You don't have to use every quotation, every observation. In journalism, quantity does not count—the quality of the quote and the observation do.

6. **Dullness.** This can be the result of overwriting. It also stems from poorly selected verbs, long sentences, lack of quotes.

Finally, here are some questions you might ask as you make the final copy check before turning in your work.

Copy Check

1. Is the lead on target or buried? If most of the body of the story is not about the theme selected as the lead, the lead is wrong.

2. If a delayed lead is used, does the quote or incident move directly into the main theme?

3. Is the story organized properly, or does it jump from one topic to another and back? Is secondary information placed above primary material in the body?

4. Does the story move? Do the nouns and verbs carry it forward? Do the facts, incidents, quotations give movement to the piece?

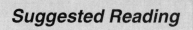

Suggested Reading

Clark, Roy Peter, ed. *Improving Newswriting.* St. Petersburg, Fla.: Poynter Institute for Media Studies, 1982.

Murray, Donald. *Writing for Your Readers.* Chester, Conn.: The Globe Pequot Press, 1983.

PART THREE Reporting

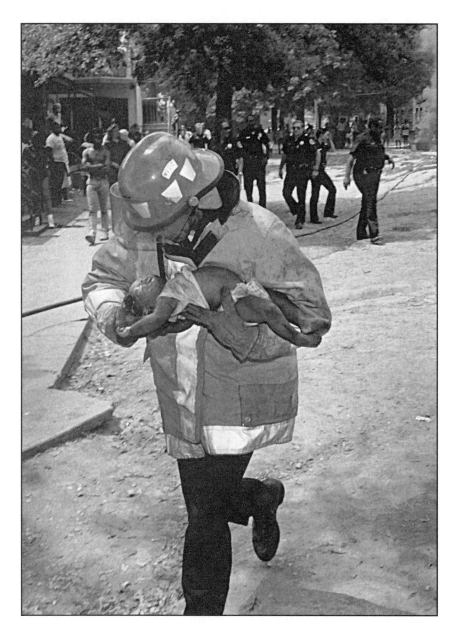

Journalists prefer first-hand observation in their reporting. The reporter's witnessing of the rescue of an infant from a burning house results in a story that has greater emotional impact than the second-hand story written from a fire department or police report. © Mike DoBose, The Tennesseean

7 Finding Information and Gathering Facts

Direct observation and direct quotes are convincing. Here, a 17-year-old is being comforted by a friend after being shot at his high school in a dispute over a girl. The principal commented: "I don't know what we're supposed to do with students who feel the only way to settle a difference of opinion is with a gun." © *Todd Panagopoulos, The Star*

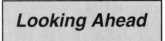

Looking Ahead

Newsworthy information is developed from observations, from interviews and through research. This material is supplemented by the writer's general and specific knowledge. The aim of the journalist is to provide the reader or listener with factual material about an event and its causes and possible consequences.

Foundations of Fact Gathering

Media writers are prodigious fact gatherers. They collect useful information with vacuum-cleaner voraciousness. Knowing that their writing can be only as effective as the factual material they gather, writers sharpen their reporting skills constantly. They teach themselves how to draw information from reluctant sources, how to put people at ease before a camera. They learn how to use research materials that range from almanacs to computer files.

Writers obtain the information they need in three ways: through direct observation, interviews and research.

Direct Observation

Informative writing stands on facts, and the facts that are most convincing are those that the reporter gathers by direct observation.

Penny Lernoux, who covered Latin America for a number of newspapers and magazines, was doing a story on Bolivian tin miners who work under difficult conditions high in the Andes. Lernoux was determined to see the miners at work, although she had heard that they sometimes threw dynamite at visitors and were especially suspicious of women, whom they believed brought them bad luck.

She disguised herself as a man and went along with an engineer who had volunteered to show her the inside of a mine. She was deep inside the Siglo Veinte mine, she recalled, "when a miner approached, a smile on his face and a stick of dynamite in his hand."

"Don't panic," the engineer shouted. "Just run."

There was a sharp bend in the corridor, which they scrambled around just as the dynamite exploded. Lernoux survived, and she had her story.

A Child's Pluck

Direct observation allowed AP correspondent Nancy Shulins to capture poignant moments in the life of an 8-year-old boy who is brain damaged but whose pluck has helped him overcome enormous obstacles.

Shulins interviewed some of the neighbors who volunteered to help with Matthew's rehabilitation and she watched the youngster struggle to use his arms, his legs. As she was leaving, the youngster, "strapped into his braces" was "hard at work practicing creeping."

Just as she reached the door, Shulins wrote, she saw Matthew "flailing one arm back and forth in front of his face. 'He's blowing you kisses,' his mother explained."

© Sid Brown, Schenectady Gazette

Direct Observation

Interview

Research

Digging Out Useful Information

The media writer uses a combination of fact-gathering techniques. Direct observation is reliable, but when it's not possible, the writer interviews participants and authorities. Research yields background and helps to put the situation or event into perspective by giving the causes and consequences.

Terror Underground   In Philadelphia, newspapers carried stories of crime, delays, fires and accidents in the city's subways. One story reported the case of a widely known Philadelphia lawyer who was beaten, raped and left for dead in the darkened track area. She was discovered 18 hours after the attack.

Mike Mallowe of *Philadelphia* magazine decided to look into the subway system. He interviewed crime victims, patrolled with the police, worked with the subway motormen and rode the subway for months as a commuter. His piece, "Tunnel of Terror," reported:

> . . . a trunk line to hell . . . 40 miles of dark, deadly terror . . . 40 miles of drunks collapsed in their own vomit; of howling teenage punks pissing in public; of hulking panhandlers, not asking, but demanding money; it's 40 miles of old people too terrified to look around them; of women alone, too scared to speak. . . .

Only direct observation could generate the tension and terror in these lines.

Going to the People   "One of the biggest problems of being a foreign correspondent in China is getting access to real people who will tell you the truth about what is going on," says Lena H. Sun of *The Washington Post*. "It's hard to reach them when you go on the official reporting trips that must be approved by

Peasant Protesters

Shi Jingxuan and his wife Pan Fuying say they were beaten after they questioned the activities of the Communist Party secretary in their poor farming village. The party boss's home is built on a 2½ acre plot, larger than the farms of most of the villagers. "His pigsty is better than our homes," says Shi, who was forced by authorities to beat his son, and whose son was forced to beat him, in retaliation for his protests against the regime. *Lena H. Sun, The Washington Post*

the local foreign affairs bureaus, which are under the supervision of the Chinese Foreign Ministry."

To get to the people, Sun and another reporter took a trip to one of China's poorest regions where a democracy activist had agreed to show them around. Sun was aware of China's history of abusing the peasants in favor of city dwellers. Under Mao Zedong's Great Leap Forward, an estimated 20 to 30 million peasants starved to death in a famine during which Chinese leaders forced peasants to ship food to the cities.

The central government's local party leaders are still disliked by the peasants, Sun found. People talked freely to her, though they knew the consequences could be serious. Sun's story begins:

> YUANZHUANG, China—No one is hated more in this poor farming village than the man who has dominated the lives of peasants here for more than a decade, local Community Party boss Shen Shaoxi.
>
> When floods devastated this village in Anhui Province in eastern China, families were forced to go begging and one villager starved to death. Shen pocketed the relief funds for personal use, peasants here said. Instead of distributing emergency grain, he allegedly sold the rice to friends and gave sacks of flour to a relative, the village accountant, who fed it to his pigs.
>
> The final straw came last spring, when villagers accused Shen of rigging local elections to keep his hold on power. . . .

When Shen found out that villagers had talked to Sun he had them interrogated and beaten. "He told the villagers," Sun said, that if she and another reporter returned, "he would break our legs and arrest us."

A Fish Story On a skyway over Tampa Bay, a couple of fishermen are trying their luck. Jeff Klinkenberg, an outdoors reporter for the *St. Petersburg Times,* and another reporter are "catching nothing," as Klinkenberg puts it, when a fisherman walks by with what seems to be about 60 pounds of equipment.

The fisherman looks at Klinkenberg and his companion and laughs. "You'll never catch anything with that," he says to them, pointing to their equipment.

Then he begins talking about a shark he is determined to catch, name of "Old Hitler." Klinkenberg manages to get in a few questions before the fisherman goes on his way. The reporters resume fishing, but Klinkenberg is distracted. He is thinking, this guy is worth a story.

Two weeks later, Klinkenberg calls the shark fisherman and makes arrangements to meet him on the skyway.

"I went back out there with him. We went to the bridge about 6 p.m. and stayed until 2 a.m., fooling around with sharks and ladyfish," Klinkenberg says.

Klinkenberg returned to the newspaper and typed up three pages of single-spaced notes for his story. Then he wrote:

Ron Swint moaned in the dark about the shark called Old Hitler, the largest shark in Tampa Bay, as traffic roared by on the Skyway Bridge. Somebody in a car shouted and Swint automatically winced. He has been hit by beer cans thrown from passing cars. A huge truck rumbled by so fast the bridge shook. Diesel fumes hung in the air.

The first shark to come along was not Old Hitler, but it was a big one, a shark Swint later estimated at 500 pounds, a shark that swallowed a three-pound live ladyfish bait and swam toward the lights of Tampa. The shark almost killed Swint. . . .

Again, we see that the reporter who has observed the event is able to make the story come alive for readers.

At the Surrender   Observations by keen journalists do not always center on the major and the momentous. Sometimes, it is the inconspicuous item that gives us a sense of what happened.

Homer Bigart, one of the great reporters of his time, was on the deck of the battleship Missouri when the Japanese foreign minister signed the document of unconditional surrender ending World War II. Here are the first three paragraphs of Bigart's dispatch to his newspaper, *The Herald Tribune:*

Japan, paying for her desperate throw of the dice at Pearl Harbor, passed from the ranks of the major powers at 9:05 a.m. today when Foreign Minister Mamoru Shigemitsu signed the document of unconditional surrender.

If the memories of the bestialities of the Japanese prison camps were not so fresh in mind, one might have felt sorry for Shigemitsu as he hobbled on his wooden leg toward the green baize covered table where the papers lay waiting.

He leaned heavily on his cane and had difficulty seating himself. The cane, which he rested against the table, dropped to the deck of this battleship as he signed.

On the Battlefield   Bigart had covered the ground war in Europe and had witnessed some of its bloodiest battles. While with the 5th Army in Italy in 1943, he had seen the war's human costs. Here is a paragraph from a story he sent back after prowling through a battlefield:

On the far side of the field sprawled some dead. One boy lay crumpled in a shallow slit trench beneath a rock. Another, still grasping his rifle, peered from behind a tree, staring with sightless eyes toward the Liri plain. A third lay prone where he had fallen. He had heard the warning scream of a German shell. He had dropped flat on his stomach but on level ground affording no cover. Evidently some fragment had killed him instantly, for there had been no struggle.

At the Coal Mine   After the *Tribune* ceased publication, Bigart worked for *The New York Times,* which sent him to Kentucky to cover unemployment among the coal miners. He took time to look at the landscape:

> Creeks are littered with garbage, choked with boulders and silt dislodged by strip-mine operations. Hillsides that should be a solid blaze of autumn color are slashed with ugly terraces where bulldozers and steam shovels have stripped away the forest to get at the coal beneath.

These word pictures, starkly painted with the pitiless word strokes of the journalist, are effective because of the details, diamonds of observation in stark settings. An admiring colleague said of Bigart, "He observed many things we missed."

Bigart, considered by his fellow reporters to be about the best ever, did not shoot into brilliance. His star was long developing. A college dropout, he took a job with the *Tribune* as a copy boy. He ran news copy to the composing room, took coffee and doughnuts to reporters bent over their typewriters and generally made himself useful—for four years. When he finally was given a chance—an assignment to cover the opening of a rail service from New York to Florida—he went to the wrong track and described the wrong railroad in his story.

Bigart dug into every assignment, seeking the causes and consequences of events. This perseverance got him into trouble in countries where truth is what authorities declare it to be, and he was thrown out of many countries, including Hungary, Syria, Vietnam, Saudi Arabia.

He was also a craftsman, spending every moment before deadline worrying about the story he was writing. A fellow correspondent in Vietnam said Bigart "worked over his copy more than any of the rest of us." When the other reporters were turning in their stories, he said, "Homer would still be at his portable, crossing off one word because he had thought of a better one."

Interviews

As we have seen, direct observation provides the writer with the vivid detail that makes writing come alive. But the truth is that the fact gatherer usually isn't on the scene at crucial moments and so must rely on eyewitnesses or participants.

The reporter who observes the flood sweeping over farms spots a collapsed bridge. To add life to the piece, the reporter will try to reach someone who saw the water's surge carry off the bridge.

A reporter will give a bank robbery story necessary detail and color through interviews with bank employees and customers who were in the bank at the time of the robbery. The reporter will interview in detail the teller who was held up.

The writer of a company's annual report will give life to endless columns of figures by interviewing the president for comments about the year's business.

No Media Monster

What kind of relationship did you develop with her? Sheryl James was asked this question about her interview with a mother who abandoned her newborn child.

James replied, "I simply tried to be straightforward about what I was doing and get her to trust me, to know that I would keep my word to her. Aside from that, when I finally did interview her, I felt as I do with many people I interview—I try to establish a relaxed rapport, to be human myself so that they know I'm not a media monster."

James, a feature writer with the *St. Petersburg Times,* won the 1991 Pulitzer Prize in feature writing for her series describing the abandonment, the arrest of the mother and her trial and subsequent developments.

The Crazy Bishops When Bonnie Van Gilder was assigned to do a story about street gangs for her journalism class, she hoped to observe a gang on the prowl. Unable to do so, she had to interview sources.

Van Gilder could have relied on the police alone for information. She did interview police officers and examine police documents, along with news clippings. But she wanted more direct contact with a gang. She located a Times Square gang, the Crazy Bishops, and she interviewed some members.

Here is how her story begins:

NEW YORK—"China," a female member of a Times Square teen gang called the Crazy Bishops, narrowed her black eyes and declared, "If you want to be a Bishop, you got to mug people and beat them up and take whatever you can."

Like most of the other Crazy Bishops, China, 15, comes from a broken home, is a runaway and has an extensive arrest record. Police have identified 60 Bishops, but suspect as many as 200 Hispanic boys and girls, ranging in age from 14 to 19, are associated with the gang.

Detective John McNamee knew where to find China. When the 42nd

Street policemen change shifts at 7:30 a.m., the Bishops come out of a nearby park where they sleep. They go to a local coffee shop or sit on the stoops of pornography and peep show businesses that line 42nd Street.

At night they work the streets and vast network of area subway tunnels. The gang has rampaged through the theater district, looting stores, mugging tourists and harassing transients.

"When you're a Bishop, you don't have no pity for people," China said, "You got to hustle to survive. . . ."

Van Gilder's story stands out because she went beyond official sources to those directly involved in the event, the gang members themselves.

A Brilliant Listener For his six best-selling books, Bob Woodward of *The Washington Post* gathered information few others were able to obtain. How? Those who have worked with him, according to a profile of Woodward in *The New York Times,* say "his trademarks are careful preparation and interviewing crucial sources again and again." His greatest gift, says Carl Bernstein, with whom Woodward wrote the book about Richard Nixon and Watergate, *All the President's Men,* "is being a brilliant listener."

A government press agent described Woodward's style as "disarming. He says things like, 'Could you help me with this?' "

Woodward does his homework, carefully preparing for his interviews. When he needed key information from an admiral, Woodward began the interview by praising the naval officer for a book he had written some 20 years before. Woodward had stayed up half the night before to read the book.

Dentists and Photojournalists When Nikon decided to replace its advertising agency, half a dozen agencies vied for the $15 million contract. The winner was Ammirati & Puris, and the reason it won, said its president, was that it spent weeks gathering information about how Nikon cameras were being used.

Ammirati interviewed dentists who use cameras in restorative dentistry. The agency also interviewed photojournalists in Saudi Arabia for the Persian Gulf War to find out what they expected from their photo equipment.

"We totally immersed ourselves in the marketplace," said Martin Puris, the agency president. Nikon decided that the agency's information gathering showed its creativity and its interest in the project.

The Youngest Mothers   Teen-age pregnancy is a grim subject. Figures are released each year that reveal the growing numbers of young, unmarried mothers, some of them just into their teens. Sharon Cohen decided to put a human face on the data about the youngest of the young mothers. She interviewed Kim, a child mother. Here is how Cohen's story begins:

CHICAGO (AP)—For Kim, the last blush of girlhood—the whir of jump ropes, playground flirtations and slumber parties—faded and went cold at age 13. Kim got pregnant.

Today Kim is a high school freshman. She has a 10-month-old daughter and a stoic streak. "I just have to take it as it comes," she says with a shrug. "Suffer the consequences—whatever good or bad comes."

Kim is a child mother. She is one of almost 10,000 girls in the United States each year who, at 14 years and younger, are wrested from the cocoon of childhood and thrust, bewildered, into motherhood.

For teen mothers, the road is tough enough.

For child mothers, the path is tougher, and longer.

Physically, emotionally, socially, America's youngest mothers are disadvantaged at every turn.

Their risks of problem pregnancies and of delivering small, sickly babies are higher than normal. They're so immature that they often treat their babies as dolls to dress up or, at best, as brothers and sisters.

Unlike older teens, it will be years before child mothers have high school diplomas, jobs or homes of their own—in short, years before they themselves will be grown up.

"Almost every (negative) consequence associated with teen pregnancy is accentuated for the younger girl. The repercussions go on and on and on," said Shelby Miller, a research associate in Atlanta for the Child Welfare League in New York and author of "Children As Parents."

Many child mothers have second babies while still in their teens, further miring themselves in a swamp of poverty, ignorance and despair where they create new generations of child mothers. Studies indicate 15 percent to 25 percent of children who bear children get pregnant again within two years. . . .

Cohen has blended her interviews with background material to gather sufficient material for a shocking, revealing story. It is well told, too.

All the ingredients for a good read are here: Everyday language. Short sentences—the average sentence length is 16 words. The story moves from a close-up of Kim to a panoramic shot of the problem of child mothers, a logical—and

Hanging Around. "One thing I am death on is the constant citation of experts which is very easy for reporters to fall into. To my way of thinking, there is no such thing as a cowboy expert. The only cowboy expert is the cowboy. And the only way you can find out and appreciate what his life is like is to work with him, and to go out with him and to be there, just hanging around. I am a tremendous believer in hanging around."
—*William Blundell, The Wall Street Journal*

Pushy and Nosy. Pushing to the front of a crowd, asking questions that embarrass sources, refusing to be put off by an uncooperative official—this can be the daily routine for reporters. Some newcomers to journalism find this behavior aggressive and discourteous. No reporter should be impolite, but the reporter's obligation is to gather information for people who want and need to know, and beginners must overcome their timidity.

cinematic—structure. The quotes and the specific details convince us that the writer has accurately captured the situation. Good writing persuades us it is accurate by introducing evidence, which we call the *buttressing facts.*

Note the use of short, almost staccato sentences when Kim's pregnancy is introduced. This is blunt talk for a grim subject. When Cohen widens her lens to take in the general picture, the sentences become longer. The sentences about Kim's predicament average 13 words; the last five sentences average 24 words.

Research

We have examined two basic sources of information—direct observation and interviews. A vast third arena beckons the journalist—the huge treasury of reports, documents, reference material. This treasure trove includes newspaper clippings, government reports like the Census, court documents, police files, tapes in television libraries, budgets, tax records. We could fill pages with the available material, much of it useful to the journalist.

Most stories combine all three types of sources. We saw how Lernoux used her observations from her trip into the bowels of the Bolivian mine. She collected detailed material about the production of these mines, the salaries of miners, the profits of the mining companies from records and documents. And she gathered information from interviews with engineers, mining officials and others connected with the mines.

Mallowe rode the subways, talked to passengers, motormen, transit officials and read all the newspaper clips he could dig up about the subway system.

A vast amount of information is filed daily—in the courthouse, in legislatures, in newspapers and magazines. It's all there. The only problems for the journalist are knowing what's available and knowing how to locate it.

What's There   There is no easy way to learn this. But the journalists who know how systems work can put their hands on records and documents. They know what has to be filed, when it is filed and where it is kept.

Getting It   Almost all information—with a few exceptions—in departments and agencies that are tax supported is available to the public. All city, county, state and federal reports, documents, studies and the like are open to the reporter. The reporter who befriends the people who keep records is likely to have access to them. Another treasure trove of material can be found in the vast array of publications. Getting at them has been simplified with the computerized data base.

Data Bases   A computerized data base is a machine-readable storehouse of information. Scores of newspapers put their contents into computers, as do magazines and research publications. Many government documents are also computerized, along with court opinions, thesis topics, dissertations and government statistics such as Census reports.

Using References

Using the Nexis Databank

Research into published material can take the writer to periodical indexes and then to the articles in bound volumes, or to a data bank that provides summaries of relevant articles and is used to call up the desired articles.

A data base saves the reporter time, provides the most recent information and allows access to information usually not available anywhere else or available only through expensive travel and telephone calls. Some newspapers subscribe to a few data bases. Most university libraries have several. A law school, for example, will subscribe to the Lexis data base for legal opinions, and the medical school may have Medline.

Computer-Aided Reporting   The computer is not only a tool for gathering information—it can be used to process the information as well. In fact, it can sort and organize so much material so quickly that knowledge of how to use the computer is a necessity for journalists.

When the Paddock papers in the Chicago area wanted to know what happened to people arrested for drunk driving, reporters fed into the computer 1,500 drunk driving arrests and their dispositions. The finding: More than two-thirds of those arrested avoided conviction. Only one in 15 was jailed or fined heavily. The Atlanta *Constitution* used local bank records to show a pattern of racial discrimination in housing loans, and it won a Pulitzer Prize for its stories.

Roberta Heiman examined felony arrests in county courts for a year for her newspaper, *The Evansville Courier*. She wanted to know:

- What percentage of cases were plea bargained.
- What percentage of blacks and whites were sent to prison.
- How heavy the public defender's caseload is.

She found: "So many people are being prosecuted that the system is strained both in its ability to keep the community safe and to provide fair and equal justice for the poor."

To keep the courts from collapse, 84 percent of cases were plea bargained. (A *plea bargain* is an arrangement whereby the defendant agrees to plead guilty in return for a lesser charge—murder is lessened to manslaughter, grand larceny to theft, etc.) Only 8 percent of felony cases went to trial.

Blacks were more likely to be arrested and sent to prison, and 80 percent of all blacks charged with serious crimes had to use public defenders because they could not afford to hire lawyers.

The public defenders in the county work on a part-time basis, but their caseload is so heavy they are overwhelmed. Heiman found that the load justified a full-time defender's office. The result of a heavy load is pressure on prosecutors for plea bargains, which results in lighter sentences, or no sentences at all, for criminals.

Government Sources   Local, state and federal government agencies pour out a vast stream of useful material. Studies are always being made, findings issued. Local planning offices examine the city's growth. The state legislature finances a legislative service that makes vital studies of state problems. At the federal level, the stream becomes a river.

Computer Limits

Helpful as the computer is, "it's not a replacement for any basic reporting skill. The data spewed out by a computer will give you the basis for a stronger story than you'd have without it. You'll have more and better questions to ask. You'll have better ideas of who to ask, and where to look for more information.

"But all of that will be of little help if you don't have good interviewing skills, if you don't have an ability to cultivate good sources, if you don't get the facts right and don't know how to organize and write a story."
—Roberta Heiman, The Evansville Courier

Keeping Up

Media workers read nationally circulated newspapers for background
and for ideas.

Record Record. When
Janet Wilson of *The
Hudson Dispatch* (Union
City, N.J.) heard rumors
about the head of a city
antidrug agency, she used
the FOIA and learned that
the man had been arrested
33 times on charges
including rape, atrocious
assault, drug use and sale,
burglary and assaulting a
police officer.

In 1966, Congress passed the Freedom of Information Act to make federal
files and reports available to the public. The Act states that the public has the right
to examine any document the executive branch of government has in its possession, with nine exceptions, among them income tax returns, intra-agency letters
and secret documents relating to foreign policy and national defense. The government has a time limit by which it must abide after a request is made. All federal
agencies and all states have Freedom of Information offices, and requests for
information should be sent to these offices. No reason need be given for asking for
the material, though a specific request helps the agency answer faster. Charges are
reasonable.

Appendix C contains the request procedure and a sample letter.

The General Accounting Office, an independent federal agency, issues
reports that make headlines. One recent report that could be localized concerned
bottled water: "Because of lax oversight by the Food and Drug Administration,
bottled water may contain levels of potentially harmful contaminants that are not
allowed in public drinking water." What's on your supermarket shelves?

Polls Public opinion polls are a major source of information for news stories. Polls are a systematic way of finding out what people say they are thinking
about at a given time. Polls are conducted by hundreds of organizations, including
advertisers and their agencies, newspapers and broadcast stations.

Used carefully, poll results can predict how people will act in the immediate
future. But since people change their minds, long-range forecasts can be misleading. Also, times change and new circumstances influence people.

Here are two cautions and five suggestions to consider when conducting polls
and when handling poll results:

1. Polls reveal only what people say they prefer or intend to do. No poll
can state that those polled are telling the truth. A candidate for the U.S.
Senate, whose background includes membership in the Ku Klux Klan and the
sale of neo-Nazi literature from his legislative office, received only 22 to 28

percent of the vote in several polls. On election day, however, he captured 44 percent of the vote. Clearly, people were unwilling to tell the pollsters they intended to vote for a racist.

2. Hundreds of individuals, groups and organizations conduct polls and are delighted to have them used by the media. Generally, the major polling organizations, Roper, Harris and Gallup, are careful about the questions they ask, the people they poll and the interpretations they make of the results.

Here are the suggestions:

1. Ask to see the questions. Examine the wording to determine whether the questions are clear and unbiased.
2. Find out when the poll was taken. On controversial issues, people change their minds with new developments.
3. Check to see how the poll was conducted: coupon, call-in, man-in-the-street? These techniques are suspect since they use what is known as a *non-probability* sample, a sample that is not representative of the population at large. Usually, reliable pollsters select telephone numbers at random and call or—better still—conduct household interviews. Ask to see how the sample was selected and who is in it.
4. Determine who sponsored the poll.
5. Find out if the margin of error is stated and if it is accurate.

Focus Groups   A brief word about a reporting technique used by advertising and public relations agencies and now and then by newspapers and stations: To find out how potential purchasers feel about a new athletic shoe, an agency will ask a representative group, or focus group, of people questions about style, price, color.

The key to the usefulness of the focus group is its makeup. It has to be representative. For its study of why 18-, 19- and 20-year-olds don't vote, an organization gathered a group of young, men and women of those ages. *The New York Times* in a story on the non-voting behavior quoted an 18-year-old Delaware member of the focus group as saying that parents and teachers are not doing enough to encourage young people to vote. "As soon as you turn 18, it's not like we can just switch on our 'vote' modes and go out and vote."

PR Sources   An important source of information is the public relations agency or news office. Whether it is a tip on a new snack that will soon be introduced to the marketplace or a press kit about the local basketball team, the work of public relations people plays an important role in the news-gathering process. From half to three-fourths of all news originates with a public relations source.

PR material is supplied in these forms:

News release—Information the source thinks would make a news or feature story.

Fact sheet—An outline of material that can be used for background.

Position paper—The source's stand on issues before the public.

Press kit—A detailed and sometimes elaborate set of materials that usually is accompanied by photos.

Guidelines

Margin of error: The more people selected at random for polling, the smaller the margin of error. Pollsters say that 95 out of 100 polls will have the following margins of error:

Number Interviewed	Margin of Error (%)
50	±14
200	± 7
600	± 4
1,500	± 3
9,600	± 1

Thus, with 1,500 polled, a result of Jones over Smith by 51 to 49 could mean 54 to 46 Jones or 52 to 48 Smith. Too close to call.

TV polls: Television stations poll viewers by asking that they call a 900 number and register their opinions on certain topics. Stations report the results as news. What isn't reported: The stations pocket the money (75 cents to $1 per minute per call), and the poll is non-scientific and notoriously inaccurate, as *USA Today* discovered when it looked into the 81 percent favorable rating callers gave Donald Trump, a New York financier in trouble with creditors. It turned out that a single source made 5,700 of the 7,800 calls.

Reference Works   Without reference material, the journalist is as prepared for his or her tasks as a Little Leaguer thrown in to pitch against the Texas Rangers. Helpless. Begin with the telephone directory and the dictionary. In cities where there is a city directory, this, too, is essential. The stylebook of the newspaper, station or agency is at the writer's elbow. (See Appendix B for a stylebook suggested for your use.)

Alongside these four are the *World Almanac,* a good grammar book, an atlas, a road map of the state and a map of the city. Many journalists carry a pocket-size dictionary as well.

Editors may excuse a buried lead or a disorganized piece. Even the best of writers have bad days. But editors snarl at those who misspell. There is no excuse for an incorrectly spelled word. Worse, editors consider the writer who consistently misspells to be indolent, too lazy to check the dictionary. The writer who hasn't the energy to turn the pages of the dictionary is not going to put his or her all into an assignment.

Scores of reference works are available. The business journalist is acquainted with the many works of Standard & Poor's, the Dun and Bradstreet directories and Moody's manuals. Advertising and public relations personnel, who need to have demographic material at hand, are familiar with Simmons reports and Census data.

Everyone in the writing trade is expected to know how to use the following basic references, many of which are available on a CD-ROM:

- *Bartlett's Familiar Quotations*
- *Reader's Guide to Periodical Literature*
- *New York Times Index*
- *Who's Who in America*
- *Dictionary of American Biography*
- *Current Biography*

Authoritative Sources   Sometimes an assignment is so complex or so unfamiliar that a reporter hardly knows where to begin. The clips on the subject prove to be too sketchy, and the references presume some knowledge of the subject. The reporter needs a crash course in the topic, but the assignment is due and there is no time for in-depth research.

On her second day as the marine news reporter for *The Gazette* in Montreal, Jan Wong was given an assignment and told to handle it quickly because her editor had another story for her to cover the next day.

Wong did what reporters do in such circumstances. She turned to people who know, authoritative sources:

"I must have called 20 people," she says. "I called everyone I could find in the marine directory. People were very helpful, but I felt I was drowning."

ALPHABETICAL DIRECTORY
WHITE PAGES

(h) HOUSEHOLDER   (r) RESIDENT OR ROOMER

correct full name — Landon Edw G & Charlotte D; servmn B F Goodrich h1215 Oak Dr

occupation and employer — Landon Fred M & Mary E; supvr Reliance Elec h60 Norman Av

complete street address including apartment number — Landon Kenneth A & Carol L; clk First Natl Bk h1400 E Main St Apt 14

student 18 years of age or older — Landon Kenneth A Jr studt r1400 E Main St Apt 14

Landon Virginia E r1641 W 4th St

cross reference of surnames — Lane See Also Layne

Lane Allen M & Joan M (Allen's Bakery) h1234 Grand Blvd

Lane Avenue Restaurant (Ernest G Long) 216 Lane Av

out-of-town resident employed in area — Lane James M & Betty B; brkmn Penn Central r Rt 1 Jefferson O

armed force member and branch of service — Lane Marvin L USA r1234 Grand Blvd

Lane Robt B & Margt E; retd h1402 N High St

Lane Walter M r1234 Grand Blvd

Layne See Also Lane

wife's name and initial — Layne Agnes E Mrs v-pres Layne Co h2325 Eureka Rd

Layne Albert M & Minnie B; slsmn Hoover Co h19 Bellows Av

corporation showing officers and nature of business — Layne Co Inc Thos E Layne Pres Mrs Agnes E Layne V-Pres Edw T Layne Sec-Treas bldg contrs 100 N High St

Layne Edw T & Diane E; sec-treas Layne Co h140 Oakwood Dr

Layne Ralph P & Gladys M; formn Layne Co h1687 Maple Dr

Layne Thos E & Agnes E; pres Layne Co h2325 Eureka Rd

Leach See Also Leech

suburban designation — Leach Wm E USMC r1209 Ravenscroft Rd (EF)

retiree — Lee Alf M & Celia J; retd h2106 Oakwood Dr

business partnership showing partners in parenthesis — Lee Bros (Louis J And Harry M Lee) plmbs 151 Abbott St

Lee Harry M & Karen L (Lee Bros) h2023 Stone Rd

husband and wife employed — Lee Louis J & Martha B (Lee Bros) h1616 Fulton

Lee Martha B Mrs ofc sec Lee Bros h1616 Fulton

Lee Minnie M Mrs h87 Eastview Dr

"r" resident or roomer — Lee Muriel E r810 LaForge St

"h" householders — Lee Sterling T & Nadine S; mtcemn Eastview Apts h202 Wilson St Apt 1

owner of business showing name of business in parenthesis — Lee Thos W & Effie M (Tom's Men's Wear) r Rt 23

bold type denotes paid listing — **LEE'S PHARMACY (Lee A Shaw) Prescriptions Carefully Compounded, Complete Line Of Toiletries And Cosmetics, Fountain Service, Greeting Cards, 1705 N High St (21505) Tel**

Leech See Also Leach

business firm showing name of owner in parenthesis — Leech Doris E tchr North High Sch h1323 W McLean St

Leech Joseph B & Lucy V; slsmn Metropolitan Dept Store h824 Wilson St

unmarried and unemployed resident — Leech Joseph B Jr studt r824 Wilson St

Leech Marcia M clk Community Hosp r1323 W McLean St

more than one adult in household — Lewis Anne M Mrs clk County Hwy Dept h914 Wilson Av

church showing name of pastor — Lewis Ernest W studt r914 Wilson Av

Lewis Harold G & Anne M; mgr Cooper Paint Store h914 Wilson Av

Lewis Robt B lab County Hwy Dept r1410 Union Hwy Rt 2

Lewistown Methodist Church Rev John R Allen Pastor 515 Maple Valley Rd

Basic Reference—City Directory

Most cities have city directories, which provide considerably more information than telephone directories. More than 20 pieces of information can be gleaned from a city directory entry. *R.L. Polk and Co.*

The people she called were patient. Gradually, she learned enough from the sources to make sense of the clippings and to take advantage of other resource material in the newspaper library.

"I learned an awful lot in that one day about sources, phone books, the library and clippings," she says.

"I worked at the story until I was sure I had it right, and when I submitted it to the editor, he looked it over and approved it with minor changes.

"The very next day, I had to write a story about the acquisition of Canada's largest shipyard by Canada's largest petroleum company. That was just as hard as the previous day's story. I had no idea what was involved.

"But again, a million calls and reading the clips saved me. The story made the front page of the business section."

Wong recalls being embarrassed by the questions she had to ask in her first days on the job.

"I'm sure my sources thought I was asking dumb questions," she says.

But there are no dumb questions for a reporter gathering information and background for a story. And sources who have an interest in seeing that the stories about themselves and their concerns are reported accurately realize this.

Taking Stock

Let's review for a minute. We've said that the foundations of information gathering are direct observation, interviews and research. The most persuasive material we can gather comes from first-hand observation, but that isn't always possible so we must fall back on reliable and credible sources to interview.

To give our information the rounded perspective it requires, we do research. In fact, given time, the first step the journalist takes on any assignment—news release, news story, advertisement, editorial or review—is to consult the clippings, the files, the record of what's gone before on this subject.

Background is important, for both the journalist and the story. But before we get to that subject an important word about gathering information.

Actually, it's a question: How do we know what facts are relevant, what information we should look for, what facts to gather?

What to Look For

We can reduce the guidelines to two:

1. Information that supports and amplifies our story idea.
2. Information we anticipate our audience will want.

Look back at the reporters we've been watching and you will notice: Penny Lernoux went into the tin mine to find out how miners worked under difficult conditions. Mike Mallowe knew before he set out that the Philadelphia subways could be tunnels of terror and he gathered documentation for that idea. Lena Sun traveled to a remote village to find the real condition of the peasants, which she knew was hardly the glowing portrait Chinese officialdom had drawn. Sharon

Cohen began to sketch her story of the youngest mothers when she read the data in her AP office.

We could go on with more examples. In each instance, we would see that the journalist was guided toward observations, sources to interview and background material by an idea, a concept, a notion that was generated prior to the fact gathering. This is guideline one.

Our second guideline is our anticipation of what readers expect from the stories they read. Here's an example. It's the beginning of a profile of an 88-year-old judge in Chicago. The story is by Ron Grossman and it appeared in the *Chicago Tribune:*

Judge Abraham Lincoln Marovitz's story could be a leftover script from the golden age of schmaltzy Hollywood movies like "It's a Wonderful Life"—but with the Jimmy Stewart part being taken over, every few frames, by a tough-guy actor like George Raft.

Abraham Lincoln Marovitz?

Grossman knows that every reader of his piece stopped dead at his first paragraph. *Abraham Lincoln* Marovitz?

And so Grossman proceeds to let the judge tell how he acquired his first and middle names:

Consider the only-in-America etymology of his name.

"My mother, God rest her, was a poor immigrant who discovered that in this country high-class Jews went to temple not synagogue," Marovitz said. "She heard Lincoln was shot in the temple and saw pictures of him with a beard, so she figured she was naming a son for a great Jewish hero."

How do you anticipate what your reader or listener wants to know? There is no simple answer. For generations editors have told young journalists that they'd better not have holes in their stories, which is a negative way to think about this guideline. The idea is to fill in the cracks. Don't leave the audience with any questions.

One way the journalist knows what is needed is through a wide-ranging knowledge. Facts have a way of associating. That is, if you observe Fact A, your background knowledge tells you that Fact B had better be used as well. So let's look at background.

Building Background

New to her education beat, the summer intern asked her reporter neighbor, "What should I know about the beat?" The reply was jolting: "Everything."

Welcome to the world of journalism. While this may have been a beginner's initiation rite, the reporter neighbor spoke from experience. But there is a starting point: Learn how the systems on the beat work.

Learn the System, Know the Community

Education—Who's in charge? Is the superintendent elected or appointed? How is the school system financed? Does the school board have control over the curriculum, the purchase of textbooks? How are principals selected? How many seniors take the SAT or ACT, and what are average scores for the city and for individual schools? What are the dropout and graduation rates? How are school purchases made—by bids or negotiated deals?

The same kind of questions can be asked about any beat, and the answers provide the new reporter with a good starting point for coverage.

The new-to-town journalist also needs to know a great deal about the community:

The political process—How are the mayor and city council elected? Who appoints the police chief? Is the mayor or the council the source of power? How does the judicial system work?

The social setting—What is the racial, religious and ethnic makeup of the community? How do people get along with each other?

The economics of the city—How do people make a living? Who are the major employers? What is the unemployment rate?

Apartment dwellers in large cities are not as interested in the setting of the property tax as are small-town and suburban residents who own homes. Twin Falls, Idaho, has an economy based on agriculture, and Sierra Vista, Ariz., is

Public Display

The student's bungling is heard by few, and the saying goes that the architect covers his mistakes with ivy and the doctor's misdiagnoses are muffled by the grave. But the journalist cannot hide his or her bloopers and blunders. *Marshall Ramsey, The Courier, Conroe, Tex.*

franchise city with its array of fast-food places and motels that cater to travelers and to service people from a nearby base.

When journalists do not have adequate background they can look foolish in print, sound ridiculous on the air:

Print—The corrupt city politician sent out an anguished plea from prison, and *The New York Times* quoted him. His 19-year prison term, he said, was longer than the terms others had received for similar crimes. When he completed his sentence, he would emerge an old, broken man, his productive years gone.

The fact is that a convict is eligible for parole after serving a third of the sentence, and the politician's 19 years actually would amount to six years, four months.

Broadcast—The million-dollar-a-year anchor had bad news for New York City residents—the city's murder toll for 11 months had exceeded the entire 12 months of the previous year, giving the city "the highest rate in the nation," he said.

A half-truth at best. New York City does have the largest *number* of murders in the U.S., around 2,200 a year. But the *rate* is something else. A rate is not a total number; it is the number divided by the community's population. New York has a murder rate of about 29 per 100,000 population. Washington, D.C., has a rate of 72, and the national rate is 8.7 per 100,000. The rate is a true reflection of a situation like crime since it takes population into account.

Study Press Law and History

Journalists also need to know press law and the history of the press. An understanding of the laws of libel and privacy helps reporters avoid troublesome legal suits and encourages them to be venturesome. (The law of the press is examined in Part 5.)

Understanding the history of the press opens the past to the journalist. Knowledge of those who helped to make the press a bastion of democracy gives the journalist courage when attacked, stamina when the routine approaches drudgery and confidence when journalism is belittled.

When Dan Rather was covering President Nixon for CBS television, the White House chief of staff accused him of inaccurate and biased reporting and tried to have him removed from the beat. Rather's tough coverage of the president antagonized Nixon and his aides. Rather did not buckle. He knew what a journalist is supposed to do, and he persevered in his job.

Rather was described by one television critic as "the only person whom the network news system of journalism has produced since Edward R. Murrow who can conceivably supply the conscience missing from television news."

Murrow's name is prominent in any broadcast journalist's hall of fame. As a radio and television reporter, he took broadcast journalism from the routine reporting of official activities to the task of digging behind the pronouncements. His tradition remains powerful in broadcast journalism.

The Wide Range of the Writer's Knowledge

History

In the 1930s a severe economic depression bankrupted many farm families and they headed west by any means possible. *Arthur Rothstein, the Library of Congress*

Religion

At the same time a religious revival is taking place, mainstream religions are split by disagreement over social and political issues. *Bob Thayer, The Providence Journal*

Poverty

Cities are drifting into widely separated classes, the well-to-do and the poor. Uneducated farmworkers and non-English-speaking immigrants have moved to the cities and added to strained welfare, health and educational systems. *Debbie Noda, The Modesto Bee*

Gather Specifics

Our intern who was assigned to the education beat did so well that when she finished her journalism studies the newspaper hired her for that beat. She was prepared. She knew that public education is under attack for failing to educate large numbers of youngsters. (General knowledge.) She wanted to know why some schools educate well and others poorly, and through her reading she established some guidelines for judging schools. (Specific knowledge.)

She has these guidelines listed in her notebook:

- Strong principal
- Disciplined atmosphere
- High expectations for students
- Plenty of homework
- Individual attention to students
- Emphasis on basic skills
- Systematic evaluation of pupil and teacher performance

On her visits to schools the education reporter bases her questions and observations on her list of guidelines.

The reporter's range of specific knowledge is especially important when he or she is sent out on an unfamiliar story or must substitute for the regular beat reporter on short notice. The reporter assigned to interview a country music singer will have to do some fast reading if all she knows is rock or jazz. When the singer says he is true to the tradition of Jimmie Rodgers and that other singers are cashing in on the bland commercial sound introduced by the Nashville record producers, the reporter should know what the singer is talking about.

A short item in a Boston newspaper went like this:

> The Civic Symphony Orchestra of Boston, Max Hobart, conductor, will present the Beethoven Piano Concerto No. 4 with Stephanie Brown, soloist, in Jordan Hall, tomorrow night at 8:30. There'll also be an exhibition of pictures by Mussorgsky.

To many readers of the newspaper, the item was hilarious. Those familiar with classical music realized that the reporter was not. Mussorgsky is a Russian composer who wrote a piece called "Pictures at an Exhibition," which was to be played in this concert along with the piano concerto.

The people who hire writers do not expect them to know everything, at least not at once. But they do want their writers to know something about the people for whom they are writing and the subjects they are writing about. Employers also expect writers to have a habit of learning, of building their storehouse of knowledge. Let's take these expectations in order.

Meet the Audience

Everything writers do is aimed at an audience, and writers who hope to reach their audience have to know something about the reader or listener. Content, language and writing style depend on the audience.

The writer for a sports weekly can use technical language without explaining *ERA, RBI* or *in the paint.* An article for *Seventeen* about the new fad in hairstyling might be given only a couple of lines inside *The Wall Street Journal* in its marketing section.

As society grows more complex, writers—who can be viewed as marketers of information—and their publications and stations are finding it increasingly difficult to identify their targets.

Misunderstandings can be costly. A major Canadian newspaper with considerable readership in the business community confronted a sharp drop in advertising revenue and decided to cut back its staff and some coverage to reduce expenses. Its deepest cuts were in the sports department. Circulation plummeted. The newspaper had ignored the fact that many of those in the business world are avid sports fans.

The New Woman What of the woman of the 1990s? Just who is she? A single professional postponing marriage until her late 20s or 30s or not marrying at all? A homemaker whose life centers on her children and husband? A businesswoman thinking of a family?

In devising an advertising campaign, American Telephone & Telegraph determined the woman of the 1990s was all three, and print ads pictured the three types. When *Good Housekeeping*'s agency showed women in the home full time, the campaign backfired. "We got a lot of criticism from women who thought a new traditionalism meant a return to the kitchen," said a member of the agency's creative team. The new ads show women at work outside the home.

AT&T has a hefty advertising budget and can show women in a variety of roles, but smaller firms have to find elements women have in common. One advertiser for pre-moisturized towels showed a woman with a towel in one hand and a cellular phone in the other. She is also putting on her jacket. Whether she is going out to work, her son's Little League baseball game or a social function isn't clear. "We try to keep it neutral," said a company official.

A pasta ad for Borden's shows a woman walking into the kitchen as her husband and children drop the pasta into boiling water. Is she returning from the office, a school board meeting, vacuuming upstairs? The hope is that the advertisement will appeal to all who see it.

The same hope underlies the work of journalists, public relations specialists and others in the mass media who seek to reach the maximum audience.

The Range of Readers and Listeners At one end of the audience spectrum are those with minimal reading ability. A study of 23,000 recruits at the San Diego Naval Base showed that 37 percent of them could not read at the 10th grade level. At the Walter Reed Army Hospital in Washington, signs were rewritten to the third-grade level because many enlisted personnel could not understand them.

At the other end are college graduates and others who would resent being written down to.

Some journalists have a specific type of reader in mind. Martin Nolan, of the *Boston Globe,* has "a sort of image of the guy who works with his hands but retains a lively interest in what's going on and doesn't need to be given clichés and comfortable slogans in the copy."

Dan Rather of CBS News thinks back to his youth in Texas.

"I know people who work with their back and hands in Texas. A number of them are in my family. And I ask myself, will they understand this story? They're the people I know best . . . good, decent, intelligent people."

All these people, whatever their economic status, however much or little schooling they have had, share many characteristics. They want to live in harmony with their neighbors, they want their children to do as well or better than they, they believe in the work ethic and that they deserve their leisure, they want a hand in making decisions about matters that affect them and their families.

Journalists owe these people the best they can do.

Research

Reference materials are rich hunting grounds for the media writer on the prowl for new ideas. A billion-dollar market was discovered by the marketing department of an advertising agency when an employee was sifting through some demographic data. The employee was astonished by the amount of money teenagers spend on food. A reporter who was looking for data on disease rates came across what was to him a startling piece of information. He found that the United States is 17th in the world in the percentage of children under 1 who are fully immunized against polio. He decided to see what the local situation was for his 7 p.m. newscast.

Studies of U.S. family life reveal that contrary to assumptions, the poor are concentrated among the children, not the aged. Almost one in four under the age of 3 lives in poverty. That's a national figure. What is it in your area? In New York, it's 22.7 percent; Mississippi, 36 percent.

Reference materials also show that most of these poor children live in single-parent homes, usually in households headed by mothers. Data indicate that the number of single-parent homes now being formed is about the same as that of the traditional husband-wife home.

And this leads to still another good local story. The U.S. teen-age pregnancy rate is the highest in the world, and unlike the rates in other countries it is not declining. Local figures can be compared to national and state data.

Another figure: Almost a third of American youth can expect to be on welfare by the age of 18. Welfare is second only to education in non-defense governmental expenses. Compare welfare, education and health expenditures locally.

Most of the material in this section was spotted in the *World Almanac*. Browse through it and see what you can pick up that could lead to an article or be used as the basis of a public service advertising or public relations campaign.

Keep on Learning

The reporter never stops learning. He or she is always replenishing the storehouse of knowledge essential to the journalist.

"A good reporter is a student all his or her life," says Joseph Galloway Jr., a veteran reporter. "Each new assignment demands a crash course in the theory and practice of yet another profession or system."

The accumulation of so wide a range of knowledge may seem to develop a journalist of great breadth and no depth. Not so. Information has a way of linking and integrating, of forming patterns so that the bits and pieces come together. David Halberstam, journalist and author, says, "The great reporter's gifts" consist of "limitless energy, a fine mind, total recall and an ability to synthesize material."

It is this synthesizing, this putting together of information that makes for superior writing.

The two supports on which the house of knowledge is built are reading and practical experience. Journalists read voraciously, and they seek out a wide range of people, groups, organizations.

Reading   "To be a good reporter, you must read," says Galloway, who worked his way up from a small daily in Texas to serve as the UPI's bureau manager in Moscow after combat correspondence in Vietnam. He then moved to *U.S. News & World Report.*

"If in this electronic era you are not accustomed to it, then you must train yourself to gulp down the printed word with the same thirst of someone who has covered the last 15 miles of Death Valley on his belly.

"Read for your life.

"Read every newspaper that comes under your eye for style, for content, for ideas, for pleasure. And the books, my God, the books. The world of modern publishing has a 500-year headstart on you and is pulling further ahead every year.

"Never mind your transcript or your résumé. Let me see your bookshelves at home and your library card."

Journalists read the specialized publications useful to their beat. The reporter covering the local university will read *The Chronicle of Higher Education,* and the court and police reporters will be on the mailing list of the Federal Bureau of Justice.

Keeping up also requires the reporter to read the interpretations and opinions of experts in the magazines of opinion. Among the magazines journalists read are *The Atlantic Monthly, Commentary, Harper's, The Nation, National Review, The New Republic* and *The New Yorker.*

Inspiration   Ask around. Ask a writer how he or she learned to write. Among the sixth grade teachers and college professors the writer names, the name of another writer will pop up. A novelist, poet, short-story writer, essayist, playwright. Even the name of another journalist.

Hemingway had a tremendous impact on journalists of a generation ago. As a young man, Hemingway covered the police courts in Kansas City, and the journalistic style he cultivated can be seen in his novels. He cut language to the bone. He left it to the reader to draw conclusions from his spare descriptions and simple but not simplistic dialogue.

Hemingway was a wide-ranging reader, but he had one favorite author and one favorite book:

> "All modern American literature comes from one book by Mark Twain called *Huckleberry Finn.* . . . It's the best book we've had. There was nothing before. There has been nothing as good since."

John McPhee, a peerless reporter and writer whose work appears in *The New Yorker* and has been reprinted in several books, is studied by journalists. McPhee says he reads Shakespeare frequently, always with awe. There is nothing, McPhee says, Shakespeare could not do.

Another *New Yorker* writer whose work is admired is E.B. White, a master wordsmith. His collections of essays are read for their precise and yet poetic prose. Other *New Yorker* writers to read in anthologies are James Thurber, William Maxwell, Lillian Ross, Joseph Mitchell and Brendan Gill.

Falloff. High school seniors spend less time reading books than fourth graders do.
— *National Assessment of Educational Progress*

Journalists utilize the techniques of fiction, and the writers they are borrowing from include Norman Mailer, Saul Bellow, J.D. Salinger. Journalists have learned style and observational techniques from Dickens, Virginia Woolf and Ralph Ellison. They have been taught sentence rhythm and conciseness by the poetry they read, from the sonnets of Shakespeare to the verse of Sylvia Plath. The journalistic work of Gay Talese and Tom Wolfe, which set in motion the liberating New Journalism, is still important.

But all is not technique and writing styles. Many writers have been influenced by the voices of conscience, voices of writers like George Orwell, whose work impaled intolerance, imperialism and racism long before it was politically correct to do so.

Dickens saw more than a century ago the horrors of homelessness and the way society made victims of the helpless, the young and the poor.

"Dickens had experience with homelessness," says Steven Marcus of Columbia University. "He'd been homeless himself as a child—and he had experience in dealing with it as a reformer who ran a refuge for homeless women."

Dickens shows in his novel *Hard Times,* a child trapped between a callous school system and a money-based society. The dialogue is between the child, Sissy, and her benefactor Louisa, who asks Sissy about her problems in school:

> "Tell me some of your mistakes."
>
> "I am almost ashamed," said Sissy, with reluctance. "But today, for instance, Mr. McChoakumchild was explaining to us about Natural Prosperity."
>
> "National, I think it must have been," observed Louisa. . . .
>
> "National Prosperity. And he said, Now, this school room is a Nation. And in the nation, there are fifty millions of money. Isn't this a prosperous nation? Girl number twenty, isn't this a prosperous nation, and an't you in a thriving state?"
>
> "What did you say?" asked Louisa.
>
> "Miss Louisa, I said I didn't know. I thought I couldn't know whether it was a prosperous nation or not, and whether I was in a thriving state or not, unless I know who had got the money, and whether any of it was mine. But that had nothing to do with it. It was not in the figures at all," said Sissy, wiping her eyes.

Develop Common Sense

No matter how wide the reporter's range of knowledge may be, no matter how assiduously he or she keeps up with the news and events in city, state and nation, all this will be wasted unless the reporter has common sense, an innate feel for the logical and the practical.

Ronald Reagan was fond of telling a moving story of sacrifice. During World War II, he said, a bomber was badly damaged. The pilot refused to bail out, he said, because the belly gunner was too badly wounded to move. In a quavering voice, Reagan told his audiences that the pilot reassured the frightened young gunner, "Never mind, son, we'll ride it down together."

The story worked for a while . . . until a few reporters noted in their stories that if the two airmen had died in the crash of their plane, no one would have known their last words.

A Passion for Justice

As a young teacher in Tennessee's segregated school system, Ida B. Wells was outraged by the separate and inferior schools for black children. As a user of the state's transit system, she refused to abide by the rules segregating black riders. Wells made journalism out of her indignation, and in 1891 her articles for the *Memphis Free Speech and Headlight* so angered school authorities that they fired her. Wells then turned to journalism full time. She expanded her range to attack racial and sexual discrimination in all forms.

A year later, she revealed the names of those responsible for the lynching of three young black businessmen in Memphis, and she urged blacks to leave the city. Those who remained, she wrote, should boycott the local transit system as a signal of protest. The boycott paralyzed downtown business. A Memphis newspaper suggested that she be tied to a stake and branded with an iron. She so angered the white community that a mob wrecked her newspaper and sought to lynch her.

But Wells had left the city to attend a meeting in the East where she remained to work at Thomas Fortune's *New York Age.* At the *Age,* she wrote about lynching and other anti-black practices. Her writing was based on high-risk reporting in Missouri, Arkansas and other states, and, as in Memphis, not many in the white community welcomed it. *The New York Times* described Wells as a "slanderous and nasty-minded mulatress."

Her daughter, Alfreda M. Duster, who edited Wells' autobiography, said of her mother, "The most remarkable thing about Ida B. Wells is not that she fought lynching and other forms of barbarism. It is rather that she fought a lonely and almost single-handed fight with the single-mindedness of a crusader, long before men or women of any race entered the arena; and that the measure of success she achieved goes far beyond the credit she has been given in the history of the country."

Sixty years after her death in 1931, the United States issued a postage stamp in her memory. *Schombury Center for Research in Black Culture, New York Public Library, Astor, Lenox, and Tilden Foundations.*

Taking Notes

In gathering information—from references, research, interviews and direct observation—reporters take notes. Few reporters have total recall, and only the suicidal would dare to trust to memory the spelling of names, exact addresses and other specific information. It's not enough to jot down notes; they must be jotted down legibly, a demanding task for journalists whose penmanship usually is at a fourth-grade level.

Some reporters put their faith in the tape recorder, which is all right for the sit-down interview. But on breaking stories and with people who might freeze up at the idea they are being recorded, written notes are best.

Take copious notes, advises a journalism textbook. Not really, say experienced reporters. Only the most inexperienced or hopelessly confused reporter jots down everything. Walter Mears of the AP says, "Having too much in your notebook can be as severe a problem as having too little. So the best reporters don't write down every word. They only write down the important ones. The best reporters know which ones those are. . . ."

The trick in gathering information is to find the story focus while reporting and to note the material relevant to the story idea.

Bill Blundell, who was an editor and reporter for *The Wall Street Journal* for many years and who holds writing clinics, says that before going out on an assignment, "I always try to have some sort of theme. . . ."

Once the theme is fixed, the relevant information is gathered. Other themes "may pop up that are even more interesting and you have to have the flexibility to grab them," says Blundell.

Without a directing idea, he says, "you are asking for trouble . . . your horizon is so wide you cannot cover it all."

Homer Bigart, considered the reporter's reporter, could write his lead at any instant he was covering a story, said a colleague. "He had a complete grasp of the story at all times."

Marking Notes

Here is a trick to help organize the story: As soon as a theme develops that you are fairly sure will be in the story, put a mark of some kind next to it—let's say an X—and put this mark as you go along next to all your notes that are related to this theme.

When a different theme or idea pops up, use another letter to identify it in the column of your notepad. Other marks can be used: #, /, *, +. You might circle the mark of the theme you believe will be your lead.

The series of marks or letters is used to organize the piece. In the office, you group similar marks. Lo and behold, the story is structured because you are putting similar material together. The piece has logic and coherence.

Pierce confab

Uk city council csdr inc sales tax nxt mtng. No idea how he'll vote on inc. 2-3%.

City Prks mgr. Herbert Smyth (eg) plans retire next .. mo to take new job in Nashville. No replacement yet. "Has done exc job. Hard to replace."

Tday ordered MTA to resume bus service to Fieldston. Will hv to find other ways of cutting MTA expenses. "Too grt hardship on residents." 750 ppl/day used line. Will resume next Monday. Same routes, same schedule as before cut on June 15.

(lots protests city council, petitions -- background)

Hopes to be able to buy 45 acres undvlp land for "wilderness park" in newly annexed area w town. Maint. cost will be minimal cuz leave as is. Cost $48,500 "within our budget." Will be new mgr's baby to dvlp. No specific plans.

A Reporter's Notepad

Here are some pages from a reporter's notepad of a news conference by Mayor Pierce. The mayor made several announcements, and the reporter indicated the subject of each with a distinct marking as the conference continued. Note the reporter's shorthand: *Uk* for understand; vowels and the articles *a* and *the* are eliminated.

The reporter checked the first item, which reads: Understand city council consider increase in sales tax next meeting. No idea how he'll vote on increase 2–3%.

The next item, marked with a circled *X*: City Parks Manager Herbert Smyth (*cq* for correct spelling) plans retire next month to take a new job in Nashville. No replacement yet. "Has done excellent job. Hard to replace."

On the second page, marked with two number signs(#), used to indicate a possible lead, the notes read: Today ordered MTA to resume bus service to Fieldstone. Will have to find other ways of cutting MTA expenses. "Too great hardships on residents." 750 people a day used the line. Will resume next Monday. Same routes, same schedule as before cut on June 15.

(Lots protests city council, petitions—background.)

The note "background" tells the reporter to be sure to check the files on the MTA item.

The third page has a marking similar to the circled *X* on the first page, indicating the two items could go together. It reads: Hopes to be able to buy 45 arces undeveloped land for "wilderness park" in newly annexed area in town. Maintenance cost will be minimal because (we intend) to leave (the land) as is. Cost $48,500. "Within our budget." Will be new manager's baby to develop. No specific plans.

The tax increase had been introduced weeks before and was not lead material but could go high up. The parks items would appear third in the reporter's piece.

On longer pieces, when the reporter has a notepad or two, perhaps some taped interviews, research notes and even a data base report, the pile can be overwhelming. Here's some good advice from Saul Pett, for many years a premier AP Newsfeatures writer:

> Try to picture this. I'm back at the office now. I've got several notebooks full of stuff. I've got clips. I've got maybe portions of a book, or magazine and taped interviews which I've transcribed. All that is done. It is my basic material. But it's all kind of in bunches. So I sit down, and this is just dull donkey work, and I hate it, but find it necessary, and I kind of outline my material. I don't outline the story because I don't know that yet. I'm outlining the material. I try to put it in piles. Here's stuff about his wit. [Pett was discussing a profile of New York Mayor Ed Koch.] Here's stuff about his independence. Here's stuff about how he can be tough with minorities. Here's stuff about his background. All that exists in my notebooks scattered throughout. So the advantage of the outline is that I've got it on paper in long segments. It's a lot of dull work. I spent two or three days on that.
>
> I'm getting more familiar with the material. So that when I'm ready to write, I don't have to pause and go fishing around in notebooks or in stacks of clips. By then I almost never have to consult my notebooks.

Summing Up

The information-gathering process begins with an assignment from an editor or supervisor or with an idea you generate yourself. In either case, the first check is to make sure that the assignment or idea is clear, that you know precisely what you are setting out to find.

The next step is to organize the reporting procedure. Is there time to look over the clips and other background before going out? Next, who are the sources to talk to, and in what order should they be interviewed? Who can be interviewed by telephone, who in person? What documents need to be examined, what records searched?

Usually, the assignment or idea needs some refining, and it's worth taking a few minutes before setting out to adjust the original concept. As good as this concept may seem at the outset, the writer always understands it is subject to change as the reporting and fact gathering proceed. Good writers have alternative ideas in reserve.

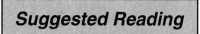

Suggested Reading

Hayakawa, S.I. *Language in Thought and Action,* 5th ed. New York: Harcourt Brace & Company, 1991.

Ross, Lillian. *Reporting.* New York: Dodd Mead & Co., 1981.

Rothmyer, Karen. *Winning Pulitzers: The Stories Behind Some of the Best News Coverage of Our Time.* New York: Columbia University Press, 1991.

Wells-Barnett, Ida B. *Crusade for Justice: The Autobiography of Ida B. Wells.* Alfreda M. Duster, ed. Chicago: University of Chicago Press, 1972.

8 Purposeful Reporting

Whether it is an assignment to follow bird-watchers on their dawn trek along the coast for a feature story, to develop an advertisement for a local fast-food outlet or to design a public relations program for the United Way, the work begins with idea formation. Information gathering is based on idea formulation; the ideas direct the fact gathering.

> ## *Looking Ahead*

Planning pays off. Whenever possible, writers develop story lines and generate thematic material that direct their information gathering. This planning is guided by the writers' general knowledge of the subject matter and their specific understanding of developments in their field.

Bias and stereotypes can get in the way of conscientious fact gathering, but strong feelings can lead to compassion and understanding.

Developing the Framework

Fred Zimmerman knew that he had a good story for his university newspaper. He had heard that an instructor at nearby Emporia State College had been summarily fired. The teacher was young and had unconventional political and social ideas. The dismissal had split the campus into angry factions.

"I raced all over Emporia, interviewed everybody I could think of," Zimmerman recalls. "I filled two notebooks. Then I sat down at a typewriter—where I found I didn't have the foggiest notion of what I wanted my story to look like."

Early in his career, Zimmerman had learned about the information-gathering process that underlies news writing. He discovered that journalists begin to conceptualize their stories as soon as they are given an assignment, even before they begin their reporting. They do this to give their fact gathering direction, and they are able to do it because of their specific knowledge and their general fund of information.

After his experience at the University of Kansas, Zimmerman went on to a career with *The Wall Street Journal,* which included covering the White House. As a reporter, Zimmerman always had an idea or two in mind when he went out on a story. These initial ideas would give him a framework from which to make his observations and to ask questions of his sources. If his observations or the answers to his questions indicated he was on the wrong track, he would ditch his original idea for one that conformed to his findings.

The reporter assigned to interview a local banker about the steep rise in interest rates may banter with the banker about the weather for a few minutes. But the reporter knows exactly what he is there to find out: How has this increase affected local home building? Can people afford to build when they have to borrow at record-high interest rates?

The reporter who has been told to find out the reaction of university officials to a bare-bones budget just adopted by the state legislature knows what the focus of her story will be: What cuts will have to be made by the university? Will some programs have to be eliminated? What about faculty and staff salaries?

The journalistic process is much like any other investigative process, whether it is conducted by a detective, a nuclear physicist or a historian. First, the investigator develops a theory. The investigator's observations will then either support or refute the theory. If the theory is not supported by the facts, the investigator develops a new theory.

In his story "The Hound of the Baskervilles," Arthur Conan Doyle describes Sherlock Holmes sitting in seclusion in his Baker Street rooms after learning of the murder of Sir Charles Baskerville. Holmes "weighed every particle of evidence, constructed alternative theories, balanced one against the other, and made up his mind as to which points were essential and which immaterial." Holmes needed a starting point for his inquiry, long before he visited the scene of the murder.

Unlike the master detective, the reporter cannot spend hours in seclusion mulling over particles of evidence. The reporter sometimes has only minutes to

---

Sturdy Legs. Every story is like a tripod, says Ken Fuson of *The Des Moines Register.* Its legs are "the idea, the reporting and the writing. While all three legs are equal, the idea comes first. If the idea is poor, no amount of solid reporting or pretty writing can salvage it."

Insights First. The editorial writer, advertising copywriter, reviewer, agency publicist—all have a plan in mind before they start writing. Kirk Citron knew before he dug deeply into his work for the California Prune Board that fiber in prunes was the key to his ad copy.

Halfway through a movie she was watching, Barbara Shulgasser knew her review in the *San Francisco Examiner* would be negative and she watched for evidence to prove her conclusion.

prepare. Remarkable as it may seem, reporters develop the ability to generate useful ideas under pressure.

Clearly, ideas cannot be generated by the barren mind. Only the well prepared, those with a general and specific range of knowledge, can develop workable theories and ideas. The reporter who asked the banker about the effect of high interest rates on home building knew from his reading and his chats with builders that the two are tightly related. The reporter covering the university knew through her knowledge of university budgets just what areas are most likely to feel the pinch.

Journalists are always reading, chatting, looking around them for information and story ideas. What is not immediately useful is stored. Their minds are like computer disks, storing material, squirreling it for later use.

Women as Victims

A reporter passes the police reporter's desk, sees a Department of Justice pamphlet on it, "Violence Against Women," and asks to borrow it. She's heard that while violence against men is declining, violence against women is not. Maybe there's a story here. She reads and learns:

- "The violent crime rate for males has decreased since 1973; however the rate for women has not." About 2.5 million women a year are victims.
- "Over two-thirds of violent victimizations against women were committed by someone known to them." Almost a third of the victimizers were husbands or boyfriends; another third were acquaintances.
- "Women who were the most vulnerable to becoming the victims of violent crime were black, Hispanic, in younger age groups, never married,

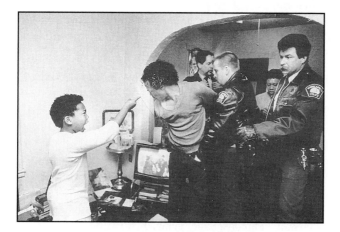

"You Hit My Momma"

The victimization of women is growing steadily each year. Although women's groups are urging battered women to file charges, many do not because they fear reprisals.
Donna Ferrato/Domestic Abuse Awareness Project

with lower family income and lower education levels, and living in central cities."

- "Almost six times as many women victimized by intimates (18%) as those victimized by strangers (3%) did not report their victimization to police because they feared reprisal from the offender."

These general conclusions are supported by a number of tables, some of which the reporter sees are useful for a story that is forming in her mind. The story is that crimes against women may be growing in her community, that there may be specific areas in the city where the crimes are numerous. She would like to interview some victims, especially those who did not report their victimization.

As she is filing her notes, Sarah, the reporter, notices an AP story she had saved. "Grandmothers step into crack's breach" is the headline over a story by Dana Kennedy about how crack has made many mothers unable to care for their children in urban centers. The burden of care is picked up by children's grandmothers, and in five years in New York the number of grandmothers and other relatives who were receiving aid for taking care of dependents jumped from 150 to 17,000.

Sarah knows that crack is not a big-city phenomenon, that it has filtered down to the smallest communities and is a problem in her town. She decides to check to see whether there is a local story on this situation.

She has two ideas for local stories now. She first turns to the victimized-women material, and questions flood in: Does the local situation reflect the national trend? Are the police tough on those who batter women, arresting them rather than trying to calm domestic fights? Are prosecutors filing the maximum charges on persistent offenders or allowing plea bargains to be made because they consider abuse of women a minor crime? Are there local assistance groups for battered women?

These questions are already shaping her reporting. She is aware of the journalistic process: Idea—Reporting—Writing. Too often, the writing phase is given priority. She recalls a statement by the columnist Dave Barry:

> I was a pretty good writer and I thought that was all that mattered. But journalism isn't about writing. You learned that what it's really about is asking the hard questions, being persistent.

Profile of a Lawyer

Sarah starts gathering material about local assistance groups and comes across the name of a lawyer who spends considerable time assisting women and children who are abused and the victims of sex crimes.

Perhaps the lawyer can help with details about some of the themes the reporter has in mind. Perhaps, Sarah thinks, her first step will be to do a profile of the lawyer. Yes, that's what her first story will be.

She knows that for any profile there are absolute essentials, and these essentials will guide some of her questions:

Appearance—What the person looks like.

Background—Education, upbringing, interests.

Occupation—Training. Length of time in the field. Reason for selecting the work. How the job is related to the theme of the profile.

Details—Anecdotes, quotes, incidents that reveal the person's personality.

Sarah has read the clippings about the lawyer and decides that her tentative theme will be the lawyer's role in the growing refusal of women to accept their victimization. She knows that she will have to ask the lawyer whether she herself was battered or the victim of a sex crime. She doesn't enjoy pushing herself into the personal lives of her subjects, but she knows that this is what Barry mean by the necessity to ask the "hard questions."

Sarah turns away from her notes and sighs. Hard work. Her eye catches the AP story about crack-addicted mothers. She reads the beginning again, possibly as much for inspiration as for information.

Missing Mothers

The AP story begins:

NEW YORK—Shirley Ceasar is 27 years old, and she's expecting her 10th child. But another baby won't be a burden for her. Like the rest of her kids, the child will be taken care of by its grandmother.

Shirley, a crack addict for at least four years, lives in Harlem with her boyfriend, the father of all her children. Her mother, Sarah Mae Ceasar, lives a 15-minute subway ride away, in a housing project in lower Manhattan.

There, in a cramped three-bedroom apartment, Mrs. Ceasar takes care of five of her grandchildren, including 11-year-old Walique, who was born deaf and mentally retarded. Shirley's other children are cared for by their paternal grandmother.

"I used to go up and see them and there was nothing in the refrigerator to eat, no clothes for them to wear, they weren't even going to school," said Mrs. Ceasar, 57, who is hoping to adopt the children. "I'd bring them clothes. Their father would sell the clothes for drugs."

In New York City and other large metropolitan areas, grandmothers like Mrs. Ceasar are the glue holding together many poor black families splintered by drugs.

In the past five years, the crack epidemic has made addicts of more young minority women than any other drug in history. In particular, experts say, it has threatened the tradition of black women who often hold their families together.

"There's a quality in crack that is so quickly addictive that people don't get away with experimenting with it," said Richard Johnson, director of the Jewish Child Care Association of New York. "Women who would normally retain some responsibility and some conscience about their children don't have the chance. They're addicted so quickly. They're just lost."

Since 1985, the number of children in New York City's kinship foster care program, which allows grandmothers and other relatives to receive aid for taking care of dependents, has jumped from 150 to 17,000.

Seventy percent of the placements of children within kinship foster care are the result of mothers' crack addiction, Johnson said.

Sarah likes Kennedy's approach to the story. The use of human interest for the delayed lead strikes her as useful for her battered women story. She notes how Kennedy used the first four paragraphs for the focus on an individual and then widened out the story for the general picture.

And she is aware of the compassion and concern that Kennedy clearly took to her reporting, which obviously made a favorable impression on her source.

Being Flexible

When Bob Rose of *The Blade* in Toledo, Ohio, was told to interview a former president of the American Cancer Society, he had a framework in mind. He would ask about the major types of cancer and their causes. When Rose arrived at the hotel where the cancer specialist was staying, he picked up a copy of the day's events at the hotel desk to see if anything newsworthy was going on.

On the schedule was a room number for the R.J. Reynolds Tobacco Co., where workers were being instructed for a local advertising campaign. Rose quickly changed his plans. He decided to focus on the connection between lung cancer and cigarettes.

Rose sums up the process of purposeful reporting: You know what you want to write and how you want to write it while you are doing the reporting. But whenever there is a hitch, be prepared to change plans.

Here is the story Rose wrote:

Surgeon, Tobacco Firm Salesman
2 Men Worlds Apart On Smoking

Both In Toledo
To Promote Cause

By BOB ROSE
Blade Staff Writer

Two men who have a deep interest in whether Americans smoke cigarettes were in downtown Toledo Tuesday morning.

They were a floor apart in the Commodore Perry Motor Inn, but they were a world apart in what they said.

One was the immediate past president of the American Cancer Society. The other was a representative of the R.J. Reynolds Tobacco Co.

In an interview on the second floor, Dr. Lasalle Leffall, Jr. talked about what a killer lung cancer is.

In a talk to 14 temporary workers one floor above Dr. Leffall, the R.J. Reynolds man talked about handing out free samples of his firm's products.

Dr. Leffall, who until last week was president of the American Cancer Society, was eager to talk, to warn people about the more than 100 types of cancer.

The Reynolds man was not so eager.

"The media is an entity that we do not deal with," he told his group in the smoke-filled room.

Dr. Leffall told about what he does when he meets a smoker. "If someone asks me if I mind if they smoke, I say, 'Yes, I do.' In doing that, I emphasize

DR. LASALLE LEFFALL
Eager to warn of cancer

that they are doing something dangerous to my health and dangerous to their health."

The Reynolds man recommended a different routine in handing out cigarettes:

"Are you a smoker or a nonsmoker?

Regular or menthol? Full flavor or lights? Longs or regular length?"

Dr. Leffall would not like the euphemism, "full flavor." He'd say "High tar and nicotine."

And he would recommend neither high nor low tar. "The American Cancer Society believes that there is no safe cigarette, but that if you must smoke, the lower tar cigarettes cause fewer changes in your system that lead to lung cancer."

Dr. Leffall said he hopes smokers will kick the habit at least on Thursday, the date of the society's annual "great American smokeout."

Not willing to fight such an effort, the R.J. Reynolds man told his people to take the day off.

Dr. Leffall, who is chairman of the surgery department at Howard University's college of medicine in Washington, D.C., said the biggest opposition to the anti-smoking drive is the person who continues to smoke in spite of all the evidence that it can be deadly.

"We're not winning the battle," he said. "We're making progress, but we're not winning the battle."

The R.J. Reynolds man, who declined to give his name, said he has no quarrel with the American Cancer Society.

"They have their job to do," he said. "And we have our job to do."

Knowing the Essentials

Breaking news stories might seem an exception to the approach of taking an idea to the event. After all, the reporter never knows what to expect on a breaking news story. The fact is that most spot news stories do fit a pattern, and if the reporter knows the pattern, he or she will find it much easier to report and write the story. We could call this pattern the **necessities** or **essentials of the story.**

In Chapter 1, you read about Lindy Washburn covering a fire for the AP. As soon as she heard that the fire in Bradley Beach was a big one, Washburn developed a framework. Her first question to the fire department dispatcher in Asbury Park was, "Any deaths?"

Washburn knew that an essential element of a fire story—as of any disaster—is the human dimension, the number of dead and injured. There are other necessities or essentials of a fire story, and if we look at Washburn's questions we can see what they are. She asked the dispatcher for the address of the building, what it was being used for, when the first alarm had been received. She wanted to know the cause of the fire and what the building looked like. Washburn knew that the answers to her questions would shape her story.

The obituary writer in Chapter 1 also had a series of questions to ask because she, too, knew that the answers would be essential to her story. She needed to know the name and identification of the deceased, accomplishments, survivors, funeral plans.

In this chapter, Sarah listed the essentials for her profile of the lawyer. She took this list to her interview.

The essentials can be established for various types of stories. Chapters 9 and 10 list the basic ingredients of or necessities for many types of stories.

The essentials are the writer's starting point. They determine the journalist's early observations and the first questions asked of sources. They shape the story, fill in the framework.

One of the most common failings of beginning reporters is that they do not cover the essentials in their stories. In the newsroom, the editor will say that the writer has left a hole in a story or that she has failed to anticipate and answer the reader's questions.

Once the essentials are gathered, the reporter moves on to more specific and detailed observations and questions. The answers to the essential questions usually provide leads for the questions that get at the unique aspects of the particular event or individual.

Every story, every release, can be fitted into a type or category. There are game stories that sports writers handle, fire and arrest stories that police reporters write, meeting stories a variety of beat and general assignment reporters cover and write, news releases about promotions and new products. Each of these types of stories consists of essential ingredients or elements.

Break the Mold. Fire stories all seem more or less the same. Good reporters can spot the item that makes the one they cover today different from last week's. Here's a lead by Emil Venere of *The Mesa Tribune:*

An 81-year-old Mesa man was burned seriously in a natural-gas fire Wednesday morning and a neighbor used slices of white bread to smother the man's smoldering skin.

An Obit Gone Wrong   An obituary, for example, obviously must include the name of the person who died. Since the reader wants to know something about the person, every obituary must also include the person's address or hometown and his or her occupation and accomplishments. There are other necessities for the obituary, one of which was left out of the following wire service story. See if you can spot the missing essential:

> AM-HOBGOOD DIES, 180<
> OLDEST WAR VETERAN DIES<
> ARKADELPHIA, ARK. (AP)—Funeral services will be held Monday for Norman Hobgood, the man the government calls the nation's oldest war veteran.
>
> Hobgood, who died Friday, enlisted in the army in 1898, serving in the third Kentucky Volunteer Infantry during the Spanish-American War. The veteran's administration said he was the oldest of 30 million veterans listed in its records.
>
> Only about 250 veterans of the Spanish-American War are living, according to the VA.
>
> The Kentucky Native also was Arkansas' oldest State Legislator. He was elected to the State House of Representatives for two terms in 1925 and 1927.
>
> Hobgood, who lived in an Arkadelphia nursing home, frequently was interviewed about his status as the oldest veteran. He also was in the limelight in the annual Veterans Day celebrations in Arkadelphia.
>
> Last year, Hobgood was awarded the Arkansas Distinguished Service Medal in a Veterans Day ceremony at Henderson State University.
>
> Hobgood was a lawyer, teacher and farmer. He farmed until he was 99 and preached the Sunday worship service at his church on his 100th birthday.
> AP-NR-03-02 1413EST<

Minutes after this story moved on the wires, an editor caught the lapse and ordered a new story written with the essential information included. The new story was identical to the first except for this second paragraph:

> Hobgood, who died Friday at the age of 108, enlisted in the army in 1898, serving in the Third Kentucky Volunteer Infantry during the Spanish-American War. The Veteran's Administration said he was the oldest of 30 million veterans listed in its records.

Ageless. The evening radio newscast of the Canadian Broadcasting Corporation reported that the dancer Gene Kelly, famous for his role in the movie "Singin' in the Rain," had suffered a stroke. His age was not mentioned. (He was 81.)

(In case you didn't catch the blooper, the news writer had forgotten to include the man's age, an essential ingredient of all obituaries.)

To sum up, there are essential elements for every type of story that are non-negotiable. You can complain about being forced into a rigid style by these requirements all you want. But forget one of them and you will face the embarrassment of the writer who neglected to put in the veteran's age.

The essentials can be placed anywhere in the story—in the lead, in the middle, at the end. Placement is up to the writer and his or her feel for the relative importance of the elements.

No list can predict the full dimensions of any story. Writers must be alert to highlight the unique aspects of the event they are describing. Often, it is the unusual, the strange fact that makes the story different from other fire, sports or speech stories. If the fact is unique and significant—the tears in the firefighter's eyes as he carries the body of the child from the smoking ruins, the mistake of the base runner in the ninth inning, the sparse attendance at a meeting of school board candidates—the writer begins the story with it.

Journalism is not mechanical. It cannot be carried out like a drill team automatically stepping out its patterns. Journalism is an art that requires its practitioners to look with a fresh eye at each event to capture its unique aspects. But the eye must have a focus, a direction in which to begin looking. The essentials point the news writer in the proper direction.

Perry Werner, The Hays Daily News

Northeastern University

The Essentials

Every message—every news story, press release, photograph, editorial or advertisement—must contain the essentials, material that answers the basic questions the writer knows that readers or viewers will have. Story of a fire: the dead, injured, cause, damages. A press release about Saturday's football game: the teams' records to date, past records against each other, last year's game, leading players.

Forming Ideas

"Let's say the mayor is going to reduce the number of policemen because the city has a budget problem. We would lose a lot of cops. Big story. My duty would be not to just take it down like a tape recorder, but to try and find out by interviewing the mayor and, more likely, other officials, and other people involved with the budget or the police force and ask what does it mean in terms of: Is he serious? Is it just a bargaining ploy to get more money out of the state? How easily would he be able to do this? What would that mean in terms of patrol? What would that mean in terms of crime?"

—Clyde Haberman, *The New York Times*

Developing Confidence

Everyone likes to criticize the journalist. This article was too condensed to give the real story. That piece was all black and white; the nuances were missing. The beginning journalist may cringe under this battering. With experience, the journalist will shrug off such criticism.

The journalist who works hard to gather and store general and specific information and whose story ideas are based on sound thinking has earned the right to be confident. He or she knows there is no satisfying everyone. Consider the rebuttal that Walter Lippmann made to critics. Lippmann, one of the great figures in American journalism, observed that there are too many facts for the reporter to gather and that even if a reporter could gather them all, nobody would want to read all of them. News stories are capsulated reality.

Fine-Tuning the Framework

This story came into the office of *Newsday* from one of its bureaus:

> Plainview—A 12-year-old newsboy died Wednesday after he was struck by a car while delivering papers by bicycle, police reported.
>
> Philip Goldstein, of 6 Ramsey Rd., left his home at 5:48 AM and rode his bike to Old Country Road, where police said he crossed the path of a car driven by Joseph Havranck, 53, of 7 Timon Ct., Huntington. Havranck, who was unhurt and was not charged in the incident, told police his car skidded on wet pavement when he attempted to stop.
>
> The Goldstein boy was taken to Central General Hospital, in Plainview, and was later transferred to Nassau County Medical Center, East Meadow, for surgery. He was pronounced dead at 2:40 PM.

An editor at the newspaper sensed there was more to the story, and he asked a reporter to dig further. Here is the beginning of the story written by Jeff Sommer:

PLAINVIEW—By 9 a.m. Tuesday, doctors at Nassau County Medical Center told Gerald and Barbara Goldstein there was little chance that their 12½-year-old-son, Philip, injured in an auto accident, would live.

The Goldsteins thought of Philip's bar mitzvah—his ceremonial coming of age as a Jew—which was scheduled for tomorrow. And they thought of a close friend of Philip's who was to attend the bar mitzvah. The friend was confined to a Manhattan hospital, where he recently received a kidney transplant from his father.

"We decided immediately to donate his [Philip's] kidneys for transplants," Gerald Goldstein said yesterday, sitting in the sunlit yard of the family's Plainview home. "Philip was a very sensitive, compassionate boy. He was very concerned about his friend. We're sure he would've wanted it this way."

The seventh-grader, who hoped one day to attend Harvard Medical School and become a doctor, died Wednesday. And yesterday at Stony Brook University Hospital two young Suffolk residents who Philip never knew received his kidneys. Philip's parents say their son lives on, symbolically.

"I hope some day my wife and I will be able to break bread with these people," Goldstein, a Manhattan lawyer, said. "We have been told that they share our grief and we hope to be able to share their joy in this gift from our son."

The kidney recipients—Kathy Kuhl, 22, of 16 Reynolds St., Huntington Station, and Robert Tagliaferro, 23, of 15 Longacre Court, Port Jefferson—were in stable condition last night at the hospital, resting after their operations performed by a team of 30 medical personnel, headed by Dr. Felix Rapaport. . . .

Why is the second account so much better than the first? Only one reason—more thorough reporting. This is what editors mean when they tell their reporters, "You don't write writing; you write reporting."

No matter how proficient a writer may become at manipulating words, there is only so much even the most gifted writer can do without good material.

Listen to the latest songs; watch the television talk shows; recall the last movie you saw. When the material is ordinary and run-of-the-mill, not even the most gifted performer can make it come alive. Not every song The Rolling Stones have recorded has gone platinum, and Madonna cannot turn a so-so tune into a hit. All of David Letterman's nimble wit cannot bring a dull guest to life. Meryl Streep and Dustin Hoffman have appeared in some lemons they and their fans prefer to forget. Marlon Brando, considered one of the greatest film actors of the last 40 years, appeared in more than a dozen bombs.

But given good material, the rock group, singer, talk show host, talented actor or actress can make us sit up and exclaim, "That's something." So can the writer who makes perceptive observations and asks the right questions.

Carol McCabe, an editor who was instrumental in improving the writing of staffers with *The Providence Journal,* has some advice:

> You ask the questions: What was it like? What did it feel like? Take the reader where he cannot go. You, reporter, go in and bring back information. What was it like in those woods? What was it like on that island? What is it like in the person's dreams? And you do that by accumulating every bit of meaningful detail and using it where it seems appropriate. It's what you leave out sometimes that is as important as what you put in.

Looking and Listening

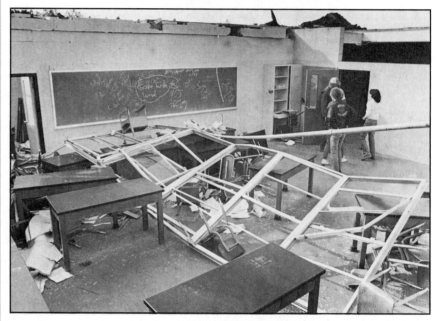

Keith Warren, The Commercial Dispatch

When Keith Warren, of *The Commercial Dispatch* in Columbus, Miss., photographed a tornado that killed six, injured 100 and caused massive damage, he looked for a scene to symbolize the event, and he sought eyewitnesses. He photographed the roofless Northeast Jones High School with the wry note on the blackboard, and he interviewed Austin Wade and his wife Willie:

> "It sounded like a train coming. It sounded awful," Mrs. Wade said. "We went in the bathroom and Austin grabbed onto the sink and I grabbed him. Then he said, 'Bill—some people call me Bill—we're gone.' And I said, 'No, we're not. The Lord is with us.' Then we started praying. And when you pray you have to pray with faith."

Knowing the Beat

The heart of news gathering is the beat. Reporters are placed at strategic locations where news usually develops—the police station, the county courthouse, city hall and the federal courthouse. Some reporters are assigned to shopping malls. The reporters assigned to these strategic locations are called **beat reporters.**

Some reporters have topical rather than geographical beats. While the police and city hall reporters spend most of their time at one location (a geographical beat), the education and environmental reporters move over a wide territory and examine a variety of topics (topical beats). The education reporter visits grade schools, looks in on community colleges, attends school board sessions and even goes to the state capital to cover education issues. The environment reporter covers local, regional, state and federal developments.

Other topical beats include medicine, science, labor, agriculture, politics, religion and the performing arts. Sports is considered a topical beat because most sports writers handle a variety of sports.

Because radio and television stations have fewer reporters than do newspapers, almost all stations make their staffers **general assignment reporters.** Only the networks and the largest radio and TV stations have beat reporters.

Most wire service reporters also do general assignment work. On one shift, Los Angeles AP writer Jennifer Bowles covered a major fire at Universal Studios and a train collision that killed four people. Then as she was preparing to leave the office for the night, a call came in from the Los Angeles Dodgers—the team was signing Mets star Darryl Strawberry to a lucrative contract. The story was an exclusive, and Bowles went to work again. At 3 a.m., she headed home.

Building Relationships

New to her beat covering religion, Melanie remembered the advice of her journalism instructor. "On a new beat, introduce yourself to everyone, not just the people in charge," he had said.

Everyone? Yes, not only the pastor of the largest church in town but the organist, the choir director and the secretary. "And give them your business card or write down your name and phone number for them."

Later, the advice paid off when the secretary of the First Baptist Church let the reporter know about a split in the church board over the literal interpretation of the Bible. Another big story developed when a cantor at a local synagogue called Melanie to tell her about the synagogue's new position on its rabbi officiating at intermarriages.

She learned to chat with people on her beat, not to seem to press for news. And she kept in telephone contact with those she could not visit as often as she wished.

"Get over and shake hands," says Kurt Rogahn of *The Cedar Rapids Gazette.* Then ask the people you have met to introduce you to others. Rogahn, the paper's education reporter, advises reporters new to a beat to seek out private individuals who have been around for a while. "The person may have an ax to grind, but he can also give you some perspective."

Mike King, science and medicine reporter for the *Constitution* in Atlanta, says the best way to build a relationship with people is to "get to know them without writing about them. It takes a while for you to get used to each other." King

An Intimate Moment

The closer journalists move to their sources, the more penetrating the information they gather. The pastor of a small church who shares with the reporter his need for spiritual guidance allows readers a glimpse into his personal life. *Joel Sartore, The Wichita Eagle-Beacon* likes to swap information with sources. "You give them some tidbit to take back to a meeting.

"Nothing you would put in the paper, but they like that kind of inside stuff." In return, he says, he often is given newsworthy material. He also finds public relations people helpful. "When you're new to a beat, you have to use PR people to find the right experts to talk to."

When Dan Rather covered the White House for CBS News, he said he survived the highly competitive race for news by relying on his personal sources. "They didn't pass me notes in invisible ink, but I made it my business to know them—secretaries, chauffeurs, elevator operators and waiters," Rather says. "I take them to dinner and keep them in cigars or whatever turns them on."

Courtesy, a cheerful word or two and personal interest often are enough to make friends of potential sources. People on the fringes like to feel they are a part of important activities. They do this by feeding information to journalists.

Reporters cultivate their sources, and the yield can be impressive. A source that AP science editor Paul Raeburn had developed on his Environmental Protection Agency beat called him: Tobacco lobbyists had succeeded in having a scientist dismissed from a panel studying the effects of secondhand smoke. Raeburn verified the tip, and his story about the dismissal led the EPA to reappoint the scientist.

A reporter cannot be everywhere on the beat. A good source is another pair of eyes.

Two Dangers   Beat reporters face two dangers when dealing with sources: writing for them and getting too close to them. Sometimes, a reporter will become so technical only his or her sources will understand the stories. A more insidious pitfall is becoming too friendly with sources, so close that the reporter may be soft on them. A reporter also may not want to risk losing a good source by writing a critical story.

The Greatest Comeback   Making a personal contact paid off in a big way for Ron Rapoport, who writes a sports column for the *Daily News* in Los Angeles. One of the better runners in his area is Gail Devers, an Olympic-quality sprinter and hurdler who for a time was training at the nearby UCLA track where she had gone to school. Rapoport had heard rumors about Devers' battle against Graves disease, a thyroid condition.

It was two weeks before the Olympics and Rapoport knew that Devers had a strong chance at winning a medal.

"I made a date and went to see her at the UCLA track stadium. We had to get in out of the rain, but there was nowhere to go so we sat on the stairs inside a training room. For two hours, the story just spilled out of her just the way it appears.

"She is an incredibly intelligent and well-spoken woman, not at all shy about telling the most intimate details of her agony."

It was a story of pain, near death and despair; of doctors unable to diagnose her, her skin turning into scales, her hair falling out, her memory loss and perhaps worst of all for a track star, her feet swollen twice, three times their normal size.

Caution: Watch out for Experts

Even the best of sources can be wide of the target when they offer opinions and make predictions. Look at these forecasts of the Persian Gulf War that were published before the Persian Gulf War broke out:

"The United States is likely to become estranged from many of its European allies and it is almost certain to become the object of widespread Arab hostility."
—Zbigniew Brezinski, former U.S. national security adviser

Neither occurred.

". . . the coalition would almost completely fall apart overnight" if the U.S. went to war, and the U.S. would be left "with not a single friend except Israel. . . ."
—George Ball, former U.S. ambassador to the U.N.

The coalition stood and only Jordan among the Middle East states supported Iraq. Later, Jordan established relations with Israel.

Iraq will use chemicals that will cause U.S. troops "to panic and run"; Israel will attack Iraq; the Arab countries will switch sides; Iraq will use anthrax; then the U.S. will retaliate with nuclear weapons, and terrorists will "attack western nuclear power plants and bomb Union Station in Washington."
—Daniel T. Plesch, British-American Security Information Council

None of the above occurred.

Now look at the following casualty estimates made before the war:

3,344–16,059—Joshua Epstein, Brookings Institution
30,000—Pat Buchanan, political analyst
45,000—Center for Defense Information

There were fewer than 500 casualties, most of which were the result of friendly fire and accidents.

"Two years of it," Rapoport wrote in a column that covered more than a page. "Blood dripping out of her body in clots the size of silver dollars."

Rapoport says that during the two days he had to write the column he was "consumed, as emotionally involved as I have been with a column in as long as I could remember.

"I kept waking up at 6 a.m.—not my usual routine—so I could spend extra time working on it."

That column appeared July 12. Three weeks later the scene shifted to Barcelona. Devers had made a remarkable comeback from her two-year battle and had qualified for the Olympics. Rapoport was there, watching her run.

Begin 12,000 Years Ago

When Carol Nation, Arlington County, Va., Department of Public Works public information officer, was browsing in the county's Historical Society, she noticed a description of a 23-mile route over historical areas and locations. Why not publicize this? she thought. Her idea was to combine a map with brief historical notes and an attractive cover. The result, this brochure, was widely copied. *Dept. Public Works, Arlington County*

Enterprise. When Howard Weinberg was doing a documentary for WABC-TV called "Scoundrels! Scalawags! and Saviors!" he wanted to visit the grave of Boss Tweed, who defrauded New York of at least $30 million and died in prison. Permission to film was denied, so Weinberg bought some flowers and visited the gravesite with four other solemn men posing as mourners—the film crew.

"I was sitting almost across from the finish line when she stuck her head across the tape," he recalls. "I couldn't be sure she had won." Nor was Devers sure. But she already felt herself lucky in one sense: She had run competitively even though, as Rapoport wrote from Barcelona, "On the eve of the Olympics," Devers "was sick all over again."

He continued: "It does not seem possible that after all she has gone through there could have been still more torment in store for her. But there it was.

"It does not seem possible that even as she was kneeling down to run in the most important race of her life her Graves' disease could be acting up again. But it was," his column continued.

Rapoport was able to blend the fascinating story of Devers' personal battle back from near death to this race with her running for the gold. He was able to do so because of his painstaking reporting the month before.

"It got so bad," Rapoport wrote from Barcelona, "she could not feel her foot against the starting block" when she was practicing for the big race. She made the qualifying races, though, and then ran in the finals.

"At first, it was impossible to tell if Devers had won the race," Rapoport wrote. Five women crossed the finish line within six-hundredths of a second of each other.

Devers won in 10.82 seconds. The time of the second finisher was 10.83.

"I'm back where I wanted to be," Devers said after the race, and Rapoport quoted her simple victory statement.

Actually, Devers' specialty is the hurdles and later in the Olympics she was leading in that race, on her way to a second gold medal, when she tripped over the last hurdle.

"She got up and instinctively started applauding the woman who had beaten her," Rapoport recalls. "A remarkable woman, really."

Showing Enterprise

The coverage of a crime is a spot news story the police reporter is expected to be able to cover. Digging into police records to find that most crimes are committed between 9 p.m. and 2 a.m. shows enterprise. Finding out that the local police department has assigned fewer officers to this period than to any other time in the day shows real enterprise. Enterprise stories, known as **enterprisers,** are the result of the reporter's initiative.

The Molars of Gambling   When Heidi Evans was a journalism student she was assigned to do a story on people who take the free buses to Atlantic City's gambling casinos. Unlike most of her fellow students who interviewed people on the buses or at the slot machines, Evans walked a few blocks to a nearby pawn shop.

"What do people try to pawn when they run out of money?" she asked the owner. He reached under the counter, brought up a pair of pliers and answered.

"They ask me what I'll take for a gold tooth," he said, "and I hand them these." Evans built her story around the quote.

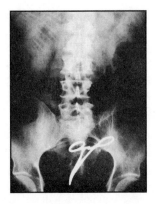

Investigating an Abuse

The Orlando Sentinel staff spent nine months investigating medical care. Florida doctors pay more for insurance than doctors anywhere else in the country, and that means their fees are high. The newspaper found two major abuses: 3 percent of the state's doctors accounted for nearly half the money paid to malpractice victims, and insurance companies exaggerated the number of suits against doctors, and on the basis of the distorted data they doubled and tripled premiums for doctors' insurance. *The Orlando Sentinel*

A Dangerous Intersection Ruth Padawer of *The Record* in Hackensack, N.J., says she has used her own experiences to develop stories. "I nearly got killed at an intersection in Fair Lawn," she said, "and when I got to the office I looked for clips on accidents at the site and planned improvements. The last story was a few years old. So I updated it." This is the result:

> After at least 13 years of promises from the state Department of Transportation, Fair Lawn's most dangerous intersection is still the most dangerous, and not a penny has been spent for repairs.

She went on to point out that each year renovations are promised and then put aside. The intersection, she wrote, is the location of 179 accidents with 120 injuries in six years.

A Formula for Death Lisa L. Ryckman of the AP was breastfeeding her daughter at a hospital when a passing nurse made a disparaging comment about nursing mothers. None offered assistance with her nursing, and when Ryckman left, a nurse pressed a formula sample pack into her hands—"even though I had not requested it." At an American Academy of Pediatrics press briefing, Ryckman learned that doctors were alarmed by the declining numbers of breastfeeding mothers.

"I decided to investigate," she said. The result was a three-part series that included the activities of infant formula companies in the Third World. The companies' peddling of formula in these countries resulted "in the deaths of more than 1 million babies each year," she reported.

In the United States, the federal government gives away $750 million worth of formula each year in a program that, Ryckman wrote, "is a big disincentive to breastfeeding," which physicians say is the best way to feed an infant.

Investigative Reporting

Once a reporter has shown an understanding of the way organizations, agencies and branches of government work in the community and has displayed enterprise in digging up stories on a beat, he or she may be given the go-ahead to do investigative reporting.

Investigative reporters seek to uncover material that people want to keep hidden. Some of the material involves activities that are illegal or legal but abusive. By abusive, we mean that the activities in some way hurt people or deny them their rights.

The Charlotte Observer won a Pulitzer Prize for meritorious public service for a series on the effects of unsafe and unsanitary conditions in southern textile mills. The paper won another Pulitzer for exposing the financial misdeeds of Jim and Tammy Bakker in the PTL religious organization. The Gannett News Service was awarded the Pulitzer for exposing the fraudulent activities of a charity run by the Pauline Fathers.

Prizes have been awarded for reporting that revealed a city's water supply was contaminated with carcinogens, that uncovered inadequate medical screening of airline pilots, that maintained the innocence of a man convicted of murder and that exposed discriminatory practices by lending institutions.

Although some reporters are assigned investigative reporting as a special beat, all reporters are expected to dig out information on their beats. The reporter who relies on the assertions of authorities without checking them fails to inform readers and listeners of the full dimension of his or her beat.

Writing Interpretive Stories

The reporter who knows his or her beat, who has good sources and who can place current events in context is often asked to write interpretive pieces. These articles, sometimes in the form of columns, are called **news analyses.**

For instance, a writer might try to show how a city ordinance came into existence—the groups that pushed for it, the organizations that unsuccessfully opposed it and the reasons for their positions. The writer will also describe the effect of the new ordinance.

Interpretive reporting is not editorial writing. Editorial writers tell readers or listeners that something is good or bad. That is, they make value judgments. The interpretive news writer puts the event in its context.

Putting an event in context means that the interpretive writer places the news event in the stream of cause and effect. An event that is isolated for a news story is plucked from a cycle or stream of related events. The interpretive story shows the news event to be part of the stream.

A city council decision to allow a developer to build homes on a small tract near the city limits can be shown to be the consequence of several factors: population pressure, people in the inner city wanting to move out of older homes into newer houses and to raise their children away from the problems of the inner city. A new high school curriculum may be the result of falling SAT or ACT scores, and pressure by the area university distressed that too many of its freshman students need remedial English and mathematics.

Negotiating the Obstacles

In our discussion of reporting, we have stressed the logical, thoughtful approach. We have talked about reporters adopting tentative ideas, then going out on the story to find supporting material, then dropping the concept for another if no proof is forthcoming.

This approach makes the reporter seem cool and detached, dispassionately jotting down data from his or her observations like a scientist tracking electrons. Most journalists don't work that way. Like everyone else, they have feelings, attitudes and personal values. No one is exempt from emotions, prejudices and biases. Some of these feelings and attitudes are positive and can reinforce good journalism.

Moral Indignation

The persistent underlying sentiment of many digging journalists is a sense of moral indignation. Many journalists want to make the world a better place, and they cannot abide the misuse and abuse of wealth and power that make life painful and arduous for so many. Not content with official statements, versions or excuses, reporters who are blessed—or afflicted—with moral indignation get things done. Look at what radio station WIND in Chicago did.

Accidents in big cities are frequent, so frequent they are not given much attention by the media. But one accident bothered the staff of the radio station. It involved a woman and her two children.

Their car had stalled on the Dan Ryan Expressway. The three waited almost two hours as thousands of cars passed, including several police cars. No one offered to help.

Finally, the mother and her 12-year-old son sought assistance. They left the other son, a paraplegic, behind in the car. But they never found help. As the older son watched from the car, his mother and brother were struck by a car and killed.

The deaths angered a staff member of WIND and the anger generated stories and editorials that revealed the need for a communications system on the 125 miles of expressway around Chicago. During the campaign, people called in with horror stories of their own. One man said his son was driving on the Eisenhower Expressway when his windshield was shot out by a passing motorist.

"The car swerved, banged into the median and threw the boy out of the car," the station quoted the father. "He lay by the side of the damaged car for nearly an hour before help came."

The campaign by WIND won a Sigma Delta Chi Award for public service by a radio station.

Personal Biases

As we have seen, news reporting and writing is rooted in the art of selection. Reporters choose what they want to observe, and then they select from those observations the elements they want to put in their stories. The reporter who believes that the poor bring about their own misery would not have recognized the story that Mary Ann Giordano of the *Daily News* saw in the plight of a family living in a tenement without heat or water.

Like many of us, reporters have strong political views. But they try to hold them in check. Some reporters are unaware of their biases, the distorted pictures they carry around with them.

Our parents, our churches or synagogues, our friends, our schools, our favorite television programs—all these and more influence us to see the world in certain ways. The aspiring journalist should remember that no one, not even those who follow a credo that calls for an open mind, compassion and a commitment to democratic values, is exempt from the prejudices of time and place.

Developing an open mind requires jettisoning some customs, beliefs and ideas that may go back to childhood: a parent's prejudice against Jews and Italians, a teacher's indifference to the slow learner, a friend's hostility to blacks and Hispanics, a church's intolerance of critics.

One of the most difficult tasks young journalists face is establishing a workable relationship with authority. The child is taught to respect and abide by authority—parents, teachers, professionals. As children, we did what others told us to do.

Then there was the period of rebellion. If my father is so smart, why can't he pay his bills? If the politicians are so wise, why can't they balance the budget? As for teachers, every high school and college student has a favorite tale about an inept instructor.

There is a middle road. The journalist must be skeptical of authority but also understand the necessity for leadership. An assertion is not true simply because someone in power or an expert said so. The journalist's task is to check statements, claims and declarations, no matter how authoritative the source.

Skepticism is not cynicism. It makes no sense to turn away from someone in authority merely because the person has a credential or a title. An open mind, a broad outlook, association with all kinds of people and the realization that although people have much in common they are different—these are useful to counter the pictures in our heads that can distort reality.

A healthy skepticism led Giordano to check with the city to see how it had responded to the Walker's plight after her story appeared. The city had promised to find city housing for the beleaguered family, but Giordano knew how slowly bureaucracy works and she kept checking. After three weeks she wrote a second story that began this way:

The plumbing is still broken, the heat is still out, the junkies and rats still roam freely through the lower floors, and the Walker family of Bedford-Stuyvesant is still looking for decent housing.

Three weeks after an article appeared in the *Daily News* detailing the plight of the seven members of the Walker family, they are still trekking through the maze of housing regulations—cruel realities that confront New Yorkers searching for livable housing. . . .

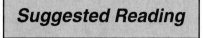

Suggested Reading

Arnett, Peter. *From Vietnam to Baghdad: 35 Years in the World's War Zones.* New York: Simon & Schuster, 1994.

Broder, David. *Behind the Front Page: A Candid Look at How the News Is Made.* New York: Simon & Schuster, 1987.

Liebling, A.J. *The Press.* New York: Ballantine Books, 1961.

Snyder, Louis, and Richard B. Morris. *A Treasury of Great Reporting.* New York: Simon & Schuster, 1969.

Woodward, Bob, and Carl Bernstein. *All the President's Men.* New York: Simon & Schuster, 1974.

9 Capturing the Spoken Word

The news that the city has a sudden cash shortfall and is in dire financial trouble sends reporters scurrying to interview the mayor. His comments make the 6 o'clock news and are on page one of the morning newspaper. *Joan Vitale Strong, City of New York*

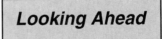

Looking Ahead

Spot news interviews develop information for a news story. Depth interviews are used for profiles that emphasize the individual. Meeting stories focus on a decision, a consensus or the most significant issue raised. News conferences are usually called for a specific purpose, and the story emphasizes the point. Speech stories focus on the speaker's major theme; audience reaction and post-speech answers to questions are often included.

Interviews

Most stories are based partly or wholly on an interview of some kind. The interview may be a few short questions asked of a police officer investigating a robbery, an extended interview for background for a piece on increases in college tuition or a lengthy interview for a profile of the new owner of the local baseball team. For almost every story, a reporter asks someone for information.

Since we know that the written account should reflect the nature of the event, we have a starting point for stories that contain or are based on interviews: Quotes.

Techniques

The key to a successful interview is knowing what we want to find out. Since the spot interview often is conducted by telephone with busy sources, the reporter has to get to the point quickly. For the profile, there is more time to report. Still, the reporter must not waste the subject's time.

Here are some guidelines for conducting interviews:

- Have a good idea of what you want to learn from the source or subject.
- Get to the point quickly.
- Listen for the pertinent comments. For profiles, watch for revealing gestures, movements and mannerisms.
- Ask if there is anything important you did not ask about.
- Ask the source if he or she can be called back should you need further information. (Some sources will not take calls at home after they leave the office. Ask for the name of another person who can be called.)

Spot News Interviews

Reporters interview police officers for information about crimes, fire marshals for possible causes of fires. Sports reporters talk to coaches and players for background material for game stories. In these spot news interviews, the reporter usually is looking for the facts that will illustrate or highlight the event being described.

All writers conduct these spot interviews. A reviewer wants some background about the singer who just joined the rock group and calls a press agent. An editorial writer calls the city clerk for information about sales tax revenues for the past five years. An advertising copywriter talks to youngsters playing basketball in a neighborhood playground to find out what they like in an athletic shoe. A cartoonist needs some background on drunk driving arrests for her Thursday editorial page cartoon. She calls the state highway patrol.

In this search for supplementary material the emphasis is clearly on the event, not on the person being interviewed. But the writer does not ignore statements from the source that can provide drama and human interest as well as the factual material that is sought.

Open to Questions

"Most people are willing to grant interviews. I've never understood why, but they are. It's always very surprising. People who have no benefit to be gained by it either want to help you or are flattered that you'll be taking time out to interview them. . . . And that includes people under very adverse circumstances. People who have had terrible things happen to them, like having members of their family killed. . . ."

—*Clyde Haberman, The New York Times*

The Talkers and the Silent Ones

Entertainers, politicians and athletes are the most frequently interviewed, and although they are accustomed to being asked questions, each requires a different approach. Some, like singer Frankie Avalon interviewed by AP reporter Anne McGraw, need no prodding. Politicians may need to be steered from the subjects of their choice to the issue the reporter considers important. Athletes are loquacious after victory, sullen and silent in defeat. *Amy Sancetta*

In the following story, a state highway patrol officer was the source of information about a fatal traffic accident:

Three people were killed in a grinding collision between a truck and an automobile last night on Highway 10, 15 miles north of Morgantown, the state highway patrol reported.

Those fatally injured were in the automobile. They were Albert Foster, 22, of 237 Western Ave.; his brother, Michael, 18, of the same address; and the driver, Bert Pierce, 21, of Tampa, Fla. The truck driver, George Allen, 48, of New Orleans, suffered minor bruises.

A state highway patrol spokesman, Robert Jackson, said the automobile apparently tried to make a U-turn off the westbound lane and moved into the path of the truck as it sped eastward.

"The car was demolished," Jackson said. "There were parts all over the road for 100 yards." Traffic was delayed on the eastbound section for 90 minutes, he said. . . .

Notice that the lead contains the major news theme—the deaths—and attribution. The next paragraph gives the names and identifications of the victims. The third paragraph describes the accident, and the fourth contains a good quotation.

This is the standard approach to the spot news story. But since we have a dramatic quote, why not use it high in the story? And while we are at it, let's be more specific in the lead about what happened. Can we make the reader visualize the scene? Let's try:

> Three young men were killed last night when the car they were in made a U-turn on Highway 10 into the path of an eastbound truck.

The reader can see the car turning around and into the path of the oncoming truck. We have had to leave out the exact location, but we can pick that up in the third paragraph after using the dramatic quotation to follow up the lead. Here are the next three paragraphs:

> "The car was demolished," said Robert Jackson of the State Highway Patrol. "There were parts all over the road for 100 yards."
> The accident occurred 15 miles north of Morgantown as the automobile tried to make a turn from the westbound lane.
> Those fatally injured were. . . .

This version is an improvement because the direct quote captures the essence of the event—a horrible traffic accident.

The patrol officer's description was given in response to the reporter's question asking him to describe the scene. Good questions lead to valuable information and can evoke responses that provide the details that animate a story.

Remember: A good direct quote is better than any paraphrase.

The questions asked for a spot news interview are based on the story type essentials. In this example, a fatal traffic accident, the reporter first asked the essential questions: names and addresses of those killed, cause, location of the accident. When the officer mentioned the wreckage, the reporter asked for more details and elicited the descriptive quotation.

For a story about a refresher course offered by the School of Nursing at the University of North Carolina at Chapel Hill, a woman who had taken the course was interviewed. She had been a nurse and then had married and spent 20 years at home raising a family. She decided to return to nursing and took the nursing-update course. Here is a quote from the story in *The Coastline Times* of Manteo, N.C. It captures the story's theme: "I would not have dared walk on a hospital floor without having gone back to school," she said. "There have been so many advances and so many changes."

Nothing earthshaking about the quote, but it does the job.

Getting Through

"Police are often very difficult to interview. Once you get going they're okay. But often they surround what they say with some bureaucratic jargon that sounds like it was made up in the police academy or something. Things like, 'As best as we can ascertain the perpetrator was a male Caucasian.' Nobody talks that way. And that makes it hard to penetrate that armor of bureaucratese which they surround themselves with. . . ."

—*Clyde Haberman, The New York Times*

Intrusive

Journalists who interview victims or people close to the victims understand that they are intruding. The public is increasingly intolerant of journalists who pry when people are the most vulnerable. *Joseph Noble, The Stuart News*

Interviewing Victims

Sooner or later a journalist will interview the victim of an accident, fire, crime, disaster or disease. Such interviews require sensitivity to the subject, who may be vulnerable at this time. Some situations have a potentially sensational aspect, such as the interview with a victim of a sex crime or the family of a person who has died in an unusual way.

The first decision, sometimes made by an editor, is whether to talk to a victim. "You have to ask yourself why you are doing the story," says Helen Benedict, who has written extensively about victims. "You should have a reason that goes beyond merely doing what your editor told you to do. You should be able to find a moral or a conclusion in the story that justifies it." Otherwise, the interview could be exploitive.

Benedict says there are good reasons for covering even a sordid sex crime. "The public has to know these things happen; we have to know how devastating they are to victims, how commonly they happen, what little is done about them, the types of people who commit them."

Kathy Seligman of the *San Francisco Examiner* gives the following advice:

• Talk to the victims right after the event. Wait too long and the victim may become too grief-stricken to talk.

• Be human. Console them. Express your sympathy any way you can. You've got to take some responsibility for the emotions that are going on. I've cried a lot at these interviews.

• Sometimes it's not necessary to talk to the victim or grieving relatives. You can often get better material from an eyewitness police officer who not only saw what happened but might know something about possible motivations for the crime or other circumstances that surrounded the tragedy. Sometimes you have to realize that calling a relative or victim is a hideous invasion of privacy. So look for a way to avoid it.

The National Victim Center is against coverage of funerals, filming bodies or body bags and interviewing or photographing child victims, unless the family approves. The Center also finds objectionable the use of innuendo about the victim and inappropriate photos and films of survivors' grief.

Profiles

We are all curious, maybe even nosy. We want to know why the brightest young woman in the class suddenly quit school, how the elderly couple around the corner can afford a new Cadillac every year, why the young couple down the street suddenly separated. We wonder how an outfielder for the Oakland Athletics spends the $4 million he is paid annually.

Most of our questions will never be answered, but some will—by a reporter writing a profile or personality feature. Curiosity about the lives of others has made the profile the most frequently written feature story. Sooner or later, every writer does a profile.

Sometimes, the profile can be a small snapshot in a long piece. In a series on Rhode Island's jewelry manufacturing business—the state's largest industry—Bruce Butterfield of *The Providence Journal* tells us about Mary, a high school student who works part-time in a jewelry factory. Butterfield lets Mary talk:

> . . . Like, what I'm doing now. I stand up the entire time. I go in there for three hours and 45 minutes a day.
>
> It's in a room and you have metal that's melted down. I think it's twelve hundred degrees.
>
> There's people who've been working in there 25 years and they're still making less than $4 an hour.
>
> And they deserve more 'cause they're such nice people that work in there. And they just can't do anything else. They either don't have a high school diploma or they just have a high school diploma and there aren't many jobs in our society today for these people. And they're over 40.
>
> They deserve more.

Guidelines

These quotes tell us something about the factory and a lot about Mary. She works hard at an arduous job, and she is concerned about her co-workers. She is a decent young woman. Her fellow workers deserve more because they, too, are decent people. But she is realistic about their lack of education. She knows there aren't many jobs for people with little education.

"They deserve more." Mary's words make the reader put down the newspaper to reflect a minute. Although we are told little about Mary, we feel we know her.

This is our first requirement for the profile: It must capture the person. A good ear for the revealing quotation and a sharp eye for the descriptive detail do the job.

Look at how much Michael Winerup of *The New York Times* gets out of a few sentences by blending observation and a quotation:

> The principal, Sister Joanna, wears a blue habit, is five feet tall and in charge. "Our purpose," she says, "is to give them the proper morals to— Excuse me. JUST STOP RIGHT NOW! I can't stand it when they throw things across the lunch table—to give them a Christian education. We're doing our best. Some of it will rub off."

Let the Subject Talk

In the heart of the Appalachian Mountains in East Tennessee, the mines and the jobs have mostly gone. In his story and photographs of life in Still House Hollow, Robert E. Kollar describes a poor but proud and resourceful people, and he lets them tell their stories. Daisy Pierce, shown here with her granddaughter, maintains a garden: "Why, I share with them, you know, and then if they have got something that I am out of, well, then they share with me. We just share back and forth. If we didn't, people up on this hill just couldn't make it."
Robert E. Kollar, Tennessee Valley Authority

Here are four guidelines for successful interviews for the profile:

1. **Prepare carefully.** Know the subject matter and the person who is to be interviewed.
2. **Devise a theme** or two from these preparations as the basis of questions.
3. **Establish a relationship** with the subject that induces him or her to talk.
4. **Listen carefully and watch attentively.** Be alert to what is said and how it is said. Look around the room, office, workplace for clues to the subject's interests, tastes, personal life.

Preparations

Careful preparations begin with the newspaper or broadcast station library that may have material that provides background and suggests questions. The next step is a quick look at references. The new college president may be listed in *Who's Who in America*. Although *Who's Who* is brought up-to-date frequently, biographical material should always be checked with the subject.

If the new president is a specialist in a field, she might have written articles that are indexed in the *Reader's Guide to Periodical Literature*. Her comments about a subject in one of her articles could be the basis of a question early in the interview. Sources are flattered by a reporter's interest in them and their work.

When Mal Vincent of the *Virginian-Pilot* in Norfolk, Va., was preparing for an interview with actress Jacqueline Bisset, he went back to an interview he had had with her 10 years ago.

Vincent had tried to interview Bisset on the set of a thriller in which she was co-starring with Alan Alda. In those days, Bisset had been cast as a sex object. She had done a nude scene in a surfing movie, and she had played a bedhopping jet-setter in another film.

At that time, Vincent had a definite personality in mind, the kind of young actress that moviegoers glance at in minor films and forget. But Bisset had surprised him then. She had taken over the interview. "The name is Bisset," she had said at the outset. "It rhymes with *kiss it*."

When Vincent had tried to ask her about her relationship with an actor, Bisset bristled. Although rumors about her living with the actor had been widely publicized, she refused to discuss the matter.

Vincent then tried women's liberation, a new phenomenon at that time.

"I have no intention of discussing women's rights with you," she had flared at him. "You wouldn't agree with me." She beckoned to her chauffeur and departed.

Bisset was a prickly subject for an interview, Vincent knew. In his preparations for his current interview he found that she was financing a movie in an attempt to convince critics she could act. As the co-producer, she had a stake in good publicity for the new film. Therefore, Vincent knew, she had to be patient with interviewers. He also remembered she had a mind of her own—as she proved in the new interview.

"I don't want to be a pinup," she told Vincent curtly. "I want to be something more than just an attractive woman. The public makes a mistake in labeling people that way."

Still bristling Bisset—but she stayed through the interview this time. Vincent knew how to approach her because of his preparations.

Devising a Theme

Vincent's preparations for his interview with Bisset point out the importance of figuring out lines of questioning from a tentative theme or idea developed before the interview.

Sometimes, the theme is the news peg, the reason the individual is newsworthy. For example, a local merchant is recognized by the city's United Way organization for his charity work. A profile of the businessman will focus on the activities that earned him the award. Bisset's new film was the news peg. But the news peg may not necessarily be the theme of the profile. In a profile of the new college president, the news peg was the appointment, but the theme of the profile was the appointee's ideas for reorganizing the college curriculum.

The news peg tells the reader, "Here is a newsworthy person." The theme says, "Here's something interesting or revealing that you ought to know about this person."

The depth interview is a confrontation between reporter-with-theme and subject-with-idea. Both interviewer and interviewee have points they want to make. In Vincent's second interview with Bisset, she was trying to tell readers and moviegoers, through Vincent, that she is a serious actress, that they should forget her as a sex object, an image that had been stamped on their minds by a movie scene in which she appeared in a wet, clinging T-shirt.

Vincent's new theme was the change from young starlet in grade-B films to mature woman making serious movies. The interview went well because both themes, Bisset's and Vincent's, were parallel and not on a collision course.

Sometimes collisions are unavoidable. The reporter sent to interview a gubernatorial candidate for a profile knows that the candidate is a political novice, a person who has never sought public office. The reporter's theme is "What makes this man think he can handle the complexities of state government with no political experience whatsoever?"

The candidate's campaign theme is "A new broom sweeps clean."

The reporter is too experienced to buy that cliché. So the reporter will be pressing and probing to make the candidate talk specifically about what he would do if elected. Reporters are not copying machines, passing on whatever sources condescend to tell them. Friction looms in interviews unless writer and subject move on the same track and the source willingly responds to the reporter's questions.

Inducing Subjects to Talk

Reporters use different tactics to induce their subjects to talk freely and to act naturally. Gene Miller of *The Miami Herald* says he tries to make himself as agreeable as possible during interviews.

"I nod a lot," he says, to appear to be agreeing with what the subject is saying and to encourage him or her to keep talking. "No tape recorder and no notetaking if I suspect I'll turn off my man. The unpleasant questions always come last, often apologetically."

Miller's technique is the opposite of the confrontation tactics used by some television interviewers. After a while, a reporter learns the technique best suited to him or her. Of course, the nature of the interview will often determine the technique used. An interview with a manufacturer whose factory has been polluting the city's air and a nearby river cannot be much else but a confrontation.

When Truman Capote was on assignment to profile the actor Marlon Brando for *The New Yorker,* Capote wanted Brando to talk about his troubled relationship with his mother. One evening, Brando did open up to Capote, who quoted him saying of his mother, "I didn't care any more. She was there. In a room. Holding on to me. And I let her fall. Because I couldn't take it any more . . . breaking apart, like a piece of porcelain, I stepped right over her. I walked right out. I was indifferent. Since then, I've been indifferent."

After the interview was published, Brando was asked why he had been so open with Capote about such a personal matter.

"Well," said Brando, "the little bastard spent half the night telling me about all his problems. I figured the least I could do was to tell him a few of mine."

Ralph Ellison, the author of *Invisible Man,* the classic novel about life in black America, was employed during the Depression by the Federal Writers Project. His job was to interview Americans of all kinds for first-person accounts of their lives and times.

Ellison's technique for making people talk was similar to Capote's.

"I would tell stories to get people going, and then I'd sit back and get it down as accurately as I could."

A gentle nudge is all some people need. But for many, the reporter has to ask questions—a lot of questions.

Asking Questions

The first questions asked in an interview for a profile may be throwaway questions designed to put the subject at ease if the source is not accustomed to being interviewed. The first meaningful questions will reflect the theme that the reporter has in mind for the story.

"What I ask gives me my story," says Jane Brazes, a reporter for the *Cincinnati Post.* "What I don't ask I won't find out."

Answers to questions suggest additional themes. "When you think you have found an answer, you'll have found another question," Brazes says. The key to interviewing, she says, is to "find questions and never stop asking them."

Questions should be simple and direct. Larry King, whose talk program, "The Larry King Show," is carried by more than 200 stations around the country, is a skilled interviewer. He says that "if it takes you more than three sentences to ask a question, it's a bad question." The point of the question is to induce the subject to talk. Complicated questions overwhelm the source.

King recalls an interview Sandy Koufax did with the winning pitcher of a baseball game. Koufax, one of the greatest pitchers in the history of the game, was an inexperienced interviewer. He asked, "In the game tonight, I noticed that in the fourth inning you took a little off your fast ball—you still had it in reserve because you had a 4-0 lead. Then, in the seventh inning, you used your curve ball. And in the ninth inning you went back to your fast ball and you still had it left."

"All that the pitcher could answer was, 'Right,' " King recalls.

King says the best question for the interviewer is "Why?" Questions such as "Why," "How" and "Give me an example of what you mean" induce people to talk.

Sometimes, silence can lead a person to talk. David M. McCullough, who interviews authors for the *Book-of-the-Month Club News*, says, "I found that a little silence often gets a better response than a pointed question."

Some experienced interviewers remain silent after a source or subject has made an unusual assertion. Except for a raised eyebrow, the reporter will not move. The interviewee has the feeling that the assertion isn't going down well, and usually he or she will feel obligated to fill the silence with an explanation that moves closer to the truth.

Generally, the tactics used and the questions asked in an interview depend on the source and the kind of information sought. A public official cannot be silent about public business, and reminding the source of this may be necessary. An inexperienced subject may require a slow, deliberate approach that is non-threatening.

The subject is not the only person a reporter should interview for a profile. Friends, relatives, employees, employers, teachers—the list of those who can provide interesting information about the subject is endless. Sometimes, these sources may have a perception of the subject that gives the reporter a fresh insight. Samuel Johnson, the brilliant 18th–century English author, remarked that "more knowledge may be gained of a man's real character by a short conversation with one of his servants than from a formal and studied narrative begun with his pedigree. . . ."

Listening and Watching

By asking good questions and by listening carefully, the reporter usually can find the one quote that best sums up the person or the event. When Wayne King was sent by *The New York Times* to cover a coal mine disaster in Colorado, King interviewed the brother of one of the 15 miners who had died. The man looked toward the western slope of the Colorado Rockies where the Dutch Creek mine is located and said, "That big mountain ate my brother."

King put the quote high up in his story. It summed up the life and death of the miner.

Gestures can speak. The narrowing of a person's eyes as he or she is talking can emphasize a statement as emphatically as boldface type. And if a source turns away while saying something, it may signal that the person is uncomfortable about what he or she is saying. Good reporters are alert to nonverbal communication—the actions of the source.

Careful Approach

"If you have a lot of information that you want to get from a person, it really makes no sense to ask as the first question when did you stop beating your wife or when did you start. Better to get everything else you want, and then, when you're ready to get thrown out, ask that question. In questions that are clearly delicate, questions about the personal lives of people, their finances, and their feelings about things that are not necessarily your business, I find it sometimes helps to preface the question with the acknowledgement that this in truth is not a very nice question, but it has to be asked, so please forgive me. That at least takes some of the sting out of the question."

—*Clyde Haberman, The New York Times*

When the interview is conducted in the subject's home or office, notes are made of the furnishings, pictures on the wall, magazines on the coffee table or desk. These details sometimes reveal a person's interests, tastes and concerns.

A well-known journalism professor covered his office walls with pictures of himself with famous people. Noticing the pictures during an interview, a reporter wondered whether the professor—famous as he was—had a sense of inferiority, that he felt a need to demonstrate his accomplishments at all times. The reporter filed his observations for later use. Reporters often do this. Some save observations, anecdotes and stories they hear until the right moment.

Howell Raines of *The New York Times* saved an anecdote a source gave him about a rising young politician. "I saved that quote because I knew that someday I would need it," Raines said. A year later he used it as the concluding anecdote in a profile of the young politician.

Taking Notes

Many reporters use tape recorders for profiles, but some prefer the note pad, finding it less obtrusive. Raines told Roy Peter Clark, who questioned him about interview techniques, "If I'm working with a notebook, I bring it out early, and I take a pen out early. I do a lot of business with them. People then lose interest in your taking notes.

"If someone really gets cooking on something and I feel taking notes will be obtrusive, I won't take notes. Then, when the person is finished on that point—I've got a good memory—I'll take out my pad and write down what he said.

"But I try to be open about taking notes for two reasons. One, it establishes your authority. No one is going to come back to you and question a quote that he's seen you write down as it came out of his mouth. And two, these are people that are used to seeing reporters."

On- and Off-the-Record

The reporter's job is to write stories. Most experienced reporters are reluctant to go off-the-record, and they almost never bring up the possibility with a source.

"I never suggest putting anything off-the-record," Raines said. Most of those he interviews are experienced sources, usually public or political figures. They know that what they say is going to be used.

"I never put anything off-the-record retroactively," Raines said. "If they say to me, 'What I just told you is off-the-record,' they can say that all they want to, but I'm not bound by it. I'll usually tell them that, but I don't feel compelled to tell them that."

Raines does accept off-the-record information. When he does, he scrupulously follows journalistic ground rules. Here are some rules that sources may set when they do not want to be quoted:

- Quotes are not to be attributed to the source but to "an official" or a similar nonspecific source.
- The statement is to be paraphrased and used without attribution.

- The material is to be used only if it is obtained from someone else and then may not be attributed to the original source.
- The material is for background use only—not for publication in any circumstance.

Master of the Interview

Her interviews led to international incidents, caused embarrassment to a U.S. secretary of state and elicited the envy of reporters. Oriana Fallaci has interviewed kings and presidents, tyrants and spies. For each interview, she used different tactics, but the underlying technique was the same: She prepared thoroughly—she read books, articles, other interviews, everything she could. She had a firm idea of her approach and the questions she would ask, and she was alert to the need to shift her approach and questions as the interview progressed.

In her preparations, Fallaci seeks the interviewee's soft spots, vulnerabilities. She says she goes into her interviews with her subjects "each time seeking, together with information, an answer to the question of how they are different from ourselves."

"Dr. Kissinger," she asked the then secretary of state, "how do you explain the incredible movie-star status you enjoy; how do you explain the fact that you're almost more famous and popular than a president?" Fallaci flattered Kissinger because she had decided that by catering to what she had concluded was his vast ego he would open up, as he did, to his everlasting regret.

Yes, he admitted, he had been a great success. Because, he said, "I've always acted alone. Americans like that immensely. Americans like the cowboy who leads the wagon train by riding ahead alone into the town, the village, with his horse and nothing else. Maybe even without a pistol, since he doesn't shoot. He acts, that's all, by being in the right place at the right time. In short, a Western."

This image of the urbane and learned Kissinger as a cowpoke-hero made headlines around the world.

Fallaci asked the Ayatollah Khomeini, "Are you a fanatic?" When he told her she need not wear the chador, the garment that women use to cover their bodies, since it was appropriate only for young women, Fallaci ripped it off. "This is what I do with your stupid medieval rag." That drove the Ayatollah out of the room, with Fallaci shouting after him, "Where do you go? Do you go to make pee-pee?" She then staged a sit-in, refusing to move until he continued the interview, which he promised to do. Fallaci had overwhelmed him.

Not many reporters can use these tactics. Fallaci is an electric personality, and sources know this when they consent to let her interview them.

Fallaci's starting point is that those in power must be answerable for their actions. She confronts them with their deeds and demands explanations. She once interrupted the Libyan dictator, Muammar Qaddafi, as he was extolling his infallibility: "Do you believe in God?" she asked.

"Of course, why do you ask?"

"Because I thought you were God," she responded.

Fast. The story should be written as soon after the interview as possible, say experienced writers. In fact, all writing should be done quickly following the event, while impressions and recollections are still fresh.

To Tape or Not to Tape

"I tape, therefore I am."

—Studs Terkel, radio interviewer

"Interviewers today . . . rely too much on the tape. They don't listen. They don't carry on a conversation. . . . They, especially the younger generation, are apt to treat words that come off the machine as gospel and feel they can't touch them when they transpose them to paper."

—George Plimpton, author

"The moment you introduce a mechanical device into the interview . . . you are creating an atmosphere in which the person isn't going to feel really relaxed, because they're watching themselves."

—Truman Capote, author

Profile Essentials

We can sum up the essential elements of the profile or personality sketch as follows:

Essentials

- Name and identification of subject.
- Theme of profile.
- Reason for profile (**news peg**).
- Background of subject.
- Incidents and anecdotes from subject as well as from friends and associates of subject.
- Physical description of subject.
- Direct quotes from subject and sources.
- Observations of subject at work, home or play; mannerisms, gestures.
- Strong ending.

Behind the Screen   Now let's look at some profiles. First, here is the way Vincent begins his profile of Bisset:

Delayed lead for first two paragraphs

HOLLYWOOD—Don't call Jacqueline Bisset beautiful. Not if you want to get along with her.

"I don't want to be a pinup," she says curtly, the famous gray-green eyes flashing. "I want to be something more than just an attractive woman. The public makes a mistake in labeling people that way."

News peg at the beginning of the third paragraph

Currently, Bisset is chairman of the board—even if she is the only person on the board—of Jacquet Productions. As such, she is co-producer of "Rich and Famous," the plush, expensively mounted new soap opera movie that stars her as a respected novelist who has affairs, sometimes casually, with younger men. The film, currently showing at the Lynnhaven and Circle 6 Theaters, gives Bisset what she calls "a

Theme at the end of the paragraph

chance to prove, once and for all, that I am capable of being a serious actress."

The last sentence of the third paragraph also serves as a transition or swing sentence. It takes the reader to a fuller explanation of the major theme of Vincent's piece—Bisset's attempts to prove she is more than a pinup. Notice that the news peg is not the theme of this profile. In his fourth paragraph, Vincent picks up the theme mentioned at the end of the third paragraph, Bisset's desire to be a serious actress:

Although she thinks she has proved herself previously, she is aware that some critics haven't observed as much. "For some reason, critics like to take pot shots at me," she said. "In that way, my career has been similar to that of Candy Bergen, my co-star. We've both had our knocks from the critics."

Over the Drums   For a profile or personality sketch, the news peg need not be momentous. It may be as simple as the one used in a profile about Sonny Greer, a famous jazz drummer playing in New York City.

The story by Timothy Weiner begins with an incident in Greer's life and shifts in the second paragraph to background. The third paragraph states the theme—that Sonny Greer at 83 is still playing the drums and enjoying life. It continues with quotes from Greer and the pianist who plays with him.

Greer is shown at the drums. We can see his "cannonball serve," the drumsticks doing a "tapdance on the high-hat cymbal."

The ending reinforces the theme with a good quote from Duke Ellington, with whom Greer played for 32 years.

All the profile essentials are here. Notice that Weiner does not try to tell Greer's life story. No profile can be any more than a glimpse into a person's life. Here is Weiner's profile, written when he was a journalism student.

NEW YORK—When jazz great Sonny Greer was a kid, back in 1910, he had a single driving ambition: to be the world's greatest pool hustler.

Had Sonny not traded in his pool stick for drumsticks, he might never have teamed up with a young piano player named Duke Ellington in 1919. He couldn't have brought the Duke Ellington Orchestra to New York in the 1920s, where it gained fame as a worldwide paragon of jazz. And he might have spent most of his 83 years behind the eight-ball instead of behind his battery of drums and cymbals.

At an age when the rhythms of most people's lives have slowed to a crawl, Sonny Greer hasn't missed a beat.

Every Monday night at 8 o'clock, an impeccably dressed Greer sets up his drums onstage at the West End Cafe in New York City. Young admirers sit at the old gentleman's feet as he spins out stories of Harlem speakeasies and the halcyon days of jazz.

"My favorite place to play," Sonny said with a smile and a faraway gaze in his eyes, "was the old Kentucky Club. Fats Waller and me used to play duets there and sing risqué songs. We'd play all night and come walking out of the club in the morning, the sun shining and all of us walking down Broadway laughing, feeling no pain. Those were good days, baby, oh yeah."

For 32 years' worth of good days, Sonny Greer's percussion was the beating heart of the Duke Ellington Orchestra. For thousands of nights he sat like a king on his throne, elevated above the rest of the band at center stage, surrounded by chimes, gourds, tympani, vibraphone and kettle drums, a great brass gong shining behind him like a halo.

In the 1930s and '40s, the Duke Ellington Orchestra was the closest thing to royalty the jazz world has ever known. But the band's fame didn't dampen the members' creative fires.

"While we were onstage," Sonny said, "as the evening progressed, we would experiment. If Duke liked it, he would keep it in. If he didn't, well, it cost nothing—throw it out, forget it.

"The guys in the band were amazing. They always had ideas, a million ideas. They were very creative. They created."

Sonny Greer is now the sole survivor of the original orchestra. He is probably the oldest jazzman active today. What keeps him going?

"Look, the drums are my life," he said, lighting a cigarette and cradling an Old-Fashioned glass of whisky. "I get a great pleasure out of playing and making the people happy."

Brooks Kerr, the 27-year-old blind pianist and Ellington scholar who plays with Sonny, said, "One thing that Sonny has that so few people of any age have is that desire to play. I think he lives to work and works to live."

At showtime, Sonny leads Brooks to the piano and seats himself at his drums. The drums, encrusted with tiny mirrors, sparkle in the spotlights. Brooks hits the first chords of "Take the 'A' Train" and shouts, "Sonny Greer, ladies and gentlemen!"

Sonny swats his snare drum with a flick of his wrist, the sound of a cannonball serve. His drumsticks tapdance on the high-hat cymbal. His bass drum pulses. Everyone in the audience is keeping time, their fingertips and feet following the drummer's beat, their bodies swaying slowly in unison.

Sonny's drums are talking. His drumming is musical syntax, giving structure to flowing musical language. And something more: echoes of Harlem, a conjuring of the past.

He's telling his life's story on the drums, distilling all those years of remembered rhythms into fluid syncopation. Listening to Sonny Greer is a trip back in time to the golden age of jazz. To hear him solo on the drums is to briefly recapture a classic style.

Sonny Greer's drum solo won't go on forever. But, as Duke Ellington once wrote, "Sonny Greer is an endless story."

Behind a Best Seller   Sitting at home one day browsing through magazines, Andrea Sachs came upon a cover story in *The New Republic* about the drug Prozac, which is used for depression. Sachs, the law reporter for *Time,* recalls: "One passage made me sit up and take notice." It was about Susanna Kaysen's recent memoir, *Girl Interrupted,* which describes Kaysen's 16-month stay in a psychiatric hospital as a teen-ager.

At first, Sachs' interest was personal as she has had a longtime interest in the poet Sylvia Plath, who also wrote a book about her stay at the same hospital. "The last thing on my mind was journalism," Sachs says. "I was just following personal curiosity." She bought Kaysen's book.

"At that point I started to wonder whether *Time* had ever reviewed it." It hadn't, and the book had become a best seller. Sachs began to think of Kaysen and her book as a *Time* story. Best of all, she found a news peg for the book that was now more than a year in print: It was to be released in paperback and Kaysen was about to go out on a book tour. Sachs wrote a proposal for the book section, and the assistant managing editor in charge of the section told Sachs to do a profile of Kaysen: How did she live now? What is it like to go public about such a taboo subject?

Sachs called Kaysen in her Cambridge, Mass., home. "I was determined to see her in action. In my experience, you can tell more about an interview subject if you see him or her interacting with other people."

Sachs met Kaysen at her home for part of the interview and then accompanied her to an Easter dinner in Cambridge with friends.

"The central theme for the profile presented itself in the first seconds after I met Kaysen," Sachs says. "I was very struck by how wary she was of me when she opened the door, as if she were both opening the door and closing it at the same time. To me, it seemed like the crux of her personality and her book."

Sachs' problem was to make Kaysen talk about a touchy subject, her mental illness, and to reveal whether she were still in therapy. "The way I got around the problem was a little verbal game that occurred to me on the spot," she says. She recalled a negative review that *Time*'s film critic had written about a friend's movie; Sachs had asked him how he had handled that unpleasant task. "He shrugged and said, 'A man's got to do what a man's got to do.'"

"I told the story to Susanna Kaysen, and every time I had to ask her an embarrassing question, I prefaced it by saying, 'A man's got to do what a man's got to do.' It was so ridiculous we both cracked up.

"We went to the Easter dinner, and it was illuminating as I expected it to be. During our interview, Kaysen had been fairly solemn, but around her friends she was sardonic and animated."

Reflection

Andrea Sachs of *Time* gives author Susanna Kaysen time to think about a question. *Richard Schultz, Time Magazine*

Sachs wrote a first draft and nothing happened. "The problem with a story like this at a newsmagazine is that it doesn't have a hard news peg." Week after week, Sachs' story was pushed aside for one of greater urgency. Finally, the editors decided to use it, with some updating.

"The editing process was give and take. In the process, I lost some lines I really liked. But I picked up some good ideas from my editors. Editing is sometimes a collaborative process, and together we came up with some new approaches." Here is how Sachs' story begins:

People ask, How did you get in there? What they really want to know is if they are likely to end up in there as well. I can't answer the real question. All I can tell them is, It's easy.

—Girl, Interrupted

Not since Sylvia Plath's *The Bell Jar* has a personal account of life in a mental hospital achieved as much popularity and acclaim as Susanna Kaysen's *Girl, Interrupted.* Published in hard cover a year ago, it immediately became a surprise best seller. The paperback edition (Vintage; $10) is now firmly entrenched on the bestseller list. Kaysen has received hundreds of letters from readers who have also been hospitalized for psychiatric problems, and on her just completed tour of 16 cities to promote the paperback, dozens of people whispered their own stories of mental illness to her. To many, the author has become a cult figure; the irony is that she actually wants to keep her life private.

Girl, Interrupted has a wary tone, and Kaysen greets a visitor at her home in Cambridge, Massachusetts, with a similar air of caution. Is the door half open or half closed? Her apprehension is understandable, given the subject she has written about: her two-year stay as a teenager on a ward for girls at McLean, a private psychiatric hospital outside Boston. Kaysen wrote two novels, *Far Afield* and *Asa, as I Knew Him,* before she began her literary journey back to McLean. In fact, she spent more than 20 years avoiding the topic. "I never discussed it. I didn't know what to say," she recalls. If she did bring it up, "it was a good way to irritate or frighten people." But in the late 1980s Kaysen found that memories of McLean kept surfacing. The result was her witty, poignant memoir.

Ending the Profile

A good idea for ending the profile is to use an incident or anecdote that reinforces the major theme. In his profile of Bruce A. Smathers, the son of a powerful political figure in Florida, Raines makes the point early in the story that Smathers' political future is dubious because he lacks the steely determination of his father, who, Raines writes, "never hesitated to backstab a friend for political advantage."

Raines puts the following high in his piece:

. . . With his fawn eyes and unlined face, he has more in common with Bambi than with the rapacious roebucks normally encountered in the political forests of Tallahassee.

Yes, Bruce Smathers says, smiling, he knows about those jokes that he is indecisive, that he would starve to death in a cafeteria line trying to choose between the Salisbury steak and the Spanish mackerel.

That rap, as Smathers tells it, is the price he must pay for having a trained mind and introspective nature.

"I have almost a repulsion of the easy answer," he says, and one hears in the scholarly tone echoes of Yale, where he won honors in economics. . . .

Bambi in the Jungle

Bruce Smathers and his wife at the time Smathers was a candidate for secretary of state for Florida. *The St. Petersburg Times*

The picture Raines draws is clear. Young Smathers is an intelligent, decent person, unfit for the raw political infighting of southern politics. Raines drives home his theme in the last two paragraphs:

Perhaps Smathers' political gifts are that great, but many who know politics as it is played at the top question whether this young man loves it enough or is hard enough. Most people who make it as high as governor or U.S. senator have something—a hunger, a fire in the gut, a toughness—that one can sense. It is not necessarily a good thing to have, but it is essential to winning and surviving in office.

This is not the picture of Bruce Smathers that emerges from a story once leaked from his office—an intimate of Smathers was quoted as saying, "Somebody offered him some money for a vote and Smathers got up and went out of the room and threw up."

This is the anecdote Raines had heard a year before and saved for the time he would need it.

Public Gatherings

We are now ready to move from the one-on-one interview to reporting the spoken word at meetings, panel discussions, symposia, news conferences and speeches.

Meetings

Much of the public's business is conducted in meetings. Important as they are, most meetings are sparsely attended. It is the journalist's job to write clear, complete stories so that people know what their appointed and elected officials are doing. Reporters are **entitled** to attend these meetings.

There are, of course, all kinds of meetings in addition to those of official bodies. The parent-teacher association holds monthly meetings. College political clubs meet every so often. Church, civic and professional organizations meet regularly. Reporters are **invited** to attend these meetings. The meetings of groups that are not financed with tax funds can be closed to the public and the press. A political club can call a closed meeting if it wishes. The board of the Kiwanis Club is not obligated to admit reporters.

Once admitted to a meeting, a reporter can report anything that is said, unless the meeting is of a private organization and admission is granted with limits on coverage. When meetings are closed, the reporter can use anything obtained from interviews with those who attended the meeting.

Meetings usually have a purpose, and often the matter at hand is resolved by agreement or vote. Sometimes, there is only general discussion. Each type of meeting is handled differently.

A story of a meeting that results in an action emphasizes the action taken:

> A bill to change West Virginia's 10.5-cents-per-gallon liquor tax to a percentage of the wholesale price was soundly rejected by a joint House-Senate finance subcommittee yesterday by a vote of 9-2.

A story about a meeting that does not result in any decisive action usually stresses the most significant part of the discussion:

> A student petition for more parking spaces on campus received sympathy but not much more at yesterday's monthly meeting of the University Board of Trustees. "We know it's a problem," said Alfred Breit, Board chairman. "But it is so complicated. . . ."

Let's examine these two types of meeting stories in detail.

Meetings with Action Taken
Essentials

- Vote, decision, agreement.
- Summary of issues.
- Reasons for action taken.
- Arguments for and against issues.
- Names of those for and against, if important issues.
- Consequences of decision.
- Discussion leading to vote or action.
- Background of issues.
- Significant additional issues discussed.
- Purpose, time and location of meeting.
- Additional agenda items.
- Makeup of audience and number attending.
- Statements, comments from audience.
- Significant departures from agenda.
- Agenda for next meeting.

Any one of these essentials can be the basis of the lead, and the story need not follow the order outlined in the list of essentials.

Here are some leads based on meetings in which a decision was reached. The leads stress the vote, agreement or decision.

Vote lead   The city commission voted unanimously last night to increase the property tax rate by $5 for each $1,000 in assessed value.

Agreement lead   The County Bar Association agreed yesterday to allow Grant County lawyers to advertise certain legal services.

Decision lead   Parents today warned the city school board they will fight the proposed closing of the Donald Vogt Elementary School "by every possible means."

Another type of lead can be used when an action is taken. Readers usually want to know the consequences of an action or what it means. The reporter who wrote the agreement lead above asked lawyers what the action would mean. She was told the advertised legal services, such as divorce actions and drawing up wills, would probably result in lower legal fees. With this information in mind, she decided to rewrite the straight news agreement lead and make it a feature lead about the consequences of the action:

Consequence lead   It may be cheaper to draw up a will or file for a divorce in Grant County soon.

When the Alabama Public Service Commission granted permission to a bus company to run bus lines from a suburb into Birmingham, the reporter had two choices: a decision lead or a consequence lead. Judge which is better:

Decision lead   The Public Service Commission yesterday granted B&B Transport and Limousine Co. permission to run bus service from Alabaster to Birmingham.

Consequence lead   People who don't want to fight commuter traffic between Shelby County and Birmingham may soon have a new way to get to work.

Let's examine a story from the *Louisville Courier-Journal* about a meeting in which an action was taken:

Decision lead	The Oldham County Planning and Zoning Commission yesterday recommended a denial of new zoning for a 68-unit townhouse and apartment complex in La Grange.
Next step	The recommendation goes to the La Grange City Council, which will make the final decision.
Summary of the issue	Terry and Donna Powell want a change from low-density residential to high-density residential zoning on 7.28 acres near Russell Avenue and Madison Street in a section of La Grange known as The Courts.
Audience, time of meeting; transition to discussion	About 50 people attended a planning commission hearing on the request yesterday. Charles Brown, county zoning administrator, said the commission cited these factors in voting against the rezoning:
Reasons for decision	√The area contains suitable land already zoned for apartments.
	√Two other apartment complexes have been approved in the past year in or near La Grange.
	√The property is not close to such services as shopping areas.
	√The proposal conflicts with La Grange's comprehensive land-use and zoning plan.
Argument against proposal	Opponents from the neighborhood argued that the development would compound traffic problems. They also expressed concern that dynamite to be used during construction might damage their homes.
Argument for proposal	James Williamson, attorney for the applicants, contended that the apartments are needed. Some of them would have been reserved for the elderly and handicapped. The developers proposed building five townhouses and six apartment buildings.

Meetings with No Action Taken   When the meeting does not lead to a decision, vote or action, the writer's task is more difficult. In this situation, the writer may want to focus on what seems to be the consensus of the participants or on a conflict or on some important statement made during the meeting.

Essentials

- Most important aspect of discussion: consensus (stated or implied), significant statement, strong disagreement.
  - Arguments for and against issues.
  - Names and identifications of those for and against.
  - Background of major issues.
  - Purpose, time and location of meeting.
  - Additional matters discussed.
  - Makeup of audience, number attending.
  - Statements, comments from audience.
  - Significant departures from agenda.
  - Agenda for next meeting.

Here are some no-action leads:

Consensus

City council members last night displayed impatience with local residents who protested a proposed increase in the property tax rate.

Conflict

City Councilman Garth Maguire last night told a delegation protesting a proposed property tax rate hike their opposition was "too strident, too narrow and too late."

Significant statement

Mayor Sam Parnass last night told the city council he opposes the proposed property tax increase.

Sometimes, the lack of action is emphasized in the lead:

No action

City council members last night argued for two hours but did not act on the property tax rate increase City Manager Harold Born proposed last week.

Panel Discussions and Symposia

A *panel* or *symposium* is actually a meeting, but one at which there is usually no intention to reach a decision. A consensus may emerge, however. If so, that consensus should be the basis of the lead.

Most of the time panelists insist on going their own way, each person giving his or her opinions or findings. Three, four or five people, each one merrily piping his or her own tune, can cause a cacophony that is difficult for the writer to arrange into a coherent story.

Sometimes, the statements of one speaker are more newsworthy than those of the others, and these statements become the lead, as in the story by Ray Cohn of *The Lexington Herald.* No other speaker but Welch is quoted until two-thirds down the story. The third speaker isn't even mentioned until the end of the story. The writer gave Welch top billing because of his experience as an FBI agent and his authoritative position as the state's top official in the justice system.

White collar crime costs the country about $200 billion a year and the criminal justice system is losing the war against it, State Justice Secretary Neil J. Welch told a University of Kentucky symposium on crime and punishment last night.

Welch, a top FBI official before he came to Kentucky last year, said there has been an overwhelming increase in this type of crime.

"Profit is the motive," he said.

To illustrate the magnitude of the problem, Welch said that tax officials estimate $16 billion a year in taxes should be collected on interest income, but that only $2 billion is actually collected.

"We have won some battles," Welch said, "but we are losing the war." . . .

But Welch's approach was opposed by another member of the symposium panel, Dr. Ernest Yanarella, UK associate professor of political science. He said law enforcement officials must avoid the "nice lure" of technology as instruments of social control. . . .

Finding a Theme When it is possible, an area of agreement should be used as the basis of the lead. It may be that the speakers' only agreement is to disagree. If so, the subject of their disagreement can be the basis of the lead.

Editors know that singling out a speaker is the easiest way to write a lead. They value the reporter who has the ability to put the statements and ideas of different speakers together, to pattern his or her observations. Every writer tries to cultivate the ability to extract a meaningful theme from separate ideas.

Here is the beginning of a story for which the writer extracted a common theme from a diversity of statements:

High schools are not attracting the best teachers, panelists agreed last night in a discussion on the future of the public schools.

The panelists were not of one mind about most of the issues facing public education. But they did agree that a series of factors has made high school teaching unattractive.

The panel, which met in the Civic Auditorium last night, was sponsored by the college's department of education.

High school teaching has suffered from the following, the panelists said:

• Women are no longer forced to go into teaching because of limited opportunities in other fields. "Whole areas of professional life and business have opened to women," said Professor Esther Josephs, associate professor of education at the College.

• The public has "little or no confidence in high schools, and morale is at the lowest point in years," said Richard Battle, principal of Horace Mann High School. "No one wants to go into a profession in which the public lacks confidence."

• Salaries are lower for high school teachers on the average than for any other field but social work, said Harry Metzger, an official of the state office of the National Education Association. . . .

Incidents and No-Shows   Sometimes what is said is secondary to an incident in the audience or even to what is not said, as when speakers tiptoe around a controversial issue.

In the following story by Karen Ellsworth of *The Providence Journal,* the low turnout for a political meeting became the basis of the lead. Had any of the candidates said anything of significance, that would have been the lead. But Ellsworth concluded that most of what was said was not new. Instead, she focused on what her eyes, and not her ears, told her. Her theme was apathy. Notice how her lead **shows** the reader public apathy.

PROVIDENCE—About half of the candidates for state general office and Congress attended a "Meet the Candidates" night at Rhode Island College last night, and they almost outnumbered the audience.

Every Republican candidate attended except James G. Reynolds, the Senate candidate. According to Doris McGarry, president of the Rhode Island League of Women Voters, his press secretary said he was ill. The league sponsored the event.

The only Democrats who attended were Robert Burns, the incumbent secretary of state, Dennis Roberts, candidate for attorney general, and Sen. Claiborne Pell. Neither independent candidate showed up.

About 30 persons, many of them students, attended the 2 1/2-hour session in the lounge of Browne Hall. Mrs. McGarry said she didn't know whether to blame the low turnout on "illness or general apathy."

The format consisted of two-minute statements and questions from the audience, with the candidates each giving an answer and sometimes rebutting another's answer. . . .

Burying the Lead   Look at the beginning of this story about a meeting of candidates for the school board. What do you think of the lead?

Mt. Pleasant's magnet schools, education for the handicapped, and the quality of schooling were the focus of debate Saturday as the six candidates for at-large seats on the school board answered questions posed by area black leaders.

The election for the three posts will be held May 15.

The candidates appeared before the Mt. Pleasant Black Civic Organization at a meeting at the First Methodist Church at 609 Claremont Ave.

Among the charges by the black leaders were that magnet schools and special-education classes were being used to defeat integration, that the quality of education is poor, and that the system allows inferior teachers to remain in the classroom.

Board members Beatrice A. Florentine, Kyle Smith and Linda Stern, who are seeking re-election, defended the school system. . . .

The story has an agenda lead. That is, it tells the reader the subjects that were discussed. But it does not state what was said about these subjects, the conclusions reached, the consensus. The reporter did not write a specific lead.

We could make a lead out of the fourth paragraph:

> Black leaders told school board candidates last night that local schools are failing to educate and that special classes and magnet schools work against school integration.

Or we could make the fifth paragraph the subject of a lead:

> Three school board members defended the school system last night against charges by community black leaders that the board is not meeting the needs of black students.

We may have even better leads than these two. Notice that the point of the rewritten leads is to pull the reader right into the meeting where there were charges and defending statements. Try your hand at putting life into this important story.

Pullout

The words and deeds of politicians during the campaign season are given considerable attention by the press. A candidate's withdrawal draws print and broadcast reporters. *Leslie Jean-Bart*

News Conferences

Essentials

- Major point of speaker.
- Name and identification of speaker.
- Purpose, time, location and length of conference.
- Background of major point.
- Major point in statement; major points in question-and-answer period.
- Consequences of announcement.

The news conference has two scenes. Scene 1, the curtain raiser, stars the person who calls the conference and usually begins with a monologue in which the speaker presents the reason for summoning the press. Scene 2 begins with many actors seeking center stage. The press asks questions usually but not necessarily related to the speaker's statement. News can be made from both scenes.

A prospective candidate for governor announces he is pulling out of the race:

State Sen. Joseph Margeretta said today he is withdrawing from the race for the Republican nomination for governor.

He pulled himself out of the contest at a news conference at the Allen Hotel.

"My plans are to seek re-election to the legislature," he said. Margeretta's withdrawal clears the way for Ben Appleman, the only remaining announced candidate for the GOP nomination.

Margeretta denied his withdrawal was the result of his wife's divorce action. Rose Margeretta filed for divorce 10 days ago. . . .

The two scenes provided the news here. Margeretta's announcement is given the lead, and the response to a reporter's question about the divorce is a major theme as well. Had Margeretta replied that he felt his wife's action put him in a difficult political situation, Scene 2 would have provided the lead:

State Sen. Joseph Margeretta today pulled himself out of the race for the Republican gubernatorial nomination because of his wife's divorce action.

"The filing of the divorce puts me in a difficult political situation," he said at a news conference at the Allen Hotel. . . .

Usually, the major news at a news conference is developed in the question-and-answer period. During a Ronald Reagan press conference, the president was asked about a super-secret airplane his administration wanted to sell to Saudi Arabia. How, a reporter asked, could Reagan be sure the plane would not fall into the hands of an unfriendly country if the Saudi government were toppled?

Reagan replied there was "no way" the United States would stand by and let that government be overthrown. The president's remark seemed casual, almost an aside and reporters went on to other issues. As the significance sank in, another reporter asked about the plane sale, and the response, again, was brief.

Should the source be quoted as he or she speaks? What do you do with these:

"We're having an international—this is not as much education as dealing with the environment—a big international conference coming up. And we get it all the time—exchanges of ideas. . . ."

"And the look on his face, as the man who was in jail and dying, or living—whatever—for freedom, stood out there, hoping against hope for freedom."

"Simply, we want you to have a very good time in this museum that we, at least in Houston, are very proudful of."

This was the language of President Bush who, columnist Mary McGrory says, enjoyed an arm's length relationship with the English language.

Some journalists insist that it is unethical to tamper with quotes. They paraphrase.

It seems senseless, and at times cruel, to quote someone's grammatical mistake or factual error. Reporters should steer around such spoken lapses and get at the point the source is making.

Although the exchange about the plane took up less than a 20th of the time of the news conference, reporters realized later it was the lead to the story: The United States was warning all nations not to step into Saudi Arabia.

Reporters had only seven sentences for their stories, so they called a White House spokesman for elaboration and asked other sources for background.

The Boston Globe began its account this way:

President Ronald Reagan said yesterday that the United States would defend Saudi Arabia against any threat to take over the kingdom and cut off the flow of oil to the West.

Reagan's remark, which his aides acknowledged afterward constituted a major foreign policy pronouncement, was delivered as an aside to a question. . . .

The news sense of the Washington correspondents was highlighted four years later when Iraq invaded Kuwait and made threatening moves south to Saudi Arabia. The United States decided to push Iraq back.

Speeches

Essentials

- Name, identification of speaker.
- Major point of speech.
- Quotes to support main point.
- Purpose, time and place of speech.
- Nature of audience; prominent people in audience.
- Audience reaction.
- Background of major point.
- Speaker's dress, mannerisms, if important.
- Speaker's comments before and after speech, if any.
- Additional points made in speech.
- Material from question-and-answer period, if any.

The key to writing speech stories is to isolate the major point a speaker is trying to make and then to select the quotes that amplify this point. The major point goes into the lead, usually in the writer's words. The quotes go into the body of the story.

Since speeches are often long and may include several themes, the reporter has to be choosy. A speech story should not include more than three or four of a speaker's points. There are exceptions—a major policy speech will be covered in detail—but the usual, everyday talk can be covered in a few hundred words.

Sometimes, something that **happened** provides the main element for the story. During a political campaign in Wisconsin, the Republican candidate for senator was reciting the failings of his opponent and closed with, "I challenge him to deny these charges."

Suddenly, from the back of the room, his opponent rose and shouted, "I deny every one of those charges," and he made his way to the stage. The **happening** obviously became the lead, and the confrontation between the two made up most of the story.

Speeches and speakers come in as many varieties as the offerings of an ice cream parlor. There is the Kiwanis Club luncheon talk given by a member of the local chapter of the Audubon Society about the need to save saltwater marshlands and the recollections of a dentist before the county dental society about the early days of dentistry when Painless Parker cruised city streets in a horse-drawn wagon and extracted molars at 50 cents a yank.

Leads

The speech story lead generally answers the question, "Who said what?" It does so in S-V-O fashion, the speaker's name or identifying label first and what he or she says next.

Some editors prefer the lead reversed: "What was said by whom?"

Rural Americans are not going to let high-voltage lines crisscross their homes, farms and ranches, two Carleton College faculty members said today.

The theory behind this O-S-V structure is that often what is said is more important than who says it. But for broadcast news writing, and increasingly for newspaper usage, the S-V-O structure is preferred.

The identification of the speaker is essential. This gives him or her the credentials to merit our attention. The identifying label usually establishes the speaker's credentials at once in the lead. We use a label when the name of the speaker will mean little to readers or listeners. With widely known people, the name alone usually establishes the person's authority to speak.

Finding the proper material for a lead can be difficult. A tipoff to the theme can be the title of the talk, if there is one. Watching the speaker's demeanor can indicate the emphasis of the speech. When the words come slowly and deliberately, the speaker is trying to stress his or her point. When the arms wave or a finger points, listen closely or follow the prepared text, pencil ready to underline.

When in doubt about a theme, ask the speaker. Post-speech interviews can sometimes turn up better leads than the speech itself.

Occasionally, the writer will find a lead in a point a speaker did *not* emphasize. The manager of a local television station may be speaking to a women's club about the merits of programming for the mass audience. In passing, he may say that his station is cutting back on public affairs programming because "nobody watches those shows anyway."

The writer knows that the change in local programming is of greater interest than a generalized defense of situation comedies and quiz shows. To gather more details, the reporter may stop the speaker on his way out or call him at the station.

Tipoff

The lead to a speech story may be discovered in an answer to a question, in the emphasis the speaker puts on a point or in a gesture. *Bob Thayer, The Providence Journal*

Using Quotes As in all the types of stories in this chapter, the speech story is built on direct quotes, the words of the speaker, but careful writers avoid direct quotes in their leads. A great orator is able to reach out and grab the audience and shake it with ringing sentences worthy of a lead. Quotes from such speakers make perfect leads. But such speakers come along once in a decade. Name one or two.

Most of the time, the writer begins with a paraphrase of the speaker's major point. This is followed closely by a direct quote that best makes the point.

A speech story is a blend of direct and indirect quotes, of a speaker's exact language and a writer's paraphrasings.

Sometimes a writer is tempted to take a clever or flashy quote and put it high in a story to attract readers' interest. Colorful phrasing may be a speaker's way of getting attention and may not relate to the news point. Placed high in the story, this phrasing would mislead readers. The same caution should be taken with the anecdotes speakers sometimes use to spice their talks. Unless they fit the news point, anecdotes should not be used high in the story.

Locations and Audiences In addition to a speaker's identification and major point, two other essentials may be placed in a lead:

- Where a talk is given—location
- To whom a speech is given—audience

It is not always possible to jam location and audience into a lead and still make it crisp:

> The head of a local architectural firm told members of the Engineers and Architects Club at their monthly meeting in the Miller Hotel last night that the proposed city hall may prove too costly to build.

To shorten such leads, we drop the location and audience to the second or third paragraph:

> The head of a local architectural firm said last night that the proposed city hall may prove too costly to build. Preston Wilcox told the Engineers and Architects Club that the cost is estimated at $22 million. He spoke at the Miller Hotel.

In our list of essentials, the word *audience* refers to those directly addressed. In Wilcox's talk, the audience is a local club. *Audience* can also mean the people the speaker hopes to reach through the press. Many speakers have the general public in mind when they speak. Wilcox obviously was intent on warning the general public about the costs of constructing a new city hall.

The writer handled this warning aspect of Wilcox's talk by including background:

Wilcox's talk comes in the midst of a controversy over whether to go ahead with construction. The increased cost of labor and supplies has sent construction costs soaring. Taxpayer organizations oppose the construction that was authorized by the city council in 1989. But local unions and the administration of Mayor Fred Partell favor going ahead.

Sometimes, as we have seen, the audience may provide the lead element. Unusually poor attendance at a presidential candidate's major speech can merit the lead, unless the candidate says something extraordinary. An unexpectedly large turnout can be the basis of the lead as well, as can the use of a small hall to make a small audience seem to be a crowd.

Audience heckling or boredom may be lead material. Audience questions may reveal more newsworthy information than the speech itself.

Follow-up   Reporters usually interview speakers after their speeches to clarify statements and to seek elaboration on something newsworthy. If a follow-up interview is impossible and an important point is vague or not sufficiently explained, the writer should write that the speaker could not be reached after his or her talk. Otherwise, the writer will be blamed for the hole in the story.

An AP reporter covering a speech at an Asian population conference quoted a member of the Islamic Consultative Assembly as saying that Iran had eliminated 114,000 prostitutes "who were the products of the disgraceful, satanic domination of America and lived at the highest level of wretchedness." The AP reporter added, "She did not say how this was done."

Prepared Texts   The texts of important speeches are often distributed to the press before the event, which gives reporters time to study the material and to write without pressure. Advance distribution also allows newspapers and broadcast stations to use the material before the talk is given—unless it is embargoed (restricted for use) until after delivery.

When prepared texts are used before delivery, the writer places in the lead or high in the story the phrase "In a speech prepared for delivery. . . ."

Reporters always cover important speeches with eyes on the text and ears on the speaker. News can be made by last-minute insertions to or deletions from the prepared speech.

Summary

Readers perk up when they see a quotation mark. They anticipate something interesting, something lively. The journalist's job is to elicit from the source or the situation the quotations that will reward the readers' anticipation. But not at the expense of truthfulness. That is, the quotation must be representative of the situation or the person.

When the sponsors of the New York St. Patrick's Day Parade refused to allow the Irish Lesbian and Gay Organization to march in the parade, a number of politicians declined invitations to march to express their sympathy to the excluded. To illustrate the reactions of marchers to the situation, a *New York Times* reporter quoted a 45-year-old Irish-American's comments about one of the politicians:

> "He's a plastic Roman Catholic, and a hypocrite. If he ever runs for another public office, I will fight tooth and nail to help destroy his political career."
>
> Homosexuality, he said, is not open to debate. "Certain things I hold in my heart. God made men and women with different characteristics."

Suppose, the reporter asked the marcher, he found that one of his children was gay. He would, the man said, react "irrationally—I'd kill the bastard." Then he paused and added, "I don't know what I would do. It would be a major crisis."

Suggested Reading

Benedict, Helen. *Portraits in Print*. New York: Columbia University Press, 1990.

Fallaci, Oriana. *Interview with History*. New York: Liveright, 1976.

Fallaci, Oriana. *The Egotists*. Chicago: Henry Regnery Co., 1968.

Garrett, Annette. *Interviewing: Its Principles and Methods*. New York: Family Association of America, 1982.

Mitford, Jessica. *Poison Penmanship*. New York: Vintage Books, 1980.

Terkel, Studs. *Working: People Talk About What They Do All Day and What They Think While They Do It*. New York: Pantheon, 1972.

10 Story Essentials

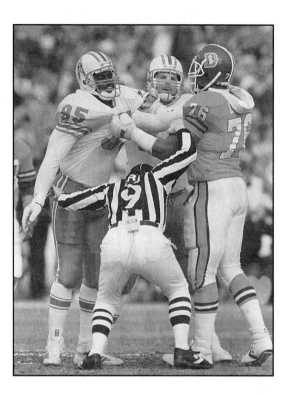

Media writers range widely, from the football field to corporate offices. They handle deadline pressure, complex subject matter and controversy with relative ease because of their grasp of the areas of their specialties. *Dave Einsel, Houston Chronicle*

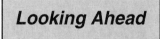

Looking Ahead

The essential elements of many types of stories are described in this chapter. These elements usually center on the individuals involved in the event—what happened to them and the special circumstances surrounding their situation. Story types covered include accidents and disasters, fires, crime, the courts, obituaries, sports, weather. The writer looks for the incidents that make this story different from others like it.

Accident Stories

New reporters are often assigned to the police beat as a way of introducing them to the community. Although covering the police beat would seem to show the city's underside, it does give the reporter a quick overview of the community since accidents, fire and crime strike all levels of society.

Let's look at the traffic accident story first. The accident story is a staple of journalism. More than a million people are killed or injured every year in traffic accidents, and all but the largest newspapers carry stories of these accidents. Only the most minor accidents—the so-called fender benders—are ignored or summarized in a column of briefs.

Accident stories must include the names of the dead and injured. They must identify the victims by age, address and occupation. Accident stories also give the extent of the injuries and the condition of the injured.

Essentials

- Names and identification of dead and injured.
- Time and location of accident.
- Types of vehicles involved.
- Cause (quote official sources).
- Source of information.
- Names and identification of drivers and of others in vehicles if relevant.
- Where dead and injured were taken.
- Extent of injuries.
- Condition of injured.
- Funeral arrangement information, if available.
- Arrests made or citations issued.

If an accident merits a longer story, add the following:

- Damage to vehicles.
- Speed, origin and destination of vehicles.
- Unusual weather or highway conditions.
- Accounts of eyewitnesses and investigating officers.

Caution: Do not try to affix blame, to attribute the cause of an accident or to write about excessive speed or drinking by a driver unless the information comes from an official source.

If an accident is minor, only the first six essentials are included, as in this story about a car striking a pedestrian:

James Oates, 46, of 447 Dartmouth Ave. suffered two broken legs Thursday evening when struck by a car while crossing Bailey Avenue near LaSalle Avenue, police said.

He is reported in serious condition in the Erie County Medical Center.

Police reported that John Rinzel, 24, of 211 Doat St., driver, said the man stepped into the path of his vehicle from a parked car. He was not charged.

—*The Buffalo News*

For fatal accidents, background about the victim is given, as is information about survivors and the funeral arrangements if available:

A 34-year-old Drexel County man, Jackie L. Boone, was killed Monday in a car-motorcycle accident near Albion Junction.

According to state police at the Corinth post, Boone, of Route 1A, Corinth, was killed when the motorcycle he was riding was struck from the rear by an auto about three miles north of Corinth on State Road 16.

Deputy Coroner J.B. Close said Boone died at the scene of a broken neck.

The driver of the auto, Marla Seay of New Albany, was not injured. No charges were filed.

Boone, formerly of Mt. Pleasant, was a maintenance machinist for the Naval Ordnance Station and a Navy veteran.

Survivors include his wife, the former Janice Goeing; a son, Jackie L. Boone; his parents, Mr. and Mrs. Witt Boone; four sisters, Miss Juanita Boone, Mrs. Norbert Carey, Mrs. Colleen Gipson and Mrs. Beth Lehner; and a brother, Robert Boone.

The funeral will be at 10 a.m. Friday at O.D. White & Sons Funeral Home, 2727 S. Third St., with burial in Resthaven Memorial Park.

Visitation will be at the funeral home after noon tomorrow.

Instead of leading with the name and identification of the dead and injured and the location of the accident, the writer can lead with an interesting angle to the story:

James D. Robinson of Opa-locka was driving in the proper lane when he died.

The car that killed him and seriously injured his wife and two small children was not.

In the next few paragraphs, *The Miami Herald* writer gives full identification of those involved in the fatal collision, the location, where the injured were taken and the extent of their injuries. The story ends with this paragraph:

Charges are pending, Broward Sheriff's Deputy Hal Samuels said. Altieri's blood was tested to determine if he had been drinking while driving, Samuels said.

Oops. Death or serious injury is not necessary for an accident to make the news. Massive tie-ups with the usual dented fenders and broken taillights interest readers, as does the accident with an unusual twist:

MUSKOGEE, Okla. (AP) —A woman who stopped on a slick bridge here to scrape off her windshield drove off without a scratch, leaving 36 dented cars behind her.

Fire Stories

Whether it is a farmhouse fire that causes $20,000 in damage or an apartment house fire that kills eight people, a fire is given thorough coverage:

HARRISBURG—A farmhouse six miles northeast of Harrisburg was badly damaged Sunday evening by a fire that began when the occupants of the dwelling were away.

Harrisburg Fire Chief Sonny Hanf said the two-story frame house, at 24661 Rowland Rd., sustained a loss of about $20,000. The building is owned by George Turney of Dallas and rented by Jim and Patsy Rosenberg, Hanf said.

According to Hanf, Jim Rosenberg returned to the house about 7 p.m. Sunday and found a bedroom in flames. Firefighters from Harrisburg and Halsey responded to the alarm.

Hanf said fire damage was confined to the bedroom area, although the rest of the house sustained smoke and water damage.

—*Eugene Register-Guard*

PATERSON, N.J. (AP)—Eight people died in a predawn tenement fire and 11 were missing yesterday after a man who had been spurned by a female resident allegedly set the building ablaze with a can of gasoline, authorities said.

Two dozen others were injured, "many of them jumping from windows," said police Sgt. Edward Hanna.

"The firemen were inside the building, crawling around on their hands and knees, feeling for people," he said. "Twenty minutes after I got there, they carried out three kids while the fire was really going. I never saw anything like it in my life."

Paterson Fire Chief Harold J. Kane said the bodies were found after firefighters gained control of the blaze that left more than 100 people homeless. . . .

Essentials

- Deaths, injuries.
- Full identification of victim(s).
- Location.
- Type of structure.
- Official cause.
- Investigation of cause.
- Source of information.
- How victims were injured or killed.
- When and where fire started and how and when it was brought under control.
- Rescue attempts.
- Where injured and dead taken.
- Extent of injuries.
- Damage to structure; cost; insurance coverage.
- Number of units and firefighters; amount of water used.
- Name(s) of fire company(ies) responding.

Mike DuBose, The Tennessean

Human Interest

There is usually a human dimension to the fire story in addition to the essentials—the cause, deaths and injuries, damages—that good reporting will uncover. Here is a lead to a fire story by Renee Elderman and Linda Moore of *The Tennessean*:

Two-month-old Brian Underwood was in critical condition in a Nashville hospital last night with burns and lung damage following a dramatic rescue from his mother's South Nashville apartment by Metro firefighters.

- Quotes of witnesses, firefighters, residents.
- Human interest details.
- Time of first alarm; who called fire department.

Go back to the fire story datelined HARRISBURG. One of the essentials is missing—the cause of the fire. If the cause of a fire is unknown at the time the story is written, say so.

Quotations add human interest to stories. In the Paterson story, notice the use of quotes that show the tragic consequences of the fire.

When there are several deaths or many injuries the lead usually will focus on these essentials. When property is the only loss, that essential usually is the basis of the lead.

In small and medium-size cities, fires are usually covered even when there is no loss of life and damage is minor.

In rural communities, coverage is thorough. The fire companies that answer the call are identified and the chief's quotes usually are used. A farm fire that destroyed a feed barn, a tractor, a hay baler and 3,000 bales of hay received front page play in the *Georgetown News,* a weekly newspaper in Kentucky. The fire was caused by lightning. Ed Moore, chief of the Scott County Fire Department, was quoted as saying, "We just call this kind of thing an act of God. I've seen farms with lightning rods go up in smoke. Once the lightning flash causes a dust explosion in the hay, there's just nothing you can do to save the barn."

Death of a Smoker

Dennis Love of *The Anniston Star* was making routine checks of the police and other sources while on weekend duty one Saturday night. "I got a tip while calling funeral homes throughout our seven-county circulation area. An employee said he was handling funeral arrangements for a 76-year-old man who died in a school bus fire the night before.

"An accidental death alone merits a brief story, but this man's age and obvious questions about why he was in the bus required further checking. I called the coroner, the sheriff's department and the fire department and pieced together the basic information.

"The old man, who lived with his brother in a rural part of the county, often slept in an old school bus he had converted into a camping vehicle. On this night he had apparently fallen asleep while smoking and was unable to escape the flames that rapidly engulfed the old vehicle. The coroner said there was no evidence of foul play."

Then Love began to try to reach relatives of the dead man to piece together the details. The coroner supplied the name of one relative who gave Love the telephone number of the family home, which he had not been able to find in the directory. He reached the victim's brother. This was a vital call.

"He gave me a first-hand account of what had happened, and he testified to his brother's love of cigarettes, which they were convinced caused the fire. He also said his brother recently had moved in with him from a nursing home and was not in the best of health and often needed assistance in moving around. I wrote down his comments and was ready to write the story."

Here is Love's story and alongside it his comments about how he wrote it:

I had some colorful quotes from the brother about his brother's smoking habits, and since that had emerged as the consensus as to the cause of death, I decided to emphasize that angle in my lead paragraph. His age was also significant, as was the school bus setting, so I incorporated all of it in what I consider a somewhat clumsy lead. But it seemed to work.

Next, the sequence of events was in order so I used the clearest and most official source I had—that of the coroner. I let him give the basic facts in the next three paragraphs, throwing in an aside about the victim's health in the third graf.

Then I came back to the smoking angle, using my best quote from the victim's brother. I let him describe the chainsmoking habits, tell about the camper and the events leading up to his discovering the fire in progress.

I let him continue to tell me what happened.

FRUITHURST—Seventy-six-year-old Tom Jenkins' penchant for chain-smoking has been blamed for the fire which engulfed the old school bus in which he slept early Saturday and in which he died.

Cleburne County Coroner Hollis Estes said he and the Heflin Fire Department were summoned to the Coldwater community near Fruithurst shortly after 4 a.m. Saturday to find the old bus—converted into a camping vehicle—ravaged by flames.

The bus was parked in the front yard of the home of the victim's brother, Hubert Jenkins. Tom Jenkins was living with his brother while he recovered from a stroke he suffered earlier this year, according to family members.

Estes said the bedding in the rear of the bus apparently caught fire from a burning cigarette and spread rapidly throughout the vehicle. The coroner said there was no evidence of foul play and no autopsy would be performed.

"Lord, he (the victim) was always careless with his cigarettes," said Hubert Jenkins Saturday night. "He would just smoke one right after the other. Only thing we can figure is he got out there in the camper and fell asleep or something with one lit."

Jenkins said his brother, who left Golden Springs Nursing Home in April, spent a great deal of time sitting in the bus, which was equipped with a stove, refrigerator and other appliances.

"Friday afternoon, he said he was going out for some fresh air, and I watched him make a beeline for the bus," Jenkins said. "I checked on him later on and he was just sitting on the side of the bunk bed, said he wanted to stay out there a while longer."

Jenkins said his brother later told his daughter "he wanted to spend the night out there."

Around 4 a.m., Jenkins said he awoke to the sound of "something popping. It sounded like his old walking cane he used—I thought he was tapping on the side of the bus to get my attention. Before I could get to the door I could see the trailer" on fire. Jenkins said he believes the popping sound that woke him was .22-caliber cartridges exploding in the bus.

Jenkins said his brother needed some help in "getting around" after the stroke, but was at a loss to explain why the victim was unable to escape the flames.

He said the bus had a front and rear entrance, but the back door was blocked by the bed on which Jenkins slept. Estes said, however, that the body was found on the floor of the bus.

I closed the story with his brother's explanation of the death.

"It just looks like when he woke up he tried to get out, but just didn't make it," said Hubert Jenkins.

Love said his story lets "the people who were involved answer the obvious questions: How and why did Jenkins die where he did, and why couldn't he avoid his death? My last phone call to the family of the deceased brought all that together, and helped to take the story a bit beyond the level of a routine item."

Crime Stories

The main job of the police reporter is to handle reports of crimes, investigations and arrests. The police reporter may also cover the police and municipal or criminal courts to follow up arrests.

Almost everyone knows someone who has been a victim of a crime or has himself or herself been a victim. Each year, a third of all households in the United States are affected by burglary or a violent crime. In towns where people never locked their doors, there are now thriving businesses in burglar alarm systems. Automobile owners search for the system that will keep a thief from taking off with their Toyotas and Fords. In some cities, people are advised not to wear jewelry on the streets. On and around college and university campuses, the number of rapes has doubled and tripled in recent years.

A property crime is committed every three seconds and a violent crime every 16 seconds. A rape occurs every five minutes and a murder every 21 minutes.

Because of the volume of crimes, police reporters would be overwhelmed with material if they weren't discriminating in their reporting. To help clear the way through the flood of police information, a police reporter usually spends more time on violent crimes than on property crimes.

Violent Crimes	Property Crimes
Murder	Burglary
Rape	Larceny
Robbery	Motor vehicle theft
Aggravated assault	

Definitions. *Violent crime* involves force or the threat of force that may result in injury to a person. A *property crime* is an unlawful act with the intent of gaining property that does not involve force or threat of force.

Perpetrators and Their Victims

A study of violent crimes reveals that half of those arrested were under the influence of drugs, alcohol or both when they committed their offenses; 46 percent were white, 51 percent black, and almost half were between the ages of 25 and 34.

Blacks and teen-agers have higher victimization rates than whites and adults. The federal Bureau of Justice reports violent crime victimization rates at 44 per 1,000 blacks, 34 per 1,000 whites, 67 per 1,000 teen-agers and 26 per 1,000 adults. About half of all violent crimes against teen-agers occur in school buildings, on school property or on the street.

Young black men and women are three and four times more likely to be handgun crime victims than young white men and women, the U.S. Department of Justice reports. Here is a chart of the annual rate of crime committed with handguns (per 1,000 persons):

	Handgun Victimization			
	Male victims		Female victims	
Age of victim	White	Black	White	Black
12–15	3.1	14.1	2.1	4.7
16–19	9.5	39.7	3.6	13.4
20–24	9.2	29.4	3.5	9.1
25–34	4.9	12.3	2.1	9.0
35–49	2.7	8.7	1.4	3.3
50–64	1.2	3.5	0.7	1.6
65 or older	0.6	3.7	0.2	2.3

Crime Reports

Few police reporters ever see a crime committed. Yet they write about crimes every day, often with the intensity and drama of an eyewitness. Most of their information comes from crime reports. These are the forms filled out by officers who have investigated the crime. The reporter supplements these reports with interviews with the officers or their superiors and with victims or witnesses of the crime.

Essentials

- Full identification of victims(s).
- Nature of crime and description of how it was committed.
- Date, time, location of crime.

- Violent crime: official cause of death or injury; weapon used; motivation; background of victim, if relevant.
  - Property crime: value of loss; method of theft or entry.
  - Suspects (no names unless charges filed); clues.
  - Unusual circumstances.
  - Quotes of witnesses, victim(s), police.
  - Source of information.

The following story about a violent crime begins with the nature of the crime and the victims. The second paragraph identifies the victims and describes their injuries. The third paragraph describes the weapon that may have been used and the questioning of two suspects.

A man and woman were shot about 10:40 p.m. Monday when gunfire erupted during what police called a "neighborhood-type" argument in a field at 34th and Forest.

The victims were identified as Tony Simmons, 20, of 5117 Woodland, who was listed in critical condition with a gunshot wound to the forehead, and Debra Williams, 21, of 3327 Tracy, in fair condition with a gunshot wound to the left hand. Both were admitted to the Truman Medical Center.

Police, who said they heard different accounts of the shooting at the scene, said they were questioning two persons in connection with the incident. A pump shotgun believed to have been used in the shooting was recovered on the porch of a home at 3329 Tracy, police said.

Comparisons. Local reporters can compare the crime rates of their cities and states with those of others nearby. Data can be obtained from the FBI's annual report "Crime in the United States" and from state legislative research councils and similar study groups. Here is the lead to such a story by Terry Woster of the *Argus Leader* in Sioux Falls, S.D.:

PIERRE—Chances of being robbed, raped or murdered are six times as great in Rapid City as in Bismark, N.D., a University of South Dakota researcher said Tuesday.

Robbery

Beginning reporters sometimes confuse robbery, a violent crime, with burglary, a property crime. *Robbery* is a crime against a person. *Burglary* is a crime against property. Robbery involves taking or attempting to take something of value from a person by force or threat of force. Here is a typical robbery story:

A gunman held up the Thrifty Liquor Store at 42 First St. this morning and got away with $1,780 in cash, police said.

The owner, Martin Nolan, said that he was closing the store when a man in his thirties bought a bottle of wine. As Nolan opened the register, the man took a revolver from his jacket pocket and told Nolan to hand over the day's receipts.

On leaving, he warned Nolan against following him. But Nolan told police he managed to see the tall, thin man drive off in a 1989 blue compact car with Arkansas plates.

Burglary

Burglary is the unlawful entry into a structure to commit a felony or a theft. State law usually distinguishes between theft, a misdemeanor, and a felony according to the dollar amount of the stolen goods. A misdemeanor is a crime punishable by a fine or a term of less than one year in a city or county jail or prison. In some states, felonies are thefts of goods amounting to more than $250;

Everywhere

The police have many responsibilities in addition to crime prevention. They protect important visitors, supervise parades, spend considerable time in courts as witnesses. Here, a police officer has just sped a medical technician with a heart for a transplant operation to an Akron hospital. *Susan Kirkman, Akron Beacon Journal*

in some states the amount is $1,000. A felony is a crime that is punishable by a year or more in a state or federal penitentiary.

When the loss in a burglary is considerable, the lead focuses on the value of the stolen goods:

Jewelry and personal items worth $50,000 were reported missing from the home of Victor Sewell, 560 Eastern Lake Ave., last night.

Police said Sewell told them he and Mrs. Sewell returned from a visit to friends about 11 p.m. and discovered the window to a bedroom at the rear of the house had been forced open.

Sewell, an attorney, told police he had purchased a matching diamond bracelet and necklace last week in London where he attended a law seminar. He said he had told no one of the purchase.

Police said the bedroom was the only room in the house that had been entered.

Investigation

Police are understandably closemouthed when investigating a serious crime, which makes it hard for the reporter to obtain material for a story during the detection-investigation stage. Sometimes, the police will provide information about a high-profile crime to the press to enlist its help in locating a suspect.

Now and then a reporter will learn something the police want to keep confidential. Most police reporters will keep such material under wraps because they risk antagonizing their sources if they use it. In the larger cities, however, the unwritten code is that a reporter may use anything he or she can learn. If the department cannot keep its people quiet, so be it.

Early information about suspects may compromise not only the investigation but the court case. A reporter must consider this possibility before running any but officially sanctioned material.

Essentials

- Progress of investigation.
- Suspects.
- Additional clues.
- Personnel assigned to case.
- Summary of crime.

Only the most serious crimes are investigated in metropolitan areas. Generally, the greater the public interest, the more likely the police are to push an inquiry. The murder of a prominent person or a police officer will be investigated. In large cities, where two to five murders occur daily, the investigation of the murder of a drug dealer or a drifter may be closed quickly. Burglaries, pot smoking and car thefts have, for all practical purposes, been decriminalized in large cities.

Arrests

Some of the best crime stories are of arrests. Again, the information usually comes from a report, in the case of arrests an arrest report. For arrests related to serious crimes, the police or district attorney may call a news conference.

Usually, charges are filed on arrest, but sometimes a suspect is held for investigation. A suspect may be detained for a limited period until formal charges are filed. The reporter does not wait for the filing to write a story and so must be careful with the wording. Notice the key phrases in this lead:

> Ralph Hunter, 24, of 167 Broad St., was arrested last night *in connection with* (or *in the investigation of*) the armed robbery of a service station last week that netted the robber $18,000.

When the charges have been filed, the lead says so:

> Ralph Hunter, 24, of 167 Broad St., was charged last night with the armed robbery of a service station. . . .

Never write this kind of lead for an arrest story:

> Ralph Hunter, 24, of 167 Broad St., was arrested for the armed robbery. . . .

This lead makes Hunter guilty of the crime.

Careful: Double check names and addresses, especially if the person arrested gives the name of a person well-known in the community. Verify by calling the suspect at home or at work or questioning police closely. Some suspects give false names and addresses.

Pursuit and Arrest

O.J. Simpson became the subject of an intense and massive police manhunt Friday after a warrant was issued for the arrest of the former football star in connection with the brutal slayings of his ex-wife and a male friend.

O.J. Simpson was arrested Friday for the murders of his ex-wife and her male friend after he had led police on an intensive two-hour chase through the rush-hour freeways of Southern California.

Double-Check. It was a good story: A local businessman was arrested for paint sniffing. The reporter copied the police report which had taken the man's name, age and address from his driver's license.

The businessman sued the reporter, the *Alamogordo Daily News* and Donrey Inc., which owns the newspaper, for libel. Turned out when he was arrested the suspect had the man's stolen license. The state supreme court said the case had to go to trial.

Extra! Extra!

When the mayor of Washington was arrested, *The Washington Times* put out this extra, the first time there had been an extra in Washington since the assassination of President Kennedy in 1963. The paper was on the street at 3 P.M., in time to catch commuters on the way home, and it quickly sold out. *The Washington Times*

Streetcorner Drug Mart

Police make a drug bust at the notorious drug trafficking corner of Fourth and Cambria in Philadelphia. Suburbanites from surrounding states drive in for their supply, and, during lunch hour, white collar workers, even mothers with infants in their cars, drop by for a quick hit. The gang that ran the operation netted $25,000 a day. *Ron Tarver, The Philadelphia Inquirer*

Essentials

- Name, identification of person arrested.
- Crime person is charged with.
- Details of crime, including name and identification of victim(s).
- Circumstances of arrest.
- Officers involved in arrest.
- Source of information.

For serious crimes, add these:

- Investigation.
- Background of suspect.
- Motive.
- Circumstances of arrest announcement.
- Booking, arraignment, any other procedures.

Newsworthiness   In Miami, Detroit, New York City, Chicago, Los Angeles and cities of similar size, a murder or the arrest of a murder suspect may merit a few lines, if that. But in smaller cities and towns, even the theft of some jeans and the arrest of a suspect are worth a story:

A Dress Barn employee was arrested Wednesday on a warrant charging him with stealing 49 pairs of blue jeans.

Joseph Scapella, 40, of 95 Trudy Lane was charged with second degree larceny in connection with the theft of the jeans valued at $1,302 and taken from a Dress Barn warehouse March 26, police said.

The jeans-theft story appeared in *The Advocate* in Stamford, Conn., and is as long as the following piece about an arrest for attempted murder in Chicago, which was carried by a Chicago newspaper only because of the grisly nature of the crime:

A resident of a West Side halfway house was charged Monday with shoving his roommate out of a third-floor window, then rushing downstairs and stabbing him 11 times as he lay in the alley where he landed.

The police charged Allen Taber with attempted murder. The victim, Fred Krumpe, was in critical condition with multiple fractures.

Analyzing the Arrest Story   Here is an arrest story with the list of arrest essentials alongside it:

Circumstances of arrest, nature of crime

A special burglary detail yesterday chased and caught a suspect the officers believe responsible for a rash of house burglaries in the Tacoma Avenue area.

Charges, name and identification of person arrested

Karl Vogt, 31, of 967 Eastern St., was charged with burglary and possession of burglary tools.

Circumstances of arrest elaborated

Police said that Vogt was spotted by a detective in the special unit going from house to house along Tacoma Avenue. When he saw the man enter 98 Tacoma Ave. he radioed for the rest of the detail. Vogt awoke a tenant, John Strong, and then tried to flee but was arrested a block from the building.

The detail was set up for round-the-clock surveillance of the neighborhood after several house burglaries were reported.

Officers making arrest

Detectives who made the arrest included Ray Miller, John Hazar and Bill Smith.

Law-Enforcement Agencies

Crime is handled by a variety of law-enforcement agencies. Local crime is under the jurisdiction of the municipal police force. More than 90 percent of all cities with a population of 2,500 or more have their own police forces. At the county level, sheriff's departments have duties similar to local police in unincorporated areas and in municipalities with no local police force. The sheriff operates the county jail. State police and highway patrols handle traffic on state and federal highways and assist local police and sheriff's departments. At the federal level, there are several law-enforcement agencies, among them the Drug Enforcement Administration (DEA) and the Federal Bureau of Investigation (FBI). They handle interstate and international matters and are sometimes called in to assist local authorities.

Booking

After an arrest, the suspect is **booked** at the police station:

A 23-year-old prison parolee, the object of a statewide manhunt, surrendered in San Luis Obispo County and was booked Tuesday in the murder of a teen-age Hollywood girl, Los Angeles police said.

Mauricio Rodriguez Silva was being held without bail in the Hollywood Division jail. He is expected to be arraigned on a murder charge Thursday, authorities said. . . .

—*Los Angeles Times*

The police reporter usually will cover the booking at the police station. The court reporter will take over for the arraignment, which is the beginning of the court process.

Criminal Court Coverage

Criminal law procedure can be roughly divided into two areas for coverage: *pretrial* and *trial*. Both areas are given considerable coverage in the case of a major crime.

Pretrial

The pretrial process begins soon after the suspect is arrested and booked. During the process, the suspect is informed of the charge and is asked to enter a plea. For serious offenses, a grand jury indictment or an information is returned against the suspect, to which he or she again pleads. Several kinds of hearings may also occur at this stage.

Arraignment   The suspect is arraigned in a local court within 24 hours of arrest, as required by law. The procedure consists of the court's advising the suspect of the charge and hearing the suspect's plea. Bail is sometimes set at the arraignment.

A 19-year-old West Roxbury man yesterday pleaded innocent to second-degree murder and assault and battery charges in connection with the death last winter of a Boston College student.

The case of Scott O'Leary was continued one month for a pretrial conference following his arraignment before Suffolk Superior Court Judge James P. Donohue. . . .

—*The Boston Globe*

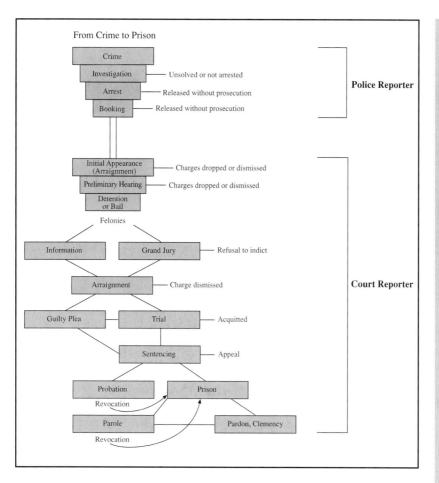

From Crime to Prison

Crime

Investigation —— Unsolved or not arrested

Arrest —— Released without prosecution

Booking —— Released without prosecution

Police Reporter

Initial Appearance (Arraignment) —— Charges dropped or dismissed

Preliminary Hearing —— Charges dropped or dismissed

Detention or Bail

Felonies

Information   Grand Jury —— Refusal to indict

Arraignment —— Charge dismissed

Court Reporter

Guilty Plea   Trial —— Acquitted

Sentencing —— Appeal

Probation   Prison
Revocation

Parole   Pardon, Clemency
Revocation

Criminal Court Coverage

Adapted from *The Challenge of Crime in a Free Society*, the President's Commission on Law Enforcement and Administration of Justice.

Few Charged. Only between a third and a half of those arrested are formally charged with a crime. For most arrests, the prosecutor decides not to draw up a charge because the evidence is inadequate, witnesses will not testify or additional information makes prosecution inadvisable.

This tendency has led some newspapers, such as the *St. Louis Post-Dispatch,* to withhold in most cases the names of those arrested until charges are drawn.

Trial Set

Judge Kathleen Kennedy-Powell ruled Friday after a six-day preliminary hearing that O.J. Simpson must stand trial on murder charges.

Preliminary Hearing   This *hearing* is sometimes called a *probable cause hearing*. The judge reviews the facts and may hear testimony. The judge then decides whether there is reasonable and probable cause to bind the suspect over for grand jury action and whether to hold the suspect in jail or to set him or her free on bail. A person without a lawyer may have one assigned at this hearing.

Where the grand jury system is not used, the preliminary hearing determines whether the suspect is to be held for further court action.

Arraignments and preliminary hearings are held in what are known as *courts of original* or *least jurisdiction*. These are municipal, police, city and criminal courts. These courts can try misdemeanors and sentence those who plead or are found guilty. A higher, state court must try felonies.

Grand Jury   This jury, which usually consists of 23 persons, hears the evidence presented by a prosecutor and decides whether to issue an indictment (*true bill*) or to dismiss the charge (*no bill*):

Re-Arraignment   In the second arraignment, called the *re-arraignment*, the defendant is informed of the charge in the indictment or information, is advised of his or her rights and is asked to plead to the charge. If the plea is *guilty* and the judge has jurisdiction, the defendant may be sentenced. If the plea is *not guilty,* the case is set for trial.

> A Cobb County grand jury returned murder indictments Thursday against two men and a woman accused of causing the death of a Marietta woman who took an overdose of cocaine in February. . . .
> —*The Atlanta Constitution*

Pretrial Hearings   A number of different hearings may be held before the case goes to trial. The most frequently held hearing is on a motion to dismiss the charge. The judge may turn down the motion but allow it to be amended and refiled or may dismiss "with prejudice," which means the motion cannot be refiled. Other pretrial hearings:

Suppression—Consideration of the admissibility of evidence or of a confession.
Sanity—Determination of the fitness of the defendant to stand trial.
Jurisdictional—Determination of whether the court has jurisdiction over the case.

Motion to Dismiss

Attorneys for O.J. Simpson are preparing to file a series of motions, including one to dismiss the case based on a lack of evidence presented by the prosecution during the preliminary hearing.

Simpson's lead lawyer, Robert L. Shapiro, said Tuesday the prosecution failed to link Simpson to the murders of his ex-wife and a male friend.

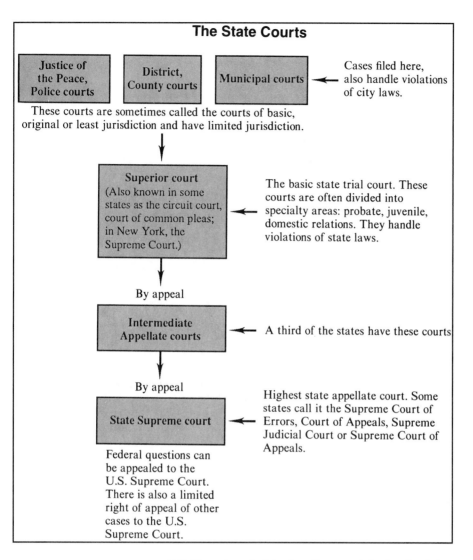

The State Courts

Justice of the Peace, Police courts	**District, County courts**	**Municipal courts** ← Cases filed here, also handle violations of city laws.

These courts are sometimes called the courts of basic, original or least jurisdiction and have limited jurisdiction.

↓

Superior court (Also known in some states as the circuit court, court of common pleas; in New York, the Supreme Court.) ← The basic state trial court. These courts are often divided into specialty areas: probate, juvenile, domestic relations. They handle violations of state laws.

↓

By appeal

Intermediate Appellate courts ← A third of the states have these courts

↓

By appeal

State Supreme court ← Highest state appellate court. Some states call it the Supreme Court of Errors, Court of Appeals, Supreme Judicial Court or Supreme Court of Appeals.

Federal questions can be appealed to the U.S. Supreme Court. There is also a limited right of appeal of other cases to the U.S. Supreme Court.

U.S. Department of Justice, Bureau of Justice Statistics,
Report to the Nation on Crime and Justice.

The State Courts

Plea Bargaining

During any of these steps in the pretrial procedure or before a trial verdict is reached, the defendant may plead guilty and the case goes directly to the sentencing stage. Often, the defendant is allowed to plead to a lesser charge than the one on which he or she has been indicted. This negotiation of a plea is called **plea bargaining** and is used to avoid costly and time-consuming trials. Bargaining clears the court calendar of the enormous number of pending cases. A study of 13 cities showed that plea bargaining occurred in 81 percent of the cases in Louisville and 97 percent in New York City. Here is a story based on a bargain struck by a prosecutor and a defense lawyer:

A 26-year-old man described by authorities as a Marine deserter has been sentenced to life in Walpole state prison after pleading guilty to second-degree murder in the Oct. 12 death of concert pianist Mary Louise Sellon, 30, of Medford.

The guilty plea last Tuesday of Steven Ballway came less than a week before he was scheduled for trial in Suffolk Superior Court on first-degree murder and rape charges.
—*The Boston Globe*

Sometimes, authorities will plea bargain with a defendant in return for his or her cooperation:

PHOENIX—A Boulder man charged with seven others in a 56-count indictment has been placed on four years' probation for possessing cocaine and selling marijuana.

Dennis J. Cimmino, 31, was sen-tenced by Judge Cheryl Hendrix of Maricopa County Superior Court after pleading guilty to the two drug charges and agreeing to help prosecutors. . . .

Should no plea bargain be offered—which often happens when the defendant is a frequent offender—the case moves to trial. In many cities, district attorneys concentrate their sparse resources on prosecuting the career criminal, the defendant with a record of felony arrests and convictions.

Trial

Trials are often dramatic, and the reporter should seek to reflect the drama. They are also complex, frequently complicated by legal jargon and technical procedures. The reporter must look beyond the technical points to the source of human interest, the tale that is unfolding.

The trial procedure begins with the selection of the jury, which can take a few hours or many weeks. During jury selection, the questioning of prospective jurors often indicates the strategies of the prosecution and defense.

Jury Selection   A jury is chosen from a **wheel** or jury box that contains the names of all registered voters in the jurisdiction. A defendant may waive the right to trial by jury and ask the judge to hear the evidence.

During the examination of potential jurors, attorneys can challenge the seating of particular jurors. A *peremptory* challenge allows the attorney to dismiss someone without giving a reason. A *for cause* challenge requires the attorney to cite a specific disqualification.

Adversarial Processes   The actual trial begins with opening statements by the prosecutor and the defense attorney. The reporter usually learns the outline of the case from these statements. Then, the prosecutor presents the state's witnesses. (In criminal trials, the state, not an individual, brings the charges.)

The defense then may cross-examine the prosecutor's witnesses, after which the prosecutor may again question the witnesses in redirect examination.

The defense then presents its case by calling its own witnesses:

CLAXTON, Ga.—Annette Moore sat in Evans County Superior Court and read from a pocket-size Bible while her son testified for more than an hour as the sole witness in his own defense.

Before 18-year-old Michael Moore was arrested Feb. 1 and charged with murder in the bludgeoning and stabbing death of his girlfriend's mother, Rebecca Futch, he was his own mother's hope for the future.

Now, in the third and last day of testimony before Judge John R. Harvey, he was staring a possible death sentence in the face and blaming his girlfriend for the crime.

Moore's girlfriend, Sherri Futch, is white. Her mother did not like her seeing Moore, Miss Futch said, because he is black. Moore testified that on the evening of Feb. 1 he and Miss Futch, 17, planned to tell her mother that she was pregnant. . . .

The prosecutor may cross-examine defense witnesses, and the defense then is allowed to make redirect examination of its witnesses.

Both sides are allowed to present rebuttals to testimony. The last step in the trial procedure is the final argument by both sides.

Essentials

- Identification of defendant.
- Original charge.
- New charge if plea bargain.
- Nature of crime; details.
- Status of proceeding:
    - What happened today.
    - Review of trial.
    - Next steps.
- Name of judge; title of court.
- Courtroom scene.

Charge to Jury   The judge charges or instructs the jury about the law as it affects the case.

Jury Deliberations and Verdict   The jury retires to a jury room to decide the facts of the case. The jurors must reach a unanimous verdict in all states but Louisiana, Montana, Oklahoma, Oregon and Texas where a majority decision stands. The jury may ask the judge for further instructions about the law, and it may request that testimony be read to it from the transcript. Since jury deliberations are secret, these occasional requests may tip off the reporter to what the jury is considering.

Free Press, Fair Trial

After the news media sought access to photographs of the bloodied bodies of O.J. Simpson's former wife and her friend, the judge in the murder case denied the request.

The judge ruled that their release would create "a virtual certainty that the defendant's right to a fair trial will be prejudiced." He continued:

The public display of these items to the news media would inevitably lead to graphic, sensationalistic, lurid and prurient descriptions, accurate and inaccurate, that would paint mental images in the minds of potential jurors that would prejudice the right to a fair trial of both parties.

Verdict stories cover the period a jury deliberates and include the reactions of those involved in the trial. When possible, jurors are interviewed. Also included are the accusation, identification of the accused and background of the crime. Notice in the beginning of this story by Beverly Medlyn of *The Mesa Tribune* that she has stressed the viciousness of the crime and the relief of the child's parents at the trial outcome:

PHOENIX—Frank Jarvis Atwood, an ex-con and a drifter, was convicted Thursday of first-degree murder and kidnapping for snatching an 8-year-old girl off her bicycle in broad daylight and then killing her in the desert northwest of Tucson.

The verdict was the emotional climax of a 2½-year wait by Vicki Lynne Hoskinson's family, which held a press conference after court adjourned to describe the long torment that had finally come to an end.

"I'm on top of the world. Today, justice was served for Vicki Lynne," proclaimed Debbie Carlson, the victim's mother. Carlson, her husband, George, and her daughter, Stephanie Hoskinson, alternately beamed and wept for joy as they faced a battery of cameras and microphones.

Carlson said she was "relieved that Frank Jarvis Atwood will never walk the streets again. He will never be able to victimize another child."

Hung Jury

When jurors cannot agree on a verdict, they are described as a *hung jury,* and a *mistrial* is declared by the judge. The jury agreed the mayor of Washington was guilty on one count—a misdemeanor possession of cocaine—and not guilty on another count. The jury was deadlocked on the remaining 12 counts. *The Washington Times*

Sentencing   If the jury returns a verdict of guilty, the judge may sentence the defendant at once or may await a probation report or schedule a presentence hearing at which evidence of aggravating or mitigating circumstances may be considered. In some states, the jury determines the sentence for capital offenses such as murder.

Judges sometimes make newsworthy comments when sentencing. Perhaps the most famous was that of a Colorado judge who presided over the trial of Alfred G. Packer, accused of murdering five of his companions while they were marooned in the Rocky Mountains during a gold prospecting expedition. The winter of 1874 was one of the worst in history. Packer survived by killing the men and eating their flesh over the winter. In sentencing Packer to life, the judge said, "Packer, there was only five Democrats in this county, and you et em all." At least that's what they say about the trial out west.

Stories can be written at any stage of the trial process. If the crime is notorious or involves a prominent person, a reporter may be assigned to follow the case from arraignment through sentencing.

Doing Time. Actual time served usually is one third of the maximum sentence. Thus, a five-to-15-year prison term means the prisoner will serve five years and then be eligible for a parole. In sentencing stories, always give the probable time behind bars along with the sentence.

Civil Court Coverage

We have been discussing *criminal law* procedures. In this area of law, the government is the accuser. In the other major area of law, *civil law,* the action is usually brought by an individual or a group.

Actions at Law

Civil law is not considered to have the drama of criminal law, and consequently coverage of the civil courts is limited, usually confined to the suits brought in *actions at law*. These suits seek the recovery of property and damages for personal injury and breach of contract.

The county courthouse reporter has the responsibility for checking the court clerk's records daily to ferret out the most interesting and significant suits filed. The reporter often chooses the suits involving large sums. But be careful: Lawyers sometimes seek huge sums for the damage allegedly done their client and then agree to a much-reduced figure in pretrial bargaining. In fact, most suits never reach the trial stage.

When a settlement is reached or an award is made by the jury, the story must contain the amount awarded, the name of the person bringing the suit, the damage inflicted, the name of the defendant, the title of the court in which the suit was heard and the incident leading to the suit:

> A 20-year-old Wyckoff woman who was injured in an automobile accident yesterday won a $405,000 jury award in Superior Court in Hackensack from the friend who was driving the car in which she was a passenger.
>
> Megan McMurtrie of 402 Meer Ave. was semiconscious for eight days of a month-long hospitalization after Kathryn Gallant lost control of the Mercedes Benz in which Ms. McMurtrie was riding, causing the car to strike a tree in Franklin Lakes. . . .
>
> —*The Record*

Equity Proceedings

The other area of civil law is called *equity proceedings*. Here, an individual or a group seeks to have the court compel an individual, the government or an organization to act or to refrain from action.

Here is the beginning of a story about a court's issuance of a temporary restraining order:

> Dr. John H. Lambette's attorney obtained a court order Friday barring state health officials from suspending the heart specialist's medical license.
>
> State Superior Court Judge Karl Krane granted the order and scheduled a hearing next Tuesday to determine whether the temporary restraining order should be made permanent. . . .

Injunctions are usually issued pending a hearing to determine whether they should be made permanent.

Criminal and *civil law* varies from state to state. The descriptions in this section may differ somewhat from those in your state.

Damage Suit Filed

Alvin Kellogg of St. James, Minn., checked into a Rochester motel room on Sept. 13, 1991, planning to have his annual checkup the next day at the Mayo clinic.

That night he suffered a stroke in his room. He claims in a suit filed in Olstead County Court that he was not found until three days later. He is suing the Chambers Corp., which owns the motel, for $500,000.

Kellogg, 67, alleges that the company was negligent because its employees at the Phillips Downtown Motel failed to discover him for three days. Medical reports filed with the suit state that Kellogg was severely dehydrated when he was found. . . .

Federal Court Coverage

There are two judicial systems: federal and state. In cities where federal courts are located, a full-time staff member is usually assigned to cover the federal court.

Federal courts hear a wide variety of cases that involve the violation of federal laws—immigration cases, constitutional issues, interstate car theft, drug shipments from outside the country into the country and across state lines, tax cases, civil rights.

NEW YORK (UPI)—The largest tax fraud case in U.S. history has ended with the conviction of four Wall Street executives and a hung jury in the case of a fifth defendant.

The nine-man, three-woman jury considering the complex trail of $130 million worth of phony tax shelters reached a partial verdict. . . .

DETROIT—One white man was found guilty and another was acquitted in federal court yesterday in a civil-rights trial stemming from the 1982 killing of Vincent Chin, a 27-year-old Chinese-American.

A jury of 11 whites and one black found Ronald Ebbens, 45, guilty on one count of violating Chin's civil rights. Chin had been bludgeoned to death with a baseball bat after a bar-room brawl in what U.S. Department of Justice prosecutors said was a racially motivated slaying.

—*Los Angeles Times*

The federal court system has three tiers. First, the district courts, where most trials are held. Second, the courts of appeals in 12 circuits, to which cases may be taken by appeal, and the Federal Circuit Court of Appeals for cases involving international trade, patent infringement and copyright and in which the U.S. government is a defendant. Third, the U.S. Supreme Court, to which cases are taken by writ of certiorari.

Obituaries

Death Sells. *People* magazine said its three best-selling issues had covers on:
1. The death of John Lennon.
2. The death of Grace Kelly.
3. The death of Karen Carpenter.

The Washington-based political reporter finished his talk to the journalism class and asked for questions. He had just completed a tour of the Midwest to sound out sentiment about the presidential candidates.

"What was the strongest impression you got from your trip?" a student asked.

The reporter paused a moment before answering. "When I was interviewing a woman in her kitchen in Iowa, I glanced over to the wall where she had some things clipped to a wallboard. At the top was a newspaper clipping behind a piece of clear plastic.

"It was the story of President Kennedy's funeral. The paper was yellow and frayed. It told me something about the woman's politics. But it also told me something about journalism. Here was the most basic journalistic story of all, an obituary, and it had been saved for all these years."

Obituaries are among the most frequently read items in newspapers. A third to half of the readers regularly look at them. Large newspapers have space for only the deaths of people prominent in the community and nation. Smaller newspapers run most deaths and ask their reporters to go beyond the essentials. This further check often results in an interesting story. "We did an obit once on a bus driver whose name meant nothing to most people," said Leon Hirtl, managing editor of *The Cincinnati Post*. "But we discovered that many people knew him as the bus driver who sang."

Newsworthiness can be an elusive guideline for an obituary. If the president of a local highway equipment firm is worth seven or eight paragraphs, why not the bookkeeper in his firm who emigrated from Hungary as a child 60 years ago? What made his family leave, and how did he fare on arrival? How did he manage to educate himself? Friends and relatives would know.

"There are a lot of missed opportunities for good stories with obituaries," says Jim Adams, city editor of *The Cincinnati Post*. "It's my philosophy that you treat the obituary the same as any other news story—get quotes and talk to people and try to give a face to the person you're writing about."

Essentials

- Name, age, address and occupation of the deceased.
- Time and place of death.
- Cause of death.
- Date and place of birth.
- Survivors.
- Funeral and burial arrangements.

These are the bare essentials. For the longer obituary, add:

- Accomplishments and achievements; education.
- Membership in organizations, religious groups.
- Military service.
- Anecdotes of friends and relatives.
- Marriage.

Usually, the basic material is made available by the mortuary. Information may be available from the advertising department, which receives paid death notices from the funeral home. Occasionally, a person identifying himself or herself as a friend or relative will call in an obituary. Be careful. Always verify the information by telephoning a relative or a mortuary. Some people call in phony death reports for the kick of seeing an obituary of someone who is very much alive.

Personal Details

Readers are interested in stories about the deaths of local people. The obituary gives readers in capsule form the biography of someone we know or have heard about. We can read that the local Chevrolet dealer grew orchids as a hobby

Deadly Dull Obits

Some newspapers are slaves to formula—all their obituaries begin with the announcement of services or burial plans.

Look at these details from a woman's life:

- She began her teaching career in a one-room school.
- She taught mathematics for 51 years in Wisconsin, Washington, Nevada and South Dakota.
- She was the first woman elected to the Rapid City city council.
- She was Teacher of the Year and founder of a state teachers' society, and in retirement she was active in state and national education groups.

Surely from these details a fascinating story could have been fashioned. But the local newspaper began its obituary this way:

Services for longtime Rapid City teacher Florence Krieger, 96, Rapid City, will be held at 2 p.m. Tuesday at the First Presbyterian Church with the Rev. Bob Garrard officiating.

With Malice Intended

Objectivity went out the window when the great editor William Allen White of *The Emporia Gazette* learned that Frank Munsey had died. Munsey had bought newspapers and folded them at a profit. The few he kept were published for the sole purpose of making money. For Munsey's obituary White wrote:

Frank Munsey, the great publisher, is dead.

Frank Munsey contributed to the journalism of his day the talent of a meatpacker, the morals of a money changer and the manners of an undertaker. He and his kind have about succeeded in transforming a once-noble profession into an eight percent security.

May he rest in trust.

and won prizes at local shows or that the retired music teacher set a national collegiate record for the 100-yard dash 50 years ago.

Obituaries balance these personal details with the obvious essentials—name, age, address, occupation, survivors, funeral arrangements.

The following obituary from the *Lexington Herald-Leader* includes the kind of detail that in just a few paragraphs reveals not only the story of a local businessman but the story of a class of people who pulled themselves up from humble beginnings:

Store Founder 'Al' Wenneker Dies at Age 76

Alex "Al" Wenneker, a prominent Lexington businessman, died here yesterday. He was 76.

With a rented storefront on Main Street measuring only 12 feet by 30 feet, eight kitchen chairs, empty boxes used as shelves and a relatively small stock of shoes, Wenneker and his wife Mary opened for business back in 1935. The business, located at 155 East Main St. until 1979, was called Wenneker's Sample Shoe Store.

Although no longer at the Main Street location, Wenneker's Shoe Stores have become a very successful business chain here with locations at three of Lexington's shopping malls.

Wenneker was a member of Temple Adath Israel.

A native of St. Louis, Mo., he was the son of William Wenneker, a Russian immigrant, and Libby McDowell Wenneker.

Besides his wife, survivors include two sons, James E. Wenneker and William R. Wenneker, both of Lexington; four sisters; and three grandchildren.

The funeral will be at 3 p.m. Tuesday at W.R. Milward Mortuary—Broadway. Burial will be in Lexington Cemetery. Visitation is from 3 to 5 and 7 to 9 p.m. today.

Cause of Death

Reporters often discover that finding out the cause of a person's death is the most difficult part of reporting for the obituary. The family sometimes feels ashamed, embarrassed or fearful that the way a person died will reflect poorly on that person's life or on the family. The family of a teen-age girl who committed suicide asks that the obituary say simply that she died "suddenly." The widow of a man who died of cancer insists that the obituary say death came "after a long illness," a euphemism that has become less frequent as the number of cancer deaths has increased. Most newspapers or stations have policies on how to handle situations in which survivors wish to conceal the cause of death.

Deaths from diseases that may indicate a lifestyle some people consider unsavory are often troublesome for the reporter—deaths caused by cirrhosis of the liver or complications from AIDS, for example. Cirrhosis is associated with alcoholism, and AIDS victims are for the most part gay men or intravenous drug users.

Many larger stations and newspapers have decided that a death from AIDS is no different from a death from cancer or from a heart attack, and they encourage funeral homes and families to list AIDS as the cause of death.

Suicides. Unless a suicide is committed in a spectacular fashion, the story of the death should be treated no differently from other obituaries. Newspapers and stations usually play down the means of death. But how a person died should be mentioned somewhere in the story.

When Thomas Schippers, a well-known orchestra conductor, died of lung cancer, *The New York Times* received several letters asking whether Schippers had been a smoker. The information should have been included in the obituary, the *Times* admitted. The newspaper had included such information in the obituaries of other heavy smokers who died of the disease, an editor stated.

The Lead

Generally, a person's occupation, accomplishments or distinctive contribution to the community is placed in the lead to identify him or her:

Occupation

> Raymond T. Baron, former president of Paxton and Baron Co., book publishers, died yesterday in his home at 75 Arden Lane. He was 78 years old.

Accomplishment

> Mortimer Heineman, an advertising executive who helped create the slogan "Promise her anything, but give her Arpège," died yesterday following a heart attack. He was 74 years old.

Contribution

> Florence Gable Cerrin, long active in the local chapter of the American Red Cross, died yesterday at her home at 65 Eastern Parkway at the age of 94.

Funeral and burial arrangements can also be the basis of the lead. Some newspapers will try to vary their leads so that instead of every lead beginning with the report of someone's death, an occasional obituary will begin with the date, time and place of the funeral and burial.

> Services for Albert D. Scott, 79, of 156 W. Central Ave., will be held tomorrow at 11 a.m. in the Boulder Funeral Home.
>
> Burial for the retired pharmacist will follow in the Piedmont Cemetery in Oberlin.
>
> Scott died yesterday at his home after suffering a heart attack. . . .

When the death has occurred a few days before the obituary is written, the lead usually will be based on the funeral and burial arrangements.

LOCAL DEATHS

William J. Bacigalupi
Pleasant Hill
Jan. 3, 1904 — Sept. 15, 1994

William Bacigalupi, who worked for Chevron USA for 29 years, died Sept. 15 at Crestwood Convalescent Hospital in Pleasant Hill. He was 90.

The native of San Francisco lived in Pleasant Hill for 26 years.

He is survived by his wife of 51 years, Angela Bacigalupi of Pleasant Hill; sons, William L. Bacigalupi of Walnut Creek and Victor J. Bacigalupi of Moraga; and four grandchildren.

Services: Were private. His ashes will be scattered at sea. Arrangements are by the Neptune Society, Walnut Creek.

Memorial gifts: Salesian Boys Club, 666 Filbert St., San Francisco, CA 94133.

John H. Bond
Walnut Creek
March 31, 1929 — Sept. 19, 1994

John H. Bond, a food and candy broker for 20 years, died Monday in Walnut Creek. He was 65.

The native of Hollywood lived in Walnut Creek for five years and before that in Burlingame. He enjoyed sailing and racing, golf, bridge and traveling.

He is survived by his wife of 24 years, Marilyn E. Bond; daughter, Melissa Anne Bond of Santa Cruz; son, John Timothy Bond of Squim, Wash.; and four grandchildren, four stepgrandchildren and one step-great-grandchild.

Services: Pending. Burial will be private. Arrangements are by Affordable Mortuary Service.

Memorial gifts: American Cancer Society, P.O. Box 4295, Walnut Creek, CA 94596-0295.

Polly Holcomb Burgess Carroll
Silver Spring, Md.
July 19, 1921 — Sept. 8, 1994

Polly Holcomb Burgess Carroll, a former board president of Bethesda-Chevy Chase Meals on Wheels, died Sept. 8 at Montgomery General Hospital in Olney, Md., from complications after surgery for an intestinal obstruction. She was 73.

The native of Berkeley lived in Silver Spring, Md., for two years and had previously lived in Walnut Creek. In the mid-1960s, she was a volunteer and trustee for Peirce-Warwick Adoption Agency. She worked for Meals on Wheels beginning in 1973 and was board president from 1984 to 1988. Beginning in 1978, she taught swimming classes at the Bethesda YMCA, including swimnastics, arthritis exercises and adaptive aquatics for people with

Contra Costa Times

Delayed leads are rarely used for obituaries, but if the delayed lead is in good taste, it is acceptable:

Margaret Wilson did get her last wish.

When she was told she had terminal cancer, the 73-year-old former high school teacher asked that she be buried in her ancestral family plot in Ireland.

Localizing the Obituary

When a widely known person dies, a local follow-up is sometimes possible. The person may have been born or gone to school in town. Here is how a Springfield paper handled the death in another state of a former Springfield resident:

Sometimes, the local connection is less specific, as when the nation mourned the death of President John F. Kennedy. Then, local observances were the subjects of many stories.

Robert Cowan, who served as governor from 1956–60, died today in a retirement home in St. Augustine, Fla. Cowan was born in Springfield and attended school here before moving to Gulfport in 1935. . . .

Sports Coverage

A sportswriter once asked Carl Furillo, the great outfielder for the Brooklyn Dodgers, how he learned to play the tough right-field wall in Ebbetts Field.

"I worked, that's how," Furillo replied.

And that, says the writer, Roger Kahn, is how a reporter learns to write sports stories. The first efforts may be as fumbling as the lead that a high school correspondent called in to a newspaper after his high school team had won a no-hit game:

In the best-pitched game these old eyes have ever seen . . . .

Or the sport being covered may be as confusing as it was to Becky Teagarden, a sportswriter for the *Columbus Citizen-Journal* when she covered her first basketball game.

"I didn't know what was going on," she recalls. But she had the good sense to corner the coach after the game. She asked him, "Tell me, what happened out there?"

The high school reporter learned, too. His first task was to learn to keep himself out of the story. The reader is interested in the athletes and the game, not in the writer.

Who's Watching Sports on TV

	Number of People (millions)	Percent of Adults
Professional football	63.2	37
Baseball	62.7	37
College football	48.9	29
Boxing	37.2	22
College basketball	36.2	21
Professional basketball	34.7	20
Professional wrestling	28.8	17

High School and College Sports

Sportswriters who aspire to cover the Cleveland Indians, Dallas Cowboys or Golden State Warriors break in on school or nonprofessional sports. Although many people follow professional sports, many more are fans of high school or college teams and they expect the same quality of reporting and writing given to the fans of professional teams.

Many newspapers hire part timers, most of them students, to cover school games. Don Watz, a junior at Florida State University, was assigned to cover a high school baseball game one afternoon and a college baseball game that evening. He describes how he went about it:

> My day started with traveling from Tallahassee to Live Oak (80 miles) for the 2 p.m. high school game. That game lasted about two-and-one-half hours. At about 5:15 I finished with my interviews and hit the highway.
>
> I then had 80 miles to travel to Jacksonville. The FSU-Jacksonville game started at 7 p.m.
>
> By the time I traveled crosstown through rush-hour traffic and reached the University field, the game was just completing the first inning. I had to finish my high school game story (I started it during the high school game).
>
> While the FSU game went on I finished up my high school story. By the sixth inning I sent it to the office in Tallahassee.
>
> Then, I had the FSU game to worry about. The game took 12 innings and had 17 runs scored. It finished at 11:30 and I had a midnight deadline.
>
> I made it.

How did he do? Judge for yourself. Here is the beginning of his high school game story:

Learn the Game. No one can predict the kinds of events he or she will be covering. Even those who have no interest in reporting sports events may find themselves in the press box at a football game or courtside for a college basketball tournament.

"If you're not a sportswriter when you begin working as an AP newsman or newswoman, you become one—quickly," the AP tells news staffers.

LIVE OAK—It was a mismatch on paper, and by the end of the game, the scoreboard reflected that. Second-ranked Leon won the District 2-AAA baseball title Friday afternoon, thumping Suwannee 13-1.

The underdog Bulldogs were no match for Leon, which has won three straight district titles and six of the last eight. The game lasted just five innings due to the 10-run mercy rule. The Bulldogs could manage just one hit off Leon starter Brad Culpepper. The single by Jason McCarl came with one out in the fourth and brought home the only Bulldog run.

"I tried to keep them off-balance," said Culpepper. "They are a good ball-club and a good hitting club; after a while they would get used to a fastball pitcher."

Culpepper struck out eight in the five innings but at times Suwannee did manage some hard shots—all of which were scooped up by the solid Lion defense.

"We played two games back-to-back and haven't made an error. We had outstanding defense," said Leon coach Ronnie Youngblood. . . .

Notice that Watz did more than give the score. He had an idea of a mismatch when he went to cover the game, and that's what he saw unfold. The mismatch became his lead. Despite his hurry, he did manage some postgame interviews.

Now, over to Jacksonville for the college game. Again, Watz wrote a lead that is imaginative. Here are the first few paragraphs:

JACKSONVILLE—When Florida State began its current three-game road swing, Chris Pollack was told he probably would be needed in a relief role. He liked the idea.

Not only did he like it, he's good at it. The senior lefthander pitched 7⅔ innings and earned the win, beating Jacksonville 9-8 in a Friday night game that took 12 innings.

"When they told me I might be coming in relief I was excited," Pollack said. "Coming in with two on and two out and the score tied is exciting. After starting all of last season and most of this one, I looked forward to it."

The leads that Watz put on his stories are informative and entertaining. Look at the game story essentials below and see how many Watz handled in his first few paragraphs.

Essentials

- The score.
- Names of teams; type of sport.
- When and where the game took place.
- Key incident or play.
- Outstanding player(s).
- League.
- Scoring.
- Effect of game on league standings.
- Strategy.

- Crowd size; behavior, if a factor.
- Statistics.
- Injuries.
- Winning or losing streaks.
- Duration of game.
- Record(s) set.
- Postgame quotes.

The quality of the written story depends on the quality of the reporting. The reporter who knows the players well, who keeps up on the strategies coaches use for different opponents and who knows the sport he or she is covering writes informative and interesting stories.

Some Statistics

The odds against a high school athlete becoming a professional ball player are 12,000 to 1.

Thirty percent of college basketball and football players are functionally illiterate.

Seventy percent of all basketball and football players in big-time college sports never graduate.

Teams that go to the Rose Bowl get $5 to $6 million each for the game.

The Lead

Any of the essentials can be placed in the lead of the story. Let's look at a few sports stories. Note that none of the stories begins with scores alone. Fans already knew the scores. The leads focus on a player and a record, a play or the length of the game along with the score.

Outstanding player and record

ANAHEIM, Calif. (AP)—Ken Griffey Jr. hit his 31st home run Wednesday night, breaking Babe Ruth's record for most home runs before the end of June and leading the Seattle Mariners to the 12-3 American League victory over California.

HOUSTON (AP)—Hakeem Olajuwon lived up to his most valuable player billing and the Houston Rockets won their first championship and gave the city its first major-league title, beating New York 90-84 Wednesday night in Game 7 of the National Basketball Association Finals.

Commercializing High School Sports

High school sports are becoming increasingly commercialized and professionalized. A cable sports network found sponsors for 25 Friday-night high school games, mostly basketball and football, despite many advertisers' fear of criticism that national television exposure and athletic scholarships will corrupt high school athletics.

Larry Hawkins, a former high school coach who is director of the Institute for Athletics and Education at the University of Chicago, says high school sports are covered as a part of the feeder system to the professional ranks. He doesn't like what he sees.

"The adoption of professional values at every level of the sports feeder system is destructive to social values," he says. "School sports should reinforce education."

Hawkins says urban high schools have particular problems. The NCAA seeks prospective student-athletes with an ACT score of 15. In Chicago at "urban high schools with a rich athletic tradition the average score for all students was 9.2 and was significantly lower for athletes.

STORRS, Conn. (AP)—Frances Savage had a tournament record 41 points as Miami extended the nation's longest winning streak in women's basketball with an 82-70 victory over Providence. Miami advanced to Monday's Big East championship game against Connecticut.

Winning plays

HAMILTON (CP)—They will be the shots Canadian basketball fans will remember forever—and not fondly.

Sergei Bazarevich's two foul shots with 30 seconds and Vasilii Karassev's layup with four seconds led Russia to a 73-66 victory over Canada in the world basketball championship before 10,000 highly charged fans at Copps Coliseum.

Length of game

Two months and 33 innings after it started, the longest baseball game in history was completed tonight when the Pawtucket Red Sox defeated the Rochester Red Wings 3-2.

Imagination and Emotion

Imagination is vital to the sports story. There are so many sports, such a multitude of games that after a while the sports pages seem to swim in team names and numbers. Stories should reflect the spectacle of men and women stretching mind and body to reach beyond their limits, of unusual people and sometimes strange events.

When Nolan Ryan pitched his fifth no-hit baseball game, the story was as much his nonchalance as the accomplishment. When the Montreal Expos couldn't win a game against the Los Angeles Dodgers in their home park, the story of still another loss was the story of jinxes and superstitions.

"People forget about game scores in one hour," says T.J. Simers of *The Commercial Appeal* in Memphis. "But a story about emotion may stick with them for two hours." Simers is being sarcastic about the durability of a news story, but he does have a point.

The writer who captures the human dimension of the event creates a story the reader will remember, and this is what we all strive for in journalism—the story that makes the reader sit up and take notice.

Behind the Score

Scores, says a sportswriter, are remembered for a few hours. But the emotions endure. By capturing the human element, a writer may tell a story that moves beyond the playing field.

This photograph by Morris Berman of the *Pittsburgh Post-Gazette* captured the moment that a battered Y.A. Tittle of the New York Giants sensed his long career as a topflight quarterback was at an end. In this game against the Pittsburgh Steelers, Tittle found he was no longer nimble enough to sidestep charging linemen. His body could not respond to the commands of his still-sharp mind. *Morris Berman, Pittsburgh Post-Gazette*

Leads can focus on the small details unseen by fans sitting in a stadium or watching a game on television:

> Paul Williams leaned a foot too far
> to his right last night, and that was the
> ball game.

This was the beginning of a story about a baseball team trailing 1-0 in the bottom of the ninth with two out. Williams had walked and the next batter had two balls and no strikes. And suddenly the game was over because Williams was picked off first base by the pitcher.

Structure

Increasingly, delayed leads are put on sports stories. The first paragraph or two may contain an incident, an anecdote, a key play or a strategic move. Then, in the second or third paragraph, the writer gives the score. Next, a few paragraphs are devoted to the important points of the game—the scoring, significant substitutions, injuries or changes in the standings:

NEW YORK—When the final buzzer sounded in Madison Square Garden last night, all eyes were on the referees who were huddling at mid-court. If Xavier McDaniel's 20-footer beat the buzzer, the Knicks would go into overtime against the Lakers. If it was late, the Knicks would lose.

After 10 seconds, a referee waved his arms—no good. McDaniel fell to the court in frustrated anger, and the Lakers hugged one another in joy.

The Lakers won 106-104 in an emotional game few in the crowd of 19,763 will forget. . . .

Don't Root. Journalists have compromised their integrity by ignoring drug use by athletes, payoffs to college players and special treatment of college athletes.

Writers seemed to want to keep their heroes and their sports part of the dreamland they believe fans prefer. The fantasy and cover-up has a long tradition. When Babe Ruth missed the first six weeks of the baseball season, sportswriters attributed his illness to a passion for hot dogs, which led to a massive case of indigestion.

They knew it was a passion for drink and sex in which he had overindulged during spring training that laid the great Babe low. But they kept the image clean by giving him an all-American ailment.

Outdoor Activities

Noncompetitive sports involve millions of people and have become the subject of increasing media attention.

Restraint

Sportswriters are enthusiasts. Sometimes they write as though they are covering the end of the world and not a game. This kind of enthusiasm leads to excesses.

Shrillness This is a common ailment, especially of some television announcers. In football, every other play is accompanied by a rise in the announcer's voice. A writer can be shrill, too. A story written with high-pitch intensity from lead to end irritates the reader. The story should not be dull, but it should not scream at the reader.

Overstatement Games sometimes are made into battles of titans, and the language of the story is exaggerated. Writing of this sort often flows shamelessly in stories about the games of traditional rivals—Green Bay Packers-Chicago Bears; Stanford-University of California at Berkeley; Red Sox-Yankees; New York Knicks-Boston Celtics; Kansas-Missouri; Rangers-Flyers; Iowa State-University of Iowa.

Mindless Emotionalism Fans do become excited by games. They have been known to hurl beer cans at players and officials. Some fans become so involved with the action that it becomes a life-and-death conflict for them. Sportswriters should reflect the intensity and the seriousness of sports, but they must also keep their distance. These are, after all, only games.

Extra Dimension

Since most of those who turn to their newspapers to read of yesterday's games already know the results, the reporter's task is to add an extra ingredient.

Emery Filmer, a sports reporter for *The Advocate* in Stamford, Conn., was covering a local team in the state baseball playoffs. On Tuesday, the team, the Stamford Catholic High School Crusaders, had upset the defending state champions, 2-1. Then, on Wednesday, Stamford lost 7-2 in the semifinal. Filmer was writing for the Thursday newspaper. *The Advocate* is an afternoon newspaper, which meant that most fans following the local team already knew it had lost.

How would you handle this situation? A story that begins this way would be barely adequate:

> Andrew Warde High School defeated the Stamford
> Catholic High School Crusaders yesterday in the semifinal
> state baseball playoffs by a score of 7-2.

There is technically nothing wrong with this lead, but it repeats what many fans already know. What about the following lead?

> The Crusaders from Stamford Catholic High School
> hung up their gloves yesterday and will have to wait
> another year before trying for the state high school

baseball championship. The Crusaders lost to Andrew
Warde 7-2 in a semifinal playoff game yesterday.

Although this lead is also adequate, it says little more than the previous lead.
All it does is add a picturesque but trite phrase, "hung up their gloves."

Filmer was able to write an effective lead because he understood the key to
the Crusaders' loss, the absence of their leading pitcher. His knowledge of the
team and the game enabled him to add dimension to his story. Here is how
Filmer's story begins:

Here are the two sides of the Stamford Catholic High School Crusaders:

On Tuesday night, they played a near-perfect game in upsetting the defending state champion Westhill Vikings, 2-1, in an FCIAC first-round playoff game. But on Wednesday, they fell behind 5-0 in the first inning and ended up on the short end of a 7-2 score against Andrew Warde, a club they had beaten 8-3 last month.

So, what's the difference?

Roger Haggerty perhaps. After all, he wasn't pitching Wednesday.

"Knowing that we did not have to face Haggerty tonight was a definite factor in our favor," admitted Warde coach Ed Bengermino after his team had qualified for its first appearance in the FCIAC championship game.

Haggerty pitched a brilliant two-hitter against the heavy-hitting Vikings on Tuesday to vault the Crusaders into Wednesday's semifinal against the Eastern Division champions, Warde. It was Haggerty's sixth victory of the year and lowered his ERA to 1.82.

But, unfortunately, he cannot pitch every day. And therein lies the difference in the Stamford Catholic Crusaders. . . .

Advice for the Novice Sportswriter

Here are some suggestions from experienced sportswriters:

- Avoid commenting in straight game stories. Often, comments reflect lazy reporting.
- Use quotes that reveal important aspects of the game. Avoid inane quotes.
- Watch out for the coach who gives the same statements every season, every game.
- Be in touch with the reader. Too often, sportswriters write for each other.
- Don't sacrifice information for style. First, give the information. The style will come naturally.
- Don't use war references, such as *battling* or *troops being sent in.* You're covering a game, not a war.
- If anything, understate. Overstatement is the sign of the beginner.
- Don't use sports jargon—*netminder, pigskin, hoop, horsehide.*
- Avoid making athletes into heroes. They're humans, not gods.

More Than Only Games

Sports reporting is not exclusively game coverage. Sports reporters have become investigative reporters and revealed payoffs to athletes and university complicity in keeping academically unqualified athletes eligible. They have written interpretive stories about how money has corrupted supposedly noncommercial sports.

They have written features about the personal lives, often tragic, of athletes:

His father left home when he was a 2-year-old. While growing up in San Bernardino, Calif., Johnson's mother battled a cocaine addiction, leaving him and his younger sister, Christine, drifting from place to place. From the time he was in eighth grade until a junior in high school, he lived in 16 different places with an assortment of relatives and friends and in welfare hotels. Overwhelmed by it all during his sophomore year at Cajon High School, Johnson attempted suicide by swallowing a handful of pills.

Quick Pick. Johnson was selected by the Pittsburgh Steelers in the first round of the National Football League draft, the third receiver they drafted in 21 years.

This is a section from Timothy W. Smith's story about Charles Johnson, an All-America and Academic All-Big Eight Conference football player at the University of Colorado, where he graduated in three years with a bachelor's degree in marketing. *The New York Times* story resumes:

"So many kids use the cop-out that I'm black, I'm from a broken home, I'm from a bad neighborhood, and they do nothing with their lives," said Jerry Buckner who took Johnson into her home in 1989 and whom Johnson now calls his mother. "But Charles took all those things and just inverted them. I don't know how he did it. But he did."

There is a darker side to the few success stories, the underside, and writers have examined it. They have shown, for example, that few minority players graduate. In fact, 44 major universities failed to graduate a single black basketball player who started as a freshman in the 1983–1987 period. Indiana graduated 75 percent of its white players but none of its blacks. The University of Florida, another basketball powerhouse, graduated half the whites and none of the blacks.

Writers have revealed that despite the assertion that big-time sports brings in needed revenues, three of four Division I athletic programs lose money.

Jocks No More

Sportswriters traditionally were thought of as the jocks of the news staff. No longer. They are among the best-read, most literate of the journalists on the beat. Some of this luster is the result of the work of writers like Red Smith, whose writing over the decades inspired many young reporters.

Red Smith was covering baseball when the Brooklyn Dodgers fell from their 13½ game league lead to a tie with the New York Giants in 1951, which was resolved in as dramatic a finish as fiction could invent. In the ninth inning of the deciding game for the pennant, the Giants were behind 4-1. They scored a run. Then with two men on base, Bobby Thomson came to bat. He hit a home run that sent the Giants announcer babbling. Smith wrote, "The art of fiction is dead. Reality has strangled invention."

It was Smith who, after watching a famous spitball pitcher display his talent, wrote that the line score should have another column after runs, hits and errors: relative humidity.

Many sports reporters write books or help athletes with theirs. For *My Favorite Summer 1956*, Mickey Mantle had the help of Phil Pepe, a New York sportswriter, who asked Mantle to recall his contract problems with the Yankees. Mantle, one of the greatest hitters in the history of baseball, recalled that the team had sent him a contract for $32,500. "To me, that was all the money in the world. My dad probably didn't make that much combined all the years he worked in the mines." (The average salary for a major leaguer today is more than $1 million a year.)

Women in the Locker Room

The emergence of women on sports staffs has changed sports coverage. "It's the great revolution in sportswriting of our generation," says Ron Rapoport, a nationally syndicated sports columnist for the *Los Angeles Daily News.* "When I started writing sports in the late '60s essentially there just were no women sportswriters. Once in a while a woman would try it, but then she would quickly leave.

"Now, 25 years later, I'm astonished to find myself the editor of a book in which 66 women sportswriters are represented." And he adds, "I'm also embarrassed not to have included a lot more who deserve to be in it." Rapoport's book is a compilation of the writings of women sportswriters.

Rapoport estimates there are more than 200 women on sports staffs, from the largest newspapers and mass circulation magazines to newspapers in smaller cities like Casper, Wyo., Monterey, Calif., and Greensboro, N.C.

"They cover every kind of men's sports—professional football, basketball, baseball, hockey and all men's college sports," he says. Most of Rapoport's selections are about women athletes. One profile is of the golfer Heather Farr, who died of breast cancer. It was written for *Golf Digest* by Betty Cuniberti, who has breast cancer.

"I've read it five times during the editing process," Rapoport says, "and I've cried five times."

The book is *A Kind of Grace: A Treasury of Sportswriting by Women,* published by Zenobia Press. The title is taken from a comment by Jackie Joyner-Kersee, the Olympic track star, who was asked whether women who compete in sports give up their inherent femininity.

"I don't think being an athlete is unfeminine," she replied. "I think of it as a kind of grace."

Sexist Incidents

Women sportswriters are accepted in most locker rooms, but they have to be ready for the sexist incident. A reporter for the *Detroit Free Press* approached pitcher Jack Morris, who was in long underwear. She started to ask a question, but he told her, "I don't talk to people when I'm naked, especially women unless they're on top of me or I'm on top of them." When the newspaper complained, Tigers president Bo Schembechler blamed the newspaper for sending a woman into the locker room.

When a reporter for the *Boston Herald* sought locker-room comments from New England Patriots team members, she was greeted with obscene comments, and several of the players exposed themselves to her. (They were later fined by the National Football League.)

Tips on Covering Games

Here is some advice from the AP on covering a few sports:

Baseball lives on numbers and that is where you'll generally find your lead: a low number (e.g., a one-hitter for a pitcher) or a high number (e.g., four home runs for a batter). Account for all scoring and remember to mention outstanding defensive plays and unusual incidents.

Basketball is a sport where points come too rapidly to mention all the scoring, so focus on the players with the biggest or most important numbers and key stretches in which the game is won or lost.

Bowling is an easy sport to describe because it basically involves two plays, a strike and a spare. Total pins and decisive plays, such as missing a key spare or covering a difficult split, are essential to any bowling story.

Football stories begin with a summary, a graf or two that disposes of the most important episodes in the game. Every football lead (and basketball lead as well) must have a key player in it. Include anything unusual.

Track and field coverage emphasizes a record-breaker, a multiple individual winner or a team's domination of a meet. Most track events are short and merely listing the performances is enough. But be sure to mention the excitement such as a shot-putter winning with a mammoth heave on his last try, or a miler coming from far back on the final lap to win by inches.

Covering Religion

Just as politics pervades our lives, so, too, does religion. And yet much of the coverage of the subject has been uninspired. The lackadaisical coverage may have something to do with a misconception of the part religion plays in America.

The assumption that Americans are skeptical, irreverent, pragmatic and secular is unfounded. The truth is that they are, for the most part, religious. Polls have shown:

- 90 percent believe God exists.
- 80 percent expect to be called to God on Judgment Day.
- 80 percent believe God works miracles.
- 70 percent believe in life after death.
- 50 percent believe in angels.
- 40 percent attend church weekly.

Garry Wills, in his book *Under God: Religion and American Politics,* writes that life in America is "a marvel of religiosity."

On many newspapers, news of religion used to be relegated to the back pages where reports of sermons, fund raising and trips to the Holy Land were routinely reported. Such reporting missed the dynamic changes in religion—the growth of fundamentalism, the changes in the Roman Catholic Church, the high intermarriage rate of Jews. Serious religious reporting was left to religious newspapers and periodicals. Now a few newspapers have recognized the importance of religion and have hired specialists in religion to cover the subject.

These reporters understand that religion is hardly confined to church, mosque, synagogue. They write stories about the social and economic reasons people turn to evangelical Protestantism, the problems of the Catholic Church hierarchy with liberal Catholic theologians in Europe and the Americas, the religious aspects of such perplexing issues as whether the federal government should give aid to parochial schools, sex education should be included in a high school curriculum, condoms should be distributed in high schools and prayer should be permitted in public schools.

A growing cadre of journalists has taken theology courses. All religion reporters read the religious magazines: *America* and *Commonweal* (Roman Catholic); *The Christian Century,* (Protestant); *Commentary, Tikkun* (Jewish).

Sources include the heads of religious organizations, members of theology faculties and lay people associated with religious groups. These contacts lead reporters to good stories about trends in the churches and synagogues such as the conflict between the so-called conservative and liberal wings of religious denominations.

Other Types of Stories

When the reporter arrived in the newsroom, he knew he wouldn't be out on his beat for a while. Piled on his desk were announcements and press releases, a couple of notes from the city editor and a telephone message. The reporter set to work on the stack in front of him.

First, he looked through the releases. One was about a regional history conference that would be held on the campus of the local college. Another concerned a skating party to be held Sunday for a charity. The third was about a speech to be given by the governor next week. He put these in one pile, took a slip of paper and wrote **precedes** on it and clipped the slip of paper and the material together.

On a release from an army base about the promotion of a local soldier, he scribbled the word **personal.** He knew that he could handle this release and the precedes quickly. The rest would take a little more time: One was an obituary, another was a wire story that required a local angle and the third required a call to the weather bureau.

"Better get the easy ones out of the way first," he decided. He turned to the advances and the personal item. These would require short, tightly written pieces called **briefs** or **shorts.**

Briefs

The trick to writing briefs, the reporter had been told his first day on the job, is to give the reader the basics. "No frills, no ornamentation. The Five W's and an

H and get out of there fast," an experienced reporter had told him. No more than two or three paragraphs, unless the personal is about the appointment of a new minister to the largest church in town, or the marriage in town next month of the 72-year-old senior U.S. senator.

Precedes

The reporter looked over the seven-paragraph press release from the local college about the history conference.

The **precede,** or **advance,** tells people about events they may want to attend or know about. A family may not want to go roller skating, but it might send a donation to the community hospital after reading the short item about the benefit.

Essentials

- Event or activity planned.
- Date, time, place of activity.
- Purpose.
- Sponsor.
- Fee, admission charge, if any.
- Background, if a significant event.

He wrote a precede for the history conference:

The eighth annual Midwestern Conference of History Teachers will be held on the Hampden College campus next Thursday and Friday.

Registration will take place in McGuire Auditorium Wednesday afternoon and Thursday. The fee is $5.

Sessions will be held in the Liberal Arts building.

The main speaker will be Professor Felix S. Woodward of Oxford University. He will speak Thursday evening on "Breaking the Plains."

The smaller the newspaper, the longer the precede. Here is how the skating benefit story was written:

A fund-raising skating party to assist the Norwalk Community Hospital will be held Sunday at the Wheels Roller Skating Center at 61 Converse St.

There will be two sessions, from 7 to 9 p.m. and from 9:30 to 11:30 p.m.

Music will be provided by "Soul Sounds." Admission is $3.

The income will be used to furnish a children's playroom in the hospital.

Personals

Names make news. In big cities, the names that make news are those of public figures—television personalities, the wealthy, politicians, athletes, the social set. In smaller towns, the names are those of neighbors. Their comings and goings are recorded in detail in news items called **personals.**

Precede

Summer concert series starts with jazz band

The Civic Arts Commission's free summer concert series kicks off today with the Devil Mountain Jazz Band.

The band will perform from 5 to 9 p.m. at Waldie Plaza on Second Street across from City Hall.

Also scheduled this summer are:
■ Sunday — Vocal Ease, big band-era music.
■ July 17 — Killin' Floor, blues.
■ July 24 — Azucar y Crema, Latin jazz.
■ Aug. 14 — Pacific Brass, show tunes and pop music.
■ Aug. 21 — Rangers, contemporary country.
■ Aug. 28 — Pan Exastasy, steel drums.

All concerts except today's will be from 6 to 8 p.m. Sundays at Williamson Ranch Park, Lone Tree Way and Hillcrest Avenue. Information is available at 779-7018.

Contra Costa Times

Here are two personal items from the Hinsdale correspondent of a Massachusetts weekly newspaper:

Airman First Class Edward G. Barrett and Mrs. Barrett have returned to their home in Hampton, Va., after spending a week with their grandparents, Mr. and Mrs. Richard Boker.

The Ladies Aid Society will have a food sale during the annual town meeting this Saturday. Ethel Perth and Julia Anderson are in charge of the event. Nancy Jenkins is in charge of the snack bar where homemade doughnuts and coffee will be available. Hours are 1 p.m. to 5 p.m.

Births, engagements and weddings, awards, retirements, promotions, confirmations, bar and bat mitzvahs, appointments—all are duly recognized.

Even *The New York Times* with its million daily circulation recognizes the general interest in personals and runs pages of engagements and wedding announcements:

November wedding plans for Charlotte Ridgely Thorp and Darryl Joseph Donohue, a son of Mr. and Mrs. Robert E. Donohue of Franklin Lakes, N.J., have been announced by her parents, Mr. and Mrs. Peter C. Thorp of Bronxville, N.Y.

Miss Thorp, 26 years old, is known as Ridgely. She is an officer in the legal department at J.P. Morgan in New York. She graduated from the University of Vermont. Her father is the manager of the university relations department at Citibank in New York. . . .

Lori Ann Duggan, the daughter of Virginia Haas of Rockaway Beach, Queens, and the late Donald J. Duggan, was married in Brooklyn yesterday to David Jonathan Gold, the son of Mr. and Mrs. Hadley W. Gold of Brooklyn. Rabbi A. Bruce Goldman performed the nondenominational ceremony at the Brooklyn Botanic Garden.

Mrs. Gold, 26 years old, is the deputy director of communications for the New York City Campaign Finance Board. She graduated cum laude from New York University. Her mother is a physical therapy assistant at nursing homes in Queens. Her father was a computer specialist at the Bank of New York. . . .

The personal cements communities. It tells people about the successes, and sometimes the tribulations, of the family down the street.

Open to All

Changes have come to one of the most traditional of all sections of the newspaper. *The Star Tribune* of Minneapolis has changed the title of the "Weddings" page to "Celebrations" and now accepts announcements from gay couples. (Two small West Coast newspapers did so first.) Also, the paper said it would accept announcements by heterosexual couples who want to announce partnerships outside marriage.

The classified advertising section is changing, too. A growing number of newspapers are accepting personal ads by gay men and lesbians seeking partners.

Essentials

- Name, identification.
- Newsworthy activity.
- Connection of individual to activity.
- Special or unusual activities in connection with the event.

Personals are usually handled in a straightforward manner. If there is a special or unusual activity connected to the event, that can become the lead—the wedding held underwater, the birthday party celebrated atop a mountain.

In wedding stories, the names of the bride and groom and the location of the wedding are carried in the lead. Also essential to the story are the background of the couple and the names of the parents.

Brights

Notice those short items that make you chuckle? To journalists, these are brights—short, humorous notes to give the reader a respite from the daily barrage of starvation in Africa, turmoil in the Middle East, political strife at home.

Look back at the beginning of this chapter. In the margin is a story from Muskogee, Okla., about a minor car accident, an accident known to journalists as a fender bender.

It's a bright. In about 30 words the writer has left the reader with a smile. Quick in, quick out. That's the work of the clever writer. But don't kid yourself. Most writers agree that humorous writing is the most difficult of all writing styles.

Localizing Stories

The logic of localizing news stories is simple. Readers want to read about people and events close to them. Proximity is a basic news determinant.

A reporter is handed a wire service story that lists the names of 11 people who were killed in Ohio when the bus in which they were riding collided with a truck. Two of those who died were local residents.

The reporter calls the AP to ask if anyone from the local area was injured. He also makes a few calls to gather background on the two local people who were killed and information about the funeral arrangements.

The reporter makes sure that the names of the victims are spelled correctly. Names are often garbled in wire stories in such situations. The reporter also verifies that the people involved are actually from the home community.

Here is the wire story given to the reporter:

> YOUNGSTOWN, OHIO—Eleven people were killed when the chartered bus in which they were riding collided with a truck on U.S. 80 last night.
>
> The driver of the truck and 15 passengers were injured. The bus had been rented by a church group, the Presbyterian Fellowship League, that was holding a conference in Akron.

Witnesses told investigating officers the truck seemed to veer into the bus as the bus tried to pass it.

Names of the dead are:

Alvin Bailey, 59. . . .

The localized version begins this way:

Two local residents were killed last night when the bus in which they were passengers collided with a truck on U.S. 80 near Youngstown, Ohio.

The dead are: Alvin Bailey, 59, of 12 Belford Place and Charlene Dearborn, 21, of 68 Topper St.

The Associated Press reports they were attending . . .

Essentials

- Name of local person or situation that justifies localizing.
- General situation or background.
- Source of information—name of wire service or organization.

Reports of national organizations and government agencies provide reporters with considerable material that can be localized. A national insurance group lists cities' fire rates; the FBI's annual publication "Crime in the United States" contains the crime rates of all major cities in seven categories of crime; there are reports for automobile fatalities by state, poverty and unemployment rates and a vast variety of social and economic data.

The U.S. Department of Education and state education offices release large amounts of information that can be used to compare your state with neighboring states and the national averages. One comparison that is often made is among state teacher salaries. A recent federal report showed Alaska with the highest average teacher salary, in excess of $42,000; Arkansas had the lowest at $22,000. Other comparisons can be made using expenditures per pupil, student-teacher ratio, the graduation and dropout rates, SAT and ACT scores.

The next step could be to make correlations between the high-scoring states and teacher salaries, student-teacher ratios and so on. Contrary to expectations, the states with the highest paid teachers and the largest expenditures per pupil do not have the highest scoring students. Utah, which had the lowest per-pupil expenditure, had the highest scoring students on the College Board's Advanced Placement Tests, studies show.

Some correlations do seem logical:

		Minority Students (%)	Students Living in Poverty (%)	Per Capita Income ($)
High Scoring	New Hampshire	2.0	8.9	19,434
	Iowa	5.0	10.8	14,662
	Wisconsin	13.0	9.6	15,524
Low Scoring	Mississippi	56.0	30.4	11,116
	North Carolina	32.0	17.8	14,304

You can obtain information about the 50 states by writing to the U.S. Department of Education, Washington, D.C. 20202–0120. Your U.S. representative's office can also request material for you.

Follow-Up Stories

A **folo** is a story that follows up on a theme of another story. If a national educational organization reports that a growing percentage of high school graduates is putting off college, the enterprising reporter calls area high schools, junior colleges and four-year schools to gather information for a folo. Folos often run the day after the original story appears.

When Congress considered adopting a budget that would have cut services to the poor, reporters sought to determine the local consequences. Here is how one newswriter began her folo:

Needy local residents would be severely hurt by proposals in Congress that would cut and restrict many federal programs.

This was the opinion of officials of several public and private organizations concerned with social, economic and health services for the poor here.

Margaret Murtagh, executive secretary of the Family and Children's Services agency, a private organization, said:

"Half of the proposed reductions affect the poor. The budget seems to single these people out."

Another local agency, the Hospital

Some people sit at home and paste stamps into albums while others fly model airplanes. Most hobbies are perfectly safe. But some people climb treacherous mountains. Why?

This question occurred to several editors after an icefall entombed 11 mountain climbers under 70 feet of ice on Mount Rainier one Sunday in June; just a few hours later five others died when their climbing party plummeted 2,000 feet down Mount Hood.

Reporters were told to find some local mountain climbers. The climbers' answers made an interesting folo to the wire stories of the tragedies:

Contrary to the view of one well-known mountain climber, climbers do not attempt to scale mountains just because they are there.

"First, you have the beauty," said John Simac, 78 Harper Ave., who has climbed Mount Rainier in the state of Washington a dozen times, as well as other mountains.

"Then you have the challenge. Sometimes, it is almost too great," Simac said.

Then the challenge defeats the climber with frostbite and frustration. But sometimes the loss is greater. Last Sunday, 11 men climbing Mount Rainier were entombed when. . . .

Notice the insertion in the fourth paragraph of the **news peg,** the reason for the folo.

Essentials

- Reaction, response, local aspect of an event.
- Event or situation that gives the folo its news peg.

The *Boston Herald* jumped on a story involving the city administration after it issued a dress code for city hall employees. The dress code contained the following provision for female city employees:

Wearing apparel must be clean, neat and of a "business look" nature. Pants suits, dungarees, slacks or shorts will not be permitted at any time.

As soon as the code was issued, the *Herald* assigned reporters to do a story on the new code. The newspaper also assigned a reporter to ask fashion designers for their reactions.

If the reaction story had appeared the next day, it would have been a folo. But since the reporter was able to report and write the story so quickly, the reaction appeared alongside the story about the code. The accompanying story became a **sidebar** to the main story.

Sidebars

A **sidebar** is a story that emphasizes an aspect of another story that is printed nearby. When Bonnie Britt did a series of articles for the *Houston Chronicle* on the dangers of insulation used in the construction of mobile homes, she wanted to get the reaction of the mobile home industry, which was being sued by a number of Texas mobile home owners.

Britt sought out the attorney for the industry. Although he was unwilling to comment, Britt dug into his background for the following sidebar that appeared next to one of her articles in the series:

One of the ironies in the formaldehyde story is the involvement of Former Atty. Gen. John Hill, who while in office obtained 440 injunctions and $5 million in civil penalties against polluters.

Hill is the lead attorney hired to defend the Texas mobile home industry in the 70 or so lawsuits filed by mobile home buyers irritated by indoor pollutants.

The second irony underlying Hill's defense of the industry is that formaldehyde irritation struck close to home. In this case, his grandchildren's home. Hill's grandchildren (ages 1 and 4) became sick after exposure to urea formaldehyde foam insulation in their parents' brick home, according to plaintiff attorneys Robert Bennett and Andy Vickery.

When asked why he would take so prominent a role in the cases if this were true, Hill would only say "No comment." . . .

The essentials for the sidebar are the same as those for the folo. The news peg of the original story and the reaction or response are placed high up.

Roundups

The **roundup** is frequently used to combine several stories into one. The roundup is based on finding an element common to two or more events and then writing a lead that reflects the common element.

Roundups are frequently used for weather and traffic accident stories. You can spot them after a busy weekend or a holiday or when bad weather has caused a number of accidents:

Crews in North Dakota found the bodies of two people yesterday who died in a blizzard that dumped up to 25 inches of snow. The same blizzard paralyzed northeastern Wyoming, where it claimed three lives. Further east, thunderstorms raged over Tennessee, leaving one man dead and another critically injured after they were struck by lightning.

—AP

Essentials

- Lead that focuses on a common element.
- Body that takes each incident or event in turn.
- Causes, consequences, quotes inserted high in story if they explain the situation.

Weather Stories

The spectators in the large auditorium were filing out after having watched the second round of competition for Miss Iowa. The lines moved slowly, and people were chatting. But they weren't talking about Miss Muscatine's chances of making it to the finals or the fact that Miss Dubuque seemed embarrassed about parading in front of a few thousand people in a bikini.

They were looking out the windows of the auditorium watching a hailstorm gather force, and the talk was about the weather.

"It'll tear up the beans pretty bad," one man said. "Wind like that is worse than hail when you come down to it."

Everyone is interested in weather, at home and away. The traveler going to California wonders what the weather is like in San Francisco, and the Florida-bound family checks to see whether the Christmas holiday will be spent under blue skies in 80-degree weather.

Most of us have friends or relatives in other cities and states. When a wind-storm hits Washington, a flood strikes the midwestern states or a drought wilts crops in the Southwest, we are concerned.

Newspapers respond to this concern. They publish half-page weather maps in color, and radio stations flood us with weather reports every 10 minutes. Television has a popular all-weather channel.

Weather stories are often routinely written but they need not be. When a heavy snowfall hit New York City, Meyer Berger, a gifted writer who covered local news for *The New York Times,* wrote that the storm "left tremendous drifts in the countryside, and in main urban avenues it veiled skylines, tufting sky-scrapers and steeples with enormous white caps."

Hot and Cold

The many faces of weather make for good stories. In the summer, the fire departments of large cities will turn on hydrants to cool off inner-city children. In winter, sudden snowstorms can block highways and leave motorists stranded.

Richard Childress, The Baltimore Sun

Jay Koelzer, The Rocky Mountain News

H. Allen Smith of the *New York World-Telegram* wrote a weather forecast that has become what may be the most-celebrated one-liner in all of journalism:

> Snow, followed by small boys on sleds.

As you can see, there are two types of weather stories: the daily forecast and the longer piece about unusual or extreme weather. Here are the essentials for both types:

Essentials

- Forecast for next 24 hours.
- Long-range forecast.
- Most recent temperatures, humidity and precipitation.
- Record highs and lows, if any.

When weather is severe, the writer must consider the consequences. The effects are included along with the basics:

- Deaths; injuries; property damage.
- Amount of precipitation (or drought).
- Strength of wind, depth of snowfall and height of drifts.
- Any record(s) set.
- Predicted duration of severe weather.
- Consequences:
    Traffic—roads, bridges blocked; accidents.
    Travel—air, bus, rail, local travel curtailed or stopped.
    Mail—any delivery or collection changes.
    Public services—power, water and telephone outages.
    Business—crops, tourism affected; business shut down.
    Schools—closings or changed hours.
    Aid—declaration of disaster area or aid from government.

Writers try to show the consequences of unusual weather by introducing human interest. When unusually warm weather settled over western Massachusetts, *The Berkshire Eagle* reporter wrote that "large numbers of baby carriages blossomed forth on North Street and mopeds were seen putt-putting about."

Rewriting Releases

For every man and woman who works at the writer's trade there are a dozen who dabble. These are the amateurs the local United Way chapter and the Boy Scout troop select to write up their activities or call them in to the local newspaper. They send in information about the progress of the current fund drive, and they dictate the names and addresses of the new eagle scouts.

Then there are the professionals: The governor's press office says he will give a talk to the Rotary Club next Wednesday; the university information office sends a release about an award a chemistry professor has won.

Much of the material makes good news stories. In fact, at least half the contents of an average day's newspaper or newscast originates with a release from a volunteer or professional press relations person. The volunteer may not be as careful and complete as the professional who knows that his or her reputation is only as good as his or her reliability. But before information from either source is used, it must be checked.

The first check is with newspaper files. The governor might be making his first visit locally since elected; the press release did not mention that. The professor of chemistry may have recently been denied tenure; the college press office neglected to mention that.

Because other news outlets in the community will also be using the news release as the basis for stories, the news writer seeks to find an aspect or angle of the story that he or she considers unique. It may be lurking in the fifth paragraph of the release, or it may be something that turns up during the checking.

The releases of local organizations often start this way:

> The local chapter of the League of Women Voters met last night at the home of Mrs. Albert Morrison. The invited guest was Rep. Frances Gilmore of Ardmore.
>
> Rep. Gilmore spoke about impending legislation in Congress. She is on a two-week tour of her district to . . .

Avoiding a gradual drowsiness, the newswriter plows through the next two paragraphs and, yes, there in the fifth paragraph is the lead: Rep. Gilmore said she intends to vote against protective tariffs of any kind. The writer knows that because some local industry benefits from such tariffs, the lead and story are here. The writer knows he has to do some more reporting at once—question Rep. Gilmore, talk to heads of affected companies, check to see what is going on in Congress on this issue.

The Roving Reporter

Some reporters' beats are chunks of geography. A Memphis newspaper has a northern Mississippi reporter. Television stations have regional reporters. Tad Bartimus of the Associated Press covers a million square miles. Her beat is the seven states of the Rocky Mountains and the Great Plains.

"I eat in the six-stool diners where all the entrées are fried and the pizza is just as likely to come blue cheese as mozzarella because that's all the cook has in the fridge," she says. "I sleep in motor courts called 'The Sands,' and frequently I interview people who've never flown in an airplane."

Her sources range from cowboys to governors. She has interviewed coal mine operators and a 65-year-old shepherd who spends five months a year alone in the Big Horn mountains.

Bartimus, who is based in Denver, travels mostly by car. One day when her car broke down in Alamosa, Colo., she went to call for help and discovered 50

AP Photo

Tad Bartimus

Guatemalan refugees holed up in safe houses rented by Catholic nuns. The nuns were running an underground railroad from Central America to the United States.

Bartimus began to write about what became known as the sanctuary movement.

She has found changes on her beat. "Gas stations are fewer and farther between, a dying town visited last year has two more vacant storefronts this year, a friendly contact isn't available on a return trip because her husband lost his job and they've moved away.

"The wide open spaces seem to be wider, the roads longer, and there's a lot more out there. America, like it or not, has its own third world."

Summary

In this blockbuster chapter, we have emphasized the essentials of several types of stories, the non-negotiable necessities the writer must include so that readers are fully informed. But the writer must keep in mind that these essentials are only a first step in the reporting and writing process.

In addition to meeting the reader's needs for basic information, the writer has to include material that shows how this death or fire, that crime or ballgame are unique. To settle simply for the basics of any event, to report only the essentials, would deprive readers of reality, for we know that no two events or situations are alike.

Another reminder: By digging, by using imagination, the writer can make seemingly routine events more revealing than the recitation of the essentials allows. That is, the writer must look beyond the essentials in reporting as well as in writing.

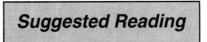

Suggested Reading

Anderson, David, ed. *The Red Smith Reader.* New York: Random House, 1983.

Denniston, Lyle. *Reporter and the Law: Techniques of Covering the Courts.* New York: Columbia University Press, 1992.

Kahn, Roger. *The Boys of Summer.* New York: Perennial Library, 1987.

Oran, Daniel. *Law Dictionary for Non-Lawyers,* 2d ed. St. Paul, Minn.: West Publishing Co., 1975.

Rapoport, Ron, ed. *A Kind of Grace: A Treasury of Sportswriting by Women.* Berkeley, Calif.: Zenobia Press, 1994.

Whitman, Alden. *Come to Judgment.* New York: Viking Press, 1980.

Wills, Garry. *Under God: Religion and American Politics.* New York: Simon & Schuster, 1990.

PART FOUR Specialties

Media workers defy classification. Public relations practitioners write news stories in the form of press releases, conduct focus groups and make presentations. Television journalists go into the field to report, rewrite the news wires and develop feature stories. News photographers write captions for their photos and practice psychology in cajoling sometimes reluctant subjects to allow their photographs to be taken.

Burson-Marsteller

11 Broadcast Writing

Broadcast journalists give viewers and listeners the latest accounts of events in the local community, from the nation's capital and from news fronts over the world. *KRON-TV*

Looking Ahead

Broadcast news is written simply and directly in everyday language and conversational style. Broadcast news writers simplify complex events, use short words in short sentences and use the present tense whenever possible. When attribution is necessary, the writer places it first in the sentence so that the listener or viewer knows at once the source of information. Broadcast journalists rewrite wire stories and report at the scene.

On-the-Scene Reporting

This morning the viewers who are tuned in to Channel 5 in Los Angeles are looking at scenes of desolation. It is seven months after the devastating earthquake hit the area. Michele Ruiz of KTLA-TV had gone out to report what has happened to L.A.'s "ghost towns," as she will describe them in her report.

The anchor of the "Morning News," Ruiz reports as well as reads.

Her report begins with her co-anchor's introduction:

> Almost seven months after the Northridge earthquake, Los Angeles is plagued by entire blocks vacant and abandoned.
> They are mostly in the San Fernando Valley—the epicenter of the quake.
> Michele Ruiz joins us from the newsroom with a report on what's being done with these ghost towns.

He looks to Ruiz and she picks up the introduction of her videotaped report:

> The City of Los Angeles has identified twelve areas as ghost towns. Most are streets lined with apartment buildings and condominiums.
> The earthquake drove out hundreds of people—now the ghost towns may take a similar toll.
> Some people who live near these areas are packing up and moving away. Some retail stores and other businesses are closing down.

The tape begins to roll and Ruiz's voice is over the scene of abandoned apartment buildings. It is a street, she reports, that is all but deserted.

> Now, vagrants and hoodlums have ransacked and vandalized the abandoned apartments, causing further damage.
> And it's not just in Northridge, but eleven other areas, too—most in the San Fernando Valley. For residents who live next to these areas they've become crime-ridden, rodent-infested nightmares.
> Lillian Wilkoff lives on Willis Street in Sherman Oaks.

Reviving the Ghost Towns

Michele Ruiz interviews an official of the Los Angeles Ghost Town Task Force about efforts to revive the earthquake-damaged communities.

The camera turns to Wilkoff, who tells Ruiz:

> I'm afraid to walk the streets in the evening. . . .

Ruiz moves on to the Hubbard-El Dorado area of Sylmar where, she reports, "when the residents moved out the prostitutes moved in." Then the tape shows a fire-damaged building. Her voice-over picks up:

> In this building, squatters started a fire that burned out some units.
> The city has hired guards and fenced off these properties to keep out vagrants and to protect residents around them.
> Some people stayed in their damaged buildings hoping repairs would be made. They are now leaving because they don't want to live in ghost towns.
> For local businesses, the situation is getting worse rather than better.

Ruiz next interviews a restaurant owner in Sherman Oaks who's struggling to keep his family's Italian restaurant open, and then she talks to a real estate broker who says some owners have walked away from their properties.

But some help is on the way for these areas, Ruiz says, in the form of the Earthquake Ghost Town Task Force. Her next taped interview is a 10-second one with an official of the task force. Then comes her close or tag:

> The city's Ghost Town Task Force is aggressively trying to get owners to make repairs to their buildings by offering financial incentives.
> With the help of the federal government, which has released 225 million dollars to be used specifically on the ghost town recovery, the task force hopes that by the end of October all these areas will be in the process of re-construction.

Next, let's move north where another TV anchor is doing some field reporting.

Human Guinea Pigs

It is an August morning in Delano, a small agricultural community in California's Kern County. Emerald Yeh and her photographer, Gary Mercer, have been on the road for three days on an assignment for KRON-TV News in San Francisco.

Yeh is a co-anchor of evening newscasts for the station, but she does more than read the news. When possible, she takes on reporting assignments. This assignment takes her to Porterville, a small town at the southeastern edge of California's San Joaquin Valley.

Yeh had heard that a chemical company was testing an insecticide called Zolone, suspected of having made 78 farm workers sick the previous year.

"The makers of the insecticide are convinced it is safe and want to prove it by sending volunteers into a field sprayed with Zolone," Yeh had told her assignment editor. Yeh was given the go-ahead to cover the experiment.

In Porterville, she interviews officials of the firm that makes Zolone, and she talks to a state agricultural official.

"I wanted to know why the state feels it's acceptable to use the human guinea pig approach and whether we can expect to see more experiments of this nature," she says.

Then she heads into the field where the volunteers are busy picking Zolone-sprayed grapes. She wants to find out who the volunteers are, how much they are being paid, why they are taking part in the test and whether they have any concerns for their health. "I needed shots of them working, too," she says.

The Story Outline The day before, Yeh had asked a pesticide expert about the Zolone experiment. "She was outraged by it," Yeh says. This comment helps balance her story from Porterville where all she has are the company's assurances the pesticide is safe.

"In my head, I had sketched out the structure of the story. In television, there are two simple rules—start with your best pictures and tell a story in a beginning-middle-end manner. There are exceptions, of course, but these effectively engage a viewer and take him through the story in a simple, clear fashion."

She lays out the story:

1. Pictures at the beginning of the volunteers in the field and Yeh's explanation of who they are and what they're doing.
2. The company's explanation of the experiment.
3. The other side.
4. Why the workers volunteered and whether they are concerned.

5. Why the state gave its OK to human subjects and whether this is the beginning of more such tests.

6. End with an indication of what the outcome of the Zolone experiment might mean for the use of the pesticide.

The Script　This is what she wrote:

(Voice-over): For the next six days, these 50 volunteers, many of them college students, will work this grapefield, exposing themselves to an insecticide called Zolone. It's part of an experiment for the makers of Zolone. Last year, 78 farmworkers got sick after working in fields sprayed with Zolone. But the manufacturer of Zolone, Rhone Poulenc, is convinced the insecticide did not cause the illness, so it's sending volunteers into sprayed grapefields to prove that.

(Sound bite. Rhone Poulenc spokesperson:) There's no conclusive evidence that exposure and illnesses were related to Zolone.

(Voice-over:) The state food and agriculture department, which gave permission for the test, believes Zolone did cause the workers to get sick, but feels that reduced amounts can be safely used. That's also what this test is for. But some health experts are appalled.

(Sound bite. Dr. Marian Moses:) You don't bring it out here and try it on human beings. You just don't do it. Period.

(Voice over:) The volunteers say they need the money—60 to 100 dollars a day. They signed a consent . . . .

Yeh then is shown interviewing a volunteer who says, "Hasn't killed any of the pickers yet, has it?" And she quotes a state official who says the state probably will do more human testing:

(Sound bite. State official:) The only way to get meaningful human data is by looking at people. There's no animal model that we can turn loose in the grape vineyard and predict what human exposure might be.

Then Yeh closes her report:

(Voice over:) It's costing the Zolone-makers half a million dollars for this test, but many growers say whatever the test turns up, they won't use Zolone again, that it's just too dangerous. Reporting in Porterville in the Central Valley, Emerald Yeh, Newscenter Four.

The report is brief, to the point and clear. Although for the most part broadcast writing is for the ear, its goals—clarity, accuracy, fairness and balance, honesty of expression—are the same as those of print writing, which is mostly for the eye. But there are, as we can see from Yeh's reporting and writing, differences between print and broadcast writing in the application of these principles.

Reporting is not Yeh's major activity at KRON-TV4. Most of her work consists of rewriting material from the news wires and overseeing the script for her newscast. For the great majority of radio and television writers, their work is in the office.

Writing news in the office or from the field, Ruiz and Yeh understand—and their scripts here demonstrate—that the television news story is a seamless creation. It flows naturally from introduction to scenes with voice-overs to descriptive matter and back to on-the-scene interviews. The tag or close sums up.

Writing for Listeners

Broadcast news has been described as a headline service. It is intended to give the listener or viewer an outline of the event. A half-hour newscast may have as many as 20 news items crammed into the 22 to 23 minutes allotted to news. The CBS "Newsbreak" program runs four to six items in 68 seconds. One day there were seven. That's a bit less than 10 seconds for each story, one or two sentences a story. Altogether, the news script for a "Newsbreak" program contains about 170 words, which is the equivalent of a three- to four-inch story in a newspaper.

In other words, there are more words in a routine traffic accident story in a newspaper than there are in the entire "Newsbreak." On the longer television news programs most stories have fewer words than a newspaper story about a noncontroversial appointment by the governor.

All the news on a half-hour newscast will not fill a single page of a newspaper. Clearly, the broadcast writer must be able to reduce news stories to their essence.

Clarity

Language—Broadcast news writers **use everyday words,** the language of conversation. Colloquialisms and contractions are acceptable. The style is informal.

Ideas—Broadcast writers simplify the complex by reducing the event to a central theme or idea and by avoiding secondary matter. The listener usually is informed at once of this theme. A story about the settlement of a long teacher strike might begin, "The teachers' strike is over."

Style—Broadcast writers think in short sentences, even in phrases. Long sentences cannot be read easily by an anchor nor understood by listeners. Most long sentences are broken into two sentences. Introductory phrases and clauses are not used. The S-V-O sentence construction is the backbone of the writing.

When a mayor and a city council disagree over a proposal to increase the city sales tax from 3 to 4 percent—a week after another disagreement over taxes—the radio copy of a local station begins this way:

Capsule introduction	The mayor and the city council are feuding again. This time, the issue is the city's sales tax.

Attitude Helps. "Good writing," says television journalist Linda Ellerbee, "is the basis of what television is about. Good writing is not insulting your audience; good writing is not talking down to your audience; good writing is not being arrogant. It is the most important thing there is because it will give you a seamless newscast."

Radio Miscellany. One of six radio stations has no employee devoted to gathering local news.

The number of radio station news employees is 15,000, the same number as in 1972.

News-talk stations have 16 percent of all radio listeners.

The typical radio station news staff consists of one full-time and one part-time employee.

After this brief introduction, the writer goes into the details:

Short sentences

> The city council last night turned down a proposal to increase the city sales tax from 3 percent to 4 percent. Mayor George Grogan told council members the city faces trouble unless it takes in more revenue.
>
> And the only way the mayor can see to add to revenue is to raise the sales tax.
>
> But the council voted six to one against the increase.

Count the words in the six sentences about the city council meeting. They have 9, 9, 20, 16, 18 and 10 words, short and to the point.

Attribution and Leads

Here's how the AP tells its broadcast writers to handle attribution:

> Attribution on broadcast circuits must be every bit as clear as on newspaper wires. But the use of titles is less formal and the attribution should be expressed in a conversational manner—usually at the start of a sentence, rather than hanging at the end, as in newspaper copy.
>
> Thus, "The National Aeronautics and Space Administration" becomes "NASA" or "the space agency" on first reference, and it's worked into the story where it falls naturally.

Consider these examples:

Newspaper style

> Seven people died and 35 were injured in a bus crash on a slippery highway outside New York City today, the Metropolitan Transportation Authority said.

Broadcast style

> A TRANSIT BUS CRASHED ON A SLIPPERY HIGHWAY OUTSIDE NEW YORK CITY, AND THE TRANSIT AUTHORITY SAYS SEVEN PEOPLE WERE KILLED. AND 35 WERE HURT.

Do not begin a story with the name of an unknown person. If you must, precede the name with the person's title or some identifying label. You can begin with a name if the person has what Mervin Block, a broadcast newswriter and writing coach, calls "star quality." That means the president, the pope, the governor of your state, a senator or congressman, your mayor.

When he was writing a story about the death of Robert Moses, Block realized few listeners would be familiar with his subject. Moses had built many of New York City's major highways and a number of its major buildings, but he had been out of public life for many years. Here is how Block begins the obituary:

> The man credited with building even more than the Pharaohs of Egypt—Robert Moses—died in a New York City suburb today at the age of 92.

Here the identifying label is an arresting description. People will listen.

Broadcast news writers not only avoid long leads and leads with unfamiliar names, they also avoid leads that begin with quotations. The listener cannot see or hear quotation marks and may think the words are those of the broadcaster.

Here is the AP's advice on leads to its broadcast writers:

> The shorter the better. The function of the broadcast lead is to capture the listener's interest by providing the essence of the story's status at that hour.
>
> Don't summarize the day's major development in a long, complex sentence. Instead, provide a short and compelling reason for the listener to keep listening.

Immediacy

Broadcast writers frequently use the **present tense** in their leads. The reason for using the present tense is simple. Broadcast news is supposed to give the listener or viewer a sense of immediacy, of events being covered as they happen.

Sometimes, the present tense would sound silly, so the writer has to use the past tense. Evening news programs use the past tense when looking back on events that occurred during the day.

If the mayor announced at a noon news conference that he will not seek re-election, the radio news account will begin this way:

> Mayor George Grogan **says** he will not seek re-election. The mayor **made** his intention clear at noon today in a news conference. He **said** he wants to go back to running the family business.

Summary

We have seen that broadcast news is written in simple, conversational language. The sentences are short, and they are usually in the S-V-O form.

Every word has a purpose. Broadcast news is timed to the word. No lengthy phrases and clauses to begin sentences. When a source is being used, the source is put at the beginning of the sentence. Action verbs. Few adjectives or adverbs.

Unnecessary introductory phrase

Weak—Stressing the increased number of cars on campus, the Student Council has asked for more parking spaces near dormitories.

Improved—The Student Council wants more parking spaces near student dormitories.

Attribution placed incorrectly	**Weak**—There are two cars for every parking space, says Student Council President Tom Jarrett.
	Improved—Student Council President Tom Jarrett says there are two cars for every parking space.
Action verb lacking	**Weak**—The Council was unanimous in its vote for the proposal.
	Improved—The Council voted unanimously for the proposal.
Unnecessary adjective	**Weak**—Dean Albert Levine reacted with strong criticism to the vote.
	Improved—Dean Albert Levine criticized the vote. (Or: Dean Albert Levine condemned the vote.)

Rewriting the Wires

News Wire	Broadcast Account
DALLAS (AP)—Grade-school children who watch two hours of television a day are at increased risk of having high cholesterol levels, and the risk climbs the more they watch, researchers said Tuesday. Children watching television four hours a day are four times as likely to have high cholesterols as are children who watch less than two hours, the researchers reported. Previous research showed that children who watched too much television exercised less, were overweight and had bad diets. "We made the next step—to look at TV and cholesterol," said Thomas K. Hei, who reported the findings at the annual meeting of the American Heart Association. "The message is if you can't get your children to stop watching TV, maybe get them to exercise more and keep them from unhealthy food," said Hei, a student at the University of California, Irvine. The study of 1,077 suburban Southern California children demonstrated that television habits are the best clue to identifying children with high cholesterol, said Dr. Kurt V. Gold of the University of California, Irvine, who directed the study. . . .	A new study says grade-school children who watch T-V two hours a day are at increased risk of higher cholesterol. And the more they watch, the study says, the more the risk goes up. The average American child reportedly watches T-V more than three hours a day. The study was done by researchers at the University of California--Irvine, and it covered a thousand suburban children.

Although radio and television stations have staff members who report, much broadcast news originates from outside the station. Except for the networks, which have bureaus in some major foreign capitals and in large U.S. cities, most stations rely on the AP and UPI for their national and foreign news and for most state and regional news.

Most stations subscribe to a broadcast wire and use the material as is. Large stations usually subscribe to both the AP and UPI main trunk wires because the stories usually provide more information than do the broadcast wire versions. The stations' writers rewrite wire copy for broadcast.

Another reason bigger stations rewrite the main or A news wires is that news directors prefer that their writers see the original story, before it has been filtered by a broadcast rewrite person at the wire service. The wire service rewrite may neglect an aspect of special interest to local listeners.

Examine the differences between the original news wire copy from Dallas and the rewritten broadcast account at the beginning of this section on the opposite page.

The news wire story continues for a dozen more paragraphs. The four sentences of the broadcast account contain 67 words, an average of 16 to 17 words to a sentence. The six sentences of the wire story have 175 words, 29 to 30 words a sentence.

When stories are rewritten from the AP and UPI wires for television newscasts, they are described as **tell stories** or **readers.** The anchor *tells* the listener about them instead of showing tape produced by the staff. Tell stories do not excite viewers, broadcast people believe. So the tell story must be as brief as possible. Few tell stories run more than 20 or 30 seconds, which limits them to 50 to 75 words, the equivalent of one newspaper paragraph.

Under Pressure: 30 Minutes to Deadline

In the CBS network newsroom in New York an urgent story—a dogfight between U.S. and Libyan jets—caught Mervin Block's attention. Block had to boil down thousands of words from wire stories to about 135 words. After his last glance at the wires for late-breaking material, he went to the keyboard. He had half an hour to write. He knew he had to tell one essential fact—U.S. planes had downed two Libyan jets.

"There are some things I would change now," he says. "Maybe I would use plane instead of craft on the first page of copy. But in broadcasting there are no second chances. I was reading a book the other day with the title *Done in a Day,* about newspapers. It describes the work to be done, all in a day, to produce a newspaper.

"But in broadcasting it's done in minutes, sometimes seconds."

Block says he tries to use ordinary language—at one point he used *taking part* instead of *participating*—and he tries to write short sentences that conform to the S-V-O pattern.

Block's script and his comments are on the next page.

BLOCK'S COMMENTS	SCRIPT
This headline--admittedly a fragmentary sentence--gives the viewer a quick preview. The wire services said "off the coast of North Africa," but I jettisoned "the coast of" as needless. Near the top, I cite the source of the story. In broadcasting, attribution precedes assertion. Again, I took pains to name the source for the second assertion. My producer, however, might have thought the second sourcing was redundant, and he deleted it. Or he thought I was running long. Apparently, no reporter saw the dogfight, so we must make clear who told us. The wires quoted the Department of Defense, but I condensed it to "Pentagon," which has more punch. The wires also quoted the State Department; I reduced that to "Washington." We're constantly struggling for tighter scripts, even on two-hour newscasts. Although a viewer can't see quotation marks, I use them so the anchor can change his delivery. I use direct quotations seldom, and I say "quote" or "unquote" rarely.	A jet battle off North Africa: The Pentagon says two Libyan jets fighters attacked two U-S Navy F-14 jets over the Mediterranean today. and the ~~Pentagon says the~~ Navy jets shot down both Libyan craft. Washington says the attack against the U-S jets was ''unprovoked'' and that it took place in ''international air space over international waters.'' Libya says the U-S jets violated air space over its waters, but Washington does not recognize
After I gave the gist of the accusation, I reported the other side's response. And I tacked on a bit of background about the territorial claim. I couldn't take time to elaborate on the claim or to report on U.S.-Libyan relations. Nor did I waste time with name-dropping or name-calling. Until now, I hadn't identified the type of U-S jet. At 11:57 a.m., most of our viewers are probably housewives, and, chances are, few, if any, know an F-14 from an F-4 or even a 4-F. The wires said the Nimitz is nuclear-powered, but I saw no need to waste words about its propulsion. The AP said the encounter was "60 nautical miles" off Libya. I know that a nautical mile is about a mile and a seventh, which would make it nearly 70 miles. I wrote "almost"; years ago, my editor on the CBS Evening News told me an anchor can get a better grasp on "almost." That editor also told me, repeatedly, that viewers are only half-listening. So I strive for simplicity. My maxim: Make it minimal. That's one reason that in the first sentence I didn't mention "F-14." But the director dug up a photo of an F-14, so he prevailed upon the producer to insert "F-14" high up. He obliged, and I was shot down.	Libya's territorial claim. The U-S jets, Ef-fourteen Tomcats from the carrier Nimitz, were taking part in Sixth fleet exercises. The Navy says its jets were almost seventy miles off Libya when the Soviet-made Libyan jets fired at them. The Navy says neither of its planes was hit. The State Department has protested, and it warned Libya against any new attack.

Let's move over to another news operation at CBS. It is 5:30 p.m. according to the wall clock of the CBS Broadcast Center at West 57th Street. It's almost an hour before air time for the "CBS Evening News" and we have to hurry to catch the preparations. Through the lobby, down a long corridor, a set of double doors opens into a two-story studio.

The "CBS Evening News"

It is quiet in the pale blue studio. At one side, behind large glass panels, is the executive producer's room. Dan Rather, the anchorman for the "Evening News," is going over the program with the producer. From time to time, Rather emerges to talk to the writers who are seated at a large desk in the middle of the studio.

The Writers

The writers have been at work since 10 in the morning. First, they read several newspapers—*The New York Times, The Washington Post, The Wall Street Journal* and the *Daily News.* Then they scanned the news wires. Each writer has a different area of responsibility: One handles national news; another, foreign news; a third, features, disasters and obituaries.

The writers look for news items that could make interesting features and takeouts. They also are conscious of the visual possibilities of each story they examine. A **tell** story, also called a **reader,** in which the anchor reads from a script is not as interesting to viewers as a story accompanied by action videotape.

Tell stories, therefore, are written tightly. A writer may collect several thousand words for such a story and reduce them to 50 words for the anchor. Stories with action videotape may run five or six times as long.

By midafternoon, the program has taken shape. The news items for the 22 minutes of air time have been selected, and the editor and executive producer discuss how much time each story will be given. Air time approaches.

Minutes to Go

5:58—Rather leaves the executive producer's office. He is holding a sheaf of papers, the items he will read for the "Evening News." He manages to chomp on his cigar as he reads the script aloud. He is trim and vigorous.

6:02—Rather turns to one of his writers and asks about a lawsuit. "You think we should explain this?" Rather asks a writer for the program. "If we do, we'll need 10 or 15 more seconds." The writer thinks for a few seconds, agrees and starts writing.

6:04—Lineup item No. 22, a tell story, displeases Rather. He discusses some of the wording with a writer. The item runs for 20 seconds and is 50 words long. They agree on new wording.

6:05—"Ten is out," someone shouts, and item 10 is scratched to make room for the additional material in the lawsuit story.

Wanted: Writers. The Help Wanted News section of *Broadcasting* magazine lists the qualifications of people stations seek. Here are some phrases from the section:

- top-notch writer
- best writing and production skills
- a reporter who can do journalism
- crisp, clear writing
- journalist first and on-air talent second
- strong writing abilities

TV News Guidelines

Av Westin, executive producer of the "ABC Evening News" wrote his staff:

The Evening News, as you know, works on elimination. We can't include everything. As criteria for what we do include, I suggest the following for a satisfied viewer: (1) "Are my world, nation, and city safe?" (2) "Are my home and family safe?" (3) "If they are safe, then what has happened in the past 24 hours to make that world better?" (4) "What has happened in the past 24 hours to help us cope better?"

Final Editing

CBS newsman Dan Rather goes over his evening newscast just before broadcast time, making changes to reflect late-breaking news. *CBS News Photo*

6:08—The camera crew begins to position itself around the room, and the two people running the prompter machines go over the script. The machines project large type directly in front of Rather so that, although he appears to the viewer to be looking directly into the camera, he is reading from the script projected in front of him.

6:10—Rather looks up from editing the lead-all, the first item in the newscast. "Very nice lead," he tells the writer and resumes reading.

6:11—A woman dashes out of the executive producer's office. "We have an emergency," she says. "We need something from the archives." File footage is necessary for a particular news item. It may not be used, but the producer wants to have it available.

6:14—Rather detects an ambiguous statement in one of the stories and asks the writer to clarify it.

6:15—A sudden hush descends on the studio as everyone studies the script.

In the control room, seven people are jammed together at a console, each one talking. In the middle front row is the director. He will cue the cameras as they focus on Rather and give other cues as the visuals, remotes and videotapes pop on and off the screen.

The goal of the control room staff is to have a tight program, to move neatly from Rather to a Washington correspondent without dead air, without cutting Rather off too soon; to synchronize the visuals that are the backdrop as Rather describes a spot in the Pacific (a map appears), a planet (a picture of Saturn looms over his left shoulder), a labor union (its emblem is shown).

6:23—Rather sits in front of a small mirror and is made up. He applies the lip rouge himself.

6:24—Rather shouts, "Sandy, you've got to pump that audio way up." Silence again.

6:25—"Five minutes," the stage manager calls out.

6:29—Rather settles into his chair, again reading the script to himself. This time his lips are immobile.

"Thirty seconds." The deep voice booms throughout the studio and over a loudspeaker in the control room where the hubbub suddenly ceases. The people at the various panels prepare countdowns to cue the announcer, Rather, the videotape recorder, correspondents and the visuals. "Ten seconds."

On the Air

Rather opens the program with a summary of the three major news items on his half hour:

> A new vaccine that may help slow the damage of AIDS.
> In the Philippines, 30,000 run for their lives as an angry volcano shows its stuff.
> Also, a new report says small cars may not be all they're cracked up to be.

Then a snatch of the music theme and Rather is into the news:

> This is the CBS Evening News, Dan Rather reporting. Good evening.
> There is encouraging word tonight about an experimental AIDS vaccine.
> It shows promise in helping to slow AIDS' attack on the immune system. I
> want to stress the vaccine is not a cure, and it cannot prevent AIDS. CBS
> health correspondent Edie Magnus has more on what the experimental vaccine
> means to AIDS patients.

Magnus takes over with an interview with an AIDS patient, introducing human interest into the report:

> No one is more hopeful about today's news on AIDS than Army Specialist
> Mitch Cantrell. Over the past two years, he's been getting injections of a
> vaccine called gp-160. Cantrell is among 19 of 30 volunteer patients in the
> early stages of the disease. . . .

Preparing Broadcast Copy

Radio and television copy are prepared in different formats. Since standard reading time is 150 words a minute and radio copy usually is written to 10 words a line, the news reader can glance at the copy and estimate how long it will take to read the story.

Preparing television copy is a more complicated affair. This is what Lauren Thierry, an experienced television journalist, does:

> I type my script into my computer, which automatically writes on one side
> of the page only, the right side. This side also has cue lines to tell the anchor to
> stop for a soundbite—it will say SOT (sound on tape)—and a line indicating
> when the SOT is about to stop so the anchor can pick up.
> On the left side are all cues for the director's use.
> The script is printed on a multi-page printer and copies go to the producer,
> the director, the audio engineer. The prompter copy is computer-generated
> directly into the camera lens.

Style Rules

These rules have been used by broadcast news writers for many years to avoid confusing the announcer reading the copy and to help listeners quickly grasp what they hear:

- **Numbers** are spelled out.
- **Abbreviations** are not used.
- **Titles** are placed before names.
- **Initials** of agencies and organizations are not used unless they are widely known.
- **Quotes** are clearly introduced as direct quotes: "As the senator put it," "In the words of the president," "To quote the prime minister."

From the Bowels of Hell

When General Patton's Third Army reached Buchenwald, the correspondents accompanying the troops were shown the Nazi death camp. They saw hundreds of bodies stacked up because in the last days of the war the Germans had run out of coal to burn their victims. The reporters saw the gold teeth extracted from bodies, the lampshades made of human skin and the piles of human hair and clothing near the crematorium where the bodies of gassed men and children had been incinerated.

One of the reporters was Edward R. Murrow, a CBS correspondent. He was escorted by a camp doctor and their first stop was a barrack occupied by 1,200 men, five to a bunk. It had once been a stable for 80 horses. One of the pajamaed figures staggered up to Murrow. "You remember me," he said. "I'm Peter Zenkl, once mayor of Prague." Murrow remembered Zenkl but did not recognize him. Others went up to him, some simply to touch him. "Professors from Poland," he recalled later, "doctors from Vienna, men from all Europe. Men from the countries that made America."

They entered a courtyard and then the crematorium; Murrow's insides rumbled and heaved. He forced himself to look and to count, and his report became one of the most famous in broadcast history:

> There were two rows of bodies stacked up like cordwood. They were thin and very white. Some of the bodies were terribly bruised, though there seemed little flesh to bruise. . . .
> All except two were naked. I tried to count them as best I could and arrived at the conclusion that all that was mortal of more than five hundred men and boys lay there in two neat piles. . . .
> God alone knows how many men and boys have died there during the last twelve years. . . . I was told there were more than 20,000 in the camp. There had been as many as 60,000. Where are they now?

Murrow had to fight his impulse to turn away. He forced himself to look at the torture chambers and, worst of all, to stand before the stacks of children's shoes—shoes in the thousands.

Later, he said that he could describe a pair of shoes or a few pair. But how could he communicate the enormity of the horror he was seeing? Somehow he managed, and he closed with these remarks:

> I pray you to believe what I have said about Buchenwald.
> I have reported what I saw and heard, but only part of it. For most of it, I have no words. Dead men are plentiful in war, but the living dead
> . . .
> If I've offended you by this rather mild account of Buchenwald, I'm not in the least sorry. . . .
> Murder has been done at Buchenwald. I reported what I saw and heard.

Broadcast Career Necessities

For those considering careers in broadcast journalism, the ability to write well under pressure is essential. But mastery of the writing craft is not enough, Block says. "The writer has to have a wide knowledge. He or she should know what is going on in the world. Also, the writer should understand how things work—government, the criminal justice process, zoning boards, state government."

Ruiz and Yeh, both graduates of journalism programs, say they have never stopped learning. They read widely and constantly monitor their performances for content. Since they are called on for a wide variety of assignments, they know they must have a grasp of many and diverse subject matters.

"The data bank in the writer's mind has to have a jillion bits of information because the writer must be able to retrieve a lot of data, and do it almost subconsciously," says Block.

For television reporters who do on-camera reports, the ability to organize a story quickly is essential. Often, TV reporters covering breaking stories have to go on the air live.

The best way to do this, says John Chancellor, a veteran NBC-TV journalist, is to make a brief outline of what is to be said. "The whole story needn't be outlined," he says, "but the lead and the closing line should be settled." He says that a few minutes on an outline will pay off with "a very well organized piece of work."

Writing skills, broad knowledge and organizational skills are important, but the successful broadcast journalist is, above all, a good reporter. Good reporting makes for good writing. Good writing cannot make up for weak or lazy reporting.

When WCPO-TV in Cincinnati learned that a hospital orderly who was accused of killing one man was also implicated in 20 other deaths at the hospital, the station decided to investigate. "We worked very hard. We worked very carefully," said Terry Connelly, the general manager. "We spent many months on it."

The result was a half-hour newscast based on the station's three-month investigation. The reporters linked the orderly to a score of deaths. "No one else had done the legwork so we were three months ahead of everybody," said the news director.

A grand jury investigation followed the newscast, and soon the orderly pleaded guilty to 24 murders and was connected to as many as 70 other deaths.

The Angel of Death, as he was described, was sentenced to three consecutive life sentences.

Suggested Reading

Barnouw, Erik. *Tube of Plenty: The Evolution of American Television.* New York: Oxford University Press, 1975.

Block, Mervin. *Rewriting Network News: WordWatching Tips from 345 TV and Radio Scripts.* Chicago: Bonus Books, 1990.

Block, Mervin. *Writing Broadcast News—Shorter, Sharper, Stronger.* Chicago: Bonus Books, 1987.

Block, Mervin. *Broadcast Newswriting: The RTNDA Reference Guide.* Chicago: Bonus Books, Inc. and Radio-Television News Directors Association, 1994.

Donaldson, Sam. *Hold On, Mr. President.* New York: Random House, Inc., 1987.

Ellerbee, Linda. *And So It Goes: Adventures in Television.* New York: G.P. Putnam's Sons, 1986.

Goldenson, Leonard H. with Marvin J. Wolf. *Beating the Odds: The Untold Story Behind the Rise of ABC.* New York: Charles Scribner's Sons, 1991.

Gunther, Marc. *The House That Roone Built: The Inside Story of ABC News.* Boston: Little, Brown & Company, 1994.

Kimball, Penn. *Downsizing the News: Network Cutbacks in the Nation's Capital.* Baltimore: The Johns Hopkins University Press, 1994.

Mickelson, Sig. *From Whistle Stop to Sound Booth: Four Decades of Politics and Television.* New York: Praeger Publishers, 1989.

Paisner, Daniel. *The Imperfect Mirror: Inside Stories of Television Newswomen.* New York: Morrow, 1989.

Rather, Dan. *The Camera Never Blinks.* New York: William Morrow, 1977.

Smith, Sally Bedell. *In All His Glory: The Life of William S. Paley.* New York: Simon & Schuster, 1990.

Sperber, Ann M. *Murrow: His Life and Times.* New York: Freundlich Books, 1986.

12 Visual Reporting

Photojournalists show us the human condition—our triumphs and our failures, our joys and our sorrows. They take us places we cannot go. Here, Bob Thayer of *The Providence Journal* puts us in the wings of the Rhode Island Festival Ballet alongside a young ballerina as she is about to make her debut. This photo has won many prizes. *Bob Thayer, The Providence Journal–Bulletin*

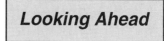

Looking Ahead

Photojournalists are reporters of a different kind. They provide us with pictures that give us information and insights about people, events and ideas that words alone cannot convey. Their photographs reflect an understanding of how people live, work and play. Through their sure grasp of the technical aspect of the craft, they provide news and feature photographs that are truthful, informative and interesting. The photojournalist's work can be educational and entertaining as well.

Pals

The photograph can help us share private moments. As evening settles in, a youngster chats with his horse after a day's ride. "The boy would spend long periods talking to his horse, and the horse seemed to know the boy had special needs and seemed particularly gentle with him," says Bob Thayer, the photographer. The photograph was part of a photo essay on the world of a blind boy. for *The Providence Journal– Bulletin*

The Picture Is Universal

From earliest times, people have used images to record their thoughts and experiences—hunters etched animals on the walls of caves, mourning women scratched figures on pottery. Modern men and women make pictures, too, millions of them. We also place them on our walls. And we send them off to distant friends and relatives. Pictures tell our stories. They are a universal language.

Pictures extend our reach. They allow us to see events that have passed into history, to travel to places we will never visit, to experience the emotions of others. They communicate feelings, set moods. Dorothea Lange's photos of migrant workers and their families take us back more than half a century to the Depression, showing us haunting faces, aged by adversity, looking into a future without hope.

Today's picture-storytellers work for newspapers, magazines and television stations. These photojournalists combine the skills of journalist and photographer. While the writer seeks to capture the essence of the event in words, the photojournalist uses the camera to capture the essence of the event in visual terms. On small dailies and weekly newspapers, reporters are expected to take photographs to illustrate their stories.

Photographs reveal as well as inform. They let us live with people different from us, experience events half a world away. They put us in touch with hidden objects, things too small and too fast for the eye and brain to capture in their natural state. They hold for us the leap of the ballet dancer, the kick of the fetus in the mother's womb, the finish of a close race.

The photojournalist's picture enables us to understand and emotionally identify with the event. By using scene or setting and the expression, gesture and body language of those in the picture, the photojournalist communicates with us at a personal level. Sometimes, a news photograph comes to symbolize the issues and the problems of a period in history.

The Ingredients of a Good Photo

The photographs in this book show us something about what makes a good picture, and they reveal something about what it takes to be a good photojournalist.

A good picture is first a truthful portrayal of an event. It is a pictorial record of the event the photojournalist is reporting. The good photograph is also interesting and informative, and sometimes it is educational. It may be entertaining as well. The good photograph has impact, a message. It is technically sound and aesthetically right. It has a point of interest, a focus.

The good photograph makes proper use of light and shadow. There is logic and there is rhythm in the good photograph.

Some photographs reach us in the same way that a song or symphony, a novel or short story touches us. The news photo of the death throes of the battleship

Arizona at Pearl Harbor portrays a humbled United States and the beginning of a struggle for survival with a powerful adversary.

Arthur Rothstein's famous picture of a farmer and his sons making their way through swirling sands became a symbol of the struggle of the country's farmers when the blowing soil made the Southwest into a dust bowl. The barefoot boys, the younger one shielding his eyes against the stinging sands, the father's shapeless clothing and the hopelessness of his slouch tell the story. Photographs like this one made the public aware of the need for rehabilitation of rural areas and led Congress to adopt new farm legislation.

Morris Berman's prizewinning photo of a sacked quarterback transcends the game and the season. The quarterback's sagging body and his agonized face tell us he knows his speed and agility are gone, that his body will no longer respond.

U.S. Navy

Arthur Rothstein, The Library of Congress

Morris Berman, Pittsburgh Post-Gazette

Three Memorable Photographs

The Tools of the Photojournalist

The photojournalist blends an understanding of people and events with technical competence to freeze a message in visual form. The knowledge of how "human beings live, work and play," said Rothstein, enables the photojournalist to portray events and ideas "in unusual visual terms."

That knowledge must be built on sensitivity, the capacity to identify with what is being photographed. "Every photographer in each situation becomes a vicarious participant in the event," says Michael Geissinger of the photography faculty at the Rochester Institute of Technology. The news photo of a woman awaiting word about men trapped in a Centralia, Ill., mine shaft is "an example of the emotion a photographer must experience in order to produce a profound picture," Geissinger says. (See next page.)

Commonality. "Our best photography of actual events . . . stress(es) a common human element in any situation, the drama, comedy or tragedy of the human condition."

—*Hans Koning*

Focus on Reality

"I'm not a photographer. I'm a journalist."

—*Robert Capa*

"He [Capa] meant that he was out to report the facts of the wars he covered in Spain, France, Italy, China, Israel, and Indochina—his life's intinerary—and not to make those facts beautiful."

—*Roger Rosenblatt*

The photograph portrays the grief and tension of one woman. But it represents all those who look fearfully into the unknown. The harsh and cutting light, the "pitiful hands that don't seem to know what to do with each other," as Claude Cookman of Indiana University says, the eyes focused on some awful scene as much in her mind as in front of her—all these prepare us for the awful news of death underground. The explosion took the lives of 111 miners.

The Face of Anguish

A photo of someone's reaction to an event can tell us as much as a photo of the event itself. Sam Caldwell of the *St. Louis Post-Dispatch* found a face in the crowd of relatives and friends waiting outside Centralia No. 5 mine. An explosion in a shaft 540 feet below the surface had trapped the miners. The toll was 111 dead. *Sam Caldwell, The St. Louis Post-Dispatch*

Content and Treatment

Cookman, a picture and graphics editor with AP Wirephoto and *The Louisville Times* and *The Miami Herald,* says, "Every photo incorporates at least two aspects: content and pictorial treatment." The high quality photo emerges when photographers know what they want to say and use their ability, techniques and craft to say it.

Photojournalists have impressive technology at their disposal. "But these techniques are used only to obtain more freedom, to make the mechanics of taking a picture so simple that they (photojournalists) can concentrate on the subject, the idea and the event," Rothstein said. Techniques and technology are not ends in themselves. Fritz Lang, the movie director, declared as a moral of technique, "Every camera movement must have a motivation, a reason."

Pictorial treatment involves "training the eye and mastering the technical side of the medium in order to organize reality into a visually interesting photograph," Cookman says. The process consists of the photojournalist deciding what is significant for content and then making decisions about light, composition, camera angle and space.

Starting Out

"Simplicity is a virtue in any type of communication," Cookman says. "It's also a good place to start in photography. Begin by recording what you see that interests you, and most often that will be people." He suggests practicing on one person and then trying to capture the interaction between two people.

"After you've learned to get them to relax and to stop worrying that your camera will make them look ugly or ridiculous, then concentrate on telling as much about them as you can through expression, body language, setting, clothing and other props. Try to record a range of emotions and experiences.

"To tell a complete story, make sure there is action in all your pictures. For every subject let there be a visual verb," Cookman recommends.

For the beginner, the task of learning begins not with shooting yards of film and spending hours in the darkroom. As with writing, the starting point is internal—thinking, feeling and looking before the shutter is snapped. Know what it is you want to show, the experts say, and then examine what you have done with that in mind. Ask yourself, "What do I want the print to say?"

Know Everything

Karl Mondon, staff photographer for the *Contra Costa Times,* says that the aspiring photojournalist needs to develop "interests as broad as the subjects found in the newspaper. You don't have to love golf, but it pays to know what a hole-in-one is. Politics may bore you, but when the indicted mayor shows up unexpectedly at the city council meeting, it pays to recognize him or her."

Photographers have to be on the scene to do their job. "This means the ears must be as sharp as the eyes," Mondon says. "You have to listen to every possible source of information—news radio, police scanners, even the clerk at the local grocery store can be a source for finding that next exciting image.

"No type of camera equipment can compensate for not being there."

The beginner looking for a position on a small newspaper may need to provide his or her own basic equipment since most small newspapers do not provide cameras. Mondon suggests buying a good system with motor drive for sports events and a set of lenses with short to medium focal lengths. "Since many professionals are converting to autofocus systems, there are good buys on manual equipment," he says.

"Finally, it is imperative for the new photographer of tomorrow to be computer literate." Mondon suggests learning how to work with Photoshop to be able to scan, crop, color-correct and dodge/burn photos.

Doing it All

One day the assignment is to photograph the Pleasant Hill alumni football game, where clearly the NFL standings are not at stake. So this is a feature photo, and Karl Mondon decides to show how these out-of-shape warriors approach their game. Next day,

Mondon has a breaking story for the *Contra Costa Times,* the removal of the wreckage of a helicopter from a power transmission tower. The crash killed the rock music impressario Bill Graham. *Karl Mondon, Contra Costa Times*

On the Job

In handling an assignment, the photojournalist goes through five steps. He or she develops an idea or concept; decides on the appropriate lenses, speed and aperture; selects locations from which to shoot; decides when to shoot; usually does the darkroom work that will enhance the story's point.

For a feature, the photojournalist moves carefully and deliberately through these stages. On a breaking news event, the thinking and the decisions come quickly, seemingly instinctively.

Prep and Shoot

The photojournalist is able to hit it off with people quickly so they are willing to be photographed. Photojournalists say they must have the talents of the psychologist and the sociologist. Karen Leff, a young freelancer, chats with a street merchant, gains her confidence and then shoots her picture. Leff graduated from the Boston University School of Public Communication in photojournalism. "Since free-lance photography is not consistent enough to pay the rent, it means working in a job, usually not related to photography. One of the reasons I stick with free-lance photography is that each assignment means a new adventure and a new set of personalities, locations and events."

Tension on Campus

For Bob Christy, the assignment from his Kent State University newspaper was simple enough, but the execution was difficult. Christy was to cover a talk by Khalid Abdul Muhammad, a spokesman for the Nation of Islam who had aroused violent controversy with a series of anti-white and anti-Semitic statements at college gatherings.

Christy was frisked, had to walk through a metal detector and was carefully watched by Muslim security aides. The security, he said, was tighter than at any event he had covered, including the presidential race and President Clinton's inaugural ball.

Robert Christy, Daily Kent Stater

Khalid Abdul Muhammad

Campus Discord

The Nation of Islam speaker aroused college audiences with his fiery rhetoric that some described as enciting racial tension.

Daisy Pierce's Okra

To illustrate the importance of home gardens to the people of Roses Creek, Robert Kollar photographed Daisy Pierce. Her face was in shadow and the background was bright, a three-stop difference in brightness levels, Kollar says. "I used just a little fill light bounced from a flash card bent backward atop my strobe. The primary exposure was basically for the sunlight, although I backed off slightly—opened up some." The exposure was f11 at 1/250 with Tri-X. *Robert E. Kollar, Tennessee Valley Authority*

As one of the few whites in the audience, Christy felt uncomfortable, especially when the speaker roused the crowd. "Some of the things he said really made them go wild," Christy said.

Christy took his photos and left. "I felt very uncomfortable, and I feared for my personal safety. I've been in many dangerous situations but I've never felt that way before."

His photo shown here was taken with a Nikon F3 with an 80-200 f2.8 lens. The film was Kodak T-Max 400, which he pushed to 800. The exposure was f4 at 1/250 under what Christy says were very harsh lights.

Poverty in Appalachia

Considerable planning went into a series of photographs by Robert E. Kollar, chief photographer of the Tennessee Valley Authority. The concept was to study the economics of Appalachia for *Forum,* a TVA publication. Kollar planned to show a proud people caught in poverty. He wanted to animate the article, to "bring it to life," he said, in a sensitive, nonsensational photo essay.

The community of Roses Creek, Tenn., was selected as representative. Kollar realized he would need the confidence of the people so that he could photograph them. A TVA employee who had worked in the area accompanied Kollar and helped him to gain the trust of Roses Creek residents.

"Roses Creek is one of many communities that grew up around the Clear Fork River on the Tennessee-Kentucky border when mining was in its heyday," Kollar wrote in an article accompanying his photographs.

"Now most of the mines are gone—and the good jobs with them. Their passing has left scars on the people and the land. The carved-up earth of unclaimed strip mines stares out from the sides of mountains like open wounds. Few people

Appalachia Mountain Family

Letta Casey and her family were among those Kollar chose for his photo essay. After he gained their trust, Kollar said, they felt comfortable with his equipment. "They were even eager to tell their story and to work with me." Kollar asked Casey and her two children to stand together on their porch. "I was trying to illustrate some of the family's surroundings. I wanted the setting to be as natural as possible. The whole idea of the series was to document the conditions the people live in without being degrading to those people." In the family photo, Kollar used a 35mm lens with 1/125 shutter speed and an opening of f11. Tri-X film was rated at 400. *Robert E. Kollar, Tennessee Valley Authority*

have jobs, and many go hungry. They wear secondhand clothes and drive worn-out cars. Many homes don't have electricity, running water, or indoor plumbing. . . ."

Small home gardens are important to the people of Roses Creek. "If we hadn't had our garden, we really would have gone hungry," Letta Casey told Kollar, who took several photos of women in their gardens.

Kollar said he found Casey "a strong-willed person, full of determination, despite her limited financial means. She may be poor in terms of money, but not in spirit. I wanted to show this.

"We were standing in front of her house talking about her hopes and plans for her two sons when her face took on a determined expression. I knew if I worked fast I had my photograph.

"In anticipation of this very thing, I had put my 180mm, f2.8 lens on one of my three cameras, a Nikon FE2."

Kollar shot half a dozen frames, checking the exposure between shots.

"This all happened in a matter of probably five seconds or less. Then, the expression was gone."

Kollar used a motor drive, and he opened the lens a little wider than the meter indicated because the light was coming from the side and back, just where he wanted it.

"I had to burn the hair and the headband slightly, but the photo turned out exactly as I had envisioned it. The highlight on her hair added drama, and there was still plenty of light on her face. The headband added interest to this photo because it seemed so out of place in this setting."

Violence at Florence and Normandie

Wedged in a news helicopter with 12 inches for himself and his camera, his 400mm f2.8 lens pointed at the intersection below, Robert E. Clark of *The Outlook* of Santa Monica, Calif., is shooting a scene of racial fury. A section of Los Angeles is erupting after the acquittal of four white officers accused of beating Rodney King.

"I could see over and around the pilot and video operator, but my camera and its lens were limited to one viewing area," Clark recalls. "I was working blind. I could see a scene for a second or two, then whatever was there was gone.

Flashpoint of the L.A. Riots

Reginald Denny lies wounded and bleeding as his attackers wave to photographers in a helicopter hovering overhead even though some people on the street were shooting at the aircraft. *Robert E. Clark, The Outlook*

"There was no second chance. No panning of the subject. I had to see, review, choose, edit, focus and shoot in less than a second." Clark turned off the motor drive and put the camera on single frame.

Night was coming on and Clark's readings were 1/60th and 1/125th with the lens wide open at f2.8. "The streets are paved with asphalt and were absorbing all my light. I had half a roll of film left," Clark remembers.

"We saw a red, double-tandem gravel truck driving west on Florence Avenue, winding its way past debris in the street, the driver oblivious to the anarchy. We orbited low, trying to wave him away.

"Using the chopper's public address system we tried to encourage him to speed up, to run the intersection. But he stopped for a red light."

"The attack was instant. Bricks, fire extinguisher, bottles. The windshield and side windows exploded like a grenade into jagged glass fragments. Someone jerked the door open, pulled the driver to the ground, and the beating of Reginald Denny began.

"One thug stood on Denny's head while others kicked him in the head, the back, stomach, groin."

Clark keeps shooting. As Denny is on his hands and knees, a man hits him above his right ear. The helicopter newsman, Bob Tur, continues to radio for police help, "to please rescue this man being killed below us," says Clark. The police do not come, but four black residents, hearing the broadcast plea, rush to Denny's rescue, saving his life.

Clark's 15 frames became a pictorial record of one aspect of the troubled race relations in the U.S. For one of his photos, *Time* paid $20,000 and spread the picture across a page and a half of the magazine.

From Vietnam to a Kansas Prison

Joel Sartore of *The Wichita Eagle-Beacon* used most of the techniques in the photojournalist's camera bag for his photographs of a Vietnamese woman convicted of paying a man to burn a restaurant. The man hired two young Vietnamese to assist him. They were trapped inside the building when the gasoline and diesel fuel ignited, and they died.

The trial attracted attention because the woman was a member of a family that had fled war-torn Vietnam and had been welcomed to Kansas by a Salina church.

Sartore was able to obtain permission from the presiding judge to photograph inside the courthouse. He was also granted permission to take photographs in correctional institutions where the woman was held.

Sartore shot several rolls of film, used several different lenses and pushed the Tri-X film to 800 and 1600 because of poor lighting conditions. To create the proof sheet reproduced on the next page of the trial of Huong Thuy Pham, the lens used was a 35mm, f2 on a Nikon F3 camera body. The film was pushed to 800, and the shutter speed was 125. Frame 8a-9 was selected to show the "curiosity and confusion Huong experienced," Sartore said.

From Proof Sheet to Publication

Photographer Joel Sartore shot several rolls of film on his assignment and made a number of proof sheets for his editor. The photo of Huong Thuy Pham peering into the courtroom at the top of this section of one of the sheets was used on the first page of the three-page article.

The page follows the maxim that good art is big art. The top photo works because of the small figure against the large and featureless background, which symbolizes the emptiness of prison life. Some of the other photos reveal portions of the trial and an aspect of the woman's home life. *Joel Sartore, The Wichita Eagle-Beacon*

The Photo Essay

The projects of Kollar and Sartore are described as photo essays or picture stories. The photo essay is a series of shots with a common theme that documents an event or tells a story about a person or a place. While single photos can be effective, the series can reveal subtleties and make distinctions that one photograph cannot.

Usually, the picture story is built around the strongest single shot, the picture that describes or defines the theme. The photographer keeps the focus in mind while shooting, always alert for the scene, the gesture or the expression that symbolizes the event.

The photojournalist understands that a variety of photos is essential for an interesting display. To accomplish this, the photographer may use a wide-angle lens for one shot, a telephoto lens for another. Photos will be taken from several different positions.

Close-ups that focus on a single aspect of the subject vary the perspective. These close-in shots, called **detailing,** make for an intimate relationship between the newspaper or magazine reader and the subject.

The photographer may use various lighting techniques—the light from windows, room light, silhouette. Pictures are cropped according to a layout that emphasizes the theme and presents the photos in varying sizes and shapes. The theme photo is placed in a dominant area and is surrounded by supporting photographs.

Writing Captions

Although some photographers are asked to write the captions or cutlines for their photos, on most publications this work is done by the reporter assigned to the story, and on a few it is handled by the photo or graphics desk.

The Associated Press advises its correspondents to write captions that are interesting, accurate, always in good taste and "whenever appropriate, in a sprightly, lively vein."

The Associated Press Managing Editors Continuing Study Committee made a list of the Ten Tests of a Good Caption:

1. Is it complete?
2. Does it identify, fully and clearly?
3. Does it tell when?
4. Does it tell where?
5. Does it tell what's in the picture?
6. Does it have names spelled correctly, with the proper names on the right person?
7. Is it specific?
8. Is it easy to read?
9. Have as many adjectives as possible been removed?
10. Does it suggest another picture?

And the cardinal rule: Never write a caption without seeing the picture.

Freed. President Truman freed press photographers from a tiny chamber they called the doghouse and let them work in the press room. Truman remarked to a foreign visitor, "I am President of the most powerful nation in the world. I take orders from nobody, except photographers."

On Patrol with the Fort Worth Police

Photographer Rodger Mallison of the *Fort Worth Star-Telegram* spent seven months with a team of reporters investigating crime in the city. Mallison took part in reporting as well as in taking pictures. He conducted interviews, did research and wrote a fourth of the extensive series. His job was to show crime up close, at the street-cop level.

Runaway

This 13-year-old is found hiding in her boyfriend's closet and resists being returned to her parents, who ask that their daughter be held in the juvenile detention home. "We're not a baby-sitting facility," an officer tells them.

Response

An alarm has gone off at the Pilgrim Valley Missionary Baptist Church and Officer S.J. Benjamin checks the maze of hallways, schoolrooms, offices and fellowship halls.

Warning

East Lancaster Avenue, on Officer R.D. Radwan's beat, is the scene of illegal evening activity, from prostitution to robbery. A passerby has just told Radwan he saw some women in a car on a side street with a man they were planning to rob. Radwan lets one of the women know she'd better not be seen again on his beat.

Suspect

Burglaries are common, arrests rare. This detective arrives soon after a burglary report and finds this man hiding under a sink next door to the break-in.

The Photo Editor

The layout and the cropping of the photographs for the photo essays we have described were done by a picture editor, whose job also is to assign photographers. On large publications, the editor is able to choose from a staff of specialist photographers. Some photographers are best at covering spot news events; others do high-quality work on features.

On large publications, photographers accompany reporters on assignments. When possible, photographer and reporter discuss photo ideas, but often the photographer works independently, especially on spot news stories.

Back in the office, the photo editor decides which shots to use. The editor must have an eye for the photograph that best symbolizes the event. At the same time, the editor must be able to resist the temptation to select the dramatic shot that may distort the event.

The Camera

Most photojournalists use the 35mm camera, a single-lens reflex (SLR) with a fast lens. The same lens is used for viewing the scene and exposing the film, so what we see in the viewfinder is what we will see in the print. The camera usually has a built-in exposure meter that measures the light on the scene and allows the photographer to determine how to expose the film. Some cameras are automated so that the proper amount of light is automatically let in.

Aperture

The lens opening or aperture affects the amount of light reaching the film. The lens opening is measured in numbers called **f-stops.** The smaller numbers have the wider apertures, letting in more light than the larger numbers: f1.4 lets in twice as much light as f2. Each lens setting on the camera indicates half the light of the preceding setting: f1.4, 2, 2.8, 4, 5.6, 8, 11, 16, 22, 32, 45.

The other element that controls the amount of light that strikes the film is the shutter speed.

Shutter Speed

The shutter speed affects the length of the exposure, the amount of time the shutter is open. The shutter openings are measured in fractions of a second. The markings of 15 and 30, for example, refer to 1/15 and 1/30 of a second. The B marking allows the photographer to keep the shutter open as long as the shutter release is pressed down.

The correct exposure is a combination of lens opening and shutter speed. Since much of the photographer's work involves action in poorly lit areas, the shutter speed usually is 125 and the lens opening is wide, f2.8 or f4. The shutter speed of 125 or 250 may not stop the action and 500 or 1000 might be necessary. To obtain sufficient light, the lens opening has to be made wide—f1.4 or thereabouts. But the wide lens opening cuts down on the depth of field, the area of sharpness. Compromises and adjustments are always being made.

28mm—Wide angle

50mm—Normal

135mm—Telephoto

300mm—Telephoto

Reciprocity   One of the adjustments photojournalists are always making involves the concept of reciprocity. Since the apertures (f-stops) and the shutter speeds double or halve the amount of light reaching the film, they can be adjusted together to accomplish the photographer's purpose. If the reading is f4 at 125th of a second and the photographer must capture high-speed action, the shutter speed should be set at 250, which lets in half the amount of light at 125. To compensate for this, the lens should be opened one stop to f2.8, which lets in twice as much light as f4.

But f2.8 has a narrower depth of field than f4, and if depth of field is essential for the photo, the f-stop will have to be left at f4 and the shutter speed at 125, which may result in a blurred image of the action. The photographer must decide what he or she wants the picture to show.

Lenses

Lenses are usually described in terms of focal length—normal, long and short. The 50mm lens is considered the normal lens because it most nearly duplicates human vision. The long lens, 100mm and up, is known as the **telephoto lens.** This lens brings distant objects close and compresses the scene. The longer the lens, the greater the magnification and the narrower the angle of coverage. The short lens is known as the **wide-angle lens.** It takes in more of the scene than the other lenses.

The shorter the focal length, the greater the area that can be photographed and the smaller the objects will appear. The photographer can move the camera toward or away from the scene or change lenses to bring about the effect desired. Sometimes, the simplest step is to change the lens. But each lens has limitations as well as advantages.

The Normal Lens   The normal lens is usually designed with large maximum lens openings, which permit photos in low-level light situations. Distant objects are small. Objects outside the area directly ahead, 47 degrees in the angle of view, are not registered on the film.

The Long Lens   Distant objects are increased in size, but the area photographed is smaller the longer the lens: 85mm, 29 degrees; 200mm, 12 degrees; 1000mm, 2.5 degrees. Also, the longer the focal length, the shallower the depth of field. Since the larger image magnifies slight hand movements, a fast shutter speed is necessary when the camera is hand held. (Use a shutter speed at least as fast as the reciprocal of the focal length—with a 200mm lens, shoot at 1/250 or faster.)

The Short Lens   This lens is useful in crowded areas where the photographer is close to the scene. The shorter the focal length the greater the depth of field. The photographer can preset the wide-angle lens and be sure distant and close subjects will be in focus. However, wide-angle lenses will make close subjects disproportionately larger than objects of the same size in the background.

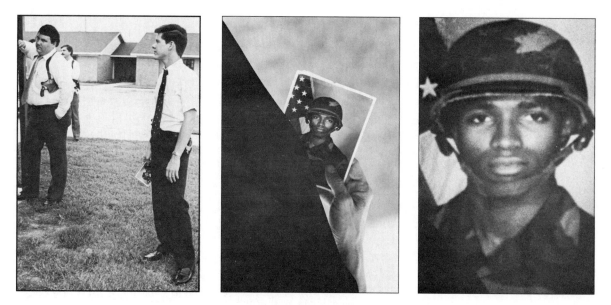

Quick Thinking

After a man stabbed a woman and fled, investigators showed the suspect's picture to people in the area. Keith Warren was shooting the scene for *The Commercial Dispatch,* using a wide-angle lens when he noticed one of the investigators was carrying the photograph in a visible position. Warren quickly switched to his 300mm lens and focused on the photograph. In the darkroom, he blew up the negative. *Keith Warren, The Commercial Dispatch*

Other Lenses   Photographers use a variety of other lenses:

Zoom—Combines a range of focal lengths in one lens. Zoom lenses have the advantage of eliminating the need to change lenses. They are not practical in extremely low light conditions.

Macro—Used for close-ups. This lens eliminates the distortion of subjects close to the lens.

Fisheye—Has an extended wide angle of view; some of them extend to 180 degrees. Objects close to and far from the lens are distorted. The image appears as a circle instead of the usual rectangle.

Different situations call for different lenses. Since the long lens compresses space, a telephoto lens is often used to convey a sense of cramped space. For portraits, the normal lens on a camera close to a subject will make the person's features nearest the camera (nose and forehead) disproportionately large. A medium-long lens (85–135mm) will give better results. Also, a longer lens allows the photographer to be farther away from the subject, which lessens the subject's discomfort.

Depth of Field

Depth of field refers to the area between the nearest and the farthest points in the picture that are in sharp focus. Depth of field is affected by three factors that the photographer can control:

1. **Lens opening**—The smaller the f-stop number, the shorter the depth of field.
2. **Focal length**—The shorter the focal length, the deeper the depth of field.
3. **Lens-to-subject distance**—The farther away, the deeper the depth of field.

In Berman's photo of the football player on page 321, the viewer's eye is directed to the player because the background is purposely out of focus. At the same time, the background is clear enough to show us spectators.

Most cameras have a depth of field scale on the lens that tells the photographer the extent of the area of sharpness at each f-stop. By using this scale, the photographer can deliberately put areas out of focus, such as a distracting background, or make sure some parts of the scenes are sharp.

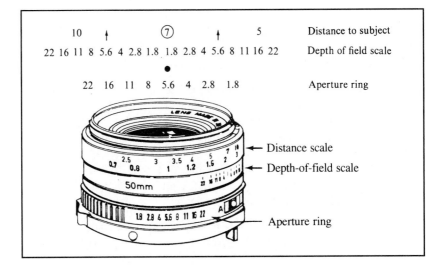

Sharp Area

The area of sharpness, the depth of field, can be determined for different apertures by reading the depth of field scale on the lens barrel. For example, when the lens opening or aperture is set at f5.6 and the distance is set at 7 feet, the area of sharpness on the scale is from about 6 to 9 feet, as indicated by the arrows at the top of the illustration.

Don Ultang, a Pulitzer Prize-winning photojournalist and a photography instructor at Drake University, suggests using the "one-third rule" to make a quick determination for the point of focus so that the various elements in a picture are sharp:

1. Estimate the distance between the nearest and farthest subjects.
2. Take one-third of the difference between the two figures.
3. Add the one-third figure to the nearest distance and set this figure on the distance scale.

For example, when the nearest subject is five feet away and the farthest is 20 feet, the difference is 15 feet. One third of 15 is five. Add five feet to the distance to the nearest subject (five feet) and you get 10. Set the camera at 10 feet.

For grab shots in quick-shooting situations, Ultang often will preset his distance scale at 12 or 13 feet. (The one-third rule does not work in low-light situations with wide-open apertures.)

Film

Film is described by its speed—its sensitivity to light. Fast films have speeds of as high as ASA 3200. The faster the film, the less exposure or light needed to produce an image. Fast films allow the photographer to take pictures in dimly lit areas, but in the prints there is some graininess and a falloff in contrast and sharpness of the image. Slow or medium-fast films show more detail.

Fast Film

The lighting was dim in the courtroom where Nancy Stone of *The Plain Dealer* was covering the trial of a man accused of murder. Stone had film with a speed of 1600 ASA in her camera but still had to open wide, f2.8, and use a slow shutter speed, 1/30. She managed to capture the victim's son in the witness box answering the judge's questions. *Nancy Stone, The Plain Dealer*

Shift to Color. Increasingly, newspapers are using color to attract readers. Also, it is more economical to assign one photographer with color film rather than two, one with black and white and the other with color. Since it is easy to make black and white prints from color negative film, nothing is lost.

At the AP, black and white film is a thing of the past. Black and white prints made from color negative film often are better than those from black and white negatives.

In some situations, even the fastest film is not fast enough. Photographers can "push" a film to the equivalent of 12,500 by using a high-energy developer for their film.

Even color film, once notoriously slow, has been speeded up to meet the demand for fast film. Previously used only on front pages of newspapers, color now is working its way into the rest of the newspaper.

Revolutionary Changes

Film may soon be a part of photography's past, says Karl Mondon, staff photographer for the *Contra Costa Times*. And when film goes, so will the traditional darkroom of chemicals, safelights and enlargers. Just as the 35mm camera replaced the 4×5 Speedgraphic, the still-video digital camera is gradually replacing the traditional camera loaded with film.

"Digitized images are now being taken and transmitted instantaneously back to the newsroom from late-night sports assignments," says Mondon. "This gives newspapers a chance to compete with television's 11 p.m. newscast."

But Mondon says some things will not change for photographers. "Photographers cover everything," he says. Whereas reporters are assigned to specific beats, photographers cover feature events, breaking news, sports, business and a multitude of other subjects. "It's not unusual to spend the morning covering the somber funeral of a murder victim and the afternoon creating a wacky food photo in the studio for the Home and Garden section," Mondon says. "The photographer does it all."

For his work, Mondon keeps a variety of clothes in his car, from a sports jacket for semiformal events to a hard hat that may allow access to an otherwise off-limits construction site.

The Photojournalist's Insight

Faster and faster film. Point and shoot cameras. New cameras, new lenses every month. There seems to be no end to the advances in photography. Yet, some of the most memorable pictures were taken with the simplest equipment, even with a shoebox with a pinhole. Some early equipment was so bulky and heavy it had to be carried by pack animals.

The key element of good photography is obvious—the photographer. No mechanism has yet replaced the man or woman who is able to see clearly the faces and events of the times and who can transfer these insights to film.

Lewis Hine's photograph of a child working in a cotton mill still speaks to us today, though it was taken more than 80 years ago. Despite the limits of the photographic technology then, the picture is technically excellent.

"The camera has a devastating effectiveness in portraying evils," said Frank Luther Mott, a noted historian of journalism. "It is the best crusader of our times. Think of any abuse—social, economic, political—and sound and honest pictures which will bring the evils to our eyes suggest themselves immediately."

Photographers continue to show us society's problems. Some of Jeff McAdory's photographs that accompanied the stories of poverty in Tunica, Miss., describe the timeless as well as the timely, as does his photograph of a child and her doll.

Hope Resides in the Young

A reporter-photographer team for *The Commercial Appeal* found poverty and ill health during their stay in Tunica, Miss., one of the poorest areas in the nation. The infant mortality rate was three times that of the middle-class white areas nearby, and 45 of Tunica's 100 families lived in poverty. Despite the overwhelming problems, the journalists found hope among the people. This photograph by Jeff McAdory symbolizes the determination and strength of the community. *Jeff McAdory, The Commercial Appeal*

Crusaders With Camera

Some photographers put their skills to social use. As we have seen, Dorothea Lange, Arthur Rothstein and other gifted photographers chronicled the Great Depression in graphic ways that have made a lasting impression. They had predecessors and they have had followers.

Migrant Pea Picker

One of the most frequently reproduced photographs of our times, this picture by Dorothea Lange has come to represent the hopelessness of the Great Depression of the 1930s. Mother of seven at the age of 32, destitute and without hope, this woman shows us the face of despair. *Dorothea Lange, Library of Congress*

Lewis Hine

From 1906 to 1918, Lewis Hine took photographs for the National Child Labor Committee that revealed the exploitation of children in factories, mines and mills. Hine, considered the pioneer American documentary photographer, saw his work as a way to educate, inform and reform. He said:

> I try to do with the camera what the writer does with words. People can be stirred to a realization of the values of life by writing. Unfortunately, many persons don't comprehend good writing. On the other hand, a picture makes its appeal to everyone.

The Photograph as Social Commentary

Some pictures do more than supplement a story. They can provide new ways of looking at the world. Lewis Hine's photograph of a child at work in a southern cotton mill is simple, yet devastating.

At first, says Claude Cookman, there is nothing so terrible about the scene depicted. "The factory does not seem particularly dangerous, and we cannot see the girl's face closely enough to tell whether she is fatigued, malnourished or otherwise ravaged by her experience."

But what is not shown is important: "Our associations of what a good childhood should be like—education and play and freedom from drudgery." The picture was taken in 1908, when children labored in mines and factories. Knowledge of child labor combines with our emotional reaction to make the picture a powerful statement.

The photo is pictorially simple. The long loom directs the eye to the picture's focal point, the girl in the foreground. The strong light from the window not only sets up an interesting pattern but reminds us of the world outside, where children are at play. The narrow corridor seems to confine or imprison the child. *Lewis Hine, International Museum of Photography at George Eastman House*

"Hine combined written documentary evidence with photographic materials to make a single powerful social statement," says Eugene F. Provenzo Jr. of the University of Miami. In one of Hine's photo essays—a form he is credited with inventing—he showed two children, no more than 10 years old, at the gate to an Alabama mill. In another photo, he showed two older boys who worked for a Massachusetts mill. Hine pointed out that the same company had differing standards for hiring young workers.

In another report on working children, he showed youngsters in a Mississippi cannery. In the text, he wrote, "See those little ones over there stumbling through the dark over the shell piles, munching a piece of bread and rubbing their heavy eyes. Children 6, 7 and 8 years take their places with the adults and are at work all day."

Hine's work and that of others led in 1916 to a federal child labor law, which a conservative Supreme Court overturned two years later. In 1941, the Court overturned the second ruling, and child labor is now illegal.

Hine, whom some consider the greatest photographer the United States has ever produced, took 15,000 pictures between 1900 and 1940. Recognition came too late. He died a pauper in 1940.

Contemporary Documentarians

Increasingly, photojournalists are giving us insights into how we live now. Subject matter once considered too stark, too controversial for the mass media is now amply illustrated, thrust before us.

Ron Tarver documented the drug culture that had overwhelmed Stella Street in Philadelphia. The first person Tarver met was the Doctor, known to drug users as a hit man. For a few dollars and a cut of the dope, he would mix the heroin and shoot it into a junkie's veins. He was an expert: He could find a rope (a vein) where it appeared there was nothing but scar tissue.

Tarver and his wife had prepared 30 peanut butter and jelly sandwiches the night before, and with these as his introduction, Tarver befriended the Doctor and others. The Doctor took Tarver into Stella Street's "shooting galleries," dens of living hell.

Ron Tarver

"Their whole being revolved around a fix," Tarver said. He made contacts, learned the rules. "Yes, it has its rules, things you can do, people you answer to, people you avoid." And so Tarver made his way deep into the zone the cops call The Badlands, and he began to document for his newspaper, *The Philadelphia Inquirer,* the people who patronized the area.

Tarver spent 12 months watching a cross-section of Philadelphia travel to The Badlands for a fix—white, black and Hispanic; rich and poor; young and old; professional and laborer.

Tarver, a journalism graduate, says his experiences on Stella Street were depressing. "No other country in the world has areas that are any worse than Stella."

In the Grip of Drugs

Drugs and needles are peddled openly in the Badlands, Ron Tarver of *The Philadelphia Inquirer* found. Now and then police throw a net around an area and move in to arrest sellers and buyers. "Put the car in park," an officer screams at a 19-year-old in a white Ford LTD. "Get your hands where I can see 'em." Within minutes, another officer points his gun at two men who have just bought vials of crack. The net took in 40 buyers, and police confiscated 28 vehicles. And this, said one officer, isn't the busiest corner in the Badlands.

Photography as Fine Art

Bob Thayer of *The Providence Journal–Bulletin* ventured into the closed world of transvestites and captured youthful infatuations as he moved his camera across the changing social landscape.

He also showed the world of a blind youngster. On a trip to Russia, he captured the faces of women factory workers dulled by endless routine.

The Transition

Tracey puts on makeup before setting out for the night. Bob Thayer's photographs documented "a tiny community on the far end of human behavior." *Bob Thayer, The Providence Journal–Bulletin*

City Lovemaking

Not under the moon and stars but under the glare of lights in a mall parking lot, this couple is caught by Bob Thayer's camera. *Bob Thayer, The Providence Journal–Bulletin*

Thayer has been influenced by Henri Cartier-Bresson, the great French photographer noted for his magnificently composed photographs. Thayer says an examination of Cartier-Bresson's work in some of the several books he published is an education. He also recommends the work of Alfred Eisenstadt, the great *Life* photographer; Margaret Bourke-White, another *Life* photographer; and W. Eugene Smith, who, Thayer says, believed that photojournalism "must approach the quality of fine art" to be effective.

Documenting Domestic Violence

As Donna Ferrato became aware of the abuse of women and their children, she noticed that, although there was a growing body of published material, no photographer had documented the subject for publication. She set out to fill the gap.

Publishers told Ferrato that domestic violence was unphotographable, but an editor of *Life* advanced expenses for her investigation. She first tried women's shelters but was rebuffed because the directors felt a photographer would violate the women's confidence. Publishing such photos also could create risks for the women. Finally, a shelter in Pittsburgh gave her permission to photograph. She moved in, gained the confidence of the women and photographed them.

Then she widened her operations, photographing police who were investigating domestic assaults. Although books and sociological studies were being published, few media editors considered the situation newsworthy.

"They said domestic violence wasn't important," Ferrato recalls. "The more I saw, the more I knew that I had to get their stories out so that people would care about them," she told Susan Thames, who describes Ferrato's struggle in the Spring 1994 issue of *Who Cares, a Journal of Service and Action.*

A breakthrough occurred in 1987 when *The Philadelphia Inquirer* ran a two-part series on domestic violence in the city and featured Ferrato's photographs.

A Healing Kind of Hurt

"I spend so much time a wreck," says Donna Ferrato of her work as a photographer of domestic abuse. "I want that to happen to other people. I see this as a healing kind of hurt." Asked how she manages to take her pictures, she replies that when a man is hitting "he doesn't care who's around." More than 2 million women are abused every year by husbands and boyfriends. *Donna Ferrato, DOMESTIC ABUSE AWARENESS PROJECT*

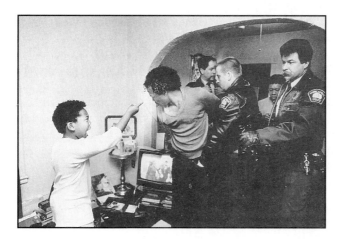

Nancy and Tonya

The big story of the 1994 winter Olympics was made on the sidelines when the husband and friends of one of the figure skating contestants, Tonya Harding, conspired to disable Harding's major competitor, Nancy Kerrigan. The Harding-Kerrigan story dominated newspapers and television.

Both qualified for the Olympics, and coverage was intense. *New York Newsday* published a page-one photo showing the two skating next to each other. It was eye-catching, exciting and phony. It was a composite, as the caption with the photo stated. Chapter 15 examines the ethical debate that followed. (Photo used with permission of *Newsday.*)

More assignments followed. In 1991, she published a book of her work, *Living with the Enemy,* and shortly thereafter a shelter for battered women asked Ferrato for permission to use her photos for a fund-raising exhibition. The shelter was amazed by the response, and Ferrato discovered what she would make of her work. She created the Domestic Abuse Awareness Project, a nonprofit organization that provides photographic exhibits to battered women's shelters for fund-raising purposes.

The Cracked Mirror

The photograph has been described as the mirror of reality or the mirror with a memory. But recent technological developments can make photographs lie.

With **digital imaging** or **computer enhancement,** the photographer can create whatever effects he or she seeks.

The *National Geographic* moved two pyramids closer together to enhance the composition of a cover photo. *Rolling Stone* erased a pistol and shoulder holster in a picture of Don Johnson, star of "Miami Vice." For its Summer Olympics photo coverage, *The Orange County Register* changed the color of the sky in all its outdoor shots to an attractive blue. (The newspaper won a 1984 Pulitzer Prize for its photo coverage of the games.) *A Day in the Life of America,* a book of photographs taken on a single day all over the country, has a cover that was made more dramatic by moving a cowboy on horseback up a hillside and enlarging the moon. For one of its covers, *Popular Science* put an airplane from one photo on a background from another.

The changes are made possible by a machine that scans the photo, creating a computer code of its shape, colors and tones. The code is entered into the computer's memory and the image can be reconstructed later in another setting or with changes.

The Ethics of Changing Reality

Some photo editors defend the practice of photograph enhancement, but others consider it immoral.

"I don't know if it's right or wrong," said an editor of what was done for the cover of *A Day in the Life of America.* "All I know is it sells the book better."

Many disagree with this approach. "I think what's happening is just morally, ethically wrong," says Jack Corn, director of photography for the *Chicago Tribune.*

If this is the future, says Andy Grundberg, photography writer for *The New York Times,* "readers of newspapers and magazines will probably view news pictures more as illustrations than as reportage, since they will be well aware that they can no longer distinguish between a genuine image and one that has been manipulated."

Nothing is wrong with devising graphics like the future city skyline that the *Courant* in Hartford, Conn., put on page one. Clearly, it is a fabrication. But unidentified changes do threaten truth telling, the heart of journalism.

"You don't cheat just because the technology is available," says Brian Steffans, graphics editor of the *Los Angeles Times.*

Nor do you mislead. *New York Magazine* features an article about AIDS among infants. The cover states, "Should it be a crime to treat this baby for AIDS?" The fetching cover photo shows a red-haired white child who, it turns out, does not have AIDS. The illustrations inside that accompany the article show dark-skinned children, for the fact is that AIDS strikes disproportionately among the minority population.

Photographers and photo editors defend manipulation of the photo image. "As artists we can do whatever we please to express our vision," says Frank Van Riper, syndicated photography columnist. But he advises caution: "When process dominates or interferes with image, it is well to ask if the manipulation is being used prudently or for its own sake. . . . There's no denying that computer imaging is becoming not merely a way to change or improve upon the silver image, but an entire art form. Nevertheless, photographers should realize that anything that removes the 'photographness' of their photographs not only can change their work, but also diminish and devalue it at the same time."

Time's Troubles   This devaluation may have occurred when *Time* magazine enhanced the police department photograph of O.J. Simpson after his arrest in connection with the murder of his ex-wife and her friend. *Time* turned the cover photo over to an artist, who made Simpson's skin look darker. The public had an opportunity to compare *Time*'s version with an untouched original as *Newsweek* put Simpson's police photo untouched on its cover that same week.

Lasting or Lost Forever?

No one can predict what "lasts and what merely occupies our present viewing," says Ken Burns, the producer and director of the highly successful PBS series on the Civil War. He comments:

> Immediately after the surrender at Appomattox, the appetite for Civil War photographs fell off dramatically. No one seemed to want them anymore. Mathew Brady went bankrupt. Thousands of glass-plate negatives were lost, mislaid or destroyed. Thousands more were sold to greenhouses around the nation, not for their images but as replacement glass. In the years after Appomattox, the sun slowly burned the image of war from thousands of greenhouse panes. Still later, some historians claim, the same glass became face-plates in World War I gas masks.

The difference was clear and startling. And *Time* felt forced the following week to apologize editorially in a note to readers. In response to a charge by the head of the National Association for the Advancement of Colored People that *Time* had darkened Simpson's face to portray him as "some kind of animal," *Time* said that "no racial implication was intended."

As to whether photographs should be altered, the magazine said its critics had a point "since only documentary authority makes photography of any value in the practice of journalism." Yet, it pointed to the obvious manipulation involved in photography all the time—photographers "choose angles, and editors choose pictures to make points. . . ." Not to mention cropping and retouching.

But *Time* apologized for not making clear "that this was a photo-illustration rather than an unaltered photograph."

Some Problems

On this page and the following two pages is a series of six photographs. Each illustrates a problem. Describe what you would do to make them better photos.

What's Wrong with These Photographs?

Wilderness Cabin

For a photo essay on life in the back country, the photographer took this interior shot. The kerosene lamp indicates the lack of electricity and the woodstove the source of heat. A saw, an ax and the books add to the feeling of the occupant's lifestyle. But one ingredient is missing. What it is?

Sam Caldwell, St. Louis Post-Dispatch   *Wilmer Counts, The Arkansas Democrat*

Momentous Events, Classic Photos

These memorable photographs could be made even better, says Claude Cookman, a photo and graphics editor. He says there is no question that the pictures, which present the human dimension of these historical events, are moving still lifes taken under enormous pressure and that probably there was little time for the darkroom to work on them. Given time, what would you do?

Interview

On a spot news assignment, the photographer took this picture of a civil rights group spokesman at a rally protesting a campus racial incident during which protestors padlocked a classroom building.

Before going on to the next page, jot down your suggestions for changes you would make to improve the six photographs on this and the previous pages. Use common sense along with the technical knowledge you have picked up from this chapter and from lectures and other reading.

Comrades

Joel Kilthau took this photograph for a class at the Rochester Institute of Technology to illustrate several basic mistakes beginning photographers make.

Strip-O-Gram

While shooting for an article about a local softball league, Joel Sartore saw a young woman sprint out toward one of the players in the infield. This was the dentist's birthday, and his friends had sent him a "Strip-O-Gram" as a gift. *Joel Sartore, The Wichita Eagle-Beacon*

What's Wrong? The Answers

Here are a few problems that photographers pointed to in the pictures on the preceding pages:

Wilderness Cabin—The dog adds some life to this photo, but where is her owner? The empty chair cries out for someone to sit in it, the person whose lifestyle is being pictured.

Momentous Events, Classic Photos—These pictures could have been improved with cropping, says Cookman. The photo of the woman at the mineshaft was run in 1947, but today it would probably have been cropped before use, he says. Many of the faces to the left of the principal subject would have been cropped or burnt down in the printing process to make them less noticeable.

A similar step would have been taken to the left of the downed man in the Little Rock photograph. The photo would have been cropped inside the left edge of the utility pole, and this would strengthen the picture by "not allowing our eye to escape from the central message to the area to the left," Cookman says. The pole would become a solid border on the left side of the picture.

Cropped for Greater Impact

These classic photographs were made with the old-style cameras that had a 4 in. × 5 in. negative and thus took in wide areas of the scene being photographed. Today's photographers use the 35mm camera, which has a significantly smaller negative, 1 in. × 1½ in. *Sam Caldwell, St. Louis Post Dispatch* (left); *Wilmer Counts, The Arkansas Democrat* (right)

Interview—The focus of the photograph is lost in background and foreground images. The student in the background is much too sharp, and the blurred heads in the foreground get in the way. The photographer used a 135mm lens to move close in. A longer telephoto lens would have helped in a number of ways. It would have eliminated the heads in the foreground because they would be out of the frame, and the shorter depth of field would have blurred the student's head in the background. Another way to rid the photo of the student would have been to increase the shutter speed and open the lens wider since the wider the lens opening, the shorter the depth of field.

Comrades—Michael Geissinger of the Rochester Institute of Technology says that all the elements necessary for a successful photograph are present in this photo, but they are assembled awkwardly. In the background, the automobile next to the boy's head is distracting. Failure to notice the background is a common beginner's mistake. Also, the bright street distracts.

The gap between the subjects is too great. The viewer is attracted by the youngster's upward glance but has to work too hard to find the adult, Geissinger says. Once the adult is located, his head is too near the top of the photo and the viewer's eye moves off the page. Also, the adult's hat is cut off.

Strip-O-Gram—When Sartore submitted this photo to his editors at *The Wichita Eagle-Beacon* it was part of a picture story on softball in Wichita. "I had brought it back thinking it might have a chance of getting into the paper. (This was during my internship, and I was still pretty green about such matters.) The picture got to the assistant managing editor level and went no further. It was too risqué to be used, I was told. In general, we don't run pictures with any nudity."

A Home Study Course

Use photos to learn photography, photojournalists advise beginners. When he was a college student, Michael O'Brien studied issues of *Life* magazine, trying to figure out the problems various shots posed and how the photographers solved them. O'Brien went on to be a photographer for *Life*.

A photography teacher suggests using the *Photography Annual,* published each year by the editors of *Popular Photography* magazine. He asks students to look at the shots and determine what the photographer wanted to say, whether the picture was planned or shot quickly, what kind of light was used, why a particular angle was chosen, what lens was used and why. At the back of the *Annual* the photographers describe their shots—equipment, film, exposure, lighting.

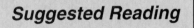

Suggested Reading

Capa, Cornell and Richard Whelan, eds. *Robert Capa: A Biography.* New York: Alfred A. Knopf Inc., 1985. Capa is considered the greatest war photographer of his time. He covered wars in Spain, France, Italy, Israel, China and Indochina. His photographs are collected in *Robert Capa Photographs,* edited by Cornell Capa and Whelan and published by Knopf.

Carlebach, Michael L. *The Origins of Photojournalism in America.* Washington, D.C.: Smithsonian Institution Press, 1992.

Chapnick, Howard. *Truth Needs No Ally—Inside Photojournalism.* Columbia, Mo.: University of Missouri Press, 1994. Chapnick, who was associated with the photo agency Black Star for 50 years, examines the work of a number of photojournalists, including Margaret Bourke-White and Donna Ferrato.

Mora, Gilles and John T. Hill. *Walker Evans: The Hungry Eye.* New York: Harry N. Abrams, Inc., 1993. Evans is considered by some to be the most influential photographer of this century. His photos of American life cover 1928–1974. He collaborated with James Agee for *Let Us Now Praise Famous Men,* taking the photos of sharecropper life in Hale County, Ala.

Willis-Braithwaite, Deborah. *Vanderzee: Photographer, 1886–1983.* New York: Harry N. Abrams, Inc., 1993. Vanderzee was a studio photographer who documented Harlem's black community. He recorded weddings, anniversaries and deaths in a straightforward, documentary style.

13 Advertising

KID: Can I be a doctor?   V.O.: Grandpa?

Advertising agencies donate the work of their employees for public service advertising, and the media donate time and space. *United Negro College Fund and Young & Rubicam*

Looking Ahead

Advertising brings sellers and buyers together. It helps sellers compete for a share of the market by encouraging people to try new products, maintain product loyalty or switch brands. Advertisements are the product of a process that involves research into consumer behavior, positioning of the product, selection of the medium preferred by the target audience and the composition of the advertisement.

The Art of Persuasion

Advertising and public relations personnel try to persuade us to think and behave in certain ways: Buy this brand of jeans, ask for that tube of toothpaste, think kindly of this candidate, appreciate the work of that organization.

Though superficially alike, advertising and public relations differ significantly. The advertiser buys time and space to reach the public. Public relations operates more quietly, behind the scene. "The advertising man must know how many people he can reach *with* the media, the public relations man must know how many people he can reach *within* the media," says the author Martin Mayer.

James Webb Young, an advertising pioneer whose ideas are still influential, said advertising works in five ways to bring seller and buyer together:

1. By making the product or service familiar to the people.
2. By reminding people about the product or service.
3. By spreading news about the product or service to the people.
4. By overcoming inertia in potential customers.
5. By adding value that is not in the product. (A sleek sports car is not sexy in and of itself. But if a person feels sexy driving such a car because of advertising, then advertising has added a value to the product that didn't previously exist.)

The Rule of Three

Advertise to people ready, willing and able to buy. Use the media that reach them. Make advertisements that win their business.

PEANUTS Characters: © 1950, 1951, 1952, 1954, 1958, 1966 United Feature Syndicate, Inc.

Charlie Brown and Pals

Snoopy, Linus and Lucy—along with their pals—help sell more than 100 products, from root beer and snack foods to life insurance. They figure in print and television advertising that amounts to more than $40 million a year, and they reach all age groups. Snoopy is used in a promotion for A&W root beer, and Lucy peers out from packages of Chex for party mix. The Peanuts gang has helped sell General Electric light bulbs and Metropolitan Life insurance policies.

Looking Back

Advertising has been around a long time. From the times of the earliest marketplaces, merchants used advertising techniques to call the public's attention to their goods. They may have spread produce on cloth or hung sample hoes or lanterns outside their shops. Some hawked their merchandise, and the loudest of the sellers often had the best sales.

The industrial revolution brought about the mass production of a great variety of goods—many brands of machine-made skirts and pants, several kinds of soap and shelves of packaged goods.

The intimacy of the community marketplace disappeared and sellers needed new ways to reach out to buyers. Also, given the proliferation of competing products, the sellers had to find ways to make the buyers ask for their particular brand of skirt, soap or cereal.

At the same time, the industrial revolution was turning the newspaper from a costly hand-produced product to a cheap mass-produced product. Rotary printing on a continuous roll of paper, a machine that would fold and count the paper and the linotype machine made it possible to produce the newspaper in large quantities quickly and cheaply. This made the newspaper an ideal advertising medium.

Some of the revolution's technological developments were especially useful to those selling goods. By 1872, photoengraving was being used by newspapers for advertisements, and in 1880, the half-tone, which made illustrations less stark, was developed.

We can track the development of the modern advertising enterprise through the history of the oldest advertising agency in the U.S., NW Ayer, which was created in 1869 when Francis Wayland Ayer decided to foresake a teaching career for one in business. An editor suggested that young Ayer sell newspaper ads, and with the help of his father, Nathan Wheeler Ayer, after whom the agency is named, N. W. Ayer & Son was launched in Philadelphia.

Newspapers hired Ayer to sell advertising. Within seven years his original 11 clients had grown to hundreds all over the U.S. and Canada. At the outset of his business, he simply bought space. Then Ayer realized he could widen his service and soon he was writing copy for his clients and engaging in research for them.

Brand Identity

As the 19th century drew to a close, competition between national products intensified. Ayer asserts that it was the first agency to make clear to advertisers that they needed to develop brand identity to differentiate their products from their competitors' goods. In 1899, Ayer helped National Biscuit Co. sell its Uneeda biscuit in the first million dollar advertising campaign in the U.S.

Ayer's idea was to identify the brand name with the product. Uneeda became synonymous with biscuits, as, later, Kleenex did with facial tissues, Xerox with photocopying and Coke with soft drinks.

Image Ads

Ayer was a pioneer in several areas of advertising. It ran the first color print ad, handled the first advertiser-sponsored radio entertainment program, "The Eveready Hour," and created the client-agency compensation system. Ayer's largest account is AT&T, which has been with the agency since 1908 and for which Ayer created a series of memorable slogans, part of what Ayer called image advertising: "The Voice with a Smile," "Reach Out and Touch Someone," "The Right Choice."

At the time, 1908, image advertising was considered radical if not absurd because it did not directly sell a product. But today the concept is secure in the advertising world.

An Ayer copywriter is credited with inventing the coffee break in an ad for the coffee trade association, and the agency is said to have persuaded DeBeers to sell its diamonds as engagement rings, a concept now part of U.S. tradition.

One of Ayer's art directors employed Picasso, Dali and Georgia O'Keefe to illustrate image ads for DeBeers, Dole, the Container Corp. and other clients.

Competition

Though Ayer had pioneered in many areas, it remained basically conservative in its approach. Two of its more adventurous employees left in 1923 to form Young & Rubicam, and other agencies sprang up to take advantage of the growing impact the media were making on consumers.

New management has made Ayer more vigorous, but it faces stiff competition. Ayer created the successful "Be All You Can Be" campaign for the U.S. Army but later lost the account to Young & Rubicam. It lost the AT&T long distance account to Foote, Cone & Belding but retains $100 million in AT&T business. When Burger King ditched the Thompson agency, it took its $200 million account to Ayer. But within 18 months, Burger King had switched agencies again, dropping Ayer.

Newspaper Ad Departments

Successful advertising is the result of team effort. Whether the task is designing an advertisement in *The Times-News* in Twin Falls, Idaho, for a local home furnishing store or designing a television commercial for Kentucky Fried Chicken, the basics are similar.

At the Idaho daily newspaper, the advertising staff is divided into five teams; each team handles a group of accounts. A team consists of two salespeople and two designers. The salespeople, called advertising representatives, work with the advertiser. Together, they plan a month's advertising program.

"The advertiser will give us ideas," says Linda Miller, an advertising representative. "Then we work with the designer in drawing up a rough advertisement, a spec, and discuss this with the advertiser. He might like what we've done and just fill in a price."

Examining Ad Proof

Advertising representatives at *The Times-News* look over an advertisement for today's newspaper.

The work at an agency is more complex, but the essentials are the same. Let's visit Young & Rubicam, one of the world's largest advertising agencies, in its Madison Avenue offices in New York City.

Advertising Agencies

Teamwork at an advertising agency involves four areas:

Account—An account executive assigned to a client helps the client define advertising needs and establish an advertising program. The account executive is the liaison between the advertiser and the agency.

Research—The agency analyzes the nature of the consumer or user through studies, focus groups and research.

Creative—A team made up of a writer and an illustrator designs the advertising to be used.

Media—The appropriate medium is selected.

Together, agency personnel search for what Larry Chiagoris, director of strategic planning for the Bozell Agency, calls the "breakthrough idea," the fresh approach that makes "a positive difference in the marketplace."

Account

David Flemister, an account executive at an ad agency in New York, says much of his job consists of helping the client define the target group. "You can't reach everyone with your product or service, so we try to find the appropriate group for the client," he says.

"Often the client wants to find the fastest, quickest ways to sales. That's understandable, but it's not always the best way to build up a product."

Wagner International

David Flemister

Flemister counsels clients that the product has to fulfill the promises advertising makes. A consumer may try a new product once, but if it does not meet the promise, Flemister says, the consumer will return to the product he or she has been buying.

Flemister says that the competitive skills he used as a rugby player at Connecticut College apply to advertising work. "You have to stand up and make a presentation in the face of competition," he says. The presentation is the result of research that defines the consumers and their spending habits, the competition's position in the market and other factors.

Research

Buyers usually have a choice among similar goods and services. Walk down a supermarket aisle: rows of detergents, scores of cold remedies, shelf after shelf of hair care products. The truth is that little differentiates the products other than packaging, pricing and advertising.

In one recent year, the manufacturers of cold and cough remedies put 48 new products on the market. These products came in 85 flavors or sizes, all aimed at a $2.4 billion market. Most of the remedies had similar ingredients. Marketers spend $360 million a year to attract consumers to these remedies.

To reach the buyer, to find a niche from which to pitch their product, advertisers engage in market research. They study a variety of buyer characteristics and behavior: sex, age, education, occupation, residence, attitudes toward the product.

On the basis of this research, an advertising program is drawn up.

Timely Research   Sometimes the research is done by an agency seeking an account. When Seiko Time was reviewing its advertising, DDB Needham New York spent months in research.

"We went into stores with cameras in paper bags with holes cut out," says Mary Lou Quinlan of the agency. DDB learned that clerks "were not able to describe to customers what made Seiko worth the money," she says.

Seiko's vice president of advertising, Jonathan B. Nettlefield, found that most watch ads are "narrow, and boring, very passive, very neutral," and he agreed that "people have to be actively told why to buy a product." Seiko awarded DDB the account.

Seiko and the agency decided to push a quality image, and replaced the slogan "The future of time" with a new one: "Built for life."

For Christine MacMaster, research is not all paperwork. "You have to be able to deal with people as well as to examine Census data, the Statistical Abstract and other research material," she says. In addition to digging into demographics and buying habits, she handles focus groups, which she describes as *qualitative* work; her data research is *quantitative* research.

"For the qualitative stage, we might show a group of women some advertisements. Are the ads talking to these women? Are the women concerned about what they see?"

Focus Group

Christine MacMaster shows a focus group an advertisement for a pain remedy. Women, she learned, more readily admit they ache than do men. Advertising reflects this finding. *Maryanne Russell*

A focus group consists of a representative group of people at whom the product or service is aimed. In addition to discussing material with the focus group, MacMaster does depth interviews as part of her research of the prospective market for the product. Her work helps the creative team fine-tune the advertisements tried out on the group.

MacMaster, a graduate of the University of Michigan, spent a year with a small agency before moving to Young & Rubicam. "If your job isn't going to get you up at 6 a.m. excited about going to work, it's not a good job," she said as she shoved papers into a briefcase and slipped into her jacket before taking off for New Jersey to work with a focus group.

Focus on Teen-Age Smokers

A focus group of California teen-agers was asked to look at some anti-smoking advertising. California had spent half a billion dollars to reduce smoking, and the campaign had been successful with all but teen-agers. Shown the ads, the teen-agers said they either lacked relevance to them or seemed to preach.

Livingston & Co. produced new ads as a result of its focus group findings, one of which shows a character named Clifford wearing a gas mask and conducting a breath test with a blindfolded girl. He asks her to identify which breath is worse: 1. A slob blowing cigarette smoke at her or 2. A dog panting in her face.

"Breath No. 2 is slightly less putrid," she says.

Voice-Over Copy

Kevin O'Donoghue types copy for a TV commercial for KFC in which a group of men are shown paying more attention to their chicken legs than to an entertainer in the background.
Maryanne Russell

Creative and Media

A floor above MacMaster's office at Young & Rubicam, Kevin O'Donoghue is working on the U.S. Army account. A veteran of a dozen years with the agency, he is an associate creative director and has been involved with Kodak, Rolaids and Kentucky Fried Chicken accounts.

For television commercials he works with a director to marry text and visuals.

"For every spot we might take 20 different approaches," he says. "For a Kentucky Fried Chicken commercial we can have people eating the chicken despite distractions—dolphins doing tricks or Magic Johnson handling a basketball. The concept is that people are too busy enjoying their Kentucky Fried Chicken to be distracted.

"For some spots we will try a celebrity, a key line or a song. The decision is made by the advertiser's marketing people, who have agreed on a strategy with us before we executed these spots," he says.

For the Army, the strategy was to sell the Army as training for a career. "The execution consisted of showing a soldier coming out of a tank in a business suit," O'Donoghue says.

"In the best of advertisements and commercials," says Henry Jacobs, chairman of the Martin Agency in Richmond, "you can't tell where the strategy ends and the execution begins.

"I admire people who can develop a simple strategy from an overabundance of marketing information. But what really excites me is the writer who 'nails it' with the right words or the art director who puts it down in a way that seems absolutely, positively perfect," Jacobs said.

Positioning   O'Donoghue's work involves finding the theme or concept that makes the product or service appealing to a certain audience. The selection of the theme and audience is known as **positioning,** and to see how it works we go to San Francisco where Kirk Citron, a senior writer with Hal Riney & Partners, is struggling with a problem.

B.O. = P.U. = $

The TV commercial shows a sweaty man walking up to his daughter after jogging. The child pulls back and blurts out, "P.U. Your shirt smells icky." The shirt then undergoes a transformation. It is washed in Surf. Daughter and father embrace.

By positioning itself in an area none of the other detergents wanted to enter—body odor—Surf shot to No. 2 in the $3.3 billion detergent market. Most detergent advertisements claim to make clothes fresh and fragrant. Procter & Gamble, makers of Tide, No. 1 in the field, monopolized the clean, white, bright claims, said an advertising man. But Lever Brothers found for Surf a niche in smell and spent more than $100 million on promotion and advertising. "Body odor isn't pleasant and detergent companies didn't really want to talk about it in the past," said the agency executive.

Putting Prunes on the Table   Prune sales had been declining for three decades despite advertising campaigns and television commercials. The California Prune Board was disturbed. "People thought prunes just weren't worth buying," says Citron. "Obviously we needed to tell people something to change their minds.

"So the first thing we did was go talk to people. Hundreds of people. And we found that one thing could make a difference: a thoughtful, reasoned discussion of the benefits of prunes."

Prunes have plenty of fiber, he found. Fiber is on the minds of people these days because medical authorities say that the typical fast-food diet (usually low in fiber) is a lousy diet, and an unbalanced diet is a cause of cancer.

"When we told people prunes have more fiber than almost any other food, it turned all the negatives about prunes into positives," Citron says. "Prunes had something people wanted—fiber. So it was easy to find what the advertising should say."

Citron had defined the objective—to increase the sales of prunes—and he had found a theme for his advertising campaign—the high fiber content of prunes. Citron had found a position for prunes in the market.

Every advertisement has a specific purpose—to move the reader or viewer of the advertisement to approval or to action. To realize that purpose, every advertisement is built on a specific idea or theme.

Distress . . . Ad . . . Relief. Psychologists who study the advertising process contend that the advertiser creates a need that is then satisfied with the purchase of the goods or services advertised.

Until the need is satisfied—that is, the purchase is made—the individual suffers distress. The purchase gives relief and puts the individual in a state of psychological well-being.

Meeting Needs   The theme selected implies that if the consumer acts on the advertising he or she will be a happier person. The theme may be the low price of beef at the local market—which promises the satisfaction of saving money. Or the theme can be the sweet smell of a wash—which promises to demonstrate a woman's love for her family.

Some advertising people say they sell emotions, not products.

"We don't buy the product. We buy the satisfaction the product will bring us. And that's what the commercial should display," said Ted Bates, head of the agency that bears his name.

"We're using a whole battery of psychological techniques—some old and some new—to understand the emotional bond between consumers and brands," says Paul Drilling, director of strategic planning for McCann-Erickson. "You have to sell on emotion more than ever because it's a world of parity products out there. The days of having a competitive edge and a special product benefit are long gone."

Rosalinde Rago, director of advertising research at the Ogilvy and Mather advertising agency, says, "Brands are not just commercial products we buy and use, they are our companions in life as well."

Automobile advertisements promise neighbor-envy. Perfume and cologne advertisements promise sexual attraction. Insurance advertisements promise a feeling of security.

Noxema shaving cream promises men a great deal. One advertisement promised too much. The commercial showed a man emerging from the woods and eyeing Farrah Fawcett. "I haven't seen a woman in nine years," he says. She returns his hungry look. Suddenly, a can of shaving cream bursts through the earth's crust, surging from the forest.

No go, said the network's censors.

Image Making   Advertisements combine information and image making. When Campbell Soup Co. entered the frozen food market—a $2 billion a year business—it faced stiff competition. Campbell chose to specialize in gourmet foods, a market that has grown enormously as consumers have become more conscious of their diets.

Campbell informed shoppers of the nutritional value and the quality of its product. And it sought to build an image of its foods to appeal to intelligent, cultured consumers.

One commercial had a string quartet in the background. Another was filmed aboard a yacht. These images differ considerably from the frozen food commercials of the 1950s, which emphasized quantity. Commercials then showed families sitting in front of television sets helping themselves to large portions of spaghetti and fried chicken.

Once the objective and the theme are set, the advertisement is composed. Illustrations are selected, copy written, the commercial recorded and shot. The advertisement is then placed in an appropriate medium.

Finding New Markets   Sellers are always on the alert for new groups of buyers. But some markets lie untapped for decades. Blacks and Hispanics were ignored until research revealed their buying power.

While teen-agers were known to be big spenders on clothing and music— about $20 billion a year—research showed that they also spend a lot on food. Not on burgers and malts and fries alone, but on food for the family dinner.

Alert Publishing Inc., a marketing research firm, found that despite a decline in the numbers of teen-agers, they are spending about $25 billion a year on food. Teenage Research Unlimited discovered that 57 percent of teen-age females and 33 percent of teen-age males cook or prepare food for the family at least once a week. They bake as well; almost half the young women and a fifth of the young men make pies, cakes, cookies and bread at least once a week.

Rejuvenating the Product   The cost of introducing a new brand in the 1990s is at least $20 million, marketing consultants estimate. Despite the investment, only a fourth of the new products makes it. The riskiness of introducing new brands leads many companies to try instead to rescue fading brands with new marketing concepts.

Cheez Whiz, Phillips' Milk of Magnesia, Barbasol Shaving Cream, Heinz Ketchup and Dippity-Do—a hair gel—were in decline. Rather than reduce advertising budgets for them and let the products die, their companies injected cash and new marketing strategies in salvage operations.

For Cheez Whiz, which has been described as the culinary equivalent of a velvet painting of Elvis Presley, Kraft tripled its advertising budget to $6 million and marketed it as ideal for the microwave. "The after-school set goes for this unique pasteurized process cheese spread—it's easy and neat . . . for instant snacks, quick pasta sauce, too."

Aqua Velva, an aftershave, had a reputation as "cheap and downscale," according to marketers. The Beecham Group lightened the fragrance and hired former pro football player Dick Butkus to give it a macho sell. Although the scent has proven popular with some young men, Beecham's marketing officials say they haven't turned the corner because, as one put it, "A lot of young guys . . . still think of it as their dad's aftershave."

Not all the advertising facelifts turn aging products into vibrant brands. Stroh's Brewery tried to rescue Schlitz through nostalgia: A young man polishes his 1956 Chevy; fans watch Willie Mays play baseball. The strategy didn't work and sales of Schlitz beer continued to decline.

Tough Sell. New products face an uphill battle. In 19 of 22 different product categories, the brand that was the leader in 1925 leads today. "In a world where every new sale has to come out of some other brand's hide, the marketer that maintains and builds distinctive, high-quality brands has the upper hand," says Alvin Achenbaum, vice chairman of Backer Spielvogel Bates Worldwide.

From Browning to Barkley

Research has demonstrated for the makers of cosmetics and toiletries that, as NW Ayer put it, "At the root of all successful brand imaging for cosmetics/toiletries is a wish.

"In the early 1930s, American women no longer wished to be jazzy, painted flappers. Yardley was English. And things English were seen as proper, refined—classic."

Ayer continued to meet this wish into the 1950s. It positioned Yardley's Orchis perfume "for the romantic gentlewoman." A snippet of poetry headlined each ad: "Where the quiet-colored end of evening smiles—Browning." The content began: "The summer wind stirs through the scented dusk. . . . There is a perfume so like an English garden that it seems the breath of a thousand blossoms, the incarnation of a hundred vanished Junes: the perfume Orchis. . . ."

Then came the 1960s and practicality replaced poetry. Utility became the theme. Also, men moved into the target area for toiletries. Ayer helped relaunch Gillette's Right Guard as Sport Stick and over the years used tough guys—boxer Marvin Hagler and basketball player Charles Barkley—to squelch perceptions of deodorants being for sissies.

The 1990s found people sensitive to issues of health and well-being, and emphasis on these themes, says Ayer, became a key factor in a brand's success. In tune with the times was the reformulation and Ayer's repositioning of Bain de Soleil, a suntan lotion. Ayer designated the product for "The Intelligent Tan," and copy for a television commercial began, "Because you go to the beach and stay all day. Because you love the water. Because you think you look great with a tan. Knowing it's not great for your skin. . . ."

Media Selection

The advertiser has a wide array of media through which to display goods and services. Direct mail is one avenue. Almost 65 billion pieces of advertising go through the postal service each year. The telephone is also used—7 million canned messages are heard on the phone every day. Agencies have placed products in movies—that Coke can on the star's end table is not the movie director's prop; it's the advertiser's. The movie "Die Hard 2" featured 19 paid advertisements.

Watch the Yankees or the Padres on television. There is usually an advertising billboard in the background as an outfielder catches a fly. The close-up of the basketball player shows the Nike logo on his shoes—a $7 million investment by the company in college teams.

Look at your local newspaper. The supermarket has a special on canned vegetables, and the large downtown men's store is offering a special: Buy three pair of Viyella socks, get a fourth pair free. Local merchants turn to their community newspaper to let the shopping public know what's special today—a white sale; fruit fresh from the orchard; four tires for the price of three. Local advertisers are the single largest source of advertising income for the newspaper.

Local Advertising

Drive Drunk And We'll See You Real Soon.

If you saw drinking and driving from our point of view,
you wouldn't drink and drive.

Goodwine
Funeral Homes
Caring For Families The Way Only A Family Can.

Flat Rock 584-3200
Palestine 586-2067
Robinson 544-2131

A huge amount of advertising is local retail—advertisements placed in newspapers by florists, fast-food outlets and funeral homes. Local merchants find the newspaper to be the most effective way to reach a wide range of people in a timely way. Department stores advertise their specials on sheets and pillow cases in their white sales; grocery stores inform shoppers that asparagus, artichokes, and rhubarb are in season and are now available.

This advertisement was part of a six-advertisement campaign designed to highlight the services of a local funeral home. Each ad emphasized a single point. The budget was limited, so an all-copy format was the most cost-effective, said Patrick Fagan, the creative director of Keller Crescent Co. who wrote the copy.

"Since prom time was right around the corner, and since the peer pressure to drink and drive would be strong during prom parties and the like, we created this ad."

Goodwine's, a family business with strong local ties, sought to demonstrate its concern for the community. "To the best of our knowledge, Goodwine's was the first funeral home to address this issue," Fagan said.

Creating an Outdoor

Billboards are everywhere about us, usually catching our attention for a fleeting instant. And that's the catch for the people who design what is known as *outdoor* in the trade.

"Outdoor is a challenge for the writer/art director," says Patrick Fagan, vice-president and creative director of Keller Crescent Co. of Evansville, Ind. "Your message has to be summed up in as few words as possible, and the graphics must communicate that message quickly and clearly."

Here's how Fagan thought through an outdoor for Citizens Insurance:

> *Rather than focus in on a single disaster—fire, flood and so on—to promote the need for insurance we chose to represent the "limitless possibilities" that are beyond one's control.*
>
> *Insurance is purchased to protect oneself from loss. If nothing bad could ever happen, there would be no need for insurance.*
>
> *However, ANYTHING CAN HAPPEN, as our copy line makes clear, and to demonstrate this we created billboards that appear to have been demolished by unforeseen circumstances—earthquakes, wind storms, falling telephone poles.*

Anything Can Happen, three words quickly grasped by the passerby, became the line for the insurance company's billboards. Under the line, appeared another three words, the sponsor's name.

For the falling telephone pole billboard shown on the left, Fagan added solar chips. "When the sun hits them, it appears as though the wires are live and sparkling."

Tots, Teens, Travelers

Children and teen-agers are supposed to influence household spending of around $1 billion a year. No wonder the classroom is no longer outside the reach of the advertiser. Whittle Communications has given 6,000 high schools satellite dishes, VCRs and TV monitors in return for permission to show a 12-minute newscast that includes two minutes of advertising.

By the time today's young people reach age 40, they will have seen at least a million ads.

If the product is frequently used at home—painkillers, soap, toothpaste—the media buyer will use network television to try to reach many of the country's 72 million households. If the product is world cruises, which only those with large disposable incomes can afford, then the advertiser might select the *National Geographic,* whose readers' income is $300 billion a year, the magazine says.

Manufacturers of fashionable women's clothing seek out *Vogue.* Indeed, so many place their ads in *Vogue* that a fall fashion issue will contain well over 800 pages. J.C. Penney, on the other hand, will advertise its inexpensive daily wear in local newspapers, and Sears will use direct mail.

Used car advertisements often are placed in the sports sections of newspapers, and laundry detergent ads appear on television during the daytime soap operas. When Young & Rubicam initiated its "Lovin' from the Oven" campaign for Pillsbury, it put on the commercials for microwave oven products—cakes, popcorn, brownies and pizzas—during the Miss America Pageant.

An Outdoor

The message on a billboard must be simple, direct and clear. An eye-catching illustration holds the passerby just long enough for the few words to be read. *Keller Crescent Co.*

Super Costly Super Bowl

The more consumers the advertiser wants to reach, the more expensive the medium used. Most expensive: the televised Super Bowl. To reach the estimated 135 million viewers who tune in the game, two-thirds of all U.S. homes, the advertisers pay close to $1 million for a 30-second commercial. Add to that another $1 million in production costs for making the advertisement.

You'd think the commercials would be superb. Not so, say advertising specialists, and they cite some duds:

- Burger King's Herb the Nerd $40 million campaign that was to have reached a climax on the Super Bowl where Herb, who'd never been to a Burger King, would finally eat a Whopper. No one cared, and Burger King left the Thompson agency.
- Pepsi-Cola's pursuit of the older generation with its "Gotta have it" commercial featuring Yogi Berra, Regis Philbin and Leeza Gibbons. Flop. The next year's Super Bowl commercial found Pepsi back selling to youthful consumers with "Be young. Have fun. Drink Pepsi."
- Reebok launched a $30 million campaign with the Super Bowl as the major effort. The company had two athletes, Dan O'Brien and Dave Johnson, pitted in competition for the title of "world's greatest athlete," the winner to be decided in the upcoming 1992 Summer Olympic Games.

Oops: O'Brien didn't make the team, and Johnson finished third, winning the bronze medal, not the gold. A Czech won the gold and although Reebok had him in its collection of endorsers it had never mentioned him in its costly U.S. advertising campaign.

The Ratings Game

Numbers aren't the whole story for advertisers. They also want to know the nature of the audience—just who's looking. This explains why a TV show rated 60th in the Nielsen ratings asked advertisers to pay more than a competitor in its time slot that ranked seventh.

The reason "Sea Quest, DSV" could charge more than "Murder, She Wrote" was that the NBC show appealed to young adults, a more lucrative market than the older audience that tunes into the CBS show.

Advertising is not sold on the basis of the most viewers but the kind of viewers, say TV sales people. "Sea Quest" had a VPVH (viewers per viewing household) of 106 for viewers from age 18 to age 49, whereas the rating for "Murder, She Wrote" was 42 per 100 households for the same age group.

Big Bucks Involved

The five leading buyers of advertising over a recent six-month period spent $1.16 billion to persuade buyers. AT&T lead the way with $280 million, followed by Ford, $252 million; Sears, $240 million; McDonald's, $203 million; Kellogg's, $185 million.

The top 15 advertiser buyers spent a total of $2.4 billion in the six-month period.

What Women Want

When Gloria Steinem, a founder of *Ms.* magazine, asked Leonard Lauder to advertise in *Ms.,* he declined. He told Steinem the magazine was inappropriate for his customers because his company Estee Lauder sells a "kept-woman mentality," Steinem recalls. She replied that 60 percent of *Ms.* readers work. Of no importance, he said. Users of his beauty products "would like to be kept women," Steinem says he told her.

Unpredictable Audiences

Advertisers are aware of certain generally accepted guidelines in positioning and in the selection of media to reach consumers. It's assumed that the more educated people read more and that low-income people watch television a great deal. Radio is attractive to young people. Women are more likely to read the food and style sections, men the sports pages and financial tables.

But, says Leo Bogart, a marketing and advertising writer, "consumer interests and audience interests can never be defined precisely in advance. Just as many individuals who have never gone beyond grade school follow the fortunes of stocks and opera stars, many of modest means buy new Cadillacs and mink coats."

Image and Reality

"It's the real thing. Coke is." Commenting on the Coca-Cola commercial, Ann Nietzke wrote in the *Saturday Review,* "In the back of our minds we are all looking for the real thing—genuine affection—and would be ready and willing to buy any products that might help us find it."

An article in *The Wall Street Journal* about a producer of television commercials for politicians said the commercials have "striking photography with almost no message about issues or ideology." In reply, the producer, Bob Goodman, said, "This tube is a very emotional thing. We measure passion, not facts. What I am trying to do is show this man the best way I can, to capture his essence. Feelings win elections. What I strive for is an emotion, not a position."

"It pays to give your brand a *first-class ticket* through life. People don't like to be seen consuming products which their friends regard as third-class."
—David Ogilvy of Ogilvy, Benson & Mather, advertising agency

"If you actually ate the 'TV diet'—with the amounts of each food you eat proportionate to the advertising dollars spent on each food—you would be dead long before your time."
—Beverly Moore, a lawyer-nutritionist

The Content

What should the copy say? What kind of pictures should illustrate the message? What should Sergio Valente have said when he was introduced to the youth market for jeans? Should he have spoken or should he simply have walked around in his jeans against a rock beat background?

The creative team must bring the advertising to life.

At Hal Riney & Partners, Citron pondered, "How many ways are there to say, 'Prunes are high in fiber'?"

"Would you believe 300? That's how many headlines we wrote. And we came up with a dozen visual ideas. We had to do more than just give people information. We had to grab their attention and capture their imagination."

Citron decided that the copy would be longer than usual. He had to give buyers a lot of information, and the kind of people he was seeking to reach would not be frightened away by a lot of text—if it was interesting.

Macho man, on the other hand, had only to saunter down the street with a sighing blonde on each arm. He was seen from the rear with the name of the jeans on his back pocket.

"Sex sells. Everyone knows that," said the manufacturer.

The Results

Did the advertising work? For Citron, "The results were astonishing. Every month since the advertising started, prune sales went up, 10, 12, 17 percent.

"*Advertising Age* named prunes as one of the 10 hottest products in supermarkets for the year," he said. Also, the advertisements won a number of awards.

Sportswear Ltd.'s Sergio ads worked wonders. The manufacturer thought it would sell $2.5 million of its jeans a month. But after the commercials appeared, orders piled up at the rate of $2.5 million a week. Sportswear's success led to a flood of television commercials for signature jeans. Companies were spending as much as 15 percent of their sales on advertising.

"The prize goes to the biggest spender," said an investment broker whose firm handles major industries. The managing director of Sportswear, Martin

---

A Vocabulary for Copywriters

The psychology department at Yale University identified these 10 words as the most personal and persuasive:

New—Human beings continuously crave novelty.

Save—Everybody wants to save something, whether it be time, energy or money.

Safety—This word indicates long-lasting product quality and personal well-being.

Proven—Documentation works.

Love—Everybody wants the inner satisfaction this word connotes.

Discover—This word stimulates feelings of adventure and excitement.

Guarantee—Today's consumers often demand a guarantee of some kind.

Results—Ultimate results are every consumer's desire.

You—This is possibly the most persuasive word of all in ad copy.

Health—Health consciousness can be applied to a wide variety of products.

Heinfling, who created the Sergio Valente jeans and suggested the macho character, takes this idea a step further.

"People don't care about quality," he told *The Wall Street Journal*. "All they wanted was this television hype."

Maybe. There is actually no solid evidence that advertising alone can sell goods. Consumers, studies show, care about quality and cost, and unless they are given both they turn their attention elsewhere sooner or later.

Helping Dreams Come True

When Marvin Waldman and Mark Shap were working on a public service television spot for the United Negro College Fund, they decided on a new approach. For the first time in the 20-year-old campaign they would show a black person whose potential or dream is lost, the Young & Rubicam creative team decided.

A youngster shows his grandfather a drawing he made in school. "Very good," the grandfather says. "The aorta, the left and right ventricles and the auricles." The youngster is impressed and asks if his grandfather wanted to be a doctor. The older man avoids the question. Then:

> ANNCR. V.O.: Being black once meant forgetting about your dreams.
> Today, the United Negro College Fund keeps these dreams alive.

The last frames show the youngster looking up at his grandfather.

> KID: Can I be a doctor, grandpa?
> V.O.: Grandpa?

Public Service Commercial

Advertising agencies donate their services to nonprofit organizations like the United Negro College Fund, and the public service advertising is placed through the Ad Council. This commercial was used by the Fund during its drive for donations. The panel of photographs shown here went to television stations to advise them of the content of the 60-second commercial. Also available were 20- and 30-second versions. *United Negro College Fund and Young & Rubicam*

Shades of Opinion

"Advertising is a meter of social and cultural change . . . though advertising is rarely controversial. Only when a new idea no longer is threatening do marketers exploit it through advertising. They oversimplify and stylize the idea in order to sell products and make profits."

—The Wall Street Journal

"In the factory, we make cosmetics; in the store, we sell hope."

—Charles Revson, founder of Revlon

"Again and again advertising has been an agency for inducing Americans to try anything and everything—from the continent itself to a new brand of soap. As one of the more literate and poetic of the advertising copywriters, James Kenneth Frazier, a Cornell graduate, wrote in 1900 in 'The Doctor's Lament':

This lean M.D. is Dr. Brown

Who fares but ill in Spotless Town.

The town is so confounded clean,

It is no wonder he is lean,

He's lost all patients now, you know,

Because they use *Sapolio*."

—Daniel J. Boorstin, historian

"Advertising can either increase or decrease the degree of sanity with which people respond to words. Thus, if advertising is informative, witty, educational and imaginative, it can perform its necessary commercial function and contribute to our pleasure in life without making us slaves to the tyranny of affective words. If, however, products are sold largely by manipulating affective connotations . . . the influence of advertising is to deepen the already grave intensional orientation widely prevalent in the public. The schizophrenic is one who attributes a greater reality to words, fantasies, daydreams and 'private worlds' than to the actualities around him."

—S.I. Hayakawa, semanticist

"Advertising . . . projects an image of what life *could* be and associates this image with its product."

—Peter B. Hammond, anthropologist

"The advertisements are by far the best part of any magazine or newspaper. Advertisements are news. What is wrong with them is that they are always good news."

—Marshall McLuhan

Speaking to Runners

After years of product advertisements that described heel counters and mid-soles, Nike wanted to re-establish itself as the company that understands how runners think and feel. The athletic shoe manufacturer asked Wieden & Kennedy of Portland, Ore., to create ads "that spoke directly to runners, that would reinforce an emotional connection, while expressing that Nike knows what it 'feels like' to run," says Katherine Gulick of the agency.

"We added that maybe we didn't even have to show a shoe in the ads. And so, we didn't. Instead, we chose beautiful 'I want to be there' running images and honest, heartfelt copy."

One color print ad showed a lone runner on a bridge at full moon. This is how the copy reads:

> Mothers, there's a mad man running in the streets,
> And he's humming a tune,
> And he's snarling at dogs,
> And he still has four more miles to go.

The copywriter, Jerry Cronin, says, "The assignment was simple enough. Show that Nike understood runners. Being an ex-runner I knew how it felt to be able to run with some degree of speed and power. And being an ex-runner, who's

The Private World of the Runner

The copy reads: "Ten million decibels loud. And it doesn't care you're tired. Or it's your birthday or some holiday honoring a saint. So though you'd rather not, you start down the road again. The road when it calls, it screams. Just do it." The copy and the color photos used in the series of advertisements for Nike were designed to reach men and women who run to escape the stresses of job and home. *Harry De Zitter, Wieden & Kennedy*

now become a fat out-of-shape slug, I became quite nostalgic about it all. Thus it was real easy to write."

Hype Is Out

When Ammirati & Puris designed advertisements for BMW cars in the 1980s, the ads featured expensively dressed people in luxurious settings. The idea was that purchasing a BMW bought status.

The 1990s are another matter. "If the '80s were the Me Decade," one agency official said, "the '90s are the Decade of Skepticism." The major market is the over-40 group, and these people are less insecure about their identity, she said.

This analysis led BMW to stress information about the car's technical points in its ads. Hype, says an Ammirati executive, is out with today's consumers. "More than 40 percent have attended college. They know hype when they see it."

The senior vice president of advertising for Gap Inc. describes the '80s as the "celebrity decade when everyone was consumed by who was doing what and what they were eating for breakfast." Now, the emphasis for Gap clothing is on the practical. The company does not use celebrities. It stresses style and fit.

As the economy of the '90s tightens, ads change their look, going from slick, expensive and opulent to stark: larger logos, more copy, greater emphasis on the product and less on lifestyle. "There has been a real return to simplicity," says Martin Fox, editor of *Print*, "to a bare and open look in design."

Risk taking has decreased. As costs have increased, the price of failure has zoomed. "A failure used to cost about $100,000," says Geoff Thompson, deputy executive creative director at Foote, Cone & Belding's San Francisco office. "Now it costs $400,000."

The Truth Works

Classified advertising is a big moneymaker for newspapers. Classifieds are used to sell all sorts of goods and services, from cars to dog walking. A rapidly growing section of classifieds is the Singles or Personals section.

Many readers enjoy the imaginative phrasing of the advertisers: *Rubenesque* or *full-figured* indicates the single is overweight; *vivacious* or *active* often means the seeker is unattractive.

Occasionally, the Singles advertiser tells the truth. This is how a classified in the singles column of *The Courier-Journal* in Louisville begins:

BIG, ugly, fat, white woman seeks slender and financially secure, good looking man. . . . I won't cook, won't clean your place, won't babysit any kids, won't hang out at any redneck places . . . don't like to be told what to do. . . .

The woman told the newspaper she received 60 replies. The classified won an award from the ATHENA organization.

Some Constants

Despite the shifts in advertising concepts, there are some constants that always occur in print ads:

Dominant element—A headline or a picture gives the ad immediate visibility. The photo usually is an action picture, and it may show actual people. The headline tells the reader how she or he will benefit from the action the ad recommends.

Then . . .

The illustrations are more dramatic, the copy more imaginative these days. But the basics remain: The message is briefly expressed in a headline, and an illustration is used to catch the eye.

More than a century ago, *The Tombstone* (Ariz.) *Epitaph* used black and white woodcuts for its illustrations, and the headlines were presented in a line of large type.

. . . and Now

Today, action photographs and color are often used to catch the reader's eye. A stop-action photo and a clever headline were used by Earle Palmer Brown of Bethesda, Md., to advertise a dog-frisbee contest. The Nike ad by Wieden & Kennedy of Portland, Ore., uses a cityscape color photo by Arthur Meyerson and copy by Jerry Cronin that appeals to an upscale audience.

Simple layout—Ample white space is used. The amount of different type faces and sizes is minimized. The design carries the eye through the message.

Distinctive treatment—The type, art and layout set the ad aside from competitors.

Honest presentation—The information is truthful and complete.

Reaching Out To Pet Owners

Headline and illustration catch the reader's eye. The message explains. These advertisements are the work of Tom Darbyshire, creative director who also wrote the copy; Terry Taylor, art director; Dan Mullen, photographer; Lou Janesko, photo retouching. *Earle Palmer Brown*

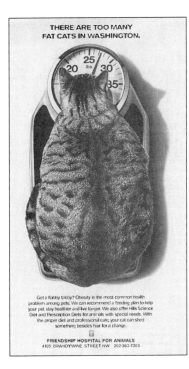

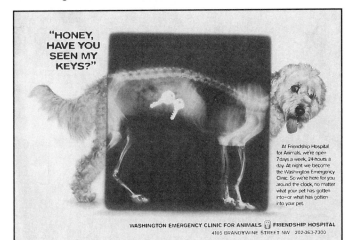

Regulation

Advertisers are regulated and checked by a variety of groups and agencies. When Miles Inc., a maker of health and household products, claimed its One-A-Day vitamins were effective in preventing or reversing the health effects of air pollution and stress, the attorney general of New York charged that the commercials were "false and unfounded." Miles agreed to pull the ads.

State attorneys general involved themselves in regulating advertising when the Federal Trade Commission became less active during the Reagan administration. Three states moved against General Mills' claims that Benefit cereal removed cholesterol from the body, and several investigated advertising that made environmental-safety claims for products.

Unforeseen General Motors wondered why it was having trouble marketing its Chevrolet Nova in Latin America. Someone finally pointed out that in Spanish *no va* means "it doesn't go." A large consulting industry that caters to international marketers and advertisers has developed.

False Classified Ads

Despite safeguards to prevent hoaxes from slipping into the classified ad sections of newspapers, even the most careful newspapers are sometimes fooled. *The New York Times* ran an ad for three days that announced sales jobs at a start-up newspaper for the National Association for the Advancement of White People and listed a phone number in Louisiana for David Duke, the right-wing politician who was affiliated with the Ku Klux Klan.

The *Sun Sentinel* in Ft. Lauderdale ran a classified offering a "bar of Jewish Human Soap" for sale and listed the telephone number of the Christian Task Force Against Antisemitism, an organization that battles religious intolerance. Spokesmen for the newspaper said the ad managed to "slip by."

A *Times* spokesperson said it is impossible to read every classified ad every day before deadline. "We don't know of a completely fail-safe method for stopping false classified ads, but the hoax is still quite rare." It is much harder, he said, to place false display ads as they are examined more carefully than classifieds.

In reaction, the Association of National Advertisers called on the federal commission to become more active so that advertisers do not "have to comply with regulations from 50 separate little state F.T.C.'s."

Beginning in the late '80s, the FTC took an active role in jumping on misleading advertisements. No longer were marketers allowed to trumpet candy bars as health food and potato chips as a source of fiber.

When the FTC questioned General Foods for implying that Kraft Singles cheese slices were high in calcium, advertisers knew the crackdown was serious. "The FTC is back in the game," said a New York advertising lawyer.

The courts exert a controlling arm. Excedrin, an advertisement claimed, is a better pain reliever than Extra-strength Tylenol. When Tylenol sued, Excedrin pulled a $10 million campaign. A judge ruled that the studies cited by Excedrin failed to substantiate its claim.

The courts also have ruled against newspapers that carry obvious or implied messages indicating preference based on race, religion, sex, place of birth, age, ancestry. *The New York Times* ran into legal trouble for using only white models in real estate advertisements.

The federal Food and Drug Administration looks into questionable claims for products in its jurisdiction. The Bureau of Alcohol, Tobacco and Firearms forced the Adolph Coors Company to stop claiming that Coors is brewed from "pure Rocky Mountain Spring water." Anheuser-Busch Inc. complained that since Coors shipped concentrated beer to be mixed with local water before packaging, the slogan was not true.

Local Better Business Bureaus, consumer groups and acceptability offices within newspapers, stations and magazines also check advertising claims.

Consumers occasionally move into the act. A group of women in Boston formed Boycott Anorexic Marketing to protest the use of ultrathin models in advertising. The Los Angeles chapter of the National Organization for Women joined the group to urge a boycott of Calvin Klein products. "Advertising has always been used to impact our society's way of thinking, and women have been paying the price for far too long," the president of the NOW chapter said.

Careers in Advertising

Advertising is one of the fastest growing majors in the journalism curriculum. The career opportunities consist of:

Account management—The handling of the agency's relations with clients. Marketing and accounting courses are helpful.

Advertising sales—Newspapers, magazines, broadcast stations and other media have advertising sales departments. These jobs are stepping stones to management.

Advertising research—Agencies, the media and research companies do vast amounts of research. Familiarity with the computer, mastery of statistics and an advanced degree are usually required.

Art direction—Artists and art directors are in demand to supply the illustrations that accompany copy.

Copywriting—Agencies, companies and the media advertising departments need writers.

The University of North Carolina–Chapel Hill warns students enrolling in its advertising sequence: "While the School of Journalism and Mass Communication has indeed placed students in lucrative and important positions, the placement record is modest in light of the large number of graduates." Some, the school states, go on to careers in law, business, mass communication. The school's advisory continues:

> Some students get their first jobs in advertising as secretaries or in clerical positions. One graduate of the School who now works for a top New York agency spent two years as a receptionist during the day and a coat checker at night. Starting at the bottom is common in the communication field and is no reflection on your ability.
>
> You are competing against yourself and your own abilities when you look at this tough job market. For example, advertising agencies don't hire new college graduates as a general rule, so it isn't a matter of beating other students to the jobs. Become exceptional and doors will open. The real competition is with yourself and your potential. . . .
>
> You need to broaden your perspective of the advertising industry as you think about career and internship opportunities. While agencies have tightened their employment, the general field of communication has lots of opportunities. There are direct marketing companies, telemarketing firms, promotion firms,

**Reaching out to
Young Women**

To cope with the
declining numbers of
women considering a
vocation, the Sisters of St.
Benedictine in Indiana
enlisted the volunteer
assistance of Patrick
Fagan of Keller Crescent
Co. He designed simple,
direct messages that were
placed in religious
publications.

direct marketing firms, company advertising departments, retail copywriting
jobs, yellow pages advertising and other new kinds of jobs evolving every year.
The study of advertising will also be a helpful preparation for jobs in other
communication fields.

Summing Up

All advertising has an objective. To reach that objective, a strategy is devised,
often as the result of research. Appropriate media are selected for the advertising
that is drawn up. Let's look in on how this worked for a public service campaign
devised by Patrick Fagan, creative director for Keller Crescent Co. in Evansville,
Ind.

The Sisters of St. Benedictine is a religious order of Catholic nuns in the rural
community of Ferdinand, Ind. The sisters live in a monastic community. Of the
250 members of the order, about half engage in nursing, teaching and social services away from their home base. The order's motto is, "Pray and work."

The Objective

Like all religious orders, the Sisters of St. Benedictine has suffered from a
massive decline in vocations. To counter that, the order ran full-page ads in vocation publications, which generated about 50 responses a year. In the best year, the
ads resulted in 13 prospects. Something had to be done to keep the order vital.

A vocation committee of nuns and lay people was formed. It established the
need to identify the order, to show how it differed from other religious orders. Few
in the lay community, says Fagan, "had a good idea of what the Sisters of St.
Benedictine were committed to."

The Strategy

Focus groups had shown a vast area of misperceptions about the order. "Since
it was nearly impossible to be specific with regards to the Sisters' mission in our
advertising, we decided to focus on the misperceptions," Fagan said. "If we can't
tell our audience what we are with any great focus, let's tell them what we are
not."

Content, Media Selection

The order had a minuscule advertising budget, around $10,000, with which to
buy advertising to get its points across. The decision was to use small space advertising in annual religious publications.

"Initially, we used straight headlines keying in on a single misperception in
each ad," Fagan says.

Then the format was modified to include testimonials that addressed the misperceptions. For each ad, a simple statement is placed in boldface type, and the
order's telephone numbers and address are given in small type.

The Results

"The results have been extraordinary," says Fagan. "Despite the dwindling numbers of religious vocations nationwide, the Sisters of St. Benedictine have increased their prospective ranks dramatically: Instead of 50 responses a year, the Sisters now receive as many as 600 a year. Their mailing list has grown from 13 to 201, and is increasing each week." Retreats for prospects, which had attracted a handful in the past, now involve 30 prospects each of the weekends they are offered.

Other religious orders are trying to learn the secret of the order's success.

Suggested Reading

Arlen, Michael, *Thirty Seconds.* New York: Farrar, Straus & Giroux, 1980.

Mayer, Martin. *Madison Avenue U.S.A.* New York: Harper & Brothers, 1958.

Mayer, Martin. *Whatever Happened to Madison Avenue? Advertising in the '90s.* Boston: Little, Brown & Company, 1991.

Ogilvy, David. *Confessions of an Advertising Man.* New York: Atheneum, 1963.

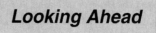

Shortly after the death of the man who had created and organized the New York City Marathon, Mercedes-Benz of North America took out this full-page advertisement in *The New York Times. Courtesy of © Mercedes-Benz AG and Mercedes-Benz of North America, Inc.*

Looking Ahead

Public relations seeks to establish goodwill for the client by creating, changing and molding attitudes. The public relations practitioner examines the interests, concerns and attitudes of the various publics that the client serves and then recommends a program to reach these groups. The practitioner carries out the program in a variety of ways—through press releases, news conferences, mail, brochures, employee publications, speeches and videotapes.

The Purpose: Advocacy

"We are advocates," says Harold Burson, of Burson-Marsteller, the largest public relations firm in the world, with 2,000 employees in 21 countries. "We are being paid to tell our client's side of the story. We are in the business of changing and molding attitudes, and we aren't successful unless we move the needle, get people to do something. But we are also a client's conscience, and we have to do what is in the public interest. I define public relations as an effort to influence opinion—to influence the attitudes of people. That's all it is. We can do three things to public opinion:

"We can try to change it, if it suits our purposes to do so.

"We can try to create new opinion, where none exists.

"Or we can reinforce existing opinion."

Joseph P. McLaughlin, president of a public relations agency, defines his work this way:

> We may speak of the PR man's role as an interpreter to his client or clients of society and events; an evaluator of the meaning and consequences of social and economic change; a prognosticator of future troubles; a prudent and imaginative preparer of programs designed to deal with problems before they descend in full force upon his employer; a transmission belt to carry the client's messages to various publics and to convey back to the client the reactions of those publics to his programs and activities. He undoubtedly, at various times, depending upon the scope of his responsibilities, is all of these. But primarily he is an advocate.

Public Relations News puts it this way:

> Public Relations is the management function that evaluates public attitudes, identifies the policies and procedures of an individual or an organization with the public interest and executes a program of action to earn public understanding and acceptance.

The purpose was put succinctly by John W. Hill, founder of Hill and Knowlton, Inc., who advised his clients that his job was to help influence the public to think well of them. Hill had a formula for what he called "lasting and substantial success" for his clients:

1. Integrity and truth. "Public opinion is entitled to the facts in matters of public concern," he said.

2. Soundness of policies, decisions and acts viewed in the light of the public interest.

3. Use of facts that are understandable, believable and presented with imagination.

The Beginnings

Historian Allan Nevins considers the band of American revolutionaries who agitated for independence as having done "the best public relations job in the nation's history" when they wrote and distributed the Federalist Papers to the newspapers of the emerging nation. Alexander Hamilton and James Madison, the major authors, accomplished what public relations workers still hope to do: set the agenda.

Madison's and Hamilton's work may be described as public relations, but modern public relations originated in 1900, when three former newspapermen established their "Publicity Bureau." Two years later, they were followed by another former reporter. Then, in 1906, Ivy Lee and George F. Parker left journalism to embark on careers in the relatively new field of public relations. The purpose and function of public relations has not changed since. (Nor, perhaps, has the motivation to leave newspaper work for public relations. Lee said he made the switch because of the low pay and late hours of journalism.)

Robber Barons and Reformers

The early 20th century was a period of public cynicism toward big business. The United States had rapidly developed into an industrial giant. But it was growth with pain: low wages; trusts and monopolies; child labor in mines, fields and factories; a 12-hour workday and seven-day workweek; resistance to collective bargaining and strikes against owners who had the help of state militia, federal troops and their own private detective forces. Factory owners posted signs on their doors: "If you can't come in Sunday, don't come in Monday."

In his book *Bitter Cry of the Children,* John Spargo described what he saw in Pennsylvania and West Virginia coal mines at the turn of the century:

> Crouched over the chutes, the boys sit hour after hour, picking out the pieces of slate and other refuse from the coal as it rushes past the washers. From the cramped position they have to assume most of them become more or less deformed and bent-backed like old men. . . . The coal is hard and accidents to the hands, such as cut, broken, or crushed fingers, are common among the boys. Sometimes there is a worse accident; a terrified shriek is heard, and a boy is mangled and torn in the machinery or disappears in the chute to be picked out later, smothered and dead.

The boys, 10- and 12-years-old, were working for 50 and 60 cents a day.

The biggest of the big businessmen were described as "robber barons," a mark of the aristocracy of wealth that had developed and a description of the means by which their wealth had been accumulated.

Jay Gould, the railroad tycoon, announced, "Labor is a commodity that will in the long run be governed absolutely by the law of supply and demand."

John D. Rockefeller had destroyed competition in the oil business and had constructed a monopoly, the Standard Oil Company, that controlled refineries, pipelines and the transportation of oil. The Ohio Supreme Court dissolved his monopoly in 1899, but he quickly formed a holding trust. Workers were exploited. Many lived in company towns where they paid high rents and exorbitant prices for food. They could not live or shop elsewhere. The Rockefeller fortune was enormous; the Rockefeller name was reviled.

The excesses of the railroads, financiers, factory owners and mine operators led to public reaction. When Theodore Roosevelt succeeded to the presidency on

William McKinley's assassination in 1901, Roosevelt began a campaign "not toward making the rich richer, but toward giving a 'square deal' to the farmer, laborer, and small business man who was being squeezed by big business," writes the historian Samuel Eliot Morison.

"The future of American democracy was imperiled by no foreign enemy," Morison continues, "but gravely menaced by corporate greed and financial imbalance when Roosevelt took from the bewildered Bryan Democrats the torch of reform."

Roosevelt's progressive reforms served to regulate big business. He took lands out of the reach of exploiters by putting them into national parks and forests; he refused to use the army to break a strike in the coalfields; he used federal powers to inspect corporations engaged in interstate commerce. Roosevelt's concern about concentrations of power in fewer and fewer hands led him to battle an attempt by financiers to consolidate all the nation's railroads under single ownership. By a narrow margin, the Supreme Court upheld Roosevelt's attack on the holding company set up as a cover for the railway takeover.

After his election in his own right, Roosevelt made it clear that the country was no longer a province for plunder by the moneyed interests. He set out to regulate big business, and he used the press to help rally public support by making such newsworthy attacks on the "few men of great wealth" such as this:

> "Our laws have failed in enforcing the performance of duty by the man of property toward the man who works for him, by the corporation toward the investor, the wage-earner and the general public."

The editorial pages of the metropolitan press condemned Roosevelt as a socialist and a subversive, but the president steadily grew in popularity. The public would no longer tolerate exploitation.

The political message was not lost on people like the Rockefellers. Power had shifted.

By 1911, his billions secure, Rockefeller—the richest man in the world—had left the business to his son, John Jr., and managers. He sought to cleanse his name. He turned to Ivy Lee, who, in that year, had formed his own public relations firm after he had engineered a huge increase in freight rates for his employer, the Pennsylvania Railroad. Lee went to work for Rockefeller.

A "Physician to Corporate Bodies"

Lee's revolutionary idea was to win public support. Corporations and industry had been hiring lawyers to fight their battles in the courts and within legislatures and Congress. Lee advanced another method to win favor for big business. "If you go to the people," Lee said, "and get the people to agree with you, you can be sure that ultimately legislatures, commissioners and everybody else must give way in your favor." Lee, who called himself a "physician to corporate bodies," believed it was in Rockefeller's best interest to win the approval of the public.

Lee, a former New York newspaperman, faced formidable tasks, not the least of which was overcoming the charge of journalists that he had compromised his integrity. Reporters felt Lee had sold out.

The Journalism Of Reform

Journalists played a major role in establishing the climate for reform at the turn of the century. Ida Tarbell exposed the ruthless activities of the Rockefeller interests in establishing the Standard Oil monopoly.

Upton Sinclair's *The Jungle* portrayed a meat packing industry indifferent to the health of its workers and to consumers of its products. Lincoln Steffens revealed municipal corruption to be the result of the alliance of business interests and crooked politicians.

Known as the age of social reform, this period saw Jane Addams in Chicago and Jacob Riis in New York seeking to alleviate the miseries of slum dwellers, Samuel Gompers extending the reach of his union, the American Federation of Labor, and W.E.B. DuBois organizing the National Association for the Advancement of Colored People.

"They saw this new occupation called public relations as a form of black magic," said Burson. Public relations, reporters decided, was "an attempt to make things seem what they weren't—to make people who behaved badly look good," said Burson, who himself left the newsroom of the *Memphis Commercial Appeal* and subsequently formed his own public relations firm.

PR became a pejorative term. Its practitioners were known as *flacks*. Some of the early practitioners resorted to their imaginations more often than to facts in their attempts to market their clients. Not all the criticism was undeserved, says Burson.

Rubber Whales and Salami Queens

The press was usually happy to use the odd feature stories that some creative public relations practitioners (often called publicity men or press agents) dreamed up. A baby elephant might be hired to attract reporters to the opening of a new business, or the manufacturer of cold cuts would announce the selection of a salami queen, who was available for cheesecake photos—pictures that showed ample female epidermis.

In the 1920s, a press agent dreamed up what he thought was a great news story to publicize a Warner Brothers movie, "Down to the Sea in Ships." He planted a fake whale atop Pikes Peak and told newspapers that a whale had been sighted on the mountain. The press agent hired a youngster to sit on the whale's back and spurt seltzer into the air.

When the agent for movie star Francis X. Bushman was trying to wrest a hefty raise for himself and his client from the studio, he told his client to walk with him to the movie company's office. Both dribbled coins out of their pockets, which attracted a huge crowd. The studio's executives were impressed with Bushman's seeming popularity, and they gave them the raises.

Code of Professional Standards

The Public Relations Society of America adopted a code of professional standards in 1988 that calls upon practitioners to conduct their "professional life in accord with the public interest," to "exemplify high standards of honesty and integrity while carrying out dual obligations to a client or employer and to the democratic process."

The code also asks members to "adhere to the highest standards of accuracy and truth, avoiding extravagant claims or unfair comparisons and giving credit for ideas and words borrowed from others."

The code contains 17 provisions and three more pages of "official interpretations" that include special sections for political and financial public relations practitioners.

Who's Out There?

Much of public relations practitioners' research is directed at obtaining information about income, household patterns, educational levels and other demographic factors. Large agencies maintain a reference library like this one used by Stacy Sperling, working on the General Electric account, and Kyle Kunz, working on the AT&T account, for Burson-Marsteller. *Burson-Marsteller*

The Quest for Legitimacy

The days of the rubber whales and other public relations excesses have faded. As the media have matured, so has the field of public relations. The growing reliability of public relations practitioners has led to a greater use by the media of information and tips from PR people than ever before.

When AT&T was split up by court order, some of the so-called Baby Bell companies invaded the turf of others. For example, Southwestern Bell tried to market its Yellow Pages in New York. Tom Barritt of Burson-Marsteller sent a "pitch letter" to a reporter at *The Wall Street Journal* suggesting these turf wars might make a good business story and offering to set up interviews with company officials.

Kyle Kunz of Burson-Marsteller distributes video news releases of the Army Reserve to television stations. One video shows Reserve troops in Ecuador helping out after a flood. Kunz's job is to give the videotapes legitimate news value. Many stations use these videotapes as news items.

As more people in public relations have journalism degrees, says Mary Huchette, one of Kunz's fellow workers, the suspicion lessens. "Since we know news values, we can talk one-to-one with journalists," she says.

Despite this mutual dependence, suspicion of public relations lingers among some media practitioners, and Burson says that public relations remains engaged in "a quest for legitimacy."

The Scope

Public relations covers a variety of activities—17 at last count—that include public information, public affairs, investor relations, corporate communications, employee relations or communications, marketing or product publicity and consumer service or customer relations.

These activities are carried out in the following ways:

• **As a staff function within a company or organization.** For example, Burt Unger supervises public relations publications for Mercedes-Benz of North America, Inc. He puts out a monthly newsletter for dealers and their employees. He and his assistant do most of the writing, much of the photography and all of the design with a desktop publishing system. We will see more of his work later. We will also look at the work of some sports information directors who are employed by universities. Finally, we will look over the shoulders of two people in government public relations.

• **As an independent firm that serves clients.** Edelman Public Relations Worldwide handled the StarKist Seafood Company account when the company broke with the industry to announce it would not handle tuna caught by methods that endangered the lives of dolphins.

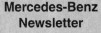

Mercedes-Benz Newsletter

PR Makes News—or Something

The constant need for news works to the advantage of public relations firms. Here is a story the AP ran that is based on a PR practitioner's brainstorm. Decide for yourself whether it is news.

NEW YORK (AP)—Give Americans an extra hour and what do they want to do? Not much, it turns out.

In a recent nationwide telephone survey, 1,283 people were asked what they wanted to do with the extra hour they'll get Sunday when daylight-saving time ends. A majority—51 percent—said they just want to be alone—or asleep.

Others were looking forward to such exciting pursuits as "appreciating simple things" (9 percent), "doing fun things . . . goofing off" (6 percent) and "watching television" (2 percent).

Eleven percent said they want to spend the time with a sexual partner or "someone special," but they weren't asked what they wanted to do with that person.

Seven percent want to spend the time with friends; 4 percent with family.

Two percent want to play sports and 2 percent want to do nothing.

Two percent wouldn't say what their plans were, but considering the other responses, nobody is likely to care.

The survey was conducted for Tissot, a Swiss watch company, by Edwards Associates of San Diego.

- **By individuals offering public relations advice.** Some of these people are engaged in image consulting. For a few hundred dollars a client is advised on clothing, jewelry, hair and the ways to enter a room, shake hands and make small talk. Image consulting has become a $150 million a year business.

Whatever the activity and however it is carried out, the basic task of public relations consists of communicating positive, favorable information about an organization or an individual. Some practitioners are geniuses at staging events that seem—and sometimes are—newsworthy: a corporation's donation of funds for minority scholarships, a beer company's annual contest for the largest fish caught during the summer, a television star's visit to the geriatric or pediatric ward of the local hospital, a transcontinental walk for nuclear disarmament. These events are accompanied by press releases, photo opportunities, background kits, videotapes.

The task of public relations is to manage relations with the public so that the reputation of the client is enhanced, the image is positive. To bring this about, public relations counselors first analyze trends, preferences, feelings and attitudes through research. They then indicate the consequences of these findings to the client and devise a program that will promote the client's interests.

The Tasks

The varied tasks of public relations practitioners can be grouped into three categories:

Technical tasks—Writing news releases, preparing publications such as company newsletters and magazines, writing speeches, setting up events for news coverage, preparing audiovisual material and advertisements.

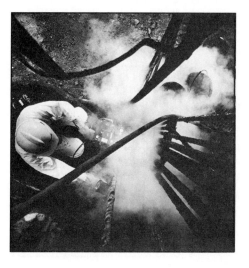

Research Information

Earth Technology Corp. learned that its major business was from repeat clients and that most of these businesses were more influenced by direct mail than by any other form of promotion. The company's public relations office mailed to its clients four handsome photos accompanied by what it describes as a "soft-sell message." *Jeff Corwin, Earth Technology Corp.*

Research work—Examining demographics, census data and consumer characteristics; conducting focus groups and interpreting the results.

Managerial activities—Setting up and conducting news conferences, maintaining relations with news personnel and the public, cultivating relationships with people in politics and other leadership positions, managing other public relations practitioners.

Let's watch some of these people on the job. First, to Long Island University where Bob Gesslein is sports information director.

Sports Information

It's a month before the men's and women's basketball season opens and Gesslein is busy preparing background media guides on the teams. He is working on profiles of the players and listing statistics for players returning from the previous season. Alongside his basketball material is a batch of paper that he is accumulating for his LIU Soccer Media Guide. Last year's soccer guide was a 56-page affair; LIU is a soccer powerhouse.

"It's a one-man job," Gesslein says. "I write, edit, design and do the layout and paste-up myself," he says. Copies go to local newspapers, radio and television stations; to newspapers in opponents' towns; to LIU soccer alumni. Photographs and a profile of the top players go to the players' hometown newspapers.

Before a game, Gesslein prepares a press kit for reporters that includes current notes on the teams, the players, the coaches, series records and history, current statistics, averages and playing time. He also notes what he calls "the highs and lows of the season."

At Northeastern University in Boston, hockey is a major sport. When longtime coach Fern Flaman decided to retire, the sports information office went into high gear. Jack Grinold, the director, knew local papers would want as much material as possible.

Grinold gathered biographical detail on Flaman (Flaman signed a professional contract with the Boston Bruins at age 15 and had a 15-year NHL career) and information about his accomplishments as a coach (in a 19-year career he won more than 250 games and several of his teams went to NCAA finals). The work paid off with a three-column photograph and a long piece in the *Boston Globe*.

Press Release

This release alerted local sports reporters to a major story. They used the release as the backbone of their stories and added quotes from the retiring coach. *The Boston Globe* began the story under a three-column headline:

Northeastern hockey coach Fern Flaman announced yesterday he will retire at the end of the season, his 19th behind the Huskies' bench.

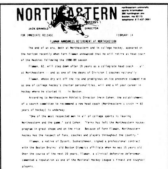

Corporate Public Relations

"You could describe corporate public relations as a desktop with an 'in' box at one end, an 'out' box at the other end and a messy bunch of papers in the middle," says Bert Unger, who supervised public relations publications for Mercedes-Benz of North America, Inc.

Selling Cars

Unger says he divides his time between in and out functions, but he believes the "in is the more important."

In—"My assistant and I spend a great deal of time reading—newspapers, consumer and trade magazines and newsletters of the automobile industry—in order to spot news of interest and importance to top management, to discern social and economic trends that may impact automobile sales and to identify any problems concerning our products that may reach the media."

Each day his office receives about 100 pages of newspaper clippings that must be scanned for the most important stories. Unger watches television news for any mention of the firm.

Out—The 10 to 20 clippings selected as important go into a daily news summary sent to executives, and a one-page summary goes to middle management and those who request it.

Unger's major job is to reach dealers and their employees with a monthly newsletter. "Although I do report on new car models, the newsletter is intended to inform about people," Unger says. It contains news of promotions, deaths, social events and anniversaries and it has feature stories about employees.

"Most of the people in professional roles in corporate public relations are former journalists," he says. "To write a decent news release you have to know how to write a news story, and it certainly helps when dealing with reporters to have the same kind of mindset they do."

The salary, he says, "is about equal to that of a reporter or editor on a major metro daily, there is lots of travel, and the fun of driving some of the finest cars around."

Selling Tuna

The goals were clear: Boost lagging sales, end the consumer boycott and establish a leadership role in the industry. How to accomplish them?

Clearly, action was necessary. Traditional efforts by the StarKist Seafood Company to promote sales of its tuna had failed. After years of ineffectiveness, the environmentalists had finally generated public concern about the decimation of dolphins by tuna fishermen. Congress was starting to react. StarKist was in trouble.

But what strategies to adopt? Edelman Public Relations Worldwide, public relations advisers to StarKist, engaged in research to figure out an approach. Edelman used focus groups, consumer awareness studies, an analysis of environmental groups.

As the strategies were discussed, the flow of postcards protesting the dolphin slaughter became a flood. An environmentalist had stowed away on a tuna boat and his film of dolphins dying was being shown widely.

The course became clear: adoption of a dolphin-safe policy to win the support of key environmentalist groups and even to emphasize the importance of saving dolphins. StarKist would become the champion of the dolphin.

To persuade the public of the company's commitment, Edelman forged a coalition of environmentalists and congressional leaders. Greenpeace, the U.S. Humane Society and other environmental groups were consulted, and arrangements were made with the government for federal observers to ride on fishing boats to verify compliance.

Media decisions were next. There would be two steps—"first unpaid (for credibility) and then paid (for sustained momentum)," Edelman decided.

Before a packed news conference in Washington, the announcement was made: StarKist would buy only tuna caught with dolphin-safe methods. A U.S. senator and environmentalists spoke and praised the action. The event was a public relations dream come true.

A videotape of the event was made and distributed widely. The conference became the lead story on ABC's evening news and it received prominent mention on NBC and CBS; it was covered in *Time* and *Newsweek* and in some 600 local newspapers. The PR videotape was seen by more than 81 million TV viewers—a record audience.

Media Event

StarKist's announcement of its dolphin-safe policy at a Washington news conference attracted major attention. Here, the chairman of StarKist, Keith A. Hauge, answers reporters' questions. To his right is Sen. Joseph Biden, who welcomed the policy. Although the event was clearly created by a public relations agency for a client, it had sufficient news value to draw extensive coverage by newspapers and television.

Kits for Kids

Edelman mailed to 30,000 fourth-grade teachers a packet containing puzzles, a parent-child pact that pledges both to work together "to keep our waters clean and the Earth free from pollution" and background information about dolphins. The protests of school children were instrumental in causing StarKist to change its policy.

Daniel J. Edelman, chairman of the agency, analyzed the situation: What had threatened to become a financial disaster instead had become a success because the company and its parent, Heinz, were willing to adopt a nontraditional approach to the problem. StarKist would not stonewall.

Edelman says that "PR people today are public opinion consultants, strategists, problem solvers." At one time, he says, PR firms "just put out news releases. Then we counseled on what should be said. Today, we advise on what should be done."

Public Affairs

Government is not a passive player in the business of trying to influence public opinion. The work of public relations firms in seeking from government favorable legislation and an amenable regulatory climate for its clients is well-known. The activities of government publicists is less visible but no less energetic.

In fact, in the earliest days of public relations, government and commerce publicists battled each other. The very first public relations agency, the Publicity Bureau, squared off against Theodore Roosevelt when he sought to regulate the railroads. Roosevelt, a master at influencing public opinion through the press, won that battle.

The work of most of the tens of thousands of government publicists is done far from any battlefield. We'll examine the work of one government public affairs specialist at the county level. Then we'll turn to a publicist who is engaged in battling the heavy hitters in industry for his boss, a congressman.

In the County

Recycling. Water conservation. Car pools. Everyone in favor, say *aye*. The vote is unanimous. No one is against preserving the environment.

But persuading people to collect leaves for mulch, to conserve water and to share rides to work is a tough job. It was the job of Carol Nation, a county public information officer.

"I am selling expensive programs that need citizen participation to succeed," she said. And to do her job she took what she calls a noninstitutional approach, which is, she said, really an advertising and newspaper approach.

"I learned that good newspaper techniques—layout, principles of type, good writing, arresting illustrations—help sell these programs," she said.

She sought to make her brochures interesting as well as informative. Take one job she was handed: to encourage Arlington residents to accept a pilot project testing a semiautomated refuse collection container called the Eagle-cart. "I was told similar campaigns in other major metropolitan areas had resulted in melees, public hearings and controversy," she says. "When I looked at the publicity put out by these cities, I noticed at once that material was 100 percent institutional.

ANSWERS

The Compleat
Public Works

Citizens Inquiry Directory

Refuse Pickup   Water   Street Lights
Leaf Collection Sewers   Bike Trails
Snow Control   Streets   Utilities . . .
Traffic Lights   Sidewalks AND MORE!

Hardhat & Kitten   Photo by Debbie Prost

We handle the small problems, too!

Irresistible

You can't pass this brochure by no matter how much mail you have to read today. For her work with the Arlington County Public Works Department, Carol Nation used human interest to attract readers to her brochures and pamphlets. An eye-catching illustration, she says, helps to sell the county programs.

"The brochures might be on fine paper and printed in full color, but on the cover would be a picture of a great big trash container, and inside would be a photo of a neighborhood street lined with these great big rolling trash containers."

The brochures were "about what citizens could do for the refuse collection system and nothing about what it could do for them," she said.

She took a two-pronged approach—an offbeat cover and a light approach to the content. Her cover, which she photographed herself, was of a young woman in an evening gown pushing the container to the curb. And the cover, which invited citizens to take part in the pilot project, stated:

PAMPER YOUR BACK
No More Lifting Heavy Trash Cans.

Nation had found through her research that back injuries are a major problem in the country. "Back pain and injuries cost the nation an estimated $81 billion a year, and are a major cause of disability and lost time at work," she wrote in the brochure. The result: "We had an amazing 97 percent response rate from people who were willing to test the lightweight carts. There was no public opposition."

Some of Nation's brochures have been used in public relations courses, and her noninstitutional approach has influenced governmental agencies around the country.

In the Capital

Reporters are by nature skeptics, if not cynics, and the Washington press corps probably has the highest quota of cynical journalists. They consider every hearing, handout, speech and debate as a possible vehicle for hype. But government relies on a cooperative press for access to the public.

Rep. Ron Wyden, D-Ore., an active member of a subcommittee on regulation, business opportunities and energy, says the press is one of the points on the "iron triangle" in Washington. The triangle consists of a powerful lobby that can put together the votes, a powerful member of the house or senate who commands a following and the press. Each point plays a role in getting things done in government.

Wyden uses the press first in making policy. When Wyden was the subcommitte chairman, his staff director, Steve Jenning, was his outlet to the reporters who cover Congress. "You've got to have a compelling story to tell to reach the press here," says Jenning.

"Without the press, a lot of what we have accomplished would have been much more difficult to achieve, if not impossible. We haven't co-opted the press; nor do we view it as a partner. The facts are that our issues stand on their own—there's very little spin control going down," Jenning says.

"We worked on an investigation involving medical fraud. To help reporters covering the hearings get past 'talking-head coverage'—which television reporters are reluctant to handle—we pointed out opportunities." Wyden's staffers cited instances of fraudulent medical practice that enabled reporters to go to the clinics for coverage.

Jenning keeps lists of reporters from major news organizations who have special subject areas. These specialists are kept up-to-date on developments.

"Much of this involves an understanding of how reporters operate, the demands on their time and knowing how, why and when events and issues are newsworthy," says Jenning, a former AP newsman.

Political Public Relations

Campaigning for public office once consisted of speechmaking from a platform set up in the city square. Or Harry Truman's famous cross-country train trip when he hustled votes from whistle-stops in his come-from-behind presidential campaign. No more. Today's campaigns are waged in the media, and the costs are astronomical.

Among the key players in these finely crafted political campaigns are a special breed, the political public relations specialist. Here's a glimpse of how two of them fashioned successful campaigns for their clients.

Too Funny

When David Garth was hired to run Edward Koch's try for mayor of New York City, Garth found Koch a funny guy, a clever man with a penchant for devastating one-liners. Koch had been a congressman from the city but was unknown outside his district. So Garth's job was to fashion an image for Koch.

Garth decided to forgo the humor. Instead, he would fashion Koch into the "issues" candidate, a somber, thoughtful candidate, perhaps on the colorless side, someone who rarely smiled.

"He was unknown," recalls Garth, "and I didn't want humor to be the opening picture they got of him, to get the idea he was a joker. When you're talking about running New York, with all its troubles, people don't want Henny Youngman." (Youngman was a stand-up comedian probably most famous for the one-liner uttered in the middle of a story about his household problems: "Take my wife . . . please.")

Too Bookish

No one gave Dawn Clark Netsch much of a chance in the Democratic primary for governor of Illinois. Bookish—she taught law for 18 years at Northwestern University—and a bit on the stuffy side, silver-haired and 67, her image didn't help endear her to the voters to whom she was promising an increase in state income taxes.

But she knew politics, having been in the state senate since 1972 until her successful run for state comptroller in 1991, and her associates knew her. They suggested for TV commercials that she shoot some pool, eight ball to be precise. In a smoky hall she made some tough shots and catapulted herself to the top spot as a straight shooter with the guts to tell tough truths.

A Reporter's View

Let's look at public relations work from another perspective. James B. Meadow is the society writer for the *Rocky Mountain News* and is on the receiving end of large amounts of material from public relations and publicity people, most of which is in the form of prereleases.

"The motives behind the diligence of these PR agency people and publicity chairs is to generate mention of the event in my column," Meadow says. Such mention helps boost ticket sales to fund-raisers. Although he does not use too many of the prereleases in his column, they do serve a purpose. They help Meadow set up his calendar of reporting. He tries to cover as many of these events as he can.

"What I like to have is the date, some background information on the event and a telephone number for a contact person I can call for a last-minute fact check," he says.

"Invitations are the grist for my mill, and I get them in all shapes and sizes. Some come rolled up in ribbon, some stuffed in plastic bottles. Some come in bags festooned with balloons and streamers. Occasionally, some are accompanied by a toy—soap bubbles, a water gun shaped like a machine gun for a 'Gatsby Gala.'

Garth's Rules. Make lots of commercials. Use cable TV as much as possible. Never reveal strategy to reporters. Don't lie to reporters "because they can catch you." Don't be afraid to confront your candidate's weaknesses head on.

Just so Far. Clever public relations won Netsch the party's nomination, but in the general election in 1994 she was swept under by the massive Republican tide.

Big Social Event

There was no way that James B. Meadow, the *Rocky Mountain News* society reporter, would turn down this invitation, and he gave over most of his column to the event that he covered for his newspaper.

"Does it work? Sometimes. But just because I read theirs first, and just because I'll smile at the creativity that went into it does not mean that I will give the event advance notice in my column or cover it and write about it," Meadow says.

He has too many invitations to handle. His choices, he says, are often dictated by the guests. "Just about any fund-raiser for the zoo, public library, botanical gardens or art and history museums invariably brings out the old guard," he says, and so his attendance at those events is important. Some events are held to raise large amounts of money, and he attends these. He also goes out of his way to attend events sponsored by minority groups. For too long, he says, these groups have been ignored by the press.

Ethics

The critics of public relations contend that its practitioners are more concerned with selling clients and their products and services than with truth telling. In their defense, people in public relations reply that the excesses of the past belong to the past and that they now practice an ethic that emphasizes openness and fairness.

Unquestionably, public relations has matured. Its developing morality parallels the gradual enlightenment of the business community. A study by Michael Ryan of the University of Houston found that most public relations practitioners agree that "developing programs that are good for society is good business; that a corporation that is socially responsible is more credible."

Public relations and advertising agency workers are usually isolated from those at whom they aim their messages, and this can cause ethical problems. When the audience is dimly seen or visualized as a mass to manipulate, the copywriter may see language as an end in itself and ignore its effect on individuals.

Some agency executives understand the dangers of this isolation from the real world, and they advise their employees to be aware of the consequences of dealing with people at a distance. They stress the need for writers to respect the people at whom their work is directed. Without this awareness, this respect, the executives maintain, the best-crafted news release and the most persuasive advertisement will be ineffective.

The Path to a Job

Most advertising and public relations agencies test job applicants. The interviewer looks over the applicant's college record, work experience and references. A journalism major is helpful. For the large agencies, experience may be necessary, but it is not always required. However, for the applicant without previous work in the field, some sign of commitment to advertising, journalism or public relations is usually essential.

Mary Huchette went to Burson-Marsteller directly after graduation from Ohio University. Though she lacked professional experience, she was able to demonstrate her commitment: in high school, she did public relations work for the school district and was the school correspondent for her local newspaper.

Arthur V. Ciervo, director of public information and relations for The Pennsylvania State University, advises public relations employers, "Always give a writing test . . . for writing style, speed and accuracy."

John Atropoeus, editorial director for Burson-Marsteller, judges the written tests taken by applicants for jobs at his agency. The test consists of several parts:

- Editing a paragraph to correct misspellings and misplaced pronouns, to eliminate unnecessary words, to improve and correct word usage.
- Writing a picture caption from a set of facts.
- Writing a 250-word press release on a new product.
- Correcting redundancies.
- Writing a news release on a speech.

"The most common mistake I see on the speech story is the lead that begins, 'So-and-so spoke last night on the subject of such-and-such,' " Atropoeus said. "Too many don't know what news is and what a lead is."

In talking about other problems that beginners have, Atropoeus says, "Some don't seem to have the energy to check so-called facts."

Required. Public relations practitioners increasingly are using social science techniques in their work. Those interested in careers in the field are expected to know about surveys, data searches and content analysis and how to conduct telephone and personal interviews.

Up the Career Ladder

Here is the pay scale (in thousands of dollars) for a large agency and the period an employee usually is on the job before being considered for promotion:

Account representative—20 to 25; six months to one year.
Assistant account executive—mid-20s; one year.
Account executive—high 20s to mid-30s; one to two years.
Senior account executive—high 30s; unlimited.
Account supervisor—unlimited.

A year or so of experience in journalism usually leads to employment as an assistant account executive.

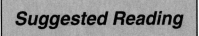

Suggested Reading

Aronson, Steven M.L. *Hype*. New York: Wm. Morrow & Co. Inc., 1983.
Dilenschneider, Robert L. *Power and Influence: Mastering the Art of Persuasion*. New York: Prentice Hall Press, 1991.
Packard, Vance. *The Hidden Persuaders*. New York: Pocket Books, 1957.

PART FIVE Laws and Codes

Offensive?

Media writers have to move through treacherous territory. They must be aware of the dangers of libel and alert to the possibility of offending their readers and viewers with language and photographs, such as this one of a suicide, that might be perceived as vulgar, obscene or distasteful. *Stewart Bowman, Louisville Times*

15 Libel, Privacy, Ethics and Taste

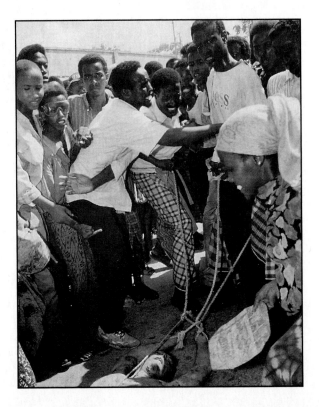

The publication of this photo of a U.S. soldier's body being dragged through the streets in Somalia caused many newspaper readers to condemn the press for violating the family's privacy. The photo won a Pulitzer Prize for photography. *Paul Watson, The Toronto Star*

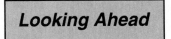

Looking Ahead

The laws of libel and privacy, the codes of ethics and the guidelines on matters of taste place limits on the media writer. Libel is the intentional publication of false and malicious material that damages a person's reputation or business. Privacy is the right of the individual to be left alone. Ethics are the understandings of the moral obligations of the media and their personnel. Taste is what is deemed proper in language and subject matter.

Some Problems

- The news story was like a dozen others that the newspaper had printed—a local resident had been arrested for drunk driving. But this one led to a libel suit.
- The reporter used a false identity to work his way into the membership of the Ku Klux Klan so that he could write a series of articles on the organization that preaches hatred of blacks, Jews and Catholics. Some journalists questioned the methods he used to gather information for his articles.
- On their 6 p.m. broadcasts, two Cleveland television stations reported that a coroner's examination of the body of a female murder victim determined that the body was actually that of a man. The victim was Stella Walsh, a former women's Olympic track champion and a well-known member of Cleveland's Polish-American community. Members of the community assailed the coverage by the two stations.
- A woman who charged she had been raped at the Kennedy compound in Florida was identified by name and her background examined in a story in *The New York Times*. Staff members of the *Times* protested the newspaper's departure from its policy of preserving the anonymity of rape victims.

What, if anything, was wrong here? In this chapter, we will look for some answers in our examination of (1) libel and privacy laws, (2) journalistic ethics and (3) guidelines for matters of taste.

Libel

A news story reported that L.D. Sylvester of 536 Western Ave. had been arrested for drunk driving the night before and had posted bond. Several weeks later, Sylvester's lawyer sued the newspaper for libel. Sylvester said he had never been arrested. In fact, he had been out of town the evening that the newspaper had him weaving down the center of town.

The reporter had made an error, the editor learned through a quick check. There was nothing to do but settle out of court for several thousand dollars. The newspaper had no defense.

What had happened was simple but devastating. In his haste at the police station, the police reporter had scribbled the man's name and address on his note pad. Drunk driving arrests are not major events, and the reporter had been hurrying to get on to more important material.

Back in the office, the reporter had not been able to decipher the scribbled address or name. He thought his notes said L.D. Sylvester, and he looked in the telephone book to verify the address. He found the address was 536 Western Ave., which went into the story. Actually, the arrested person was T.D. Sylvester of 561 Eastern Ave.

The incident reveals the cause of most libel suits: sloppy reporting and careless writing, the failure to check or verify potentially dangerous material.

Libel Defined

Libel is the publication or broadcast of material that injures a person by causing:

1. Financial loss.
2. Damage to reputation.
3. Humiliation.
4. Mental anguish or suffering.

Newspapers do publish stories that cause people to lose their jobs and that damage their reputations and humiliate them. The Ohio congressman who put his mistress on his Washington payroll in a do-nothing job was exposed by reporters and defeated in his bid for re-election. No job and a tarnished reputation. Even so, the congressman did not sue for libel because the story was true. He knew a suit would be hopeless. The reporters had the sworn statement of the woman and proof from the payroll records.

A true story can be printed or broadcast without fear. When the story is untrue, however, there is trouble. The story of Sylvester's arrest was the only erroneous one of a dozen arrest stories that weekend. The people mentioned in the other stories undoubtedly were humiliated by the news of their arrests. Unlike Sylvester, they had no grounds for a libel suit because the printed reports of their arrests were accurate.

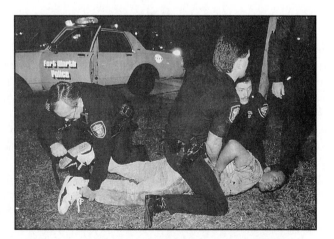

Humiliation and Embarrassment

The man being subdued in a tussle with arresting officers is clearly identifiable. His reputation is damaged by the publication of this photograph. But he has no hope of winning a libel suit since the damaging photograph is a truthful account of an actual event. *Rodger Mallison, Fort Worth Star-Telegram*

Libel Defenses

There are three basic defenses against libel suits:

1. **Truth**—If the writer can show that the defamatory material is true, the offended person still may sue but usually won't win. It is not enough for the reporter to say he or she believed the material was truthful or that someone said it was true. There must be proof of its truth. Truth is almost always an absolute defense in a libel suit.

2. **Privilege**—Anything said in a **public** and **official** legislative or judicial situation—whether it is true or false—can be reported. Legislative bodies include the city council, county commissions, state legislature and congress. In the courts, statements by attorneys, the judge and witnesses and any documents filed with the court are privileged.

3. **Fair Comment and Criticism**—Critics may comment on the work or performances of artists, authors, performers, sports figures and others who offer their services to the public. Criticism must be based on facts and must not attack the personal life of the individual whose work is being assessed. Comments must not be malicious.

In all of these defenses, the reporter is on safe ground if the report is a full, fair, impartial and accurate account of the event. If the story is so one sided that it could be proved that the reporter intentionally singled out the critical or defamatory material, the reporter could be in trouble if sued.

The Sullivan Ruling   In 1964, the U.S. Supreme Court granted reporters some leeway for their mistakes. In a famous case, *The New York Times v. Sullivan,* the Court ruled that if a **public official** is the victim of a libelous story, the official must prove that the account was published with "actual malice." To prove actual malice, the plaintiff must prove in court that the material was published with:

1. Knowledge that it was false or
2. Reckless disregard of whether the material was true.

The Sullivan decision took away from the state courts their total control over libel actions. In its ruling, the Court said that a constitutional issue was involved—freedom of the press.

For a while, the Court's ruling about "actual malice" was extended to **public figures** and to **private individuals** involved in public or official matters.

However, recent court decisions have restricted the definition of a public figure, so that now some public figures and most private individuals need only prove that the defamatory material was published or broadcast because of carelessness or negligence. They need not go so far as to meet the more difficult task of proving actual malice.

It Began on a Montgomery Bus

When Rosa Parks refused in 1955 to vacate her seat on a Montgomery bus for a white passenger and was then arrested, southern black resistance to segregation and discrimination began on an organized scale. Newspapers sent reporters to cover the sit-ins and freedom marches, some of which resulted in violence. To counter the poor image the south was receiving, officials in several cities brought libel suits.

By 1964, $300 million in such suits had been filed, including one by L.B. Sullivan, a Montgomery city commissioner responsible for the city police department. An Alabama court found that *The New York Times* had published material about the police that was exaggerated and erroneous and awarded Sullivan $500,000. The southern authorities had discovered an effective weapon against press coverage.

Nevertheless, the *Times* appealed the case to the Supreme Court, which in 1964 granted the press wide latitude in reporting and commenting on the actions of public officials.

Police told the reporter for a Michigan newspaper that a factory worker had been arrested for rape. The newspaper printed the man's name.

The man was held in jail overnight, but no arrest warrant had been filed and he was not charged or arraigned for the crime. He sued for libel and was awarded $2.5 million.

The lesson: Oral statements are not protected. Use only official documents.

Key Supreme Court Rulings on Libel

New York Times Co. v. Sullivan, 376 U.S. 254 (1964)—This historic ruling required public officials to show that the defendant printed a defamatory statement knowing that it was **false** or **with reckless disregard for the truth.** These conditions constitute "actual malice," which must be proven by the plaintiff.

Curtis Publishing Co. v. Butts and *AP v. Walker,* 388 U.S. 130 (1967)—In deciding these two cases together, the Court established its meaning of "reckless disregard of truth." Justice John Harlan applied three criteria to the problem: (1) Was publication of a story urgent—a rush news item—or was there time for a reporter to check facts? (The Butts case involved a magazine; the AP case involved a fast-breaking news story.) (2) Was the source of a story reliable or suspect? (3) Was a story probable on its face or improbable enough to warrant further investigation? Butts won his case; Walker lost his.

Gertz v. Welch, 418 U.S. 323 (1974)—The Court held that a **private person** could win a libel suit without showing actual malice. The court returned to an emphasis on the status of a libel plaintiff rather than on the subject matter involved. But **public figures** as well as **public officials** still must meet the actual malice liability standard. Public figures, the Court said, are of two types: **public figures for all purposes,** those who "occupy positions of persuasive power and influence," and **limited public figures,** who voluntarily step into the public spotlight in order to influence the resolution of a public issue.

Avoiding Libel Suits

Material that might injure someone's reputation should be treated carefully. Hasty, careless reporting and writing are dangerous. Here are some suggestions:

1. **Confirm and verify all possibly defamatory material**—A writer should double-check anything that
   (a) Questions a person's fitness to handle his or her job.
   (b) Alleges a person has committed a crime or has performed some act that constitutes a crime.
   (c) Implies or directly states that a person is mentally ill or has a loathsome disease.
2. **Make sure that questionable material can be proven.**
3. **Be especially careful of arrest reports, damage suits and criminal court hearings**—These stories cause more libel suits than all others, and almost all the suits are the result of careless reporting or writing. Check names, addresses; make sure the defendant and plaintiff are properly identified.
4. **Watch out for charges, assertions, claims**—Just because you quote a person accurately does not mean you have avoided libel. If a district attorney

tells you he is investigating a business that has a long string of lawsuits, and you quote the official, you may lose a libel suit if the owner of the business proves he has never been sued. If the district attorney makes the same statement in a court proceeding, or if he files charges and makes any allegations in them, you can use the material because it is protected by the defense of privilege.

5. **Don't try to sneak in defamatory material with such words as** *allegedly,* or *reported*—These words are not protections against libel.

6. **When charges and accusations are made in a privileged situation, it is a good idea to check with the person being defamed**—This extra check demonstrates your fairness.

7. **Watch out for words that a court may hold to be libelous:**

Subject	Dangerous Words
Commission of a crime	Swindler, thief, loan shark, shoplifter, bigamist, gangster, ex-convict
Inadequate performance in job or profession	Incompetent, failure, quack, shyster, hack, slick operator
Diseases that would cause a person to be ostracized	Wino, leper, sickie, AIDS victim, addict
Damage to a person's credit	Unreliable, bankrupt, gambler, cheat, failure
Sexual conduct including promiscuity	Loose, sleaze, hooker, seducer, immoral, streetwalker, adulterer, prostitute, gigolo, pimp, pervert
Lack of mental capacity	Screwy, nutty, strange, incompetent, out-of-it
Characterization that incites ridicule or contempt	Phony, coward, hypocrite, communist, fascist

8. **Don't color an article with opinions**—Watch out for personal enthusiasms that cause you to lose control of the writing.

9. **Be careful of statements made by police or court officials outside court.**

10. **Truth is a defense, but good intentions are not**—You may not have meant to defame someone, but when your well-intended writing proves to be untrue, your intention is no defense.

11. **A retraction of an error is not a defense**—At most, it could lessen damages and eliminate punitive damages.

Another danger area for reporters is the private lives of individuals. Reporters cannot indiscriminately pry, peek and probe into the personal affairs of anyone they choose to single out.

Privacy

In their search for news, reporters gather material that can be embarrassing or unpleasant to those involved. Newspapers routinely carry any reports of hospital admissions, divorce actions, arrests and traffic violations. Reporters search out and interview the parents of children killed in automobile accidents and fires. Sunday supplements and magazines detail the sex lives of pop artists and the drug habits and alcoholism of athletes. Television carries into millions of living rooms the shame and the grief of people involved in crime and tragedy.

These stories can be published and broadcast without fear of a damage suit because the people are involved in legitimate news events. The drunk driver has no claim to privacy when he or she is arrested. The details of a divorce case may be published. The horrors of a nursing home fire and the sorrow of relatives may be shown on television.

A Florida newspaper published the picture of a scantily clad woman being led by police from an apartment house where she had been held captive. The woman sued, claiming the picture had embarrassed and humiliated her. Her lawyer told a jury that there was no argument about the truth of the incident but that the picture had invaded her privacy. The jury agreed and awarded the woman $10,000 in damages. The verdict was appealed and the appeals court reversed the decision. It found that the photograph was part of a legitimate news story and that its publication was not so outrageous as to show intentional "infliction of emotional distress."

However, when the press digs into private acts that are of no public interest or that are of no legitimate concern to the public, there can be trouble, even when the account is accurate. The law of libel protects a person's reputation and character. The right of privacy gives the person the right to be left alone, unless he or she is involved in a legitimate news event.

Danger Areas

The right to privacy protects people from several kinds of activities that journalists engage in:

1. **Publicizing private matters**—Public disclosure of sensational material about a person's love life, health, business affairs or social activities can constitute an invasion of privacy. If the acts are private and of no legitimate concern to the public, the material is dangerous.

If an athlete has been suspended for drug use or alcoholism, information about that suspension can be publicized. The courts have ruled that personal material can be used if it **concerns a newsworthy person, is of public concern** and **is not "highly offensive to a reasonable person,** one of ordinary sensibilities."

If an event occurs in public or if information is contained in a public document, it can be publicized, no matter how sensational or offensive it may be. Thus, the victims of sex crimes can be named if a publication wishes to do so.

Sam Upshaw Jr., The Courier-Journal

Public Event

The White House

Public Figure

The public arena is the journalist's domain. Activities that are carried out in public—such as this woman's reaction to slayings at her workplace—and personalities characterized as public figures cannot be draped with the veil of privacy.

2. **Intrusion**—If a reporter forces his or her way into a private area to gather news, it is called intrusion. Intrusion need not be physical. Using tape recorders, cameras and any other kind of electronic recording equipment without the subject's permission constitutes intrusion, even if the material gathered is not publicized. Also, when a reporter misrepresents his or her identity to gain entrance, eavesdrops on personal affairs or trespasses, intrusion occurs.

3. **Publicizing false material**—When a reporter tries to dramatize an event by inventing material, or when a television station produces a docudrama (a fictionalized account of an actual person or event) and defamatory material is used, a person or an event may be placed in what the law calls a "false light." A documentary on drug dealers, for example, may show an innocent person walking by a crack house, inadvertently putting the person in a false light.

4. **Appropriation**—Using someone's name or picture for advertising, for commercial purposes or for private use without the consent of that person constitutes appropriation. No permission is needed from those involved in legitimate news events.

An excellent guide to the laws of libel and privacy is *Synopsis of the Law of Libel and the Right of Privacy* by Bruce W. Sanford, published by

Scripps-Howard Newspapers. The paperback edition is distributed by World Almanac Publications, 200 Park Ave., New York, N.Y. 10166.

Most journalists manage to walk unscathed through the thickets of libel and privacy, probably because the dangerous areas are so clearly marked. In matters of ethics and taste, however, the markers are not prohibitions but suggestions and recommendations. The libel and privacy signs warn, DO NOT ENTER. The signs marking the areas we are about to examine advise, BETTER NOT.

Our first foray will be into the field of ethics where we will attempt to find some standards we can use as guides to our work. Then we will move on to the realm of taste where the standards and guidelines are fast changing and a source of angry discussion.

Ethics

Throughout the textbook you have seen references to accuracy, balance and fairness, impartiality, objectivity, verification. You have read about the journalist's quest for some workable, relevant truths that are useful for the public welfare. You have seen journalists in action who are independent of pressures from those who would use them or suppress their work.

These concepts, these actions constitute the moral underpinnings of journalistic practice. They suggest an approach to work, a state of mind, a commitment to ideals that make journalism more than the sum of its techniques and craftsmanship.

Together, they constitute the journalistic ethic. Not that everyone agrees on how to put these principles into action in everyday work. They are goals and goads, the ends that journalists strive for, prods to keep them from wandering off.

Some of these ethical principles have been collected into codes by journalism organizations and by individual newspapers, stations, public relations associations and other media groups. They all have common elements, and we can begin our study of the morality of journalism by examining a few of these agreed-upon principles.

Plagiarism

The journalist is expected to do his or her own work. Passing off another's work as yours is "dishonest and unacceptable," says the Code of Ethics of the Society of Professional Journalists. When using another's work, attribute it. The penalties for plagiarism are severe:

• A reporter for a California newspaper wrote a column that was almost a word-for-word copy of a column by Art Buchwald. He was asked to resign.

• A sports writer wrote an article that contained material that had been published in *Inside Sports*. He was suspended.

Dishonesty

The writer John Hersey, author of books and many famous *New Yorker* articles, said, "The writer must not invent. The legend on the license must read: None of this was made up." This, he said, is the sacred rule of journalism. Again, the violations can lead to punishment:

- A columnist for the *Daily News* in New York invented characters and quotes in a story about a street clash between British soldiers and youths in Belfast. He was forced to resign.
- A *Washington Post* reporter who won a Pulitzer Prize for her moving story of an 8-year-old heroin addict was fired when it was discovered she had invented the child and the events. The *Post* returned the prize.

Conflict of Interest

The journalist is expected to avoid any activity that would raise questions about his or her integrity and independence. "The newspaper and its staff should be free of obligations to news sources and special interests. Even the appearance of obligation or conflict of interest should be avoided," says the Code of Ethics of the Associated Press Managing Editors.

The sports writer who wants to earn extra money is hired to write news releases for the local baseball team. He compromises his integrity if he accepts the offer. Even working for good causes can pose problems: The reporter who serves on a neighborhood improvement council might be asked by his editor to resign from the council because the newspaper is actively seeking rezoning reforms.

Abortion Marchers

Reporters for *The Washington Post* and *The New York Times* who marched in an abortion-rights demonstration were told by their newspapers that they had crossed the line between their rights as citizens and their obligation to avoid the appearance of conflict of interest.

The *Times* reporter had been covering the legal aspects of Roe v. Wade; the *Post* reporter covered banking. The editors of the newspapers said that even those not involved in covering the abortion issue should not participate in such demonstrations. But other newspaper editors were less restrictive. Their prohibition would apply only to those engaged in related coverage.

Paid For

The travel writer whose airfare, hotel bills and travel abroad are paid for is open to the suspicion of writing favorably of his or her hosts.

Gifts

"Gifts, favors, free travel, special treatment or privileges can compromise the integrity of journalists and their employers. Nothing of value should be accepted," says the Society of Professional Journalists. *The Des Moines Register* says, "staff members pay for their own meals. . . . no staffer accepts any free ticket to any event." When a staffer accompanies a team or an official on a trip, "the company will send a check covering our staffer's share of the transportation."

The temptations are many, and often accepted: Travel writers accept junkets. Business writers are wined and dined at commercial events. Journalists reply that even though they may accept, the giver buys no special favors. But the American Society of Newspaper Editors asks, "Would knowledge of the exchange give my readers the *impression* that I have somehow sold out?"

Ethical Behavior

The ASNE identifies six categories of ethical behavior:

Responsibility—The task of the journalist is to serve the general welfare by informing people so they can make judgments about the issues confronting them. Journalists should not abuse their power for selfish motives or unworthy purposes.

Freedom of the press—Journalists must make sure public business is conducted in public so that people can make informed decisions about public issues. They must be vigilant against those who exploit the press for their purposes.

Independence—Journalists must avoid conflicts of interest. They should accept nothing from sources nor engage in any activity that compromises or might seem to compromise their integrity.

Truth and accuracy—The journalist must seek to keep the good faith of readers by assuring them that news is accurate and free from bias and that all sides are presented fairly.

Impartiality—News reports and opinion should be clearly differentiated. Opinion articles should be identified as such.

Fair play—Journalists should respect the rights of people in the news and be accountable to the public for the fairness and accuracy of their reports. Persons accused in the news should be allowed to respond to the accusations made against them.

The Code of Ethics of the Society of Professional Journalists is included in Appendix D.

Personal Guides

Written codes do not go far enough as guides to ethical behavior. They do not cover the personal factor, the personal ethic that underlies journalistic decision making. NBC and *The New York Times* gave the name of the woman who charged she had been raped by a Kennedy relative. *The Miami Herald* spied on Sen. Gary Hart to confirm that he had a woman visitor overnight.

Newspapers and stations carried accusations in a *Penthouse* article by a woman who said she and Bill Clinton had an affair.

At a *Times* meeting, the newspaper's executives sought to explain why they had used the rape victim's name—because other media had disclosed it. The 300 staffers present jeered.

For Anthony Lewis, a *Times* columnist, the *Herald*'s ambush journalism of Sen. Hart left him "degraded" in his profession.

The reporting of alleged Clinton's infidelities drew a drumfire of attack and defense, not only from the public but from journalists as well.

Some journalists said their stations and newspapers might be able to defend their actions on these stories, but they said that they personally would not have accepted the assignment. Their personal ethic made such activity impossible.

This choice takes us to the bedrock of ethical behavior, the journalist's personal code. Personal standards vary, but they are based on four ethical principles: (1) journalists have a social responsibility to seek truths and to communicate them; (2) journalists have an adversarial relationship to power; (3) journalists operate out of concern for the powerless; (4) journalists are obliged to scrutinize their work and their motives.

Socially Responsible   Most of us know right from wrong. Our moral sense might have been influenced partly by our parents, schools or religious training. Some of our guidelines come from literature and the media. For many young men and women, friends exert a powerful influence in establishing what is right and wrong.

For two days, a 16-year-old student at Milpitas High School in California bragged to his classmates he had raped and strangled his 14-year-old girlfriend. He then led several friends to a remote spot in the foothills near San Jose and showed them her body.

Eight teen-agers saw the body of the girl. Some covered it with leaves to hide it. One dropped a rock on the girl's head to make sure the corpse was really that of a human.

Not one of the friends informed the police.

One of them did show the body to an adult. He called the police.

When word got out that the body had been recovered, some of the high school students criticized the man for notifying the police. One described him as a "snitch . . . a fucking narc." After being harassed by students, the man said, "I don't know if I'd do it again."

Sheriff's Sgt. Gary Meeker wondered, "What the hell has happened to these kids?"

Sgt. Ron Icely of the Milpitas Police Department thinks he knows. "Usually when people are witnesses to a homicide, they come forward right away," he said. "But you have this code of honor (that says) forget about the girl on the side of the ravine and let's protect our buddy."

Although loyalty to friends is an honorable quality, we must respond to a greater demand on our loyalty—our responsibility to society. Journalists can use their social responsibility as a basis for establishing a personal code of behavior.

Re: Gennifer Flowers

Peter Jennings, according to media critic David Shaw, told him that Jennings was initially against running the assertions Flowers made about Clinton, but Jennings said, "It was made clear to me that . . . every affiliate in the country would say, 'What the hell's going on? Don't they know a story when they see it?' "

Passive Press

Newspapers lack "sustained outrage over basic injustices and fundamental idiocies," said W.E. Chilton III, publisher of *The Charleston Gazette*. "We hit an issue and then pass on to something else. We show the attention span of a postal clerk. . . . We're sitting on our mountains of money and our tremendous power, and we might just as well be silent for all the impact we're having on our society."

Journalism is a public service. Its practitioners are independent of commitments or obligations to any special group. The journalist places responsibility to the public above and beyond loyalty to an employer, a political party or friends.

If a source or a friend asks that something be withheld from print or broadcast, the journalist must weigh the request against his or her commitment to inform the public. If an editor, publisher or news director kills a story or removes information from a story on the ground that it will hurt business, advertising or friends of the newspaper or station, the journalist must confront the situation from the same moral perspective—the obligation to report truths.

In both cases, the action the journalist must take is clear: See that the information reaches readers and listeners. Journalists have lost sources and some have quit their jobs rather than be party to a cover-up.

Truth Seeking   Most reporters understand that they should seek out truthful material. But what is truth? At one level, it is the accurate reporting of the record, what a source says in an interview, the contents of a public document. But the truth seeker must do more. On important stories, the reporter is obligated to dig into causes and consequences, to peel away the layers that may conceal the truth. Sources lie. Records mislead. Documents are incomplete.

A tenement burns down. One person is killed. The reporter quotes the investigators about the cause—faulty wiring. Other buildings in the neighborhood have been damaged by fire. The reporter senses a pattern and checks records, looks at property transfers, examines insurance claims. She finds that most of the fires are listed as being of suspicious origin, that the buildings have been heavily insured and that they are owned by local police officers.

Her stories expose the sordid affair of arson for insurance. Some of the officers sue for libel, but a New Jersey court tosses out the suit after finding the stories are accurate.

Adversarial to Power   Journalists serve their readers and listeners by checking on power. They maintain an adversary relationship to power. The power may be held by a dean, a corporation president, the mayor or the president. The founders of this country made sure that journalists would be free of government interference or supervision so that the press could be a check on power.

If we go back to the first part of this chapter where we discussed libel, you can see the willingness of the federal courts to grant journalists wide freedom, even the freedom to make mistakes that libel officials. In the Sullivan ruling, the Supreme Court said that the press needs to be free of restrictions so that it can provide "the opportunity for free political discussion to the end that government may be responsive to the will of the people. . . ."

Reporters and their newspapers have confronted power at the highest levels, even at the risk of compromising what officials have said is "national security."

Given such power, the press can be an unchecked power itself. If government has no control over the press, what then is to protect the public from a freewheeling, irresponsible press? Very little. And this is precisely why codes and guidelines—whether they are written and handed to reporters along with a stylebook or are the reporter's personal beliefs—are so important.

Compassionate   Reporters have little tolerance for any person or action that harms the defenseless. This is the third point in our personal code. Journalists have concern for the victims of unfair, illegal or discriminatory actions. They consider such actions pollutants in the community that must be exposed.

Journalists have revealed the miserable working conditions of migratory farm workers. They have shown the disparity between education for the children of the poor and for the children of the well-off. Journalists have gone into prisons, mental hospitals and homes for the aged to expose mistreatment of the helpless.

A reporter for an Arkansas paper showed how some county officials had conspired to take the property of a poor family when the officials learned that the state was planning to pay a high price for the land, which was to be used for highway construction.

In Chapter 5, we watched Heidi Evans reveal how New York City health officials mishandled Pap smear tests that endangered the lives of many women. Evans' work was propelled by her compassion for the women, mostly poor and members of minority groups, who were victims of the city's negligence.

Stimulus to Action

Photographs like this of a migrant farm worker's child in a tent in Corpus Christi, Tex., told the public about the sordid conditions of these workers and their families. *Russell Lee, Library of Congress*

Self-Examining Some final words on developing a personal code. Much attention is given in ethics discussions to case studies: Was the *Times* right to name the woman who alleged she was raped? Should the press have paid so much attention to charges women made about Bill Clinton's alleged sexual proclivities?

The emphasis in these discussions usually is on errors of commission. But this emphasis is insufficient as a basis for an ethical journalism. We need to look at the sins of omission as well. Are reporters and their editors giving their best? Are they digging into the real nature of the community? Or are they taking short-cuts, taking the easy way? Readers and viewers won't know.

The actor James Earl Jones was commenting about the performers in a prize-winning play. "We were only getting four out of eight performances right, and the producer said the audience doesn't always know. In fact, they probably never know," Jones said.

"But we knew, and it made a difference."

This striving to give one's best always is a moral necessity.

Journalists are always checking themselves: Is this story telling people all they need to know about the event? Is this editorial, review, column fair to the other side? Should I make one more telephone call, check another document, talk to another source to make this complete?

Is this the precise word, or should I keep trying to find the word that describes this situation more accurately? Are all the facts here, or am I hiding behind glitzy writing? Do I remember to keep in mind the warning of the journalist Paul Sann: "If you've got the story, tell it. If you don't have the story, write it."

Am I being honest with the reader or viewer in the way I've structured this piece, or have I emphasized a secondary element because it is more dramatic?

Am I silent when conscience and duty demand that I speak out? Men and women have given their lives in the cause of truth. In repressive regimes, they have written articles for underground publications and broadcast from portable transmitters, always on the move to evade the authorities.

No one asked the writers in China to risk imprisonment and torture by speaking out. There were no financial incentives to the journalists in Latin America to write about the brutal regimes there.

The striving to speak out, to tell truths about the human condition, is a moral necessity that guides many journalists in their work. William Safire, *The New York Times* columnist, says the very purpose of writing is "the revelation of some truth."

There is a practical side to the moral demands society places on the journalist and that the profession accepts as its duty. Society understands that it needs the fearless writer who resists the blandishments of the powerful and the pressures of cronies to go along with the status quo. Democracy requires openness and robust debate, which the journalist promotes. In return, society honors the honest messenger with its respect and occasionally with awards.

Journalists understand that their work is public, on the record. This record— be it a news story, editorial, review or advertisement—is a visible legacy. It is by this work that journalists judge their effectiveness.

The Cost of Silence

"In Germany they came first for the Communists, and I didn't speak up because I wasn't a Communist. Then they came for the Jews, and I didn't speak up because I wasn't a Jew. Then they came for the trade unionists, and I didn't speak up because I wasn't a trade unionist.

Then they came for the Catholics, and I didn't speak up because I was a Protestant. Then they came for me, and by that time, nobody was left to speak up."

—*Martin Niemoeller, German Protestant clergyman imprisoned by Hitler 1938–1945.*

Guidelines for a Personal Code of Ethics

Here are some additional points for the beginning journalist to consider for a personal code of ethics:

1. **The willingness to admit errors.**
2. **The determination to follow the facts,** even if they lead toward a conclusion you personally dislike or disagree with.
3. **A commitment to improve** your talents to serve better those who rely on you as their eyes and ears.
4. **Resistance to praise, the attractions of money, popularity and power** if any of these should stand in the way of your writing the truth.
5. **An identification with those who suffer.**
6. **The desire to make the community a better place for all its people**—children in school, the sick, the poor, the unemployed, the sick and the elderly with little hope, the victims of discrimination.
7. **Resistance to injustice.**

Poses and Disguises

At the beginning of this chapter, we mentioned the reporter who adopted a false identity to expose the Ku Klux Klan in his state. The use of poses and disguises is an old device frequently used by investigative reporters. A *Wall Street Journal* reporter obtained a job in a factory in Texas and then revealed the company's harsh personnel practices and anti-union bias. A reporter for *The Washington Post* feigned mental illness and was admitted to a large mental hospital. She described the inadequate care given patients.

The use of undercover techniques in journalism is being questioned. If journalists feel free to criticize others for illegal and underhanded actions in business and public life, is it proper for them to use questionable tactics to gather news?

Spies, snoops and informers are not respected in our society. Yet the journalist uses poses and disguises to spy and snoop and then tell the story. It seems unethical, and it is. It can be justified, but only under certain circumstances.

The reporter who is trying to formulate a personal ethical code might want to consider this point: When a critical condition exists in which lives are endangered by a person or an organization, the journalist may use a tactic or a technique that otherwise would be considered unethical.

The journalist has a responsibility to the general society to serve as its watchdog, and sometimes this requires the warning bark of a brief story. At other times, it may be necessary to bite deeply into the situation. We punish the dog that bites unnecessarily, but we reward the watchdog that grabs an attacker by the arm.

An Indictment

"Every journalist who is not too stupid or too full of himself to notice what is going on knows that what he does is indefensible. He is a kind of confidence man, preying on people's vanity, ignorance or loneliness, gaining their trust and betraying them without remorse."

—Janet Malcolm in her book, The Journalist and the Murderer

Misleading

The Ontario (Canada) Press Council ruled that a reporter for *The Daily Mercury* in Guelph had acted improperly when he obtained information from a hospital admitting clerk. The reporter had failed to identify himself while gathering information about admission policies. The clerk said the reporter told her his mother was in a nursing home affiliated with the hospital.

Members of the Klan have advocated violence against minority groups, and some Klansmen have been sentenced to prison for murder. The reporter who joined the Klan by using a pose may be thought of as providing a public service.

When undercover techniques are used, the reader or listener should be so informed. A tactic or technique that a reporter is ashamed to describe in print or on the air should not be used in reporting.

Taste

Public Frankness

Placards in New York subway cars show two teenagers talking. One of them says:

Boys can be a real trip. They'll tell you anything to get you to do it, like, "You don't need a condom when you have sex." Yeah, right. I'm just glad somebody told me the real deal.

The public-service announcement was placed by the New York Planned Parenthood Federation.

Reread the **Socially Responsible** section. Was there something in this material that offended you, some word that bothered you? What about some of the photographs in this chapter?

Read back still farther. Look at the photographs about the executions in Liberia. Were you uncomfortable when you looked at any of them?

I have used in this textbook material that some people may consider offensive, a word and photographs that are in questionable taste. A youth describes someone as a "snitch . . . a fucking narc." Some of the photographs are grim, if not horrifying.

Most people are bothered by obscene language and by explicit representations of death. Why, then, was the material used? Why did some newspapers that ran the story of the youngsters in Milpitas change the quote to read, "f------ narc," whereas others printed the word in full? And why did the Pulitzer Prize jurors think so much of the Liberia and Somalia pictures that they awarded the photographer prizes, while others turned away from the photographs in horror, condemning their use as another example of journalistic bad taste and sensationalism? Such questions are easier to raise than they are to answer.

Many people, and even some editors, have declared, "Nothing obscene, profane or indecent should be published or broadcast. We risk losing readers or listeners, so we'll play it safe."

Some newspaper advertising departments worried that the picture in the display advertisement for a James Bond movie might annoy readers. It showed the barely covered behind of a rifle-toting female. Some newspapers put their artists to work, painting short pants on the woman. And a few covered the area with copy.

The Double Standard

If the journalist is supposed to give the public a picture of reality, then a head-in-the-sand attitude deprives the public of essential information. Not only that, it is hypocritical. At the same time that some readers and listeners (and some editors as well) condemn the gossip columnist and are appalled by the picture of the dead child lying in the street, they applaud the talk shows, movies and soap operas that routinely parade incest, adultery, murder and nudity. They tune in the schlock jocks whose radio shows are a string of sexual innuendoes.

Here's a week on the soaps: In "General Hospital," Damian seduces Bobbie, a married woman, to win a bet. What did Tony expect when he married an ex-hooker, a character asks, and anyway, Bobbie says, Damian made her feel young

Mixed Messages

After the surgeon general in 1987 called for the use of condoms to promote "safe sex", TV and newspapers advertised the sale of prophylactics. Soon, however, interest groups flooded the stations with angry letters, and some politicians protested. The three major networks today do not accept paid contraceptive advertising, and FOX does but only for disease prevention messages. However, the networks have run public service announcements produced by the Department of Health and Human Services that advocate safer sex with condoms or abstinence to prevent the spread of HIV. Newspapers and magazines are more open to ads like these of the Planned Parenthood Federation that advocate the use of condoms to prevent pregnancy as well as disease. The media that turn down these advertisements contend their readers and viewers complain they are offended by the ads. Polls, however, show that most people are not opposed to such advertising. *Planned Parenthood Federation of America*

and sexy. In "The Bold and the Beautiful," James loses his virginity to aggressive Taylor. In one soap, Vivian steals Kate's embryo; in another, Mac and Felicia split, which enables Felicia to have a one-night stand with Frisco. In "One Life to Live," Blair seduces Max in the stable. In "Guiding Light," Dylan tells Bridget he'd like to spend the night with her. She doesn't hear his plea; she's fallen asleep. Later, they make love at the farm.

Many viewers do their housework—and homework—with one eye on these daily dramas. College students schedule their classes around their favorite soaps. And vacationers insist that their cottages come equipped with color TV sets so they can follow "Days of Our Lives" and "Another World."

Clearly, there are words, subject matter and pictures that should be off-limits. But how do we determine the limits? Do we refrain from using any material that would offend someone even though it is essential to a full description of the situation or event? Benjamin Franklin remarked, "If all printers were determined not to print anything until they were sure it would offend nobody, there would be very little printed."

These days much of what is newsworthy involves unsavory matters. Sources use profane and obscene language, and many of the crimes we report are unspeakably violent and vicious. Do we refrain from describing the brutal rape, the beheading of a 5-year-old, the robbery gang that drove ballpoint pens through the ears of helpless patrons of a supermarket?

We need guidelines for the use of frank language, subject matter that is offensive and pictures that are gruesome.

Frank Language

Vital. *The New York Times* permits the use of obscenity or vulgarity "only when the printing of the objectionable word or words will give the reader an obviously essential insight into matters of great moment—an insight that cannot be otherwise conveyed."

Most people find profanities and obscenities that refer to the sex act or to bodily functions to be unsavory. Much of the hostility to such language stems from the desire to keep this kind of language from becoming acceptable speech. Taste is the sum of many value judgments about what is acceptable language or behavior. If such language is seen and heard frequently by young people, it becomes a part of their vocabulary and, possibly, will influence their behavior. Thus, many adults—who are responsible for establishing values for their children—are anxious to hold the line against obscenity and profanity.

On the other hand, such language is part of everyday life. How do newspapers, radio and television stations tread the thin line between the extremes without falling on either side—offending well-intentioned people or cutting readers and listeners off from reality?

Audience and Relevance Let's start with the quote from the youth angry at the man he described as a "snitch." *The Miami Herald,* which carried the quote as "f------ narc," tried to walk the line. It did not run the obscenity, but by using the first letter and the exact number of dashes it was obvious to nearly all readers what the teen-ager actually said. The *Herald*'s readers range from grade school students to senior citizens. Some of the adult readers have strong feelings about obscenities. The newspaper prefers not to risk offending them. Yet the word *fucking* appears in this section. Why? Primarily to convey the intensity of the youth's feeling, and also because the audience of this book is likely to be acquainted with such language. To have used dashes would have been insulting and condescending. In addition, students are entitled to know the precise details of subjects they are studying.

To sum it up, the word was used because it was **essential to the situation** and because the **nature of the audience** was such that the word would not be considered offensive. These concepts are put in boldface because they are important guides in deciding whether to use certain kinds of language.

If the publication or station desires to set a policy on matters of taste, then editors and news writers must follow the policy. We now have a third guideline for determining what should be used: **the policy of the publication or station.**

Changing Guidelines

Up to this point, we have been assuming that everyone agrees on what is offensive. But what is in poor taste to one person may be acceptable to another. A rap singer and an Episcopal minister probably do not share the same definition of what is profane and what is obscene, and even among rappers and ministers there will be disagreement about what is tasteful and what is tasteless.

The truth is that there is little agreement on what is considered acceptable and what some believe to be in bad taste. There never was, and there never will be. For years, people enjoyed Shakespeare's plays. Then along came Thomas Bowdler who in 1818 found some parts of the plays unfit. He was dismayed by Juliet's young passion and changed her to a 17-year-old. He found Hamlet's vehement distaste for his mother's remarriage too graphic and eliminated the famous section.

In 1818, Bowdler produced a 10-volume version of the plays, *The Friendly Shakespeare,* and went on to clean up Gibbon's *Decline and Fall of the Roman Empire* and the Old Testament. His name has outlived his works. Bowdlerization or the verb *to bowdlerize* describe the revision or elimination of material for reasons that are absurdly circumspect.

Mark Twain had fun with bowdlerizers.

Mark Twain and Morality　In 1905, the Brooklyn Public Library decided to ban from the children's room Twain's *The Adventures of Huckleberry Finn* and *Tom Sawyer.* The librarians decided that the books were "bad examples" for children. (The guardians of public morality often contend that their actions are intended to protect the young from contamination.)

When Twain heard about the action of the librarians, he was facetiously contrite:

> I wrote *Tom Sawyer* and *Huck Finn* for adults exclusively, and it always distresses me when I find that boys and girls have been allowed access to them.
>
> The mind that becomes soiled in youth can never again be washed clean. I know this by my own experience, and to this day I cherish an unappeasable bitterness against the unfaithful guardians of my young life, who not only permitted but compelled me to read an unexpurgated Bible through before I was 15 years old.
>
> None can do that and ever draw a sweet breath again. . . .

Twain was poking fun at the aggressive guardians of public morality. *Huckleberry Finn* and books by J.D. Salinger, Kurt Vonnegut, Judy Blume and others are constantly under attack by zealots who seek to ban books even though the courts have held that book banning is unconstitutional.

Offensive Subject Matter

Subject matter that was once deemed unfit for use in the media is now daily fare. Nudity has increased in advertisements. Unsavory details in trials are daily fare on television. Newspapers carry material about the activities of a child pornography ring.

Even *The New York Times,* which promised on its founding that it would not "soil the breakfast table," reports the details of the latest survey of the sexual behavior of adults.

Because the *Times* is considered a model of circumspection in its use of stories and illustrations, readers were shocked when the cover of the Sunday *Times Magazine* carried the photo of a woman exposing her scarred breast where a surgeon's scalpel had performed a mastectomy. The photograph illustrated an article about the dangers of breast cancer.

Some readers objected, but most felt that the newspaper had performed a service by making the public take notice of an important issue.

The Associated Press carried on its wires and several newspapers ran a story about two 6-year-olds and an 8-year-old raping a 7-year-old girl in the back of a school bus.

These examples take us to another guideline for consideration: **the cautionary and informative nature of the potentially shocking material.**

Material that warns us, serves as a deterrent or informs us of important matters we should know about may be used despite its tastelessness. Indeed, it is the shocking nature of the material that helps to drive home the point.

We now have four guidelines to help us evaluate material we think warrants a closer examination because of questions of taste. But what do we mean by *essential,* for example, and *relevant?* And how can one judge the *nature of the audience* when it clearly is so diverse?

These questions came up with the story we mentioned at the beginning of this chapter: the murder of Stella Walsh, the Olympic track champion and a prominent member of Cleveland's Polish-American community.

After two television stations reported the coroner's finding that the examination revealed the body of 69-year-old Walsh was that of a man and not a woman, the community became angry and hostile. People called and wrote to protest the station's revelation.

The only local television station that did not mention the result of the autopsy was WJKW-TV, whose news director said that although the station knew of the sex angle it did not use it because "we didn't think it was germane to the story. It was essentially a story of crime and violence."

Cleveland's two daily newspapers agreed with the news director's sentiments. An editor of the *Plain Dealer* added that the paper "felt there should be dignity in death." To these objections, the assistant news director of WEWS-TV countered that the coroner's findings were the story. The full story was run by *The*

Philadelphia Inquirer, The Boston Globe and *The New York Times.* Only then did the Cleveland papers use the details.

Unquestionably, the coroner's findings were relevant: It is newsworthy that a female Olympic gold medal winner was actually male. The local newspapers and WJKW were overly sensitive to their audience, the Polish-American community. In the balancing of these legitimate claims, the journalist usually decides to use the material, for, after all, the journalist's job is to tell truths, no matter how unpleasant.

Why were the coroner's findings "unquestionably" relevant when clearly that's only my opinion? Because journalists are paid to make judgments—about what to cover, what to ignore, whom to trust as sources, what to play up and what to play down. The nature of the calling is risk taking, and along with that comes the self-assurance to stand by judgments.

Questionable Photographs

Pictures, particularly photographs of bodies, are the source of more reader complaints than are articles. Paul Watson's photo of the defilement of the dead U.S. serviceman in Somalia led to many complaints. In fact, Watson says he did not expect the pictures to be used because they were "too graphic." But he says he took the picture because "if they were my soldiers and I were back home, I'd sure as hell want to know about it so I could do something about it."

Thousands did. They called the White House to demand that U.S. troops be withdrawn from Somalia, and even more people called the newspapers and wrote letters saying that use of the photos had been tasteless.

Public Service or Irresponsible?

When the *Columbus Citizen-Journal* published this photograph of the body of a 9-year-old child who had been struck by a car, many readers wrote to protest. They described the picture as tasteless, irresponsible, an invasion into the family's grief. The newspaper editor replied that the picture was a stark reminder to parents and to children of the danger of city streets. *Hank Reichard, Scripps Howard Newspapers*

At a seminar at the Poynter Institute for Media Studies, 12 of the 22 print and broadcast journalists said they would have used the photo on page one, five would have used it inside, three would not have used it, one was unsure and another did not answer. A study of 34 major daily newspapers showed 11 used it on page one, 15 used it inside and eight didn't use it.

The photo the *Columbus Citizen-Journal* ran was stark and tragic. A child's body, half covered by a blanket, lay in the street where she had been struck and killed by a car.

As soon as the newspaper arrived in the homes of readers, the complaints began. Callers, then letter writers, complained that using the picture was irresponsible, that it was sensational journalism. Richard R. Campbell, the editor, said that "the most common accusation was that the picture was tasteless.

"One reader called us coldhearted and tasteless and urged us not to forget discretion and compassion." Another reader said, "You have won first prize in the journalistic bad taste contest. Your price for achieving this distinction is an all-expense paid trip to 'Sensational City' for the photographer and the editor who saw fit to print the picture."

Documentary   Campbell said that the decision to run the photograph was his. His reasons, he said, were these:

> There could be no more dramatic way to point out to mothers and fathers and children, to drivers and pedestrians, the danger of carelessly stepping into the street. The proverb says one picture is worth more than 1,000 words. Here was such a picture.
> Secondly, it was part of our role of writing history.
> One father who appreciated our reason for using the photo said he showed it to his small sons, separately, and took the time to explain to each what happened to the little girl and why. That is what we expected the reaction to be.

If we look back at the guidelines for using material that may be in questionable taste, we can see that one of the reasons editors use such pictures is the hope they will serve as warnings, deterrents. The horror of the picture might register, as no written warnings can, the dangers of playing in the street or darting out into the street.

Campbell also mentions the fact that this incident was part of local history. **The ability to capture history** is another guideline for the use of photographs. Of course, not every incident and accident is recorded by newspapers or television. The newspaper or broadcast station, like the historian, is selective. The editor chose to run this picture because it was a graphic documentation of a part of every community's history—the appalling toll of traffic deaths.

"We gave our readers a slice of Tuesday's life in Columbus that they did not want to see," a reporter said about the protests. "Hank Reichard took the image of that broken little girl and hurled it in our faces so that we would have to look at her, too.

"Hank made us care that a little girl had died when she should not have died, in a place that was terribly wrong for a child's death. He made us suffer."

Some of the same reasons can be given for the other photographs in this book that might have offended readers—the pictures by Larry C. Price of the executions on the beach in Liberia. These pictures did indeed show us history in the making, and they showed us the dark and lethal side of life.

News Value Sports pictures do not usually provide problems of taste. But Harry Baumert's photograph of an angry basketball coach caused problems for editors at *The Des Moines Register.* The photograph was of Iowa State University coach Johnny Orr gesticulating toward a referee—it was dubbed the "finger photo."

Although the editor of the newspaper approved the picture for publication, the sports editor killed it. "While it was a dramatic photo, it was clearly obscene. I didn't feel there was sufficient news value to risk alienating the bulk of our readers," the sports editor concluded.

An associate editor of the *Register* decided to ask editors across the country whether they would have used the picture. The result: 129 said no, 31 said yes and 61 said perhaps.

Of those who would have turned it down, 32 said they had used the photograph of Nelson Rockefeller, then vice president, making the same gesture to heckling students. AP Newsphotos ran the Rockefeller picture, but not the Iowa State shot. Why?

Rockefeller was widely known, his actions covered by the press. The coach, says Hal Buell, AP assistant general manager for Newsphotos, is hardly in the category of well-known. Buell says, "A picture of nobody giving nobody the finger is still a picture of nothing. So we wouldn't carry it, basically because it lacks news value." Our final guideline for the use of photographs is **news value.**

Summary

Here are some guidelines for questionable language, subject matter and photographs:

1. **The material must be essential to the story being told**—Without the material, the point would not be made or would be diluted.
2. **The audience must be taken into consideration**—If the great majority of readers or listeners would be offended, the material should not be used.
3. **The policy of the medium determines usage.**
4. **If the material serves as a warning or a deterrent, then it may be used despite its offensive nature.**
5. **If the event has historical significance and involves a well-known person in a news situation, it should be used.**

No to a Nobody

Harry Baumert, The Des Moines Register

Yes to a Somebody

Don Black, Binghamton Press and Sun-Bulletin

When the Associated Press transmitted top photograph it asked editors whether they would use it: 129 said no; 31, yes; 61, maybe.

But when the photograph below of the same gesture made by Nelson Rockefeller, then vice president, was distributed, many papers gave it page-one space. The difference, said editors, was in Rockefeller's prominence, the coach's relative anonymity.

Suggested Reading

Hulteng, John. *Playing It Straight.* Chester, Conn.: The Globe Pequot Press, 1981.

Sanford, Bruce. *Synopsis of the Law of Libel and the Right of Privacy.* New York: Newspaper Enterprise Assn. Inc., 1986.

The *Associated Press Stylebook* contains a Libel Manual of more than 20 pages. It is an excellent guide.

Stylebook

addresses Abbreviate *Avenue, Boulevard, Street* when used with specific addresses: *1314 Kentucky St.* Spell out when not with specific addresses: *construction on Kentucky Street.*

Use figures for address numbers: *3 Third Ave.; 45 Main St.* Spell out numbers under 10 in street names: *21 Fourth Ave.; 450 11th St.*

age Use figures. To express age as an adjective or as a noun, use hyphens: *a 3-year-old girl; it's for 5-year-olds.* Unless otherwise stated, the figure is presumed to indicate years: *a boy, 4, and his sister, 6 months.*

Further guidelines: *infant,* under one year of age; *child,* ages 1–13; *girl, boy,* under 18; *youth,* 13–18; *man, woman,* over 18; *adult,* over 18, unless used in specific legal context for crimes such as drinking; *middle-aged,* 35–55; *elderly,* over 65, but try to avoid.

a.m., p.m. Lowercase with periods.

amendment Capitalize when referring to specific amendments to the U.S. Constitution. Spell out for the first through ninth; use figures for 10th and above: *First Amendment, 10th Amendment.*

brand name A nonlegal term for a trademark. Do not use a brand name as a generic term or verb. Use *soft drink* instead of *Coke* or *coke; photocopy* instead of *Xerox.*

capitalization Generally, follow a down style. Use capitals for proper nouns: for names of persons, places, trademarks; for titles when used with names; for nicknames of people, states, teams, titles of books, plays, movies.

century Lowercase, spelling out numbers less than 10, except when used in proper nouns: *the fifth century; 18th century;* but *20th Century-Fox* and *Nineteenth Century Society,* following the organization's practice.

The purpose of a stylebook is to uniformly present the printed word. It sets standards for the use of abbreviations, capital letters, titles, punctuation and dates.

The stylebook eliminates arbitrary decisions. It is the guide that newspapers and the wire services use routinely to settle questions of usage.

423

chairman, chairwoman Use instead of *chair* or *chairperson;* use *spokesman* or *spokeswoman* instead of *spokesperson* and similar constructions unless the *-person* construction is a formal title.

Use *chairman* or *spokesman* when referring to the office in general. To avoid sexism, a neutral word such as *representative* is often the best choice.

co- Use a hyphen when forming nouns, adjectives and verbs that indicate occupation or status: *co-star, co-written.* No hyphen for other constructions: *coeducation, coexist.*

congress Capitalize when referring to the U.S. Senate and House of Representatives. The term is correctly used only in reference to the two legislative branches together.

Capitalize also when referring to foreign governments that use the term or its equivalent.

Constitution, constitutional Capitalize when referring to the U.S. Constitution, with or without the *U.S.* modifier. When referring to other constitutions, capitalize only when preceded by the name of a nation or state. Lowercase *constitutional.*

court names Capitalize the full proper names of courts at all levels. Retain capitalization if *U.S.* or a state name is dropped.

dates Use commas: *July 6, 1957, was her birth date.* Use no comma between month and year: *She was born in July 1957.*

Abbreviate month with specific date: *Feb. 19.* Spell out all months when standing alone. With dates, use abbreviations: *Jan., Feb., Aug., Sept., Oct., Nov., Dec.* Spell out *March, April, May, June, July.*

directions and regions Lowercase *north, south, northeast,* etc., when they indicate compass direction: *Police followed the car south on Route 22.*

Capitalize when referring to regions: *Southern accent; Northeastern industry.*

Lowercase names of nations except when they are part of a proper name or are used to designate a politically divided nation: *tourism in southern France;* but *South Korea* and *Northern Ireland.*

fireman Use *firefighter* since some women hold this job.

fractions Spell out amounts less than 1, using hyphens: *one-half, two-thirds.* Use figures for amounts larger than 1, converting to decimals whenever possible: *3.5* instead of *three and one-half* or *3½.*

Figures are preferred in tabular material and in stories about stocks.

holidays and holy days Capitalize them. In federal law, the legal holidays are New Year's, Martin Luther King's Birthday, Washington's Birthday (President's Day), Memorial Day, Independence Day, Labor Day, Columbus Day, Veteran's Day, Thanksgiving and Christmas. States are not required to follow the federal lead in designating holidays, but federal employees must receive the day off or must be paid overtime if they work.

Jewish holy days are Hanukkah, Passover, Purim, Rosh Hashana, Shavuot, Sukkot, and Yom Kippur.

initials Use periods and no space: *H.L. Mencken; C.S. Lewis.* This practice has been adopted to ensure that initials will be set on the same line.

nationalities and races Capitalize the proper names of nationalities, peoples, races, tribes, etc. Lowercase *black, white,* etc. Lowercase derogatory terms such as *honky* and *nigger* and use them only in direct quotations.

See **race** for guidelines on when racial identification is pertinent in a story.

non- Hyphenate all except the following words, which have meanings of their own: *nonchalance, nonchalant, nondescript, nonentity, nonsense, nonsensical.*

numerals Spell out *one* through *nine* except when used to indicate age or with dates. Use figures for *10* and above.

Spell out a number when it begins a sentence unless the figure is a year: *Fifteen members voted against the bill; 1980 began auspiciously.*

Use figures for percentages and percents.

For amounts of $1 million and more, use the *$* sign and in figures up to two decimal places spell out *million, billion, trillion: $1.65 million.* Exact amounts are given in figures: *$1,650,398.*

When spelling out large numbers, separate compound numbers ending in *y* from next number with hyphens: *seventy-nine; one hundred seventy-nine.*

percentages Use figures—decimals, not fractions—and the word *percent,* not the symbol: *2.5 percent; 10 percent.* For amounts less than 1 percent, place a zero before the decimal: *0.6 percent.*

When presenting a range, repeat *percent* after each figure: *2 percent to 5 percent.*

policeman Use *police officer* instead.

political parties and philosophies Capitalize the names of parties and the word *party* when it is used as part of an organization's proper name: *the Democratic Party.*

Capitalize *Communist, Conservative, Democrat, Liberal,* etc. when they refer to the activities of a specific party or to members of a party.

Lowercase the name of a philosophy in noun and adjective forms unless it is derived from a proper name: *communism; fascist;* but *Marxism* and *Nazi.*

prefixes Generally do not hyphenate when using a prefix with a root word starting with a consonant: *rewash; ultrafast.*

Except for *cooperate* and *coordinate,* use a hyphen if the prefix ends in the same vowel that begins the root word: *re-elect,* not *reelect.*

Use a hyphen if the root word is capitalized: *pan-American; anti-Catholic.*

Use a hyphen to join doubled prefixes: *sub-subclause.*

president Capitalize only as a title before an individual's name: *President Bill Clinton,* but *The president said he would spend New Year's in Maine.*

race Race, religion and national origin are sometimes essential to a story but too often are injected when they are not pertinent. When in doubt about relevance, substitute descriptions such as *white, Baptist, French*. If one of these descriptions would be pertinent, use the original term.

religious references Lowercase *heaven, hell, devil, angel, cherub, apostle, priest*.

DEITIES: Capitalize the proper names of monotheistic deities, pagan and mythological gods and goddesses: *Allah, the Father, Zeus*. Lowercase pronouns that refer to the deity: *he, him, thee, who*.

Lowercase *gods* when referring to the deities of polytheistic religions. Lowercase such words as *god-awful, godlike, godsend*.

RITES: Capitalize proper names for rites that commemorate the Last Supper or signify a belief in Christ's presence: *the Lord's Supper; Holy Eucharist*. Lowercase the names of other sacraments.

HOLY DAYS: Capitalize the names of holy days: *Hanukkah*.

seasons Lowercase *spring, summer, fall, winter* and their derivatives. Capitalize when part of a formal name: *St. Paul Winter Carnival; Summer Olympics*.

senate, senatorial Capitalize all references to specific legislative bodies, regardless of whether the name of the nation or state is used: *U.S. Senate; the state Senate*.

Lowercase plural uses: *the Iowa and Kansas state senates*. Lowercase references to nongovernmental bodies: *the student-faculty senate*.

Always lowercase *senatorial*.

sexism Avoid stereotyping women or men. Be conscious of equality in treatment of both sexes.

When writing of careers and families, avoid presuming that the wage earner is a man and that the woman is a homemaker: *the average family of five*, instead of *the average worker with a wife and three children*.

Avoid physical descriptions of women or men when not absolutely relevant to the story. Personal appearance and marital and family relationships should be used only when relevant to the story.

Use parallel references to both sexes: *the men and the women*, not *the men and the ladies; husband and wife*, not *man and wife*.

Do not use nouns and pronouns to indicate sex unless the sex difference is basic to understanding, or there is no suitable substitute. One way to avoid such subtle sexism is to change the noun to the plural, eliminating the masculine pronoun: *Drivers should carry their licenses*, instead of *Every driver should carry his license*.

state names Spell out names of the 50 states when they stand alone in textual matter.

The names of eight states are never abbreviated: *Alaska, Hawaii, Idaho, Iowa, Maine, Ohio, Texas, Utah*.

Abbreviate other state names when used with a city, in a dateline or with a party affiliation. Use the following, not Postal Service abbreviations:

Ala.	*Kan.*	*Nev.*	*S.C.*
Ariz.	*Ky.*	*N.H.*	*S.D.*
Ark.	*La.*	*N.J.*	*Tenn.*
Calif.	*Md.*	*N.M.*	*Vt.*
Colo.	*Mass.*	*N.Y.*	*Va.*
Conn.	*Mich.*	*N.C.*	*Wash.*
Del.	*Minn.*	*N.D.*	*W.Va.*
Fla.	*Miss.*	*Okla.*	*Wis.*
Ga.	*Mo.*	*Ore.*	*Wyo.*
Ill.	*Mont.*	*Pa.*	
Ind.	*Neb.*	*R.I.*	

statehouse Capitalize all references to a specific statehouse, with or without the state name. But lowercase in all plural uses: *the New Mexico Statehouse; the Arizona and New Mexico statehouses.*

suspensive hyphenation Although suspensive hyphenation looks somewhat awkward, it guides readers, who may otherwise expect a noun to follow the first figure: *The 19- and 20-year-olds were not served alcoholic beverages.* Use in all similar cases.

teen, teen-ager (noun), **teen-age** (adjective) Do not use *teen-aged.*

temperatures Use figures for all except *zero.* Use the word *minus,* not a minus sign, to indicate temperatures below zero. *The day's high was 9; the day's low was minus 9.*

time Exact times often are unnecessary. *Last night* and *this morning* are acceptable substitutes for *yesterday* and *today.* Use exact time when pertinent, but avoid redundancies: *8 a.m. this morning* should be *8 a.m. today* or *8 o'clock this morning.*

Use figures except for *noon* and *midnight: 12 noon* is redundant.

Separate hours from minutes with a colon: *3:15 p.m.*

titles ACADEMIC TITLES: Capitalize and spell out formal titles such as *professor, dean, president, chancellor, chairman,* etc. when they precede a name. Lowercase elsewhere. Do not abbreviate *Professor* as *Prof.*

Lowercase modifiers, such as *journalism* in *journalism Professor John Rist* or *department* in *department chairwoman Kim Power,* unless the modifier is a proper name: *French Professor Ann Marie Jones.*

COURTESY TITLES: Do not use the courtesy titles *Miss, Mr., Mrs. or Ms.* on first reference. Instead, use the person's first and last names. Do not use *Mr.* unless it is combined with *Mrs.: Kyle Scott Hotsenpiller; Mr. and Mrs. Kyle Scott Hotsenpiller.*

Courtesy titles are used on second reference for women in most newspapers. Use these guidelines:

1. Married women: On first reference, identify a woman by her own first name and her husband's last name: *Betty Phillips.* Use *Mrs.* on first reference

only if a woman requests that her husband's first name be used or her own first name cannot be determined: *Mrs. Steven A. Phillips.*

On second reference, use *Mrs.* unless a woman initially identified by her own first name prefers *Ms.: Rachel Finch; Mrs. Finch* or *Ms. Finch.*

If a married woman is known by her maiden name, precede it by *Miss* on second reference unless she prefers *Ms.: Sarah Wilson; Miss Wilson* or *Ms. Wilson.*

2. Unmarried women: Use *Miss* or *Ms.* on second reference, according to the woman's preference.

For divorced and widowed women, the normal practice is to use *Mrs.* on second reference. Use *Miss* if a woman returns to her maiden name. Use *Ms.* if she prefers it.

If a woman prefers *Ms.,* do not include her marital status in a story unless it is pertinent.

A number of newspapers drop *Mrs., Miss* and *Ms.* as well as *Mr.* on second reference. The *AP Stylebook* states, "If the woman says she does not want a courtesy title, refer to her on second reference by last name only."

GOVERNMENTAL TITLES: Capitalize when used as formal titles before people's names. It is not necessary to use a title on second reference: *Gov. Fred Florence; Florence.* For women who hold official positions, use the courtesy title on second reference, according to the guidelines for courtesy titles: *Gov. Ruth Arnold; Miss Arnold, Mrs. Arnold, Ms. Arnold.* Some newspapers do not use the courtesy title on second reference.

Abbreviate *Governor* as *Gov.* and *Lieutenant Governor* as *Lt. Gov.* when used as a formal title before a name.

Congressional titles: Before names, abbreviate *Senator* as *Sen.* and *Representative* as *Rep.* Add *U.S.* or *state* if necessary to avoid confusion.

Short form punctuation for party affiliation: Use abbreviations listed under **state names** and set off from the person's name with commas: *Sen. Nancy Landon Kassebaum, R-Kan., and Rep. Charles Hatcher, D-Ga., attended the ceremony.*

Capitalize and spell out other formal government titles before a person's name. Do not use titles in second references: *Attorney General Jay Craven spoke. Craven said . . .*

Capitalize and spell out formal titles instead of abbreviating before the person's name only in direct quotations. Lowercase in all uses not mentioned above.

OCCUPATIONAL TITLES: Always lowercase: *senior vice president Nancy Harden.* Avoid false titles: Make it *Helen P. George, Sioux Falls bridge tourney winner,* not *bridge champion Helen P. George.*

TITLES OF WORKS: For book titles, movie titles, opera titles, play titles, poem titles, song titles, television program titles and the titles of lectures, speeches and works of art, apply the following guidelines:

Capitalize the principal words, including prepositions and conjunctions of four or more letters.

Capitalize an article or word of fewer than four letters if it is the first or last word in a title.

Place quotation marks around the names of all such works except the Bible and books that are primarily catalogs of reference material, including almanacs, directories, dictionaries, encyclopedias, handbooks and similar publications.

Translate a foreign title into English unless a work is known to the American public by its foreign name.

Do not use quotation marks or italics with the names of newspapers and magazines.

TV Acceptable as an adjective but should not be used as a noun.

vice Use two words, no hyphen.

vice president Follow the guidelines for **president.**

well- Hyphenate as part of a compound modifier: *well-dressed; well-read.*

words as words Italicize when possible. Otherwise, place in quotation marks: *Rep. Ellen Jacobson asked journalists to address her as "congresswoman."*

years Use figures. Add an *s* without the apostrophe to indicate spans of centuries: *the 1800s.* Use an apostrophe to indicate omitted numerals and an *s* to indicate decades: *the '80s.*

Years are the only figures that may be placed at the start of a sentence: *1959 was a year of rapid city growth.*

Punctuation

Keep a good grammar book handy. No stylebook can adequately cover the complexities of the 13 punctuation marks: apostrophe, bracket, colon, comma, dash, ellipsis, exclamation point, hyphen, parenthesis, period, question mark, quotation mark, semicolon. The following is a guide to frequent problems and usages:

apostrophe Use to (1) indicate possession, (2) indicate omitted figures or letters and (3) form some plurals.

1. *Possessives:* Add apostrophe and *s* (*'s*) to the end of singular and plural nouns or the indefinite pronoun unless it has an *s* or *z* sound.

The woman's coat. The women's coats.
The child's toy. The children's toys.
Someone's pistol. One's hopes.

If the word is plural and ends in an *s* or *z* sound, add an apostrophe only:

Boys' books. Joneses' farm.

For singular common nouns ending in *s,* add an apostrophe and *s* (*'s*) unless the next word begins with *s:*

The hostess's gown. The hostess' seat.

For singular proper nouns ending in *s,* add only an apostrophe:

> *Dickens' novels. James' hat.*

2. *Omitted figures or letters:* Use in contractions: *Don't, can't.* Put in place of omitted figure: *Class of '88.*

3. *Some Plurals:* When figures, letters, symbols and words are referred to as words, use the apostrophe and *s.*

   a Figures: *She skated perfect 8's.*

   b. Letters: *He received all A's on his finals.*

   c. Symbols: *Journalists never use &'s to substitute for the ands in their copy.*

The pronouns *ours, yours, theirs, his, hers, whose* do not take apostrophes. *Its* is the possessive pronoun. *It's* is the contraction of *it is.*

Compound words and nouns in joint possession use the possessive in the last word:

> *Everybody else's homes.*
> *His sister-in-law's book.*
> *Mondale and Kennedy's party.*

If there is separate possession, each noun takes the possessive form:

> *Carter's and Kennedy's opinions differ.*

bracket Check whether the newspaper can set brackets. Use to enclose a word or words within a quote that the writer inserts: *"Happiness [his note read] is a state of mind."* Use for paragraph(s) within a story that refer to an event separate from the datelined material.

colon The colon is usually used at the end of a sentence to call attention to what follows. It introduces lists, tabulations, texts and quotations of more than one sentence.

It can also be used to mark a full stop before a dramatic statement: *She had only one goal in life: work.* The colon is used in time of day: *7:45 p.m.;* elapsed time of an event: *4:01.1;* and in dialogue in question and answer, as from a trial.

Should the word immediately following a colon be capitalized? Only if what follows is a complete sentence.

> *He found three pens: red, blue and black.*
> *Tourism looks promising next year: Construction of motels/restaurants is booming.*

comma The best general guide for the use of the comma is the human voice as it pauses, stops and varies in tone. The comma marks the pause, the short stop:

1. *He looked into the hospital room, but he was unable to find the patient.*

2. *Although he continued his search on the floor for another 20 minutes, he was unable to find anyone to help him.*

3. *He decided that he would go downstairs, ask at the desk and then telephone the police.*

4. *If that also failed, he thought to himself, he would have to give up the search.*

Note that when reading these sentences aloud, the commas are natural resting points for pauses. The four sentences also illustrate the four principles governing the use of commas:

1. The comma is used to separate main clauses when they are joined by a coordinating conjunction. (The coordinating conjunctions are *for, nor, and, but, or.*) The comma can be eliminated if the main clauses are short: *He looked into the room and he froze.*

2. Use the comma after an introductory element: a clause, long phrase, transitional expression or interjection.

3. Use the comma to separate words, phrases or clauses in a series. Do not use a comma before the coordinating conjunction in a series: *The flag is red, white and blue.* Use it in a series of coordinate adjectives: *He was wearing a long, full cape.*

4. Set off nonessential material in a sentence with comma(s). When the parenthetical or interrupting nonrestrictive clauses and phrases are in the middle of a sentence, two commas are needed: *The country, he was told, needed his assistance.*

Other uses of the comma:

1. With full sentence quotes, not with partial quotes: *He asked, "Where are you going?" The man replied that he was "blindly groping" his way home.*

2. To separate city and county, city and state.

3. In place of the word *of* between a name and city: *Jimmy Carter, Plains, Ga.*

4. To set off a person's age: *Orville Sterb, 19, of Fullerton, Calif.*

5. In dates: *March 19, 1940, was the date he entered the army.*

6. In party affiliations: *Bill Bradley, D-N.J., spoke.*

7. To set off a title: *Jane Tyrone, the chairwoman, spoke at the meeting.*

The comma is frequently misused between two main clauses when a period or a coordinating conjunction would be correct. This error is called comma splice:

WRONG: *The typewriter was jammed, he could not type his theme.*

RIGHT: *The typewriter was jammed. He could not type his theme.* Or: *The typewriter was jammed; he could not type his theme.* Or: *The typewriter was jammed, so he could not type his theme.*

dash Use a dash to (1) indicate a sudden or dramatic shift in thought within a sentence, (2) set off a series of words that contains commas and (3) introduce sections of a list or a summary.

The dash is a call for a short pause, just as are the comma and the parenthesis. The comma is the most often used and is the least dramatic of the separators. Parentheses set off unimportant elements. The dash tends to emphasize material. It has this quality because it is used sparingly.

1. *He stared at the picture—and he was startled to find himself thinking of her face.*
The man stood up—painfully and awkwardly—and extended his hand in greeting.
2. *There were three people watching them—an elderly woman, a youth with a crutch at his side and a young woman in jeans holding a paperback— and he pulled her aside out of their view.*
3. *He gave her his reasons for being there:*
    — He wanted to apologize;
    — He needed to give her some material;
    — He was leaving on a long trip.

This third form should be used infrequently, usually when the listing is followed by an elaboration.

The dash is also used in datelines.

ellipsis Use the ellipsis to indicate material omitted from a quoted passage from a text, transcript, play, etc.: *The minutes stated that Breen had asked, "How many gallons of paint . . . were used in the project?"* Put one space before and one space after each of the three ellipsis marks. If the omission ends with a period, use four ellipsis marks, one to mark the end of the sentence (without space, as a regular period), three more for the ellipsis.

The ellipsis is also used by some columnists to separate short items in a paragraph.

Do not use the ellipsis to mark pauses or shifts in thought or for emphasis.

exclamation point Much overused. There are reporters who have gone through a lifetime of writing and have never used the exclamation point, except when copying material in which it is used. The exclamation point is used to indicate powerful feelings, surprise, wonder. Most good writers prefer to let the material move the reader to provide his or her own exclamation.

When using the exclamation point, do not place a comma or period after it. Place it inside quotation marks if it is part of the quoted material.

hyphen The hyphen is used to (1) join words to express a single idea or (2) avoid confusion or ambiguity.

1. Use a hyphen to join two or more words that serve as a single adjective before a noun: *A well-known movie is on television tonight. He had a know-it-all expression.*

Do not use the hyphen when the first word of the compound ends in *ly* or when the compound follows the noun: *He is an easily recognized person. Her hair was blonde black.*

2. Use a hyphen between prefixes or suffixes and the root word to avoid (a) ambiguity or (b) an awkward joining of letters:

    a. *He recovered the chair. He re-covered the chair.*
    b. *Re-enter, macro-economics, shell-like.*

parenthesis Generally, avoid. Parentheses may be necessary for the insertion of background or to set off supplementary or illustrative material.

Use a period inside a closing parenthesis if the matter within the parentheses is a complete sentence. Other punctuation goes after the closing parenthesis unless the punctuation refers to the material in the parentheses: *Abbie Hoffman (remember him?) was a Sixties radical.*

period Use a period at the end of declarative sentences, indirect questions, most imperative sentences and most abbreviations.

A period is placed inside quotation marks.

question mark A question mark is used for direct questions, not indirect questions.

    DIRECT: *Where are you going?*
    INDIRECT: *He asked where she was going.*

A question mark goes inside quotation marks if it applies to the quoted material: *He asked, "Have you seen the movie?"* Put it outside if it applies to the entire sentence: *Have you seen "Phantom of the Opera"?*

quotation marks Quotation marks set off (1) direct quotations, (2) some titles and nicknames and (3) words used in a special way.

1. Set off the exact words of the speaker: *"He walked like a duck," she said. He replied that he walked "more like an alley cat on the prowl."*

2. Use for book and movie titles and titles of short stories, poems, songs, articles from magazines and plays. Some nicknames take quotation marks. Do not use them for nicknames of sports figures.

3. Use for words meant in a special sense: *If you were "it," you had to try to tag the other players.*

Punctuation with quotation marks:

The comma—Use it outside the quotation marks when setting off the speaker at the beginning of a sentence: *He said, "You care too much for money."* Use it inside the quotation marks when the speaker ends the sentence: *"I just want to be safe," she replied.*

The colon and semicolon—Always place outside the quotation marks: *He mentioned her "incredible desire for work"; he meant her "insatiable desire for work."*

The dash, question mark and exclamation point—Use them inside the quotation marks when they apply to quoted matter only and outside when they refer to the whole sentence: *She asked, "How do you know so much?" Did she really wonder why he knew "so much"?*

For quotes within quotes, use a single quote mark (the apostrophe on a type-writer) for the inner quotation: *"Have you read 'War and Peace'?" he asked.* Note no comma is used after the question mark.

semicolon Usually overused by beginning reporters. Unless there is a special reason to use the semicolon, use the period.

Use the semicolon to separate a series of equal elements when the individual segments contain material that is set off by commas. This makes for clarity in the series: *He suggested that she spend her allowance on the new series at the opera, "Operas of the Present"; books of plays by Shaw, Ibsen and Aristophanes; and novels by Tolstoy, Dickens and F. Scott Fitzgerald.*

Speaking Punctuation

Russell Baker, the writer, says that "when speaking aloud, you punctuate constantly—with body language. Your listener hears commas, dashes, question marks, exclamation points, quotation marks as you shout, whisper, pause, wave your arms, roll your eyes, wrinkle your brow." Here are some of Baker's tips for punctuating on paper:

Generally speaking, use a comma where you'd pause briefly in speech. For a long pause or completion of thought, use a period.

The semicolon separates two main clauses, but it keeps those two thoughts more tightly linked than a period can.

The dash SHOUTS! Parentheses whisper. Shout too often, people stop listening; whisper too much, people become suspicious of you.

A colon is a tip-off to get ready for what's next: a list, a long quotation or an explanation.

Too many exclamation points make me think the writer is talking about the panic in his own head.

Don't sound panicky. End with a period. I am serious. A period. Understand?

Well . . . sometimes a question mark is okay.

Appendix A
Preparing Copy

On a Typewriter

1. Use copy paper, newsprint or some other nonglossy paper. Triple space. Use wide margins left and right.

2. Make a copy of all your work. Keep the copy.

3. In the upper left-hand corner of the first sheet of all assignments, place your name, slug of story, news source and date. Thus:

```
Chamberlain
PHA-attended
12/21/96
```

4. Begin one-third down the first page. Write on one side of the paper only.

5. If the story consists of more than one page, write and circle *more* at the bottom of the page that is being continued. On the next page, put your name, slug and "2" at the top left. Thus: Chamberlain-PHA-2. On the next page, make it 3, and so on.

6. End each page with a complete paragraph, not in the middle of a sentence.

7. Do not correct mistakes by backspacing and typing over. Cross out and retype. Never write over.

8. For simple errors, use copy editing symbols. (See Appendix F.) Do not confuse these symbols with proofreading marks. Use pencil to edit your copy.

9. Never divide words at the end of a line. Hit the margin release and continue, or cross out and begin the word anew on the next line.

10. Keep the copy clean. Retype hard-to-read sections and paste over.

11. Do not write more than one story on each sheet of paper.
12. End stories with an end mark: 30, #, or END.
13. Follow the stylebook.

On a Video Display Terminal

Newspapers have traded in their typewriters for electronic equipment. The video display terminal (VDT) consists of keyboard and screen. The keyboard is used much like a typewriter, although it also has keys with special instructions for setting the type, moving copy around and editing.

The screen displays the copy as it is typed. Depending on the terminal model, 14 to 30 lines of copy can be seen on the screen.

The copy may be stored on a magnetic disk, a magnetic card or in some other storage device. It can then be called up for copy editing, which is also carried out on the screen of the terminal.

The edited version is sent to the phototypesetter, which sets the story according to the instructions of the news writer or editor. The story is produced on photosensitive paper that is placed in a processor.

In the processor, the paper is developed and a positive image or print is produced. The printed material is proofread and then placed on sheets for makeup.

For the newswriter, keyboarding a story is faster and easier than using the typewriter. Since most systems have a program that justifies lines and hyphenates words, the writer does not have to return the carriage but types in an endless line. Corrections and other changes are made with the use of a cursor, a patch of light that can be moved anywhere on the screen.

On newspapers whose terminals connect to a large storage computer, newswriters can call up various reference materials, such as the newspaper's clippings on a subject. Reporters also can store their notes or partially completed stories, and with the use of their personal codes can retrieve them.

When the story is finished, a copy editor reads it on the screen and puts into the terminal the instructions about how the copy is to be set. These instructions are called *formats* or *parameters*.

Appendix B
Moving the Story

Newspaper Copy

After a local story has been written, it is turned in to the city desk. If it has been written on a video display terminal, the city desk calls it up for examination on the screen.

The city editor or assistant city editor reads through the copy to see that it is satisfactory, that the lead contains the main news point and that all questions the reader may have are answered. If the story is inadequate, it is sent back to the newswriter for further work. If acceptable, the story moves to the next stage, the news desk, where the type of headline and the story's length are determined. Then the story moves to the copy desk. On smaller newspapers, the city editor decides on the type of headline and the story length.

At the copy desk, the story is given a thorough reading. Grammar, punctuation and spelling are checked. The writing is made to conform to the newspaper's style—*Street* may be abbreviated to *St., fourteen* changed to *14.*

If the paper is tight that day, the copy editor trims the story, usually from the bottom. Unnecessary adjectives and adverbs are removed, even when the paper is open—meaning there is plenty of room for news. Redundancies (*true facts, circulated around, 7 a.m. in the morning*) are corrected. Sentences in the passive voice are changed to the active: *The burglar was seen by one of the children* becomes *One of the children saw the burglar.*

A copy editor may spot something the city editor missed. If the problem is minor, the copy desk will solve it, but if it is major the story may be sent back to the writer. If the education reporter used too much education jargon—the specialized language of educators—the copy editor replaces the technical wording with everyday words and phrases. When the editing is completed, the copy editor writes a headline for the story.

How a Newspaper Story Moves

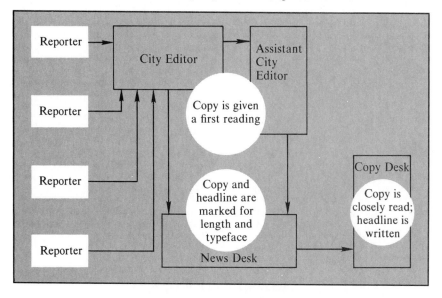

Before a story reaches production, it is checked at several points by various editors to insure its accuracy, clarity and correct length for the assigned space.

Central Nervous System

The computer is the vital link in the newsroom. It joins reporters, editors and the production unit into an integrated system. Reporters type their stories, editors call them up for editing and headline writing. The finished matter is sent to production. *Joel Sartore, The Wichita Eagle-Beacon*

Nonlocal stories are usually taken from the wire service machines—AP, UPI or others. If the newspaper subscribes to more than one wire service and the news editor wants to combine the dispatches of two or more of them into a single story, the news editor may ask the managing editor to assign the job to a newswriter.

On large newspapers, such as the one diagrammed below, a regional editor goes over news from correspondents in nearby communities, the business editor handles news from the business staff and from the wires that the news editor or wire editor has turned over to the business desk, and the sports editor handles sports copy.

Each of these specialized departments may have a copy desk of its own. On smaller newspapers, all copy is channeled to a single copy desk.

Newsroom Organization

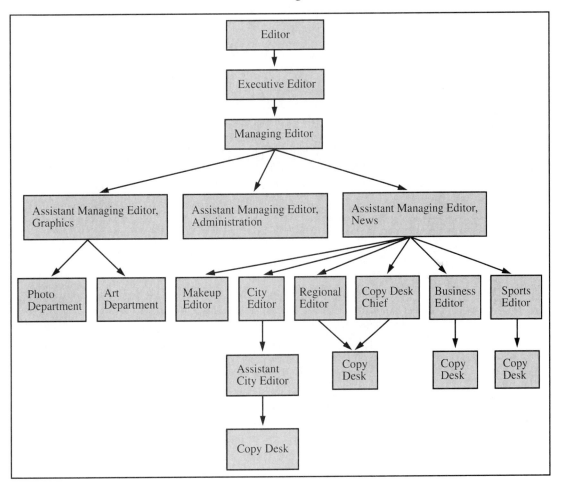

This diagram illustrates the way large newsrooms are set up. Smaller newspapers may have just one copy desk, called the universal desk, that handles all copy but sports and social news.

As the news day develops, the makeup editor decides how to lay out the newspaper—where to put the stories. Material for the inside pages—columns, editorials, comic strips and secondary stories—is laid out first.

On large newspapers, the decision about where to put, or **play,** stories is made at a story conference or news conference. There, the editors of the various sections present the best of their stories to the managing editor. The city editor discusses last night's city council meeting, the national news editor mentions a story from Washington about the federal budget. On some newspapers, a foreign editor is also present.

The managing editor decides what stories will go on page one and which will be given top play. The number one story is usually placed in the upper-right-hand side of the page.

On smaller newspapers, the decisions on play are less formal. The managing editor and the city editor discuss story play during the day and then instruct the makeup editor about their decisions.

In both cases, the photo editor, or assistant managing editor for graphics, informs the managing editor or another editor about the local and wire photos or graphics and charts that are available to accompany the major stories.

Once the decisions have been made about play, it is up to the makeup editor to produce a pleasing display of the news for page one and for other section pages—those pages that begin different sections of the newspaper.

Increasingly, newspapers are being edited and made up on video screens. Just as the terminal keyboard has replaced the typewriter, the terminal is replacing the copy editor's pencil and the layout sheets, called **dummies,** of the makeup staff.

When the newsroom work is completed, the laid-out stories are placed on plates, which are usually made up by photocomposition, and then are sent to the pressroom.

Broadcast Copy

Broadcast news stories move from the writer to the news editor or to the person who will be reading the copy. The copy is edited to see that it can be read aloud without difficulty. Factual errors are corrected, and the copy is checked for broadcast style. Some numerals are written out: The number *20* becomes *twenty; 500,000* becomes *500 thousand.*

Correspondents in the field write their own copy, but sometimes they "wing it," meaning they speak without written copy.

In smaller stations with no news staff, announcers take wire copy directly from the AP or UPI Teletype machines and read it with little advance checking. This is called "rip and read," and it is the cause of many of the bloopers that are collected and sold as entertainment.

Local TV Newsroom Organization

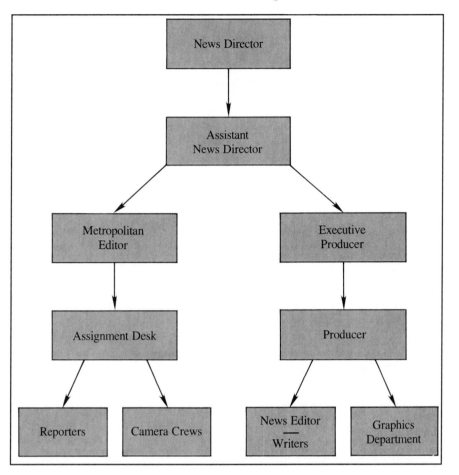

This system is used by CBS-owned stations for their local news staffs. The metropolitan editor directs the reporting staff and camera crews. The executive editor oversees the actual broadcast. At stations where there are several major newscasts there will be different executive producers and producers for each newscast.

Appendix C

How to Use the Freedom of Information Act

Who Can Make a Request?

The FOIA permits "any person" to request access to agency records. In practice, "any person" includes U.S. citizens, permanent resident aliens and foreign nationals, as well as corporations, unincorporated associations, universities, state and local governments and members of Congress.

How Quickly Will an Agency Respond?

The FOIA requires an agency to respond to an initial request within 10 working days and to an administrative appeal within 20 working days.

An agency may take an additional 10 days to respond to either the initial request or the administrative appeal in "unusual circumstances" involving the agency's need to obtain records from field facilities, process separate and distinct records, or consult with another agency or two or more of its own components having a substantial interest in the request.

If the agency fails to comply with the applicable time requirements, the requester is deemed to have exhausted his administrative remedies and may seek satisfaction in court. In such a case, however, if the agency can show that "exceptional circumstances" exist and that it is exercising due diligence in responding to the request, the court may retain jurisdiction and allow the agency additional time to complete its review of the records.

Otherwise, upon any determination by an agency to comply with a request, the FOIA requires that the records "shall be made promptly available" to the requester.

Where to Write

The first order of business in making an FOIA request is to determine which agency should receive it. If you are uncertain about which agency may have the information you seek, go to the library and check the records you want and find out the specific mailing address for its FOIA office.

Describe What You Want

The FOIA requires that a request must "reasonably describe" the records being sought. This means that the description must be sufficiently specific so that a government employee who is familiar with an agency's filing system will be able to locate the records within a reasonable amount of time. There is no requirement that you explain why you are seeking the information, but such an explanation might be necessary if you want the agency to waive its fees or comply more fully with your request. The more precise and accurate the request, the more likely you are to get a prompt and complete response, with lower search fees. If you do not give a clear description of the information that is being requested, the agency will contact you for clarification.

Plan Your Request Strategy

Try to limit your request to what you really want. If you simply ask for "all files relating to" a particular subject (including yourself), you may give the agency an excuse to delay its response and needlessly run up search and copying costs.

If you know that the request involves a voluminous number of records, try to state both what your request includes and what it does not include.

Try to be specific about the "search logic" you want the agency to follow. Use *and/or* to describe the different subject matters under request. By using the word *and* between different topics—for example, "mail openings *and* surveillance"—you may receive information that falls into both categories but receive none of the documents that relate *only* to "mail openings" or *only* to "surveillance."

If you want material released to you in an order of specific priorities, inform the agency of your needs; for example, you might want to have materials reviewed and released to you in chronological or geographical order, or you may simply not want to wait for *all* of the records to be reviewed before any are released.

Decide whether you want to write a local or regional office of a given agency instead of (or in addition to) the headquarters. Headquarters will ordinarily have policy-making information, plus information of a more general nature than the local officials have chosen to report; the field offices ordinarily have the working files.

STATEMENT OF WITNESS

2 December 1981
(Date)

I, WAYNE G. SHELTON, Special Agent, AFOSI, hereby state that KARL L. GULBERSON, SPECIAL AGENT, as has identified himself to me USAF.
(Special Agent AFOSI, Security Police, Other-Specify)

I do hereby voluntarily and of my own free will make the following statement without having been subjected to any coercion, unlawful influence or unlawful inducement.
On 30 Nov 81, at approximately 2200 hours, I arrived at Manzano Weapon Storage Area (MWSA) with [6X] and we reported for duty. Earlier in the night I had been with [6X] when he rolled two "joints" (marijuana cigarettes) and he stated they were for tonight and placed them in his shirt pocket. While standing in the Armory of MWSA, prior to guardmount, I approached [6X] and asked him what post he has tonight and he replied he's going to be posted on India-4 with [6X] asked me where I was going to be posted and I told him India-6 with [6X]. I had originally been scheduled to be posted with [6X] but that night when [6X] reported for duty the Armory personnel said he was no longer qualified to carry the M-203 grenade launcher, so a post change was made, [6X] was placed on India-5 with [6X] and I told him [6X] asked me who's going to be on Bravo-3 and I. He then stated that later in the shift we would rendezvous at the bravo sector pumps and smoke the joints he has. At approximately midnight, after we were posted, Bravo-3 [6X] came to the bravo sector pumps and parked their vehicle [6X] and I exited our jeep walked to Bravo-3's vehicle and got into the back seat. We sat there and talked for a while. [6X] were debating whether or not they would "toke up" (slang: a puff on a marijuana cigarette) when [6X] arrived. [6X] stated the last time he had gotten high was about a month ago with [6X] then stated the first time he had ever gotten high on duty was with [6X] At approximately 0100 hours, 1 Dec 81, [6X] arrived at the bravo sector pumps and [6X] pulled his jeep alongside the six-pack we were sitting in, within arms reach of the right side of our vehicle. [6X] jeep was facing towards the fenceline and ours was facing the opposite direction. Almost as soon as [6X] who were sitting in the passenger seat of both vehicles, rolled their windows down, [6X] I told [6X] to light up one of his joints. [6X] removed one of the joints from his shirt pocket, lit it, took a toke from the joint and then passed it to [6X] took a toke and then passed the joint through the open windows of the two vehicles to [6X] placed the joint on my "key clip" which I handed to him, took a toke from the joint, and then passed it over to [6X] who was driving the six-pack. After [6X] took

AF FORM 1169   ☆ U.S. GOVERNMENT PRINTING OFFICE: 1977-241-130/1208   Page 1 of 2 Pages

QJCN 3-52/7017-7027

FOIA Payoff

After a year of failing FOIA requests, David H. Morrissey of the *Albuquerque Journal* learned that 14 security police at the local base where nuclear weapons are stored had been convicted of drug use. Some had used drugs while on duty. Morrissey also used the FOIA to reveal that the bomb accidentally dropped in the United States by a plane was the largest hydrogen bomb built. Morrissey's advice:

> When you file FOIA requests you often receive hundreds of pages in response—most of it of marginal value. There are seldom any individual "smoking gun" pages. When writing a story based on FOIA documents, it's common to spend hours sifting this material, pulling out a line here, a written comment in the margins there, and then piecing it together like some crazy jigsaw puzzle.

Identify What You Want Clearly

If there are published accounts—newspaper clips, articles, congressional reports—of the material requested, these should be cited specifically. If they are brief, it may also be helpful to enclose copies of relevant sections.

If you know what portions of the requested records have already been released, point this out. (It may eliminate or reduce search fees.) Give information, if possible, to identify that release (i.e., date, release number, original requester).

If you know the title or date of a document, who wrote it, the addressee or the division or field office of the agency in which it originated, include such information.

Sample Request Letter

Tel. No. (business hours)
Return Address
Date

Name of Public Body
Address

To the FOI Officer:

This request is made under the federal Freedom of Information Act, 5 U.S.C. 552.

Please send me copies of *(Here, clearly describe what you want. Include identifying material, such as names, places and the period of time about which you are inquiring. If you wish, attach news clips, reports and other documents describing the subject of your research.)* . . .

As you know, the FOI Act provides that if portions of a document are exempt from release, the remainder must be segregated and disclosed. Therefore, I will expect you to send me all nonexempt portions of the records that I have requested and that you will justify any deletions by reference to specific exemptions of the FOI Act. I reserve the right to appeal your decision to withhold any materials.

I promise to pay reasonable search and duplication fees in connection with this request. However, if you estimate that the total fees will exceed $———, please notify me so that I may authorize expenditure of a greater amount.

(Optional—substitute for previous paragraph) I am prepared to pay reasonable search and duplication fees in connection with this request. However, the FOI Act provides for waiver or reduction of fees if disclosure could be considered as "primarily benefiting the general public." I am a journalist *(researcher or scholar)* employed by *(name of news organization, book publishers, etc.),* and intend to use the information I am requesting as the basis for a planned article *(broadcast or book)*. *(Add arguments here in support of fee waiver)*. Therefore, I ask that you waive all search and duplication fees. If you deny this request, however, and the fees will exceed $———, please notify me of the charges before you fill my request so that I may decide whether to pay the fees or appeal your denial of my request for a waiver.

As I am making this request in the capacity of a journalist *(author or scholar)* and this information is of timely value, I will appreciate your communicating with me by telephone, rather than by mail, if you have any questions regarding this request. Thank you for your assistance, and I will look forward to receiving your reply within 10 business days, as required by law.

Very truly yours,

(Signature)

Appendix D
Code of Ethics

The following is the code of ethics of the Society of Professional Journalists (Sigma Delta Chi, 1987):

The Society of Professional Journalists, Sigma Delta Chi, believes the duty of journalists is to serve the truth.

We believe the agencies of mass communication are carriers of public discussion and information, acting on their Constitutional mandate and freedom to learn and report the facts.

We believe in public enlightenment as the forerunner of justice, and in our Constitutional role to seek the truth as part of the public's right to know the truth.

We believe those responsibilities carry obligations that require journalists to perform with intelligence, objectivity, accuracy, and fairness.

To these ends, we declare acceptance of the standards of practice here set forth:

I. RESPONSIBILITY: The public's right to know of events of public importance and interest is the overriding mission of the mass media. The purpose of distributing news and enlightened opinion is to serve the general welfare. Journalists who use their professional status as representatives of the public for selfish and other unworthy motives violate a high trust.

II. FREEDOM OF THE PRESS: Freedom of the press is to be guarded as an inalienable right of people in a free society. It carries with it the freedom and the responsibility to discuss, question, and challenge actions and utterances of our government and of our public and private institutions. Journalists uphold the right to speak unpopular opinions and the privilege to agree with the majority.

III. ETHICS: Journalists must be free of obligation to any interest other than the public's right to know the truth.

1. Gifts, favors, free travel, special treatment or privileges can compromise the integrity of journalists and their employers. Nothing of value should be accepted.

2. Secondary employment, political involvement, holding public office, and service in community organizations should be avoided if it compromises the integrity of journalists and their employers. Journalists and their employers should conduct their personal lives in a manner which protects them from conflict of interest, real or apparent. Their responsibilities to the public are paramount. That is the nature of their profession.

3. So-called news communications from private sources should not be published or broadcast without substantiation of their claims to news value.

4. Journalists will seek news that services the public interest, despite the obstacles. They will make constant efforts to assure that the public's business is conducted in public and that public records are open to public inspection.

5. Journalists acknowledge the newsman's ethic of protecting confidential sources of information.

6. Plagiarism is dishonest and unacceptable.

IV. ACCURACY AND OBJECTIVITY: Good faith with the public is the foundation of all worthy journalism.

1. Truth is our ultimate goal.

2. Objectivity in reporting the news is another goal, which serves as the mark of an experienced professional. It is a standard of performance toward which we strive. We honor those who achieve it.

3. There is no excuse for inaccuracies or lack of thoroughness.

4. Newspaper headlines should be fully warranted by the contents of the articles they accompany. Photographs and telecasts should give an accurate picture of an event and not highlight a minor incident out of context.

5. Sound practice makes clear distinction between news reports and expressions of opinion. News reports should be free of opinion or bias and represent all sides of an issue.

6. Partisanship in editorial comment which knowingly departs from the truth violates the spirit of American journalism.

7. Journalists recognize their responsibility for offering informed analysis, comment, and editorial opinion on public events and issues. They accept the obligation to present such material by individuals whose competence, experience, and judgment qualify them for it.

8. Special articles or presentations devoted to advocacy or the writer's own conclusions and interpretations should be labeled as such.

V. FAIR PLAY: Journalists at all times will show respect for the dignity, privacy, rights, and well-being of people encountered in the course of gathering and presenting the news.

1. The news media should not communicate unofficial charges affecting reputation or moral character without giving the accused a chance to reply.

2. The news media must guard against invading a person's right to privacy.

3. The media should not pander to morbid curiosity about details of vice and crime.

4. It is the duty of news media to make prompt and complete correction of their errors.

5. Journalists should be accountable to the public for their reports and the public should be encouraged to voice its grievances against the media. Open dialogue with our readers, viewers, and listeners should be fostered.

VI. PLEDGE: Adherence to this code is intended to preserve and strengthen the bond of mutual trust and respect between American journalists and the American people.

The Society shall—by programs of education and other means—encourage individual journalists to adhere to these tenets, and shall encourage journalistic publications and broadcasters to recognize their responsibility to frame codes of ethics in concert with their employees to serve as guidelines in furthering these goals.

Appendix E

Grammar

Agreement

A verb must agree in number with its subject. Writers get into trouble when they are unsure of the subject or when they cannot decide whether the subject is singular or plural.

Uncertainty often arises when there are words between the subject and the verb:

WRONG: **John,** as well as several others in the class, **were** unhappy with the instructor.

RIGHT: **John,** as well as several others in the class, **was** unhappy with the instructor.

The subject is *John,* singular.

WRONG: **The barrage** of traffic noises, telephone calls and similar interruptions **make** it difficult to study.

RIGHT: **The barrage** of traffic noises, telephone calls and similar interruptions **makes** it difficult to study.

The subject is *barrage,* singular.

A collective noun takes a singular verb when the group is considered as a unit and a plural verb when the individuals are thought of as separate:

RIGHT: **The committee** usually **votes** unanimously.

RIGHT: **The family lives** around the corner.

RIGHT: **The family were** gathered around the fire, some reading, some napping.

The pronouns *anybody, anyone, each, either, everyone, everybody, neither, no one, nobody, someone* and *somebody* take the singular verb.

A pronoun must agree in number with its antecedent:

WRONG: **The team** has added two players to **their** squad.
RIGHT: **The team** has added two players to **its** squad.
WRONG: **Everyone** does **their** best.
RIGHT: **Everyone** does **his** or **her** best.
WRONG: **Each of the companies** reported **their** profits had declined.
RIGHT: **Each of the companies** reported **its** profits had declined.

Dangling Modifier

Another trouble spot is the dangling modifier—the word, phrase or clause that does not refer logically or clearly to some word in the sentence. We all know what these look like:

Walking through the woods, the trees loomed up.

The phrase in boldface is a dangling participle, the most common of these errors. There are also dangling infinitive phrases:

To learn to shoot well, courses in marksmanship were offered.

The way to correct the dangling modifier is to add words that make the meaning clear or to rearrange the words in the sentence to make the modifier refer to the correct word. We can easily fix the two sentences:

Walking through the woods, **the runaway boy** felt the trees loom up at him.

To learn to shoot well, **the police** were offered courses in marksmanship.

Misplaced Words

Related parts of the sentence should not be separated. When they are separated, the sentence loses clarity.

Adverbs such as *almost, even, hardly, just, merely, scarcely, ever* and *nearly* should be placed immediately before the words they modify:

VAGUE: He **only** wanted three keys.
CLEAR: He wanted **only** three keys.
VAGUE: She **nearly** ate the whole meal.
CLEAR: She ate **nearly** the whole meal.

Avoid splitting the subject and verb:

AWKWARD: **She,** to make her point, **shouted** at the bartender.
BETTER: To make her point, **she shouted** at the bartender.

Do not separate parts of verb phrases:

AWKWARD: The governor said he **had** last year **seen** the document.
BETTER: The governor said he **had seen** the document last year.

Avoid split infinitives:

AWKWARD: She offered **to** personally **give** him the note.
BETTER: She offered **to give** him the note personally.

Read the sentence aloud if you are unsure about the placement of certain words. Generally, the problem can be solved by placing the subject and verb of the main clause together.

Parallel Construction

The parts of a sentence that express parallel thoughts should be balanced in grammatical form:

UNBALANCED: The people started **to shove** and **crowding** each other.
BALANCED: The people started **to shove** and **crowd** each other.
UNBALANCED: The typewriter can be used **for writing** and **to do** finger exercises.
BALANCED: The typewriter can be used **for writing** and **for doing** finger exercises.

Pronouns

A pronoun should agree with its antecedent in number, person and gender. The most common errors are shifts in number and shifts in person.

WRONG: **The organization** added basketball and hockey to **their** winter program.
RIGHT: **The organization** added basketball and hockey to **its** winter program.
WRONG: When **one** wants to ski, **you** have to buy good equipment.
RIGHT: When **one** wants to ski, **he** or **she** has to buy good equipment.

A common error is to give teams, groups and organizations the plural pronoun:

WRONG: **The team** played **their** best shortstop.
RIGHT: **The team** played **its** best shortstop.
WRONG: **The Police Department** wants recruits. **They** need 1,500 applicants.
RIGHT: **The Police Department** wants recruits. **It** needs 1,500 applicants.

Sentence Fragments

A phrase or a subordinate clause should not be used as a complete sentence:

FRAGMENT: The book was long. **And dull.**
CORRECT: The book was long **and dull.**
FRAGMENT: The score was tied. **With only a minute left to play.**
CORRECT: The score was tied **with only a minute left to play.**
FRAGMENT: He worked all night on the story. **And then collapsed in a heap.**
CORRECT: He worked all night on the story **and then collapsed in a heap.**

Sometimes writers use sentence fragments for specific writing purposes, usually for emphasis: **When in doubt, always use the dictionary. Always.**

Sequence of Tenses

One of the most troublesome grammatical areas for the beginning journalist is the use of tenses. Improper and inconsistent tense changes are frequent. Since the newspaper story is almost always told in the past tense, this is the anchoring tense from which changes are made.

WRONG: He **looked** into the briefcase and **finds** a small parcel.
RIGHT: He **looked** into the briefcase and **found** a small parcel.

Not all changes from the past to present are incorrect. The present tense can be used to describe universal truths and situations that are permanently true:

The Court **said** the Constitution **requires** due process.

When two actions are being described and one was completed before the other occurred, a tense change from the past to the past perfect is best for reader comprehension:

The patrolman **testified** that he **had placed** his revolver on the table.

Broadcast writers, who tell most of their stories in the present tense, can handle similar situations with a change from the present tense to the present perfect:

The company **denies** it **has paid** women less than men for comparable work.

In the course of the story, the tense should not make needless shifts from sentence to sentence. The reader is directed by the verb, and if the verb is incorrect, the reader is likely to be confused:

Moore said he **shot** the animal in the back. It **escaped** from the pen in which it was kept.

The reader wonders, did the animal escape after it was shot, or did it escape and then it was shot? If the former, inserting the word *then* at the start of the second sentence or before the verb would help make it clear. If the animal escaped and then was shot, the second sentence should use the past perfect tense:

It **had escaped** from the pen in which it was kept.

Appendix F
Copy Editing

Although most professionals use the word processor and make corrections on screen, many students prepare copy on a typewriter. Those whose copy spins out of a typewriter should use copy editing marks to correct errors.

On the following pages are examples of copy editing markings and three examples of how copy editing marks are used. Story A is the news writer's original version. The numbers refer to the errors that the reporter caught before handing the story to the copy editor. Story B shows the reporter's copy editing of the story. Story C is the way the story appeared.

Copy Editing Marks

capitalize	U.S. <u>district</u> <u>court</u> <u>judge</u> Frank
transpose/ insert word	J. Broyles will hear arguments oral ∧ *Monday*
delete word and close up	on a suit ~~Monday~~ filed by a woman
correction	who wants to build a new Mont͜e̩ssori
new paragraph	School in east Freeport. ⌐Jane
lowercase/ separate	Fraker Levine, /President of|a
insert apostrophe/ insert comma	childrens group∧ filed suit last week
delete letter and close up	alle(d)ging that city officials illegally
separate/ bring together	revoked|a building permit she said s⌣he
spell out	obtained last July from the (CHA) for
abbreviate	the school at 301 Oregon (Avenue.)
abbreviate	In January, the (City Housing Authority)
use figures	said it had (eleven) objections but
retain/ addition	decided ~~to~~ (stet) issue ∧ anyway. *the permit*

U.S. District Court Judge Frank J. Broyles will hear oral arguments Monday on a suit filed by a woman who wants to build a new Montessori School in east Freeport.

Jane Fraker Levine, president of a children's group, filed suit last week alleging that city officials illegally revoked a building permit she said she obtained last July from the City Housing Authority for the school at 301 Oregon Ave.

In January, the CHA said it had 11 objections but decided to issue the permit anyway.

Drunk Driver

A

1.
A man who spend through Brockton with his car hood up

2.
was arrested Sunday morning after losing control of his

3.
car and crashing into the front lawn of a North Brockton

4.
home, Brockton police said today.

5.   6.
Arrested was Josehp Small, 45, of Rockville. He was

charged with drunk driving. His car came to rest on the

7.
law of the home of Peter Ronney, 16 Eastern Avenue. There

8.

was no damage to the Ronney home, police said.

B

1.
A man who spend through Brockton with his car hood up

2. he had lost
was arrested Sunday morning after ~~losing~~ control of his

3. landed on
car and ~~crashing into~~ the front lawn of a North Brockton

4.
home, ~~Brockton~~ police said today.

5.   6.   was arrested and
~~Arrested was~~ Josehp Small, 45, of Rockville. ~~He was~~

charged with drunk driving. His car came to rest on the

7. n
law of the home of Peter Ronney, 16 Eastern (Avenue.) There

8.

was no damage to the Ronney home, police said.

C

A man who sped through Brockton with his car hood up was arrested Sunday morning after he had lost control of his car and landed on the front lawn of a North Brockton home, police said today.

Joseph Small, 45, of Rockville, was arrested and charged with drunk driving. His car came to rest on the lawn of the home of Peter Ronney, 16 Eastern Ave. There was no damage to the Ronney home, police said.

Stabbing

Explanation of Editing Marks

1. No need for her name in the lead. No one has heard of her, and it clutters the lead. Save it for the second paragraph.

2. This phrase is a repetition of material in the lead. Tighten up and put a period at the end.

3. This sentence is too long. Begin a new sentence here and put in her name.

4. Oops. Murder is the finding of a jury after a trial, or a charge. She's only been booked. Call it a "death."

5. Hard to call what seems to be a killing an "incident." I can't say "death" because I've used that. Major surgery necessary.

6. Do I really need this on what may have been a drunken brawl? Might as well let the desk decide. Our newspaper does not use courtesy titles on second reference. So *Miss* is deleted.

A

A Brockton man died from stab wounds Monday night after a dispute with his former girlfriend, *1.* Barbara Garth, 39, 25 Elm St., had turned violent.

Lee Sam Bensley, 42, died at Bayfront Medical Center *2.* *3.* Monday evening after the fight, and his former girl-friend was later arrested and booked for investigation *4.* *5.* into the murder. The incident occurred in Bensley's apartment at 423 W. 120 St.

6. Police said the two had been seeing each other but split up two months ago when Miss Garth learned he was married.

B

A Brockton man died from stab wounds Monday night after a dispute with his former girlfriend, *1.* ~~Barbara Garth, 39, 25 Elm St.,~~ had turned violent.

Lee Sam Bensley, 42, died at Bayfront Medical Center. *3.* The woman, Barbara Garth, *2.* 39, 25 Elm St. was ~~Monday evening after the fight, and his former girl-friend was later~~ arrested and booked for investigation *4.* death, *5.* Bensley was fatally into the ~~murder. The incident occurred in Bensley's~~ stabbed in his apartment at 423 W. 120 St.

6. Police said the two had been seeing each other but split up two months ago when ~~Miss~~ Garth learned he was married.

C

A Brockton man died from stab wounds Monday night after a dispute with his former girlfriend had turned violent.

Lee Sam Bensley, 42, died at Bayfront Medical Center. The woman, Barbara Garth, 39, 25 Elm St., was arrested and booked for investigation into the death. Bensley was fatally stabbed in his apartment at 423 W. 120 St.

Police said the two had been seeing each other but split up two months ago when Garth learned he was married.

Boots

A

1.
For 5 weeks they have been walking, despite the summer heat, the mosquitoes and their aching, blistered feet.

2. **3. 4.**
Up over hills. Down sharp rocky hillsides. And along

5. **6.**
narrow ledges. From 6 a.m. in the morning until 4 or 5 P.M.

7. **8.**
in the evening they walk. The fifteen soldiers have hiked

15 miles a day, even more. They are on the road to . . .

9.
Nowhere!

10. 11.
The soldiers have been walking in circles, since the middle of July they have been walking over a test course.

12.
They are testing a newlydesigned combat boot. By the time

13.
they have completed their rounds the men will have walked

14. 15. **16.**
nearly 750 miles. "Its wild, wild", said one of the soldiers.

The tests are being conducted on the Aberdeen Proving Ground in Maryland. The new boot is made of a brown suede.

17.
"No more boot polishing, that's the only thing that makes

18.
this worthwhile," said another.

B

1.
For ⑤ weeks they have been walking, despite the summer heat, the mosquitoes and their aching, blistered feet.

Explanation of Editing Marks

1. Spell out numbers from one through nine. Stylebook rule.

Boots

2. Insert a comma between adjectives.

3. *And* does not work. It spoils the parallel structure and rhythm set by the previous two sentences.

4. Capitalize the *a*.

5. Redundancy; *A.M.* means before noon.

6. Lower case *P.M.*

7. Redundancy; *P.M.* means after noon.

8. Use numerals for numbers 10 and above.

9. Delete the exclamation point. Let the reader supply it.

10. There are two sentences here. Use a period instead of a comma.

11. Capital letter for beginning of sentence.

12. Separate.

13. I want the reader to pause here. There may or may not be a grammatical reason for this, but commas can be used to stop the reader for an instant.

14. New paragraph. The quotation introduces a new idea.

15. Troublesome word. Here I need the contraction for *it is*. Insert apostrophe.

16. Transpose. When ending quotations, the comma goes inside the quote mark.

17. Delete the comma, put in a period and capitalize.

18. Another what? The prior reference to a soldier is too far away.

Up over hills. Down sharp, rocky hillsides. ~~And~~ along narrow ledges. From 6 a.m. ~~in the morning~~ until 4 or 5 p.m. ~~in the evening~~ they walk. The ⬭fifteen⬭ soldiers have hiked 15 miles a day, even more. They are on the road to...

Nowhere!

The soldiers have been walking in circles, since the middle of July they have been walking over a test course.

They are testing a newly designed combat boot. By the time they have completed their rounds, the men will have walked nearly 750 miles. "Its wild, wild," said one of the soldiers.

The tests are being conducted on the Aberdeen Proving Ground in Maryland. The new boot is made of a brown suede. "No more boot polishing, that's the only thing that makes this worthwhile," said another soldier.

C

For five weeks they have been walking, despite the summer heat, the mosquitoes and their aching, blistered feet.

Up over hills. Down sharp, rocky hillsides. Along narrow ledges. From 6 a.m. until 4 or 5 p.m. they walk. The 15 soldiers have hiked 15 miles a day, even more. They are on the road to . . .

Nowhere.

The soldiers have been walking in circles. Since the middle of July they have been walking over a test course.

They are testing a newly designed combat boot. By the time they have completed their rounds, the men will have walked nearly 750 miles.

"It's wild, wild," said one of the soldiers.

The tests are being conducted on the Aberdeen Proving Ground in Maryland. The new boot is made of brown suede. "No more boot polishing. That's the only thing that makes this worthwhile," said another soldier.

Glossary

Print Terms

These definitions were provided by the press associations and working reporters and editors. Most of the brief entries are from the *New England Daily Newspaper Study,* an examination of 105 daily newspapers, edited by Loren Ghiglione (Southbridge, Mass.: Southbridge Evening News Inc., 1973).

add An addition to a story already written or in the process of being written.

A.M. Morning newspaper.

assignment Instruction to a reporter to cover an event. An editor keeps an assignment book that contains notations for reporters such as the following:

> Jacobs—10 a.m.: Health officials tour new sewage treatment plant.
>
> Klaren—11 a.m.: Interview Ben Wastersen, possible Democratic congressional candidate.
>
> Mannen—Noon: Rotary Club luncheon speaker, Horlan, the numerologist. A feature?

attribution Designation of the person being quoted. Also, the source of information in a story. Sometimes, information is given on a not-for-attribution basis.

background Material in a story that gives the circumstances surrounding or preceding the event.

banger An exclamation point. Avoid. Let the reader do the exclaiming.

banner Headline across or near the top of all or most of a newspaper page. Also called a *line, ribbon, streamer, screamer.*

B copy Bottom section of a story written ahead of an event that will occur too close to deadline for the entire story to be processed. The B copy usually consists of background material.

beat Area assigned to a reporter for regular coverage. For example, police or city hall. Also, an exclusive story.

body type Type in which most of a newspaper is set, usually 8- or 9-point type.

boldface Heavy, black typeface; type that is blacker than the text with which it is used. Abbreviated *bf.*

break When a news development becomes known and available. Also, the point of interruption in a story continued from one page to another.

bright Short, amusing story.

bulldog Early edition, usually the first of a newspaper.

byline Name of the reporter who wrote the story, placed atop the published article. An old-timer comments on the current use of bylines. "In the old days, a reporter was given a byline if he or she personally covered an important or unusual story, or the story was an exclusive. Sometimes if the writing was superior, a byline was given. Nowadays, everyone gets a byline, even if the story is a rewrite and the reporter never saw the event described in the story."

caps Capital letters; same as uppercase.

caps and lowercase Initial capital in a word followed by small letters. *See* **lowercase.**

clip News story clipped from a newspaper, usually for future reference.

cold type In composition, type set photographically or by pasting up letters and pictures on acetate or paper.

column The vertical division of the news page. A standard-size newspaper is divided into five to eight columns. Also, a signed article of opinion or strong personal expression, frequently by an authority or expert—a sports column, a medical column, political or social commentary, and the like.

copy Written form in which a news story or other material is prepared.

copy desk The desk used by copy editors to read copy. The *slot person* is in charge of the desk.

copy flow After a reporter finishes it, a story moves to the city desk where the city editor reads it for major errors or problems. If it does not need further work, the story is moved to the copy desk for final editing and a headline. It then moves to the mechanical department.

correction Errors that reach publication are retracted or corrected if they are serious or someone demands a correction. Libelous matter is always corrected immediately, often in a separate news story rather than in the standard box assigned to corrections.

correspondent Reporter who sends news from outside a newspaper office. On smaller papers often not a regular full-time staff member.

crony journalism Reporting that ignores or treats lightly negative news about friends of a reporter or editor. Beat reporters have a tendency to protect their informants in order to retain them as sources.

crop To cut or mask the unwanted portions, usually of a photograph.

cut Printed picture or illustration. Also, to eliminate material from a story. *See* **trim.**

cutline Any descriptive or explanatory material under a picture.

dateline Name of the city or town and sometimes the date at the start of a story that is not of local origin.

deadline Time at which the copy for an edition must be ready.

dirty copy Matter for publication that needs extensive correction.

edition One version of a newspaper. Some papers have one edition a day, some several. Not to be confused with *issue,* which usually refers to all editions under a single date.

editorial Article of comment or opinion usually on the editorial page.

editorial material All material in the newspaper that is not advertising.

enterprise copy Story, often initiated by a reporter, that digs deeper than the usual news story.

exclusive Story one reporter has obtained to the exclusion of the competition. A beat. Popularly known as a *scoop,* a term never used in the newsroom.

feature Story emphasizing the human or entertaining aspects of a situation. A news story or other material differentiated from straight news. As a verb, it means to give prominence to a story.

file To send a story to the office, usually by wire or telephone, or to put news service stories on the wire.

filler Material used to fill space. Small items used to fill out columns where needed. Also called *column closers* and **shorts.**

flag Printed title of a newspaper on page one. Also known as *logotype* or *nameplate.*

free advertising Use of the names of businesses and products not essential to the story. Instead of the brand name, use the broad term *camera* for Leica or Kodak.

futures calendar Date book in which story ideas, meetings and activities scheduled for a later occurrence are listed. Also known as a *futures book* or *tickler.* Kept by city and assignment editors and by careful reporters.

good night Before leaving for the day, beat reporters check in with the desk and are given a good night, which means there is nothing further for the reporter from the desk for the day. On some newspapers, the call is made for the lunch break, too. Desks need to know where their reporters are in case of breaking stories.

graf Abbreviation for *paragraph.*

Guild Newspaper Guild, an international union to which some reporters and other newspaper workers belong. Newspapers that have contracts with the Guild are said to be "organized."

handout Term for written publicity or special-interest news sent to a newspaper for publication.

hard news Spot news; live and current news in contrast to features.

head or **headline** The display type over a printed news story.

head shot Picture featuring little more than the head and shoulders of the person shown.

HFR Abbreviation for *hold for release.* Material that cannot be used until it is released by the source or at a designated time. Also known as *embargoed material.*

identification Personal, relevant data used to identify a person: name, title (if any), age, address, occupation, education, race, religion, ethnicity. Generally, the relevant characteristics are name, age, occupation, address. To lend authority to the observations or statements of sources, we give their background. Use race, religion, national origin only when relevant to the story. In obituaries and crime stories, the readers want as much identification as possible. In general news stories, logic should indicate relevancy: Toledo readers are not interested in the home address of the North Carolina senator who collapses in a hotel and dies. But the newspaper in his home town of Raleigh will insert the address in the press association copy.

insert Material placed between copy in a story. Usually, a paragraph or more to be placed in material already sent to the desk.

investigative reporting Technique used to unearth information sources often want hidden. This type of reporting involves examination of documents and records, the cultivation of informants, painstaking and extended research. Investigative reporting usually seeks to expose wrongdoing and concentrates on public officials and their activities. In recent years, industry and business have been scrutinized. Some journalists contend that the term is redundant, that all good reporting is investigative, that behind every surface fact is a real story that a resourceful, curious and persistent reporter can dig up.

italics Type in which letters and characters slant to the right.

jump Continuation of a story from one page to another. As a verb, to continue material. Also called *runover.*

kill To delete a section from copy or to discard the entire story; also, to spike a story.

lead (pronounced *leed;* sometimes spelled *lede*) First paragraph in a news story. A direct or straight news lead summarizes the main facts. A delayed lead, usually used on feature stories, evokes a scene or sets a mood. Also used to refer to the main idea of a story: An editor will ask a reporter, "What's the lead on the piece?" expecting a quick summary of the main facts. Also, a tip on a story; an idea for a story. A source will tell a reporter, "I have a lead on a story for you." In turn, the reporter will tell the editor, "I have a lead on a story that may develop."

localize Emphasize the names of persons from the local community who are involved in events outside the city or region: A local couple rescued in a Paris hotel fire; the city police chief speaks at a national conference.

lowercase Small letters, as contrasted to capitals.

LTK Designation on copy for *lead to come.* Usually placed after the slug. Indicates the written material will be given a lead later.

makeup Layout or design. The arrangement of body type, headlines and illustrations into pages.

masthead Formal statement of a newspaper's name, officers, place of publication and other descriptive information, usually on the editorial page. Sometimes confused with **flag** or *nameplate*.

morgue Newspaper library.

mug shot *See* **head shot.**

new lead *See* **running story.**

news hole Space in a newspaper allotted to news, illustrations and other nonadvertising material.

obituary Account of a person's death; also called *obit*.

offset Printing process in which an image is transferred from a printing plate to a rubber roller and then set off on paper.

off-the-record Material offered the reporter in confidence. If the reporter accepts the material with this understanding, it cannot be used except as general background in a later story. Some reporters never accept off-the-record material. Some reporters will accept the material with the provision that if they can obtain the information elsewhere they will use it. Reporters who learn of off-the-record material from other than the original source can use it. No public, official meeting can be off-the-record, and almost all official documents (court records, police information) are public information. Private groups can ask that their meetings be kept off-the-record, but reporters frequently ignore such requests when the meeting is public or large numbers of people are present.

op-ed page Abbreviation for *the page opposite the editorial page*. The page is frequently devoted to opinion columns and related illustrations.

overnight Story usually written late at night for the afternoon newspapers of the next day. Most often used by the press services. The overnight, or overnighter, usually has little new information in it but is cleverly written so that the reader thinks the story is new. Also known as *second-day stories*.

play Emphasis given to a news story or picture—size and place in the newspaper of the story; typeface and size of headline.

P.M. Afternoon or evening newspaper.

pool Arrangement whereby limited numbers of reporters and photographers are selected to represent all those assigned to the story. Pooling is adopted when a large number of people would overwhelm the event or alter its nature. The news and film collected by a pool are shared with the rest of the press corps.

press release Publicity handout, or a story given to the news media for publication.

proof Reproduction of type on paper for the purpose of making corrections or alterations.

puff or **puffery** Publicity story or a story that contains unwarranted superlatives.

quotes Quotation marks; also a part of a story in which someone is directly quoted.

rewrite To write for a second time to strengthen a story or to condense it.

rewrite man Person who takes the facts of stories over the telephone, puts them together into stories and also rewrites reporters' stories.

rowback A story that attempts to correct a previous story without indicating that the prior story had been in error or without taking responsibility for the error.

running story Event that develops and is covered over a period of time. For an event covered in subsequent editions of a newspaper or on a single cycle of a wire service, additional material is handled as follows:
New lead—Important new information.
Add and insert—Less important information.
Sub—Material that replaces dated material, which is removed.

sell Presentation a reporter makes to impress the editor with the importance of his or her story; also used as a verb: Editors *sell* stories to their superiors at news conferences.

shirttail Short, related story adapted to the end of a longer one.

short Filler, generally of some current news value.

situationer Story that pulls together a continuing event for the reader who may not have kept track as it unfolded. The situationer is helpful with complex or technical developments or on stories with varied datelines and participants.

slant To write a story so as to influence the reader's thinking. To editorialize, to color or misrepresent.

slug Word or words placed on all copy to identify the story.

source Person, record, document or event that provides the information for a story.

source book Alphabetical listing, by name and by title, of the addresses and the office and home telephone numbers of persons on the reporter's beat and some general numbers—FBI agent in charge in town, police and fire department spokesmen, hospital information, weather bureau.

split page Front page of an inside section; also known as the *break page, second front page.*

stringer Correspondent, not a regular staff member, who is paid by the story or by the number of words written.

style Rules for capitalization, punctuation and spelling that standardize usage so that the material presented is uniform. *See* **stylebook.**

stylebook Specific listing of the conventions of spelling, abbreviation, punctuation, capitalization used by a particular newspaper, wire service. Most newspapers and stations have stylebooks. The most frequently used is the stylebook of the Associated Press. Broadcast stylebooks include pronunciations.

sub *See* **running story.**

subhead One-line and sometimes two-line head (usually in boldface) inserted in a long story at intervals for emphasis or to break up a long column of type.

text Verbatim report of a speech or public statement.

thumbnail Half-column-wide cut or portrait.

tight Full, too full. Also refers to a paper so crowded with ads that the news space must be reduced. It is the opposite of the wide-open paper.

tip Information passed to a reporter, often in confidence. The material usually requires further fact gathering. Occasionally, verification is impossible and the reporter must decide whether to go with the tip on the strength of the insider's knowledge and reliability. Sometimes the reporter will not want to seek confirmation for fear of alerting sources who will alter the situation or release the information to the competition. Tips often lead to exclusives.

titles Mr., Mrs., Miss, Ms., Secretary of State, Police Chief and Senator are formal designations and may be used before a person's name. Usage depends upon the station's or newspaper's policy. False titles—Vietnam war hero, actress, left fielder—are properly used after the name: *Patrick Ewing, the center,* instead of *Center Patrick Ewing.*

trim to reduce or condense copy carefully.

update Story that brings the reader up-to-date on a situation or personality previously in the news. If the state legislature appropriated additional funds for five new criminal court judges to meet the increased number of cases in the courts, an update might be written some months later to show how many more cases were handled after the judges went to work. An update usually has no hard news angle.

VDT Video display terminal, a part of the electronic system used in news and advertising departments that eliminates typewriters. Copy is written on typewriterlike keyboards, and words appear on attached television screens rather than on paper. The story is stored on a disk in a computer. Editing is done on the terminals.

verification Determination of the truth of material the reporter gathers or is given. The assertions, sometimes even the actual observations, do not necessarily mean the information is accurate or true. Some of the basic tools of verification are the telephone book, for names and addresses; the city directory, for occupations; *Who's Who,* for biographical information. For verification of more complex material, the procedure of Thucydides, the Greek historian and author of the *History of the Peloponnesian War,* is good advice for the journalist: "As to the deeds done in the war, I have not thought myself at liberty to record them on hearsay from the first informant or on arbitrary conjecture. My account rests either on personal knowledge or on the closest possible scrutiny of each statement made by others. The process of research was laborious, because the conflicting accounts were given by those who had witnessed the several events, as partiality swayed or memory served them."

wire services Synonym for press associations, the Associated Press and the United Press International. There are foreign-owned press services to which some newspapers subscribe: Reuters, Tass, Agence France-Presse.

Broadcast Terms

actuality An on-the-scene report using the voice of the person involved in the news event.

audio Sound.

close The end of a story or newscast.

close-up (broadcast) Shot of a subject's face that dominates the frame so that little background is visible.

cover shot A long shot usually cut in at the beginning of a sequence to establish place or location.

cue A signal in script or by word or gesture to begin or to stop. Two types: incue and outcue.

cut Quick transition from one type of picture to another. In radio, a portion of an actuality on tape used on broadcast.

cutaway Transition shot—usually short—from one theme to another, used to avoid **jump cut.** Often a shot of the interviewer listening.

dissolve Smooth fading of one picture for another. As the second shot becomes distinct, the first slowly disappears.

dub The transfer of one videotape to another.

FI or **fade in** A scene that begins without full brilliance and gradually assumes full brightness. *FO* or *fade out* is the opposite.

graphics All visual displays, such as artwork, maps, charts and still photos.

jump cut Transition from one subject to a different subject in an abrupt manner. Avoided with **cutaway** shot between scenes.

mix Combining two or more sound elements into one.

montage A series of brief shots of various subjects to give a single impression or communicate one idea.

O/C On camera. A reporter delivering copy directly to the camera without covering pictures.

outtakes Scenes that are discarded for the final story.

pan or **pan shot** Moving the camera from left to right or right to left.

remote A taped or live broadcast from a location outside the studio. Also, the unit that originates such a broadcast.

SOT Sound on tape. Recorded simultaneously with picture on tape.

V/O Reporter's voice-over pictures.

VTR Videotape recording.

zoom Use of a variable focus lens to take **close-ups** and wide angle shots from a stationary position. By using a zoom lens an impression can be given of moving closer to or farther away from the subject.

Credits

Literary

pp. 4–5, reprinted by permission from the Associated Press; pp. 41, 43, reprinted by permission from *The Commercial Appeal,* Memphis, Tenn.; pp. 51, 52, reprinted by permission from *Contra Costa Times,* Walnut Creek, Calif.; p. 55, reprinted by permission from *The Journal-Bulletin,* Providence, R.I.; pp. 66–67, from Charles M. Young, in *Rolling Stone* #266, June 1, 1978, © 1978 by Straight Arrow Publishers, Inc., All Rights Reserved, reprinted by permission; p. 101, reprinted by permission from *Working People Talk About What They Do All Day and What They Think of While They Do It,* by Studs Terkel, copyright © 1972 by Pantheon Books, a Division of Random House, Inc.; p. 103, reprinted by permission from *The St. Petersburg Times;* p. 108, reprinted by permission from *Birmingham Post-Herald;* pp. 133–134, reprinted by permission from *The Daily News;* p. 139, reprinted by permission from The Associated Press; p. 140, from *New York, New York,* edited by Donald H. Johnston, copyright © 1981 Arno Press, New York City, reprinted by permission; pp. 144–145, reprinted by permission from *The Anniston* (Ala.) *Star;* pp. 146–147, reprinted by permission from The Associated Press; pp. 147–148, reprinted by permission from *The Blade,* Toledo, Ohio; pp. 158–159, reprinted by permission from *The Advocate* (Stamford, Conn.); p. 162, reprinted by permission from The Associated Press; pp. 167–168, reprinted by permission from *The News and Observer;* p. 178, from *New York, New York,* edited by Donald H. Johnston, copyright © 1981 Arno Press, New York City, reprinted by permission; p. 179, reprinted by permission from The Associated Press; p. 205, reprinted by permission from The Associated Press; p. 206, reprinted by permission from *The Blade;* p. 208, reprinted by permission from The Associated Press; p. 210, from *Newsday,* copyright 1981 Newsday, Inc., reprinted by permission; pp. 220–221, reprinted by permission from *The Daily News,* © 1980, New York News, Inc.; p. 235, reprinted by permission from *The Virginian-Pilot* (Norfolk, Va.); pp. 235–237, from *New York, New York,* edited by Donald H. Johnston, copyright © 1981 Arno Press, New York City, reprinted by permission; pp. 241–242, reprinted by permission from *The Louisville Courier-Journal;* p. 244, reprinted by permission from *The Lexington Herald;* p. 245, reprinted by permission from *The Providence Journal-Bulletin;* p. 254, reprinted by permission from *The Buffalo News;* p. 255, reprinted by permission from *The Louisville Times;* p. 256, reprinted by permission from *Eugene* (Ore.) *Register-Guard;* p. 256, reprinted by permission from The Associated Press; p. 258, reprinted by permission from *The Anniston* (Ala.) *Star;* pp. 258–259, reprinted by permission from *Kansas City Times;* p. 266, reprinted by permission from *The Los Angeles Times;* p. 266, reprinted by permission from *The Boston Globe;* p. 268, reprinted by permission from *The Atlanta Constitution;* p. 270, reprinted by permission from *The Boston Globe;* p. 276, reprinted by permission from *Lexington* (Ky.) *Herald-Leader;* p. 278, reprinted by permission from The Associated Press; pp. 279–280, reprinted by permission from *Tallahassee Democrat;* p. 284, reprinted by permission from *The Advocate* (Stamford, Conn.); p. 295, reprinted by permission from *The Boston Herald;* p. 295, reprinted by permission from *Houston Chronicle;* p. 310, reprinted by permission from The Associated Press; p. 312, reprinted by permission from CBS; p. 434, from *News Reporting and Writing,* by Melvin Mencher, copyright 1981 Wm. C. Brown Publishers, Dubuque, Iowa, All Rights Reserved, reprinted by permission.

Photo

p. 2, Susan Pollard, Lesher Communications/*Contra Costa Times;* p. 3, John Titchen; p. 6 (top), Ron Tarver, *The Philadelphia Inquirer;* p. 6 (bottom), © Lonny Kalfus; p. 8, Lesher Communications/*Contra Costa Times;* p. 9, Lesher Communications/*Contra Costa Times;* p. 11 (top), Mark Avery; p. 11 (bottom), Jerry Margolycz; p. 15, Jerry King; p. 16 (top), Marshall Ramsey; p. 17, Robert E. Clark, *The Outlook,* Santa Monica, Calif.; p. 25, Keller Crescent Co.; p. 27, Roy Karten; p. 30, Michael Lipack, *The New York Daily News;* p. 36, Paul Watson, *The Toronto Star;* p. 37, Phil Sears, *Tallahassee Democrat;* p. 40, Maurice Rivenbark, *St. Petersburg Times;* p. 42 (top, bottom left, bottom right), Jeff McAdory, *The Commercial Appeal;* p. 44, *Scripps Howard News;* p. 46, Lena H. Sun, *The Washington Post;* p. 47, Lena H. Sun, *The Washington Post;* p. 51, Greg Stidham, *Contra Costa Times;* p. 54, Bob Thayer, *The Providence Journal–Bulletin;* p. 59, *Scripps Howard News;* pp. 61–62, Larry C. Price, *Fort Worth Star-Telegram;* p. 69, © Michael du Cille; p. 70, Bill Turnbull, *Daily News;* p. 71, Jean Pierre Rivest, *The Gazette;* p. 76 (top), John Walker, *The Fresno Bee;* p. 76 (bottom), Marc Ascher, *The Home News,* New Brunswick, N.J.; p. 78, Rafael Trias, *The San Juan Star;* p. 80, *Livingston & Co.;* p. 82, Bob Thayer, *The Providence Journal–Bulletin;* p. 87 (right), Maryanne Russell © 1991; p. 87 (left), Charlie Riedel, *The Hays* (Kan.) *Daily News;* p. 88, *The Outlook;* p. 90, Joseph Noble, *The Stuart* (Fla.) *News;* p. 93 (left), Michael Patrick, *The Knoxville News-Sentinel;* p. 93 (right), Joel Strasser; p. 96, Bill Frakes, *The Miami Herald;* p. 99, Craig Lee, *The San Francisco Examiner;* p. 104, *St. Petersburg Times;* p. 106 (top), Charlie Riedel, *The Hays Daily News;* p. 106 (bottom), Ken Elkins, *The Anniston Star;* p. 110, Mike McClure; p. 118, Rodger Mallison, *Fort Worth Star-*

(top right), Ron Tarver, *The Philadelphia Inquirer;* p. 342 (bottom left), Bob Thayer, *The Providence Journal–Bulletin;* p. 342 (bottom right) Bob Thayer, *The Providence Journal–Bulletin;* p. 343 (both), Donna Ferrato, DOMESTIC ABUSE AWARENESS PROJECT; p. 344, © 1994, *Newsday, Inc.* Reprinted with permission; p. 347 (top left), Sam Caldwell, *St. Louis Post-Dispatch;* p. 347 (top right), Wilmer Counts, *The Arkansas Democrat;* p. 348 (bottom), Joel Sartore, *The Wichita Eagle-Beacon;* p. 349 (left), Sam Caldwell, *St. Louis Post-Dispatch;* p. 349 (right), Wilmer Counts, *The Arkansas Democrat;* p. 352, Advertising Council, United Negro College Fund and Young & Rubicam; p. 353, UFS, Inc.; p. 355, *The Times-News;* p. 356 (bottom), Wagner International; p. 357, Maryanne Russell; p. 358, Maryanne Russell © 1991; p. 364, Keller Crescent Co.; p. 368, United Negro College Fund and Young & Rubicam; p. 370, Harry De Zitter photo, Wieden & Kennedy; p. 372, Earle Palmer Brown (top right); Wieden & Kennedy (bottom right); p. 373 (both), Earle Palmer Brown for Friendship Hospital for Animals; p. 376 (both), Patrick Fagan; p. 378, Courtesy of © Mercedes-Benz AG and Mercedes-Benz of North America, Inc; p. 383, Burson-Marsteller; p. 385, Jeff Corwin, Earth Technology Corp.; p. 397, Stewart Bowman, *Louisville Times;* p. 398, Paul Watson, *The Toronto Star;* p. 400, Rodger Mallison, *Fort Worth Star-Telegram;* p. 405 (right), The White House; p. 405 (left), Sam Upshaw Jr., *The Courier-Journal;* p. 411, Russell Lee, Library Congress; p. 415, Planned Parenthood Federation of America; p. 419, Hank Reichard, *Scripps Howard Newspapers;* p. 421 (top), Harry Baumert, *The Des Moines Register;* p. 421 (bottom), Don Black, *Binghamton* (N.Y.) *Press and Sun-Bulletin;* p. 438, Joel Sartore, *The Wichita Eagle-Beacon.*

Name Index

ABC, 63, 125, 389
Achenbaum, Alvin, 361
Ad Council, 368
Adams, Jim, 275
Addams, Jane, 381
Adolph Coors Company, 374
Adventures of Huckleberry Finn, 195, 417
Advertising Age, 367
The Advocate (Stamford, Ct.), 158, 265, 284
Aerospace Daily, 63
Agee, James, 351
AIDS, 276, 315, 345, 404
Akron Beacon Journal, 262
Alamogordo (N.M.) *Daily News*, 263
Albuquerque Journal, 444
Alert Publishing Inc., 361
Alice's Adventures in Wonderland, 81
All the President's Men, 178, 221
Allen, Rose Harriet, 14, 141–42
Altman, Robert, 21
America, 289
American Cancer Society, 206
American Society of Newspaper Editors, 126, 408
Ames, Aldrich H., 46
Ammirati & Puris, 371
And So It Goes: Adventures in Television, 318
Anderson, David, 300
Anheuser-Busch Inc., 374
The Anniston (Ala.) *Star*, 106, 144, 257
"Another World, " 416
Anquoe, Bunty, 48
Anthony, Susan B., 33
The Arab News, 15
Argus Leader (Sioux Falls, S.D.), 261

The Arkansas Democrat (Little Rock), 122, 347, 349
Arlen, Michael, 377
Arlington County, Va. Department of Public Works, 216
Arnett, Peter, xvi, 221
Aronson, Steven M.L., 371, 396
Around the World in Eighty Days, 7
Ascher, Marc, 76
Ashe, Arthur, 404
The Associated Press (AP), v, 4–5, 12, 13, 63, 72, 73, 75, 79, 81, 94, 106, 107, 113, 115, 126, 128, 129, 132, 135, 139, 143, 146–47, 153, 162, 179, 205, 208, 255, 256, 278, 279, 281, 282, 288, 292, 296, 308, 309, 310, 311, 331, 337, 384, 418, 421, 439, 440
The Associated Press Managing Editors, 67
The Associated Press Managing Editors Continuing Study Committee, 331
The Associated Press Stylebook, 422
AP Photo, 299
AP v. Walker, 402
Association of National Advertisers, 374
AT&T, 193, 355, 365, 383
ATHENA, 371
The Atlanta Constitution, 181, 268
The Atlantic Monthly, 195
Atropoeus, John, 395
The Autobiography of Lincoln Steffens, 68
Avery, Mark, 11
Ayendegan (Teheran, Iran), 92
Ayer, Francis Wayland, 354–55
Ayer, Nathan Wheeler, 354

Babel, Isaac, 97

Bagdikian, Ben, 68
Baker, Russell, 106, 434
Ball, George, 215
The Baltimore Sun, 297
Barkley, Charles, 362
Barnes, Eugene, 18
Barnouw, Erik, 318
Barritt, Tom, 383
Barry, Dave, 204, 205
Bartimus, Tad, 299–300
Bartlett's Familiar Quotations, 184
Bates, Ted, 360
Batten, James K., 38
Baumann, David, 17
Baumert, Harry, 421
Bazarevich, Sergei, 282
*Beating the Odds: The Untold Story Behind
    the Rise of ABC*, 318
Beaufort (S.C.) *Gazette*, 113
The Beecham Group, 361
Beethoven, Ludwig van, 33
*Behind the Front Page: A Candid Look at
    How the News is Made*, 148, 221
Bellow, Saul, 196
Benedict, Helen, 226, 252
Berger, Meyer, 297
Berkow, Ira, 68
The Berkshire Eagle (Pittsfield, Mass.), 298
Berman, Morris, 283, 321, 336
Bernstein, Carl, 178, 221
Bernstein, Theodore, 95
Berra, Yogi, 365
Best Newspaper Writing, 117
Beyer, Shula, 164
Biden, Joseph, 389
Bigart, Homer, 32, 176–77, 198
Bill of Rights, 32
Birmingham (Ala.) *Post-Herald*, 107, 421
Bishop, Jim, 97
Bisset, Jacqueline, 228–29, 235
Bitter Cry of the Children, 380
Black, Don, 421
The Blade (Toledo, Oh.), 53, 107, 138,
    147–48, 166, 206
Bliss, Ed, 74
Block, Herbert Lawrence, 15
Block, Mervin, xviii, 75, 91, 101, 115, 308,
    311, 312, 317, 318
Blume, Judy, 417
Blundell, William, 179, 198
Bly, Nellie, 6, 29
Bogart, Leo, 26, 27, 363, 366
"The Bold and the Beautiful, " 415
Boorstin, Daniel J., 369
The Boston Globe, 112, 248, 266, 270, 386,
    419

Boston Herald, 287, 295
Boswell, Thomas, 131
Bourke-White, Margaret, 343, 351
Bowdler, Thomas, 417
Bowl of Hygeia, 178
Bowles, Jennifer, 213
Bowman, Stewart, 397
Boxer, Barbara, 80
Boycott Anorexic Marketing, 375
Boylan, James, 89
The Boys of Summer, 300
The Boys on the Bus, 68
Bradstreet, Anne, 81
Brahms, Johannes, 132
Brando, Marlon, 211
Brazes, Jane, 230
Breslin, Jimmy, 39
Brezinski, Zbigniew, 215
Britt, Bonnie, 295–96
*Broadcast Newswriting: The RTNDA
    Reference Guide*, 318
Broadcasting, 313
Broder, David S., 148, 221
Brooklyn Public Library, 417
Brown, Sid, 173
Buchanan, Pat, 215
Buchenwald, 316
Buchwald, Art, 406
The Buffalo News, 254
Burger King, 355, 365
Burns, Ken, 345
Burson, Harold, xviii, 379, 382
Burson-Marsteller, 64, 301, 383
Bush, George, 124, 248
Bushey, Peter, xvii
Bushman, Francis X., 382
But We Were Born Free, 95
Butkus, Dick, 361
Butterfield, Bruce, 227

Cackley, Phil, 56
Cage, Nicholas, 21
Caldwell, Sam, 322, 347, 349
California Prune Board, 202, 359
The Camera Never Blinks, 318
Campbell, Richard R., 420
Campbell Soup Co., 360
Canadian Broadcasting Corporation, 208
Cannon, Jimmy, 81
Capa, Cornell, 350
Capa, Robert, 322, 350
Capon, Rene J., 117
Capote, Truman, 230, 234
Carlebach, Michael L., 351
Carpenter, Karen, 274
Carroll, Lewis, 81

Cartier-Bresson, Henri, 343
Catledge, Turner, 50
CBS, 27, 389, 441
CBS "Evening News, " 313–15
CBS News Photo, 314
CBS "Newsbreak, " 307
Center for Defense Information, 215
Challenge of Crime in a Free Society, 267
Chambers, Marcia, 35, 84, 85, 87
Chancellor, John, 68, 317
Chapnick, Howard, 351
The Charlotte (N.C.) *Observer*, 218
Chesterton, G.K., 94
Chiagoris, Larry, 356
Chicago Tribune, 187
Childress, Richard, 297
Chillon, W.E., III, 409
China, 11, 46–47, 174–75, 412
The Christian Century, 289
Christian Task Force Against Antisemitism,
       374
Christy, Bob, 325–26
Chronicle (San Francisco), 63
The Chronicle of Higher Education, 195
Chrysler, 33
Ciervo, Arthur V., 64, 395
Citizen Hearst, 29
Citizens Insurance, 364
Citron, Kirk, xviii, 111, 202, 359–60, 366–67
City & State, 102
City of New York, 222
Civil War, 91, 345
Clark, Robert E., 17, 328–29
Clark, Roy Peter, 117, 170, 232
Clinton, Bill, 75, 94, 325, 409, 412, 425
The Coastline Times (Manteo, N.C.), 225
Coca-Cola Co., 354, 366
*Code of Ethics of the Associated Press
       Managing Editors*, 407
*Code of Ethics of the Society of Professional
       Journalists*, 406
Cogley, John, 289
Cohen, Sharon, 179–80, 186–87
Cohn, Ray, 243
Coles, Robert, 406
Columbia College, 387
Columbus, Christopher, 33, 113
Columbus (Oh.) *Citizen-Journal*, 419, 420
Come to Judgment, 300
Commentary, 195, 289
The Commercial Appeal (Memphis, Tenn.),
       41, 339
The Commercial Dispatch (Columbus, Miss.),
       212, 335
Commission on Freedom of the Press, 29
Commonweal, 289

Confessional of an Advertising Man, 377
Connelly, Terry, 317
Connery, Sean, 21
*Contemporary Newspaper Design . . . A
       Structural Approach*, 29
Contra Costa Times (Pleasanton/Walnut
       Creek, Calif.), 2, 7–9, 50, 51–52, 277,
       290, 324
Cookman, Claude, 322–23, 340, 347
Coolidge, Calvin, 80
Copernicus, Nicolaus, 33
Corn, Jack, 344
Corwin, Jeff, 385
Counts, Wilmer, 122, 347, 349
Courant (Hartford, Conn.), 345
The Courier (Conroe, Tex.), 188
Coward, Noel, 89
Crime in the United States, 261, 293
Crippen, Bruce, 59
Cronin, Jerry, 370, 372
Crouse, Timothy, 68
*Crusade for Justice: The Autobiography of
       Ida B. Wells*, 200
Cuniberti, Betty, 287
Current Biography, 184
Curtis Publishing Co. v. Butts, 402
Cusack, John, 21

Daily Kent (Oh.) *Stater*, 326
Daily Mercury (Guelph, Ont.), 413
Daily News (New York, N.Y.), 70, 132–33,
       220–21, 313, 407
Daily Press (Newport News, Va.), 34
Dali, Salvadore, 355
Dana, Charles A., 121
Daniel Deronda, 81
Darbyshire, Tom, 373
Darnton, Robert, 121
Davis, Elmer, 94–95
Davis, Miles, 26
A Day in the Life of America, 344
"Days of Our Lives, " 416
DDB Needham New York, 357
de Tocqueville, Alexis, 92
De Zitter, Harry, 370
*Deadline Every Minute: The Story of the
       United Press*, 29
Deciding What's News, 148
Decker, David, xvii
Denniston, Lyle, 300
Denny, Reginald, 17, 328–29
The Des Moines Register, 408, 421
Detroit Free Press, 287
Devers, Gail, 214–16
Dhonau, Jerry F., 27
Dickens, Charles, 196

Dictionary of American Biography, 184
Dilenschneider, Robert L., 385, 396
Ding Zillin, 46
Dockers, 28
Doe, Samuel K., 59
Domestic Abuse Awareness Project,
    203, 343
Donaldson, Sam, 230, 318, 410
Done in a Day, 311
Douglas, Frederick, 33
*Downsizing the News: Network Cutbacks in
    the Nation's Capital*, 318
Doyle, Arthur Conan, 202
Drilling, Paul, 360
Du Bois, Enid, 101
Du Cille, Michael, 69
DuBois, W.E.B., 381
DuBose, Mike, 171, 256
Duke, David, 374
Duster, Alfreda M., 197, 200
Dwyer, Jim, 38

Earle Palmer Brown, 373
Earth Technology Corp., 385
Edelman, Daniel J., 388, 390
Edelman, Renee, xviii
Edelman Public Relations Worldwide, 77,
    384, 388–89
Editor & Publisher, 112
Edward R. Murrow Award, 17
Edwards Associates, 384
The Egoists, 252
Einsel, Dave, 253
Einstein, Albert, 33
Eisenstadt, Alfred, 343
Elderman, Renee, 256
Elements of Style, 117
Eliot, George, 81
Elkins, Ken, 106, 144
Ellerbee, Linda, 307, 318
Ellison, Ralph, 196, 230
Ellsworth, Karen, 245
Engram, Sara, 22
Epilogue, xvii
Epstein, Joshua, 215
Essays of E.B. White, 95
Eugene (Ore.) *Register-Guard*, 113, 246, 256
Evans, Charlotte, 116
Evans, Heidi, 28, 132–33, 216, 411
The Evening Bulletin, 232

Fagan, Patrick, 25, 363, 364, 376–77
Fallaci, Oriana, 233, 252
Farr, Heather, 287
Farrakhan, Louis, 147–48

Ferrato, Donna, 203, 343–44, 351
Fields, W.C., 58
Filmer, Emery, 284–85
First Amendment, 32, 423
Flaman, Fern, 386
Flaubert, Gustave, 111
Flemister, David, 356–57
Flowers, Gennifer, 409
Floyd, Liam C., 100
Flynn, Kevin, 159
Fog Index, 98
Follette, Wilson, 115
Foote, Cone & Belding, 355
Ford, Gerald, 33
Ford Motor Company, 365
Fort Worth (Tex.) *Star-Telegram*, 61, 118,
    332, 400
Fox, Martin, 371
Frakes, Bill, 96
Frank, Reuven, 123
Franklin, Benjamin, 416
Fratianne, Linda, 141
Frazier, James Kenneth, 369
A Free and Responsible Press, 29
Freedom House, 92
Freedom of Information Act (FOIA), 182,
    442–45
French, Tom, 40
The Fresno (Calif.) *Bee*, 76
*From Vietnam to Baghdad: 35 years in the
    World's War Zones*, 221
*From Whistle Stop to Sound Bite: Four
    Decades of Politics and Television*,
    318
Furillo, Carl, 278
Fuson, Ken, 202

Gage, Nick, 31, 32
Galbraith, Bob, v
Galbraith, John Kenneth, 82
Gallagher, Ron, xvii
Gallon, Sabrina, 75
Galloway, Joseph, Jr., 194–95
Gannett Company, 67
Gannett News Service, 218
Gans, Herbert, 148
Gao Xin, 11
Gap Inc., 371
Garcia, Mario, 29
Garrett, Annette, 252
Garth, David, 392–93
Gay, Peter, 122
The Gazette (Montreal), 71
Geissinger, Michael, 321, 350
Gelb, Arthur, 31

General Foods, 374
"General Hospital, " 414
General Mills, 373
General Motors, 373
Genesis, 420
Georgetown (Ky.) *News*, 257
Gertz v. Welch, 402
Gesslein, Bob, xviii, 386
Gibbons, Leeza, 465
Gill, Brendan, 195
Giordano, Mary Ann, xviii, 220
Girl Interrupted, 237–38
Gobright, Lawrence A., 91, 143
Goddess Of Liberty, 11
Goldenson, Leonard H., 318
Goldman, Ari L., 289
Gompers, Samuel, 381
Good Housekeeping, 193
"Good Morning America, " 26
Goodman, Bob, 366
Gordon, George, xvi
Gorney, Cynthia, 82
Gould, Jay, 380
Graham, Bill, 324
Great Depression, 339
Greene, Bob, 212
Greenpeace, 388
Greer, Sonny, 235–37
Griffey, Ken, Jr., 281
Griffith, Thomas, 92
Grinold, Jack, xviii, 386
Grossman, Ron, 187
Grundberg, Andy, 344
"Guiding Light, " 415
Gulick, Katherine, 370
Gunther, Marc, 318
Gurnon, Emily, 9

Haberman, Clyde, 63, 135, 210, 223, 225, 231
Hagler, Marvin, 362
Halberstam, David, 29, 77–78
Hamilton, Alexander, 380
Hammond, Peter B., 369
Hanks, Tom, 21
Hanley, Charles J., 153
Hard Times, 196
Harding, Tonya, 344
Hardwick, Elizabeth, 7, 170
Hargrove, Mary, 93, 105
Harper's, 195
Hart, Gary, 408–9
Hartgen, Stephen, xviii, 23, 64
The Hasidic Anthology, 71
Haswell, Clayton, 51–52
Hauge, Keith A., 389

Hawkins, Larry, 281
Hayakawa, S.I., 200, 369
Hayes, Elizabeth, 164
The Hays (Kan.) *Daily News*, 87, 106, 129, 209
Heiman, Roberta, 150, 181, 184
Heinfling, Martin, 367–68
Hellinger, Mark, 97
Heloise, 21
Hemingway, Ernest, 58, 165, 174, 195
Henderson, Paul, 95
Henry, Sharon, 8
The Herald Tribune, 176
Hernandez, Teri, 51
Herrick, Jean, 24, 28
Hersey, John, 407
The Hidden Persuaders, 396
Higgins, Donald H., 379
Higgins, Richard, 140
Hill, Gladwin, 136
Hill, John T., 351
Hill, John W., 379
Hine, Lewis, 338, 340–41
Hipsman, Barbara J., xviii
Hirtl, Leon, 275
Hobgood, Norman, 208
Hoffman, Dustin, 211
Hold On, Mr. President, 318
Holiday, Billie, 132
The Home News, 76
The House That Roone Built: The Inside Story of ABC News, 318
Houston Chronicle, 253, 295
How I Wrote the Story, 68
Howarth, W.L., 117
Huchette, Mary, 383, 395
Hudson, Berkley, 53–55
Hulteng, John, 422
Humane Society, 388
Huston, Anjelica, 21
Hype, 396

Iacocca, Lee, 33
Icely, Ron, 409
Imperfect Mirror: Inside Stories of Television Newswomen, 318
Improving Newswriting, 170
In All His Glory: The Life of William S. Paley, 318
Ingersoll, Ralph, II, 81
International Museum of Photography at George Eastman House, 340
Interview with History, 252
Interviewing: Its Principles and Methods, 252
Irish Lesbian and Gay Organization, 252

Isaacs, Stephen, 72

Jacobs, Henry, 359
James, Henry, 106
James, Sheryl, 36, 38, 177
Janesko, Lou, 373
J.C. Penny, 364
Jean-Bart, Leslie, 154, 246
Jefferds, Chester, 54–55
Jenkins, Simon, 82
Jenning, Steve, 50, 392
Jennings, Peter, 409
Jensen, Rita, 159
The John McPhee Reader, 117
Johnson, Charles, 286
Johnson, Dave, 365
Johnson, Gerald, 121
Johnson, Lyndon, 15, 25, 33, 35
Johnson, Samuel, xvi, 156, 231
Jones, James Earl, 412
The Journal-Gazette (Fort Wayne, Ind.), v
Joyner-Kersee, Jackie, 287
The Jungle, 381

Kael, Pauline, 21–22
Kahn, Roger, 278, 300
KAIT-TV (Jonesboro, Ark.), 63
Kallus, Lonny, 6
Kansas City (Mo.) *Star,* 128
Karassev, Vasilii, 282
Karten, Roy, 27
Kaysen, Susanna, 237–38
Keaton, Diane, 21
Keaton, Michael, 21
Keller Crescent Co., 25, 364
Kellogg's, 365
Kelly, Gene, 208
Kelly, Grace, 274
Kempton, Murray, 188
Kennedy, Dana, 204, 206
Kennedy, Edward, 28
Kennedy, John F., 39, 86, 97, 124, 143, 264,
    274, 278
Kennedy, Robert, 36
Kennedy-Powell, Kathleen, 268
Kentucky Fried Chicken (KFC), 63, 87, 355,
    358
Kerrigan, Nancy, 344
Khadafi, Moammar, 49, 233
Khomeini, Ruhollah, Ayatollah, 15, 92
Kilthau, Joel, 348
Kimball, Penn, 318
*A Kind of Grace: A Treasury of Sportswritings
    by Women*, 287, 300
King, Jerry, 15–16
King, Larry, 230–31

King, Martin Luther, Jr., 33
King, Mike, 213
King, Rodney, 17, 21, 88, 328
King, Wayne, 231
King Features Syndicate, 21
Kirkland, Jack, 153
Kirkman, Susan, 262
Kittredge, Kevin, 41, 43
Klein, Calvin, 375
Klinkenberg, Jeff, 74, 103, 175
Knight-Ridder, 67
The Knoxville (Tenn.) *News-Sentinel*, 93, 153
Koch, Edward, 392–93
Koelzer, Jay, 297
Kollar, Robert E., xviii, 227, 326–28, 331
Koning, Hana, 321
Koufax, Sandy, 231
Kramer, Linda, 140–41
Kroeger, Brooke, 6–7, 29
KRON-TV (San Francisco), 302, 306
KSAT-TV (San Antonio), 309
KTLA-TV (Los Angeles), 303
Ku Klux Klan, 399, 413–14
Kunz, Kyle, 383

L.A. Gear, 280
Lady Godiva, 420
Lang, Fritz, 323
Lange, Dorothea, 320, 339
Lange, Jessica, 21
Language in Thought and Action, 200
Lash, David, 250
Lauder, Leonard, 366
Law Dictionary for Non-Lawyers, 300
Lederer, Edie, 132
Lee, Craig, 99
Lee, Ivy, 380, 381
Lee, Russell, 411
Leff, Karen, 325
Lenin, Vladimir, 92
Lennon, John, 274, 278
Lernoux, Penny, 173, 180
Lesher Communications, Inc., 7–8
Letterman, David, 211
Levitt, Leonard, 22
Lewis, Anthony, 409
Lewis, C.S., 425
Lewis, Michael, 72
Lewis, Paul, 94
The Lexington (Ky.) *Herald*, 128, 244
Lexington (Ky.) *Herald-Leader*, 276
Lexis, 181
Liberia, 59, 414, 421
Lieberman, Joseph, 63
Liebling, A.J., 86, 221
Lipack, Michael, 30

Lippmann, Walter, 7, 19, 29, 56–57, 89, 92, 210
Livingston & Co., 80, 358
Los Angeles Ghost Town Task Force, 303
Los Angeles Times, 77–78, 129, 266, 274
Louisville Courier-Journal, 241, 371, 405
Louisville Times, 397
Love, Dennis, 257–59
Lowell, Robert, xvii
Lucky, 31, 56
Luper, Joe, 163

McAdory, Jeff, xviii, 41, 43, 339
McCabe, Carol, 212
McCarthy, Joseph, 94–95
McCartney, Paul, 278
McClure, Mike, 110
McCullough, David M., 231
McDonald's, 365
McEwen, Arthur, 121
McGraw, Anne, 224
McGrory, Mary, 210, 248
McKinley, William, 381
McLaughlin, Joseph P., 379
McLuhan, Marshall, 369
MacMaster, Christine, 357–58
McPhee, John, 58, 117, 195
Madison, James, 380
Madison Avenue U.S.A., 377
Madonna, 75, 106, 211
Magellan, Ferdinand, 33
Magnus, Edie, 315
Mailer, Norman, 196
Malcolm, Janet, 413
Mallison, Rodger, 118, 332, 400
Mallowe, Mike, 174, 180, 186
Mantle, Mickey, 287
Marcus, Steven, 196
Margolycz, Jerry, 11
Marovitz, Abraham Lincoln, 187
Marquette University, 280
Marsalis, Wynton, 26
Martin, Fletcher P., 97
Martindale, Colin, 89
Maxwell, William, 195
Mayer, Martin, 29, 353, 377
Mays, Willie, 361
Meadow, James B., 393–94
Mears, Walter R., 68, 127, 134, 198
The Media Monopoly, 68
Medline, 181
Medlyn, Beverly, 272
Meeker, Gary, 409
Mencken, H.L., 425
Mendelson, Mitch, xviii, 107
Mercedes-Benz of North America, Inc., 378, 384

Mercer, Gary, 304
Mertens, Bill, 7
The Mesa (Ariz.) *Tribune*, 207, 272
Meyerson, Arthur, 372
The Miami Herald, 73, 96, 104, 109, 164, 255, 408–9, 416
Mickelson, Sig, 318
Miles Inc., 373
Miller, Gene, 229–30
Miller, Linda, 355
Mills, Kay, 68
Milwaukee Journal, 112
Minnesota Newspaper Association, 114
Minor, Bill, 60
Miss America, 160, 364
The Missoulian (Missoula, Mont.), 121
Mitchell, John, xvii
Mitchell, Joseph, 195
Mitchell, Kirk, 23
Mitford, Jessica, 252
The Modesto (Calif.) *Bee*, 191
Mondon, Karl, 323–24, 338
Moore, Beverly, 366
Moore, Linda, 256
Mora, Gilles, 351
Morison, Samuel Eliot, 381
Morris, Jack, 287
Morris, Joan, 10
Morris, Joe Alex, 29
Morris, Richard B., 221
Morrissey, David H., 444
Moses, Robert, 308
Mott, Frank Luther, 338
Moyers, Bill, 228
Ms., 366
MTV, 28
Muhammad, Khalid Abdul, 325–26
Mullen, Dan, 373
Munsey, Frank, 276
"Murder, She Wrote," 365
Murray, Donald M., 80, 151, 170
Murray, Jim, 22
Murrow, Edward R., 189, 316
Murrow: His Life and Times, 318
Mussolini, Benito, 174
My Favorite Summer 1956, 287

Nasrawi, Salah, 35
The Nation, 195
Nation, Carol, xviii, 31–32, 216, 390–91
Nation of Islam, 326
National Assessment of Educational Progress, 195
National Association for the Advancement of Colored People, 345, 381

National Association for the Advancement of White People, 374
National Biscuit Co., 354
National Child Labor Committee, 340
National Football League, 287
National Geographic, 344, 364
National Organization for Women, 375
National Review, 195
National Victim Center, 226
NBC, 389, 408
NBC News, 126
"NBC Nightly News, " 129
Nellie Bly: Daredevil, Reporter, Feminist, 29
Nelson, Willie, 124
Netsch, Dawn Clark, 393
Nettlefield, Jonathan B., 357
Neuman, Charlie, v
Nevins, Allan, 379
New England Patriots, 287
The New Republic, 72, 195
New York City Marathon, 378
New York Magazine, 345
The New York Review of Books, 131
The New York Times, 20, 32, 71, 72, 73, 77, 78, 80, 93, 94–95, 112, 126, 177, 183, 227, 252, 277, 286, 291, 313, 374, 378, 387, 399, 401, 407, 408–9, 412, 416, 418, 419
The New York Times Index, 184
The New York Times Manual of Style and Usage, 86
New York Times v. Sullivan, 401, 402, 410
The New Yorker, 20, 101, 195
Newman, Louis I., 71
Newman, Paul, 21
The News and Observer (Raleigh, N.C.), 167
The News Business, 68
The News Tribune (Perth Amboy, N.J.), 84
Newsday (Melville, N.Y.), 210, 344
Newspaper Guild, 461
Newswatch: How TV Decides the News, 148
Newsweek, 72, 345, 389
Newton, Isaac, 33
Nexis, 180
Nielsen Ratings, 365
Nieman Reports, 75
Niemoeller, Martin, 412
Nietzche, Friedrich, xvii
Nietzke, Ann, 366
Nike, 280, 370, 372
Nixon, Richard, 15, 25, 35, 178, 189
Noble, Joseph, 90, 226
Noda, Debbie, 191
Nolan, Martin, 193
Noonan, Melinda Vercini, 105
Northeastern University, 209

N.W. Ayer & Son, 83, 89, 354, 362

Oak Ridger (Oak Ridge, Tenn.), 178
O'Brien, Dan, 365
O'Brien, Michael, 350
Ochs, Adolph S., 356
O'Donoghue, Kevin, 107, 358, 359
Ogilvy, David, 366, 377
O'Keefe, Georgia, 355
Olajuwon, Hakeem, 281
"One Life to Live, " 415
O'Neill, Eugene, 31–32
Ontario (Canada) Press Council, 413
An Oral History of World War II, 117
Oran, Daniel, 300
Orange County (Calif.) *Register*, 344
The Origins of Photojournalism in America, 351
The Orlando (Fla.) *Sentinel*, 217
Orpheus, 420
Orr, Johnny, 421
Orwell, George, 82, 97, 98, 196
Othman, Frederick C., 98
The Outlook, 17, 88, 328

Packard, Vance, 396
Packer, Alfred G., 272
Padawer, Ruth, 217
Paisner, Daniel, 318
Pan Fuying, 174
Panagopoulos, Todd, 172
Parker, George F., 380
Parker, Marcia, xviii, 8–9, 51–52
Parks, Rosa, 401
Patinkin, Mark, 57
Patrick, Michael, 93
Patton, George, 74, 316
Peck, Robert, 97
Peeping Tom, 420
Penthouse, 409
People, 274
Pepe, Phil, 287
Pepsi-Cola, 365
Perlman, Ellen, 27, 102
Perlman, Lisa, 105
Perlman, Merrill, xviii, 48–49
Perón, Eva, 188
Persian Gulf War, 32, 35, 153, 179, 215, 230
Personal History, 68
Pett, Saul, 200
Pfeiffer, Michelle, 21
Philadelphia, 174
The Philadelphia Inquirer, 6, 264, 342, 343, 419
Philbin, Regis, 365
Picasso, Pablo, 355

Pierce, Daisy, 227
Pierce, Robert N., 29
Pitts, Beverley J., 198
Pittsburgh Post-Gazette, 283, 321
*A Place in the News: Women's Pages to the
    Front Page*, 68
The Plain Dealer (Cleveland), 37, 337, 418
Planned Parenthood Federation of America,
    120
Planned Parenthood Federation of New York
    City, 414–15
Plath, Sylvia, 196, 237–38
Playing It Straight, 422
Plesch, Daniel T., 215
Plimpton, George, 234
Plunkett, L. Dennis, 94
Poe, Edgar Allan, 106
Poison Penmanship, 252
Poitier, Sidney, 21
Pollard, Susan, 2
Pope, Edwin, 36
Popular Photography, 350
Popular Science, 344
Popyk, Lisa, 59
Porter, Susan J., xviii
Portraits in Print, 252
*Power and Influence: Mastering the Art of
    Persuasion*, 396
The Powers That Be, 29, 77
Poynter Institute for Media Studies, 429
President's Commission on Law Enforcement
    and Administration of Justice, 267
Presley, Elvis, 110, 278, 361
The Press, 221
Price, Larry C., 59–62, 63, 421
Provenzo, Eugene F., Jr., 341
The Providence (R.I.) *Journal*, 54, 82, 149,
    161, 190, 227, 245, 249
The Providence (R.I.) *Journal-Bulletin*, 319,
    320, 342
Providence (R.I.) *Journal Sunday Magazine*, v
Public Opinion, 29
Public Relations News, 279
Public Relations Society of America, 382
Pulitzer, 29
Pulitzer Prizes, 15, 22, 36, 38, 44, 45, 61, 177,
    181, 218, 337, 344, 398, 407, 414
Puris, Martin, 179

Qaddafi, Muammar, 49, 233
Quaker Oats, 359
QUILL, 60
Quinlan, Mary Lou, 357

Raeburn, Paul, 214
Rago, Rosalinde, 360

Raines, Howell, 232, 238–39
Ramsey, Marshall, 16, 188
Rapoport, Ron, xviii, 214–16, 287, 300
Raspberry, William, 21
Rather, Dan, 27, 35, 58, 189, 193, 214,
    313–15, 318
Reader's Digest, 146–47
Reader's Guide to Periodical Literature, 184,
    228
Reagan, Ronald, 38, 77, 86, 196, 247
The Record (Hackensack, N.J.), 217, 273
Red: A Biography of Red Smith, 68
The Red Smith Reader, 300
Reebok, 365
Reeves, Keanu, 21
Reichard, Hank, 419, 420–21
Rembrandt van Rijn, 33
Report to the Nation on Crime and Justice,
    269
*Reporter and the Law: Techniques of
    Covering the Courts*, 300
Reporting, 200
Reston, James, 113
Reuters, 73, 74
Revson, Charles, 369
*Rewriting Network News: WordWatching Tips
    from 345 TV and Radio Scripts*, 318
Riedel, Charlie, xviii, 87, 106, 129
Rigdon, Joan E., 100
Riis, Jacob, 381
Rivest, Jean Pierre, 71
R.J. Reynolds Tobacco Co., 206
R.L. Polk and Co., 185
Robbins, Tim, 21
Robert Capa: A Biography, 350
Roberts, Gene, 45–46, 105, 218
Roberts, Steven V., 77
Robinson, Jackie, 81
Rockefeller, John D., 380, 381
Rockefeller, Nelson, 421
The Rocky Mountain News (Denver, Colo.),
    125, 297, 394
Roe, Sam, xviii, 52–53
Roe v. Wade, 407
Rogahn, Kurt, 213
Rolling Stone, 66, 344
The Rolling Stones, 211
Roosevelt, Theodore, 380, 390
Rose, Bob, xviii, 138, 164–66, 206
Rosenblatt, Roger, 322
Rosenthal, Abe, 289
Ross, Lillian, 195, 200, 232
Rothmyer, Karen, 200
Rothstein, Arthur, 122, 190, 321, 322, 339
Rowan, Paul, 59–61, 63
Rowland, Cathie, v

Ruiz, Michele, xviii, 303–4, 307, 317
Russell, Kurt, 21
Russell, Maryanne, 87, 357, 358
Ruth, Babe, 281, 283
Ryan, Michael, 395
Ryan, Nolan, 282
Ryckman, Lisa L., 217–18

Sachs, Andrea, xviii, 237–38
A Sacred Trust: Nelson Poynter and The St. Petersburg Times, 29
Safire, William, 412
The St. Louis Post-Dispatch, 267, 322, 347, 349
St. Petersburg (Fla.) *Times*, 104, 158, 239
Salinger, J.D., 196, 417
Salisbury, Harrison, 50
The San Diego Union-Tribune, v
San Francisco Examiner, 63, 99, 113
The San Juan Star, 78
Sancetta, Amy, 224
Sandburg, Carl, 99
Sanford, Bruce W., 405, 422
Sann, Paul, 412
Santa Claus, 119, 135, 145–46
Santee, Wes, 72
Sardinha, Carol, 18, 64
Sartore, Joel, xviii, 213, 329–31, 348, 350, 438
Saturday Review, 366
Saudi Arabia, 15, 247–48
Savage, Frances, 282
Savannah (Ga.) *Morning News*, 112
Savoia, Stephan, v
Scanlan, Christopher, xviii, 57, 68
Schembechler, Bo, 287
Schenectady (N.Y.) *Gazette*, 173
Schippers, Thomas, 277
Schoenberg, Nara, 53
Schomburg Center for Research in Black Culture, 197
Schultz, Richard, 237
Schumann, Robert, 132
Schwartz, Donald, 18
Schwartz, Jennifer, 18
Scripps Howard News, 44, 59
Scripps Howard Newspapers, 406, 419
"Sea Quest, DSV," 365
The Search for God at Harvard, 289
Sears, 364, 365
Sears, Phil, 37
Selcraig, Bruce, 228
Seligman, Kathy, 226
Sergio Valente, 366–68
Seventeen, 192
Shakespeare, William, 195, 196, 417

Shap, Mark, 368
Shapiro, Robert L., 268
Shaw, David, 126, 409
Sheean, Vincent, 68
Sheehy, Gail, 36
Shen Shaoxi, 175
Shi Jingxuan, 174
Shilton, Wendy, xvii
Shulgasser, Barbara, xviii, 20–21, 27, 202
Shulins, Nancy, 173
Sidey, Hugh, 228
Sigma Delta Chi, 219, 446
Simers, T.J., 282
Simon, Carly, 66–67
Simpson, O.J., 6, 16, 129, 262, 263, 266, 268, 271, 345
Sinclair, Upton, 77–78, 381
Sisters of St. Benedictine, 376–77
Sluder, Rick, 167
Smathers, Bruce A., 238–39
Smith, H. Allen, 298
Smith, Merriman, 143
Smith, Red, 29, 68, 82, 286–87, 300
Smith, Sally Bedell, 318
Smith, Timothy W., 286
Smith, W. Eugene, 343
Snipes, Wesley, 21
Snyder, Louis, 221
Society of Professional Journalists, 408, 446
Solomon, George, 36
Somalia, 35, 132, 398, 414, 419
Sommer, Jeff, 211
Sommers, Christina Hoff, 53
Southwestern Bell, 383
Spargo, John, 380
Sperber, Ann M., 318
Sperling, Stacy, 383
Sports Illustrated, 26
Stacks, David, 144
Stanton, Mike, 161
The Star, 172
Star Tribune (Minneapolis, Minn.), 291
StarKist Seafood Company, 13, 77, 384, 388–90
Starr, Douglas P., xvii
Steffans, Brian, 345
Steffens, Lincoln, 68, 381
Steinbeck, John, 89
Steinem, Gloria, 366
Stern, Jim, 158
Stidham, Greg, 51
Stinnet, Caskie, 111
Stone, Emerson, 100
Stone, Nancy, 337
Strasser, Joel, 93
Streep, Meryl, 211

Streisand, Barbra, 106
Strong, Joan Vitale, 222
Strunk, William, Jr., 117
The Stuart (Fla.) *News*, 90, 226
Sullivan, L.B., 401
Sun, Lena H., xviii, 45–48, 174–75, 186
Sun-Bulletin (Palisades Park, N.J.), 421
Sun Sentinel (Fort Lauderdale, Fla.), 374
Super Bowl, v, 26, 365, 388
Swanberg, W.S., 29
Swint, Ron, 103, 176
Sylvester, T.D., 399–400
Synopsis of the Law of Libel and the Right of Privacy, 405, 422

Taco Bell, 28
"Take Back the Night," 53
Talese, Gay, 196
Tallahassee (Fla.) *Democrat*, 37
Tammeus, Bill, 21
Tarver, Ron, 6, 264, 341–42
Taylor, Janet L., xviii, 25
Taylor, Oliver, 280
Taylor, Terry, 373
Teagarden, Becky, 278
Tedesco, Kevin, xviii
Teenage Research Unlimited, 361
Tellis, Gerard, 367
The Tennessean (Nashville), 171, 256
Terkel, Studs, 101, 117, 234, 252
Thames, Susan, 343
Thayer, Bob, v, xviii, 54, 82, 149, 161, 190, 249, 319, 320, 342–43
Thierry, Lauren, 11, 40, 315
Thirty Seconds, 377
Thomas, Helen, 38
Thomas, Isiah, 282
Thompson, Geoff, 371
Thompson Agency, 355
Thoreau, Henry David, 111
Thurber, James, 195
Tikkun, 289
Time, 17, 63, 237–38, 329, 345–46, 389
The Times-News (Twin Falls, Ida.), 23–24, 355
Tissot, 384
Titchen, John, 3
Tittle, Y.A., 283
Tolstoy, Leo, 92
Tom Sawyer, 417
Toth, Steve, xvii
The Tombstone (Ariz.) *Epitaph*, 372
The Toronto Star, 36, 398
Treasury of Great Reporting, 221
Trias, Rafael, 78
Trowbridge, Nicholas, 64–65

Trudeau, Gary, 56
Truman, Harry, 331, 392
Trump, Donald, 183
Truth Needs No Ally—Inside Photojournalism, 351
Tube of Plenty: The Evolution of American Television, 318
Tunica, Miss., 41–44, 339
Tur, Bob, xviii, 16–17, 57, 329
Tur, Marika, 16–17
Turnbull, Bill, 70
Twain, Mark, 75, 83, 100, 195, 417
Tweed, William "Boss," 216

Ultang, Don, 337
Under God: Religion and American Politics, 288, 300
Unger, Burt, xviii, 384, 387
United Negro College Fund, 352, 368
United Press International (*UPI*), 12, 13, 94, 124, 129, 143, 274, 310, 311, 439, 440
United States, Army, 32, 355, 358, 383
United States, Bureau of Alcohol, Tobacco and Firearms, 374
United States, Bureau of Justice, 203, 260, 269, 270
United States, Constitution, 104, 123
United States, Department of Defense, 215
United States, Department of Education, 17, 293, 294
United States, Department of Justice, 260, 269
United States, Drug Enforcement Administration, 266
United States, Federal Bureau of Investigation, 53, 266, 293
United States, Federal Trade Commission (FTC), 373–74
United States, Food and Drug Administration, 374
United States, General Accounting Office, 182
United States, House of Representatives, 72, 95
United States, Library of Congress, 122, 190, 321, 339, 411
United States, Navy, 120, 321
United States, Senate, 72, 95
United States, Supreme Court, 122, 274, 341, 381, 401, 402, 403, 410
United States, Tennessee Valley Authority, 227, 326–27
United Way, 28, 201, 229, 298
University of North Carolina–Chapel Hill, 375
Upshaw, Sam, Jr., 405
USA Today, 18, 183, 404

Vadehra, Dave, 354
Van Gilder, Bonnie, 178
Van Riper, Frank, 345
Vanderzee: Photographer, 1886–1983, 315
Vanneman, Ray A., 84
Venere, Emil, 207
Verne, Jules, 7
Videla, Alejandro, 128
Vietnam War, 32, xvii
Vincent, Mal, 228–29, 235
Vogue, 364
Vonnegut, Kurt, 417

Wagner International, 356
Walden, Geoff, 140
Waldman, Marvin, 368
Walker, John, 76
Walker Evans: The Hungry Eye, 351
The Wall Street Journal, 106, 164, 192, 313, 366, 369, 383, 413
Walsh, Stella, 399, 418
Warner Brothers, 382
Warren, Keith, xviii, 212, 335
Washburn, Lindy, 3–6, 36, 207
Washington, Denzel, 21
The Washington Post, 46, 47, 98, 112, 174, 313, 407, 413
The Washington Times, 264, 272
Watch Your Language, 95
Watergate, 33, 178
Watson, Paul, 35–36, 398, 419
Watz, Don, 279–80
WBBM-AM (Chicago), 309
WBZ-TV (Boston), 11
WCPO-TV (Cincinnati), 317
Weaver, Sigourney, 21
Weinberg, Howard, 216
Weiner, Timothy, xviii, 45–46, 235–36
Wells, Ida B., 197, 200
Welsome, Eileen, 44
Werner, Perry, 209
West, Jessamyn, 58
West Point, 94
Westin, Av, 148, 313
WEWS-TV (Cleveland), 418
Whatever Happened to Madison Avenue? Advertising in the '90s, 377
Whelan, Richard, 350
Whipple, Ed, 165
Whitaker, Leslie, 18–19
White, E.B., 95, 117, 141, 195
White, Paul, 74
White, William Allen, 276
White House, 15, 35, 405, 419

Whitman, Alden, 300
Whittle Communications, 364
Who Stole Feminism? How Women Have Betrayed Women, 53
Who's Who in America, 28, 184, 228
The Wichita (Kan.) *Eagle-Beacon*, 213, 330, 348, 438
Wieden & Kennedy, 370, 372
Wilde, Oscar, 404
Wilkinson, Mike, 147
Williams, Celeste, 41–43
Williams, Terrie, 25, 26
Willis-Braithwaite, Deborah, 351
Wills, Garry, 131, 288, 300
Wilson, Janet, 182
Wilson, Kurt, 121
WIND-TV (Chicago), 219
Winerup, Michael, 227
Winger, Debra, 21
Winning Pulitzers: The Stories Behind Some of the Best News Coverage of Our Time, 200
WITI-TV (Milwaukee), 309
WJKW-TV (Cleveland), 418–19
Wolf, Marvin J., 318
Wolfe, Tom, 27, 162, 163, 196
Wong, Jan, xviii, 10–11, 71, 184, 186
Woodstock, v
Woodward, Bob, 178, 221, 230
Woolf, Virginia, 196
The Word, 117
Working: People Talk About What They Do All Day and What They Think While They Do It, 117, 252
World Almanac, 184, 194
Woster, Terry, 261
Writing Broadcast News—Shorter, Sharper, Stronger, 318
Writing for Your Readers, 170
Wyden, Ron, 392

Yeh, Emerald, xviii, 304–7, 317
Young, Charles M., 66
Young, James Webb, 353
Young & Rubicam, 63, 352, 355–56, 358, 364, 368
Youngman, Henny, 393
Yount, Karen, 130–31

Zenkl, Peter, 316
Zerwick, Phoebe, xviii, 50, 250
Zhang Lin, 47–48
Zimmermann, Fred, 202

Subject Index

Abbreviations, 106, 315, 427
Accident stories, 253–55
Accuracy, 28, 30, 56, 70–73, 74, 79, 94, 96,
    100, 180, 306, 406, 408, 447
Addresses, 71, 86, 275–76, 423
Adjectives, 83, 91, 99
Advances, 289–90
Adverbs, 83, 99
Adversarial process, 270–71, 410–11
Advertisements, 28, 80, 186
Advertising, 24–27, 183, 352–77
    accounts, 356–57, 375
    careers, 375
    classified, 371, 374
    content, 366–73, 376
    copywriters, 27, 28, 101, 375
    creative, 356, 358–62
    definitions, 369
    essentials, 372–73
    history, 354–55
    local, 362–63
    media selection, 356, 362–66, 376
    regulation, 373–75
    research, 356, 357–58, 375
    Super Bowl, 26, 364, 388
    tips, 353, 367
Age, in identification, 85–86, 275–276, 423
Agreement, subject/verb, 449–50
All-points bulletin, 4
Anecdotes, 96, 127, 140–41, 162, 169, 234,
    238, 239, 250, 275, 283
Announcements, 289
Anonymous sources, 75
Aperture, 333, 336
Appeals process, 269
Appearance, 205

Appropriation, 405
Arraignment, 266, 268
Arrests, 263–65, 267
Art, 8
Assertions, 70, 95, 231
Attribution, 33, 70, 73–76, 79, 90, 95, 225,
    302, 459
    in broadcast writing, 308–9
Audience, 192, 250–51, 307, 366, 416–17
Authorities, 86, 184, 215

Background, 70, 77, 79, 151, 152, 154, 168,
    173, 187–97, 205, 234, 459
Balance, 28, 30, 70, 77–80, 306, 406
Baseball, 288
Basketball, 288
Beats, 106, 187, 191, 195, 212–14, 299, 459
Bias, 20, 56, 79–80, 89, 201, 219, 220
Bill of Rights, 32
Billboards, 25–26, 364
Billing, 362
Black & white photography, 337–38
Body, 27, 83, 162
Booking, 266
Books, suggested reading, 29, 68, 95, 117,
    148, 170, 200, 221, 252, 300, 318,
    350–51, 377, 396, 422
Bowling, 288
Brand identity, 354, 361, 363, 423
Breaking news stories, 143
Brevity, 70, 80–82, 134, 169
Briefs, 289–92
Brights, 292
Broadcast stations, 183
Broadcast style vs. print style, 74, 106, 155,
    249, 308, 440

Broadcast writing, 302–18
   attribution, 308–9
   clarity, 307–8
   copy, 315–16, 440–41
   immediacy, 309
   leads, 308–9
   rewriting wire copy, 310–11
   style rules, 315
   terms, 464
Brochures, 84, 391
Burglary, 259, 261
Buried leads, 184, 245

Cameras, 333–38, 405
Captions, 301, 331, 344
Cartoons, 15–16
Chain-owned newspapers, 67
Chronologies, 158–59
Circulation, 67
Claims, 70
Clarity, 70, 82–83, 110, 134, 169, 251, 306
   in broadcast writing, 307–8
Classified advertising, 371, 374
Clichés, 111, 114–15, 229
Clippings, 28, 77, 180, 186, 205, 444
Clutter, 110
Codes of conduct, 19, 57, 446–48
College press, 27, 325
Colloquialisms, 307
Color photography, 337–38
Colorful writing, 97
Columns/columnists, 19, 21–22, 27, 77, 92,
   218, 414
Commercials, 26, 28, 80, 365–66, 388, 393
   Super Bowl, 26, 364, 388
Commitment, 44–50
Common sense, 196
Compassion, 411
Completeness, 50–53, 70, 83
Composure, 36–38
Computer-aided reporting, 181–82
Conflict, 118, 122–23, 126
Conflict of interest, 407
Conjunctions, 83, 99, 156
Consistency, 49
Consumer reporting, 20
Content, 80–81, 192
   advertising, 366–73, 376
Contractions, 307
Contrast leads, 134
Conviction, 97, 100–105
Copy, 8
   broadcast, 315–16, 440–41
   editing, 14, 48–49, 453–58
   newspaper, 437–40
   preparing, 435–36

Copywriters, advertising, 27, 28, 101, 375
Correction, 34, 73, 460
Courage, 58–63
Court stories
   civil, 272–73
   criminal, 266–72
Courtesy, 214
Courts
   federal, 274
   state, 269
Creativity, 30, 38–40
Crime stories, 259–66
   essentials
      arrests, 264–65
      investigations, 263
Critics/criticism, 19, 20–21, 401
Cropping, 346, 460
Curiosity, 30, 31–32, 38, 227
Currency, 118, 122, 124–25, 126, 161
Cutlines, 331
Cynicism, 220, 392

Dangling modifiers, 450
Data bases, 28, 180–81
Dateline, 5, 427, 460
Deadlines, 13, 36–37, 253, 311–13, 460
Death, 276–77, 298
Delayed leads, 108, 127, 134–35, 138–41,
   146–48, 149, 235, 278, 283
Dependability, 56
Depth interview, 229
Depth of field, 336
Desktop publishing, 17–18
Detailing, 332
Details, 104, 106, 116, 162, 169, 180, 181–82,
   205, 275–76
Dialogue, 96, 97, 162, 250
Dictionary, 71, 184
Digitized images, 338, 344
Direct address leads, 135
Direct leads, 107, 127, 134–35, 138–40, 143,
   146–48
Direct quotes, 225, 250
Disaster stories, 253–55
Discipline, 58, 89
Disguises, 413
Dishonesty, 407
Dummies, 440

Ear, writing for the, 306–9
Editorials, 19, 23, 28, 92, 186, 218, 460
Editors, 49
   photo, 333
Emotions, 93, 171, 219, 282–83, 284
Enhancement, photo, 344
Enterprisers, 38, 216–18, 460

Equity proceedings, 273
Errors, 72, 111
Ethics
 journalism, 406–14, 446–48
 public relations, 382, 394–95
Exercises, 111, 114
 photography, 348–49
 writing leads, 136–41
Experts, 86, 184, 215
Explanatory stories, 45–46, 161
Exposure, film, 337

Fact sheet, 183
Fact-checking, 79
Fact-gathering, 28, 30, 72, 85, 116, 172–200,
 202
 direct observation, 173–77, 187
 guidelines, 186
 interviews, 177–80, 187
 research, 180–85, 187
Facts, 49, 56, 79, 89, 91, 108, 115, 223
Fads, 38, 49
Fair comment, as a libel defense, 401
Fairness, 30, 70, 77–80, 306, 394, 406, 408,
 447–48
False light, 405
Feature stories, 9–10, 38, 86, 118, 126, 130,
 135, 140–41, 146, 161–64, 324,
 460
 leads, 134, 144–48, 162, 241, 286
 news, 109
 structure, 164, 168–69
Federal courts, 274
Felony, 261
Film, 337–38
Fire stories, 3–5, 11–12, 116, 253, 256–59
First Amendment, 32, 423
Fisheye lens, 335
Five W's and an H, 108, 136, 137, 289–90
Flacks, 382
Focal length, 334, 336
Focus, 87, 127–30, 149, 162–63
Focus groups, 183, 301, 357–58
Fog index, 98
Follow-up stories, 294–95
Folos, 294–95, 296
Football, 288
For cause challenge, 270
Formula, journalism, 68
Freedom of Information Act (FOIA), 182,
 442–45
Freedom of the press, 32, 92, 271, 408, 446
Free-lancers, 6, 15, 18–19
F-stop, 336

Gatekeeping, 125–26

General assignment reporters, 213
Geographical beats, 213, 299
Gifts, 408
Gossip columnists, 414
Grammar, 14, 83, 100, 111, 429, 449–52
 adjectives, 83, 91, 99
 adverbs, 83, 99
 nouns, 81, 85, 99, 449
 parallel construction, 452
 pronouns, 85, 449–50, 451
 sentence fragments, 452
 verbs, 81, 99, 132, 135, 162, 302, 449,
  450–51
 action, 97
 of attribution, 75
 tenses, 452
Grand jury, 266, 268

Hack writing, 115
Hard leads, 135, 146–48
Headlines, 8, 37, 83, 120, 372
History, 48, 49, 79, 189–91
 advertising, 354–55
 public relations, 379–82
Hoaxes, 94
Holidays, 424
"How, " 108, 136, 137
Human interest, 70, 83–85, 96, 121, 140, 162,
 165, 207, 223, 256–57, 283, 298

Identification, 70, 75, 85–86, 128, 249, 254,
 260, 272, 292, 461
Illustration, 8, 127, 346
Image advertising, 355
Immediacy, 107, 161
 broadcast writing, 309
Impact, 118, 120–21, 125, 126, 141
Incidents, 96, 162, 167, 234, 238, 283
Independence, 30, 32–33
Indictment, 266, 269
Infinitives, split, 451
Information gathering, 28, 72, 172–200, 202
Infotainment, 298
Ingenuity, 38–40
Initials, 315, 425
Initiative, 56
Inspiration, 195–96
Integrity, 35–36
Interpretative reporting, 77, 218–19
Interviews, 1, 28, 80, 172, 173, 177–80, 181,
 187, 222–52, 249, 272
 asking questions, 230–31
 depth, 229
 guidelines & tips, 227–28
 listening, 231–32
 on- and off-the-record, 101, 232–33

profiles, 227–39
spot news, 222–27
taping, 198, 200, 230, 232, 234
techniques, 223
telephone, 73, 178
victims, 226
Interpretation, 56–57
Intrusion, 405
Inverted pyramid, 108, 159–60
Investigative reporting, 218, 286, 461
Involvement, 57

Jargon, 49, 285
Journalese, 115–16
Journalism, 29
as a business, 63
education, 7
essentials, 70
ethics, 406–14
codes, 19, 413, 446–48
formula, 68
muckraking, 381
rules, 99
visual, 6, 61, 301, 319–51
Journalism, New, 196
Journalistic process, 28–29, 202, 204
Journalists, 19, 27, 30–68, 213
commitment, 44–50
completeness, 50–52
composure, 36–38
courage, 58–63
creativity, 38–40
curiosity, 30, 31–32, 38
dependability, 56
discipline, 58
independence, 30, 32–33
ingenuity, 38–40
initiative, 56
integrity, 35–36
minority, 67
perseverance, 40–44
salaries, 45
savvy, 34–35
skepticism, 30, 33–34, 35, 220, 392
stamina, 58–63
women, 67, 287
Jurisdiction, 268
Jury selection, 270

Kicker, 126, 164
Knowledge, 34, 172, 190, 194, 201

Labels, 128, 129, 308
Language, 36, 48, 49, 79, 82, 97–99, 179, 192
broadcast, 302, 307, 311

frank, 416–17
offensive, 397
Law-enforcement agencies, 265–66
Leads, 4, 27, 75, 83, 108–9, 116, 131–48, 243,
461
attribution in, 73–74
broadcast writing, 308–9
buried, 184, 245
contrast, 134
delayed, 108, 127, 134–35, 138–41,
146–48, 149, 235, 278, 283
direct, 107, 127, 134–35, 138–40, 143,
146–48
exercises, 136–41
features, 134, 144–48, 162, 241
meeting stories, 240–41, 243
obituaries, 277–78
panel discussions/symposia stories, 244–46
speech stories, 249–51
sports stories, 281–84
straight news stories, 130, 134, 141–44,
165, 241
summary, 153–55, 158
two-elements, 151
Lens opening, 336
Lenses, 334–36
Lens-to-subject distance, 336
Lexis, 181
Libel, 71, 397, 399–403
avoiding suits, 402–3
dangerous words, 403
defenses, 401
Listeners, 82, 89, 108, 126, 143, 149, 151,
155–56, 192, 193, 302
writing for, 306–9
Listening, 231–32
Local news, 12
Localizing, 278, 289, 292–94, 461
Long lens, 334

Macro lens, 335
Malice, 401
Margin of error, 183
Mass media, 27
Mathematics, 34, 49, 71, 72
Media, the, 25
Media selection, 356, 362–66, 376
Medline, 181
Meeting stories, 239–43
essentials
action taken, 240
no action taken, 243
leads, 240–41, 243
Metaphors, 85
Misdemeanor, 261

Misplaced, words, 450–51
Misspelling, 71, 72, 111, 184, 292
Mistakes, 72, 111–14, 116
Muckraking, 381
Multi-element stories, 150, 156

Names, in identification, 86, 128, 234, 248, 254, 275, 292
Narrative leads, 134
Narrative techniques, 97
Natural style, 106–8
New Journalism, 196
News, definitions of, 119, 121
News analyses, 218
News conference stories, 239, 247–48
News determinants, 120–26, 138, 141
News features, 109, 138, 141, 161, 164–68
News peg, 229, 234, 235, 295, 296
News point, 70, 87, 139, 250
News releases, 28, 32, 63, 103, 159–60, 167, 183, 186, 289–90, 298–99, 301, 378, 385
News sense, 31, 33
News stories, 27, 92, 93, 120, 138, 186
News values, 118–31
News wires, 301, 302, 306, 310
Newsletters, 17–18
Newspaper style vs. broadcast style, 74, 106, 155, 249, 308, 440
Newspapers, 12, 49, 135, 155, 183, 297, 409
    advertising departments, 355–56
Newsworthiness, 118–19, 123, 125, 172, 229, 251, 264, 292, 404
Nexis, 180
Nonverbal communication, 231
Normal lens, 334
Notes, 150, 198–200, 230, 232
Nouns, 81, 85, 99, 449
Novelty, 70, 89
Numbers, 315, 425, 440
Nut graf, 87

Obituary stories, 13, 94, 106, 141–43, 207, 274–78, 308–9, 462
    causes of death, 276–77
    essentials, 208–9, 275
    leads, 277–78
Objectivity, 19, 56–57, 58, 70, 89–93, 283, 406, 447
Obscenity, 104, 397, 414, 418–19
Observation, 28, 33, 56, 87, 89, 96, 97, 171, 173–77, 180, 187, 227, 234
Occupation, in identification, 86, 205, 275–76
Off-the-record interviews, 232–33, 462
One-third rule, 337

On-the-scene reporting, 303–7
Opinions, 22, 27, 56, 75, 90–92, 369
O-S-V sentence structure, 249
Ownership, 67

Panel discussions stories, 239, 243–46
Paraphrasing, 99, 101, 248, 250
Percentages, 425
Peremptory challenge, 270
Perpetrators, 260
Perseverance, 40–44
Personals, 289–92
Photo editor, 333
Photo essay, 331
Photoengraving, 354
Photography, black & white vs. color, 337–38
Photojournalism, 6, 61, 301, 319–51
    captions, 301, 331, 344
    content & treatment, 322–23
    equipment, 333–38
    ethics, 344–46
    exercises, 348–49
    picture enhancement, 344
    taste, 8, 36, 51–52, 121, 350, 398, 419–21
    tips, 331, 421
Photoshop, 323
Phrases, 85
Placement, 74–75
Plagiarism, 406
Planning, 28
Plea bargaining, 269–70
Polls, 182–83, 228, 406
Portraits, 335
Poses, 413
Position paper, 183
Positioning, 359
Precedes, 289–90
Preliminary court hearings, 268
Prepared texts, 251
Press agents, 382
Press conference stories, 247–48
Press freedom, 32, 92, 271, 408, 446
Press kit, 183
Press law, 189
Press releases, 28, 32, 63, 103, 159–60, 167, 183, 186, 289–90, 298–99, 301, 378, 385, 462
Pressure, 203
Pretrial process, 266–70
Print style vs. broadcast style, 74, 106, 155, 249, 308, 440
Print terms, 459–64
Privacy, 51, 398, 404–6
Privilege, as a libel defense, 401
Probable cause hearing, 268

Production, 29
Profanity, 416
Profile stories, 86, 106, 162
    endings, 238–39
    essentials, 205, 234
    interviews, 227–39
    preparation, 228–29
Prominence, 120, 124, 125, 141
Pronouns, 85, 449–50, 451
Proof sheet, 330
Property crimes, 259, 261
Proximity, 118, 122–26, 292
Public affairs, 390–92
Public gathering stories, 239–52
Public officials, 401–2
Public relations, 24, 26, 77, 183, 301, 353,
        378–96
    careers, 395–96
    corporate, 387–90
    ethics, 382, 394–95
    history, 379–82
    political, 392–93
    process, 379
    public affairs, 390–92
    salaries, 396
    scope & tasks, 384–86
    as a source of information, 183
    sports information, 386
Pulitzer Prizes, 15, 22, 36, 38, 44, 45, 61, 177,
        181, 218, 337, 344, 398, 407, 414
Punctuation, 83, 111, 429–34

Question & answer stories, 101, 247, 248
Questions, 230
Quotation marks, 433
Quotes, 54, 73, 85, 86, 96, 99, 101–3, 142,
        162, 167, 169, 180, 234, 248, 252,
        254, 257, 261, 285, 296, 315, 462
    direct, 225, 250
    paraphrasing, 99, 101, 248, 250

Race, as identification, 86, 425, 426
Radio, 307
Rape, 52–53
Rarity, 120, 126
Rates, 26, 39, 41–43, 45, 52–53, 67, 71, 95,
        203–4, 260, 279, 281, 288, 294, 307,
        365, 367, 388, 396, 406
Ratings, 365
Readability, 98
Reader stories, 311, 313
Readers, 48–49, 67, 82, 89, 99, 101, 104–6,
        108, 126, 135, 141, 142, 143, 149,
        151, 155–56, 192, 193, 252, 285
Reading, 96, 195

suggested books, 29, 68, 95, 117, 148, 170,
        200, 221, 252, 300, 318, 350–51, 377,
        396, 422
Reciprocity, 334
Record, the, 49, 79, 94, 101
Redundancies, 113–14
References sources, 28, 73, 180, 184
Regulation, advertising, 373–75
Religion, as identification, 86
Religion stories, 288–89
Reporters, 19, 27, 30–68, 213
    commitment, 44–50
    completeness, 50–52
    composure, 36–38
    courage, 58–63
    creativity, 38–40
    curiosity, 30, 31–32, 38
    dependability, 56
    discipline, 58
    independence, 30, 32–33
    ingenuity, 38–40
    initiative, 56
    integrity, 35–36
    minority, 67
    perseverance, 40–44
    salaries, 45
    savvy, 34–35
    skepticism, 30, 33–34, 35, 220, 392
    stamina, 58–63
    women, 67, 287
Reporting, 27–28, 85, 201–21
    building relationships, 213–16
    computer-aided, 181–82
    consumer, 20
    interpretative, 218–19
    investigative, 218, 286, 461
    obstacles to, 219–21
    on-the-scene, 303–7
    straight, 20, 109
    visual, 319–51
        content & treatment, 322–23
        ethics, 344–46
        exercises, 348–49
        picture enhancement, 344
        tips, 331, 421
Research, 28, 173, 180–86, 194
Responsibility, 408–10, 414, 446
Restraint, 284
Retouching, 346
Revenue, 26
Reviews/reviewers, 19, 20–21, 28, 92, 186
Rewriting, 111, 298, 301, 302, 306, 310
Rhythm, 98, 169
Robbery, 259, 261
Rough, 24

Roundup stories, 296
Rules about writing news, 108

Salaries
   journalists, 45
   public relations, 396
Sanity, 268
Savvy, 34–35
Sentences, 81, 83, 85, 97–99, 106, 107, 110,
     136, 179, 180, 302, 311
   balance, 98
   fragments, 452
   parallel construction, 452
   structure
      O-S-V, 249
      S-V-O, 82–83, 98, 136, 137, 140, 249,
        307, 309, 311
   transitional, 156–58, 235
Sentencing, 269, 272
Settlement, 273
Sexism, 79–80, 93, 287, 426
Short lens, 334
Shorts, 289–92
Showing vs. telling, 103–5, 141, 167
Shutter speed, 333
Sidebars, 64, 295–96
Similes, 85
Single-element stories, 150–52
Skepticism, 30, 33–34, 35, 220, 392
Soft leads, 135, 146–48
Sources, 68, 70, 71, 73, 261
   anonymous, 75
   direct observation, 173–77, 187
   documentation, 33
   human, 33, 36, 75, 80, 90, 93, 184, 186,
     212, 248, 252
   interviews, 177–80, 187
   public relations, 183
   references, 28, 73
   research, 180–86, 187
Spec, 24
Speech stories, 36–37, 147–48, 239, 248–51
Speed, film, 337
Speedgraphic, 338
Spelling, 71, 72, 111, 184, 292
Spiked, 63
Split infinitives, 451
Sports stories, 36, 278–88
   leads, 281–84
   structure, 283
Spot news stories, 28, 141, 151, 152, 159, 225
Staccato leads, 134
Stamina, 58–63
State courts, 269
Stereotypes, 79–80, 201, 228

Stories
   accidents & disasters, 253–55
   advances, 289–90
   breaking news, 143
   briefs, 298–92
   brights, 292
   crime, 259–66
   enterprisers, 38, 216–18, 460
   features, 9–10, 38, 86, 118, 126, 130, 135,
     140–41, 146, 149, 161–64, 324, 460
   fire, 3–5, 11–12, 116, 253, 256–59
   folos, 294–95, 296
   interpretative, 77, 218–19
   meetings, 239–43
   multi-element stories, 150, 156
   news conferences, 239, 247–48
   news features, 109, 138, 141, 161, 164–68
   obituaries, 13, 94, 106, 141–43, 207,
     274–78, 308–9, 462
   panel discussions/symposia, 239, 243–46
   personals, 289–92
   precedes, 289–90
   profiles, 86, 106, 162
   question & answer, 101, 247, 248
   religion, 288–89
   speeches, 36–37, 147–48, 239, 248–51
   spot news, 28, 141, 151, 152, 159
   straight news, 109, 118, 126, 135, 137,
     150–61, 168
   tell, 311, 313
   two-element stories, 150, 152–57
Story, moving the, 437–41
Story essentials, 207–10, 253–301
   accidents & disasters, 253–55
   advances, 290
   advertising, 372–73
   courts, 253
      criminal, 271
   crime stories
      arrests, 264–65
      investigations, 263
      reports, 253, 260–61
   fires, 253, 256–59
   folos, 295
   localizing, 293
   meetings
      action taken, 240
      no action taken, 241
   news conferences, 247
   obituaries, 208–9, 275
   personals, 292
   precedes, 290
   profiles, 204–5, 234
   roundups, 296
   sidebars, 296

speeches, 248
sports, 253, 280–81
weather, 253, 298
Story structure, 28, 108–9, 127, 149–71, 180
features, 164, 168–69
inverted pyramid, 108, 159–60
news feature stories, 168–69
sports stories, 283
Storytelling, 109–11, 159
Straight news stories, 109, 118, 126, 135, 137, 150–61, 168
leads, 130, 134, 141–44, 241
Straight reporting, 20
Straight-line narrative, 160
Street smarts, 34–35
Style, 49, 96, 161–62
broadcast, 315
natural, 97, 106–8
print vs. broadcast, 74, 106
Stylebook, 106, 423–34, 463
Summary leads, 153–55, 158
Super Bowl, 26, 364, 388
Suppression, 268
S-V-O sentence structure, 82–83, 98, 136, 137, 140, 249, 307, 309, 311
Symposia stories, 239, 243–46
Synonyms, 75, 115–16

Tabloid journalism, 97
Tabloids, 120
Talking-head coverage, 392
Tape recording, 198, 200, 230, 232, 234, 405
Taste, 414–21
frank language, 416–17
guidelines, 417–18, 421
offensive subject matter, 418–19
photojournalism, 8, 36, 51–52, 121, 350, 398, 419–21
Telephone directories, 71, 184
Telephone interviews, 73, 178
Telephoto lens, 334
Tell stories, 311, 313
Telling vs. showing, 103–5, 167
Three-element stories, 150, 157–61
Timeliness, 118, 122, 123, 125, 126, 138
Tips & guidelines
advertising, 353
interviews, 223, 227–28
photojournalism, 331, 421
Titles, 315, 427–29
Topical beats, 213
Track & field, 288
Transitional sentences, 156–58, 162, 169, 235
Trends, 38–40, 49
Trial process, 270–72
Truth, 68, 94, 401, 408, 410

Two-element leads, 151, 153
Two-element stories, 150, 152–57
Typewriters, 435–36

Unusual, 120, 126

Verbs, 81, 99, 132, 135, 162, 302, 449, 450–51
action, 97
of attribution, 75
tenses, 452
Verdicts, 271–72
Verification, 28, 33, 49, 70, 71, 74, 77, 79, 89, 93–95, 150, 263, 292, 406, 463
Victims, 52, 203–4, 254–56, 260, 404
interviewing, 226
photographing, 343–44
Video display terminals, 436, 463
Viewers, 89, 101, 156, 302, 307
Violent crimes, 259–60, 261
Visual reporting, 319–51
content & treatment, 322–23
ethics, 344–46
exercises, 348–49
picture enhancement, 344
tips, 331, 421
Vulgarity, 397

Weather stories, 296–98
"What," 108, 128–29, 133, 136, 137, 249
Wheel, 270
"When," 108, 110, 136, 137
"Where," 108, 110, 136, 137
"Who," 108, 128–29, 133–34, 136, 137, 249
"Why," 108, 110, 136, 137
Wide-angle lens, 334
Wire copy, rewriting, 310–11
Wire services, 301, 302, 306, 310, 464
Women, 193, 203, 287
in journalism, 67
Words, 71, 97, 99–100, 111
advertising, 367
broadcast terms, 464
misplaced, 450–51
potentially libelous, 403
print terms, 459–64
Writer's block, 165
Writethru, 5, 147
Writing, 29, 69–117
broadcast, 302–18
colorful, 97
ingredients, 97–108
problems, 170
rudiments, 70–95
tips, 108, 169, 285, 288

Zoom lens, 335